MARY WELSH HEMINGWAY

AND HOW IT WAS...

HOW IT WAS

Mary Welsh Hemingway

BALLANTINE BOOKS • NEW YORK

Hail to R. A. G. and his tribe

Library of Congress Catalog Card Number: 76-13672

ISBN 0-345-25432-5

Manufactured in the United States of America

First Ballantine Books Edition: November 1977

Contents

1

My Father in Minnesota

OF THE FIFTEEN thousand lakes which gladdened the forests of northern Minnesota in the teens of this century, my father's and my favorite was Leech Lake where, summers, he worked and I explored, dawdled and daydreamed. Our other lakes were better named. Lake Bemidji where we lived in the winters means Shining Waters in Chippewa; Tenmile Lake, Cut-Foot Sioux, Bowstring, Kabekona Lake. But they were small and feminine, beginning to be bourgeois resorts with summer cottages along their beaches.

Leech Lake, with its six hundred forty miles of shoreline, its deep, irregular bays and sudden shallows, its twelve islands, floating bogs and big storms, seemed masculine and stimulating to a she-child who was born in a cottage overlooking it and whose first journey was across one of its bays at the age of one month.

Among the nation's waters, Leech Lake had one distinction. On a stretch of its shoreline less than ten years before I arrived in Walker, Minnesota, Chippewa Chief Bug-o-nay-ge-shig and his braves fought and won one of the very last battles against troops of the United States government. It was a small firecracker burst in our country's noisy history but still memorable among us local children who learned about it with our breakfast wild rice and milk, and my father—who was a born iconoclast, political liberal and friend

1

of the Chippewas—used to recall it with pleasure whenever his boat, *Northland,* passed Sugar Point, where the battle had flared. He would pull the whistle cord and *Northland* would shout out a couple of throaty salutations.

Lumbering, with its attendant depredations of Indian lands, was the cause of Bug-o-nay-ge-shig's battle. He had seen how white lumbermen, my father not yet among them, had ravaged the rich timberlands of the White Earth and Red Lake bands of Chippewas, leaving them fields of stumps and dispersing their indigenous populations of animals and birds. He refused to sign a paper authorizing the cutting of timber on his band's holdings on Bear Island, the biggest island in Leech Lake.

"Obstructing progress," the lumbermen complained to committees in St. Paul, the state capital. "Interfering with business."

The federal marshal at Walker was ordered to pick up Bug-o-nay-ge-shig and bring him to court to explain his willful defiance of standard business practices. The marshal caught the old chief at the Indian agency at Onigum, across the bay from Walker, and was hustling him down to a waiting boat when Bug-o-nay-ge-shig called out in Chippewa, "Where are my young men?" His braves quickly surrounded him, pushed the marshal away, and the Indians slipped into the thick shadows of their forest. Resisting arrest was an insult to the Great White imponderable Father in Washington. The federal government dispatched General John M. Bacon and a covey of soldiers to Walker to capture the chief and his young men.

Hiring local tugboats at Walker on October 4, 1898, General Bacon, his second-in-command, Captain Wilkinson, and eighty soldiers steamed to Bear Island, found it deserted, and moved on westward to Sugar Point, where Bug-o-nay-ge-shig had a cabin and a potato patch. Unable without tenders to unload their supplies, the little army went ashore anyway, rifles loaded, found the cabin deserted and explored paths through the forest. They may have seen a branch move or a bird fly off unreasonably. They saw no Indians and returned to the cabin where they were

2

ordered to stack their rifles. As they did so a gun went off. From the thick surrounding woods a fusillade poured onto them, and several soldiers were wounded as they grabbed their rifles, fired into the trees and jumped for cover.

The battle continued sporadically that afternoon and the next day, with Captain Wilkinson and six soldiers killed and ten others wounded before General Bacon took his army back to Walker and, with what dignity he could muster, offered to parley. Chief Bug-o-nay-ge-shig's force had been twenty braves with flintlocks.

Other chiefs of Leech Lake Indian clans attended a parley at Walker that year. But Bug-o-nay-ge-shig never surrendered, never parleyed and was never caught by federal marshals. One of the few photographs of him, a thin man with high cheekbones, a firm mouth and straight gaze, shows him wearing a necklace of Krag-Jorgensen shell cases from the rifles of General Bacon's troops. He lived peacefully a number of years more, fishing, hunting, counseling young people and smoking his long straight pipe of kinnikinnick, the Indian tobacco made from the dried inner bark of the red osier willow. Its rich, acrid scent said "Indian" to me throughout my childhood.

The Chippewas built oval wigwams of birch-bark around Leech Lake and there lived in a natural abundance of fish, game and wild rice. Rivers running into and out of the lake were populated by muskellunge, walleye pike, great northern pike. In the forests—a conservationist's dream—deer, elk and moose could be trapped or snared for food and for their hides which made clothing. Bear roamed their circuits among the pines and hardwoods, and marten, raccoon and foxes made the area their homes. Muskrats, otters, mink and beavers lived in swamps or in streams they dammed.

Hunting for the source of the Mississippi River, U.S. Army Lieutenant (later General) Zebulon Pike, who later discovered Pikes Peak, happened upon Leech Lake in 1806, noted the fur trading post and the lake's contours and reported its existence to the War Department in Washington. Eventually the state

3

of Minnesota rewarded him by naming the lake's smallest, nothingest island for him.

In the 1890s there remained at least 600,000 acres of unsurveyed timberland in northern Minnesota, and my father, not yet turned twenty-one, decided to acquire 160 acres of that virgin forest under what he recalled as the Squatters' Rights Law. With rough maps to guide him, a man blazed a tree, paced off 160 rods east, north, west, and south from the tree, posted a notice claiming the land, built a shelter and thus, with few further formalities, became a landholder with title to the tract.

My father favored the heavily timbered area of Itasca County, about one hundred fifty miles south of the Canadian border, for the first piece of the earth's surface he would own. He built his cabin sixty-five miles from the nearest village on a railway, and learned about his neighborhood of forest, animals, birds and people eight or ten miles away who were claiming land as he was, by living on it. Then he went home to the village of L'Anse, Michigan, a cluster of houses at the base of the smaller thumb of the state which sticks up from Wisconsin into Lake Superior. There he succumbed, he always pretended, to the blandishments of a little blue-eyed girl, Adeline Beehler, and married her in the L'Anse church on July 9, 1902.

My father had staked adjoining claims for my mother and for his sister Katherine not far from his own property north of Bemidji, and my parents' wedding journey took them first to Bemidji, which was then a town of temporary refuge for lumberjacks hunting jobs for the winter, homesteaders hunting supplies for their cabins and shoestring entrepreneurs hunting wares to buy cheap and sell dear. The second stage of their honeymoon journey was a bone-cracking wagon ride over roots and rocks to a clearing in the forest where, with the help of an Indian, my father built their first home, a one-room log cabin.

The cabin was completed well before the first snow flurries of autumn and it was snug and comfortable in the below-zero Minnesota winter, my parents declared. For income that winter my father worked as a clerk and scaler with a logging outfit whose camp, he said, was about ten miles from his and Adeline's cabin. He snowshoed the distance happily every morning and thudded back in the white twilight of late afternoons. Many years later his legs were as full of springs as a kangaroo's.

The more he learned about it, the more my father was lured by the challenges and possible rewards of logging. He was learning the skills of a cruiser—particularly to estimate the lumber footage in a stand of growing trees, eyeing heights, girths and the thickness of growth with such precision that there would never be more than a ten percent difference between his estimate and the bank scale, which was the buyer's measurement of the cut logs.

In 1904 my parents decided that the village of Walker, looking over the empty blue reaches of Leech Lake, should be the base of my father's lumbering operations, and they bought a cottage on the lake's high bank where I was born on a Sunday morning in 1908. Awaking from a nap that day my mother felt around for me in her bed and could not find me. She could hear my father pedaling their player piano and called out, asking him where I was. "I have her here," my father called back, still pedaling. He was holding me head down, feet up, so that he could see my face while he trundled. My mother remembered the upside-down position with all the stupidities I committed.

Although my father continued his logging enterprises around Leech Lake, and bought an 800-acre farm edging up from one of its bays, my parents moved their domestic headquarters from Walker to Bemidji in a big sunny clapboard house on a corner of Bemidji Avenue and Twelfth Street, in time for me to go to kindergarten in the larger town. But Leech Lake, either at the farm or aboard *Northland,* was home in the summers, and I thought the isolated, compact world of the boat incomparably preferable to living ashore.

When *Northland* was plying the lake on errands, the pilothouse on her top deck was the mind and heart of my summertime world. The pilothouse was a barefloored, Spartan room entirely enclosed from a man's waist upward by square panes of glass, and my father was often alone there steering. When I rapped on the glass-paned door he would call out, "Come in, come in, Dearidoo," and we might soar together on a flight of song, "When you wore a tulip, a bright yellow tulip." Or, "Just a little bit of heaven dropped from out the sky one day." He might tell me about the great artist Edwin Booth whom he had seen play *Hamlet* in Chicago. Or about the Pacific Ocean, which he had found cold and gray near San Francisco, but BIG and thus alluring to a landlocked Midwestern man.

He was a man of instant blooming temper, but his patience, answering my questions to help me understand the ferocious world of grownups, daily nourished my devotion to him. I learned what made the bogs grow, why birds chose one nesting site instead of another. When I was perplexed by Chapter 34 of Exodus, the Lord "forgiving iniquity . . . [but] visiting the iniquity of the fathers upon the children," my father explained the history of the Bible and the fanaticism of its early compilers.

One evening as we were splashing softly through the twilight, he pointed out the chair-shaped formation of stars emerging from the blue of the northern sky. "That constellation is Cassiopeia. It is about as far to the right of the North Star, see, as the pointers of the Dipper are to the left. Now, Dearidoo, if you were up there sitting on the North Star looking at Cassiopeia, it would look like an *M* to you, *M,* for Mary. And if you could see it from a million miles to the northeast of us, it would look like a *W* to you. So your initials are written in the stars." I remembered Cassiopeia, and did not question his astronomy.

Watching the blue and gray lake and our landmarks on distant shorelines, we talked about ideas. What was justice, really? Or charity, because one of my favorite bits of the Bible was the thirteenth chapter, the one about charity, in the First Epistle of Paul to the Corinthians. "Not the easiest to follow, though," my father would say, and then would tell me about Corinth and its long bloody history.

One of his favorite aphorisms, which we often discussed, was from *Hamlet:* "There is nothing either good or bad, but thinking makes it so." He had first read *Hamlet* at Valparaiso University where he was a student, and kept his copy of the play with other favorite books in his stateroom on *Northland*. Like bees hunting nectar, we searched and savored the proposition. Mr. Shakespeare was a frequent companion in our talks on the boat.

Of the knowledge and thought my father poured over me those summers, one gift came as we were walking toward the big white boat across a pasture full of sheep. We watched them run witlessly ahead, aside and astern of us, and I thought them hilarious, squeezed my father's hand and said, "Aren't they silly, Papa? They could hurt themselves running so blindly."

My father laughed and as we escaped the milling animals said, "Remember this, Mary. Never be a sheep. Never follow a leader only because he is ahead of you. Take time to look around and see for yourself if you are going in the right direction." I must have been eight or nine years old that morning.

The *Northland,* which had been built near Walker, was a Mississippi River type of boat, 120 feet long, with a 36-foot beam, and the paddles of the wheel at her stern were 24 feet long and four inches thick. Although she was three decks high, her flat bottom drew only four or five feet of water, a requirement on our lake with its many stretches of shallow water. When she was in operation her lower, engine-room deck offered entrancing occupations to a child. My friend Ole Helgerson, the engineer, a piece of "waste" forever in his hand, would give me some of it and let me polish nonmoving parts of his purring machines. He gave me good advice too. One time when I moaned to him over some inflated childhood problem, he said, "Don't worry. Never worry. If it is something that you can fix, fix it. If it is something impossible to fix, all your worrying won't help it."

When Ole was busy I could go and sit on the steps leading down to the black iron door of the boat's furnace and chat with Axel Strand, our softspoken fireman, and shiver with awe whenever he opened the door to toss four-foot pieces of cordwood onto the raging yellow flames inside.

7

Bob Cloud and Jim Thunder, Indian boys about twice my age, were among the logmen in our crew for several years, and my heroes. They called me Manee, Chippewa for Mary, were from the band of my father's friend Chief Kau-kau-kan, and had learned to speak English in the missionary school but patiently taught me Chippewa phrases to augment the vocabulary I'd picked up by ear.

"Boujou Nitchie. On in a kom a gut?" (Good day, friend. What is the news?), we used to greet each other. Years later I wondered if the first phrase with the same meaning had been adopted and adapted from French explorers or traders who wandered through our part of the country in the eighteenth century.

When I learned a new phrase or a new rope knot from Bob or Jim, I used to scramble up the pilothouse to report to my father. Sometimes he taught me another phrase to carry below. One time it was *"Dinne mo shai a, wetch i web."* When I repeated it to my heroes in the engine room, they fell silent and looked solemnly at their hands. I hurried back up the two steep companionways to my father who said, "They're nice boys, Dearidoo. Perhaps they didn't understand that I was making a joke. It means, 'My sweetheart, I love you.'"

When we were slowly towing or dawdling along a shoreline, Bob and Jim sometimes fished from the lower deck, with a piece of meat on a hook at the end of a string which they tied to a willow stick. One day as I watched, Bob's stick nodded, he flung it upward and a shiny brown-green pickerel flopped on the deck beside us. Bob picked it up by its tail and bashed its head against the deck and then it lay there inert. Except for flies, I had not seen many creatures killed. I took my consternation up to my father.

"It was so alive and shining," I said. "And then, so quick, it was dead and the shine faded."

My father nodded.

"Let's let things live, Papa. I don't shine, but I like living."

"You shine in your way, Dearidoo," my father

said. "But to live, even shining, is not enough. You must also learn to give."

Water seemed as natural a habitat as land, I thought in my childhood, especially since, as my mother told me, she had taken me across a bay of the lake on my first journey away from home. She wanted to show me to her friend Miss Pauline Colby, who was one of the missionaries at Onigum. In the month of May my mother made the three-mile crossing from Walker in a public launch. A storm whirled down upon the ferryboat from the big lake, northwest. The Indians aboard grew nervous and sick and the launch shipped water and spray into its passenger section. My mother, inured to the cold and inhospitable shores of Lake Superior, remained unperturbed.

With lifelong experiences on the lake, I was excited and delighted at the age of seven or eight when, as dusk was falling, *Northland* grounded herself on a patch of bog. (I don't know why boats are usually, if not universally, female.) We had passed through the Narrows into the Big Lake, from which waves, growing steadily in turbulence, came pounding against our starboard side. In the east, dark cumulus clouds were foaming, lightning splintering them, and mutters of thunder rolled toward us. My father and his crew tried every trick they knew to release us from our bog trap—paddle wheel churning, capstan whirling. Without success. They had special reason for concern that night because the bog had caught us only about two hundred yards from a hunk of granite rock jutting up almost to the surface and as big as a two-storied house. The rock was marked on our charts, but floating bog was never chartable.

It must have been ten o'clock, long beyond my normal bedtime, when my father noticed me among the crew on the workdeck and ordered me to bed. I couldn't obey. I slipped behind one of the big sliding doors of the forward deck and listened, shivering, to my father and his Irish foreman and Ole Helgerson discussing tactics against the storm and the rock, their voices higher-pitched than usual. They tried once more the maneuver of dropping the anchor and pushing with the paddle wheel and pulling with the capstan.

9

To no avail. Then I heard my father saying, his voice definitive, "Very well. I'm going to bed. You, Bill, and you, Sven, stand watch, one here, one in the pilothouse. When anything happens, come up and tell me."

Rain was sliding down onto the forward deck and for a moment it made the only sound. My father ran up the outside companionway to our living quarters while the assembled crew stood silent. Then the Irish foreman shouted out, "Tom Welsh, you are a damned fool."

In the dusk behind the sliding door I prayed my father had not heard. He was a quick man with his fists. I prayed too that I could slither into my own stateroom without alerting him. Somebody found me and took me up to our second-deck sitting-room-lounge from which opened the doors of our private staterooms. I made the passage without mishap.

The next morning my father, steering up top, told me that they had awakened him at about two o'clock, reporting that a big wave had lifted *Northland* off the bog, that the helmsman had steered us clear of the rock and that we had anchored for the remaining hours of the night in a tranquil bay. We were heading for Portage Bay that morning and my father pinpointed our position for me on his chart. (I had learned to read charts almost as soon as sentences.) I told him that I had disobeyed his "to-bed" order the night before, and waited, teetering between fear of his anger and hope of forgiveness. My father frowned, looked forward steering and said nothing, and in a few minutes I understood vaguely that the matter was finished. That day I felt lonely.

We had plenty of space in our second-deck lounge with its reading lamps, wicker furniture and bright cretonne cushions. Its bookcases bulged with Tolstoy, Ernest Thompson Seton—who hadn't yet switched his name around—the Bible, Galsworthy, *Ben Hur, Ramona,* and a few volumes of our set of Shakespeare, small-sized books of thin paper and beautiful type bound in wine-colored leather with gilt edgings, a summer lending from our principal library in Bemidji, because my mother felt it would be as slovenly

10

to send a child off on a holiday without a book as without a toothbrush.

We had books of state history and navigation and the Chippewa Indians, and our phonograph scratched out Chopin études and Mozart sonatas and "I love you truly, truly dear." (The Chopin was the same that I practiced, winters, in Bemidji). We spent few evenings in the lounge. We were nearly always too busy on the workdeck, or too tired, and my official bedtime, after supper in the dining room astern of our lounge, was 8:30 P.M. Not much evening, I used to feel, climbing into my bunk with my outside door on the starboard side still awash in sunlight.

The year 1916 brought heavy, though temporary, economic losses to my father and a summerful of wonders to me. From four different logging camps around Leech Lake his lumberjacks during the winter had cut and skidded down to the shores enough white and Norway pine to make up twenty different booms for *Northland* to tow to Federal Dam at the far eastern end of the lake. With our crew working ten to fifteen hours a day, as my father did, he had towed two booms to the dam and sent them on their way to a sawmill on the Great Northern Railway. Out on the surface of the lake the boom might measure a quarter of a mile in diameter, its shape changing from round to teardrop when we started towing, *Northland* moving backward so that her paddle wheel's splash would not disturb the logs, at the stately pace of one mile an hour.

In mid-May that year a tremendous three-day storm blew in from the northwest. It tore apart all the other booms, already made up and anchored in eighteen different coves and bays, and tossed forty-five thousand logs—three million feet of lumber, my father said— high onto sandy beaches, or wedged between rocks or mired in swamps around the lake's long shoreline. Every log had to be retrieved, reassembled into booms and delivered to the sawmill, if the winter's investment in timber and labor were to be saved.

My father ordered extra bunks built along the walls of *Northland*'s engine room and expanded his logging crew from three to twenty-five. From late May until

11

June 3, we slowly cruised the shore, our crew combing logs out of exile and herding them back inside their boomsticks. I explored miles of shoreline new to me. As we were edging along Bear Island at the eastern end of the lake I got a ride ashore in our workboat and, on the high bank which remained after a storm had chewed away the foreshore, came upon a treasure-trove of arrowheads, rusted flintlock guns, Indian pipes and wooden bowls. Then, in the high grass I found an Indian grave, a wooden box from which waves had torn away a side plank.

I peeked into the grave, and startled, found a skull from which coarse black hair was still growing. The skeleton had been a man, I saw from the carved, straight-stemmed pipe which his friends had placed beside his hand. I ran back to our crew and got myself ferried to my father.

When I had told him my adventure, my father wondered aloud if I had not imagined the hair growing after skin and flesh had disappeared. He was too busy to go back with me and confirm my discovery, and when I suggested that I collect some of the artifacts I'd found, he vetoed the notion. "They are probably from other graves which have been destroyed," he said. "Go back and memorize them and the place where they are. Get a bearing on a couple of trees or bushes, and I'll mark it on my chart. But you must not take away anything, Dearidoo. They belong to someone else." Weeks later my father told me that he had described my discovery to his friend Daniel DeLury, who was a lawyer, an important man in Walker, and a student of local Chippewa culture. He would see that the Bear Island relics were properly collected, with permission from the Indians who owned them, if owners could be found, and preserved in some official place. (I never possessed so much as one arrowhead from northern Minnesota, and the beautiful beaded jackets and moccasins the squaws used to make as presents for us are long gone. Their bright beading always took curved designs, imitating the contours of their forests, wildflowers and waves, in contrast to the angular patterns of our country's Southwest Indians who live among the straight lines and angles of mesas and rimrock against flat desert floors. A

12

small birch-bark box entirely embroidered with porcupine quills has surprisingly accompanied me through time and space. My mother used it as a sewing box. So do I.)

Occasionally groups of people chartered *Northland* for a day's excursion and a fish fry at Ottertail Point, with its sandy beach sloping up to pine forests. I did not enjoy those days. It seemed to me demeaning to my father that he should allow strangers to intrude upon our privacy, just for money. Seeing people climbing my railings and white-painted iron struts, or peering into our staterooms, gave me cramps in my head. Perhaps my father shared my distaste for the excursions. One time when we had taken four hundred and twenty-five state senators, congressmen and their wives to picnic at Ottertail Point, my father decided he should visit a small crew of men he had working at Goose Island, nearby. He assigned a pilot to take the big boat back to Walker and we set off in our working launch for the island. The sun was setting when we pulled away from Goose Island and headed for our farm ten miles away across the silky water, and we had an evening's leisure to watch the sky and the lake fade from pink to lavender to deep, dark blue with a new star blooming every minute. I had heedlessly left *Northland* wearing only my summer cotton "bloomer suit," my uniform those summers, with the bloomers hugging my legs just below the knees. No sweater. Ernest Blackburn, one of our Indian crew, offered me part of his blanket. I clung close to his warmth, and for the first time stayed awake all night.

Each early spring when the first crows arrived at Leech Lake, the Indians left their houses at Onigum and moved across the ice to their sugar camps around Hardwood Point on Sucker Bay, and during several years their sugar-making season coincided with Easter vacation from school in Bemidji. I would go down to our farm on the train, my father would discover that he must talk to a fellow about the coming summer's operations, the fellow always living near the sugar camp. One morning we would set off in our buckboard with its high red wheels behind Mike and Dan, our span of Kentucky bays. We wanted wheels rather than sled runners

13

since the ice along some shorelines might have melted. Wheels negotiated the strip of open water and slushy sandbanks better than runners; they did well on the ice too, and on any trails ashore that were melting into mud.

Singing in rhythms to match our team's trotting, we used to whisk over the ice of the Narrows, past Squaw Point and out into the Big Lake, I always awed by its emptiness of mauve distances undefined by shoreline. The sap for maple sugar came from hard maples which lived, tall and dignified, among Norway pines with their uncluttered pink trunks and the dark green of white pines. Once my father staked the horses on the ice, he would hop ashore from rock to rock, carrying me. Ashore, we stopped to smell the forest, the leaf mold emerging from the snow and the faint green smell of new life emerging, and to listen to the silence, sweetly emphasized if wind whispered in the treetops. Sometimes I found the fragile pink and lavender flowers of wild arbutus blooming in the snow and picked sprigs for my mother.

Children of a clan roamed their areas of forest emptying the sap from each small *mokahk* (Chippewa for "dish") into a larger one they carried back to the wigwam. The squaws dumped the sweet sap, thin as water, into huge blackened copper kettles, *ak-ik* in Chippewa, and probably an early acquisition from the Hudson's Bay Company in Canada. The kettles hung from chains over a fire of long hardwood logs, hardwood rather than pine, to keep the fire slow and almost smokeless. The squaws knew, but I never learned, just when to empty the boiled-down sap onto a yard-long wooden platter where the syrup cooled and solidified. When it was hard and cold they scraped it with wooden paddles into granules of sugar.

Each time my father took me to visit the sugar camps, the Indians, all old friends, hospitably invited us to lunch with them. But lunch was fish stew which always proclaimed that the Chippewas could take salt or leave it alone. Although the squaws put bits of salt pork into the stews, they did not bother with salt, if they had it, and to me the food on my tin plate tasted sickeningly as though it had been cooked with sugar. Hunger drove

14

me to swallow, but I longed for a salted peanut from our little sack in the buckboard.

My father always bought a thirty-pound *mokahk* of maple sugar from our hosts before we unstaked Mike and Dan and headed homeward. But he would not make a visit to the clan to collect the *siz-ah-bah-quit* (sugar) in its clean new *mokahk* with a peaked roof sewn over it, until the sugarbush season was finished and the lake was again liquid. That would be when the first robins returned north to spend the summer with us.

We early Minnesotans had freedoms that are now almost extinct. Freedom from public music, radio and television, from air and water pollution, from noise. Of course we did not appreciate them. We were entranced by each new mechanical device. I remember the awe with which I heard my father announce at our house in Bemidji that he would telephone a man in Cass Lake, about eighteen miles eastward. Alice and Emma, our maids in the kitchen, were warned to keep silent, as was I. The switchboard operator downtown made the connection, my father yelled into the mouthpiece at the top of his baritone voice, and the whole household quivered at his discovery that he could hear the yelling from the other end of the line.

Unabashed, we had heroes. My father, nearly six feet tall, slim, wiry, quick of movement and of blue eye, was top man on my hero hill. Lesser heroes adorned its slopes. When I was five, I fell in love with red-headed Jack MacGregor who lived across the street with five other children, all more disciplined than I. Like a pullet finding corn I proclaimed my new attachment so vigorously around the neighborhood that Jack retreated blushing into his family's barn for a day or two. His mother saved him by banishing me from her yard because, she said, I yelled louder than all her six children together when we played pom-pom-pullaway on her lawn. With only one child, my mother was more lenient than Mrs. MacGregor. A proper Victorian lady who arranged her hair and adjusted her hat upon it with hatpins before she dressed herself for her weekly round of "calling" at other houses and leaving her engraved calling cards, my mother was dedicated to the practice

15

of stiff-starched self-discipline in children as well as adults. But her sweetest memories of her young womanhood concerned the couple of years she stayed with family friends in Lansing, Michigan's capital city, worked in the office of a state senator—"very advanced for those days"—and, always chaperoned by her elder brother, waltzed at the city's fancy balls.

She waltzed alone, her cheeks pink, in our Bemidji sitting room whenever she could entice my father to pedal Strauss on our player piano, or with me pedaling when my legs grew long enough. She allowed me to play marbles on our dining room carpet in the wintertime, and if she were not expecting visitors, she let me build imaginary houses for my paper dolls in the sitting room, using as foundations the oblong boxes of the piano's music rolls. From her discarded copies of the *Ladies' Home Journal* I cut out whole casts of characters from babies up through school-children and flappers to grandparents. With my imaginary friend, Margaret, I played out afternoon-long matinees, some domestic contretemps the recurring theme, I plunging people into horrifying and evil ways and Margaret gradually restoring them to decency and happy endings, the series often continuing with the same cast for days until we grew tired of those people and created new families.

For a year or two Margaret lived with us, my constant companion and my opposite. Unlike my curly, tangly yellow hair, hers was smooth, straight and black. She was obedient and polite and seldom screamed, as I did. She was bright and sweet and the same size as I, which was fortunate because she and I decided each day what she would wear of my clothes before my mother and I chose my day's dress, and Margaret and I together agreed what we would eat and what games we would play. As one of my mother's women visitors was about to seat herself in our living room, I suddenly yelled at her, "You're sitting on Margaret!" I remember nearly provoking a faint.

Although Margaret must have caused my mother vexation sometimes, or worry, I do not remember her ever attempting to extirpate my friend. As I went to school and made friends with real children, Margaret

16

gradually disappeared. She never made it to school, but for some time I felt disloyal at abandoning her.

One bitter winter day the year I was in first grade, my father telephoned to say that Tom Smart, the Bemidji drayman and iceman and later the mayor, was going to deliver a dog he had bought for me. That day my mother was entertaining the North End Sewing Society. The dog arrived, a patterned gold and white Newfoundland weighing a hundred and fifty pounds. My mother weighed ninety-five pounds, but she managed to tug the dog to a place near our front door where she chained it to a post. When he growled and menaced her sewing society guests, she maneuvered him onto our back porch, which was screened from floor to ceiling. There he remained quietly until he saw a cat on our fence and rushed straight through the screening after it. Mother leapt away from her guests and into the icy backyard where she grabbed the dog's chain and was consequently dragged all over the yard before some of the other ladies went out and helped her subdue him. Like a dozen other dogs in Bemidji he was baptized Rex and gradually turned my mother's disapproval into affection, one reason being that he escorted me to school in the frosty mornings and waited all morning in the schoolyard to take me home for lunch. We children welcomed him, playing tag in our front yard, but most grownups declined the fun. Rex's idea of a good game was to knock everybody down, one after another, licking the faces on the grass.

When I was six or seven, with my leg muscles more or less following orders, my mother bought me a pair of ice skates and with her own skates, her mink hat and muff, took me the block and a bit down to frozen Lake Bemidji and, whirling miraculously backward as well as forward, gave me beginner's classes in the joy of skating.

Ice skates became as much an appurtenance of life for Bemidji children as winter was, and each autumn we petitioned our respective Powers that the first hard freeze of autumn would arrive on a night of no wind. In that circumstance Lake Bemidji would freeze smoothly and, with further luck, we would have weeks

17

of skating after school before snow covered the ice too thickly for good going. Skimming along looking for lake trout and bass beneath the ice, we used to head up past the private boathouses of the town, past Diamond Point, where we swam in summer, and along the seven miles to the top of the lake with its boarded-up summer cottages, some of us singing, "When Francis dances with me, Holy Gee"—a swingy song for skating. On the return flight we would be cheered in the dusk by the glow of little fires the boys built along the beach in front of the town.

One of Bemidji's two red sawmills leaned out to the lake at its southeast corner, and during several autumns it became imperative among a dozen of us to be the first to get across the lake to scratch our initials and the year on one sawmill's door which hung out over the ice. The infant Mississippi River runs through the lake and with its ice coating slower to form, and thinner, it provided us a most satisfactory hazard. As our crowd approached the river they would appoint me, being the smallest, to make a running dash across the river ice. If I made it, they probably could. There came the year when I fell in, of course, and got pulled out onto the thicker ice of the lake, but had to ask friends around a shore fire to help me undo the frozen laces of my skating boots.

Those skating years were also the years when I celebrated my birthday on April 5 by making the first swim of the season in Lake Bemidji. Usually the winter's ice had retreated only a yard or two from the beach at Diamond Point, but there was enough open water for swimming fifteen or twenty strokes and whoever accompanied me came out of the water pink and giggling.

Up to the late teens of our century we lived in a world that was then remote and now has vanished at the insistence of lumbermen, plowmen and road-builders. Swamps have been drained, farmhouses painted and gas stations planted everywhere in northern Minnesota. But in my childhood it was a world of forest, water-laced, where growing up was almost as untrammeled for children as for the birch trees that lumberjacks ignored. It was my father, more than anyone, who helped me to recognize and appreciate my personal freedoms.

I remember him paddling, slim and straight, in the stern of a canvas canoe. I had early learned how to paddle an Indian canoe of birch-bark, more fragile and fickle than canvas, so that, aged twelve, I could be expected to work my way as bow-paddle when he invited me to go with him on a five-day trip, sliding down rivers through our wilderness.

Our trip had a business purpose. My father's lumber company had been losing too much pulpwood, he judged, between the cutting camps and the mill. His intention was to discover for himself whether the missing logs had been stranded by careless driving on their journey down the Bowstring River, or had, by some connivance, been diverted to other ownership.

The day was overcast and greenish-gray when we slid our canoe into Round Lake River, tucked in our food, axe, tea-pail and blankets and headed downstream. Since this was a slow river, I could sit on the small cane seat, forward, to paddle, rather than kneel as I had been taught to do in swift water or a choppy lake. But when we emerged into Squaw Lake, my altitude on the seat availed me nothing and even my father could see no open water, for we were hedged in and dominated by the tall thin grasses of wild rice which grew like a giant's lawn from shore to shore. Now it was June and the rice grains had not filled. But in the fall this lake would give a wondrous harvest to the Indian women who would come, paddling with difficulty as we were, to knock the small beige- and lavender-streaked grains into their canoes.

While we worked our way toward an opening he saw in the trees of the shoreline, my father told me how the squaws went to the lakes before the rice had ripened, to tie it in bunches, to protect it from the autumn flights of southbound ducks.

Then my father found that the opening we approached could not be the outlet he was seeking. He consulted his map, hummed a wandering little tune which signaled to me that he was pondering. "We've made a mistake," he said. "We've got to go back."

I was beginning to yearn for a recess from paddling,

my arms and shoulders being unaccustomed to it so early in the year, and aching. My book for that journey was *As You Like It,* and I longed to lie on my tired back and burrow into it. But we had hours to travel before we could pitch camp before dark.

"It would be wonderful to see a rice harvest," I said. "Maybe we could come back here."

"We might go over to Bena. I always get our rice from a woman who lives near Winnibigoshish Dam. She makes the cleanest rice."

"How do you tell the rice is clean, Papa?"

"By smelling. Ordinary rice smells of fish or animal blood, or kinnikinnick, because the canoes or the blankets have not been washed."

We found our way out of Squaw Lake into the Bowstring River and the long summer twilight was beginning to sift down before my father found a place he liked for our night's camp. A grassy little park lifted out of the river's bank there, spreading inshore until it was stopped by the fallen needles of fir and balsam trees and the thick shade of birch trees and sumac and hazel bushes. We quickly gathered enough dry twigs and branches to get a little Indian fire burning brightly enough to light our unloading of the canoe. My father chopped a few lower branches off some of the balsams and together we stripped the smaller panicles from their ribs and spread them over the grass and leaves between the birch trees. They were our sweet-smelling springs and mattress, and after the first day of paddling I resisted falling onto them only because of the enticing fragrance which was drifting up from our frying pan. No two aromas complement each other better than those of freshly crushed balsam and of frying bacon, I thought that evening.

In our spicy bed we rolled up like cigars in our blankets and I hunched close to my father, for love, for his warmth, and to revel in the familiar, comforting smells of him. Noting them all, I floated toward sleep. Then, as had happened before and I had forgotten, came a struggle of cadences to unsettle me. Going to sleep my father breathed long and slowly, a relaxed man, and I tried to stretch out my breathing to match his tempo. Then I lay there attentive to my breathing,

20

breathing in, holding the air in my lungs, and slowly exhaling as my father was doing. I began to cheat, gulping small swigs of air between the long ones. I tried hurrying, to fit two of my breaths to one of his. I could find no way either of synchronizing my breathing with my father's or of ignoring the jagged rhythms. I shifted away a few inches, and immediately the night was busy with sounds I had not noticed before. Twigs snapped, two footfalls touched the soft earth, a branch flapped quite near us.

"Papa, are there bears here?"

"Go to sleep, dear. Nothing will harm us."

"There are so many noises."

"They've come to see our fire." And my father settled his shoulders with finality.

I knew that bears, timber wolves, foxes, coyotes and lynx with their eerie, terrifying screams lived in most parts of the country, and that my father had slept hundreds of nights like this, with no weapon against animals. He had evaded answering my questions about bears. Maybe it was that, like worrying, against which Ole Helgerson had counseled me years before, being frightened was a waste of time.

"Let us go softly," my father said in the morning when we were on the river again. "We may see something." I dipped my paddle sharply to minimize splashing, and held it low on the forward swing to soften the sounds of its dripping.

Where a small stream joined the Bowstring we found a patch of reeds and cattails and a fine upstanding muskrat house with mud from the bank slapped solidly over its reed supports. We watched it as long as the river allowed without catching sight of any inhabitants.

"What are they doing now, this time of year?" I whispered.

"They're busy raising a family. Feeding them and teaching them how to find food, and to protect themselves."

"Feeding those poor children raw fish?"

"No, at first their mother gives the babies milk. You know about mammals," my father said softly. "Then, by and by, they eat the roots of lily pads,

21

and wild rice that has fallen to the bottom of the river. They're gluttons for rice."

"I hope we see some otters. They're wonderful, my books say. Or some beavers. Would they be in this river?"

"Maybe, Dearidoo, maybe."

As we turned a bend, we came sharp upon a doe and her fawn as they stood in the shallow water, drinking. Both they and we were too surprised to move as the current carried us smoothly and silently toward them. It took us so close that I felt I could reach out and touch them, and hesitated, feeling the gesture would be presumptuous. Across the closing gap of water the doe and I looked straight into each other's eyes, her great eyes questioning, deep blue-black in the pupils, polite and interested. Then we were passing them. The mother caught our scent and soundlessly signaled to her fawn. They turned and moved without haste up the low bank and into the forest, the doe turning her head to watch us. I looked back too, saw their slim brown shanks disappear in the shadows and watched the place until the river carried us around another bend. Even though my father had forewarned me, I was unprepared for the towering excitement of so close a meeting with a creature so beautiful, and then so quickly snatched away.

"Did you ever see anything so beautiful, Papa? And did you smell them? They smelled awfully strong to me. They smelled more like rabbits than like horses. And she didn't look frightened."

"You see now, Mary, why I do not hunt them."

I remembered my father's refusal to go deer hunting with friends. I also remembered slowly, the flavor coming strong and salty into my mouth, the taste of roasted venison, and it was like a mouthful of pebbles that had to be swallowed.

"What have we done? We've eaten them." There on the happy river I could not admit such treachery, and with female guile found a whipping boy for my conscience. "How could we? You brought the meat home. How could you?"

"Yes, I like it very much. When an Indian offers me some, I always take it."

"Gee, Papa, I am ashamed."

This was the kind of growing-up problem that my father so often helped me resolve. Now that he was a protagonist in the tangle, it seemed more grievous. From the blue canopy above us the sun was giving a joyous sheen to the traveling river and to every leaf and blade along its bank. It cheered me only a little.

A mile or two later my father said, "You must not feel too bad that you have eaten deer meat. You hadn't made their acquaintance, you know."

"But, Papa, you had."

"Yes."

"I don't know, Papa. I don't know at all." I was feeling lonely.

"You will later."

That night in a new balsam bed I kept my ears alert for the sound of a deer moving and stayed awake to look again and again to the rim of our firelight. I hoped to find a pair of bright eyes there and to apologize.

By the next afternoon our river was entering country that had been cut over by lumbermen, spoiled country compared to that we had left. We had more sky but the forests were thin and empty of their shadows and mystery. Our paddling muscles moved smoothly and comfortably, but it saddened me to be approaching civilization so soon again. "Let's turn around and go back. Let's just live on the river and in the forest," I said. There was still a sore place inside me from our perfidy to the deer, but I had a store of less painful ideas needing to be discussed. Some had come from *As You Like It.* "My age is as a lusty winter, frosty, but kindly," I had read, and "his big manly voice, turning again toward childish treble." I hadn't known any old man with a childish voice.

"You haven't changed at all since I first knew you, Papa," I said. "Have you changed?"

"You have."

"But I don't want to grow up."

"You only do it a little bit each day. The world is full of good things to learn."

"Did you want to grow up, when you were little, Papa?"

23

"Partly, so that I could work and buy presents for my mother."

Downriver there was a big gap in the right-bank trees, the first clearing we saw. Some outpost of civilization, and I still had the distressing problem of the deer needing to be resolved.

"I wish we could turn around and go back," I said. "Even against the current."

"Wait. We have the best part of the river ahead of us."

In the clearing the profile of a cabin roof was just visible above the grasses of the bank where we pulled ashore. This was the fellow, my father said, who could tell us what chances we had of running Dead Man Rapids which were just ahead of us. If the water was too low, we should have to portage a couple of miles around the rapids, a ponderous task. My father went to talk to the homesteader and the man returned to the riverbank with him and looked me over doubtfully.

"Water's not too low," he said, "but it's mighty fast. You got plenty boulders. A couple of fellows, river men, turned over, must be about three weeks ago."

"What do you say, Mary?" my father asked, flattering me.

I knew what he wished me to say and I said it. If grownup men stopped to consider the peril of the rapids, the possible broken bones, or cracked skulls, I thought, how satisfying it would be for us to get through.

"Keep to midstream," the homesteader advised as we shoved off.

As we turned into the current again we could feel its pace quickening. Ahead of the clearing the forest rose like the forest of our first two days but thicker and higher-walled on each bank. The water which had borne us amiably and silently for fifty miles or more now began hurrying forward, folding and sliding in deepening eddies, its voice rising to a murmur and then quickly to a rumble. My father stretched his back high in the stern of the canoe to pick a course among the rocks which we already saw were scattered recklessly everywhere between the banks, many of them

24

looming above the surface. The more dangerous ones, I knew, were those only slightly submerged.

I was kneeling in the bow to give my paddle leverage and speed for fending us off rocks on either side, when we reached the first big boulders. Around their sides the river roared, creaming and frothing white and splashing onto us. Then we were sliding among them, dropping as fast, I thought, as a toboggan on an icy hill. We rushed close around the edge of one big stone and my straining eyes failed to see another one just below the surface and straight in our course. We brushed its top and it held us. I saw the heavy flow of water pushing almost to the top of our gunwales.

"Pull deep," my father shouted and we pulled hard to starboard and slipped off the rock. I did not take time to turn around to see if the rock had opened a hole in our canoe. If it had, I would know soon enough.

We had two miles more of foaming, runaway water to cover, with the river taking undisputed charge of our speed and my father seeking the deeper channels second by second before we were in them. Working against the nearest dangers I swung my paddle breathlessly, pushing us off rocks on one side then on the other of our fragile bow. In a short, straight, briefly uncluttered stretch, I looked up from the racing water and was frightened by the drop in our horizon.

From its stony banks to the long, dark line of treetops against the sky, our world slanted downward like an enormous ramp. My back was wet with splashings and once I noticed that my arms were growing tired and slow. But the river hurled us forward, bouncing us into the swiftest narrow channels between the boulders until ahead we saw, happily, a reach of smooth, dark, untroubled water. When we arrived there my father settled into his seat and lighted his pipe. "Take a rest," he said. "You did well."

From inside my tiredness I saw that the shadows of late afternoon were beginning to seep from the forest out over our river which was moving serenely and softly again, and we could hear birds and frogs starting their evening songs.

"You never paddled such a long and steep rapids before," my father said. "Didn't you like it?"

25

"It was wonderful. Isn't it wonderful to win?" The fast work had brought hunger rising in me, and with it, my problem. "And now, Papa, could you tell me, if you once decided not to hunt deer, why did you eat it?" I didn't realize I was being a nag.

"It was simple hunger, once or twice. But it's really not as easy as that. It's partly a thing called inertia. You must look that up in your dictionary. Partly something else. Call it expediency, or call it compromise. You are too young to understand these words or the ideas they stand for."

My father spoke about new concepts I would learn some day and how they would be easier for me to accept and practice after my conscience had grown older and weaker. (I understood something of my conscience. It was a part of me which was forever causing trouble, disappointing my mother who expected from it much more vigor and devotion to duty than she found.)

"I'm sorry, Papa. But I don't see yet what my conscience—or 'compromise'—has to do with eating those beautiful deer. It would be like eating one of my kittens. If it's wrong now, won't it be just as wrong when I'm older and have learned all those new ideas?"

"Perhaps. But then you may not *think* it's so wrong." There was Shakespeare again. "There is nothing either good or bad, but thinking makes it so."

"You mean that people don't grow better as they grow up, that they are just as naughty just as often?" This was dangerous territory. In northern Minnesota good children did not question aloud the precepts of their elders.

"I'll tell you a secret," my father said. "In many ways you don't grow better as you grow up. Or know better. But you keep that to yourself."

It was a lightning flash of revelation. How could an adult, even my father, smash the old rule so easily? The superiority of grownups had been an absolute, undisputed boundary of my thinking. If adults could be doubted with impunity, who were the new authorities?

Now the forest was a dark gray wall on both sides of us, with the strip of sky above and the moving silver of the river giving us the only light. I wished again we could stay there on the shining river, our world simple and sufficient unto itself and us. But I noticed that my ache about the deer had receded a little. It seemed a lifetime since we had started paddling through the wild rice.

When I was almost asleep that night a new question drifted into my head. Had my father belittled grown-ups, I wondered, in order to help me become one?

Conscience with its despotic demands and disciplines continued causing me trouble. I was the hymn-player on the piano in our small Sunday school, and one morning I arrived earlier than usual to practice a hymn I didn't know. Opening the door, I was stopped and staggered by the violence of two voices in argument, my mother's and that of another Sunday school teacher. The dispute was about each lady's status in the school, or who was boss, or some such detail, too minor, it seemed to me, to bring out the vehemence I was hearing. When they saw me, the pair lowered their voices, those two proper small-town matrons who were about to interpret for us children the gentle words of God and Mary Baker Eddy: "Love thy neighbor."

Sunday school went off as usual with the young voices earnestly following the ancient music and the rest of the program falling into place. When my mother reached home after church services, I told her that I was resigning from Sunday school and would no longer attend or play the hymns. I was ungrateful and cruel, she said. I was callously breaking her heart, she said that day and other days. But I never went to Sunday school again.

Another time it was I who suffered from the demands of conscience: Our family fortunes declined while I was in high school. We sold our big comfortable white clapboard house, with its hot air furnace which consumed ten tons of coal each winter. The local teachers college bought it and made it the residence of the college president, Mr. Deputy. We moved to an apartment downtown.

To Bemidji youngsters, graduation from high school was a major event, every detail of ceremony, paraphernalia and attendant customs heavy with importance. Girls became young ladies and we tried to speak grammatically. The senior class gave a dinner at the town's best hotel, the Markham, where few families of the town ever sat at table except on a rare Sunday noon. The dinner was one of the social events of the year and brought out, in debut, a class-wide assortment of boys' new suits and girls' new dresses.

We could not afford that year to buy me a new dress for the class dinner, my mother told me. But we could afford the cloth for one, and weeks early she started work on a length of blue-and-white dotted swiss. The style she chose was sweet-girl-graduate, with a high, demure neckline and ruffles of lace edging the collar. After vowing secrecy about them, I had seen the dinner dresses of some of my friends, their choices being gay, jazzy confections of chiffon with satin bows and sashes, store-bought.

When my mother brought out my dress for me to try on, gently pleased with her fine stitches and with the dress's neat fit and ingenue style, I admired it and thanked her and then ran the couple of blocks to the lake shore to sob away my chagrin. I wished I could burn the dress and attend the class dinner in my gym suit, better for me than the dress's dainty affectations. "As glamorous as a pincushion," I blubbered to myself. "I *can't* wear it."

"Yes, you can, and will," my conscience ordered.

My sense of humor having taken flight, I went to the dinner a bundle of self-pity in the sweet, lovingly made dress, but in half an hour forgot my sorrows.

My mother happily accepted compliments about her work from her friends. "So appropriate," they said. "So sweet." The dress was one of her hundreds of generous gifts to me, too many of them not in their time sufficiently appreciated.

Among our conventions was that of parents giving a present to their graduating children, also of attending the graduation exercises in our high school auditorium. I had written my father who was out of town on business. Clifford's father was giving him a Ford roadster, imagine. Winston's father was taking him on a holiday way out to San Francisco.

My father telephoned to say that he hoped to get back to Bemidji for the night of the festivities but not early enough to attend them. My mother decided that she could not attend such a function unescorted.

After the emotions of the ceremonies we teenagers strolled to town, a dozen blocks in the soft evening, to calm down, then took our time over sodas at our favorite ice-cream parlor. My parents had retired for the night when I got home and when I knocked on their bedroom door my father's voice answered warmly with congratulations and questions about that night's big event in my life. When I had finished describing it through the slightly opened door, I summoned up bravado and asked if he had brought me something.

"Yes, yes, Dearidoo. It's in my bag. You'll find it." His voice suddenly sounded tired. I found his black valise in the dining room and searched through it. There were papers and letters. There was the round leather case which held my father's stiff shirt collars and collar buttons, some shirts and socks. There was nothing wrapped as a present, nothing for the use of a girl.

"Look again. You'll find it. It's round and red," my father said.

Hunting through the valise a second time I came upon my graduation present, round and red as my father had said. An apple.

2

An Overpraised Season

Youth is like spring, an over-praised season.

—Samuel Butler
The Way of All Flesh

SOMETIMES I WONDER if writers realize the far-reaching influences of their work. With his poem "Chicago," Carl Sandburg changed the ambiance of my youth. Since my childhood, when the editor of the Bemidji *Pioneer Press* and his wife came to our house for dinner, I had known that I would like to work on a newspaper. While I devoted a year to higher algebra, calculus and history at our local state teachers college, still run by President Deputy who was still living in our old house, I hunted for reasons which would be satisfactory to my parents for establishing myself in Chicago. Without hearing the din of its streetcars and police whistles and feeling the heat of its inherent combat, my life would be zero, I felt.

Northwestern University in Evanston, just north of Sandburg's city, included a school of journalism, and I persuaded my parents to send me there, even though its high tuition rates would require me to earn part of my expenses.

Along with the wonderful elms of the school's lakeside campus, Professor Melville Herskovits, the anthropologist, captivated me. He was a student of primitive economies and the folkways of Negroes in West Africa and a number of countries of the Americas, and the scholarship he poured out about them was an irresistible force. In his abrupt, uncompromising manner he ordered exercises for our pulpous brains, exhorting application of the eye to the page, urging us to learn the ways of learning. He made crucial openings in my ignorance of our planet and its life.

It was my misfortune to encounter no other teachers comparable to Professor Herskovits, and only a few ideas I thought worth attention. One sallow-faced instructor in English composition declared his life's project was the establishment of a colony of true socialists on the shores of Lake Balkhash in middle-southern Russia. How far he made it from Evanston to Lake Balkhash, or if disciples joined him, I never learned.

My roommate in the threadbare dormitory in Evanston was a go-getting girl named Helen Vind, also from Minnesota, and in her junior and my sophomore year her father died. Helen went home briefly for the funeral and came back with her normal exuberance much subdued. Until then none of my friends' fathers had died, and Helen's misfortune sent me into a slough of doubts and fears. I was, I realized, entirely unprepared and defenseless against such disaster. I took inventory of my resources and concluded that no friends my age or older could provide the wisdom my father gave me or the loyalty of his support, that nobody could take his place.

Seeking a future solace I began to go into Chicago Saturday afternoons to look at the pictures in the Art Institute. The collections of those days were nothing like so splendid as they are now, and until, later, Virginia Woolf helped in *A Room of One's Own*, nobody had taught me how to look at pictures. But there were guidebooks, and on the walls were some good Italian and Flemish Renaissance paintings, some exhilarating Monet, Manet, Matisse, Cézanne, and the strong water-colors of Winslow Homer. I began to find the paintings instructive and also comforting, since they were not mortal. My father lived another quarter century.

But Northwestern with its snobbery and pretensions did not seem the best school for me, and I hated my shoddy dormitory with its smells and sounds and petty cliques of females, even though many of them were my friends.

During the summer after our sophomore year I took a crash course which might have been called Modern Living. One of my classmates, a tall blond soft-voiced girl from the East, Helen Silverberg, planned to drive her Dodge coupe back home for the summer vacation and wanted a companion. My treasury contained only a bit more than twenty-five dollars. I wired my father explaining and suggesting supplementary funds. My father replied, "You have enough to get you there. Earn enough to get back. Love. Dad." I was frightened and proud that my parents trusted me to an adventure so far away from them. The summer turned out to be more educational, as well as entertaining, than I had anticipated.

In Boston I found the office of the YWCA, where they said there was a job as "hostess" at the St. Clair tearoom in Federal Street. Did I have any restaurant experience? "Yes, indeed," I lied, having done a couple of weeks' stint as a soda-jerk at Bemidji's best summer hotel. Inside the tea-room, then in the middle of

31

Boston's financial district and patronized by stock salesmen, I found the room where waitresses changed into their uniforms. "I'm the new hostess," said I to a couple of the girls. "What am I supposed to do, and what is a 'station'?" They took me in tow, and for the rest of the summer I hostessed.

For a cheap but decent room the YWCA woman sent me down to the Italian district where an amiable landlady led me up five or six flights of stairs to a neat nest under the eaves. It had a window, a cot, a table with lamp, a clothes closet, a door. I could stand erect in it beside the bed, and there were a couple of clean towels. Then the landlady led me downstairs to the bathroom, also clean, and containing a tub such as I had never seen before. It was made of wooden planks, bent upward fore and aft as a dinghy is, its white paint twenty coats thick.

I would have to work for a week before I was paid anything, and, with a week's rent paid in advance, my financial resources demanded stringent budgeting. The tearoom provided lunch, but it closed before dinnertime. There was no room in my week's budget for dinner. I decided to walk to and from work, about a couple of miles, and made up my week's supper menu. From a little shop near my rooming house I could buy half a cantaloupe and a nickel Hershey bar. Supper totaled fifteen cents. By the time I got away from the tearoom, the museums were closed, but I could detour on my way home into the Common and the Gardens, watch the summer sky fade to turquoise and then silver, and listen to the strange speech of the people I passed. Awaiting me beneath the lamp in my slanted room were three or four books I had brought with me, one being a volume of Sandburg's *Abraham Lincoln, The Prairie Years*. It was a week of unbureaucratic health, education and welfare.

I was only beginning to soften with the luxury of riding a streetcar to and from work and sup on spaghetti and meatballs when one of our waitresses took me out of our traffic stream backstage in the tearoom and invited me to dine with her and her two brothers in the apartment they shared in Commonwealth Avenue on the outskirts of town. My waitress friend and her brothers, younger than she, were the children of missionaries who were in Africa. They had sent these children back to the United States to be educated, and all three were working that summer to earn pin money before they started school in the fall. Their apartment, with a piano in the entrance foyer, was simply furnished, airy and spacious. My friend's bedroom was big enough to allow a cot to be added to its furnishings. I would pay that kind and hospitable girl whatever modest sum I was paying for my aerie in Boston's Little Italy and my share of the food. I moved in.

The five o'clock or five-thirty trollies bumping out Commonwealth Avenue were invariably crowded, and I usually hung onto a center pole, reading a tabloid evening newspaper. On several occasions a tall blond man with smiling blue eyes and a ferocious mustache also stood and hung onto the pole. There came the afternoon which was an anniversary of the convictions or electrocutions of Sacco and Vanzetti, and my newspaper denounced the action in boldface type. I muttered indignations and my mustached fellow passenger joined me. When I disembarked at my stop, he got off too, and we walked chatting to my apartment house. His name was Sebastian Littauer, he said, and he worked at M.I.T. in mathematics. (He has been the mathematics genius of Columbia for many years, solving problems of volume and incidence that bewilder me.)

One evening on the streetcar Sebby invited me to the nearby apartment of some of his Russian friends for tea, served in tall glasses, conversation and singing, all of which were new to me and beguiling. The Russian songs reminded me of winds sighing in deep shadowed caves, the tunes somehow somber, the words mysterious, as, many years later, Basque songs rang in my ears. We saw each other occasionally until I returned to school in Evanston, and ever since then a tenuous, gentle communication sometimes reopens— a postcard, a letter, a telephone call and, lately, evenings at the opera—one of the small friendships which provide grace notes to the decades.

Some weekends friends motored me to Cape Cod, and a Midwesterner learned to eat lobster and steamed clams. Other weekends we scorched ourselves on beaches and swam in the Atlantic, which seemed to me colder than the spring-fed lakes of northern Minnesota. By the summer's end I had gained a few drops of understanding of Boston and New England and its local history, that Faneuil Hall had good acoustics and frequently stimulating speakers, that—I was still young enough to make big, slovenly generalizations—New Englanders were different from Midwesterners in speech and mannerisms, but similar to us in their hopes, projects, prejudices and poetry. I had saved enough money to buy my ticket back to Chicago on the New York Central's Twentieth Century Limited, then the best train, and a pair of I. Miller lizard-skin shoes—$22. I also had a new perspective on Northwestern University.

In less than two years I chose to forfeit the security of a liberal arts degree in order to work as editor of a magazine, *The American Florist,* a puny little thing intended to spread news of the trade among Chicago's retail florists. It was a job and paycheck in a wasteland of unemployment and breadlines. When the publishers of the magazine declined to pay me what I thought I was earning, working ten-hour days and six-day weeks, I quit and got a job in a newspapering sweatshop on Chicago's North Side, an outfit that published five different weekly neighborhood newspapers which were delivered free on each area's doorsteps. Their revenue came from local advertising, and the staff, all beginners like me, were paid beginner's wages. It was nearer to being "on a newspaper" than the florist magazine had been.

(Ever since my infatuation with Jack MacGregor at the age of five I had been succumbing to fevers of joy about the glories of one or another boy in our crowd, some of the seizures lasting a couple of years. In high school it was Dick Simons, captain of our football team. At Northwestern it was Lawrence Miller Cook, a drama student from Ohio whose poetic eyes, superior tennis serve and gentle manner fired in me a desire almost painful. When his parents invited me to drive down for a weekend with them, we stopped on the way and were married by a justice of the

34

peace in his sitting room. Gradually we noticed that we had made an innocent mistake—the sort young people seldom make these days. Our separate projects and purposes differed too widely for accommodation, and a check from Larry's father helped to put our problems in focus. Larry spent his present on a sports jacket, some books he needed and a bottle of sherry for mutual celebration. A few weeks later it occurred to me that he might have invested fifty cents of his present in a flower for me. Without memorable hard feelings we eventually parted formally.)

When Colonel Frank Knox bought the Chicago *Daily News,* he installed Miss Leola Allard, an energetic Hearst reporter, as women's editor, and she agreed to give me a chance on her staff as assistant in the society department. I wanted to be a real reporter, covering City Hall and the courts and politics rather than extolling the charms of women's hats or tiaras. But Miss Allard's offer gave me a chance on the paper of the distinguished Henry Justin Smith and Lloyd Lewis, who together had written my cherished book *Chicago.* It was the paper on which John Gunther started his career, for which J. Vincent Sheean had worked and Bill Stoneman and Ben Hecht and Charles MacArthur —those two, I heard, concocting parts of *The Front Page* in the grimy little bar across Madison Street from the office, the oasis to which much of the City Room gravitated after work.

Mr. Smith and Mr. Lewis were still contributing their abundant talents to the *Daily News* when I got there, and so was Robert Casey, amateur anthropologist, raconteur and prolific manipulator of words, whose book *Easter Island* I had devoured as a puppy absorbs a biscuit. Howard Vincent O'Brien was writing his gay and compassionate column for the editorial page. Carl Sandburg used to come in from the country once a week bringing a verse or paragraphs of aphorisms to Hal O'Flaherty, the debonair captain of our team. Sometimes Mr. Sandburg came into our female retreat to sit on a desk and josh with us, and sometimes he invited me, whom he named "Minnesota," to stop in at his hotel for a drink and a bit of sing-song on the way home. In the second-class hotel room he would

35

have a bottle of whiskey open and be sitting and strumming his guitar in the room's only armchair, the rest of us dangling from the sides or end of the bed. Those sessions were a happy jumble of song and chat, and it was only hunger which pulled me away from them.

Our noisy, lively troupe on the editorial floor of the *Daily News* simmered down on a bleak December day and gathered around somebody's radio to hear King Edward VIII, "I have found it impossible . . . without the help and support of the woman I love." Time after time when a fast-moving gangland-police story broke I would sneak into the City Room and beg Luke Hunt, the assistant city editor, to let me go and help gather information. Invariably he said, "You'd be in the way." One of my heroes of the City Room, Edwin Lahey, would have been there working quietly, almost invisibly, his story on whatever event emerging as the best in Chicago, which had five newspapers then, and I would *not* have been in the way.

Leola Allard was a taut-nerved, lonely woman, determined when she got her job as chief of the *Daily News* women's pages to make them the most beautiful and readable in the country. From the Hearst building across the Chicago River she lured away her former boss's two best women reporters, Adeline Fitzgerald and Sarah Brown. From Memphis she brought up a high-geared girl, Martha Sweeney. She planted us all together on the society page and then declared war, almost every morning dropping a bomb on one or another of us. Perhaps a couple of us had worked until 2 a.m. covering the opening of the opera or somebody's ball. When we got in half an hour late that morning, one of us would be summoned to Leola, her face lavender with wrath, the published story torn to pieces for its gaucheries or its unlikely observations or possibly its exuberance. She loathed the word "person" we knew, but we never knew what other words were banned until after we had used them.

It may have been Miss Allard's theory that a girl in tears, rebellion or despair would write a better story than a girl content. It may have been her conviction that a roomful of women suspicious and distrustful of one another would work harder and produce better

36

copy than would a group of friends. With imagination and guile, favoring first one of us and then another, taking one to lunch to deplore the work—or the clothes or the hairdos—of the others, she sowed doubts and mistrusts and produced the best women's pages of her time.

If she treated her employees as mercenaries hired out to fight and stepped impatiently on their supine and bleeding egos on her climb to success, Miss Allard also taught us how to work and something of how to write. Especially she taught us fortitude. In a five-year battle she wore down to a skeleton my boon companion, sloth. She also—despite her divisive tactics—forged among us four girls on the society page a chain of mutual esteem and affection which still exists, much like that of fellow soldiers who have survived a long and bitter siege.

One day in 1935, a pudgy, beguiling Frenchman had stopped in our office to chat. He was Jules Sauerwein, political writer for *Paris-Soir*, and he invited us all to visit him when next we got to Paris. None of us had been to Paris and M. Sauerwein's invitation was a challenge. Martha Sweeney and I agreed that whoever got to Paris first would receive on her return to Chicago a prize of ten dollars. The following spring I boarded a small Canadian Pacific boat of the duchess class in Montreal for a voyage to Belfast; Dublin where I traced ancestors; London and Paris.

Puppies let out of a house on a spring morning would frolic with no more delirium than I did exploring London for the first time, floating down Piccadilly, then to Trafalgar Square, up past the Law Courts and "Oranges and Lemons, the bells of St. Clements," to Fleet Street, lines from Shakespeare and Dr. Johnson bubbling in my head, Boswell and Andrew Marvell, Pepys and Samuel Butler and Charles Lamb. When I got back to my hotel near Bond Street, drunk on the sights and sounds of London, the desk clerk said, "Oh, no, Miss. The dining room has been closed for two hours. . . . I'm afraid there are no cafés in this part of London." In 1936 there were none. I had been deceived by the long twilight of London's 51 degrees north latitude. I drank three glasses of water and went to bed.

37

Jules Sauerwein was not in the Paris office of *Paris-Soir* when I went to call. He was in Berlin inquiring about the sinister occurrences in the streets and beer halls of Munich. The *Paris-Soir* staff had evaporated into the spring evening, but the small Paris bureau of the London *Daily Express* on the same floor was alight and busy and verified what I had heard of M. Sauerwein's whereabouts.

The pleasant young *Express* bureau chief was just finishing work for the day, he said. He was dining with some colleagues, and would I care to join them? Indeed, I would. Several of the four or five British journalists stationed in Paris had covered Nazi rallies in Austria, and at dinner they were glad to fill in details for me about Adolf Hitler and brown-shirt programs and practices, all of them menacing and more than I knew from the Chicago papers. It was a long, leisurely dinner with much wine, and after it we stopped in at one or two *caves* on the Left Bank and danced in the stale smoke to jiggy French versions of passé American jazz. To finish the evening they took me to Les Halles for onion soup, and when I lamented my imminent return to Chicago, the young man of the *Daily Express* said, "If you're so keen about the news in Europe, why don't you quit that paper in Chicago and stay on here?"

"My French isn't good enough yet."

"You could work in London. The London papers send their local chaps all over the continent, you know."

"But how could an American female squeeze into Fleet Street?"

"Nothing to it, my girl. Just call the Beaver in the morning. He's always looking for kicks."

"You mean Lord Beaverbrook?" I was awash in awe.

The young man gave me the telephone number of Lord Beaverbrook's house overlooking Green Park. After a few hours' sleep in the Grand Hotel in the rue Castiglione, I rang the number and Beaverbrook came to the telephone.

"Josephine, Josephine?" he asked.

"No. My name is Mary Welsh and I want to work for you on your newspaper." Beaverbrook had recently

38

met Josephine Patterson, the daughter of Joe Patterson of the New York *Daily News* and, like the rest of us, admired her. But now he felt imposed upon.

"Who?" he yowled in irritation. "I've no time to talk to job hunters."

"Oh, sir, I've got a good job on one of the best papers in America, the Chicago *Daily News*," I said, pouring honey into my vocal cords. "I'd just like to come and see you before I return home."

"But we've got an American on the *Express* already," said Beaverbrook grudgingly.

"I think I could get over there for tea and still catch my boat," said I. What could I lose, I thought.

"I'm a busy man," said the Beaver. But his voice had grown less scratchy. In those days not many girls flew from Paris to see him.

"Ah, too bad for you, sir. You don't know what you're missing." Lord Beaverbrook was amused. (He was not missing anything at all, of course. My clothes, coiffure and savoir-faire were all untutored Midwest.)

"All right. All right. I'll give you tea and fifteen minutes."

My ship was leaving Le Havre that noon and I had my ticket for the boat-train. But she was not sailing from Southampton until late evening. With my hangover in faithful attendance, I managed to get a seat on a two-motored Air France plane to London and reached Lord Beaverbrook's house, Stornoway, five minutes past tea time at four o'clock. Except for tip money, my exchequer was a vacuum.

Lord Beaverbrook allowed me some minutes in which to look over his round tea table loaded with goodies, and perhaps to repent my quixoticism. The butler poured me tea and I sipped. Since the onion soup twelve hours before I had had nothing but a quick cup of coffee and I was starving. But I could not risk having my mouth full when my host appeared.

Lord Beaverbrook came down his marble staircase, a benign host, and appeared amused by my account of the previous evening. But when I said that I wanted to be on hand in London "to cover the war" his pale blue eyes grew stony.

"There will be no war, mark you," said he.

39

"I hope you're right, sir," I said. I thought, the usual astigmatism of rich and powerful men when confronted with unwelcome prospects.

Despite this difference of opinion, he instructed his secretary to call Arthur Christiansen, his famous Fleet Street editor, and announce that an American girl was arriving to be interviewed for a job. The butler got me and my hangover and my hunger a taxi.

Christiansen in his office in the black-glass edifice of the *Express*, so inimical to its staid pseudo-Gothic or plainly Victorian neighbors in the street, was harassed, harried, impatient and irritable that he should have to receive this latest sample of the boss's whim.

"I've got one very good woman reporter. I've got an American. I couldn't possibly use you," he said, looking miserable.

I felt sorry for him.

"All right, all right. Please don't worry about it," I said. "I'll go quietly." He was not amused.

On the ship heading for New York I wrote thank-you notes to Lord Beaverbrook and his nervous editor. In Chicago Martha Sweeney gave me ten dollars and the atmosphere of Leola Allard's office seemed to have thickened in acerbity, like an overdone onion sauce. I had been away from camp too long. Nonetheless, Adeline Fitzgerald having got married and gone off to Tahiti, Miss Allard, in some disarray of reason, boosted me to the top of our small department, thereby undermining temporarily my friendships with all the other women under her tutelage.

Confidentially, and not for Miss Allard's information, I had a couple of chats with Hal O'Flaherty, our managing editor. "Let me work in the Paris office, let me work in the London Bureau," I begged. "You can cut my salary. There's going to be a war and I must be there. I should be there now, learning background."

Darling Mr. O'Flaherty smiled.

"Your French isn't good enough for Paris, Mary dear," he would say, "and anyhow Edgar Mowrer doesn't need anything more than clerical help. Stoneman is doing a great job in London. He doesn't need anybody."

In February or March Palm Springs telephoned me

40

at the office. Lord Beaverbrook's secretary-valet would like to know if I would join His Lordship for dinner in his suite that evening at the Blackstone Hotel. His Lordship was being flown up in his private plane.

I picked a path through fellow reporters outside the Beaver's door to find Himself telephoning London, Montreal, Quebec, New York. He declined an invitation from Colonel Bertie McCormick to lunch the next day, inviting me instead. On my way home I detoured to the office and wrote a squib about what he appeared to be doing in Chicago.

The Beaver allowed me to choose the place for our luncheon, and I picked a room at the Drake Hotel which overlooked a curve of beach and Lake Michigan, wild in the wind. Since I had to scurry quickly back to the office, Lord B. decided that we should dine in the same room that evening.

After an exhilarating dinner my host decided to walk me home to my flat on the top floor of a gray stone house in Elm Street, a couple of blocks from the Drake, and at the front door asked me to invite him up for a look at my habitat. I was thankful that a fire had been laid in my living room and quickly lit a match.

Lord Beaverbrook seemed to me to be restless in my sitting room, which was bright and comfortable but hardly elegant. He inspected my bookshelves without interest and a Matisse print and an old pewter plate above the fireplace without comment. He was busy telling me about British politics, how he had helped maneuver Bonar Law, another New Brunswick boy, into the place of Prime Minister, campaigning for Law in his three newspapers, and how Law, once in office, had abandoned Beaverbrook's cherished political tenet of Empire and Commonwealth first and foremost in all Downing Street decisions, especially trade. It had been perfidy. I didn't know until later that all this had happened fourteen years before, but I was impressed by the bitterness of Beaverbrook's grudge against the dead man who had betrayed him.

Hunting for happier talk, I asked him how and why he had acquired the *Daily Express* and what it meant to him. He skittered around an answer, announcing, "No other newspaper tells the British people about events in their country and the world as well as we do. It pleases me to do so." He was describing one of the then yellowest and most sensational daily newspapers published in the English language.

"What does it mean to me?" he repeated thoughtfully. "Some men in their pride of possession insist upon showing off a great horse of theirs—hunter or racer—drag you down to their stables. The *Daily Express* is my great horse." True, it had the largest circulation in Great Britain. Beaverbrook picked up his hat, and I accompanied him down the stairs to the front door and yelled at a passing cab.

"If you get short of editorial staff, I hope you'll ask someone to let me know," I said.

"Mmmmmmmm," said Lord Beaverbrook.

A week later he rang me at the office from the Waldorf Astoria Hotel in New York and cackled, "Come and see me. I will pay your fare."

"I'm pretty busy, sir," I said. "If it's to discuss a job on your newspaper, I'll go to New York and pay my own fare. If it isn't for that, I'm afraid I can't make it."

"Come along, girl. We'll discuss the job."

I didn't know that he had again succumbed to his chronic asthma and was perhaps bored. I trotted down the hall to our airplane editor and in a few minutes had a ticket assured to New York for Saturday and a return assured for Sunday afternoon. Free.

A late winter wind was roaring around the Waldorf Towers, biting their corners, when I was admitted to Lord Beaverbrook's big chilly suite, having left my suitcase in a small room on a court twenty or more floors below. I was inspecting with awe the sitting room's extravagance of flowers and baskets and urns of fruit when the valet showed me into the bedroom where the boss lay flat in bed, his thin little legs looking like sticks beneath the counterpane, his great head, round as a basketball, propped on a hill of pillows. We would dine together there in his bedroom, His Lordship announced. But first he had to see some people. They were shown in—the manager of Lord Beaverbrook's pulpwood factory in Canada and the chief of his newsprint factory, a nephew perhaps, a couple of others. They all presented themselves in the same manner, bright, smiling, deferential, sleekly barbered, each the glass of fashion, and stood at a respectful distance from the foot of the bed. Beaverbrook did not invite them to approach closer. Rising slightly from his pillows he launched at each young man in turn a barrage of questions which, if they had been shotgun shells or even marbles, would have demolished each target.

He wasted no time on such straightforward matters as last month's volumes and values. Rather it was the percentage of a chemical they were adding to the stewing pulpwood, or what percent improvement was another chemical achieving in the paper-making process, or precisely what increase in costs resulted from the new, higher Canadian freight rates. Beaverbrook knew the answers, I felt sure. He was simply drilling his troops, enjoying their floundering with figures, delighted by rapping out corrections of their errors, reading terror in the hint of perspiration on their foreheads, amused at their looks of relief upon being dismissed. An instructive hour for me. I had never before seen power exerted from a horizontal position or any other stance with such force and intelligence and irony—asthma or none.

When the last of the young men exited, shoulders inclining downward, Beaverbrook informed me that we would now dine and that afterward I would read something to him. "I'm going to travel up the Nile, I'm shipping my plane over, and I may employ you to come along as a reader."

He caught me as much off balance as he had caught his executives.

"But I'm not a reader, sir. I'm a reporter. I've had no speech training."

"We shall see."

"I can't afford to voyage up the Nile. I have to earn my living."

"You know nothing about the world. You should begin to learn."

"I'd rather learn first about London." I was thinking of two or three young men I knew in Chicago, without asthma. I also realized that Beaverbrook was

43

not accustomed to stolid, stubborn opposition from youngsters.

"You really had fun, upsetting those young men," I said, while we ate our dinners, he in his bed, I from a tray.

The Beaver's ice-blue eyes glinted with glee, but he said, "You must learn to observe and retain, but to restrain your tongue." He had no idea how much I was restraining my tongue. But good counsel, I thought, shivering in my blue woolen suit in the cold drafts of his bedroom.

My voice had never acquired the loose-string guitar twang of Midwestern voices, and the Beaver registered no objections to it when I had found the hotel's Gideon Bible (King James Version) and began to read, as ordered, the Twenty-third Psalm.

"The Lord is my shepherd; I shall not want. He maketh me to lie down in green pastures: he leadeth me beside the still waters," I read, trying to enunciate decently. If I didn't take this reading-up-the-Nile job, it was not going to be because of my ineptitude at pronunciation.

"He restoreth my soul: he leadeth me in the paths of righteousness . . ."

"PAHTHS," Lord Beaverbrook shouted from his pillows.

"*Paths,*" I shouted back. "Like *baths.*"

"BAHTHS," he shouted.

"How about *laths?*" I was giggling. "You see, you couldn't stand me as a reader. Or *maths*—you know, algebra. But please don't let me incite your WRAHTH."

My host's grin was friendly, but the reading exercises died abruptly and I went downstairs to my hole in the cliff.

As I was breaking fast in bed the next morning, Lord Beaverbrook telephoned. Our visit had so improved his health that he would entertain me at lunch in his suite. He was walking around his big sitting room overloaded with gifts when I arrived, dreaming of London. (I was supposed to have spent the night thinking about the Nile.)

44

"As you know, I should like to work for you in London," I started, "but . . ."

Beaverbrook, master of surprise, was placing a short dry kiss on my forehead. From the kindness of his heart and the depths of his worldly wisdom he delivered to my incredulous ears a ten-minute oration, a sexualized distillation of *The Prince* and the *Discourses,* restricting his precepts to the strategy and tactics of the War between Men and Young Women. The speech was a pastiche of a Sunday morning sermon on the glories of innocence and virtue in young women. "Total rubbish," said Lord Beaverbrook, with an amused smile, "and totally impractical." I listened so dumbfounded that I was unable to store away the phrases, or later to recall more than a few of them.

His principal arguments were that as a Midwestern dolt, there was much that I must learn, if I was to be a successful woman of the world; that there was only one way in Europe in which a woman might advance toward whatever objectives she had and that was with the patronage of an important and influential man; that romantic love was a waste of time and that the single, essential goal of a young woman should be to learn how to please men in every aspect of physical living and then to perfect her practice of those sorceries.

After the resounding climax to his speech, the only voice in the cold room was that of the snarling wind. Trying to compose a reply, I let Himself wait, and he walked around impatiently.

"My father told me one should never mix business with affections," I said finally. He could not frighten me. I was bigger and stronger than he was. "Besides, sir, I don't have any faith at all in my abilities to please a man. But I do have faith in my capacities as a reporter."

"Haruuuuuuuumph. Haruuuuuuuumph. I shall ring for the menu."

As I was leaving after lunch I said that the weekend had not been very satisfactory, since he had not persuaded me to go up the Nile and I had, evidently, failed to persuade him that I would be an effective employee on one of his papers.

45

"I see you don't forget your purposes, Mary," said Lord Beaverbrook. "We have no need for any more reporters on my newspapers, as Mr. Christiansen told you. However, if you come to London, I shall try to help you find work." His eyes were saying, "You stupid, unappreciative, ignorant, stubborn wench."

I started scurrying, writing letters and telephoning to my parents, flew to Detroit to consult my favorite cousins, Homer and Beatrice Guck (he an executive with Hearst), sold and gave away furniture, saved enough money for one Atlantic crossing but not enough for the return trip, reported my plans to Miss Allard who appeared annoyed but never let me know whether she was relieved or delighted about my departure. An attack of doubts and jitters overwhelmed me during my last week on the *Daily News* and I took it in to Hal O'Flaherty. What if I got over there, couldn't get a job, couldn't get back to Chicago? What if I couldn't learn the British style of journalism? What if Beaverbrook wouldn't help me? "Maybe I'm a fool," I wailed, thinking of my friends in Chicago at the ballet, the symphony, the theaters, the Art Institute, the Arts Club. Mr. O'Flaherty gave me a seven-word piece of advice I never forgot. "Never reverse a decision because of fear," he said.

A young man named Bill Hawkins who was working on the *News* invited me and some other people to drive down through a Friday night to the Kentucky Derby and after the big race herded us through the railway yards to the private car which his father and mother had chartered from New York to Louisville together with Mr. and Mrs. Roy Howard. In the hubbub of bet-settling, mint juleps in silver mugs, rejoicings and despairings, Bill Hawkins told Mr. Howard of my London project and that I did not have enough money to get home again if I failed there.

"I know Beaverbrook," Roy Howard proclaimed. "I was at Cherkley with him last fall. You're a brave girl. You'd better take along a letter from me." The adorable, tough-minded sprite sat down and wrote a letter which would have convinced Beaverbrook to hire an American chimpanzee. "Mary is one of the very best girl reporters in the U.S.A.," he wrote, never before having set eyes on me or my copy. I sent the letter to Beaverbrook at Cherkley as soon as I got to London, crossing aboard another small Canadian Pacific boat. It brought me an invitation to lunch at the country place in Surrey with its view over misty green downs and garlands of wisteria dripping from the front loggia, together with Beaverbrook's offer of a job on any one of his three newspapers. He recommended the *Sunday Express* or the *Evening Standard.* "The pace is not so fast as at the *Daily Express.*" His American reporter had departed.

"I'd prefer the *Daily Express,* sir. And that is really better for you and your editors since, if I fail there, I'll be off your hands faster, and if I succeed . . ."

"Mmmmmmmm, I know," said Lord Beaverbrook.

British immigration authorities had allowed me into the Isles because I had said I hoped to take some summer courses at Oxford. Now the *Express* had to extract from the Home Office a labor permit before I could draw a threepence of wages. My treasury drained off to rock bottom before I called Beaverbrook to announce that I had either to work or starve. The permit came through.

News of Amelia Earhart's disappearance over the Pacific reached London on the first day I showed up for work, and my assignment, to be completed in an hour, was to do a one-thousand-word story about her, to be used as a square-shaped feature in the middle of the editorial page. I didn't know that the hour deadline was a bluff. I checked the Earhart file in the morgue, found two or three items of a couple of paragraphs each, remembered the admiring recollection which my cousin Homer Guck had of her after sitting next to her at a luncheon in Chicago, and wrote my thousand words within the hour. I was in for another day.

Behind its flamboyant glass façade the London *Daily Express*'s editorial floor much more resembled the overcrowded, ill-lit, underheated office of the throwaway newspapers on the North Side of Chicago than that of the Chicago *Daily News,* where we had space, light, individual desks and where the prevailing air was donnish and accuracy more welcome than sensationalism. Some people on our *Express* floor had their own desks—the horse-racing chief and Trevor Evans, the top political writer. Lucy Milner, a swan-necked sparkling beauty who did fashion and befriended me with typewriter, paper and pencil on my first day, had her own desk in a cubicle. But we general news reporters were afforded no such amenities. At a long, unvarnished, unscrubbed wooden table standing on the bare wooden floor, we each had only enough semi-private space for a typewriter, notes, pencils, erasers. We worked as people eat at a quick-lunch counter. Hildy Marchant, the tiny, bubbling, brilliant girl reporter who had been there working successfully long before I appeared, and I put our handbags and any other gear on the floor beneath our chairs.

Our London news staff covered whatever was happening over the whole of the city and the country south of Birmingham, and when we had our stories, puny or silly or overstuffed as they might be, we telephoned them in to the men with the earphones in City Room cubicles if we were too far away to get back and write them ourselves. I bewildered the telephone men with my American accent during the first few months. Bit by bit we worked out compromises. I would dictate something such as, "The imitation Tudor vicarage is half a mile from the church." My American "half a mile" sounded gibberish and I learned to say it *'ahlf*. Neither could they make sense of "council is convening." In Great Britain the council or the government or the party "are" convening.

My best assignments were those for which Mr. Wilson, our city editor who looked like a pink-cheeked bishop, decided that photographs were required, which meant I got a ride with the photographer in his car to the scene of the news (or what passed for news on the *Express*). The photographers were jolly companions and I learned much more about the countryside, the British and their customs than I could on solitary assignments. Also I got a ride back to London.

The *Daily Express*'s custom in that era was to run a feature story with a double-column "intro" down the middle of page five and whoever wrote it got his by-line in lovely boldface type, and sometimes in letters two feet high on the posters plastered on the paper's delivery vans. I was eased into a part-time occupancy of that slot with such "color" stories as Trafalgar Square rallies protesting against British policy on the Spanish Civil War, or frothy, frivolous pieces—Champagne-Drinking at the Derby, Britain's Cold and Clammy Beaches, Top Hats in Buckingham Palace Garden, Hyde Park Is for Lovers on Sunday, the Stiff-Necked Credo of Suburbia and Small Towns: "We Keep Ourselves to Ourselves."

When the president of France and his wife on a state visit in 1938 gave the mayor of London a gift of money "for the poor of the City of London," nobody thought any poor could be found, since the City was the financial district behind St. Paul's Cathedral, the habitat of the Bank of England, the Stock Exchange, the elegant Guildhall of the Corporation of the City of London and the rich treasure-trove halls of the City's many Companies. I was assigned to hunt down some poor in the City, and I found so many of them living in rat-infested, overcrowded, malodorous misery on nothing but the dole, within a hundred yards of the coffers of the Bank of England, that we published a series of stories on this inconsistency, and I made friends who for years afterward helped me sample London opinion.

Early in 1938 Mr. Christiansen, our managing editor, whose initial irritability toward me had by then eased away, summoned me to his office and told me to get over to the Netherlands where the then Princess Juliana was expecting her first baby, due soon. In Amsterdam and immediately afterward at the pleasant countrified Baad Hotel, a mile or two from Soestdijk Palace where Juliana was installed, I found that the Dutch definition of news and that of the *Daily Express* were a couple of centuries apart. To the press corps assembling at the hotel from all over Western Europe, a government representative who courteously came to see us would say only that the princess was in good health and that when the child was born we would be informed.

I sent descriptions of the palace, a pleasant, airy-looking, unpretentious white building, as one could see from outside its closed gates; of the small demure village of Soestdijk nearby; of Queen Wilhelmina bicycling along a country road, her lady-in-waiting cycling a yard behind; of the frock-coated doctors who would attend the princess. Of the decorous official plans for welcoming the baby, even of the lovely beech forest with its lime-green tree trunks. Then, along with some forty other journalists and photographers, I waited, captive in the hotel or outside the palace gates. As the days edged by we all grew fidgety and, lacking facts, I sent a few stories of fantasy—twins might be born—which the *Express* published, thereby causing some of my colleagues' editors to send them wrathful inquiries. One Scandinavian girl reporter had a nervous breakdown and was recalled home. To alleviate the boredom, the rest of us drank too much every night and put on such carefree displays of singing and dancing in the hotel dining room that we filled it steadily with amused local burghers and their wives until January 31, when Princess Beatrix was born. We wrapped up our stories in half an hour and departed.

We city staffers usually managed to weave some pleasure into business. Alan Moorehead, who was to have the most distinguished career of any of us, George Millar, brilliant and beautiful, who later accomplished fabulous feats for British Intelligence in occupied France, a wild Irishman named Gallagher, Noel Monks, a big, gentle-mannered athletic fellow, Hildy Marchant and others of us used to report for duty in the mornings, receive our assignments and then rendezvous at a pub across Ludgate Circus to sip one or two of its nourishing champagne cocktails and make an early lunch on Scotch Woodcock, a piece of bread with a smear of cheese toasted on top of it. There must have been thirty pubs within a two-block radius of the *Daily Express* and all of us Beaverbrook employees, from the business offices upstairs to the pressmen in the basement, diligently did our best to help them stay in business.

Alan Moorehead, who sat next to me at the wooden table, did not stay long on the city staff. They promoted him to Paris as chief of the bureau there and the following spring, when I had gone over for a weekend, Alan bought me a drink at a café on the Champs-Elysées and complained that his busy life as a bachelor in Paris was beginning to pall. He had not found a Parisian girl who suited his taste for long. I reminded him of my wise, witty and lovely friend, Lucy Milner, whom of course he knew. Alan was flying to London that evening. The next day he stopped in at Lucy's cubicle on our editorial floor. They were married within the year.

Early on I found a place to live in a rather artsy-craftsy basement—strings of garlic hanging above an ancient but functioning black iron stove—in Glebe Place, Chelsea, with King Henry VIII's one-time hunting lodge at the corner and Thomas Carlyle's house in Cheyne Row around the corner. The house was a career-girl nest, with Nan, in advertising, on the top floor, a succession of models on the second floor and Joy, in film production, on the first; and since I was almost never in my basement during daylight, I did not feel oppressed by my sitting room with its window extending only about halfway above the level of our handkerchief-sized front lawn. A darling "char," Mrs. Gordon, kept the place and my clothes clean and orderly, and at night I had absolute silence after the clatter of the *Daily Express*.

When my big black stove was exuding warmth and the pleasant smells of soups and stews and sauces, my basement was a cheerful place, although desperately inelegant, and I abandoned it only when, as Mrs. Noel Monks, I moved with my husband to a doll's house nearby in Upper Cheyne Row.

A native Australian, Noel had worked on a leading newspaper in Melbourne before coming to London and getting himself assigned to cover the Spanish Civil War for the London *Daily Mail*. He was big and bulky, having been a champion swimmer in Australia, prematurely gray, and with his ruddy complexion he looked more scrubbed and shined and better pressed than any other London bachelor I knew. After nine or ten months of our going about together, he began acting protective toward me, an alluring attitude,

51

I felt. We were married in the Chelsea Town Hall and my friend Joy, by that time Mrs. Moore Raymond, gave us a jolly reception in her new apartment just around the corner in Glebe Place from our old all-girl dormitory.

As a husband Noel was abstemious, conservative, a gentle man, delighted with our doll's house even though it was too small and fragile for him with its fantasy of gilt chairs and red velvet cushions and carpets, its upstairs windows overlooking a walled garden bright with flowers and singing birds. Only the exigencies of World War II caused us to give it up.

Neville Chamberlain, Prime Minister of Great Britain, sporting his stiff collar and scraggly mustache, broke all precedents in the autumn of 1938 and had himself flown to Germany to confer with Adolf Hitler. Mr. Christiansen sent Hildy Marchant to cover the first conference, a debacle. I was finishing a story on the evening of September 28, 1938, when the authoritative punch of Chris's heels came down the hall from his office to the City Room. He came over to me and said, "The P.M. is flying to Munich tomorrow. Get yourself a plane and get there ahead of him. You'll have rooms at the Regina Palast Hotel. I may send somebody with you. Send back everything."

I got on the telephone in search of private planes that could fly the distance, found one that would not need to refuel before Frankfurt, engaged it to leave Heston Airport sometime after midnight. Webb Miller, chief of the U.P. office in London, called to ask if he could share our flight and I said, "Sure." Mr. Christiansen telephoned around London, found C. V. R. Thompson, the *Daily Express*'s New York correspondent who was back in London on a holiday, and persuaded him, a large, jovial, fast-thinking man, to join our party. Beaverbrook's afternoon half-sized newspaper, the *Evening Standard,* sent along a young man, Ossian Goulding. Keen, but inexperienced, I judged.

By the time I reached the German embassy and consulate in London, it was closed for the night. No visa. But when we put down at Frankfurt for immigration, customs formalities and refueling, Webb

Miller persuaded the Germans that I was harmless and on duty as a correspondent. The only German I knew was *Gesundheit*.

As an English-speaking bellboy was depositing our bags in our elaborate suite at the Regina Palast Hotel, I asked, snuggling into his hand a generous tip, if he had any friends who spoke English as well as he did.

"My brother," the boy said.

Would his brother like to come to the hotel to read English over the telephone to London?

Yes, indeed.

Telephone traffic between the continent and London was feeble in 1938 and would be frantic, I surmised, when news broke at this conference. I had a copy of *Punch* in my handbag and a volume of William Hazlitt's essays in my luggage. Our suite had a Bible in English. With Tommy Thompson's approval, I set up the classic ploy of keeping a line to London constantly occupied, the bellboy's brother reading to our *Express* telephone operators until we broke in on him, reading our stories—Chamberlain's arrival at the airport, Mussolini's pomposities at the railway station, a band playing and red flags with their black swastikas waving for him, Edouard Daldier arriving from France looking glum.

I talked my way into Chamberlain's suite, directly below ours on a corner of the hotel, for a peek—pink toilet paper, blue wallpaper in the bedroom, a battered suitcase, girl secretaries typing, nothing much, no balcony—then rushed around the city for a color story. I tapped out the piece on my portable, read it to London and went out to interview the female automaton who was chief of the Nazi women's organization, wrote a piece swimming in malice, figuring the censors were so busy they would not break off my reading it to the office, and they didn't.

That night the boss-men held a meeting at the Braun Haus and in the street we watched Hitler acknowledge the crowd's *"Heil, heil,"* as he drove there with a handwave that looked bored, languid, foppish, faggy. While Tommy waited with most of the press of Europe outside the Braun Haus, I chatted in the streets with anybody I could find who spoke English.

The Braun Haus meeting lasted until after midnight, and after watching the heads of state ride homeward looking noncommittal, I pushed through the crowds back to the hotel, did my final story and fell into bed. It was 3 a.m. Munich time and forty-two hours since last I had been horizontal.

The next morning we had a wire from Christiansen bestowing U.S. citizenship on Tommy. "You Americans surely can write," it said. With our private open wire—the *Daily Express* never skimped on expenses —we were also beating everybody to London with what news there was.

We probed for news from Chamberlain's staff and from M. Daladier's aides and pried loose a few tidbits amid clouds of hot air, then at noon went out onto our terrace to watch multitudes of people standing in a light rain applauding Chamberlain who appeared at his window below us. We took bows for him.

The British P.M. and the other nobs held further talks that afternoon, October 1, and then Chamberlain's staff summoned the press to a conference in his suite. The P.M., a scarecrow in his wing-collar, was saving his "peace in our time" phrase for his arrival in London. Instead he gave us the news, camouflaging the sellout in a voice of squeaky hauteur, that Britain and France had agreed to Hitler's demand for annexation of Czechoslovakia's Sudetenland (with its important Skoda armament factories and three and a half million people), adding, "in future any questions that may concern our two countries will be settled by arbitration."

When we had finished telephoning our stories, the *Express* told us to get over to the Czech border and cover the march-in of the German army. If anyone predicted that Britain and France would be at war against Germany within a year, I did not hear it.

Without delay we set off in a comfortable car with chauffeur to drive in fog and rain over twisty mountain roads to Salzburg where, on a restaurant door, we saw the first sign—JEWS NOT SERVED HERE—dined on Wiener schnitzel with paprika and noted that the

54

local diners listened with no show of interest or emotion to a roaring, lying broadcast concerning the jubilation in Sudetenland over the outcome of the Munich conference.

The roads from Salzburg to Linz, Austria, our destination, were free of troops or any heavy traffic, but in the fog the going was slow. We sang the stock gamut of British and American folksongs, sentimental to bawdy, and when we tired of singing, played the alphabet game, British accents and slang definitions prevailing, plus some inventions:

A-fer-orses	L-fer-leather	U-fer-mism
B-fer-brook	M-fer-sis	V-fer-La France
D-fer-dumb	N-fer-mation	X-fer-breakfast
F-fer-vescent	P-fer-relief	Y-fer-husband
H-fer-himself	T-fer-two	

When we reached Linz about 3 a.m., we found every hotel jammed with officers of the Austrian army. Tommy Thompson, who had the largest vocabulary in German among us (a dozen words) and the money, conducted prolonged negotiations with the night clerk of the best hotel and finally got one room for the three of us. It had a sofa as well as twin beds. No bath. We turned out the lights to undress and I was instantly asleep in one of the beds.

When I awoke the next morning my companions had disappeared and my bladder was within minutes of bursting. I loped as gently as possible down the hall, found the bathroom occupied, returned to our room where two washbowls stood side by side. Gratefully I perched on one of them. Gratitude turned to bewilderment and then to panic as I found myself sloping into midair and my roommates began pounding on the door. Like a tulip in a breeze, my washbowl had parted from the wall and was advancing steadily into the room. I prayed, and its pipe refrained from breaking.

Soon after we crossed the mustard-colored Danube that morning we ran into troops standing along the narrow country road, nice-looking youngsters about twenty-two years old, their tin helmets camouflaged with leaves as were their machine guns and a few anti-aircraft guns standing in cornfields. The beer lorries and sightseeing buses in which they had crossed the border were pulled to one side.

At the head of the column only a mile or two from the border sat General Dollmann, commanding that sector of the invasion from an armored car. An officer of the Austrian army, he was dressed in blue semi-dress uniform, with gay cerise stripes on his pants and a gallant manner. He kissed my hand, said, "Glad to see you here," and sent me to a country house where I could wait, until his troops reached the hamlet of Guglurold, their day's objective.

The country was autumn-lovely, yellow valleys glowing between the hills, red roofs brightening peasant cottages, the peasants figures from the classic painting *The Angelus*. The whole business had gone off so correctly and courteously that we found it difficult to write into our stories any sense of bullying and menace.

Our return to London was gradual. With our unexpected expenses we ran out of money and cabled for more. By the time it arrived, we had run up more bills. A week passed before the *Express* sent sufficient funds to get us back home. Meanwhile we dawdled in Alpine villages, missed the reports of Winston Churchill appraising the Munich agreement in the Commons: "All is over. Silent, mournful, abandoned, broken, Czechoslovakia recedes into the darkness."

In March 1939, having no plan or program for implementing his pledge, Chamberlain informed the Polish government that if Poland were attacked by Germany, the British and French "would at once lend them all the support in their power." London newspapers happily headlined the unrealistic news.

In April the government announced it would institute compulsory military service. My impoverished and unemployed friends in the East End of London were nearly unanimous in their reactions. "So whotsher, maittey? I get me clothes and bed and board, an the ol' laidy gets the dole, same as ever. Whotev we got ter lose?" A million men were still unemployed around the country.

When Noel and I returned to London in late August after a swimming and sunning holiday at St.-Jean-de-Luz, we stopped whatever we were doing to listen to the BBC news reports. The morning broadcasts of Friday, September 1, announced that German troops had crossed the Polish frontier and that Warsaw had been bombed. The British cabinet met in Downing Street and I wasted time standing outside Number 10, until evening when the Prime Minister went to the House of Commons.

Saturday being a half holiday, London's streets were crowded, and thousands stood or strolled outside the House of Commons, unaware that inside Arthur Greenwood, one of the Labour Party leaders, was pleading for decision: "Every minute's delay now means the loss of life, imperiling our national interests . . . imperiling the very foundations of our national honour." Chamberlain and his cabinet still hesitated.

Mr. Chamberlain's voice came out of our wireless set on September 3, while I was assembling our Sunday breakfast. The British ultimatum—promise to withdraw from Poland or we are at war—delivered to the Nazis at 9 a.m., had evoked no reply. At 11 a.m,. the ultimatum expired. We were peacefully at war. It was a sunny, tranquil morning in London and on the way to the office we saluted the roses and red geraniums outside of Buckingham Palace. In the *Express* office we heard London's sirens wailing their five-toned, wavering first warning. Docilely, we walked down to the basement where the presses were. I decided that I preferred being clobbered in the company of typewriters rather than those two-ton presses. Except in a few mistakes, London's sirens were not to howl again until after Dunkerque at the end of the following May. Going home in the twilight of that first day of war, I made two footnotes to the day's events: in the blackout of artificial light, London became shades of gray in its twilight. I saw the shapes of road signs and hedges and flowers in small front gardens, no color. And for the first time I realized that my unconscious had observed the lines of roofs and chimney pots against the sky, so that now I recognized the profiles of my neighborhood. In mutual confessions several friends confirmed that our personal reactions to the declaration of war had been attacks of diarrhea. Clearly psychosomatic, we agreed.

With the help of Noel, who was covering the R.A.F. in France, and other friends, and the approval of the *Express*, I finagled my way across the Channel to do stories on the British Expeditionary Force's housekeeping. The R.A.F. units to which I was specifically assigned had done fairly well for themselves in villages near their airstrips, and some regiments of guards had maneuvered into comfortable quarters in villages, with indoor mess halls. One regiment of guards exuberantly planned to bring over their horses and a pack of hounds for drag hunting. But other units, neither elite nor fully trained, were tented down in the empty, harvested beetfields, and although with Cockney humor they had named the lanes between tent rows after Piccadilly and the Strand, their tents were pitched open to the prevailing west wind. No officer had told them to dig ditches around the outsides of the tents, and when the November rains came, they would be very wet. Their kitchen and mess areas were set up in a mud-distilling hollow. When I wondered aloud to an officer about the setup, he answered jovially, "No matter. They're not getting killed. Actually, we could do with a bit of action, to take their minds off Home and Ma."

In France, Christmas Day was dour and dreary. Then came the word that Gracie Fields—"Our Gracie" —was coming to Reims to give a concert. Officers were not invited. Only petty officers, Tommies and aircraft maintenance crews could attend. Spirits ballooned. Hours after the arrival of the good news there arrived also a murderous storm which coated the roads with ice and camouflaged ditches with snowbanks. "She'll never make it," soldiers muttered. But she did and so did her company and her small orchestra. (Her chauffeur told me the drive from Paris was a "horror"; but Gracie said, "It was nothing, ducks.")

The Reims Opera House, its cup running over with Tommies, must have quaked the town with the racket of welcome when Gracie hurried onstage. After the nasty drive, she looked fresh as a peach, cheerful as Father Christmas, bright as a tulip with her blond hair shining, and loving, loving. She was the happy essence of home.

Afterward, outside in the freezing air, soldiers climbed into the open backs of lorries, squeezing themselves together for a twenty- or thirty-mile ride, like upended planks. One after another of the lorryfuls of young men picked up the tune and sang, "Roll out the barrel, we'll 'ave a barrel of fun," their voices echoing diminuendo in the frosty night.

Back in London Joseph Kennedy, a solid, florid man, was presiding over our embassy, and the *Express* sent me to ask him his views on Great Britain's status in Europe, her military potentials compared to those of Germany, and the probabilities of support from France. In our ambassador's office, I smelled anxiety. Mr. Kennedy had been in Germany, had seen exhibitions of its military might, and had been duly impressed. He did not say it outright, but he gave me the sharp impression that he had no faith in the capacities of Britain and France to withstand any onslaught by Germany. (And indeed, London then showed little evidence of its indigenous courage and endurance.) Mr. Kennedy kindly telephoned his wife, asking her to show me around their house in Knightsbridge for my story, and she introduced me to a number of their children who came stampeding through like a herd of Western ponies. In the *Daily Express* office that evening I wrote a fat story about Ambassador Kennedy and his family, and the sub-editors cut it to bits. Our readers did not wish to learn that the American ambassador had little faith in Britain, the sub-editors apparently decided, and so we did not force-feed it to them.

Except for debates in the House of Commons, London was not producing news that winter. Like everybody else, I felt restless and persuaded the *Express* to send me to France to do odd stories about the British forces there and also general news. (Noel was still with the R.A.F. in northeastern France.) They had transferred Alan Moorehead to Rome and George Millar was running the Paris bureau, covering French news. It took him out of Paris frequently, and I filled in around the edges, one of which, to my amusement, turned out to be Lanvin's showing of her new spring clothes in her elegant dove-gray salon, with Edith Piaf in her scraggy black dress moaning her Paris waif songs.

I found a pleasant studio flat overlooking the freshly showing leafiness of the Avenue de Breteuil behind the Invalides, enrolled in a French-speaking course at the Alliance Française, learned to use the Métro as transportation and the Ritz Bar as a place of rendezvous, and to take a book to read while waiting to see French officials with whom I had appointments. Both military and civilian, they knew how to be as evasive as the British, how to use twenty sentences to express a simple negative. None of the stories I sent to London was much more than decorative, and my conscience murmured that I was going nicely through the steps of a minuet in a house that was about to burn down.

The Paris newspapers contributed to the illusion. In early April they quoted Mr. Chamberlain, having reviewed some progress in British rearmament, as saying, "Hitler has missed the bus." After May 10, 1940, when the Germans simultaneously bombed and moved into Belgium, Luxembourg, and the Netherlands by parachute and surface transport, the Paris press continued to give me the impression of fantasy within the carnage. *"Nos canons,"* it would say, have repulsed an enemy attack *"féroce"* and are pursuing them. I imagined the cast-iron cannon with their little piles of black grapefruit balls on the courthouse lawns of the United States. The following day *"nos canons"* performed equal heroics in the newspapers, but at some place twenty or thirty kilometers farther southwest toward the heart of France. Seldom has a reading public been so hoodwinked by its press. But as I would learn later, the fault was less that of the press than of the military where fact was then difficult to distinguish from wish.

With the French army steadily retreating southwestward, the British Expeditionary Force cut off in northern France, ordinary Parisians growing daily more morose and disconsolate, I nonetheless continued tripping through the steps of the mindless minuet. Lunch in the flowering garden of the Ritz. Dawdling in the galleries of the rue Bonaparte. A fitting in the walkup flat of my "little" dressmaker. When the rumor got around that the government was moving south from Paris, I made inquiries of an acquaintance in the French Ministry of Information. *"Non, non, non, absolument. C'est défendu de parler . . ."* If I had hung around another hour I could have seen his office staff beginning to put their archives into cardboard boxes.

Noel and some friends came back to Paris from the French front and we drove out to La Cascade restaurant in the Bois and dined handsomely and wined with a bottle or two of Château Mouton Rothschild I have never forgotten. That night we heard the faint thud of heavy artillery in the distance. We believed in miracles. I went to sunbathe and swim at the Tennis Club in the Bois and that night was visited by a fever of alarming intensity. An elderly neighborhood physician diagnosed it as sunstroke, warned me that my hair would probably fall out and advised rest and liquids. I was incapable of anything else. I lay on the sofa listening to the shouts of children playing under the trees outside. It was a lulling, languorous Sunday afternoon.

That evening my husband left to catch a train back to R.A.F. headquarters, still near Reims. He could not find a taxi, missed his train and instead went to his Paris office to learn the latest news. It was that the Nazi breakthrough of the French lines appeared to be in such strength that Paris was threatened. In spite of my fever and weakness, we packed in twenty minutes, miraculously found a taxi and moved through heat of eighty-five degrees to the Austerlitz railway station. Through the taxi windows Paris in twilight looked like a dream city. A slim slice of moon was mirrored in the satin of the river and silhouetted the shapes of ancient stones. All about was silence, the peace and gentle sounds of a summer evening. Except at the station, where the whole world was clamoring at ticket windows, train barriers, and finally at the doors of the jammed trains.

We ran blocks down a platform trying each door, but the doors could not be opened, the humanity inside was so thickly packed. Finally we wrenched a door open and wedged ourselves inside, my fever and I sitting on one of our bags between the haunches of a spaniel dog and the knees of a sad, haggard, old man who mentioned to me that he was one of the curators of the Louvre. We rebreathed our breaths as we jogged along, stopping frequently in the darkness for reasons we did not know.

Noel and I disembarked at Blois, to which we had heard the French government had moved. Peace, again, in the moonlight, and we walked down a road, pounded on the door of a small inn and got a room. My fever persevered and my hair was beginning to fall out, as predicted, but we felt we must try to find remnants of the R.A.F. and the French Ministry of Information. We found them in hotels on the main street, which was flooded with harassed humanity, but the finding availed us little. Nobody knew anything in the chaos, and if we had learned any news, we could not have sent it back to London. The French censorship office was clogged with mounds of cables waiting to be sent and only one censor to read them in English. The town's wireless office emitted a half-block-long queue of correspondents who had elected to bypass censorship and try to bribe the wireless men. I decided that Blois was not for me, and, in a life dictated by chance, found, while lunching on the terrace of a hotel, means of escape.

A rich American woman, Persis Woodward, and her daughter, Ruth, whom I'd known for six months in Paris, were motoring down to Biarritz with the intention of returning to the United States through Spain or Portugal. They happened to stop for lunch at the same terrace in Blois and generously invited me and my diminutive luggage to join them for the rest of the journey. I did so. Twice on the road southward that afternoon our column of cars stopped. People flung themselves into the roadside ditches and a pair of fighter planes flew over. They were Messerschmitts, we heard, and had been strafing the column behind us. At Biarritz I installed myself in the sitting room of the Woodward Suite at the Hôtel Miramar, and went to sleep with my fever for a couple of days. When I woke up, feeling slightly less burning, I tried to assess the situation. Perhaps my placid assumption that I would soon be back in Paris, with the French government governing, was poppycock. Perhaps Noel, who had stayed behind in Blois, would join me in Biarritz, perhaps not. I had left two fur coats, twenty-seven sweaters, my grandmother's silver teaspoons and thirty or forty favorite books, insurance policies, bank books and all other papers in Paris. I had with me my portable typewriter, a tweed topcoat, a large bottle of Indiscret toilet water, a couple of changes of clothes and very little money. Conclusion: I had to get busy earning my living, and England was the nearest country, if accessible. General Gort and British sailors in every size and type of craft had successfully saved more than half a million Allied soldiers, including French and Poles, ferrying them across the Channel from Dunkerque to the English coast. The French news was so sketchy that guests clustered around the lobby radio at the Hôtel Miramar were scarcely aware of the miracle.

Word seeped down the French coast from Bordeaux that British and Americans were gathering there in the hope of escape to England, and I looked about the empty streets of the one-time summer resort for some sort of transportation northward. Buses were curtailing their travel schedules because shortages of *essence* and diesel oil loomed ominously. My fallen-out hair leaving me with a half-inch of fuzz to cover my baldness, I went to a hairdresser near the hotel to ask what might be done about it—a wig, maybe? The hairdresser had little to offer except advice about oils and massages. But as I was returning to the hotel, a friendly face smiled at me and a hand waved from inside a car. The man was a Basque, the same one who had driven Noel and me on many nights from St.-Jean-de-Luz during peacetime holidays to Biarritz for an hour or two of gaming at the Casino. Chance was taking over again. We exchanged news. He earned his living by chauffeuring people in his car on short hauls between St.-Jean and Biarritz. They were more profitable than the longer journeys to Bordeaux. "If you can find the *essence,* let me pay you double the rate," said I.

"We shall arrange it," said he. I thanked heaven we had tipped him heavily in happier times.

That evening the few guests in the lobby of the Miramar stood around its only radio, listening. M. Reynaud, the French prime minister, had resigned. The aging Maréchal Pétain had formed a new government and was asking the Germans for a conclusion of hostilities. Some people in the little group wept. I was bewildered.

The next evening as my American friends and I were preparing to go down to dinner, my husband burst in, wild-eyed, tattered, be-whiskered, dirty. He had commandeered a railway locomotive, a hearse, and other vehicles, and even so, it had taken him three days and two nights and some walking to reach Biarritz from Blois. My good news was that we had transportation from Biarritz to Bordeaux. And, marvel, there was our Basque taxi friend waiting outside the hotel the next morning.

Anthony Drexel Biddle of Philadelphia, the United States ambassador to Poland until its collapse, the most meticulously dressed man in all the U.S. Foreign Service, had somehow made his way to France and on June 22 and 23 sat at a small desk in a shed in Bordeaux, himself inspecting British, American and French passports and allotting boarding tickets to a small Peninsula and Orient passenger and cargo ship, the *Andura*. She had been ordered into Bordeaux to pick up refugees on her journey to England. With the precious boarding permits in our hands, we hunted around Bordeaux's port area, as instructed, for food for the voyage to England. Nearly all the tinned-food shops were closed and shuttered. When we found one open the proprietor would sell us only four tins of inferior sardines, nothing else of his visible hoard of goodies. He had his reasons, said the *épicier*. We found a *charcuterie* where the proprietor permitted himself to sell us one pork sausage, and we found a loaf of bread and a bottle of whiskey. Not enough food, but we dared not use more time away from the line of people waiting for the launch which was ferrying us refugees from shore to ship. We need not have hurried. The ferry chugged back and forth all night.

When we weighed anchor the following evening, fifteen hundred extra people jammed the decks of the little ship built to carry two hundred and fifty passengers.

Almost all the journalists we had known in France were aboard—Red Knickerbocker of Hearst. Ed Beatty of U.P., Bill Stoneman of the Chicago *Daily News,* Quent Reynolds of *Collier's,* Bob Low of *Liberty* and a score of Fleet Street people including our friends George and Nettie Millar with whom we set up an enclave on two square yards of deck. Eve Curie and Henry Bernstein, the playwright, had their camp on the starboard side of our deck next to a large family of fat rich-looking Frenchmen. Virginia Cowles with her mink jacket settled in with a group of Englishmen. What a shakeup there would be in British and U.S. newspaper offices if this ship went down, I thought. A generous-hearted sailor gave the Millars and us an air mattress, and we four stretched out on it crosswise and shared a single blanket in the same way. Although we had the constant threat of being torpedoed as we zigzagged up the Atlantic Ocean, for five nights I never slept better.

The ordered greenery of England never looked so hospitable and comforting, verdant hills sloping down to the neat town of Falmouth, as it did in that June morning when we drew into the quiet harbor. In London a decent place was available for subletting in Chesil Court, a big block of flats near the Thames Embankment in our old Chelsea neighborhood. I could still deal with my former greengrocer, also my old butcher and the tinned-goods people in the King's Road—an ancient provisioner's firm—whom I asked to hunt around in London's markets for American peanut butter. Any amount would do, I said, thinking that animal fat might grow scarce.

On the voyage from France I had decided, for reasons murky around their edges, that I must stop working for a British newspaper and switch to something American. The *Daily Express* accepted my resignation with equanimity.

For a couple of weeks I lounged, rejoicing in London's staunch and stalwart air after the sickly resignation of France. I indulged in reunions with old friends, swimming at Roehampton, massaging the inch-long fuzz on my head, doing a story for a Fleet Street editor about the evacuation of children from the city to strange new homes in country towns. They were a touching spectacle with their little knapsacks holding a change of socks, their printed names and addresses pinned to their lapels and their gas masks in cardboard boxes hung around their necks.

From my diary, June 24, 1940: "Diana [Greenlee] says farmers near their place in Berkshire are making little bombs from eggs. They carefully blow out the eggs, then fill them with ammonia and seal them up. They are also making petrol bombs from bottles and digging up their thousand-year-old lawns to make tank traps."

A few days later I suggested to Ronald Tree, the debonair and gentle grandson of Marshall Field of Chicago, who was working for Duff Cooper at the Ministry of Information, that I do a radio column to America. He was interested but indefinite. I made a list of the American outfits in London for which I would like to slave: *The New York Times,* which already had a woman reporter, Tanya Long; the *Herald Tribune,* its London bureau headed by a pal, Geoffrey Parsons; A.P., U.P., I.N.S.; and as an afterthought, *Time* magazine, whose bureau chief, Walter Graebner, I had known since we both worked in Chicago. For a lark I started my telephoning from the bottom of my list.

"Can you come in this afternoon?"

"No, but tomorrow."

That afternoon I got in touch with the British Red Cross. Through the International Red Cross in Geneva, they would send my permission to the branch of our Paris *arrondissement* to use all of the clothes I had left behind, my husband's permission to use the fourteen suits he had left, and my request that our private papers be kept intact for us. Three changes of clothes hung in the wooden cupboard of our Chelsea flat, and they pleased me every time I noticed them. I had freedom from wardrobe and from the waste of time of deciding each morning what to wear.

The next afternoon Walter Graebner installed me in a little room with a big desk and a window in *Time's* jumble of offices overlooking Dean Street, Soho. With Air Chief Marshal Sir Hugh Caswall Tremenheere Dowding's fighter pilots protecting us, engaging the enemy above England's southeastern counties, we Londoners would have another few weeks of comparative tranquility before the advent of the Blitzkrieg.

3

A Fury Slinging Flame

And Time, a maniac scattering dust,
And Life, a Fury slinging flame.
　　　　　　　—Tennyson,
　　　　　　　　　"In Memoriam"

JULY 10, 1940, DISTINGUISHED ITSELF as the opening day of the Battle of Britain, the miraculous defense of its homeland by the Royal Air Force against the invading Luftwaffe. (It was also the day I started to work in the London bureau of *Time, Life,* and *Fortune.*) As a sandy beach retains the shells and other small marvels of the highest wave of a storm, my memory holds intact assorted relics of those crucial weeks.

Despite the censors' haphazard bridling of the London newspapers and news services, and despite the gravity of the circumstances, the London press whooped up R.A.F. victories in huge headlines, as though it were acclaiming the winner of a cricket match, regaling readers with blow-by-blow accounts of the dogfights in the skies above the southeast counties whenever R.A.F. pilots triumphed. Since that summer was the driest and least cloudy in memory, the battle was a spectacle unprecedented in human warfare, and for those of us who had friends among the fighter pilots it was as personal as a heart tremor.

Londoners were beginning to show their mettle. The opalescent summer air of London was aglow with staunch spirits, a kind of undaunted "We'll muddle through." It was lucky, perhaps, that they did not know what the fall and winter would bring them or the following spring or the following few years.

Hunting a quick, cheap place for lunching, I happened on a tearoom just off Oxford Street and went there whenever I had shopping to do during my lunch hour. One day in late July as I was paying my bill to the proprietress I noticed a twelve-inch-long butcher's knife beside the cash register. The spare, middle-aged maiden lady with her dangling jade earrings explained. "Those Germans are coming down all around us. I live in Kent, you know. So I carry this morning and evening. If I ever meet one of those Germans, I'll swish his head off." She must have weighed all of one hundred pounds.

When Churchill reported to the House of Commons that the Germans were amassing barges in the ports of Holland, Belgium and France, I joined a class of women learning to shoot rifles, all of us lying on our bellies, holding a gun and squinting through open iron sights at a target. As no ammunition was available, I quit the class after a few sessions, deciding to throw face powder or salt into the eyes of any invaders I met.

In London we worked with dedication at prosaic jobs. Since returning from France I had broadcast a couple of thirteen-and-a-half-minute talks for the BBC, and now they asked if I would join a program of short-wave broadcasts to America and the empire. My talks would not be propaganda; they would be straight reportage about London. I told somebody at our embassy and it was agreed that the talks would not put my U.S. citizenship in jeopardy as though I were "working for a foreign government." The program was to be broadcast two or three nights a week for thirteen weeks. The mike talking began at 2 a.m., but we had to arrive earlier for script editing and rehearsals. My talk was wedged between J. B. Priestley's and Leslie Howard's and a more interesting working slot I had never known.

My diary for July 12, 1940, notes: "A long talk last night at the BBC with Priestley. He told me that the single most important thing in speaking, aside from decent enunciation, is to be and sound sincere."

The BBC had moved its cafeteria at Broadcasting House deep into its underground roots. It reminded me of a railway station lunch counter with the air removed. Mr. Priestley, Mr. Howard and I used to sit at the long midnight-empty counter fussing with our scripts, chatting and reminiscing. One of Mr. Howard's memories was of being shoved under a heavy kitchen table at his parents' house somewhere near the Straits of Dover during World War I when German long-range guns bombarded the British coast. Seeing his sharp, clean profile, I found it had to believe he had been old enough then to remember.

That fall and winter, when the Luftwaffe dumped tons of bombs and firebombs on London for fifty-seven successive nights, everybody who worked at the BBC after dark gave special thanks—and tremendous tips—to the grizzled old cabbies who maintained their taxi rank and their telephone box (Welbeck 1721)—outside Broadcasting House all night long all winter. Theirs was the only cab rank in business at night. Tightly bundled and wrapped like an awkward package, one or another of them used to come down to Lansdowne House, Berkeley Square, where we lived from mid-September onward, to pick me up and trundle me back to the broadcasting station, maneuvering around incendiaries and sometimes bouncing into the air in the blackout from a not-far-away-enough high-explosive bomb.

Most of us were too busy to give much thought to dying, but privately I opted for any sort of wound, a leg or arm chopped off, rather than loss of sight. Whenever I was caught in the streets by bombs sounding too close for comfort, I flopped face downward with my arms around my head.

I heard about some girl dispatch riders working for the navy and made an appointment at the Admiralty. There in a scruffy little office were some of them, all from Britain's first families, many of them keen fox hunters, with a cheesecloth sack of sour milk dripping gently into a navy ashtray. "Cottage cheese, you know," said one girl. This small cadre of prewar privileged girls zoomed on their motorcycles day and night from London to coastal naval stations carrying dispatches—secret orders. I suggested it must be rough going on black and rainy nights. "Of course," they said with composure. In the blackout their motorcycle headlights shone through an aperture about the size of a U.S. quarter.

In a spasm of much criticized hysteria, the Home Security forces and Scotland Yard tracked down and imprisoned batches of aliens. Many were German Jews who were musicians, psychologists or physical scientists. Also imprisoned was a small colony of Japanese who were the only workers in the British poultry markets who could determine the sex of young chicks. Simple expediency got them out of prison earlier than many other innocent aliens.

My former employer, Lord Beaverbrook, was appointed minister of aircraft production and *Time* assigned me the job of gathering information about him and his operations for a cover story. With the Beaver's permission I scuttled around to aircraft factories outside London, discovered that the workers were on a ten-hour day, seven days a week, and still cheerful about it, also that no factory owner, manager or straw boss was immune from telephone calls day or night, the scratchy voice of the minister demanding, "Why not?," harassing, insisting, inventing short cuts, ignoring standard business procedures. His byword was "Action this day," and he got it.

Having dug up whatever I could find about Beaverbrook's *modus operandi,* I went to see him in his office on the Embankment for a few words of wisdom and anything he would tell me about how he was doing personally. Lord Beaverbrook was brisk, chipper, obviously enjoying his enormous job, and no more than normally uninformative. He evaded commenting on his campaign to get British housewives to turn over their aluminum pots and pans for his aircraft construction. (A couple of chemists had told me the kitchen utensils could serve no purpose other than propaganda—"Too many alloys.")

As he escorted me through the outer office between rows of young men secretaries, he asked in the sand-paper voice, clearly audible through the room, "And tell me, is your husband giving you sexual satisfaction?" I assumed he remembered my declining his invitation to float up or down the Nile with him.

Everybody I knew anticipated a German attempt at invasion any day. Yet, buoyed by Churchill and by some ancient, ingrained obstinacy, the Londoners con-tinued placid. The Cockneys—truck drivers, stockroom workers, janitors and waitresses—who patronized the Bath House, our pub across the street from our office, continued their after-work banter over " 'alf-and-'alf"— "Me plates o' meat [feet] are crumblin' away inside me boots."

More and more frequently in London the sirens were bleating out their five-note, minor-scale "alerts," caus-ing whether-or-not-to-take-shelter problems in offices everywhere. Our building in Dean Street was newer and looked stronger than most of its three- or four-story old brown-brick neighbors which housed rather shoddy shops and eating places, with living quarters above. Our building could withstand anything but a close big bomb, we felt, not then really knowing. (Nobody, in-cluding the army and the Civil Defense bosses, really knew in those days. No definitive laws concerning de-gree of protection against high explosives had been formulated, one reason being that bomb damage was highly capricious, the same-sized bomb devastating half a square block of ordinary London buildings or only a dozen houses of the same construction and vin-tage. Was it humidity, wind velocity, angle of approach, variation in the condition of the high explosive? No-body then had the answers.)

Our bureau chief, Walter Graebner, said he felt he could not insist that the staff ignore the sirens and keep on working through raids—too heavy a burden on his conscience—and during the first few of the early raids we trooped obediently to the basement leaving cables unfinished, telephones unanswered. Very soon we decided individually that ducking to shelter was a wasteful maneuver, and maybe shameful. The air-raid wardens were out in the streets with only their tin hats

71

for protection. The R.A.F. were fighting overhead in total risk. We waived precautions and got back to our usual heavy load of work. Six or seven of us on the editorial staff of *Time* and four or five in the adjoining office and darkrooms of *Life* were producing a volume of cables and pictures which would hardly be exceeded, later, by three times the number of people.

The bombing was creeping closer to the heart of London, but, despite casualties, London's spirit held steadfast. As August waned, however, so did Air Marshal Dowding's resources—drastically. Much later we learned the figures. Between August 24 and September 6, Fighter Command lost 103 pilots killed, including some of our friends, and 128 seriously wounded. The loss in Spitfires and Hurricanes was 466 destroyed entirely or badly damaged. What we clearly saw among our friends who came to stay with us in London on a day's leave was bone-deep exhaustion. No British publication would hint at it and give the enemy comfort.

In London we half prayed for a miracle which would instantly transform us into experienced fighter pilots, and continued to pound typewriters.

On Saturday, September 7, a warm and gracious evening, Noel and I taxied from Chelsea up to Marble Arch to see a Claude Rains film, *Here Comes Mr. Jordan,* an amusing picture with a ghost as its hero. Sometime during the run the picture stopped and a notice appeared on the screen. AN ALERT HAS SOUNDED. IF YOU WISH TO LEAVE, WALK, DO NOT RUN, TO THE NEAREST EXIT. Then the film resumed. There was very little movement in the big house, and when we heard the sirens wailing behind the film's soundtrack, people remained seated.

Outside the theater we found that traffic had disappeared. No taxis or buses shuffled along Oxford Street, normally so busy. Only a few private cars hurried past. My high heels clacking, we walked down Park Lane, behind Buckingham Palace and along the King's Road to the Chelsea Embankment, a couple of miles.

That night began the Luftwaffe's long nighttime Blitz on London, giving particular attention to the

East End docks, killing about a thousand people and wounding many more, and it may well be that Goering's decision to attack London instead of the R.A.F. airfields was the fulcrum on which Germany's final defeat balanced. For the succeeding fifty-six nights, without surcease, London shuddered and burned from high-explosive bombs and firebombs.

Since my earliest days in London I had been looked after by the same "char," Mrs. Gordon, who lived with her husband and two children in a block of workers' flats, without hot water or private bathrooms, just up the Thames Embankment from us. She used to bring me morning tea in bed. She kept the house shiny clean and my clothes washed, cleaned and pressed. We had been friends and co-workers for three years, and neither then nor later did I learn her or her husband's Christian name.

On Monday morning, September 9, after a day of waiting hour by hour for word that the Germans had invaded British soil, Noel and I welcomed Mrs. Gordon as usual. She was looking smart in a black suit I had given her, and after a polite "good morning" burst into tears. Her building had been hit during the night, the bomb penetrating to the shelter. Old ladies she had known were dead, and worse, a little girl. We did what we could for consolation—arms about shoulders, a cup of tea. Neither she nor her husband nor children were hurt, but she was in shock.

The next day, in conferences both in the air force and at the War Office, briefing officers predicted "invasion this week."

I was having increasing difficulty getting from the *Time* office in Soho back to Chelsea. Either I had to leave work unfinished in the office in order to catch the last bus or I walked the three-some miles in the twilight and noise. On Monday, September 16, we moved to Lansdowne House, Berkeley Square, into a luxurious flat at £ 12 a week, nearly $60.00, which was extravagant for us. That night we dined in the building's basement restaurant with Quent Reynolds and some other friends. A bomb landed on the other side of the square. It scattered soot all over everything and sucked out Quent's windows on the front of the building. When we went upstairs, his curtains were blowing in and out.

On the night of September 17, German bombs landed in Oxford Street, half a mile to the north of us in Berkeley Square, mutilating two of the street's big department stores and burning the John Lewis store almost entirely. (There went our inexpensive fall hats and handbags and underwear.) In Lansdowne House water faucets and electric lights and telephones were still operating, and at the office, our switchboard girl, a voice-pal with the operators in a dozen London exchanges, worked out miraculous telephonic detours of wounded or destroyed exchanges to reach the numbers we wanted from Soho. "It will be a minute," she would say. "To get you Knightsbridge, I've got to go up through Primrose" (miles north).

Among the girls with whom I sometimes lunched was Virginia Hall, whom I'd first met in Paris. She had been in the United States consular service in Ankara when, at a partridge-shooting party in the country, she had been shot in the leg. Turkish surgeons operated inadequately, the leg became infected, and American surgeons could not save it. Now, from above the knee down, her leg was metal. The loss of her leg meant the loss, also, of her career, because a clause in the contract for people of Virginia's rank in the diplomatic corps said something about "personal obligation to protect state papers." It meant you had to be able to run. I surmised that Virginia was doing something for our Intelligence service as she had done in France but did not ask what, and when once she suggested that I might like another kind of work "more rewarding" than journalism for *Time*, I said, "No thanks." I hadn't the slightest talent for dissembling and for the moment I felt my work sufficiently rewarding. It was not until much later that one of her colleagues told me of her tremendous valor, of the risks she took constantly and the physical strength she expended in behalf of the Allies.

From the fall of France onward she secretly landed at one port or another, made contact with French partisans, helped in their schemes or suggested new ones, sent messages back to London, helped Allied prisoners escape. One snip of achievement, told me perhaps by someone else, remains still precise in my mind. One day when she was driving in France, pretending to be delivering eggs in a small lorry, a German road patrol stopped her, demanding papers, which she produced casually, together with the order for the eggs. The two soldiers wanted to go to the town for which she was headed and she invited them to squeeze into the vehicle's small seat with her, explaining she did not wish to disturb the eggs. After she unloaded the soldiers in the town she drove on to a rendezvous with French partisans, where she unloaded her eggs and, from beneath them, a sizable cargo of guns and ammunition.

She asked me one day in London if she might bring a friend to tea and appeared at my door standing beside an R.A.F. uniform surmounted by a protrusion of hair and flesh, hardly to be described as a head. Aluminum hooks extended from the coat sleeves. He was Flying Officer Somebody. Having introduced him, Virginia hurried away on another errand. I had had no training for dealing with that kind of inescapable visible tragedy. But this R.A.F. pilot's eyes had escaped the fire in his cockpit. He could handle a cup and, with difficulty, he could speak.

He had been shot down, burning, over France and had been rescued by partisans. But the country doctor who would call on him to do something for his charred face and hands, slipping through the night at irregular hours, had only the most elementary notions concerning the treatment of burns, and this young man, who did not speak French, could not protest when the Doctor, removing bandages, also removed, week after week, further bits of his face which had begun to heal into the bandages. He was savagely bitter. "You go into a bar and conversation stops," he said. I hunted around inside my head but could find no truthful drop of consolation. When we taxied together to his club in Piccadilly, I asked blessings for the old cabbie who appeared not to notice anything strange about the frightening apparition I was accompanying.

75

Again among the people with whom I had business at our embassy was our ambassador, Mr. Joseph Kennedy. A year before, his estimates of French and British capacity to withstand a German attack were near zero. Now I found his pessimism deeper and darker. He had sent his family back to the United States, he had moved most of the departments of his embassy to a house in the country, for safety against the Blitz—and inaccessibility to U.S. citizens in England. He considered the British government and people bewitched or mad in their resolve to hold out against the Nazis. "They haven't got a hope," said he.

They need you like a broken back, thought I, and in my cable to New York urged that our Washington office check with the State Department to discover how much credence was being given there to Mr. Kennedy's surely gloomy, and possibly not objective, reports.

On the evening of September 23, after Noel and I had finished dinner, Lansdowne House shuddering occasionally from too-close bombs, the building's telephone operator rang us to say, "You must go outside. We have a firebomb." We could not smell smoke, but we picked up coats and my handbag and slipped downstairs. From our mutual seventh floor, Quent Reynolds, Bob Low and my former editor on the *Daily Express,* Arthur Christiansen, were already out in Berkeley Square tossing sandbags on firebombs, the half-meter-long tubes hissing white-hot fire from one end. A whole clutch of the bombs had fallen on Berkeley Square as well as into our building and on surrounding roofs, and while we worked to save our grass and trees, the local fire brigade went after the more inaccessible sparklers. All around the square, we could see tin-hatted figures silhouetted against the flames, pushing open trap doors, swinging sandbags and quickly disappearing. Our Lansdowne House bomb had set one apartment afire, but firemen were so quick putting it out and sealing off the rooms that we did not stand long in the chilly acrid air. Long enough, however, for Christiansen to remember that he had stashed a bottle of Scotch near a tree trunk before he went to work fire-fighting. He passed the bottle around, to warm us all up, and Quent mumbled in his dear, gravelly voice, "Here's to the differences between editors and reporters."

All over her one hundred seventeen square miles London blazed that night, and on the next two nights, the bombers droning over to drop high explosives into the fires and thus spread them. We prayed that water mains would not be hit, and at Lansdowne House we were remarkably lucky that fall and winter. Our water supply was never interrupted, although electricity and telephone service were cut sometimes. Our bathroom became a way-station for friends from the services on twenty-four-hour leave and, since we did not lock our door, we found on many mornings one or two soldiers, sailors or airmen asleep on the sitting room sofa or the floor. Mrs. Gordon cheerfully made them morning tea, if we had any, or coffee, which was not rationed.

We were all growing protective coloration for our morale that autumn. Walking to work one morning— Bruton Street to Bond Street to Regent Street to Wardour Street to Dean Street—I passed an ordinary-looking gray van parked in the street, its back doors open. From a jumble of broken bricks, shredded timbers, shattered plaster and dust, which yesterday had been a house, men were carrying objects covered with canvas on litters. These were some of London's dead of that night. They looked nameless, and very still. I wept only a few tears for those strangers and was ashamed to be so little affected. But there was vast work to be done, and bouts of emotion would delay it. I cabled a short piece about the walk, and *Time* in New York spindled it. "Too grim," they said.

Time's New York editors were sporadically wanting to know what Londoners thought or felt about one aspect or another of the Blitz or British politics. Rather than depend on the opinions of the doormen and barmen at the Dorchester and the Savoy, I ventured into the two- or three-floored houses of the East End. Within the sound of Bow Bells—Eliza Doolittle country— and away down the Thames in workers' flats. I encountered the warmest hospitality. Grandmothers who inhabited the kitchens at the backs of the houses, warm from a little fire in the coal range, pressed on me "a cuppa" (tea). Mothers and daughters who worked in factories and fathers and sons who worked at the wharves or markets generously paused in their off-work pursuits—the corner pub, packing for the night which they would spend in a Tube station—to decide what they thought about the new food-rationing restrictions, about the new proposal that every sizable building and group of small workers' houses should have on the roofs a fire watcher, on duty all night, about the government's urging all who were not essentially employed in London to move to the country. In the houses of my working-class friends, that would mean the grandmother and the younger children, and the ten or twelve families I knew solidly rejected the idea. Husbands and wives had been born and raised within a street or two of each other, and this was their territory. They might go sleep *ensemble* on the Tube platforms, for safety and to escape the noise. But nothing could lure them from their own private bits of London.

"I imagine I'd go off my rocker," I said to Harley Street psychiatrists, "if I had to sleep underground and dream of being buried under our building." (After a couple of nights in the Lansdowne House sleeping basement, Noel and I had returned to the privacy of our own beds and the noise of the bombs and the ack-ack.) "How do your psychotic patients react to all of this?"

The answers were surprising. "My claustrophobes go with docility to their shelters. One fear supersedes the other—death or being mangled, over a resistance to being shut inside an enclosure."

The one night of October 6 was a glorious reprieve for us in Lansdowne House. For whatever mysterious reason, the Luftwaffe paid almost no attention to London. We floated like lazy clouds in a windless sky of sleep. We needed it. But about that time the main sewage exit of London took a direct hit and the vast city's sewage had to be diverted into the Thames.

At 6 a.m. on October 30 I scrawled: "Bad, bad night. We're missing too much sleep." Later we learned that nearly three hundred German bombers had been harassing London, attacking especially the railways and their stations and doing them grievous damage.

Of the very next day Churchill later wrote, "By nightfall the Battle of Britain was over. . . . For all the effort they put into this phase, the Germans achieved singularly little of strategic value." But the nightly Blitzkrieg continued shaking the island.

In the West End, the most desirable peacetime penthouse and top-floor apartments were steadily losing their desirability. The management of Lansdowne House mentioned that a top-floor flat was available at about one-third of what we were paying for the furnished seventh-floor place we occupied, and early in 1941 we moved upstairs.

Visually, the fire raid of December 29, the last Sunday of 1940, was the single most awesome one. On dozens of mornings I had climbed to the roof of Lansdowne House and seen the gray face of London ringed with fire, unreasonably, eerily beautiful, like an old lady saint with a halo of roses. The dazzling pyrotechnic display of December went up both sides of narrow Ludgate Hill, around St. Paul's and on into the City, flames leaping from one ancient roof to another that evening. Bill Stoneman, Ingrid Martins and I watched it together, marveling at the firemen crawling like black beetles up the flame-garlanded walls, marveling at the familiar dome of St. Paul's riding the sea of flame like a buoyant ship, I listening with apprehension to the drone of bombers overhead. As usual, the enemy was setting fires and then coming back with high explosives to spread them. St. Paul's escaped that night, but five million books were burned in Paternoster Row where twenty-seven publishing houses had their offices. Simpkin Marshall Ltd., the single largest distributor of English books then in the world, lost four million books and its irreplaceable one-hundred-fifty-year-old cataloging system. How could such successful publishers be so stupid as to fail to evacuate the system, I wondered. Nineteen churches in the square mile of the City were reduced to leaning shells that night, and thirty-one of the thirty-four ancient and beautiful Halls of the City Companies were damaged or destroyed. High explosives abolished national treasures at Buckingham Palace, the House of Commons, the Temple and in hundreds of other places; but the fire of the City was the most spectacular.

Our New York office decided to allocate one page of *Time*, titled "People's War," to the Blitz, and some of the responsibility for filling the page fell to me. It was an assignment I welcomed and, finding ordinary Londoners now in the front line, I was awed and entranced by their courage and fortitude.

When the Germans took the trouble to aim their bombs, my friends in the East End, especially those living near the Thames docks, took the brunt of the blows. By mid-October, the block of workers' flats near the Prospect of Whitby pub had still escaped damage, but when I went to call and have "a cuppa," one family said that some friends down the road had copped it the night before, and someone offered to take me there. These victims were a churchwarden and his wife and two children, and their casualty was their small two-story house only a few yards from the church, where they had taken shelter for the night. A bomb had hit the house squarely and what remained were little more than splinters of furniture and dust. But the housewife, smiling, pointed out to me a small china jug, intact, sitting on what had been a kitchen shelf. "Cor," said somebody. "You cahn't believe it." I wondered if someone had not placed the jug there, a sliver of Cockney wit in the gloom of loss, to ease the family.

"I'll miss the wireless," the housewife said. "We dug it out, but it's just bits and pieces."

"Where will you live now?"

"Well, we'll stay sleeping in the church, I fancy. It shook last night, but not a brick fell."

"But for cooking and washing and that?"

"Well, 'Enry's got a sister in Camberwell. And my sister lives over near Limehouse [London's Chinatown]. Somebody'll take us in." They would not know until they could take the Tube or bus to see their relatives. London's lower classes had no telephones in their homes. Those of us who did have telephones adopted the habit of calling friends in the morning to check on their welfare after a bad night.

To the British every bombing was an "incident," and the most distressing incidents were those in which the people were buried, usually wounded, under the debris of their houses. The government summoned to London the most practiced people in the kingdom, crews of miners from Wales, to work at rescue efforts. Even though *Time,* New York, was little interested in stories of personal disasters to Londoners, I walked sometimes in the clammy gray dawns toward the pillars of rising dust I could see from the roof of Lansdowne House and hung around the edges of an "incident," my nose prickling with the acrid molecules of cordite still hanging in the air, my throat contracting against a mixture of cordite and fury and grief, my ears struggling to understand the grunted orders or comments which the men from Wales gave each other as they removed a brick, a stick, a plank, always carefully, lest some support be jarred, to the doom of those still alive below.

On one October morning a bit northeast of the BBC, and of Ed and Janet Murrow's apartment, a big block of flats had been hit and dust and fumes were still spoiling the air when I reached there. A variety of private possessions were still scattered about, a brassiere, a bottle of Epsom salts, half of a pair of pliers, a dusty, bent imitation parchment lampshade, a man's bedroom slipper. How chagrined those dead or wounded people would be, I thought, to know that their private possessions were out in public view. What insupportable indignities does total war impose on humanity.

At another "incident" up near Paddington Station, a neighborhood of aging five-story houses with domestic belongings still scattered about and papers limping in the dust-laden breeze, a little boy four or five years old ran sobbing from the women in the tea wagon to me and clutched my knees. When I knelt down, I could understand his words between his gasps for breath. "My mum's down there, my mum's down there," he kept saying. He was wearing socks and some kind of sleeping costume with an outsized sweater over it.

"And where's your dad, darling?" I asked.

He looked at me, surprised. Maybe he had never heard the word "darling." "Where's your dad, ducks?" I asked.

"In the army," the child sobbed. "My mum's down there." Sitting on some broken bricks, I held him for a bit, nuzzling his dirty hair with my nose, murmuring placebos in his ear, "It's going to be all right, buddy, don't you fret. It's going to be all right," and after a bit I thought I felt the small body begin to relax beneath his wrappings. An air-raid warden came to take him away, assuring me they had his name and address and that they would soon be getting his mother out of her underground trap. "She's not in too bad shape," the man said, which could be anything short of dead, I thought, and headed for the Dean Street office, to be a mediocre worker that day.

A score of pictures bounce through my head, the way landscape and figures jerk past the eyes of a forward-facing passenger in a train. Someone discovered that a hamlet named Churchill existed in Somerset, and Walter Graebner dispatched Cecil Beaton and me to do a picture story for *Life*. As we settled into the car behind the chauffeur, heading out of London for Bristol, Mr. B. drew from a bag an enormous piece of gros point needlework and bent over his stitches. The gros point canvas inundated me in my winter coat. I asked the chauffeur to stop and moved up front with him.

At Churchill, Mr. Beaton photographed laundry flapping on a line, the unrewarding village square with church tower, the local squire in his large bourgeois drawing room, and the home guard digging a hole in the ground, protection against air raids. I accumulated bits of history, native traditions, habits, and the chilling discovery that the population of Churchill regarded the Blitz on London and Britain's other large cities with only the faintest interest. London might have been another planet.

On a story concerning women's rights, I went to see Viscountess Nancy Astor at her London house near Green Park. The front of the house had been bombed to rubble, but Her Ladyship, one of the Langhorne sisters of Virginia famed for their wit and beauty, whom Charles Dana Gibson had immortalized in his drawings, was at work with her secretary in a neat, clean room at the back, perhaps once a maid's bedroom. She chatted with enthusiasm and precision about the women's rights project, whatever it was, and at the end of half an hour invited me to spend the weekend at Cliveden, their famous country place on the Thames. For years it had been a Tory rendezvous and sub-official headquarters. I demurred. There were many political issues on which I disagreed with Tory policy, I explained, and besides, having left my wardrobe in Paris, I had no clothes suitable for a Cliveden weekend.

"Haven't you *anything* long?" asked Lady Astor.

"Only a housecoat," said I, remembering that I had just bought a long burgundy-red woolen housecoat at Fortnum and Mason.

"Well, then, bring that out. Come for tea on Saturday. I'll have so-and-so pick you up."

My husband was out of town and I welcomed the idea of a weekend in the country. So-and-so picked me up on time, and we reached Cliveden while people were still sitting haphazardly around the tea table at one end of the great hall—deep-cushioned sofas, a sedan-chair case full of silver, masses of flowers, full-suited armor and tapestries and dark portraits of scowling ancestors. Lady Astor had been investigating me. As I approached the tea table she cried, "You traitor. You've been seen with that monster, Aneurin Bevan." Nye Bevan was a giant of the Labour Party, a Tory bogeyman.

"Yes, m'am."

"You consort with all those other Labour monsters."

"Yes, m'am. With anyone who will give me news. I am a reporter, as you know." I had lunched that week with another Labour monster, Ernest Bevin, and would dine the next week in a group which included Harold Laski, the economist and steadfast critic of British conservatives, politics, and one of my heroes.

After I reached my room and saw that a maid had unpacked my small bag, there was a soft knock on my door. It was one of the Astor boys, saying, "You know Mother won't allow any alcohol. Would you like

83

a drink?" I was happy to accept a few sips of whiskey. A few minutes later my hostess came in to inspect the room with its big china washbowl inside of which stood a flowered china jug, big enough to hold a gallon of water. On the floor near the washstand was a china bucket, a "slop jar." Lady Astor found the room satisfactory, mentioned that the bathroom was down the hall, looked at my housecoat with its big navy-blue cummerbund and approved it. With some imitation pearls and a sparkly pin added, I didn't look too bedroomy, I hoped, going downstairs to the beige sitting room for a glass of cider before dinner with some twenty other guests.

When she wished to have a guest's glass refilled, our sprightly hostess summoned the butler by whistling with two fingers, the whistle being one of her favorite tricks. On the various occasions when I was a guest at Cliveden, I never saw a place card on the long oval dining table with its surface enameled to resemble green marble. From her end of the table, far from the doorway, Lady Astor called to the guests, assigning chairs that first evening. She ordered me to sit at Waldorf's, Lord Astor's, left. My housecoat caught her eye, and, while we all stood waiting, she informed the assembly that I did not have an evening dress, that I was wearing a housecoat and that housecoats were acceptable that year because of the Blitz. Somebody told me later that by the end of the speech my face was almost the color of my robe. Lord Astor helped me onto the less personal territory of war gossip and we got on comfortably through dinner until he interrupted to call to his wife, "Stop that, Nancy. Stop it." In the excitement of some controversy she was enjoying, our hostess was jabbing her dinner knife into the table top in front of her.

On the top floor of Lansdowne House, Noel's and my home life continued the same—friends from the forces dropping in to bathe, shave and sleep on the floor, giving us whatever new military "gen" they had, knowing we would not repeat it and certainly that I would not attempt to slip it past the censor, or Noel try to get it published in the *Daily Mail*. Friends came up for dinner, something simple prepared by me—corned beef from South America was still available in tins, and I had learned how to make corned beef hash.

On Saturday, March 8, I wrote: "We saw for the first time the new parachute flares which hang in the sky for what seemed like ten minutes, with their long tails dotted with lights. . . . The bombs all fell in the West End last night. They hit the Café de Paris, killed scores of dancers and all of Snake-Hip Johnson's band except the drummer. Today they were still digging them out and some twelve cars waited, still ownerless, on the other side of the square. Two hits on Buckhouse [the palace], one on Signal House in Curzon Street."

Somebody told us the story, apocryphal, of Mr. Churchill's taking a taxi to the BBC to make a broadcast. Winston asked the taxi man to wait until he came out. The driver said he wanted to go home to hear the Prime Minister. Winston tipped him ten shillings. The taxi man looked at the note in the darkness and said, "For a good fella like you, I'll wait. Bugger the P.M."

At the American embassy, re-established in its building at the southeast corner of Grosvenor Square at Grosvenor Street, there had been building up for some time a corps of military, diplomatic and business people, who were "observers" under our newly appointed ambassador, John Gilbert Winant. On March 11, the U.S. Congress had authorized the Churchill-Roosevelt scheme of Lend-Lease. Averell Harriman came over to London to administer the British end of the agreement and whenever he was not being entertained at Chequers, the P.M.'s country place, slipped into the moving stream of the town's after-office-hours cheerful, if not elegant, conviviality.

Life wanted a picture story on the new revitalized U.S. embassy in London and assigned me to do the text which would accompany Cecil Beaton's pictures. Mr. Beaton got excellent portraits of Ambassador Winant, looking as he preferred, like Abe Lincoln's younger brother, complete with tweeds, shaggy eyebrows, brooding eyes and furrowed cheeks.

On April 5, as Mr. Beaton was photographing

Averell Harriman, he mentioned that it was my birthday. Averell promptly produced an outstanding present, a book of Walt Whitman's poems, my constant companion for years thereafter. Among the more exuberant of the U.S. Army observers at the embassy was Major Arthur MacCrystal, a Montana boy, a man with the manner of mountain breezes still blowing about him. Golddigging, I mentioned my birthday and that he could, if he wished, buy me a drink. He invited me to lunch at his flat. That was about 11:00 a.m.

At about one o'clock, when I reached Major MacCrystal's flat, there, glory be, was an assemblage of friends, both from inside and outside the embassy, together with a table laden with buffet goodies and chilled champagne in buckets of ice. I was overwhelmed by my casual friend's kindness, my faith bolstered in the U.S. Army's capacity for quick organization, and became unfit for more than token devotion to duty that afternoon.

For the BBC's "schools program" I was doing a series of broadcasts about American poetry. I did a program about Vachel Lindsay, Negroes in America and Africa, and their exclusive rhythms in speaking, music and dancing, and read into the microphone a part of the poem "The Congo." For another program I hoped to read part, or all, of Stephen Vincent Benét's poem "Metropolitan Nightmare," a dramatic treatment of termites chewing away an American city because they had adapted themselves to digest specks of steel. My volume of those Benét poems was in Paris, but I found a copy at the British Museum, and, scribbling lines from the work, reflected that poetry had frequently kept abreast of stalking violence—Homer, Héloïse and Abélard, Dante, Sir Walter Scott, Siegfried Sassoon, Walt Whitman, Erskine Childers, Rupert Brooke.

The violence arrived soon enough on May 10. Three R.A.F. friends were having a drink with Noel and me in our flat when the sirens yelled and the guns started bopping. The young men started off for a nightclub and Noel and I were undressing when we heard the whoosh of a bomb coming very close. Half undressed, I ran into the hallway, yelling to Noel to follow. Lansdowne House jumped up, our windows shattered inward, the trajectory of the flying glass restrained by our floor-length window draperies. The electricity went off. We groped around, found an electric torch, and wormed our way a couple of floors down to the mattresses we had left by the staircase, haven for such a night as this.

Our friends came back, found us as they climbed the stairs, and explained that the taxi they had just hailed had caught fire from the bomb. They had helped put the fire out and were now dispiritedly ready to go to sleep on the floor. On Sunday, May 11, I wrote: "Today has brought the usual post-bomb misery—the taste of powder in the mouth, burglar alarms ringing incessantly, glass crunching under our shoes in the flat and also outside, clothes in the closets and drawers heavy with dust, my eyes red and face old looking and feeling as though it were burning, and a terrible job to concentrate my thinking.

"The sun was soft rose through the smoke which covered the sky the whole day. Jim Seymour came along and called it 'Bloody Sunday.' The bomb which broke our windows hit just behind our building. It was one of the new 'Daisy Cutters.' It made a tiny hole, only about 3' by 2' and about one foot deep through the pavement. But it broke every window in the block." Five hundred German bombers had struck at London on the tenth. Their bombs and incendiaries had lighted 2,200 major fires, had killed 500 people and wounded about 2,000. The most remarkable result of that night was that anything of value was left standing. In Trafalgar Square Nelson's monument still towered.

Walter Graebner and the manager of *Time*'s London business office had decided to rent a house in the country as a rest-relax haven for over-exhausted staff, and they had found a house in the rolling hills of Buckinghamshire, near High Wycombe northwest of London. On a weekend there I wrote: "Read *For Whom the Bell Tolls* until lunchtime—excellent book."

Noel and I were living in our top-floor flat in the chill English spring without windows or any prospect of getting them and the concomitant necessity of keeping our house lights very low in case a breeze ruffled the heavy window draperies and so allowed light to shine out. We were not much upset when the Lansdowne House management informed us that the government wanted the building for offices and that we must move. We found a new flat at 55 Park Lane, right behind the Dorchester Hotel, and moved in easily since our lares and penates were mostly in Paris or broken in the window blow-in of May 10. Material possessions meant little to us then.

French windows of the sitting room and master bedroom of the new flat overlooked the back gardens, with greenery and flowers, of some embassies facing on South Audley Street, and we had large patches of sky between us and the embassies' roofs. The sitting room was upholstered in clean beige tapestry—correct if not stimulating—and there were a dining room, a guest bedroom and two baths. "I feel like a chatelaine," I wrote, "but the bank balance shrinks."

On June 19 I was sitting on top of a hill overlooking Ross-on-Wye in Herefordshire marveling at the John Constable scenery with full-bosomed tree-tipped hills rising from valleys silvery with a haze of heat, maroon patches of newly plowed earth stitched onto curving green pastures with frothy hedges at every seam. "I've been annoying a caterpillar expertly camouflaged in two shades of green," I wrote. "He ducked when I moved a lighted cigarette near him and retreated down his stalk of grass. But he still has not abandoned the stalk. He wiggles when he is threatened, but he sticks. He reminds me of the British people."

In July Mr. and Mr. Julian Huxley gave a cocktail party at their wonderful house at the Regent's Park zoo, and rumor, gossip, even fact, filled the air thicker than cigarette smoke, above the Huxleys' elegant heirloom furniture. Ritchie Calder, long a pillar of the *Daily Herald,* had taken leave to do a hush-hush job at the Foreign Office, and now reported that he was so full of secrets that he was bodyguarded from the moment he rose in the morning until he went to bed. "Tell me half a dozen," I suggested, which amused him. All through the war I found the "tell me some secrets" gambit a good opener for a chat with generals, admirals and Intelligence people. Uttered openly with a smile in crowded rooms, it evoked diverting replies and warmed the atmosphere. When, through whatever devious channels the "no" finally reached me, I could always say, "Ah, well, at least I can report to my New York office that I have been trying." (Military secrets were the least and last of any sort of information I coveted, an unwelcome burden to conscience and a tiresome restriction of my freedom of speech.)

On a September Sunday, a cable from New York arrived at the Dean Street office, asking for a story on H. G. Wells's speech to the London branch of P.E.N., which he had made a day or two earlier. Walter Graebner was out of town, my friends at the British Ministry of Information were busy looking after John Dos Passos, who was visiting, my friends at the BBC were engaged. Having no one to provide an introduction, I rang Mr. Wells's house, and was explaining my plight to a maid when Mr. Wells got on the telephone asking who was I. Why did Luce want his speech, he asked, and I let him keep the impression that it was Luce who had cabled, rather than some minion. Did I know Luce? Yes, sir. Mr. Wells suggested I get up to see him in half an hour.

Wearing house slippers and tweeds, Mr. Wells greeted me at his door in his light slight voice and his slippery indistinct enunciation. He took me upstairs to his big sitting room, its front windows looking onto Regent's Park and the pond lying silvery quiet beneath autumn mists, its rear windows looking onto a tree and vines in his back garden, its large "very valuable" carpets rolled up into sausages for easy evacuation in case of fire or a bomb. He lit a fire behind polished andirons in the fireplace near his small mahogany desk. I noticed the rich ruby velvet draperies at his windows, and a wall cupboard full of what must have been museum pieces of china. Then he led me downstairs, on the way showing me his *cabinet pour dames* on the stair landing. The cabinet was paneled in pink glass and contained a small library with Dostoevsky among the authors. I tried unsuccessfully to imagine a woman guest sitting on the potty reading *The Brothers Kara-*

mazov while flutings of chitchat and laughter seeped under the door.

Mr. Wells told me about his P.E.N. speech, and moved on to complaining about the Royal Family— "German immigrants—this king is the only one who speaks without an accent, perhaps because he stutters," a complaint by then time-worn to the point of shabbiness.

When he could not remember the name of Thomas Mann, Mr. Wells apologized: "I've just finished a heavy lunch." He smelled of whiskey.

When I was finally leaving, he took me to the door, blocked my way out, and stuck out his cheek suggestively. I paid toll with a chaste kiss. Then he let me out and walked down the driveway with me explaining that his two maids were wardens and fire watchers for the whole row of beautiful Regency houses. "They love climbing over the roofs, particularly one of them. She has a Boy Scout propensity."

From my diary, Sunday, October 12: "It was four months last Friday since the last blitz on London. Our nights are ecstatically quiet."

On November 19 I wrote: "I looked in the mirror and discovered I'm growing old with lines between my nose and mouth. I'm going to be hideous. . . ."

On Friday, November 21, Ronnie Tree gave a supper dance at the Savoy, a blithe evening in an autumn in which conspicuous gaiety was generally considered bad form. Two days later at Cliveden when Lady Astor heard I had attended the party she severely rebuked me and criticized the absent Mr. Tree for our frivolity. "Nobody dressed up very much," I said, trying appeasement.

"The very least they could do," huffed our hostess, tugging at her second-best daytime pearls.

John Gunther, who, like Dorothy Thompson, had been much entertained around London, was at Cliveden that weekend, together with the three Astor sons and a Frenchman who mourned that the Comte de Paris had failed to seize his opportunity to call the French people to his aid, overthrow Pétain and establish himself as monarch. Sir James Grigg of the War Office was there, suave and noncommittal on every subject except bass fishing. David Astor was full of ideas for the reorganization of the British military forces, putting all services on one team under one chief and thus curtailing duplication of effort. Lady Beatrice Pole-Carew, whose grandmother, the Duchess of Westminster, built Cliveden, remembered a day in her childhood when Winston Churchill, "an obnoxious and hideous child," came to visit in her nursery and objected to sitting with girls. "I hit him with a ruler and he cried," she said, "and then I called him a crybaby which made him cry louder."

Because the United States was growing increasingly interested in the British prosecution of the war, *Time* was devoting an increasing number of cover stories to key administrators of the war, and I was learning how best to reap the extensive facts, figures, procedures and personalities which went to New York in cablese. The greatest help to the London bureau's endeavors with such voluminous jobs was the recent change of heart about the press by the British establishment. Now the British wanted publicity in America, and lowered their defenses against U.S. reporters.

Any competent journalist knows the first step toward a successful interview. You read everything already published about your subject. Nothing so irritates a man, great or small, as being asked for facts which he knows are already in the public domain. But if, having the facts ready to tongue, you ask for amplification, or verification, the fellow is usually happy to supply them. You are on his ground, and if, in London during the war, he revealed intelligence which should have been kept secret, the censors caught it for him.

Early on I tried a formula for dealing with ministries and their chiefs on cover stories which proved consistently useful. After assembling the germane information, I wrote notes on *Time*'s letter paper to the head man, listing the departments of his outfit I should like to visit and asking both for his additions to the list, if any, and that he send around word that I would be appearing. After I had learned what I could of his department and the way it worked, I hoped to talk to him himself.

Having the boss's approval, department heads amiably gave me what I asked for, or so deftly concealed some details that I did not guess I was missing anything. Starting with the outer echelons of the enterprise, I worked inward through more and more spacious offices and commands to top advisers and policy makers and parliamentary secretaries. It was peeling an onion, layer by layer.

The head man, when I got to him, usually allotted me an hour for a chat, and nearly always at the hour's end made an appointment for a further hour or two. Lord Woolton, minister of food, who organized the plowing up of nearly four million acres for growing grains and vegetables instead of cattle, and fed the whole of the people better than before the war, if not so tastily, twice invited me back to his office. Some department chiefs asked me to interview their secretaries, some invited me to lunch or home to tea with wives and to see photos of absent children or grandchildren.

The interviews were inevitably fun. Often when I asked a fellow what, at some turning point in his career, had persuaded him to take route C or D rather than A or B, was it Schopenhauer—he *had* then been reading Schopenhauer—or Machiavelli, or had it been the influence of a friend or a professor, or of his wife?

"I don't remember," a man used to say. "Let me think. I really can't remember. If you think it's of consequence to your article, you'd better come back." They confirmed the ancient maxim that to an appreciative audience, people delight in talking about themselves.

Noel and I were dining alone in the restaurant of 55 Park Lane when an old friend of mine from the *Daily Express*, Percy Hodgkins, stopped by to say that the Japs had bombed Pearl Harbor. It was an American naval base in the Pacific, he said. Bill Downs of the U.P., who was dining there, confirmed the story, and we hurried upstairs to hear the BBC's nine o'clock news report, an infuriating newscast without detail, only that President Roosevelt had announced the raid on the naval base near Honolulu. One or the other of us kept busy on the telephone all evening hunting tidbits of news. Some three hundred fifty United States sailors had been killed, we heard. Roosevelt would speak at

11:15 British time that evening. Western Union said they were snowed under. Fleet Street had gone mad and was not meeting deadlines. Lacking facts, we stirred up a maelstrom of speculation, planning two-ocean strategy, tactics and supplies. I remembered that Elmer Davis, in a radio commentary the night before, had said that a declaration of war by the United States would cause a rapid increase in the production of war materials. That would partly compensate for the diversion of some materials from England.

Since Christmas arrived on a Thursday that year, and since *Time* in New York would welcome news from London much as they would a flood of flu viruses, we arranged a long weekend at *Time*'s country house, Time Out. For four days we tramped empty roads and paths over hills, stopping to watch sheep grazing in frozen fields, their chomping on icy grass a thunderous hum in the countryside hush. So 1941 ended quietly. But it had not been a quiet year. From July 10, 1940, until the end of 1941, about thirty thousand British, mostly civilians, were killed by German bombs or in fires, about half of them in London. The bombs damaged or destroyed over three and a half million houses and more than a million people were made homeless. The statisticians figured out that there had been thirty-four million changes of address in England and Wales. But, like ourselves, many people had moved several times.

4

Combined Operations

IN JANUARY 1942 I received orders to proceed on Date Given to Place Given, with a change of clothing and passport and identity card at the ready. Not

since France in 1939 had I endured the privilege—
"hurry up and wait"—of being herded about by the
military. I dug out my Western Union credit card and
followed orders. At the London railway station I saw
some old newspaper friends and also some of the new
American faces which had begun to appear at press
conferences around town, Big Name reporters and col-
umnists who had been sent over to assure their U.S.
editors better coverage than we old hands had been
providing from the European theater.

At Fishguard we boarded a boat festooned with a
euphemism of life jackets, and headed out into the
Irish Sea on the overnight passage from England to
Ulster. The jackets might keep us from drowning, but
in January they would not prevent us from freezing to
death.

The night ride made for big business in the ship's
bar, and having deposited my typewriter and bag on
an upper bunk below deck, I paused in the bar for a
glass or two, then moved to the deck to smell the sea
air.

A number of the deck strollers and standers were
young men dressed in what looked to me like English
rather than Irish clothes, nearly all of which were ill
fitting, too long or too short in the sleeves, too baggy
or too tight in the pants. When one of them offered
to light my cigarette, I asked, "Are you in bombers or
fighters?"

"Squadron two hundred something," he said without hesitation.

"Hurricanes," said I, having not the foggiest idea
what his squadron flew.

"Mmmmm," said the young man. "And who are
you?"

"I'm just a reporter going over to North Ireland to
cover some I.R. troop movements. I'm an American.
You going to see your parents?"

"My mother."

"I imagine she doesn't like your fighting in England.
Unless you're from the North."

"She hates it, right-o. She's in Mallow. Near Cork,
ye know."

The young man's mother ran a newspaper and stationery shop in Mallow, and among the greeting cards she sold was one advocating victory against the Germans. Among several hundred boys from Eire, he had joined the R.A.F. just after the fall of France and had been with his squadron—"the best"—for more than a year.

"You really hope Britain will win?" I asked.

"You can be sure of that."

"Don't most Irish hope so too, or those you know?"

"Oh, yes."

"Then, tell me, how is it that Eire doesn't help the British more? With port facilities, that sort of thing?" It was a position I couldn't understand.

"And fight on the side of the Godless Russians!" Indignation slurred the words. "Not bloody likely."

I excused myself and went to bed. The next morning, January 26, 1942, a small group of British army officers, some officials from the Ulster government and we press people were assembled at a Belfast dock when a small troopship tied up to disembark the first units of the American Expeditionary Force committed to defeat the Axis. It was only fifty days after Pearl Harbor, and although the contingent was a small token force, as a sign of U.S. intentions for the European war theater, it made good publicity.

The press group agreed that we should go down to Eire to tap its reaction to the U.S. troop landing. We booked places on the comfortable old-fashioned train which chuffed southward to Dublin. A dining car was one of the glories of that train and we promptly installed ourselves at a couple of white-linened tables. There were kippers and steak and bacon and eggs, the waiter said. Bacon and eggs, said we. We had not seen two eggs together on a plate, and rarely one, in a year or more.

The next day Mr. de Valera, Prime Minister since 1937, received some twenty or thirty journalists, mostly Americans, at his office in the Dail—I was struck by his resemblance to Neville Chamberlain, perhaps because of his stiff wing-collar—to give us a thoroughgoing lecture on Irish history. For eight centuries the British had hounded, harassed and abused the Irish, Mr. de Valera concluded, and he could not condone this military intrusion upon the soil of Ireland by the Americans. In conscience and in loyalty to its many sons made martyrs by the British, Eire could give no assistance in this war to her age-old oppressors. His government would express strong disapproval. A few days later his government sent a protest to Washington.

With Dublin's bounty available for mere money without ration cards, we happily succumbed to sybaritism—butter with our morning toast or scones, sugar with our morning tea, unrationed shopping, a walk in the garden at the U.S. ambassador's pretty residence, big triumphant steaks at Jammet's, which was Dublin's best restaurant. Before boarding the rickety train for Dún Laoghaire and the boat to England I took a quick nostalgic walk with my old friend Harry Kennedy of the Irish *Times* through St. Stephen's Green where we had walked, hands nestling, in 1936.

Sometime during that winter of 1942 Mr. Luce came over to London to sample its air for himself. He gave a luncheon for our small staff and for a week or more stopped in at the office in Dean Street between his appointments with the people who were running the country and the war. After a weekend at somebody's country house, a Tory fortress, he stopped in my office and gave me a quick résumé of the information and opinions he had harvested. His companions had been financiers, bank and insurance and railway directors, and the views they gave Mr. Luce of Britain's economy, present and future, seemed to me unduly pessimistic. I scuffled around among whatever documentation I had available in my head and on my desk and offered him some contrasting opinions. We could not measure the course of any economic trend, we agreed, unless we had a survey of Britain's prewar economy to use as a standard. But that afternoon we could not track down a general survey.

"If you can't find one, make one," said Mr. Luce to me, thereby launching me on the longest single job of research I had attempted.

Mark Abrams, of the London School of Economics, suggested remedial reading for my ignorance, friends who worked for *The Economist* gave helpful hints and I made a work chart. My husband was with Australian

96

troops tracking the Japanese through the jungles of New Guinea and my evenings were free for reading and notemaking. I got in touch with various chiefs of production and government departments of finance and labor. While completing my usual chores for *Time* daytimes, I worked on the long-haul job nighttimes for three or four months and finished finally some thirty-six thousand words and figures reviewing the changes in the British economy caused by the war. When people at *Time* and *Fortune* in New York read my long research job in the summer of 1942, they professed approval, and they used pieces of it here and there. They did not publish the whole survey. It was too long and diffuse. But I was proud of it.

Throughout 1941 and early 1942 I continued writing and speaking broadcasts for the BBC, accepting only £10, the minimum rate for a thirteen-and-a-half minute talk, because I thought of it as a contribution to the war effort. The work took me frequently to the BBC, and on a couple of days there I saw my colleague of the 1940 early-morning empire broadcasts, J. B. Priestley, who had become one of the major personalities of the corporation.

Down in the joyless, tasteless cafeteria of Broadcasting House, I noticed one day that upon entering the big smelly room, Mr. P. walked to the head of a rather long queue of employee-customers, demanded something and bore it away. No squeak came from any mouse in the queue.

Later, at a staff meeting with some of the directors, Lady Violet Bonham-Carter among them, I listened while Mr. P. made an eloquent but, to my mind, irrational argument about a change of programming which he favored. He was not giving his opinion, as one of the corporation's most valuable and highest paid employees; he was telling the directors what to do. I sent a short cable to New York. Maybe the radio section of *Time* could use a couple of paragraphs on Mr. Priestley's "lording it" over the BBC. Some rewrite chap in New York added spice, and the story announced that Priestley was growing "too big for his britches."

Our London office received notice from Mr.

Priestley's lawyers that he was suing *Time* and me for £1,000,000 for libel and defamation of character.

British libel laws are much more stringent than those of the United States and are carefully concerned with such ancillary muddles as "malicious intention," loss of prestige or income by the libelee, degree of anguish arising from the libel. Walter Graebner and I had a solemn conference with the London bureau's solicitors.

Couldn't we blame the New York rewrite fellow and switch the whole business to Time Inc., New York, I asked.

Since the action would be instigated in London, the lawyers thought not. With my pencil I figured my chances of paying half the sum Mr. Priestley was asking for his wounds by *Time*. My share would require about five hundred years of work in the London bureau, I figured, if I lived that span on nothing but air. I was getting about £20 a week—and was worth about four times as much, I judged.

"Let us see if we can't talk to Mr. Priestley," said I. Walter agreed.

By telephone we got on to Mr. Priestley and made an engagement to take him to my flat for "tea." We might be able to clarify the ghastly situation.

One minute before the appointed time, Mr. Priestley's doorman signaled that we were waiting. As we walked the few hundred yards from his house to my building, Mr. Priestley was stiff-necked and polite. We talked of the damage the Blitz had done to those streets.

In my flat I poured modest to generous whiskey-and-sodas into our three glasses, then sat at Mr. Priestley's feet and told him, truthfully, how profoundly and for how long I had read and admired his work. I had read *Angel Pavement* ten years before in Chicago. I recalled scenes and characters and dialogue from some other books and plays—*Laburnum Grove, Let the People Sing, Duet in Floodlight*. It was the best and most instructive reading I had ever found in English, I said, sincerely, and I hoped that he, Mr. Priestley, whom I esteemed so highly, would not attribute that idiotic story in *Time* to me. I had sent a short cable about his going to the head of the food queue at the BBC; but, a lifelong admirer, I simply could not have written anything denigrating about him.

Mr. Priestley allowed ominous sounds to rumble about in his throat, then said, "I have an appointment."

"Would you not, sir, please reconsider our mutual dilemma? Your time is so valuable." We were leaving my flat.

"Oh, those law fellows. I'll call them off," said Mr. Priestley.

"Thank you very much indeed, sir," said Mr. Graebner and I.

We escorted Mr. Priestley to his doorway and skipped and sang back to the office.

Time's foreign desk in New York decided that I should now be matriculated in the New York office and serve a term there, presumably learning its ways and working habits. I acceded joyously. I hadn't seen my parents since 1938. For the first time I crossed the Atlantic in its skies.

In New York there occurred a day or two of welcoming interviews, I for the first time the subject, one of which took place over luncheon at Toots Shor's place. I could not concentrate on that conversation because I was appalled and my digestive apparatus upset by the quantities of food appearing on the plates. Even more distressing was the sight of plates only half empty being returned to the kitchen. Whole neighborhoods of London could flourish on the leavings from Shor's, I complained. My host thought Mr. Shor might be able to placate me. He came to our table and assured me that the leftovers were not being wasted, they were being sent to a pig farm in New Jersey.

My parents were living in Thief River Falls, Minnesota, and I hurried out there to find them comfortable in a white clapboard house with the customary household machinery, ample lawns and flower and vegetable gardens. They were concerned about supplies of gasoline for their car and oil for their furnace, and in chats with county officials, as a payer of federal income tax, I managed to arrange provision for their future needs. My parents stood on the station platform, waving and smiling, as my train pulled away, and for a long time I mulled over the good luck which had provided me acquaintance with them.

In the old Time-Life building overlooking Rockefeller Center with its blossoming terraces, Content Peckham, who was chief of the female research staff of *Time,* took me to a corner office on the seventeenth floor which was inhabited by a fellow. William Walton, his shirtsleeves rolled up above his elbows, his tie loosened, his blond hair lying flat against his head like a collapsed sheaf of wheat, was tapping a typewriter at one of the two desks. He interrupted his work to chat a minute, during which I became his faithful admirer.

I had been assigned to do a rather frivolous piece about the effects of United States military forces on British manners and morals, the troubles in country pubs between Americans and Tommies because the newcomers had so much more money to spend than the natives, the cheerful deceptions in which American Negro troops indulged, telling the untraveled village girls that they were native American Indians, the hustle-bustle in country hedgerows during the long northern evenings.

The story was not signed, as was *Time*'s custom; but it ignited a small intramural brushfire. In the war between men and women inside *Time*'s antiseptic jungle, the lines and ranks were strictly drawn, the pecking order inviolate. On the editorial staff men were "writers" (associate or contributing editors in the masthead) and women were "researchers," and never the twain would exchange crafts. Seeing my first ingenue story, some of the girl researchers huffed, "Unfair." How could an outlander without even basic training be accorded such unseemly prestige? The men writers closed ranks. It struck me as a bit odd that none of the fellows around the office invited me to lunch or a drink. None except Mr. Luce and a few of the inhabitants of top notches.

Charles Wertenbaker, who was foreign editor in those days, apparently shrugged off criticisms and complaints with a few "hurrumphs" and continued assigning me jobs writing stories coming in from abroad. One of them was on the death of Haile Selassie's eldest daughter, whom I'd met with her father in London. Having heard from correspondents who had covered the Italian war against Ethiopia long tales of life in Addis Ababa, I wrote such a nostalgic obit that that nice, shy young woman got a column of biography in *Time*.

Essie Lee, the jolliest of Miss Peckham's research girls, took no umbrage about my men-only employment, and some of the other girls befriended me, teaching me something of the pleasures and cuisines available in New York. Whatever discomfiture I might be causing on the seventeenth floor, I consoled myself, it would not last long. I was heading back to London any day.

Mrs. Helen Shipley, the virago who headed the State Department's passport division and appeared to gain comfort from disrupting peoples' lives, was no more responsive than an amoeba to *Time*'s requests for my clearance to England. From Washington came the report that she seemed to question my various journeys to the continent. I listed the journeys and sent them to our Washington office—weekends in Paris, holidays at St.-Jean-de-Luz, a week in Rome, the expedition to Munich, crossing to France in 1939 and 1940. No response. By chance in London I had seen the plump folder which British Military Intelligence—M.I. 5— had compiled about my every movement. M.I. 5 was Big Brother and thorough, and I suggested that Mrs. Shipley's office ask for copies of the British reports. No response. *Time*'s New York office was stuck with me for three months more than we had anticipated.

I had a few weekends in the country. One of them was at the Luces' abode in Connecticut, their place being called, simply and succinctly, "The House." Behind its colonial façade with white columns one entered a large roofed patio from one side of which ascended a skeleton iron staircase, rather like the companionway of a merchant ship. I was shown to a pleasant room and bath and presently went down to

101

join the other guests on a veranda overlooking misty green glades where the talk was of politics and war, the phrases scrupulously ordered, the voices rich, resonant and confident, reminding me of life-insurance salesmen. Mrs. Luce recounted a recent journey to India, the presentation to her of a uniquely beautiful sari—she rang for a servant to bring it downstairs so that her guests might enjoy it—and how, since she could not send *Time* the true story of the then political situation in India, she had sent no dispatches. Not hearing from her, the New York office had been distraught. From her small audience issued clucks of consternation and approval.

Mr. Luce, who had been largely silent, began to fidget. Dinner was to be served on the dot and three guests, Mr. and Mrs. William Benton and their house-guest, Carl Sandburg, had not arrived. After a few minutes' waiting, our hostess signaled us to arise and led the way to the dining room. As we entered the roofed patio from the veranda side, the delinquent guests arrived from the front door, Mr. Benton looking apologetic, Mr. Sandburg amiable. As he approached us Mr. Sandburg's wide mouth slid into a wide smile.

"Mary, Mary," he yelled, pushing past our hostess to give me a hug. "Minnesota. I'm glad to see you. Where have you been?" I introduced him to Mrs. Luce, then we babbled a moment on the way to our chairs. As we were seating ourselves, Mr. Benton on my left explained that this was a birthday party for Mrs. Luce's daughter, Ann, in her late teens, on Mr. Benton's left. She showed me the present she had received from her mother. It was a small lump of lead, or tin or pewter, a widow's mite, which Mrs. Luce had picked up somewhere in the Middle East.

I made an instant search for something not too consoling to say, and found nothing. None of the birthday girl's guests were her age, and none of them, busy being articulate and meaningful, appeared to notice her. None except Mr. Benton and me. It may have been the dining room itself which aroused my sense of angst. It was an oval room, as I recall, with an oval table, and its walls, floor to ceiling, were

102

padded with tufted pink satin, like a rich kid's bassinet.

From Australia came unexpected good news. Noel was being reassigned from the clammy jungles of New Guinea to the European theater and had managed to arrange his return journey by way of the U.S.

From my modest cell in what was then the Beekman Towers in East Forty-ninth Street, a nearly all-female dormitory for working girls, I moved upstairs to a room with a pillar in the middle and a view of roof-tops. It would do as temporary digs, since after Noel arrived, about mid-December, we used it only as a sleeping and locker room. I was doing a rag-bag of assignments at *Time*, a book review, the People column, other trivia, since nobody knew when I would be leaving. After my stints at the office, Noel and I did the town as far as our purse allowed, a drink at the Stork Club or at "21," theaters and pinball machines on Broadway, both of us enjoying the girls eyeing Noel in his British uniform, handsome with his height and breadth, his pink cheeks and pewter hair and shy smile.

Walter Graebner was in the U.S. and he and his wife invited us for Christmas weekend to their house in Connecticut, which was then still Grandma Moses country with scattered houses and sledding children visible from the roads across empty, snow-clad valleys. A peaceful, pleasant holiday that ended in an eruption of endings and beginnings. Noel was ordered aboard a ship bound in convoy for the United Kingdom. My reinstated passport arrived and I was ordered onto a flying boat for London which was leaving early in the morning of January 1, 1943.

When in the safety of the U.S.A. I had read with alarm of the resumed but sporadic bombings of Britain, the "Baedeker raids," I had reassured myself that danger and destruction loomed more and more forbidding in direct ratio to one's distance from them. Back in London I was appalled to find that I had been mistaken about that formula, at least temporarily. I was dismayed too at the grayness of face among my friends and their air of weariness in speech, thought and movement, feeling my own rude health after six months of protein almost an affront to them. But when the Hyde Park guns commenced blasting away during a small dinner party in a friend's apartment, I could scarcely control my fright. Conversation continued around me casually and cheerfully. I had to sit on my hands to hide their shaking.

Roosevelt and Churchill were meeting under the trellised bougainvillaea at Casablanca to produce their byword for victory, "Unconditional Surrender." In the offices around London's West End I found cleared-off desks and vacant chairs. The people who had presided there, British and American, military and civilian, were busy in the sunshine and confusion of Algiers.

Since the U.S. land and naval forces which were establishing themselves in Britain could produce little news, our London office decided to learn something of the U.S. Army Air Force in England and assigned me the pleasure. The U.S.A.F. could not have been more generous in its hospitality. They gave me plane lifts to air bases which were a half a day's travel from London by surface transport—thirty minutes by air—bunks in the long Nissen huts which had been made into dormitories for the WAFs, food including the required helpings of raw carrots and raisins at breakfast (good for eyesight, the doctors said) and information.

General Tooey Spaatz, whom I had first met in 1940, invited me occasionally to dine at the long table in his headquarters south of London, and there we all sometimes conducted ferocious debates on the procedures and possible profits of air combat, all of them theories, our agreements tentative, our conclusions dubious. Like General Spaatz himself, the table service and food were modest and unpretentious and if any one of the officers at the table mentioned any project, past or future, which sounded interesting, I always asked if I might telephone the next morning to verify or amplify the story. Sometimes the answer was yes and I had a story, but more often the stories could not then be used.

After a nasty, uncomfortable Atlantic crossing by ship, Noel joined me only briefly in my little flat at

32 Grosvenor Street before he took off for an R.A.F. headquarters in the Midlands and soon thereafter for the Mediterranean to cover the maneuvers of General Montgomery's army in the North African desert. With our working interests increasingly divergent—Noel's with the British military, mine with the Americans and with Allied strategy, politics and economics—neither of us could work up much enthusiasm for the other's projects. For economy's sake I had taken a one-room apartment at the end of an outdoor runway on the top floor of the Grosvenor Street building. From small, unrationed materials I had done up the room with a grass-green carpet, bright yellow-and-white striped satin curtains, a comfortable settee in front of an electric fire, handsome mahogany antique tables and chests and an exuberant Florentine gilt mirror. It was the first place in my own taste I'd had in London and I enjoyed it. But it was too small for two people.

Noel and I considered hunting for a larger flat and decided against it. We had no idea how long the war would last or where we would be working or whether we would survive it, or where we might wish to go after it. A year or two before, we had hoped to start a family. Now the time seemed inopportune. We seemed to have other problems with time. No time for long companionable walks together. No time for quiet evenings together. No time for close confidences, or inclinations to define the changes in us.

London was a Garden of Eden for single women in those years, a serpent dangling from every tree and streetlamp, offering tempting gifts, companionship which could push away respective lonelinesses, warm, if temporary, affections—little shelters, however makeshift, from the huge uncertainties of the hovering, shadowy sense of mortality. Among my London women friends I had few "war widows" who had not made friends from overseas. Word drifted up from Cairo, and was pressed upon me by solicitous pals that Noel was squiring a pretty girl there. After a day or two of gloom I decided not to worry about it. Complications in private lives would have to wait until after the war to be resolved.

From Minneapolis, Minnesota, came a dismaying letter from my parents. They were on their way to Chicago, they wrote, driving their car which was packed with their more important possessions. They had sold their house in Thief River Falls and were moving permanently "nearer to civilization." Their health was good. They would hunt for an apartment in Chicago and send me their new address. In Chicago, my father thought, he might find some work in which he could contribute, better than he could in Minnesota, to the United States' war effort. It seemed to me a gallant gesture and foolhardy. I waited for the new address, which, when it came, was in Chicago's South Side, an area about which I knew nothing.

Our London bureau had switched its Time Out headquarters from High Wycombe to a much more spacious and comfortable ivy- and rose-sheathed house overlooking sloping green-blue pastures studded with tranquil, grazing cows. Weekends there grew into marathons of diversion. Somebody found a Russian lady, an actress in her homeland, she said, who had learned how to make miraculous meals out of what puny scraps of food we could bring from London, gifts from local traders, and imagination. She became our cook at Time Out. Wandering about in the adjoining copses, she collected mushrooms and wild herbs and made crusty little hot pies from them. She conjured stews out of herbs and a sheep's heart the village butcher was about to toss away. She evolved triumphant desserts from dreams and the blackberries we gathered from the farm's bushes, and we toasted her almost every night.

Some of us used the house during the week to do long cables or stories for mailing, away from the clangor of London. But on weekends the decibels mounted, Dorothy Dennis and Jacqueline Saix and I and the fellows in the office inviting assorted friends out there. As our boss in town, Walter Graebner was nominal host in the country, but the uninitiated guest could hardly have guessed, since Walter piloted our craft with the lightest possible touch. As the climbing roses on the walls presented us with cardinal-red new leaves and deep pink hawthorn buds unfolded around us, a family of bicycles began to grow around the front door and along the graveled driveway. We climbed the hills for miles around, found and followed paths through patches of oak forest, discovered ancient pubs at country crossroads where we drank 'alf-and-'alf before hiking home through the patchwork fields and pastures. We sang in the chill moonlight outdoors, and kept a tennis game of dialectics going on and on through politics, war and postwar hopes as long as anyone kept awake in the sitting room.

In another part of the country, as some of us walked through a bomber station commanded by Colonel Pete Quesada, we heard rich, warm American voices singing in harmony in a Nissen hut.

"Some of our construction boys," the press relations officer said. "They sing in the evenings."

I thought the voices wonderful and later urged Colonel Quesada to do something dramatic to encourage the music-making. It turned out that I was promoting a project already launched.

The old red brick Royal Albert Hall, one of the graces of Queen Victoria's reign, was crowded on the night of September 28, 1943, with London's then elite of music and fashion, together with the top and middling brass of SHAEF and a few of us press. Conducting a small orchestra of servicemen, the composer Marc Blitzstein opened the concert with the symphonic poem he had just finished, "Freedom Morning," dedicated to American Negro soldiers. It was based on the melodic and rhythmic cadences he had heard in the singing around the Eighth Air Force bases. To my ears it brought a sense of eerie and sustained passion.

After the interlude the house lights dimmed and so did those of the stage. The curtains parted and all we saw were rows of polished brass buttons. Then, softly as wind soughing through a mountain canyon, the voices rose together in crescendos, moved through melody and subsided, all as one. Some of the a cappella music was martial in the picturesque Sousa manner, some of it religious. From the darkness the rolling liquid song which could only be American emerged, "Joshua fit the battle of Jericho, Jericho,

107

Jericho . . . Joshua fit the battle of Jericho. And the walls . . . came tumblin' down." Tears poured out of me.

The weather remained warmly benign that autumn. The small refrigerator in my kitchen had ceased functioning and the company which had made it, I discovered, was engaged in other work (military) and could not repair it. I succumbed to a few days of digestive upset which restrained me from investigating the "fridge." When I got around to an inspection I found that my cheese ration of that week, two or three ounces of the wartime cheese, a lowest common denominator of all English cheese, was veined and caverned with black lines and holes from which was growing green fuzz. I threw it in my trash can.

This was a time of drastic food shortages and restrictions. (A woman who had been seen throwing bread crumbs to the swans on the Serpentine in Hyde Park had been arrested.) One morning a man rang at my doorway in the sky to announce that I had violated the food regulations. I had thrown away some cheese, had I not, he asked.

Yes I had.

He handed me a summons to appear in a local court near our office in Soho. For a modest fee a young solicitor in the neighborhood went to the court with me to explain my misdemeanor. He had barely finished his short recital about the refrigerator and my efforts to have it repaired when the judge dismissed the case, saying with a fatherly smile that, although the British had done well in their kitchens for centuries without mechanical refrigeration, they now understood how important it was to Americans.

For a couple of years food, in all its aspects, had been the third most belabored topic of conversation among us civilians, only the war and politics superseding it. The whole island sounded like a club of dieting women, the emphasis of chat being on the acquisition of nourishment other than that in potatoes and Brussels sprouts and cabbage, rather than on the loss of pounds. (I remember walking down Piccadilly holding an orange in my hand and attracting as many glances, both forward and backward, as if my orange

108

were a human head. Some newly arrived Americans had given it to me, and I wondered what memories it might have stirred up in the people I passed.) Nearly all of us drank more nourishing alcohol before dinner than we had prewar, and into nearly every social evening someone, otherwise matter-of-fact, interjected a dream of plenty, the menu, complete with black olives and sauce Mousseline, of an exotic postwar dinner.

In the autumn of 1943 I had a telephone call from the elegant, old-fashioned provisioner's shop in the King's Road, Chelsea, where I had bought jams and tinned hams, wines and plum puddings during my Chelsea days and afterward when we lived at Lansdowne House until they had very little left to sell.

"We have found some peanut butter for you, madam," said the dignified voice on the telephone. I had entirely forgotten that before I had gone to the United States I had rung them to order peanut butter.

"How marvelous. Can you send it along?"

"Yes, madam, but . . ."

"Oh, I don't care about the price."

"No, madam; but it's rather large."

"Oh, that's all right. Thank you so much."

A day or two later there arrived at my wingtip flat a shiny tin barrel about fifteen inches high and a foot in diameter. Its label gave no indication of its origins, only its contents—twenty-one pounds of peanut butter. Inside—the glory of it—an inch or more of oil rested on top of the mixture. I could *fry* something.

That tin provided presents for my friends more welcome than anything else I could buy them. After dozens of "promises" dinners—all form, no substance—at Claridge's around the corner, or other hotels, it provided the snacks which rescued a dinner party from going home hungry. For the rest of my time in London it provided me with bargaining leverage, getting me such unbelievable prizes as a half pound of bacon, or four lemons, or a tin of dried egg powder, things sent to my London friends by their families in America.

By early 1944 coveys of interesting new people,

United Statesers, were alighting in the streets and restaurants and pubs of London's West End. After a North Atlantic crossing aboard a refrigeration ship, the S.S. *Talapa,* Connie Ernst landed at the Office of War Information building in Wardour Street to brighten the Soho landscape. My old friend Mark Abrams brought her to my cubbyhole at *Time* and we were instant allies. She reminded me of a family of ponies bouncing around a field of daisies, and she still does. She introduced me to some of the newcomers from New York, Henry Hathaway, the film director; good, gray, gritty Sam Boal who also worked for OWI; William Saroyan; Irwin Shaw; and others. I introduced my favorite Londoners such as Michael Foot to her, also some Time Inkers such as Bill Walton, who had arrived to cover the U.S. Air Force, and joyously we developed the nucleus of a new cell of London life, our aims being wit, wisdom and entertainment-in-the-home, however haphazard the home. (It frequently had to be "home," including my little flat in Grosvenor Street, because London's posh drinking clubs, of which I belonged to a dozen, did not admit private soldiers and, despite their impressive civilian accomplishments and status, my new acquaintances were mere G.I.'s in the U.S. Army's documentary film unit.)

Most London restaurants were not so stuffy and John Stais at the White Tower could smell a good customer as easily as he could a juicy young rabbit. The White Tower, unprepossessing and ramshackle in those days, became our club, and Connie and I took to gathering together six or eight people there for expansive, expensive Friday lunches so spirited that word of them seeped around town and a variety of characters, generals, admirals and government bigwigs asked to be invited. Week after week we invited the newcomers, including Alexander Fleming, the penicillin discoverer, not yet a "Sir," who lunched with us at the big corner table of the ground floor and cooled the party fifteen or twenty degrees with his solemn, scholarly manner. Somebody else paid for that lunch; when other out-of-the-cell guests asked for the bill, Connie and I demurely permitted them to pay it. For months we lunched well and free on Fridays.

The office in Soho bulged with new forms and faces. Dave Scherman, a skinny, volatile electric tube, appeared to photograph the war, and riveted me with his New York accent and lingo, of which, no matter how conscientiously I tried, I could understand very little. Bob Capa came to photograph the war and one could almost hear the upswing in female heartbeats around the office. Lee Miller came to photograph the war and with her crusty, cool intelligence smoothed down the office airwaves, but not the heartbeats.

After his swing through South America, Khartoum, the Caucasus, Moscow and New York, Walter Graebner was back piloting us in Dean Street and along came Charles Wertenbaker, rumbling kindly in basso profundo, directing, often by not much more than a lifted eyebrow, *Time*'s coverage of the imminent second front and the Allied efforts in France. If any of us knew precisely when or where the attack would occur, we did not communicate. Nobody in the office told me anything, and I carefully refrained from passing along the suave hints bestowed on me by military friends.

One after another of the English Channel ports was being sealed off from civilian business, and I got an idea. I went to Foyles' old bookshop in Charing Cross Road and bought an almanac. In it were listed the high tides in the English Channel for each month of 1944. In February, March and April there was not enough concentration of vehicles and men along the south coast to merit attention. By May and June there were some days of high tides. But I had not the slightest urge to suggest to New York that they consult almanacs. Instead I trotted down to the Admiralty where I had a genial friend, my almanac under my arm. I showed him the high tide dates for June—June 4, 5, and 6.

"Interesting, aren't they?" I asked.

"Mary, you're under arrest," said my friend. His WREN secretary looked up with camouflaged surprise.

"But, sweetheart, you can't arrest me for showing you some figures in an almanac."

"I bloody well can, and do."

We sat down in the small anteroom to his office.

(Before World War II the Admiralty had never condescended to include a public information officer on its staff, but my friend was it.)

"Have you ever looked at my M.I. 5 file?" I asked.

"Of course I have, though that's not your business."

"And still you are assuming that I might try to send some message to New York, against our interests?"

"This is a curious time, a suspicious time."

"Foyles' did not hesitate to sell me this book. They have many more."

"You are *not* under arrest."

"You have verified something," I gloated. "But I hereby promise not to tell on you." A man of his rank probably did not know precise dates any more than I did.

"Would you please keep your almanac facts to yourself?"

"Yes, sir. I promise to do that." I did.

From my diary, March 2, 1944: "I'm getting terrific, fulsome compliments from New York on the King George cover. Luce is editing it. Four cables so far."

On March 3: "Georgie Patton is back here, and there may be a yowl raised at home. [He had insulted a wounded soldier in Italy.] Another bad raid last night. I got up and went downstairs. Even the poor little Admiral did, although he's ill."

On Saturday, March 4: "I had to horse around for hours with the censors about a silly story about pictures of B-26's. Telephones are out of order. I got the Admiral's lunch, chicken from home, creamed on toast."

U.S. Admiral George Barry Wilson headed Ike's aquatic division and was a neighbor in my building.

Members of the U.S. Army taught me new jargon and language short cuts. "Food" became "chow," "bed" became "sack," office statuses became "T.O." (table of organization)—"He's high in my T.O." Bosses became "C.O.'s." The classic tangle of military operations—misguiding orders or orders mistakenly written or misaddressed or misread or mistimed or misapplied or misunderstood or misanthropic, the whole wild array leading to inefficiency if not to de-motion or death—acquired three time-saving adjectives. They were "Snafu," "Tarfu" and "Fubar"—Situation Normal, All Fouled Up; Things Are Really Fouled Up; and Fouled Up Beyond All Recognition, a serious state of affairs.

There was the morning when Saroyan knocked on my door at 32 Grosvenor Street, a bunch of watercress in his hand, offering it in 7:30 a.m. amiability. He waited on my runway to the main building while I quickly got into my uniform. Then we walked along Grosvenor Street and Grosvenor Square to a newly established G.I. mess hall in the basement of Grosvenor House fronting on Park Lane. Saroyan saluted some, only some, of the many officers we passed.

"How come you don't salute them all?" I asked, still sleepy. My custom was to breakfast in bed at 9:00.

"I salute the looks on their faces," said Saroyan.

In the noise and clatter of tin trays and tin utensils and the ugliness of food, even precious bacon, slung onto dishes, I lost my appetite for this adventure, and in the general uproar somehow lost communication with Saroyan. We had to yell at each other across the table in the din, and the yelling was not conducive to thoughtful conversation. But the watercress survived the warm spring day, and I shared it with friends as hors d'oeuvres before dinner that night.

Bill Walton came back to town, from whatever bomber base he had been brightening, and into my office and consumed another hors d'oeuvre. On my bookcase there reposed a bouquet of those purple and white orchids with which debutantes used to load their shoulders, inappropriate, I felt, for uniforms or the spartan civilian clothes I wore. They were a symbol of generosity from some high brass friend, but Bill looked at them with pretended abhorrence.

"Welshie, you *cannot* wear these," said he, and while I hollered possessive pronouns, he ate my orchids, all but the pin and the stem-protecting paper.

In spite of the deafening refresher course of the Blitz the Luftwaffe was giving us, showering thirteen major raids that spring, with nearly three hundred bombers in each, I decided to observe my birthday, April 5, with a small cocktail party. When I mentioned it to the secretaries of the big brass people, I warned them that my guests would include some G.I.'s or, to the British, "other ranks." I scoured the small Italian grocery stores of Soho and found a few bottles of Scotch at £5 to £6 a bottle, and engaged a barman from one of my drinking clubs. I expected twenty to twenty-five people. Fifty or sixty friends appeared and crowded into my small room. Those who couldn't burrow inside managed to get drinks from the kitchen and filled up my runway, not uncomfortable in the tranquil evening. Charlie Wertenbaker brought in General Bradley, who stood in front of my electric fireplace and chatted amiably with G.I. Saroyan. A few other American generals of lesser rank than Bradley carefully chose only pretty girls for their attentions. My friend James Fergusson from the BBC moved around oblivious of ranks, and Bill Stoneman and Drew Middleton and other American journalists stood leering at that incongruous mixture of people. Major General Sam Anderson of the U.S. Air Force remained, as usual, cordially interested in what his companions were saying, himself seldom embarking on discourses. I thought it was a good party. Nobody got visibly drunk or vituperative. After it, Connie Ernst and I and a few fellows walked along Oxford Street toward the White Tower, saying, "Anderson is a nice—TAXI!—fellow; that girl with the red—TAXI!—hair, what a—TAXI!—smasher."

Our weekends at Time Out, near Penn, Buckinghamshire, were becoming overpopulated. Everybody in the office felt free to invite at least one house guest and late arrivals accommodated themselves on the sofa or window seat of the sitting room or on its floor. Capa had a sweet-natured, pretty, strawberry-blond girl, Pinky, whom everybody liked and who frequently came for weekends at Time Out. In April or May, Pinky had an appendectomy and came out to convalesce at the house, where I was already established in the best bedroom, taking a four- or five-day leave from work. The house filled to the brim that weekend, Alice Astor Harding, Bill Walton, Bob

Landry, perhaps Maggie Stewart (Lady Margaret S.), Sam Boal, Walter Graebner and surely other girls among the company. In the rationing of sleeping arrangements Capa drew Pinky and me in the bumpy double bed of the best bedroom and all of us spent a miserable night, little Pinky on the right, Capa breathing softly but furiously in the middle, I hanging over the left edge until my right side atrophied.

The new bombing of London was making me nervous. It was due in part to fatigue, I thought, and also to new philosophical perspectives which had been developing in my private landscape. The British Isles were reverberating to the turning of wheels carrying tonnage never before imagined. The Allies were going to invade Europe and win the war. To get killed and miss the chance of observing history, not only military victory but also what political and economic triumphs might accompany it, or to be mangled into uselessness seemed more than usually unwelcome that spring.

As I was saying good night to someone at my doorstep one evening I picked idly with a fingernail at a brown brick of my front wall. I had dug a little hole an inch square before I realized how fragile the bricks were, my confidence in the building ebbing. A few evenings later a few of us were winding up a party eating my peanut butter on biscuits when the Luftwaffe seemed to be aiming its packages specifically at our corner of London. I urged my guests downstairs to the ground floor entrance hall, something I had never done before. It was new and exciting to the American newcomers, but with succeeding nearby thuds their elation subsided and, with many of the other residents of the building, we sat in desultory ennui until the noises indicated that the Krauts had shifted their target area. Connie Ernst mentioned that evening that during the night raids her service flat in Brick Street off Park Lane seemed to her to be made of papier-mâché, and we agreed that it was more disturbing when one was alone.

I had noticed that my neighbor Admiral George Barry Wilson, who had a top-floor flat in the main building at number 32 and who once gave me some

115

lemons from which I made a pie and who occasionally invited me in to scramble real, glorious, fresh eggs for him and a friend or two, had failed to join the company downstairs during the mean-sounding raid. When I told him how I had herded my guests below, he chided me. "A girl like you, who's been through so much worse. If it gets too noisy, come in and sit with me. I'll be up." On a couple of subsequent nights I did that and we chatted—families, homes, comforting memories—until the raid abated.

Noel had not worn his civilian clothes for a couple of years and, my clothes-ration coupons having disappeared, I wrote him asking if I might convert one of his suits into something for me. His suit was good, solid British wool, dark blue with a white pinstripe, and our mutual tailor created a nifty, top-of-the-then-fashion suit for me, complete with watch pocket. It and my dark glasses impressed Irwin Shaw when he came to take me to lunch on a bright May day. "Fresh from Hollywood," said he, "if a bit shy on makeup." We walked the mile to the White Tower, cheerful in the sunshine and the circumstance that his C.O. usually failed to notice when he took a couple of hours for lunch.

John Stais gave us a tiny table by the door of his second floor where half a dozen friends were already roosting, and Shaw murmured that the big fellow lunching alone across the room was Hemingway. In his heavy woolen R.A.F. uniform he looked much too warm and uncomfortable. I remembered a cocktail party for Martha Gellhorn Hemingway months before, during which Miss G. had devoted her entire attention to a couple of Polish pilots, and Helen Rogers Reid of the *Herald Tribune* had conducted a brisk bout of chat which left me agape with admiration for her.

Mr. Stais's upstairs room was too hot for my smart new jacket and I removed it, prompting Shaw to predict we would have too many stoppers-by for his taste. Ever since I was twelve or thirteen years old and my mother had tried to harness me into a brassiere, I had never owned one. "God bless the machine that knit that sweater," said Shaw.

"Haven't you ever been inside a museum?"

"A matter of texture," said Shaw. "Paint is not skin."

Two or three friends paused on their way downstairs to mumble, "Nice sweater" . . . "The warmth does bring things out, doesn't it?" . . . "Mary, I'd like to see more of you." Mr. Hemingway stopped hesitantly and said, "Introduce me to your friend, Shaw," and shyly invited me to lunch the next day. Above the great, bushy, brindled beard his eyes were beautiful, I thought, lively and perceiving and friendly. His voice struck me as being younger and more eager than he looked. I sensed an air of solitude about him, loneliness perhaps, and dismissed it. He was a newcomer with few friends. We found a day when both of us were free for lunch.

As Hemingway left, Shaw said, "Well, it's been nice knowing you."

"You off somewhere?"

"A monopoly has just been born, you dummy. The Soho answer to De Beers diamonds."

"You're off your rocker."

London's astonishingly warm spring continued and John Stais put a few little tables on the sidewalk in front of his restaurant. He assigned Ernest and me to one and it helped our first date not at all. Snorting taxis kept whizzing around the corner into Charlotte Street, blotting out words, and the waiters only occasionally remembered us outdoor customers. Ernest was lyrical about his few encounters with the R.A.F. and comic about the planes' intercoms and his incomprehension both of accents and flying phrases. He was accredited to SHAEF and working for *Collier's*. But he seemed to me signally uninformed about the general organization of the R.A.F. and its achievements in the Battle of Britain and the defense of London and about the British and American bombing offensive against Europe. I filled in some gaps in his background knowledge and suggested remedial reading, he writing down titles and references, while I noticed how well shaped his hands were, neither thin and bony nor fat and pudgy, the fingers long and square-tipped. More than anything his manner seemed diffi-

117

dent during that hour, and serious, and I missed the comfortable raillery of my other friends. He had met Noel during the Spanish War, he mentioned, and thought he was a great guy, "classy." It was a business talk luncheon and I hurried off to brighter encounters not expecting to see Mr. H. again.

With the Luftwaffe continuing its nightly visits to London, Connie Ernst and I decided to share a room at the Dorchester Hotel. Somebody had said it had a roof of lovely thick concrete, and we both found it comforting to share complaints and trepidations. Charles and Lael Wertenbaker had a room there too, on the Hyde Park side, and one evening invited me in for drinks with a fellow who was taking me to dinner. Finding Hemingway filling one of the few chairs, we flopped onto a bed and listened to him regretting that he had lost his "lucky stone" which he had brought all the way from Cuba. Lael gave him a champagne cork as a substitute, and I noticed with surprise a feeling of antagonism toward him budding inside of me. Or perhaps it was resentment that he did not seem to be as stimulating as his books.

Big events were impending any day, we all knew, and our talk that hour turned to casualties, which we treated lightly in the London fashion. General Tooey Spaatz had personally and specifically forbidden me to persuade any of his pilots to cart me along on their forays over France, and I had reluctantly and sheepishly promised. Neither Charlie nor Lael nor my boyfriend were much concerned about D-Day exploits, but Ernest was hoping to go to France with one or another American unit and mused, "My mother never forgave me for not getting killed in World War One, so she could be a Gold Star Mother." A sad joke, I thought, and noticed the antagonism again. In subsequent years I saw in many strangers' faces signs of the same disapproval I was feeling and not understanding.

As my date and I left for dinner, Ernest said something about dropping in later on Connie and me. "I must get to bed early," I said.

Miraculously I did get back early to Connie's and my big, twin-bedded room and found her and our friend Michael Foot sitting on top of her bed. With the evening warm outdoors they had wanted fresh air and had opened the windows to the blackout, leaving the lights off. I bunched up my pillows and stretched out and we were chatting comfortably when Ernest knocked. He made himself at home beside me in the twilight and soon was embarked on a long, diverting account of his family in Oak Park, Illinois, including his sister Marcelline with her precious mannerisms. When no boy invited her to a school prom, Marcelline and their mother maneuvered Ernest into taking her —his overbearing mother, who refused to cook for the family and bought fifty-dollar hats from Marshall Field's when his father's patients were not paying his fees. He had been disappointed by his father who allowed his mother to dominate him; but his sister Ursula saved the family from mediocrity. She was quick and bright as well as pretty and a very good artist in clay. It was a bittersweet bedtime story, we three of the audience grunting approvals, when Ernest abruptly veered onto a new course.

"I don't know you, Mary. But I want to marry you. You are very alive. You're beautiful, like a May fly."

Silence.

"I want to marry you now, and I hope to marry you sometime. Sometime you may want to marry me."

A long silence.

"Don't be silly," I said finally, "if you're not joking. We're both married and we don't even know each other."

"This war may keep us apart for a while," Ernest plowed on softly. "But we must begin on our Combined Operations." His voice was calm and, I thought, sad. Resigned, maybe.

"You are very premature," I said.

Ernest stood up. "Just please remember I want to marry you. Now and tomorrow and next month and next year." How could he possibly be so sure so quickly, I wondered.

We closed the windows and curtains and turned on the lights and let the men out. I was exhausted.

"Wow," Connie said, coming back from the door. "Wow. Why were you so tough on him? Why couldn't you be a little bit graceful, at least? Kind? The guy's lonesome. You don't get invited to marry a guy like that every day. Why don't you be nice to him? You might be sorry."

We had brushed our teeth and turned off the lights again. "He's too big," I said, thinking both stature and status.

Allied morning bombing of northern France was proliferating daily with thousands of aircraft assembling in the sky above England and roaring in concerted force across the Channel to pound German defenses as a giant fist. General Sam Anderson, of U.S.A.A.F. medium bombers, offered me the chance to swoop up and watch the formations gathering. At dawn one morning they stuck me in the bombardier's seat in the very nose of a radial-engined Mitchell. I was strapped into the low chair and except for the intercom over my mouth and my earphones was entirely isolated from the rest of the aircraft. It was like sitting in a bubble propelled by a skyrocket.

We shot upward and upward at, I thought, a much too sharp angle, and suddenly were throttled back, tooling around the edge of a flock of circling geese, more and more mediums, all moving in formation waiting for the order to thrust southward to the coast of France. We climbed again and I yelled, "Lancasters? Lancasters?, Blenheims?, Wellingtons?, which are they?" A rumble of shredded wheat biscuits crackling came into my earphones. Unintelligible.

"Aren't there any Flying Fortresses?" I hollered.

"Above," crackled the shredded wheat. We were flying at about twelve thousand feet, but I could see, much higher in the clear turquoise sky, a school of moving mottled silverfish, as large, it looked, as the island below us, and, flickering along their flanks, other quick specks of sardines, fighter planes. It was an armada, all right, the highest powered and most dangerous and expensive England had ever known, and it looked to me like a mackerel sky, signaling a change of weather. We flew over half of the English Midlands.

My pilot decided it was time to go home and rumbled through the intercom. He had no need to tell me.

We slid down a forty-five-degree curve, I wildly searching for something to hang on to and, as a green field swooped up toward us, thinking there would be only small pieces of me to gather for a funeral. But we straightened out and, apparently for fun, hedge-hopped all the way home, lifting over trees, swinging around a farmhouse, without, amazingly, knocking off its chimney, clearing a hawthorn bush by inches, and our home runway's fire truck by millimeters. The pilot grinned at me and went to report that he had accomplished his mission. The only thing I could report was a gasp. But it had been an instructive morning.

On a mid-May afternoon Bill Walton and I were lying on our stomachs on the warm grass of the front lawn of Time Out at Penn, I reading aloud from a paperback version of *Das Kapital*. In the pastoral tranquility of Buckinghamshire, Karl Marx's strong-to-violent phrases sounded anachronistic and supercilious. Bill stopped the reading.

"You think I should jump into France with the 82nd?" he asked. Whether or not he really wanted my opinion, it struck me as a terrible question.

"Gees, Willie, let me think." Nobody knew whether or not our strike against the coast of France, wherever or when it might be, would succeed. Our surface forces might be pushed back into the sea. But paratroopers would be captured. A man dangling from a parachute was an easy rifle target. *Time* could not demand that Willie jump. Unlike the 82nd Division, he had free choice and could, with clean conscience, decide against it. But.

"However it goes, you'll be sorry if you don't," I said, feeling like a bird mother pushing her fledgling to the edge of the nest, apprehensive and guilty. "Unless, by chance, you're dead."

"That's what I like about you, Welshie. You're so cheerful."

About May 20, my office telephone rang and it was Noel's excited voice announcing his arrival in London. I telephoned Connie, rushed to the Dorchester to terminate my stay and gather up the few things I had been keeping there, picked up what groceries I could with my one-citizen coupons, in time to welcome Noel to our small foothold in Grosvenor Street. His gear took up nearly a quarter of our floor space, but we paid no attention. He anticipated moving away soon. He was determined to get into the invasion force, for the *Daily Mail*. Turkey, where he had been sent from Cairo, and being delayed so long there, had been a tiresome bore, and now he wanted all the local news.

I told him what I knew of our British friends. "Filthy" Gardner was still a bomber pilot and alive. George Millar (British Intelligence, *Waiting in the Night, Isabel and the Sea*) had escaped from France, as he had earlier escaped from Italy, was back in town reunited with his wife Nettie or, maybe, again in France. Alan Moorehead was still with Montgomery's forces now moved up to England. He paid polite attention to the news of my new American friends. They were all alien to him. He listened to my account of the difficulties of getting the *Time* cover story on King George VI, and how I had ascertained that the King did not consider his habit of stuttering an "infirmity" but rather as a triumph over his private nervousness. I found it delicious, snuggling close to him in my narrow bed, even with bombs snorting outside. But something was missing in one or both of us.

On June 4, I wrote my parents a V-Mail letter, putting on a happier face than I really was wearing. "The last two weeks have gone by like a flash, chiefly because Noel got home, after being away nearly a year, and I was busy looking after him and getting him ready to move out again. He was so much more silent and reserved than I had remembered him. Now he has gone off again, I can't tell you more than that; but I hope to see him in another three or four months."

Neither Noel nor I mentioned his girl in Cairo or any carryings-on of mine in London about which he may have heard. Maybe we hoped for simple dispersion of our difficulties.

On June 1 or 2, he left the crowded little flat for a secret destination, the sector of the British army which would hit the French beaches on the appointed day. About a month later he was back in London, primarily because military communications from Normandy were so chancy that it was easier for a man to come back across the Channel to write his stories in London than to try to send them from France. Noel wrote of heavily loaded British Tommies, ordered off the landing craft, stepping into water above their helmets and drowning ten yards from the beach. The censor took a dim view of it.

Somebody had told me that Hemingway had been in a car accident and was at St. George's Hospital, and I took him a bouquet of daffodils and tulips wrapped in newspaper (decent wrapping paper was long gone). There was appalling dust in the corridors of the hospital and also in the corners of his big bare room, without any other flowers. His brown eyes were lively and focusing steadily as I moved around the room getting the flowers into a vase which he could see from his bandages and bed.

"I'll be back at the Dorch in a day or two," he said. "Come and see me."

"I will."

"Thank you for the flowers."

"Flowers are good for everybody."

"You're good for me."

I had finished and sent off to New York a rather pedestrian piece about the U.S. Army's arrangements for handling casualties during the invasion. *Life* titled it "Invasion Surgeon—General Hawley Provides Quick Care for Wounded." It was bylined Mary Welsh and datelined London. It happened to be the only signed piece from the European theater in *Life*'s edition of the week of D-Day, June 6.

I had an arrangement with a military friend, who would know, that he would telephone me as soon as he knew that the invasion was launched. We were joshing one evening about what confrontations would "curl our hair" and, since he thought his telephone was probably tapped by either British or American sleuths, we decided that his message to me would be something about hair curlers.

Meanwhile on June 3 I sent Cable No. 402 to "Press Hulburd, Time, Inc. New York." It was a "think piece" intended to remind whoever was writing that

123

week's air actions of facts he might be overlooking. Excerpt:

"Note preponderance of tonnage dropped paruni-states airplanes despite fact raf heavies carry heaviest bombloads stop of total allied one hundred thousand tons dropped may comma which best may weatherwize in ten years comma raf bomber command dropped thirtyseven thousand tons stop total hundred thousand during mays 744 hours equals 135 tons sur-europe every hour stop but merely unistates mediums who now flying couple sorties daily etcan uppush four daylight sorties daily in emergency flew 38 major operations on 24 days etdropped 14500 tons most antitransport stop." And on and on. "Charge Time, Gerrard 6335," I wrote after my name, together with a note for the censor, "I will be at Mayfair 2568 until 8 p.m., after that at Grosvenor 2560 this evening." For weeks both the office and the censors had insisted upon knowing my whereabouts day and night.

At about 4 a.m. on June 6 my military friend rang to say, "Take the curlers out of your hair and get going." I had no curlers but I got going. The U.S.A.A.F. had prearranged a tour of fighter and tactical bomber bases around England, our transport being a C-47, dear old dependable workhorse of our air fleet. Bill Hearst, of the news chain, looking uncomfortable in his new uniform, and Erika Mann, daughter of the exalted Thomas, looking beetle-browed and doubtful, were among our party which was composed mostly of wire-service fellows. *Life's* photographers, Frank Scherschel, George Rodger, Bob Capa, Dave Scherman and maybe some others were all in aircraft or ships getting the most important medium of communication that day, pictures. Walter Graebner and Charlie Wertenbaker were somewhere close to the action. Our safe conducted tour of air bases was second class in news value, a possible wrap-up of local air action which might make page ten in a newspaper, I decided.

My story was written in cablese and Shaw, the office chauffeur, was on his way with it to the censor by nine o'clock that night. I walked home, turned on the radio, all the news in the familiar voices very cautious, and fell into bed.

The next morning Allied infantry were still holding their precarious footing, and landing operations continued. As Field Marshal Erwin Rommel had said in April: "The first twenty-four hours of the invasion will be decisive . . . the fate of Germany depends on the outcome. . . ."

From my diary, June 8: "Wrote a story about our wild Indian paratroopers with their brass knuckles for a newscast and found Noel's first story from France in the *Daily Mail*. Tea with Pam Churchill who emphasized the stupidity of overoptimism about our chances in Normandy. The weather is being terrible and we are having trouble landing supplies."

In the Dean Street office we did not expect dispatches from our volunteer soldiers. Their stuff was being pooled in France to go direct to the U.S.A. Bad news would reach us quickly, we surmised, but, except for the near chaos of communications, none came. Willie Walton, surviving in the Normandy mud with his section of the 82nd Airborne Division, was amazed to hear, he later told me, that an inquiry as to his welfare had come from Number 10 Downing Street, the P.M. no less. Pamela Churchill had been concerned about him.

Nearly everybody in the office was so concerned with the invasion that we were paying no attention to local news. Walter rallied us. There was a murder story, grisly and juicy enough to merit a few paragraphs in *Time,* and I bussed to an East End police station in whose district it had been discovered, to find that British police were as politely tight-lipped in 1944 as they had been when I first encountered them on behalf of the *Daily Express* seven years earlier; there were also squabbles in the House of Commons requiring our attention and cables to New York.

On June 13, the first flying buzz bomb fell on England but in the first days few of the monsters reached the heart of London, and we paid them little attention. Those I heard reminded me of an Evinrude engine chugging noisily across the silences of a lake in summer.

We quickly learned that the moment of danger was when the thing cut off its motor and its one-ton explosive head dropped off. The quality of its explosive was high, we noted, seeing the damage the warheads were doing, the destruction more intensive and also more widespread in London's built-up areas than that from the old-time one-ton bombs. In the initial days of their intrusions we found the buzz bombs an irritating nuisance. Hearing one in the distance, its snorting penetrating our normal noises, we tended to halt work, trying to determine whether or not the intruder's insistent route in London's sky was in our personal direction, to wait for its sudden silence and the bang which meant it had fallen somewhere else. London's sirens were on the alert day and night, as about one hundred bombs came in daily. There was something macabre about this wholly mechanical enemy and about the idea of being killed by an insensate, innocent machine.

As local politics moved from stable to changeable, the economic climate for consumers slid steadily downward from tolerable to terrible. The sensible utility clothes which the government had dreamed up were so dreary that only desperate people would buy them. Those of us who had long favored durable tweeds coddled them and lived in them. When I had bought unrationed yellow-and-white striped satin for window draperies in my little flying buttress flat in Grosvenor Street, there had been enough satin left over from the draperies to make me a floor-length housecoat. Rather smart, I thought, if a bit bold. Not long after it had been delivered to me I took it to a weekend at one of the country's most estimable houses.

On Friday evening the maid, an old crony who had escaped work in a factory, unpacked me, and on Sunday evening packed me for my late return to London. It was not until Monday morning that I found my flashy striped housecoat was missing. I telephoned my weekend hostess.

"Darling, that's impossible," said she. "I shall make a thorough investigation, forthwith." But the housecoat never returned to me. Months later a friend of mine who had weekended at an entirely different country house mentioned that she had seen a housecoat of exactly the same material as my Grosvenor Street draperies.

When I was in New York in 1942, I'd had the sense to acquire a couple of years' supply of stockings for myself and some of my London friends. But, I had overlooked underwear; and now, in 1944, it became, for most London women including me, a crucial problem. Nothing much was available in the shops. I took to holding up my stockings with rubber bands, of which the Dean Street office had still a modest supply. Shoes were my larger problem.

On June 22, 1944, I wrote my parents in Chicago: "I hope you haven't forgotten the shoes. Shoes are by far my biggest problem, since the British simply don't make any shoes that are narrower than B—and if I get them long enough, they fall off my feet." My size, in the U.S. idiom, was 6½ AAA.

Ernest was apparently devoting much of his time and attention to R.A.F. stations and their endeavors and their people outside of London, but he called me sometimes at the office. One day when Charlie Wertenbaker and I had arranged to lunch at the White Tower—he wanted me to do a behind-the-lines housekeeping story from France, a survey of the effectiveness of food supplies, sleeping possibilities, sanitation, as well as that of the army's medical services, which was my primary job—Ernest telephoned and we invited him to join us. He and Wert were already friends and Ernest was picking up our tribal mannerisms of speech, I noticed—the low-keyed friendly insults, our "nothing sacred" deprecation of institutions, folkways, mores, heroes, including our own. The stranger was becoming amusing in our fashion.

"Never get mixed up with writers," Ernest was advising me that day.

"Speak for yourself, boy," Wert rumbled.

"They're all jerks," Ernest said, "some jerkier than others. Some jerk themselves off—they're too stingy to pay for it. One way or the other. They're misers. They don't pay back loans. They're so in love with themselves they can't appreciate girls. Not even a beauty like you."

"Just let her be useful," Wert suggested.

"I run as a brain." Me.

I was still waiting to get to France with the Medical Corps when Ernest invited me to lunch again. It would be fun, I thought, and said into the telephone, to amble out to Chelsea where I would show him some of my favorite streets and we could lunch, standing up probably, at one of the pubs, such as the Six Bells and Bowling Green.

He said, "Yes, sure," but his tone was cautious.

"You don't know anything but the West End," said I, "and that's not London," then realized that he did not care a hoot about learning about London. We settled for a table in a French restaurant in Jermyn Street, where they cooked unrationed vegetables quite well.

"I'd like to know about you," Ernest said. "You said you liked boats."

I told him about some boats I had known, and he told me about his beloved *Pilar*—"I only know one womany who really liked her"—and about the dawn's pinkening above the Gulf Stream.

"Your legs are like Prudy Boulton's," he said. "Strong." He told me about the brown Chippewa girl who was the first female he had ever pleasured. I told him about my adored Chippewa friends, Bob Cloud and Jim Thunder, and how agile they were aboard *Northland,* but could not carry my tale as far as his went. Kinnikinnick, which we called Chippewa tobacco, was one of the loveliest and easiest-to-remember smells in the world, we agreed.

If the luncheon was the beginning of a courtship, it was in the most old-fashioned manner. Each of us, like birds, kept darting forward for a better look, a firmer impression of form and context. Since the night in the Dorchester Hotel of his forthright statement of his wish to marry me, Ernest had not mentioned it again. Now after a couple of drinks and a bottle of wine with our luncheon, he said, grandly, "I'll dedicate a book to you."

Was that his way of getting the devotion of all his

girls, I wondered, and thought of some limp wisecracks about it. If I remembered correctly, he had not written many books.

"With love?" I asked.

"I've never done that," he said, immediately on the defensive. "But yes." Six years later he did it in what I thought his poorest book.

After the magically good weather of the 1944 springtime, June and July moved in with nasty, evil days. I remember going across the street from the office in Dean Street to lunch at the Bath House on Sawdust sausages, in my merely comfortable civilian clothes, my tightwoven pepper-and-salt tweed suit, with a black sweater beneath the jacket and a white cotton shirt beneath the sweater.

"Shouldn't you be celebrating somewhere?" Dorothy Dennis, our Dean Street executive officer, asked. "Such as your embassy?"

"Good God, have I forgotten something?"

"The date. It's July fourth."

"Impossible, with this weather."

In mid-July I discovered why General Hawley's Medical Corps had delayed so long taking me to France. Since I was going, they might as well take a few others of the female correspondents who had been petitioning them for the same kind of jaunt. With my officer's little mummy-shaped sleeping bag, a present from one of our high brass, I could have nestled into a corner of any field hospital; but with five or six women to look after, they felt it necessary to arrange more formal space. I had expected to munch my K-rations wherever I might be. Five women had to be catered to from an army kitchen. It was a conducted tour.

In Normandy I went off with my adjutant general's identity card, my gear and my indignation. The Medical Corps had shortchanged *Life* magazine and would now have to rearrange their plans for me. Even non-journalists could understand that *Life*'s requirements for a story were quite different from those of the wire services. I wanted to see Hawley's chain of service from the front lines to the coast. I said so to a surprised and uncomprehending aide to the Normandy C.O., and then to the C.O., who was luckily available, startled and then cooperative. He was an old army pro and had read my *Life* piece. We agreed that I would go back to the transit camp for the night and in the morning would go forward to a few battalion aid stations and later along the chain of evacuation with its division clearing stations and hospitals. He would alert the aid posts. The night at the transit camp seemed interminable, partly because the materials for a good story were waiting, much more because the damp earth of Normandy near Ste.-Mère-Eglise breathed blasts of cold air upward like an air conditioner, the chill penetrating my sleeping bag, my full uniform, my personal padding, my nervous system, my bones and their marrow. The dried scrambled eggs we got for breakfast helped me thaw, but the tepid coffee was so *un*coffee that I wondered why they bothered with it. What were the G.I.'s doing in their cotton uniforms, I wondered.

With a driver young enough to be my son who could with difficulty read the army road signs, I jolted and jogged southeast in the heavy military traffic, I navigating, amazed that such great rollers of dust as we encountered could rise in the damp air. We stopped sometimes so that I could look at abandoned battlefields with their broken and discarded objects, pieces of paper moving jaggedly everywhere like wounded birds. It was bizarre emptiness overhung by a miasma of desolation. Why had so many soldiers, both German and American, thrown away their gas masks, why had they discarded helmets, canteens, food rations, even rifles which looked intact, I wondered. I picked up some bullet cases which were made of wood, but I did not venture far from the road. Everywhere along the ditches German signs announced, MINEN.

Our route following a slightly lifted plateau, I suggested to my driver that we break away from the crowded main highway, and take a narrow gravel road between high hedges bending off to the right.

"What about mines?" my baby driver asked.

"Look at the track. Somebody has passed here this morning. Look at the splatters from the rain on the sides."

"We couldn't turn 'round."

"We won't have to, unless we come to something blown up." The road was marked, a very thin line, on my map. "You a city boy?"

"From Newark, New Jersey."

The Newark boy was afraid of this strange country road and he drove slowly. So slowly that I caught a whiff of a smell that was strange here, but familiar. We stopped and I tiptoed along the sloping bank of the ditch, and came upon an American soldier dead there in the ditch, his young blue eyes staring up at the folded gray clouds. The burial detail had not yet passed along this road, and this boy was beginning to give off the smell of the dead. It was of vinegar and sugar boiling together on a stove when my mother put up homemade dill pickles for the winter. Too early in the year for that smell, I thought. August was the month for pickling in northern Minnesota.

Ahead of us there were two other dead boys in the ditches, one with the top of his head missing. They were beyond comforting now. I did not try to touch them or ease their awkward positions. I saw no wires, but they might have been booby-trapped.

At the battalion aid station, doctors worked under tents with the sides rolled up, two or three high tables for temporary repairs in each tent, the trodden ground beneath their feet trembling sometimes from the impact of heavy artillery shells falling in front of them. The young surgeons were quick, dextrous, totally concentrated on their work, and answered my few questions without turning their heads. In these first-aid tents the doctors were from Illinois, Utah, Maine, Delaware, had studied and trained at the usual universities and hospitals, were uniformly grateful that, except for occasional patrols, the fighting subsided at night and they could rest from work. On those days, July 12 and 13, they predicted the Germans would soon mount a counteroffensive. "They've doubled their artillery fire in the last twenty-four hours."

In a blood-spotted white coat, a doctor was cutting away the back of a wounded boy's dark green jacket, the boy lying face down on the table. "Shrapnel," the surgeon said.

"Doc, I've got to crap," the boy said, his voice hoarse

131

with embarrassment. "I can't help it." I stepped back a few feet.

"That's okay," the surgeon said. "Everybody does. Go ahead, in your pants."

Those few nights in France I stayed in one or another of the medics' quarters and mornings gratefully accepted their offers of a few whiffs of oxygen before the K-ration-breakfasts. Walking between the long rows of beds in the rear evacuation hospitals, I was struck by their terrible anonymity. Name, serial number, blood type, army unit. Nothing could indicate what these silent wounded boys had been before they learned the regulations of the U.S. Army, got shipped to England and Normandy and in a flash were partially destroyed. Ganglions of tubes and bottles hung above many cots, pulsating plasma or blood into the quiet stretched-out bodies. Nobody knew, and who cared, which of the bodies had been high school football captains or presidents of the local drama club, or hot men on the guitar. I wanted, idiotically, to gather them all into my arms to drone some words of comfort. How could myself, being whole, comfort a boy with a lost leg?

Back in London I mentioned the smells of the dead to Ernest while we drank whiskey in a fetid bottleclub, Frisco's, one night and he agreed with me. He liked the club because its phonograph blasted out scratchy American tunes—"St. Louis Blues," "Thanks for the Memory"—and, apparently, because the proprietor was a smiling, easygoing American Negro. "Like home," said Ernest, fingering one of the wooden bullets I had given him.

"Not like my home. My home never smelled like this dump."

Ernest had shaved off his beard and I thought his natural face much more becoming. He had been invaded by London society, he grumbled. Emerald Cunard was often leading a gaggle of beautiful and famous-named ladies to his room at the Dorchester for drinks and flirtations.

"The upper—uppest—classes of London are the worst," he said. "Immoral."

132

"I trust you didn't lure any royalty."

"No, but those others. They want to stay all night and then have you take them home just in time to meet his Lordship leaving for the office in the morning."

"You poor, innocent country boy. What about that Bible thing, 'He who is without . . . let him cast the first stone'?"

"They're amoral. There's that one who has to telephone some friend just at the moment of . . . total exhilaration."

Noel had returned to France and this was a farewell drink, since Ernest would be off in a day or two. Lady Cunard had left small mementos of herself around Ernest's room, I had noticed, notes and trinkets, rather like an animal staking out its territory.

"Too bad you have to go off to France, dusty, dangerous France, and leave your fascinating friends."

"I'm the five-day wonder for them. Next week, somebody else. Could I ask you something, a favor? Would you write me a letter, any small thing, to France? I've got the address here."

"Sure, any favor for the troops."

"Those shits at *Collier's* don't forward my mail. Haven't had anything in two weeks. No word from my kids."

Maybe he was a conscientious father, in spite of all his wives, I thought, and remembered a casual girlfriend of his telling me, promoting Ernest, "You should take him seriously. He's serious about you, and he's so *responsible*." I wrote a short whimsical letter to Ernest in France.

With General Montgomery holding the German armored divisions immobile on the northeast front, the U.S. Army thrust through the enemy defenses in late July and began a fabulous sweep toward central France, encircling the Germans at Falaise and taking fifty thousand prisoners, then pushing on toward Paris. I was the only member of *Time*'s London bureau who had left Paris and possessions there just ahead of the Germans, and I was getting restless. I was researching a *Time* cover story on the U.S. Army's supply lines and the two-star general who ran that department, and I discovered that, one, supply had a big base camp somewhere near Argentan and, two, they shuttled personnel-carrying planes, C-47's or smaller craft, back and forth to Britain almost daily.

With Air Marshal Roderic Hill's anti-aircraft guns bunched together on the southeast coast knocking down more than half of the daily buzz bombs, life in London was becoming more tolerable. I didn't care. In mid-August, when Allied forces, mostly American, landed in the south of France, marginal comments needed to be sent from London. I didn't care. Looking up from some work I was doing in my flat in Grosvenor Street, I watched London's sky outside my big north window slowly change from 9:30 p.m. French blue to bachelor button blue to ten o'clock navy blue, and realized that I would not be working there much longer or watching that patch of sky metamorphose.

When I had finished pounding out the last couple of thousand words of cablese about the U.S. Army supply service with its infinite attention to detail—down to the two cigarettes in the cardboard K-ration boxes—I went in to Walter Graebner to say, "I've got to go to France."

"Yes, I know France is exciting now," Walter said. "But it doesn't mean that London is being erased from the map. Important political decisions are going to be made here. You should be here."

"Yes, I know. But Paris, Paris." I was like a cat in heat.

Walter smiled and said, "Come back as soon as you can."

My "travel orders" were cut and on August 24 I got a lift to the airfield. At the base camp of U.S. Army supply in France they told me I would have to wait until morning for a jeep which was taking a major in the adjutant general's office to Paris. The major, from Ohio, seemed reluctant to make this journey. He was a diffident and inarticulate man that morning. It soon turned out that he didn't know how to read an army road map. Maybe he was confused by all that greenery of forest and fields on the maps. After we had halted at two or three crossroads, looking for signs in English which had been haphazardly posted, I suggested that I take over the navigation, since I read French. We had wasted half an hour with indecisions. The driver had caught the major's sense of reluctance, and we moved forward in the comparatively light traffic at the stately pace of thirty-five to forty miles per hour, my private steam steadily rising.

Lunchtime arrived and the major began to look for an American army post where he might present his credentials and receive food. We slowed down for that. We were passing villages where cafés were open, French flags and people waving. I was longing for a drink. Finally, I persuaded the major and the driver to stop at a café beside the road, and was babbling joyously to the *patron* in my long-neglected, comic French when I noticed the major move toward the door. We were not sufficiently respecting his rank. The *patron* made lovely Gallic gestures to the major, called his wife, poured glasses of Calvados, long saved for this day and, scurrying among the other clients, all of whom I was hugging, was about to set two little tables —one perhaps for the major and the other for the driver and me, or one for the major and me and the other for the driver—when I begged them to save time. "We can eat *à pied*," said I.

The major did not like the idea, even when the *patron* brought us half a sweet-smelling loaf of bread, some cheese, salt and legs of roast chicken. Maybe they did not eat standing up at bars in Ohio. But maybe Ohio had never been under four years of occupation by an enemy. The Calvados was delivering its message to me, and for the first time since June 1940 I felt I was deliciously, deliriously back in real France.

On the road again I had to caution the driver to keep on the right side and, gritting my teeth, ask him not to try to pass convoys of eight to ten big lorries, tail-trunking like elephants. He had been emptying the Calvados too. I had never seen so many people on the roadsides or such unbridled jubilation. By the time we passed Versailles and through the St.-Cloud gate to the city and up to the Place de l'Etoile, the sky was dimming. With my typewriter, knapsack and bedroll I bid farewell to the major and walked the few blocks to the Hôtel Scribe in the noisy, happy dusk, or, rather, was propelled from one to another group of roistering, singing, shouting unburdened Parisians, hugging and kissing me and my knapsack when they saw my uniform. The city had gone crazy with rejoicing. Everybody was eighteen years old, free of shackles, bursting with joy. Somewhere in the distance I heard an accordion playing in the open air.

I had observed something of the French people in other years. In Paris they had been courteous, cool and friendly for the purposes of business. Except for hotel owners and staff or in famed restaurants, they had generally shown a hard-shell xenophobia. But here they were in a maelstrom of joy, crying, *"Liberté, égalité, fraternité,"* singing snatches of *"La Marseillaise,"* presenting me with many-flavored wet kisses.

At the Hôtel Scribe, which was to be the headquarters of the Allied press, chaos reigned supreme. Charlie Wertenbaker had registered there, but his room, which would presumably be our Time-Life office for a while, was empty. The censors were in residence but not yet in business. The Western Union office was a shambles and a dozen or more fellows were waiting, typed cables in hand, to send their dispatches with or without censor's stamp. I decided that Walter Graebner would have to wait until the morning for any news from me.

Old friends were everywhere in the hotel, but not my husband Noel. He was with Montgomery's forces somewhere in the north. The Scribe was "full up" for that night, but they assigned me a room in a large dowdy hotel across the street.

On the pretext of hunting for Wertenbaker I set out with friends to inspect the bars or any lighted places in the vicinity, and even toward midnight we found no Wertenbaker, but Parisians, still exhilarated, still wanting reassurance that we were there in force and that *les boches* would not return.

"Le général de Gaulle arrivera demain, on me dit," I kept saying.

"Mais, vous étiez ici avant la guerre?"

"Oui, et pendant le premier an."

"Bienvenue. Mille bienvenues."

I was exhausted. I brushed my teeth in the bedroom washbowl of the shoddy, musty-smelling hotel and went to bed. I knew I should have walked to Nôtre-Dame to see what, if anything, was happening there. I didn't.

Next morning I packed my kit bag and left it and my typewriter and bedroll with the concierge of the second-rate hotel; and at the Scribe found Wertenbaker, Dave Scherman and other London office pals getting to work in Wert's room. "Go get us a piece on Paris fashion," Wert said. I left and noticed the atmosphere of the Scribe on my way through the lobby. It was noisy, badly ventilated and crowded. I walked around to the Place Vendôme entrance of the Hôtel Ritz and asked the concierge, my acquaintance from 1940, if M. Hemingway was by chance in the hotel.

"*Bien sûr*," the concierge said, and directed me to Room 31. I rode up the coquettish little lift, the lift-boy in his proper uniform and white gloves, knocked at No. 31, and asked the freckled soldier who opened the door if Mr. Hemingway was in.

"Papa, there's a dame here," Pfc. Archie Pelkey yelled into the room. Ernest emerged into the hallway, a whirlwind of good cheer, and gave me a welcoming merry-go-round bear hug, my feet succumbing to centrifugal force and nearly bashing in the walls. Inside the room a couple of his friends from the French underground, who had been with him since Rambouillet, were sitting on the bare floor intermittently cleaning rifles and sipping champagne. Yes, he had received my letter in Normandy and had read it every day until he lost it. We had a month's news to exchange and we babbled it out in a fruity mixture of English expletives, French and French slang while we slaked our thirst with champagne from a tray on top of the delicate Empire-gray painted desk in front of the French windows. One of Ernest's mob, having finished his work, lay down and went to sleep on one of the twin beds, his dusty, dirty boots quite at home on top of the Hôtel Ritz's pink satin coverlet. Ernest outlined the excitement of his taking and holding Rambouillet with his volunteer French troops, and wanted us to set out to check "the town."

But I had work to do and took off, promising to be back soon.

"At least, let's dine together," said Ernest.

"Sure." A promise, that August day in Paris, Saturday, the twenty-sixth, could not be expected to be a full commitment. On my way out of the hotel I asked the Place Vendôme concierge if he could find a room for me there.

"Certainly, madame," said he.

"I will bring my luggage rather late this afternoon," I said.

"You will have Chambre Quatre-vingt-six," he said.

Quatre-vingt-six, with its chaise longue covered in gold patterned rose brocade, its brass bedsteads, its dove-gray walls and its bronze medallion of an Empire lady's graceful head on the front of the marble mantelpiece, its small, accurate electric clock on the wall, its large gray dressing table with mirror and a pink lacy pincushion, its view over the gardens behind the Ministry of Justice and its special sound of children's voices ringing out during recesses from their studies in their school in the rue Cambon, would be my home from the next morning until late the following March. But with complications.

I walked through that lane of enchantment, the Ritz's passage from its Place Vendôme side to the rue Cambon, and after years of seeing drab London shop windows was more intoxicated by the gaiety and imagination of the stylish showcases along the walls than I had been by the champagne. The House of Chanel, across the street from the Ritz's back door, was shut as tight as a vault, but at the end of the rue Cambon, at the corner of the rue St.-Honoré, a man was decorating Vera Boréa's windows with scores of small tricolors. The shop was closed, he said. *"Personne n'est venu,"* he said ambiguously.

"Did Mme. Boréa have good patronage from *les boches* these recent years?"

"Ah, mademoiselle, I don't know. I am only the window man. But I believe not. *Bienvenue, mademoiselle. Bienvenus à tous les alliés.* Today Paris begins again to live."

Prancing up the rue St.-Honoré I beheld for the

first time the device with which wealthy Parisiennes had outwitted the long petrol shortage. A man on a bicycle was pulling a small upright box, a prettily painted palanquin on two wheels with neat curtains inside its small windows. They stopped near me and an elegantly dressed woman with an enormous flowered hat disembarked.

Up along the Avenue Matignon some of the great dress houses were open and I was able to collect a quick history of the strains and stresses of French couture in the past four years—the shortages of all materials including metal hooks and eyes, the shortage of leather which caused shoe manufacturers to build their shoes on top of high wooden clogs, the platform sole. Rushing along the Champs-Elysées I was putting together phrases in my head when my beloved old boyfriend from Chicago, Herbert Clark, hove into sight, and stopped the phrase-making. When he had been working on the Paris *Herald Tribune* and I in London, we had walked and danced those same blocks on various weekends.

"There's my girl—right where she belongs," Herbie yelled and we waltzed down the block while the French around us applauded. We had a drink in the sunshine outside an old favorite café before I hurried to pick up my typewriter and bat out my story in Wert's room, my first story from Paris in fifty-one months.

De Gaulle was due in town any minute, they said at the Scribe, and General Leclerc's division, with elements of the U.S. 82nd Division, was going to parade down the Champs-Elysées that very afternoon. Hurry, hurry. Somebody had brewed coffee and I snatched food from a K-ration between sentences before confronting the censors, and joining a mercifully short queue at Western Union's office. *Time* in New York closed the book on Sunday night and with luck in transmission we could make that week's edition at the last minute.

With about a thousand words in cablese of description, the sights, sounds, songs and passing phrases of the day sent homeward, I raced back to the Place de la Concorde. From there, the Champs-Elysées was a moving mass of people all the way up to the Etoile. Collecting half a thousand embraces and avoiding the Paris police who were pushing the crowds to each side of the street, I made it nearly to the Arc de Triomphe before Leclerc's men began their descent of the glorious avenue. Onto the wad of copy paper in my hand went the names and towns and occupations of the marchers, French and American, together with the names of the dignitaries who surrounded de Gaulle and a U.S. general on the reviewing stand in the Place de la Concorde, asking and asking like a cub reporter, noting the unceasing roar of shouts and applause, a million of *"Vive la france!"* a great many *"Vivent les américains!"* Somehow in the wild elation of that afternoon, I made friends with four or five Parisians whom I saw later that year and in subsequent years and with whom I corresponded for a long time.

The parade disbanded at Nôtre-Dame and many of the military moved away, but thousands of French people wanted to attend the mass of thanksgiving in their great cathedral, more than its large spaces could hold. My SHAEF sleeve patch got me into the cool twilight of the interior, within earshot of the choir and also of a couple of rifle shots which burst out to enliven the service. They were accidental, apparently, and did no harm to anyone. I went back to the Scribe and batted out another long cable, cleared it with the censors and gave it to the weary Western Union fellows. Then I had to get back to Ernest and found him waiting alone in his room in the twilight.

Marcel Duhamel, his French translator, had insisted on his going to dine at some place on the Left Bank where there was good food.

"I don't want to go anywhere except to bed," I said.

"Have a little of this nourishing champagne. Pelkey got your stuff from that hotel. It's here."

"I won't be any help to this dinner party," I said. My head was filled with mush from having spoken French all day. But I washed and repaired makeup and we went out and along the rue Castiglione to the Tuileries and across the river. All I remember of that dinner was that M. Duhamel was very voluble and very possessive about Ernest, that we were served some red wine of poor quality, and that as we bid good-byes in the narrow street, a few rifle shots clattered in the silent, silvery night. The moon was lighting the roofs above us. We moved into the shadow opposite the restaurant and walked slowly home in the soft night air, with very little of the past few days' smell of gunpowder remaining in it. Ernest chatted softly about his early days in Paris, "The greatest town in the world." He had found a new private name for me, "Pickle."

"Could you be my Pickle? Sour but pungent?" he asked.

"Dill pickle," I said. "And since you are Heming-stein, kosher." There might be some snipers about, but I was enjoying the freedom from buzz bombs.

By the time we reached the Ritz, only the night watchman was on duty at the door. (After midnight the hotel has always behaved rather like a boarding school for young ladies.) I felt I no longer had the strength to organize myself in my Quatre-vingt-six room, climbed up to Ernest's first-floor room with him and in my underwear promptly slid into his bed and plunged into sleep. The other bed was entirely oc-cupied with Garand M–1 army rifles, hand grenades and other metal objects.

Rather early the next morning I heard the soft swish of a champagne bottle giving up its cork.

"Good morning," I said. "Thank you for the sleep-ing space. I'll move upstairs today."

"You snored all night. You snore very well." Ernest's voice held no resentment. It was cheerful. He had not run all over Paris for fifteen to sixteen hours as I had the day before.

"The hazards of romance for you, especially in Paris in August." I happily accepted a glass of Perrier-Jouet Brut champagne and rang the bell for coffee. I had not observed that Archie Pelkey was silently brewing coffee on the little G.I. stove he had installed in the empty fireplace.

Among Ernest's letters to me is one dated August 27, the first one typewritten since he had reached

France. The piece of thin paper is torn, worn into holes in some places, unfinished and unsigned.

Since I reached Paris on the night of Friday, August 25, slept in the sleazy hotel across the street from the Scribe, and went to make the brief reunion with Ernest on the morning of Saturday, August 26, he must have begun the letter that same morning, predating it by one day, and tucked it in his pocket after our joyous encounter. He seldom threw away any piece of paper.

"Just came in Ritz now and there was letter and am very happy," he had written. Long before we had made some vague, hopeful plans for a reunion at the Ritz, I had been writing him regularly, about the banalities of life in London, together with insipid sentimentalities.

He wrote me about his adventures with the French Maquis on the approach to Rambouillet and, again elliptically, of his entry into Paris by the Etoile and the Place de la Concorde, in tandem with Lieutenant Colonel S.L.A. Marshall, the official war historian, formerly a newspaperman in Detroit, ending with "Why don't you come over here?" For several months the circumstances of almost everybody's lives in the E.T.O. had been too confused to provide adequate personal communication.

Since César Ritz formally opened his hotel with a grand gala in the main dining room on June 5, 1898, he and his son Charles and his aides have expected their guests to behave with classical or conventional propriety and have always managed to maintain the appearance of it. Gentlemen did not entertain ladies in their rooms unless they occupied suites, and no departures from the rules were condoned. But Charles Ritz, our proprietor and sprightly and affectionate friend, appeared not to notice when Ernest, his own room being overcrowded with his troops, weapons and action, moved his extra shirt, two neckties and himself up to the orderly spaces of my room for a few days of repose and recreation. We *did* have separate rooms on different floors.

(During the seven months I lived in Room 86,

Charles's mother, Mme. César Ritz, never saw me. Entering the main dining room where Ernest and I would be already seated, she bowed and smiled to him. After her first entrance, when I smiled at her, I looked down at my plate. It was only when we returned to the Ritz after the war, having been properly married according to the Napoleonic Code in Cuba, that Mme. Ritz acknowledged my existence, and then she was entirely gracious.)

Ernest was taking a brief holiday from his self-made job of scouting with his French friends ahead of various elements of the 4th Infantry Division, seeking information about enemy dispositions and strengths. I, deaf to Wertenbaker's rumbling, half-approving objections, took French leave from Time Inc. chores. When we were not rejoicing and ruminating, we prowled, in glowing nostalgia, the streets of Paris. We had scores of favorite places to show each other.

Horizontal, we rediscovered what we each had known, that too much laughter quells the initiatives of bedding, and we did not care. I might murmur, "Nice, er, what did you say your name is, darling?" thereby instigating mutual collapse. We pretended that we would have endless time for our private life without wars or alien responsibilities. We lived those few days far out beyond the usual reaches of our senses. "This is it," Ernest said solemnly one morning. "Our one and only life."

Vertical, we walked across the Seine to the Invalides and along the Avenue de Breteuil to the building of studio apartments where I had left most of my worldly goods in June 1940. I recognized some of the passing figures in the clothes I had given via Switzerland to the Red Cross chapter of that *arrondissement*, the 7th, and made inquiries of the concierge of my old building, the same woman who had been there four years earlier. She had the address of the Red Cross administrator, who showed me what she had saved for me: an imitation chinchilla coat, some Irish lace doilies, my grandmother's silver teaspoons, a few books of poetry.

Ernest's favorite parts of the town were the 6th and

143

5th *arrondissements,* further southeast, Montparnasse, and we re-explored them joyously. The Louvre was closed and the Musée Rodin and also the Musée Cluny in one of my favorite street names, the Place of the Raised Bread. Those first days the bookstalls along the Seine were, most of them, closed. In the Left Bank bars the bartenders wearily repeated, *"Pas de gin, pas de whiskey, pas de 'fine'."* There was some ordinary wine and some weak, boring beer, nothing more. But the quais were there and the streets with their remembered names, and the unchanged shapes of buildings against the outstretched Paris sky. We walked miles in Montparnasse and along the river, sometimes shaken by old private memories, frequently pausing for hugs of delight at the appearance of old-acquaintance streets and vistas or just for the fun of it.

On Sunday, August 27, after my night of snoring, Ernest decreed that we would not patronize any of the black market restaurants which, on that day's walk, we found already opening for business. I agreed. The Hôtel Ritz had accommodated the Germans—what else could it do?—but its meager menus now offered only the current legitimate rations—vegetable broth sometimes, rice dishes, gnocchi, potatoes, a dollar-sized piece of fish perhaps. But its wine cellar still contained untapped treasures which we sampled gratefully.

We lunched and dined there consistently, even after the U.S. Army had opened the Correspondents Mess in the basement of the Scribe, preferably alone, or with a succession of imaginary guests, shadowy, transitory offspring of our imaginations. Marshal Michel Ney, who commanded the rear guard in Napoleon's retreat from Russia (1812) and who also commanded Ernest's respect, was one guest.

"Didn't they behead you for some stupid reason?" I asked, hunting around in my head for a kernel of fact.

"No. They shot me," Ernest said, speaking for Ney. "They couldn't forgive me for supporting Bonaparte in the Hundred Days, or for my command at Waterloo."

"What did you do to keep up morale on that march from Moscow?"

"Morale? It is a term we did not use in the Emperor's army."

We had Cézanne to lunch one day, a shy, slow-speaking man who was unhappy with the autumn light of Paris after the opalescence of Provence, and Lady Mary Wortley Montagu who was witty about Constantinople in the early eighteenth century and indignant that she was not visiting Paris in 1944.

"Did you see the Turks carrying pianos on their backs?" Ernest asked.

"Not pianos, monsieur. Pianos had not then reached Constantinople. But harpsichords, yes. They may have been as heavy as pianos."

"With your talents, can't you devise a means of reincarnation, and join us in the flesh?"

"Would that one could, monsieur. Voltaire and Alfred Nobel have been working on the problem for ages, Voltaire with particular vehemence because he is so furious to be silenced, Mr. Nobel because he feels the funds he left for peace have been so ineffective. He would like to rescind his bequest."

We had Benjamin Franklin, who loved Paris too, and Stendhal and Eleonora Duse and Thomas Jefferson, through whom we discovered that our respective political philosophies ran parallel and to the left together. The only man he had ever voted for, Ernest said, was Eugene V. Debs, one of my father's heroes. The only time I had ever voted was for Franklin Roosevelt, instead of for my boss Frank Knox of the Chicago *Daily News* and Republican Alf Landon.

We made a few calls on Paris friends, some for courtesy, some for fun. One afternoon Ernest went to Sylvia Beach's bookshop for a cheerful reunion, and another day we went to a working-class *banlieue* new to me. One of Ernest's FFI (French Forces of the Interior) mob which had maneuvered into Paris with him was a gaunt man named Marcel, whose accent and vocabulary were so alien to mine that he and I managed only limited communication. He invited Ernest and—by haphazard extension, me—to visit him and his wife in his flat, and, since he was the kind of man who would feel personal insult if Ernest eluded

145

the invitation, we went along. Marcel had arranged a jeep of the Free French for transportation.

I had seen many flats of working people in England, their common characteristics being untidiness and good cheer. Marcel's small flat was a spaceship of cleanliness, despite the soap shortage, and of austerity, its wooden floors scrubbed as clean as plates. His wife, not so gaunt but as stern-looking as he, brought out four cups and saucers and a pot of tea and gestured us to chairs. It was easily apparent that they disapproved of me, to whom they referred as "the mademoiselle," which amused me, and quickly apparent that Marcel wished to show Ernest off to his local cell of the FFI. As soon as we had finished tea, other working men and women pushed into the flat, about a dozen, perhaps, to talk about their partisan achievements of the last few days. They were handshakers, not back slappers.

I watched Ernest's face for a sign of impatience, and saw none. He understood their accents and gave them compliments and, if I understood correctly, small witticisms, some of which they failed to comprehend. After about an hour we escaped. From the front seat of the jeep on the way home Ernest turned to me, scowling, and muttered, "You goddamn, smirking, useless female war correspondent. Why didn't you help me?" It was an unexpected slap in the face.

"This was your show and you did it very well," I said. "In future, just remember not to invite me." I had never before been catapulted into the role of whipping boy, a part which I would play, unexpectedly, from time to time for years. I never learned to play it as gracefully and dispassionately as I should have liked.

One evening we walked to 27 rue de Fleurus. The concierge was there and told us that Miss Stein and Miss Toklas were still in the country, and Ernest scrawled a message. Another evening we went to the studio of M. Picasso (the French pronounced it with the accent on the last syllable, I learned) and M. Picasso was at home. He welcomed Ernest with open arms and while Picasso's girl, Françoise Gilot, a slim,

146

dark, quiet girl with serpentine movements, and I kept ourselves behind them, Picasso showed Ernest the big, chilly studio and much of the work he had done in the past four years. *"Les boches* left me alone," P.P. said. "They disliked my work, but they did not punish me for it." (I was getting a good story for *Time*'s art department.)

He showed us what seemed to be half a thousand canvases, abstractions, two- and three-profiled portraits, some more or less representational landscapes, some few paintings on cardboard or wood, many compositions which I did not even dimly understand. "There were some problems with the canvas and the paints, *tu sais*," he said. He and Ernest were *tu-toi*-ing each other. "But I managed to resolve them."

The Paris sky was turning violet and Picasso took us to an open window overlooking the roofs and chimney pots on his level and just below. It was a tightly knit composition of lines and shapes, beautiful in tranquil colors. "There," said Picasso. "That is the best picture in my studio." He painted it at least once, I discovered later.

On our way outside, we came upon the skeleton of a bicycle, with the handlebars turned forward. *"Mon taureau,"* Picasso said. Several of the canvases we had seen that evening had been reminiscent of fighting bulls and hectic action in bullrings. We made a rendezvous for dinner a few evenings later at Picasso's favorite café close by his studio.

Walking home to the Ritz, I thought out loud to Ernest, considering my story. "His colors are bolder and stronger than I remember. No Blue Period. No longer the soft sand colors. But many of the forms I don't understand at all."

"He's pioneering," Ernest said. "Don't condemn them just because you don't understand them. You may grow up to them." We walked arm in arm through the Tuileries. "If you understand easily, the thing may be spurious." I did not have to pretend to be an art critic to send my story to *Time*. I merely reported the findings in Picasso's studio.

Later Ernest wrote me some of his views on understanding art. "There is a sort of real esthetic blindness in some people . . . I suppose like true tone deafness in music . . . But a certain amount of knowledge and appreciation of pictures, writing, and music makes a fine backlog of civilized understanding between people."

With Picasso and Mlle. Gilot we dined in a froth of goodwill and wit, about a third of which I missed, my ears being too slow, at one of the places in the Boulevard St.-Germain, Ernest for once abandoning his principle of patronizing no black market restaurants because he could not offer Picasso our boarding school fare at the Ritz nor the noisy, badly ventilated U.S. Army food at the Correspondents Mess in the Hôtel Scribe. Picasso's face, as sensitive as litmus paper, showed a dozen reactions of amusement, concern, delight at Ernest's accounts of his adventures with the U.S. Army in France, and they reminisced rather solemnly together about the early days in Paris. Françoise Gilot and I mostly held our tongues, she, it seemed to me, watchfully or critically, I, because I had little but goodwill to contribute.

When Ernest asked Picasso if he would consider doing a bust of me, a portrait from the waist up, nude, Picasso's enormous black radar eyes turned onto me, shrouded in my uniform, for a moment, smiled and said, *"Bien sûr.* Have her come to the studio."

A week later Ernest began shuttling back and forth between Paris and his favorite outfit in the U.S. Army, Colonel Buck (Charles T.) Lanham's 22nd Regiment of Foot in the 4th Infantry Division, when they were up near the Belgian border. Without him to prod me, I kept postponing my return to Picasso's studio. It seemed so presumptuous of me. Besides, the weather was turning chilly, and if the maestro were to paint me representationally, as he had assured Ernest he would, he would have to paint me with goose pimples as big as grapes. I never saw Picasso again.

As I was hurrying past the Opéra about a week after we reached Paris I noticed a hand-scrawled *affiche* fluttering from a front column. It announced that Yehudi Menuhin would play a concert there that afternoon. The box office confirmed the astonishing news and sold me a ticket. The front doors were open and I peeked inside. Scores of people with pails and mops, hand-run carpet sweepers and dust cloths were hastily cleaning. "Who are they?" I asked a figure in the indoor twilight.

"They are the musicians of Paris," the figure said. "We heard only this morning. That monsieur there is one of our clarinets." The building had been closed for more than a year.

When I returned half an hour early in the afternoon, the big theater was already nearly full, the great stage showing only a couple of wings and no backdrop so that from my place at the rear of the orchestra I could see the small Gothic windows in the rear wall. Only a few dim lights showed on the walls and ceiling of the auditorium.

"Is it true that it was the musicians who cleaned the Opéra today?" I asked the white-mustached gentleman standing beside me. Everybody was standing.

"Yes, mademoiselle. The older ones who are still in Paris."

"But how could word of this concert get around Paris so quickly, please?"

"By the telephone, and also by people on foot. It is a very grand occasion."

"Truly. For Paris music."

"Yehudi has come back to us to make an act of presence."

"Many French musicians have not been inside this opera house for four years, is it not so?"

"Yes, mademoiselle." His voice was muffled.

A single shaft of bright light broke from the left of the stage and poured diagonally down. Mr. Menuhin walked into it, slight and slim in his civilian suit, simple and unpretentious, the beam of light making his blond head a small patch of gold there on the dark, empty stage. He put the violin to his shoulder and played, a bird singing without orchestra accompaniment, "*La Marseillaise.*"

When he had finished, the house remained absolutely silent for what seemed to me an age. My white-mustached neighbor's cheeks glinted with dampness in the dim light. From the upper tiers came a rustle of applause, slight and faint at first, but spreading and growing and blooming into a storm, deafening and thundering on and on. The Opéra of Paris had been returned to France.

In the dusk I could not read my watch, but it must have been ten minutes before the pandemonium subsided and Mr. Menuhin, still standing in the single streak of light, played the Mendelssohn Concerto in E Minor, familiar and comforting, a marvelous choice after that great surge of emotion, the orchestra tenderly escorting his every note. Then we had Lalo, French and appropriate, and finally Beethoven. It was not an afternoon for artistic innovations; it was simply, to my ears and sensibilities, the most emotional performance I had ever attended.

"The long applause made me nervous," Mr. Menuhin told me, years later. "The U.S. Air Force had flown me over and were waiting in the wings. We had to get back to London in daylight, because the Germans were still holding the Channel Islands."

One morning in September I awoke, looked out the French windows to see the day beginning bright and calm, looked for Ernest in the other bed. Usually he was there, reading and sipping champagne from a bottle brought up in a bucket of ice the night before. I went into the big white-tiled bathroom with its side-by-side handwashing bowls, large tub and a bidet big enough to hold a week's laundry. Ernest was sitting on the potty with his army raincoat over his shoulders.

"Good morning. How are you, my dog? I'm writing more on your poem," he said, standing up. He had started the poem earlier with the army.

"I'm not a dog. I'm a female, don't you remember?"

His poem, straggling over the tiled floor, was written in pencil on toilet paper. He had probably chosen it rather than paper he could have found in my desk drawers, but they might have scraped, being opened, and so awakened me. He respected other people's sleep.

"Sure. Now I remember. You *are* a female."

"And you're a dog," I said, hugging his chest, which

150

was about as high as I could make it with my arms. "Shall I type it for you?"

"If you have time. Shall we have breakfast?" He rang for another bottle of Perrier-Jouet Brut, with which they also brought what passed for coffee and a piece of bread for me.

Somebody in the office had found some sleazy pink typing paper and before I left for the day's business I batted out six pages, with a carbon copy of "Poem to Mary (Second Poem)" and left the copies on my desk. "It's not finished," Ernest said as he was leaving. The last two of the lines I copied that morning were,

> Throw away your own true love
> Walking up a hill.

It didn't read finished.

When Ernest was in Paris, our daily operational procedure prescribed a drink or two at the Ritz Bar on the rue Cambon side before lunch, and, wherever I was, I usually managed the rendezvous. At drinks after my poem-copying morning, Ernest pulled the folded pink paper out of his pocket and began to read it to me at his favorite small table in a corner of the inner part of the bar. "You've missed something, I think," he said, interrupting his reading.

"I don't think so. But maybe."

"Only a couple of lines. We can check it."

"Check it?" I echoed, dismay descending like a thundershower upon me. As I always did with my own notes, I had thrown his toilet paper original writing into my wastebasket as soon as I had finished getting the words in type. "Sweet Jesus, I forgot about your immortal first drafts," I croaked, and rushed down the panoplied hallway to the Vendôme side and up to my room. The brass wickerwork wastebasket in my room was pristine empty. I rushed into the hall yelling, "Mademoiselle, mademoiselle." The *femme de chambre* was about fifty, and friendly and a grandmother, and liked being addressed as mademoiselle. She emerged from another room, now suspicious.

"The papers I left in my wastebasket, *ma corbeille à papier*," I gasped. Her face relaxed.

151

"Of course, mademoiselle, I sent them down." She smiled. "Don't be worried." My wastepaper would not reach the enemy, or worse, the French Sûreté.

"Are you sure? Could we not find them, still untouched? I find I need them."

"It is some hours since I cleaned your room," she said, but she called downstairs on the service telephone. The papers from the fifth floor had efficiently been burned. If Ernest was disgruntled over the destruction of his original manuscript, he refrained from indicating so.

A few days later I found a sheaf of folded paper in my letterbox, a note written in pencil in his round, large handwriting and more of the poem. "I saw you running away from me down the hall," he said. "Couldn't you have waved, or given me at least a wink with your ass? Some friendly signal?"

I had seen him talking to the concierge and ducked down the alleyway to the Cambon side, intent on some job I thought urgent for the office. I had no time for a midmorning *quart de champagne* with light conversation in the bar. Ernest kept forgetting that I lived by deadlines. Moreover I was beginning to feel that I was being swallowed by him. The heat of exuberance he engendered in any group around him seemed to me to melt away my identity, I reflected occasionally, and although I was entirely enthralled by him, especially when we were alone, I felt dubious about the wisdom of any formal commitment between us. I was happy with our short-term celebrations, but must have looked sour and doubtful when he spoke of our future together. With his extrasensory perception—he called it his "built-in shit detector"—Ernest identified my apprehension and attempted to alleviate it with small gestures. One was the gift of a white imitation angora sweater. We saw it in a window as we were walking down the Boulevard des Capucines. "Wimmeys love presents, I've learned," he said. "Let me buy you this as a 'token of my esteem.'" His tone of voice created the quotation marks.

"Thank you, I'd love it. It looks warm."

When we got back to the Ritz I tried it on. "It reminds me of you at the White Tower," Ernest said and we hugged each other in memory of that silly first meeting. As I removed the sweater, I saw that Ernest's khaki jacket was dusted with white, and found wisps of sweater in my hair and eyelashes. Muttering epithets we brushed and picked. "The White Thing," Ernest named it and we tried living with it for another day or so before I buried it in a paper sack on a top shelf.

In early September when Ernest rejoined the 4th Division on its way north of Paris to the Belgian border, he found it "lovely in the forest country," listening to the wind in the treetops as he did as a boy in Michigan, "so I did not feel cheated out of a fall as one often is when living in the city or in strange countries with different climates." He was happy with the division, "although I think not very useful as we will be away from where I know people."*

It was a letter rich in love—"Loved you last night, this morning and now this noon"—and also in requests. "Please write if you have time or maybe even if you haven't." He wanted his mail put in a big envelope and forwarded, but there was no mail for him. He wanted me to get him a pair of bedroom slippers, size 11.

Three days later he wrote again, still buoyant and delighted with the clean blue fall weather and his fine full happy useful days in "Indian country" although they had nearly reached the limit of "where my Ojibway runs." For once he had found paper strong enough to support his pencil, which made his handwriting big

* After Ernest's death in July 1961, we found in the library safe at the Finca Vigía a paper dated May 20, 1958, stating: "It is my wish that none of the letters written by me during my lifetime shall be published. I hereby request and direct you not to publish or consent to the publication by others of any such letters." The paper was addressed: "To my Executors." In his will, dated September 17, 1955, he had appointed me executrix of all his property "of whatever kind and nature . . . real, personal, literary or mixed, absolutely."

The prohibition on letters has caused me continuous trouble, and disappointment to others who wished to publish mutual correspondence. I have no explanation, although several guesses, why Ernest chose to impose the restriction. But, being both recipient of the letters and legatee of his will, I deviate a bit from his twenty-year-old wish to publish here for the first time some excerpts.

enough to read. "But Pickle this has been the truly happiest month I've ever had in all my life." He repeated that phrase about once a day or a week or a month most of his life. "On account of you it hasn't been desperate happy it's been straight, good really happy—know what you fight for and when and why and to what ends. Not lonely. Not disappointed—not disillusioned. Nothing phony. No message . . . We loved each other very much with no clothes at all, no lies, no secrets, no pretenses, no underwear and only one shirt apiece. . . . When I wake in the night and cannot sleep I just think about Tom Welsh's kid. . . . I'm keeping a notebook because I have such a good time might not remember and one day of Indian country drives another day of Indian country out of your head. . . . Small friend—I like to remember us in the dining room at the Ritz with our own world and the others could keep theirs. . . . Capa never came with my mail nor my money. People have borrowed most of the money."

In Paris I had observed Ernest's manner with money. He behaved as though no one else had any, as though gremlins were operating a little factory inside his pants pockets, resupplying French francs as fast as he withdrew them. If anyone else picked up a bar bill, it would have been news to me. His tips to his hotel valet, and waiters upstairs and downstairs, were unnoticeably about double the average tip. He was a soft-as-eiderdown touch, handing over whatever he could without hesitation. I was totally devoted to his fiscal policy and practices. Later on Marlene Dietrich and I both lent him sums to flesh out his local resources.

In a letter dated September 11 he outlined his personal bookkeeping for my reassurance, the monies he expected that year and the next. "We will have clear dough ahead to see us through writing a novel. . . . We have good future, Pickle—the best I've ever had. Hope to write very fine, good, grownup novel of which all I have so far is the dedication

TO MARY WELSH

"If you don't like the novel you can dedicate it to anybody you want as it is your property (Deal-

154

ing in novel futures bad gamble.) Let's take our towns one at a time. . . . And if you've left me and are living with the Shah of Persia will dedicate it to you altho might add F—K her the Persian Harlot in parenthesis."

Ernest wrote to me in Paris steadily through September as the 22nd Regiment with his admired friend Buck Lanham moved northeast through Belgium and the fine weather and into Germany, bad weather, heavy murderous fighting to and through the Siegfried Line and into the nasty weather and treacherous country beyond it. Of the surviving letters there are two written on September 13, one after a dinner he had given for Lanham and other officers in an abandoned farmhouse he had "requisitioned." "We had a fine chicken dinner from off-head shot pistol chickens . . . and we drank up everything we had to celebrate the day. It was a fine day, following tank tracks through the woods and flushing them finally. . . . This country is all a succession of wooded hills and rolling country with some bare heights from which you can see everything that moves. . . . Sometimes there is thick forest like at home or in Canada and it seems as odd to be killed as it would be in Upper Michigan. . . ."

In the after-dinner letter he wrote: "I hope you were quite serious Pickle because I am as committed as an armoured column in a narrow defile where no vehicle can turn and without parallel roads . . . and in favour of you sitting up straight in bed lovelier than any figurehead on the finest tallest ship . . . and in favour of kindness, permanence. . . ."

On September 15 he wrote instructions about what mail of his to send forward and what to hold and "am now down to a battle jacket held together by safety pins—socks worn through—same two shirts—both on —no raincoat."

From inside Germany on September 23 Ernest wrote thirteen half pages saying he did not like to leave the regiment when things were bad, but hoped to get back to Paris to cure his head and chest cold. "Here in the rain and the mist and fog in the woods it doesn't get well. . . . It makes me sick that all this time you might think I didn't write or did not know how I love you and how I miss you. . . . Buck Lanham is the finest and bravest and most intelligent and able Regimental Commander I have ever known. . . . Pickle I wrote you all about us and the novel and interesting things and about the flora and fauna and you never got any of them. . . . It would be wonderful to have a letter. . . . I could come back anytime now if I'm not in trouble about Rambouillet [where he had worked with French Resistance forces and, against the Geneva agreements, was carrying arms]. . . . You have to do what you have to in an emergency. There can be a rule forbidding journalists from jumping into the Seine. But are you supposed to follow that rule when someone is drowning? . . . When I told my pal, Buck, there was some talk of trouble he said 'I've got an extra pair of eagles and if there's any trouble you stay here and we'll have two goddamn colonels to this regt, a regular Col. and an irregular Col.' . . . I think we will have big ballroom bananas again. So I might as well write to you as you are what I have. . . . I've never seen you in a house. I like a house and to wash my head and take a bath and have a pile of shirts, not just shirt, and lots of socks, not this pair, and say 'Don't wake up, Pickle there's no need,' instead of 'You've got ten minutes Pickle. Sleep till then.' . . . I want to get out of this hawk and cough and spit area and somewhere where we can sleep good and talk and put our loneliness out of business. . . . I tell you true and straight I have never been happier, true, solid, knowing, confident happier . . . than I ever was in all of my life, and all of the town I knew and loved I wanted only to share with you. . . ."

Reading his letter of September 24, I noticed the back of my neck prickling. For the first time discernible in his phrases there was a premonition of disaster, oblivion. He gave no indication of its source, but something was spooking him. Paris and a holiday from danger must have seemed very far away that day. "Will be here a while now, my dear beloved," he wrote, "love me very hard and very much and take good care of me for a while because all my fine projects of coming back right away are cancelled for a little while. . . . It is bad writing letters to someone who loves and understands facts and just have to write ballroom bananas—melodramatic sounding and chickenshit seeming . . . and not even be able to say goodbye to your true love for fear of sounding wet.

"So Pickle just please know I love you very much and whoever loved you, and everyone should have loved you much, I love you more.

"Poetry

> So now,
> Loseing the three last night,
> Takeing them back today,
> Dripping and dark the woods . . .

"Can't write poetry from too much talking . . . it started to come out as chickenshit Hiawatha. . . . I am like old steeple-chase horse back in training—ugly and only horse left—with so many races in last two months and now big races ahead and now don't know. Dirty to say—But very happy—So it comes. So it comes. . . . So keep this for comic Valentine if everything ok and if not ok, read it for a joke and burn it or keep for our grandchildren. . . . But chest better, head better, everything else, big picture, worse." On the back he wrote the address and a note, "Please Deliver in case of casualty."

I read the letter first in the microcosmic clamor of the office, and then took it back to the tranquility of Room Quatre-vingt-six at the Ritz. Remembering cherished friends in the R.A.F. and in British tanks and infantry who had been destroyed, I reread Ernest and stepped out onto my balcony overlooking the gardens of the Ministry of Justice, the summer flowers faded and shriveled, listened to the subdued late afternoon sounds of the city, a mumble of feet on cobblestones (the Métro was functioning), noticed wispy clouds in the big patch of sky between me and a slightly higher office building at the end of the block. There was no way to barricade and protect oneself from such possible disaster, or to head it off, I decided, and remembered the wedding vows Ernest had made up and spoken for us only about twenty days earlier.

157

In bed one quiet midnight he had asked, "Will you marry me, Pickle? Will you, Mary Welsh, take me, Ernest Hemingway for thy lawful wedded husband?"

I had demurred. "It's not orderly. I should settle, I should conclude my affairs with Noel first."

"They are really finished, aren't they, in your mind and your heart?"

"Yes."

"Then I'll marry us. You know I *mean* this?"

"Yes."

We would be faithful and true to each other, Ernest said. We would seek to understand and support each other in all times, troubles or triumphs. We would *never* lie to each other. We would love each other to the full extents of our capacities. I felt, drifting toward sleep, I could keep the promises—faithful, understanding, I hoped, not lying, loving. Ernest had been solemn.

"Gees," I grumbled. "I'm just an old married woman again. No more pretty flatterings. No courtship displays." Ernest's left hand found my right hand and he kissed it. "My poor Pickle, bride," he mumbled comfortably.

The "casualty" letter had uncovered my tucked away memories of our private wedding night. There on my balcony in the dimming September light, I prayed that he would survive the ballroom bananas, however our personal alliance developed.

The September 11 issue of *Life* reached us a week or more late in Paris and provoked a few interoffice acerbities. *Life* had given Wertenbaker, Walton and me a double-page spread for our stories of the Allied return to Paris, but had cut them so drastically that they read as porpoises' underwater chatterings, my piece shatteringly inconsequential. We were embittered, but not for long. Too much work demanded our attention.

I had been living too long with only one change of shirt and underwear and when I regretted it to my old medium bomber friend, General Sam, No Middle Initial, Anderson, he remembered that his private transport, a four- or six-seater unarmed airplane, was going to London in a couple of days and had room for me. His pilot and I bucked a dastardly headwind across the Channel, I gathered some clothes and a few books from the little flat in Grosvenor Street, and rented the flat to our London bureau's business office which was hungry for living space for the growing influx of experts and specialists and sightseers who were converging on Paris via London. I flew U.S. Air Force manuals, some civilian clothes and my fine, warm, army topcoat back to Paris. Our Paris bureau established itself temporarily in the *Herald Tribune* building in the rue de Berri, which provided me with a brisk walk across the Place de la Concorde and up the Champs-Elysées, never since so empty and beautiful, two or three mornings a week. Our little office space was so crowded, smoky and noisy that Wertenbaker agreed with visible relief when I suggested that I continue working in my room at the Ritz, attending the office only for conferences on each week's proposed stories. Wert passed around assignments with the delicacy of a dry-fly fisherman casting, and if I had doubts about a cable, would run an eye over it while we lunched in the Correspondents Mess in the basement of the Hôtel Scribe. Usually I followed his suggestions, "Just bung it off," and took a carbon copy to the office. With no regrets I remembered the steel reins with which Leola Allard drove her team in Chicago.

A printed notice appeared near the concierge's desk in the Ritz front entrance, saying something such as "The Hôtel Ritz provides accommodations for V.I.P. (Very Important Persons) personnel only." Alarming news to me. I hunted down the affable Major Eddie Doerr who was in charge of U.S. Army housekeeping arrangements in Paris and made plaintive inquiries. I was certainly not a V.I.P., but?

"You're an original inhabitant," the dear major said. "That doesn't apply to you."

"You're not risking your neck for me, I hope?" I did not wish to feel more than slightly indebted to him.

"Naw," said he.

Among the early V.I.P.'s to settle into the hotel on my floor was Marlene Dietrich, as sinuously beautiful in her khaki uniform and the knitted khaki helmet liner she wore askew on her head as in the see-through sequin dresses she wore in the winter's cold when she played on a carpenter's saw with a violin bow entertaining the troops. Among the high brass at the rue Cambon bar or in the newly established dining room on the Vendôme side, she made no noticeable effort to glorify the air around her. At one hen luncheon, she ate both her and my dessert, a concoction of baked meringue heaped with fruit and whipped cream. She was a business woman concerned with every detail of her program from transport to accommodations, to sizes of stages and halls, to lighting and microphones. Business seemed to be her religion and in that stolid respect she reminded me of my Rhineland-ancestored mother. When Ernest returned to Paris in late September, they had a joyous reunion—they had once crossed the Atlantic on the same ship—he proclaiming her glories to one and all and she proving them by elaborate vocal praises. "Papa, you are the most wonderful. . . . Papa, you are the greatest man and the greatest artist."

The three of us went one day around the corner to Prunier's, the saw-dusty ground floor almost empty, so that we went upstairs which was also almost empty. The elderly waiter pretended to remember Ernest and apologized for the meagerness of the food he could provide us but announced that they still had a good supply of wines. He recommended a Sancerre, the round rich white wine of the Loire, and, whatever its year was, we found it so welcome on our palates that we drank two bottles.

For Ernest's amusement, Marlene made up ingenue pleasantries. When we were talking about the sea and fishing, she asked, "What is wanting, Papa? Is it pearls, or some kind of fish? I could never understand it."

"Wanting, it's a verb, daughter. An Irish waiter would say, 'What would ye be wanting.' "

"No. No. I meant that thing I've heard—wade and found wanting. That must be in the sea." Laughter and explanation of "weigh."

Marlene used to wander down to Ernest's room to sit on his bathtub and sing to him while he shaved, and they both generously forgave me when I mimicked her, especially her habit of approaching a note cautiously, wavering up and around it before she hit it solidly. That habit, and the occasional slightly flatted note, were among her musical signatures particularly noticeable in such songs as "Peter" and "Falling in love again . . . Never wanted to . . . I can't help it," and we honored them. We restricted the singing to our rooms, Marlene being a pro who did not sing in public for nothing. I did a column about her which *Time* published; we two sitting in my room for the note-taking while Ernest lolled in one of my beds. She patiently explained to me the gastronomic spelling of her name, "diet-rich" and her long and unremitting efforts to entertain the U.S. military.

Marlene did not mind repeating "Lili Marlene" for us and out of Ernest's and my private exuberances came other songs. I loved to sing "You're in the Army, Mister Jones." Ernest used to drone, "I don't know why, I love you like I do," knowing he was a bit off-key and not caring. His favorite and most frequent song was "*Auprès de ma blonde, qu'il fait beau, fait beau, fait beau.*"

With me singing alto harmony, he performed with gusto his version of the old French song,

> *Après la guerre finie.*
> *Tous les soldats partis,*
> *Mademoiselle a une souvenir*
>   [cradled arms moving]
> *Après la guerre finie.*

Almost the only music we had that autumn was what we made ourselves.

One of Marlene's choice topics of exposition was her plans for her funeral, which she had worked out in elaborate detail. She was not lugubrious about the program.

Nôtre-Dame would be the setting and the time late afternoon, so that flickering candles would embellish the scene. One corner of the cathedral would be curtained off.

"For your girls?" Ernest asked the first time around.

"For what would you think, Papa?"

Marlene's husband Rudy Siebert would be in charge

161

of transportation, arranging planes and trains and limousines from many parts of the world to Paris in behalf of her lovers, friends and admirers who would be assembling from everywhere.

"Enough to fill the church?" I might ask, in awe.

"Who knows, darling? It is quite a big cathedral, isn't it?"

Marlene imagined herself lying, beautiful as always, in her coffin, appropriately placed somewhere below the high altar, and her long-time hairdresser arranging her hair for the final time, but maladroitly combing the one swirl of hair over her forehead, which was her favorite coiffure in 1944.

"I would rise up, take the comb from her and arrange the dip the way it should be. I should be looking my very best for my friends' last view of me."

"There'll never be such a show," Ernest might say. "You're immortal, my Kraut."

Immediately on his return to Paris, Ernest and I must have had a serious spat, for I was prompted to write him on the flimsy pink paper more than two pages of preachery ruminations. I had just received a note from Noel saying, "I'm sorry I had not the necessary qualifications to stay the distance with you."

"That makes me shaky and sad and needing to check my navigation," I wrote Ernest. "It makes me proud of him, and also as though I had sailed through a minefield, having missed the buoys and markers, finding myself far at sea beyond where I thought. . . ."

A quarrel exploded between Ernest and me when three or four of the 22nd Regiment's battalion commanders came to Paris on short leave. The officers—one from New England, one from one of the Virginias or Carolinas—and a couple of others were well-groomed, hair and hands and boots cleaned and polished, when they presented themselves at the Ritz to accept, finally, Ernest's frequent invitations.

Summoned to help with his hosting, I looked forward to meeting his heroes and refreshed my modest makeup. Ernest had also summoned Marlene, who happened to be in town.

The preprandial champagne was to be served in my room, I learned, and two or three bottles of champagne were waiting in nickeled buckets of ice—the Hôtel Ritz never ran out of ice—when the guests arrived. I noticed with dismay that they were already half drunk. Marlene, wearing something civilian and modest, chatted with one after another of the officers, who kept insisting they were more terrified of her than they were of the enemy, until one bold fellow announced that his dearest dream would be to write home that he had lain on a bed with her. She promptly stretched out on top of one of my rose satin coverlets and the blushing officer warily arranged himself, as stiff as at attention beside her. Ernest's joy surged over us all.

Eyes were becoming a bit glazed and speech a bit slurred by the time we went downstairs to a big table Ernest had reserved in the dining room. Since the hotel had become a V.I.P. hostel, the Ritz's food, its raw materials coming from the U.S. Army, was perhaps the best in town. With some trepidation I noticed that my boss's wife, Clare Boothe Luce, one member of a visiting U.S. congressional investigating committee, was dining with an air force officer nearby.

We got food and wine ordered and I was trying to elicit some sobering concentration from the officer on my left when, like a sapling bending in the wind, his head sank down into his soup. A brother officer escorted him away and they returned with surprising speed in time to reply to questions about their work from Mrs. Luce who had joined us. She had come from Italy, with the rest of the investigators, and was much impressed with the contributions made to the campaign there by the air force. But, she suggested, in Belgium and Germany the infantry must surely be of some use.

"You're darned right, babe," said my neighbor to the left. "And don't you put your mouth on it."

"The infantry, they pinpoint an advance, don't they?" asked Mrs. Luce.

"Pinpoint, sweet Jesus. You ought to read a book, you dumb broad. What are you doing here anyhow?" He did not listen to the explanation.

I could see the short note in my mailbox the next morning: "Your service with Time Inc. is terminated." Ernest's hero on my left had not the faintest idea that he was addressing a U.S. Congresswoman who was also the beautiful wife of Mr. Luce. There were a few further blood-curdling confrontations before coffee was served, and I hurriedly said good-byes and escaped upstairs.

I was readying for bed, having cleaned up the mess left by someone who had thrown up all over my bathroom, when Ernest knocked on the door, and prowled silently, glumly around my room.

"Well, I have to go to bed now. I'm tired, if you'll excuse me," said I. I was one-third tipsy and two-thirds exhausted.

"You insulted my friends," Ernest said. "All evening and without cess, you insulted my friends. You could not have behaved more horribly."

For a moment I held it, the fury inside me igniting and burning like a fuse.

"Your friends are drunks and slobs. They threw up all over my bathroom. They probably lost me my job. They drove Marlene away. They may be heroes in Germany, but they stink, stink, stink here. But I DID NOT INSULT THEM, your boorish friends." I was yelling. Reason and control had flown out the French doors.

My phrase "may be heroes" probably tipped over Ernest's temper. He stepped forward and gave me a slap, a slight slap on the jaw. It was the first physical attack I had ever received since my mother used to spank me with the back of a hairbrush, and I fell on a bed, a hand on my smarting skin. I thought for a moment and decided on the foulest insult possible, rose from the bed and chanted, now softly, "You poor coward. You poor, fat, feather-headed coward. You woman-hitter." I pranced around, chanting.

"Knock my head off, you coward. Why don't you knock my head off? Show what a big strong coward you are? Take it to the twenty-second. On a platter. Show 'em you won't let me insult 'em, you bully."

"Hold it," Ernest said, his eyes bulging. "Hold it now." He put his hands behind him.

"You think you can frighten me, you big blob? Why don't you break my jaw in self-defense? Knock my head off?"

He sat on a bed and I pushed him back, straddled

164

his hips and pounded his chest. "You big bully. You fly-blown ego."

"You're pretty when you're mad," said Ernest, infuriating in his detachment.

"This is the end of this," I said, and found his tie and a shirt and socks and handed them to him, and ushered him to the door. "Good night and good-bye." Ernest left silently. I brushed my teeth and went to bed, slept well and woke up still angry but composed and determined to pursue my life without that man.

I was finishing my coffee the next morning when the first of Ernest's emissaries arrived to plead his case. The peace offensive reinforced my distaste for the alliance. The young company or battalion commander whom Ernest had sent upstairs to begin negotiations was woefully inadequate to this situation. "Papa really feels bad," he said. "He's sorry."

"Papa be damned."

"He wishes you could see his side of it."

"Tell me about your outfit. Have you got some smart Joes in it? Is your ammo freezing up on you, nights? Tell Papa for me he's a coward."

Ernest sent up another officer, equally unable to deal with my anger and my decision to leave him to whatever companions and career he might blunder onto. Finally came Marlene.

"He loves you, as you know," she said. "You know this man? You must know he is a worthy man. He is good. He is responsible."

We were leaning against the mantelpiece of my fireplace, and I reflected that Marlene knew very much more about men than I did. But I wondered what caliber of men she had known.

"Any man worth his salt would come up here himself," I said, "instead of sending apologists. He's a coward and a bully, as I told him last night, and I've had enough of him."

"You're making a mistake," Marlene said.

"I don't think so."

"He's a fascinating man. You could have a good life, better than being a reporter." She was loyally pulling for him.

"Not with this kind of nonsense."

I had a story to do, got at it and about noontime was finishing it when my doorbell rang. Ernest stood in the hallway looking blissfully ebullient.

"You were absolutely wonderful last night, you magic Pickle," he said.

I let him in, doubtfully.

"You small fighting cock," he said. "Dancing around, giving me hell with your courage."

"Let's not repeat that performance," I said. I was entirely unprepared for this display of admiration. Ernest opened his arms for an embrace and I backed off. "Didn't you get my messages of last night and this morning?"

"Yes, and I love you more, you bantam brave. You were wonderful. But you don't know how to hit. I must teach you."

"No thanks. I've learned all I wish to learn from you."

He sat down on the rose satin chaise longue at the foot of my bed. "Pickle, I finally discovered what was wrong last night. Please listen." I was pacing. I had to finish my story.

"You had your hair done yesterday, didn't you?"

"Yes." My friend the coiffeuse at the Ritz did it every week.

"Something she did to your hair made you look mean and malicious. She really changed the expression of your face. I didn't know what it was last night. But that was it."

"What nonsense." I remembered suddenly, a non sequitur, that this day, a Saturday or Sunday, was the day we had hot water in the pipes, the once-a-week hot water, some weeks.

"Pickle, with me around, or without me, you should really let me teach you how to hit. You could break your thumbs, hitting like you hit me last night."

Insidious persuasion. My father had never taught me any of the tricks of self-defense, never imagining I might require them. But some of the contretemps I had recently encountered had turned me sufficiently pugnacious to welcome a course in hitting.

My nose told me that Ernest needed a bath, even if

166

he returned from it to his worn war-weary uniform, and I said so.

"I always wash," he said defensively.

"You may, if you wish, get into my tub and take a hot bath with plenty of soap," I said. "Otherwise, good-bye."

Ernest soaked in my large old-fashioned tub, I soaked some of my underclothes in one of the two side-by-side washbasins, and scrubbed his back, and our peace conference stumbled forward.

"You drink too much," I kept saying.

"You carp too much."

"You drink so much you lose your mental balance."

"No too-much-drinking, no too-much-carping," said Ernest.

"I only carp because I abhor drunks."

"Can I depend on that?"

"No."

"All right, Pickle, carp if you must. I'd rather have you, carping, than anybody."

Ernest had told me at length about his satisfactory marriage to Pauline Pfeiffer, who had been an editor or reporter at Paris *Vogue,* and who had sneaked him away from his first wife, Hadley. Pauline had run a shipshape gracious house in Key West and borne him two fine sons. She was educated and smart and read books. I knew something of his regard for her because I found, one day on my desk, a letter to her in which he had reported his new attachment to me—the letter was left spread out there beside my typewriter—with something about my being sensible and reliable, and that I would look after him and the children.

Now that he was captive in my bathtub, I took the time to remember his accounts of Pauline and also the letter.

"You must be still very attached to her. You're a bloody fool not to go back to her," I said. "You could start again more or less where you left off. Your children would have their own mother instead of a phony. It seems merely good sense to me. And I'm easily disposable. I had a good life before I met you."

With the water up to his neck, Ernest looked glum and thoughtful, and stared for a long time at his feet, shaped like a baby's feet with the toes spread out and the arch and the heels rounded.

"We made too many cruelties to each other," he said finally. "We couldn't erase them."

"You poor fools. If you can write her the letter about me—the Practical Nurse for you in your old age and your kids—why can't you be big enough to make a rapprochement? Why don't you try, at least?" That seemed to me the only sensible solution to Ernest's wife-tangle.

"There are things you don't know, Pickle. And from this tub I can't explain them to you. You are a beautiful and wonderful Pickle. And all I can say now is that I love you truly, and that I need you, and will love you always, and need you always."

"Always? Shit." With a shroud-sized Ritz towel I was rubbing his back hard, a service he welcomed.

"Not shit. Shitmaroo." That meant with wit and resignation added.

For a few days we treated each other with the wary diplomacy of spiders and scorpions, and one evening after ample champagne Ernest persuaded me to try a first lesson in the art of hitting, choosing my bathroom as the ring. "Thumbs out, right arm hanging free, weight on your left foot, look at his jaw, swing." Ernest muttered such phrases, demonstrating again and again, I feeling the breeze of his fist missing me by half an inch, noticing with new respect the fine old hard porcelain and marble on all sides, and wondering whether in his serious and concentrated effort to instruct me he might not innocently knock my head off, as I had suggested earlier. It was a little bit like tennis, I suggested, in its body requirements. Ernest snorted, "It's tougher."

When Marlene discovered that I was getting bathroom boxing lessons, she demanded instructions too and got them. Later she demonstrated what an apt pupil she was. She knocked Jean Gabin into a snowbank.

Along with his favorite nearly monotone-droned songs, some of Ernest's favorite phrases were beginning to settle comfortably in my ears. He applied his quotes to multiple subjects. *"Fraîche et rose, comme le jour de bataille"* he might say of a girl, a book, a wine, an aphorism. *"Un peu de trop, c'est juste assez pour moi,"* he might say on ordering another bottle of wine, or of some patently overblown compliment, or of an unexpected long walk home when transportation vanished, or sometimes in bed.

We were lunching at the Ritz on a pleasant Sunday afternoon in late October when appeared Prince (Lieutenant) Poniatowski, a member of Lieutenant Jack Hemingway's outfit, which was Intelligence (espionage, really, and counterespionage) of General John (Iron Mike) O'Daniel's 3rd Infantry Division, then struggling northeastward through the Vosges mountains of eastern France. Poniatowski's news sent Ernest's usually restless angst soaring high. His son Jack (nicknamed Bumby) had been wounded and captured on October 28 while Jack and another agent were reconnoitering at dusk inside enemy lines. As a courtesy to Ernest, the commanding general had sent the news by courier. They had already ascertained that Jack's wound was unlikely to be fatal. He had been treated temporarily at a Kraut forward medical post and was, at last word, being moved to a hospital in the enemy's rear echelon. To Ernest's dozen questions —Where was Jack hit? How much blood had they found? What German outfit captured him? Was he carrying true or false identification papers? Could we make a drop and lift him out? Precisely where was he? —Poniatowski had no definitive answers. From a couple of feet distant I could feel Ernest's temperature, blood pressure, anxiety, anger and frustration rising to some point of explosion with no safety valve apparent.

With Poniatowski we drank more and more wine, combing over the meager information, some of it acquired at the risk of lives or capture of others of Jack's unit.

"Haven't we got a plan of their hospital system there?" Ernest fumed. He was beguiled by the idea of landing a small plane near Jack's hospital and miraculously ushering him out of bed and the hospital, into the air-craft and back over Allied lines. "If we made a quick, surprise drop, we could get him out. A heist,"

Ernest said. "We ought to be able to make a heist." He liked the old gangster word.

Poniatowski remarked coolly that some action of that sort had been considered at his division headquarters and rejected as unworthy of the risk and effort. We began to understand that to the U.S. Army, Lieutenant Jack Hemingway was merely one of tens of thousands of Allied wounded captives.

The dining room had long emptied and the couple of remaining waiters were looking dour and as though their feet hurt. Having accomplished his mission, Poniatowski excused himself, and as we moved sadly upstairs, I hunted in my head for an escape from the misery. As Ernest was opening yet another bottle of champagne I suggested, "I'll bet you one hundred dollars I can make it from here to the Place du Tertre in ten minutes."

"With the Sunday strollers, impossible."

"I know the short cuts." It would simply be too bad form for Ernest to get drunk, mourning his son's capture. But what else would he do, cooped up and ineffective in the Ritz? "From the rue Cambon door to the first step inside the Place. You'll have to time me, of course."

"One hundred, no odds?"

"Even money," I said, and we straightened our jackets, checked our watches and went along the many-splendored alley to the rue Cambon door. With Ernest trailing closely at first I walked, pushing through clusters of other walkers in the rue Halévy to the right of the Opéra, up the rue La Fayette, the rue Henri Monnier to the Boulevard Rochechouart, Ernest a hundred yards behind. Noticing my haste, a Parisian fell in beside me to ask, "Is he molesting you, mademoiselle, that large American soldier back there?"

Non. Merci, monsieur. C'est une course.

I had less than two minutes to go when I reached the bottom of the long flight of the rue Foyatier steps and was running up them, dizzy and gasping, when Ernest yelled from below. I had lost my bet, but I had got Ernest exercising in fresh air. The air of Paris was clear and clean all that autumn because there were no civilian and few military cars emitting fumes.

We descended to the Place de Clichy, festive in the late sunlight with open shops offering ancient French jazz records, or bad paintings or paper flowers, and street stands offering cooked sugar beets or hand-made shoes with soles from inner tubes, or paper lampshades. But the day was rapidly cooling and Ernest, having sweated in the race earlier, began to complain of the chill. He had carried his raincoat on his arm and now put it on. But the evening chill penetrated it, he grumbled. He would catch pneumonia. Pneumonia was his deadliest enemy, always lying in wait for him, always ready to pounce if he went off guard for a moment. His throat was a rendezvous place for germs. They might be holding a convention there right this minute.

"You seem to have blocked them off for years. Why don't you use the same tactics now?" And I proposed that we walk quickly back to the Ritz, to keep his blood coursing smoothly, and immerse him in hot water, if there was any. I had not carried a raincoat and was happy to walk fast against the chill.

Ernest put himself to bed with apprehension as his companion that night, and the next morning awoke cheerful and with budding plans, as he did three hundred and sixty mornings a year in the seventeen years I shared with him.

"I can't go over there," he said. "If the Krauts learned of it, they might put the bite on Bumby. But you could go. You're an innocent *Time* reporter. You could go and recheck and see if there is anything we don't know now, and reconnoiter some and find out the true gen."

"I can't speak any Kraut. Send Marlene. I have no training in espionage."

"No. No. You wouldn't be any good behind the lines. But you could talk to Bumby's outfit people. Poniatowski is only one of them. And to his general. You've got so many friends who are generals."

A company of Japanese-American infantry in the Vosges mountains had recently overrun and captured a large group of Germans, and against a counterattack had with will and courage defended their farmhouse HQ. Knowing the true reason for my interest in that

171

front, Charles Wertenbaker agreed that its coverage by *Time* had lately been too meager. I would surely find some sort of pertinent story.

I went through a couple of days of standard army red tape and emerged with sympathetic and ambiguous travel orders cut in triplicate, a jeep and a driver. The travel orders read:

RESTRICTED
SUPREME HEADQUARTERS
ALLIED EXPEDITIONARY FORCE

AG 201-Welsh, Mary (War Co) (U.S.)
MAIN, APO 757
7 November 1944

SUBJECT: Orders
TO: Miss Mary Welsh, War Correspondent, (U.S.) Public Relations Division, Supreme Headquarters Allied Expeditionary Force.

You will proceed via government motor transportation on or about 7 November 1944, from present station to Headquarters, 6 Army Group on temporary duty of approximately seven (7) days, to carry out the instructions of the Director, Public Relations Division, SUPREME HEADQUARTERS, AEF, and upon completion thereof return to proper station.

By command of General Eisenhower

Milton H. Ellison
Captain, AGD, for
Henry C. Chappell
Lt. Colonel, AGD,
Asst. Adjutant General

RESTRICTED

With Ernest fussing around on the margins of my last-minute packing, I got myself, my pack and my bedroll down to the front door of the Ritz a minute or two after my jeep had parked in the Place Vendôme outside. Ernest was leaving a day or two later to rejoin his friends of the 22nd Regiment in Germany, so our personal communications would be slow and chancy, although the interarmy mail service was improving. I promised to report promptly any significant news I might find about Bumby.

We had good, "you-can't-miss-it" army maps of the route, and I reveled in the tranquility of the countryside, lavender hills in the distances glowing like candles with clusters and exclamation points of golden trees. As we moved further eastward we encountered fewer French farm carts and more army roadside checkposts, at each one of which they inspected my travel orders and my AGO card. We drove the last dozen miles with the jeep's light dimmed in the darkness before we reached Major General John Ewing Dahlquist's headquarters of the 36th Division in a small battered hotel well up in the six-thousand-foot mountains, with other closed and abandoned summer hotels as its neighbors in patches of pines and yellow-leafed hardwoods. In the HQ company's kitchen they gave us chow and then Dahlquist, whom I had known in London when he was one of the U.S. Army observer group, invited me to the wooden trailer he used as bedroom and office and with the aid of a few whiskeys we planned my sightseeing among his rifle companies.

By the time I got back to the HQ hotel, the floor of what must have been its lobby was covered with oval-shaped bundles, from some of which emanated soft or loud purrings. In dim light I found a space big enough for my bedroll, folded my trousers and Major Eddie Doerr's flying jacket beneath it, and was awakened the next morning only by an army boot stepping an inch away from my ear.

From the 36th Division my silent child-driver and I moved north to the approaches to the town of Nancy and the HQ of Iron Mike O'Daniel, where Jack, Ernest's son, had been wounded and captured. Having moved forward a few miles across the mountains from the copse of trees where Jack was taken, the division's Intelligence section, headed by Captain Robert Thompson, could drive me easily in the mud and snow to the precise spot where he had been ambushed. A sloping cluster of pines and hardwoods with low underbrush, it looked undistinguished to me, who had not been captured there. Once again, in the usual ritual of war, we clawed in the frozen grass and bushes for torn-off dog tags or a button or a shred of clothing which might signify something, and found nothing. We already knew that Jack had been identified by the Krauts and been treated correctly. Captain Thompson invited me to dine, on raw bacon among other things, at his small mess one evening and afterward drove me back to HQ, past a crossroad which was being interdicted by enemy fireworks—large, ditch-digging shells.

I had not learned much more than we already knew of the circumstances of Jack's capture, but I managed to collect enough local color and information to justify a couple of cables to *Time,* and a report to Ernest.

From Room 86 at the Ritz, on flimsy pink paper I wrote on November 14: "Got back late yesterday too frozen and weary to write you. . . .

"I have a fine careful three-page report for you from Thompson as well as exact and complete answers to the questions you wrote out. But I am holding the full report here because, that front being what it is, I think it would be wrong to send the report through the mails. Instead, let me tell you what I can.

"First, it was definitely in the shoulder, not touching the lung, and not serious.

"Second, it was because of the other one, seriously wounded, that Bumby failed to escape as he might well have done otherwise.

"Third, from a prisoner we took, who happened to have seen them just afterwards, Thompson had much thorough information including where they would go and complete description of the place and when they would be in various places.

"Fourth, Thompson and his boys thought of the same possible operation you did, going on the information they got from their prisoner. They turned down the idea on the ground that if it failed, it would attract attention to our two guys, whereas there is now a good chance they will get only routine treatment. From all Thompson told me, and his report to you, I am convinced that they were being neither unimaginative, unenterprising nor neglectful of their duty to Bumby, in their decision.

"Fifth, Bumby was wearing his dogtags but had no other identification. Whatever the other was wearing, he had four or five hours under haphazard guard during which he could dispose of things.

"I feel encouraged about the whole business and more optimistic than we did here. . . . One thing you know, I'm not soft-soaping you to save you anguish. I know we understand each other about that. . . . Any kind of anguish is preferable to evasion or deception. . . ." Ultimately, Bumby was released with other prisoners as the war ended.

I remember walking a faintly discernible path along the brow of a snow-frosted hill one translucent afternoon with the captain of B Company of the 3rd Division, a sinewy, tough Jewish boy who had been a shoe salesman in Paterson, New Jersey. The snow looked deeper in the valley between us and the next hill, about a quarter of a mile away, where the Krauts were entrenched and invisible. The captain called out occasionally, "Joe, you okay?" or "How're your feet, Bud?" or "Hot chow tonight, Jake." The responses were low-pitched, the voices resigned. Without warning, a piece of our hillside above us blew up, scattering earth and stones, then silence across the peaceful-looking valley, then ahead of us another explosion of earth, and again silence. "Mortars," the captain said. "Have you seen enough?" In our dark khaki clothes silhouetted against the white hill we were alluring targets.

"This is stupid," I said. "We might get somebody else hurt." As we walked back toward the cover of some pine trees, the Krauts sent over a couple more mortars, but only the hillside was damaged. That time. It seemed to me incongruous that people should be trying to kill each other across that pretty, tranquil valley; that bones and boys' blood might at any moment disfigure the Christmas-card scenery.

The progress of Allied forces eastward toward the German Fatherland, sometimes slow and always bitterly painful, indicated eventual military victory in the "Big Picture," and in November, if not earlier, began to generate governmental infighting. In Paris I was listening to French radio broadcasts, reading newspaper editorials, talking to British and American diplomats and to the sub-secretaries of the Quai d'Orsay, French officialdom still equating nearly all journalists with earthworms. For *Time* I was trying to organize a sort of mountaintop survey of the ambitions, deceits, purposes and ploys being pursued by the top-level policy makers for the U.S.A., the Russians, British and French. In November 1944, nobody with a known name would say anything specifically relevant to the political struggle for power. The small Russian delegation which had come to Paris and stayed at the Ritz—we had hot water for two days—were the most circuitous and mealy-mouthed of all government representatives, and next, offering wordy non-information, were the sub-secretaries of the French Foreign Office. It was an infuriating assignment.

Down at the Ministry of Justice on the Ile St.-Louis I was also covering the trials of accused traitors—collaborators—provincial officials, proprietors of small hotels, informers to the enemy, charged with crimes against the state. From the press gallery at one end of the long high-ceilinged courtroom, lit only by the gray daylight of November filtering through windows high in one wall, faces of the accused, of witnesses and lawyers looked uniformly gray, and the droning voices uniformly sounded more pathetic than either outraged in self-righteous patriotism or humbled by guilt.

Exposed before us were cupidity, scaled and skinned weaknesses, the broken spirits of men who succumbed to coercion. In its ritualistic prosecution of the wrongdoers, the court in its sentences seemed to me excessively severe. To sublimate their private contritions, I felt, the lawyers and the judges were sending their penitents, the small, gray malefactors, to unjust servitude, and I wrote it that way in my piece for *Time*, a longish cable. When Ernest read it the first time he frowned. When he read it again he said something like, "You son-of-a-bitching Pickle, you're right. You're a straight reporter, good for you." The lordly editors in New York cut some of my story but printed it in a couple of columns, and subsequently I was never warmly welcomed in a French court.

Whenever he was in Paris, Ernest took a too brotherly-fatherly-husbandly interest in my work and sometimes tried to take command of it. One morning he answered the telephone in my Room 86. Wertenbaker was at the other end, wanting me to do something or other. I listened as Ernest explained his views to Wert about how I should handle the assignment and, glancing at me, stopped in midsentence.

"Mary's here. You better talk to her," he said abruptly, and handed me the telephone.

Wert and I resolved the matter in a minute and as I replaced the piece in its cradle, I muttered, "You backed off pretty fast."

"You looked disapproving. Your face changed."

"I sure as hell disapproved. Or has Wert hired you to work for *Time* and *Life*?"

"Please, Pickle. I was only trying . . ."

Reasonably or otherwise, I was overheated. "Why don't you mind your own business, whatever that may be? I've earned my living for a long time without any help from you, and I neither need nor want any from you now, or from now on."

"Pickle, Pickle, you don't understand."

"The hell I don't. I will not have you intruding into what is my own personal, private work. Do you hear? Do you understand? It's not so difficult, mere child's play. Just keep your nose out of it. Just remember this is how I earn my living."

"Pickle, I'm sorry. Please." He stretched out his arms to me, my anger flew away, and I jumped toward him.

"Darling, darling, do excuse me. I love you. But I like my job." We walked downstairs and through the chic displays in the *vitrines* to celebrate another resolved dispute.

On a cold, forlorn November evening I wrote myself: "So won't forget: Water sliding icily from the hot tap six days a week; weary repetition by barmen, 'no gin, no whiskey, no *fine,* no aperitifs' and the beer is bad; tonight have only candied ginger for stimulation; telephones compared to which any little instruments the Borgias invented for the bedevilment of their friends were as children's toys; thousand franc fees for non-army repasts; adroitly doubled prices for anything to people in uniform; the cold. I'm thankful for the human circulatory system, but it wastes time buttoning and unbuttoning." Although we had hot water most Sundays, I recall showering with cold water in my refrigerated bathroom, hoping it would strengthen my fortitude.

Ernest was already talking about our leaving Europe and starting "our one and only life" anew in Cuba. I wanted to see the war closer to its conclusion, and I had long and short, deep and shallow reservations about leaving my work—my lifetime companion—and entrusting my being to the philosophies and habits and whims of such a complicated and contradictory piece of machinery as Ernest. But I agreed to ask Wertenbaker about a leave of absence during which we might make a trial run of living together in Cuba. On November 14 I wrote Ernest, still on the flimsy pink paper, "I talked to Wert about my going home, told him that we thought we had something that we feel deserves a chance. He was sweet and sympathetic and darling, agreed that we shouldn't wait with you going home and my staying here, and said he would press New York about the matter. . . . We may be on a path of our own, our own and nobody else's special, fine, crazy good life."

December 1944 seemed bleaker and colder even than November with all of Paris pulling the covers up around its neck against the drafts and dark, simulating hibernation. For seven years in England my feet had been cold, but after the first two years I lost awareness of them and was comfortable. Now in Paris I was always cold all over, except in bed, and constantly conscious of it. The cold diminished my efficiency about thirty percent, I figured, so that a cable already outlined in my head would cost me an hour and twenty to twenty-five minutes to tap out, instead of the customary, not-so-cold hour. Showering, mornings, continued to be a torture, but I warmed myself a bit by jumping up and down, fast, on the rigid bathroom floor and thinking of the Parisians both nearby and in the *banlieues* who were also at the mercy of the winter, and the men in the foxholes and the 22nd Regiment's huge casualties.

Ernest came back from the Hürtgen Forest battles with a fever and a rasp in his throat like that of a cracked accordion, and went to bed in his own room, his cheeks too pink, his temper variable. Someone had given me a miniature bottle of cognac and, dressed in civilian clothes for some small festivity, I took the bottle down to him, for lack of better remedies. Jean-Paul Sartre and Simone de Beauvoir had been in to visit, he said.

"Did they have anything interesting to say?" I asked, inattentive, merely pleased for the moment with my civilian dress.

"No," said Ernest. "Did you know you look like a spider poised there?" It was news to me. I took off.

Even though his virus clung to him devotedly, Ernest conducted *levées* in his room, receiving his old friends from the Maquis who were having various troubles rejoining the life of Paris, offering champagne to everybody, among them smiling, gesticulating Marcel Duhamel who had then appointed himself chargé d'affaires, Ernest's business with the Paris publishing world then being minimal. Some of the people from the newly re-established U.S. embassy dropped in, together with R.A.F. and U.S. Army types and such old friends as Janet Flanner. Willie Walton and Marlene and I hovered, sometimes trying to disguise our disapproval. If the man would not rest, he would never recover. In the evenings when the visitors had disappeared, Ernest looked exhausted and turned irritable. "His manners to the public are better than his manners at home," I complained in my diary. "When he is good he is more endearing, more stimulating . . . with gaiety and wisdom than anyone . . . but when he is bad he is wildly, childishly, unpredictably

179

bad. . . . Is it the ego or eagerness which prevents him from allowing me to pass first through a door?"

None of us had any inkling of von Rundstedt's mid-December counter-attack, which became the Battle of the Bulge. I happened to be among the guests at Tooey Spaatz's dinner table the night of December 16 and by midmeal realized that I must get out of the way as smoothly and quickly as possible. Three or four aides had come in to whisper in our host's ear and as soon as the dinner was finished I excused myself. Tooey insisted upon sending an armed airman with me and the chauffeur, back to the Ritz. The counterattack had thrust against a flank of Ernest's favorite infantry division, the 4th, and since no one knew the enemy's strength or potential or ultimate target, we speculated to the limit of our imaginations. The Krauts might cut off all the Allied armies in the north. They might launch parachute troops. They might reach Paris. I remembered the burning of official papers in Paris four years and six months earlier.

Still feverish, Ernest was packing at the Ritz and jumping to and from the telephone. He had to get up to the division, he said, and gave me a canvas sack full of papers with instructions to burn them before I left, if I had to leave Paris. Our friend General Red O'Hare, who happened to be at the hotel, had offered him transport, and after a nightmare night with little sleep, he took off, still feverish and sweating.

While the army public relations officers at conferences at the Hôtel Scribe assured us that the attack was contained and we were going to push forward, the word we got, we correspondents stuck in Paris, was gloomier. The Krauts were rushing toward Antwerp and we weren't stopping them, fellows said at the bar, correspondents who had come back to file stories because the facilities in Luxembourg were impossible. In Paris the censors turned heavy-handed. They did not want us to tell the enemy how far off guard they had caught us.

I foresaw a self-contained, restrained, but no more Spartan than necessary Christmas. In a street off the rue du 4 Septembre I found a shop which sold logs of wood for fireplaces and invested about a week's salary in enough sticks to burn for one evening. Ernest had left me an envelope with instructions not to open it until Christmas. But I peeked and on Saturday, December 23, wrote him three single-spaced pages of thanks and drivel. Besides a Merry Christmas note there was a check for $2,000 on his New York bank, and an Iron Cross he had removed from a dead German soldier.

In spite of the Battle of the Bulge and its eventual 59,000 casualties (6,700 killed) most of the U.S. Army and Navy headquarters outside of Paris were giving Christmas Eve or Christmas dinner parties, to some of which I was invited. They smelled to me like the British before Waterloo and I made excuses.

At Dunhill's I had bought for Ernest an outrageous jackknife, an ivory-coated contraption with twenty-some well-tooled instruments hidden in it, ready to pop out, including scissors, a leather punch, a gold toothpick, a corkscrew and a nail file besides the knife blades. But Marlene's Christmas present to him was more impressive. "Useful as well as beautiful," he said when he returned to Paris from the Bulge battle in mid-January. It was the double bed from her room down the hall on my floor, and it took a bit of doing, since neither the mademoiselle nor our floor valet approved of the transfer. Together Marlene and I yanked mattresses onto the floor and had my twin beds nearly dismantled before our floor staff acceded to the inevitable and completed the exchange.

We were still learning to appreciate so much lovely sleeping space when I woke myself one night violently scratching an arm. In the morning Ernest diagnosed. "Recruits disease. Seven-year-itch. A disease of dirt," he smirked. "Very old disease. Napoleon's troops had it. You'd better see a medic." The nearest army doctor confirmed Ernest's word, calling my affliction "scabies," and mentioned that it was widespread that year both in our army and among French civilians.

"It's highly contagious," the medico said. "You must have been sleeping in strange beds," and when I spluttered denials he conceded that it could be acquired from infected bed linen or other "inanimate materials."

In the Vosges I had borrowed blankets a couple of times, I remembered with dismay.

I could feel worms crawling all over me beneath my skin, I reported, and they were maddening. They were mites, the doctor said. The females of their tribe invade the skin, make themselves comfortable, warmed by the host's body, build themselves nests and produce offspring. "Not on me. Never," I yelled, scratching.

The army had a remedy which involved coating one's self with thick white goo, a benzyl benzoate, from neck to between the toes. Following instructions, I bought three new pairs of army long johns and, after showering, coated myself lavishly each morning, pulled on the heavy clean underwear and asked our mademoiselle to burn without delay the discarded pair.

At the army clinic I mentioned that the violent itching was keeping me sleepless, and the doctor wrote out a prescription. I swallowed his capsule the first night, slept badly, and the next morning discovered open, running, itchy sores on my face and neck, looking like the last stages of a venereal disease, or whatever might be more repulsive. I ran back to the doctor.

"You're very allergic to barbiturates," he said. "Why didn't you tell me?" I couldn't have told him since I had never until then taken a sleeping pill.

"I'm sorry, not to mention ashamed," I said to Ernest the first day of my tribulation, "but you had better sleep downstairs." He was singularly undaunted, refused to move out of our Christmas-present bed, and remained free from attack by the mites.

Early in the New Year I wrote my parents: "I finally must tell you that I have left Noel. We grew apart." (When we were both in Paris, just after the reoccupation, I had finally got around to telling him.) "There is a man to whom I am devoted, for all the things he is and some of the things he isn't. . . . I did not meet him until after I had decided to leave Noel. . . ."

Tom and Adeline Welsh wired me that they were surprised at the turn in my personal affairs but reserved judgment.

In late January Walter Graebner ordered me back to London, *Time* being drastically short of staff there, and between sessions of doing whatever it was for the London bureau, I found it sweet to live again among my gaily colored Gustave Doré prints of the *Fables de la Fontaine,* my teardrop Waterford wineglasses, and the enduring solidity of my old mahogany chests. My personal things, I thought. Since I wouldn't be needing my London civilian clothes any longer, I invited the girls from the office to an auction without money, opened my closets and unburdened myself of suits, dresses, handbags, hats, all useful to them. My army uniforms and the few civilian clothes I had in Paris were all I needed. Nobody knew when Britain's stringent clothes rationing might end.

When I went to the Bank of Australia in the Strand to pick up £100 or more for anticipated expenses, they told me that the balance was twelve shillings, sixpence. Noel and I had maintained a joint checking account there for years, my weekly deposit consistently larger than his, since I was earning more. Mr. Monks had withdrawn all but this small balance, the bank man said smoothly. Four or five hundred pounds of my earnings vanished without a syllable of explanation. I telephoned Noel's editor at the *Daily Mail.* He had sent Noel back to Australia and Southeast Asia to cover the budding counterattack against the Japanese. Had no idea where he might be just then. A month or two later I learned from *Time*'s business office in London that Noel had broken my agreement with them about the subletting of the flat, furnished, had removed all the furnishings including my small library with some signed first editions and canceled the lease. I was thankful that I had kept with me the three volumes of my parents' red-leather-bound Shakespeare, which I had taken with me to London in 1937.

In Paris in February 1945, Ernest had reverted to his bachelor style of living. "I can't stand your room without you," he explained, opening a bottle of Lanson Brut champagne to welcome me back. (We had finally consumed all of the Ritz's stock of Perrier-Jouet.) He was jubilant—and I was apprehensive—about the forthcoming arrival in Paris of his hero and friend,

Colonel Lanham, and also the 4th Division's most recent hero, Colonel Bob Chance, whose battered regiment had stemmed one prong of von Rundstedt's December attack. They had both been in active combat, or close behind it, since June 6 in Normandy.

"They must be bored with war and action. Let's find something civilized for them to do, or see," I suggested. "Henri downstairs will have something. A concert, maybe. Theater?"

Ernest decided, "No. We'll make our own divertissement. You don't know their tastes." As it turned out Ernest provided them with something else.

I had expected to meet a couple of officers subdued in their manner and their dress by so many fatiguing months of exchanged murder. Instead I found, down in Ernest's room, fresh young men, pants pressed sharp, every hair in place, eyes bright, if wary, tongues alert. Colonel Chance reminded me of a small-town banker, a bit pudgy, and conservative all around, I imagined. Colonel Lanham was a sprightly, prickly, sharp-witted elf. Ernest's cheeks were already pink from excitement and champagne, and we all had a drink.

Colonel Lanham had brought Ernest a present, two German pistols in a velvet-lined case, together with suitable ammunition for them. The boy from Oak Park, Illinois, decided he must demonstrate his appreciation of the present by shooting at least one of the pistols, if not both, from the hip. He loaded one and pranced around the room regretting there were no Krauts within range, aiming through his French windows at an imaginary enemy in the back garden of the Ministry of Justice, and was on the point of shooting into his fireplace when Colonel Lanham restrained him. I hopped around trying to keep out of his direct line of fire, my irritation mounting.

Ernest spied a photograph he had borrowed, a pleasant photograph of Noel Monks and me, taken in London a year or two before, picked up the photo and ducked into his bathroom. I followed him muttering, "Don't be a bloody fool," and watched in feeble, hypnotized revulsion as he set the picture into the bowl of his toilet and shot it with half a dozen bullets. He destroyed his toilet and some of the hotel's plumbing.

Such pieces of porcelain were then nearly irreplaceable. Members of the hotel staff came running, and I departed for the sanity and order of my own room.

On February 27, 1945, I wrote my parents: "This afternoon I'm going to ask for my travel orders, permission from the army to go home. The War Department in Washington has already granted permission.

"Apparently there are stories circulating that I am going to marry Ernest Hemingway. . . . Until I get home and we can talk it over, please say nothing about it. . . . It is not settled yet."

With events rushing one after another in the E.T.O. Ernest felt it futile to attempt stories which might get into print in *Collier's* six weeks after he had cabled them. Although he felt sure the war would be ending with an Allied victory, he could not write a forecasting piece that far in advance. His wounded head was stuffed to its walls with actions, landscapes, people, gestures and conversations, material he felt too important to spend in a weekly-forgotten magazine. He was homesick for Cuba and the airy Finca Vigía and his cats. He wanted to see his two younger sons. He wanted very much to get his civilian life and his writing going again and to arrange it so that I could fit into it. He hitched a ride across the Atlantic with General Orville Anderson, who was returning on assignment. I stripped his walls of the French Impressionist prints I had tacked up in August and helped him pack. Besides his canvas sack of army handout papers, some of them classified, which he would carry under his arm, and his beat-up typewriter, he had little luggage. He got off on March 6.

At the same time I flew east for a couple of chats with Major General Pete Quesada, chief of one of our medium bomber outfits, who was integrating the operations of his 9th Bomber Division with artillery fire by the VII Corps of the First Army. On March 7, patrols of the 9th Armored Division got across the Ludendorff single-track railway bridge at Remagen before the Krauts could blow it up and quickly established a bridge-head inside Germany. They were the first foreign troops to cross the Rhine since Napoleon in 1805, and the 9th Armored and their neighboring divisions took instant advantage of their luck. Five U.S. Army divisions crossed the bridge with all their matériel before March 17 when the bridge collapsed.

"How is your reconnaissance around here?" I asked General Quesada.

"Fine. Weather has been improving. We've been getting good pictures."

"Mmmmm. I suppose a plane that carries a photographer and his gear wouldn't have room for anyone else."

The general caught my lead. "We don't always send photographers. You want to go along for a look-see?"

On a gray Sunday morning I took off in a Piper Cub on the longest low-level flight I had ever made, a wad of the Paris sleazy pink paper on my knee. The scrawls on the pink paper remain, suggesting that day's montage of observations:

"Aachen, thousands of roofless walls. Only cemeteries still untouched. Red earth. Bomb holes water filled. Forests burned. Langrebe a dead village. Gun emplacements and the guns yellow. Moated gray castles, drab gray farmhouses. Long trenches, U-shaped foxholes . . .

"Düren, a bridge with buttresses broken, half shapes of buildings, zigzag trenches in the fields beyond. Flat green-brown fields, green now from sewing of other springs. Burned haystacks. A macabre blackened tree . . .

"Herrem, mills still burning. Smoke of forest fires . . .

"Cologne, untouched orchards, cathedral floating on a cloud of battle smoke. People on roads in patterns like lace placemats on a table. Gun flashes and white smoke. Black piles of shell cases. The rust color of powdered brick. Smokeless chimneys. Guns blinking like fireflies . . . Like a city dump . . . [We turned back.]

"Düren, willow trees turning yellow. A bedstead on a roof. Farm carts loaded with hay but no animals, no people . . .

"Eschweiler, patches in the hotel roof. Tree bursts worked like shears, snipping off heads of trees . . .

"Aachen, a Belgian train working. Sunday wash

186

hung out on a roof and another one, including a brown shirt, bleaching on a grass plot . . ."

My pilot was T.Sergeant Charles C. Cooke from Cleburne, Texas, hospitable and genial in his bouncy little craft.

A few days later I was picking through the ruins of Cologne with Major General Terry Allen's 104th Infantry Division, happy that Allied bombers had spared its Gothic cathedral, undismayed as I watched the Rhine River wash through the fallen girders of the city's Hindenburg Bridge, destroyed by the Germans. Back in Paris I sent off a long report for Time Inc.'s radio program *March of Time*, emphasizing the continuing work of the Nazi underground forces, even behind the Rhine:

"From what I saw jeeping slowly through bomb rubble in scores of villages and towns I am convinced we do not understand the thinking and feeling patterns of German people . . . whose standards of ethics, right and wrong, have been gradually eaten out, as by radium, both by Nazification of their educational system and by daily propaganda fed out on radio, posters, party meetings, church services. . . .

"You want to see whether or not the German people have really suffered from our bombings, you check on the cellar of any German house you enter. . . . The roof may be blown away, some walls may be down. But in the cellars there are rows of neatly put up glass jars holding chicken, vegetables, fruit, fruitcake. There is always the big earthenware jar holding eggs in waterglass. There are the makings of considerable comfort, rugs, the radio, couches, an air intake system, the family pewter or china, the best clock. In the town of München Gladbach they were able to distribute milk onto the broken doorsteps two days after the 29th Division passed through there. One woman there was complaining because the milkman had overlooked her. . . .

"In a dozen different towns I saw what the German looting of the Continent meant—nylon or real silk stockings, shoes better than England or France have seen for four years, thick, warm coats. In Eschweiler a pretty young woman, sunning her baby in front of her house, was wearing a mink coat with a Paris label.

Children looked healthy, their knees plump, cheeks pink, unlike the bony babies with puffy stomachs in the poor districts of Paris. . . .

"Everywhere the Germans were cheerful. They called hellos to friends in front of our jeeps. They smiled in conversations on the street corners. When you asked them why they felt so good, they said 'Now we can repair the electricity for the last time,' or 'My wife has been looting in the other end of town. We have a fine new chair.' No hint of compunction in the voice . . .

"They still retain their Nazi mannerisms, greet you with an upward hand wave and 'Heil.' Grammar school boys still wear their Hitler Jugend caps. Two of them, passing a group of GI's I was with, waited until a couple of soldiers passed them, then turned and spat at the backs of the Yanks. . . . The rest of us saw that. . . . We did nothing. . . .

"How can American troops live among people on the streets, in their shops, notice their gardens, their dogs, their clean, cheerful children, and obey their orders not to fraternize? . . . Near Cologne the other day a lanky boy from Oklahoma was chatting with three children, teaching them how to count in English and, as he'd done in England, France and Belgium, giving them gum. I reminded him that an M.P. might happen along. 'Yeah,' he said. 'Yeah, I know. But lookit that one. He's the perfect copy of my kid brother, the little jerk.' . . .

"The German girls . . . with high, healthy bosoms, stout limbs, their hair clean and shiny . . . grin and say *Wie geht*'s to our wandering dogfaces. . . . Our ground and air generals have seen all this too. . . .

"In his trailer-office near Cologne, Brig. Gen. Dick Nugent of the 29th Tactical Air Command, said 'Maybe our G.I.'s are too healthy in their own hearts to understand a nation or a girl without a conscience.' "

That was one of the last stories I sent as a working reporter.

Charles Wertenbaker had arranged with the New York office that I should take a year's sabbatical leave beginning the end of March and I got travel orders which would get me across the Atlantic on a troopship. Ernest was urging me to Cuba and I had seen enough of conquered Germany. I begged the press office to put me on a British ship, aware that U.S. troopships were desert dry. "Can't guarantee," he mumbled. My old friend Herbie Clark provided a welcome recess from my packing in Room 86 at the Ritz. The day was precociously warm and we sipped champagne sitting in the sunshine on my balcony, reviewing at random the past months and probing the uncharted future. He would rejoin his wife in London and then perhaps head for South America to be a correspondent there for one of the U.S. news services. I would visit Ernest in Cuba, but the toil and tumult, trouble and trepidations of the past year had been good for us, we concluded. We had lived it more profoundly than any year we were likely to know.

My ship sailed from Glasgow and was, indeed, British, the dear *Aquitania*, on which I had crossed a couple of times before, but now miserably converted to a troopship and leased and under the orders of the U.S. military. No alcohol, not even wine.

We docked at Halifax and some of the Red Cross girls and I made a modest shopping excursion, buying unrationed stockings and chocolate, before we boarded a train for Boston and New York. In the train's chair car—such luxury—a master sergeant of the U.S. Army stared disapprovingly at the hash marks on the left sleeve of my Eisenhower jacket and also at the floppy tip of my cloth belt with its splash of English hunting pink satin. Since he did not ask, I did not tell him that both small displays had been approved by the chief of SHAEF personnel.

I was repacking at the then pleasant Ambassador Hotel on Park Avenue, on April 12, when somebody called from the *March of Time* office. "Roosevelt has died," the voice said. "Can you do something about the reaction in the army, for tonight's show?" In a numb fog, feeling the sudden insecurity of an earthquake, I cracked out what I hoped were truthful comments, and in the studio that evening, the announcer said into the microphone, "In our studio here tonight is Mary Welsh of *Time* magazine. She is a woman war correspondent, and only returned day before yesterday from the European war theater. Be-

189

fore that she had worked as one of our correspondents in London. We believe that few journalists are as qualified . . ."

To the microphone I began, "Sudden, unexpected death is nothing new to American soldiers by now. . . ."

My parents' little apartment in Chicago's South Side was crowded with memorabilia from northern Minnesota, especially beaded gifts from Chippewa friends, and comfortable enough for them with its one bedroom. My parents were in good health and spirits, I was relieved to observe. They had hacked away at their respective disapprovals of each other for so many years that the differences had bound them together and their feuding had subsided into routine, a daily play of sharp- and soft-tongued repartee. I slept on the sitting room sofa for a few nights before I moved to a flat in East Delaware Place on the near North Side where my favorite and beloved cousins Homer and Beatrice Guck lived.

No longer a man of property or command, my father was nonetheless enjoying himself in his work at the accounting department of some war materials manufacturing firm. He could not abstain, and did not, from questioning some of the working rules decreed by the management, and also the flabby efforts of some of his co-workers.

"You'll get into trouble," I warned.

"Trouble? How can a man get into trouble by advocating simple efficiency?"

When Beatrice invited my parents to dine in Delaware Place, my mother declined, feeling not strong enough for the journey by taxi. But my father accepted, and our dinner abounded in good spirits and affection. Afterward I wanted to send him home by taxi. "No," he said. "Unnecessarily extravagant."

I walked with him westward to Clark Street where a streetcar would take him directly to a stop some fifty or sixty blocks south, not far from their apartment. Along came the car, clanking complaints, and my father swung onto its open, unglassed stern. He turned and waved a big smiling good-bye. I dallied a long time in the dim-lit streets on my way back to my cousins' flat with its radiant, unquestioned security. A whiff of my father's mortality had crossed my face, stirring my love for him. He was seventy-five years old.

Since he had returned to Cuba Ernest wrote me almost every day to New York or Chicago. Many of the letters got lost, but somehow I saved those written on April 9, 1945, and subsequently April 10, 11, 13, 14, 16, 17, 18, 19 and 20. On April 9 he wrote: "It's a month and three days since I saw you last, and this fine imitation of purgatory and limbo and those other whistle stops is building up on me. Children [on their spring vacations from school] left a week ago yesterday [and] yesterday there was a fiesta in the village with wonderful music and all the country people in on their horses and riding races in the street and tilting at rings. Lots of rockets and general festivities . . . I was alone and read the life of Nathaniel Bedford Forrest . . . I ought to get so I can be alone. . . . But I miss you as though they had cut my heart out with one of those things you take the cores out of apples."

Although I had written him three long letters during the tedious Atlantic crossing and continued writing every few days, Ernest's letters to me, so often beginning with lamentations, "I counted on some sure this morning but none came," read to me like a man gasping for breath. No letter that morning but he would somehow manage to get through the day until the evening post arrived. No letter that evening, but he would swim in the pool or go to the jai alai match in Havana and get tired enough to sleep and there would surely be a letter in the morning.

"Stayed in last night instead of going out to dinner," he wrote on April 17, "because thought there might be mail. But there wasn't. And then was sure there would be some this morning. There had to be. Today was the 17th and you got it on the 12th. But guess what? There wasn't any mail." I was flattered to be missed so fervently both in being and its written extensions, but also disquieted. The importunings seemed to be putting a lien on my independence, and I couldn't understand how a man in his own house with his books and animals and friends and sports could feel so frantic.

"I don't know how to get through fourteen days," he wrote. "I'm not impatient. I'm just desperate." He provided one explanation for my incomprehension. "You know how some people are allergic to things? . . . People don't say to them: Now be sensible. Just stop being allergic."

While I stitched together dangling ends of business at Time Inc., Ernest was making good use of Cuban diversions to leaven his loneliness. He was refurbishing *Pilar* after her overcrowded submarine hunting service, having the forward cockpit rebuilt, canvas side curtains replaced and mattresses and cushions on the afterdeck recovered, and incidentally looking over the Gulf Stream on fishing forays.

"There are some damned interesting things going on in the ocean. A new species of shark has turned up in 600 fathoms in great quantities. They have no fin on their backs, are black with a horrible ugly mouth and their stomachs are full of swordfish swords, marlin bills and they eat each other if you don't get them right in. Also one of the Cojimar fishermen caught a Great White Shark that weighed 7,000 (seven thousand) pounds. . . . The biggest shark I ever caught weighed 798 pounds and even a tiny fish of that sort offered considerable resistance. . . ."

He was pigeon shooting with friends. "I shoot miserably. Win money consistently but only by miracles. If I were managing a ballclub, would sell myself quickly; but if even smarter would hold myself knowing would clear up. Will clear up wonderfully for you."

He was getting the Finca grounds cleaned of the debris left by the severe hurricane of the fall of 1944 and planting trees, eucalyptus around the pool to shade it, and Persian lime trees, "so that eventually [can] open a Tom Collins factory," and having the loggia at one end of the swimming pool rethatched with palm branches. His newest command consisted of four gardeners, a cook, a butler, a maid, two small boys and a chauffeur. "Cook sits in kitchen all day long cutting radishes and onions into artistic compositions." He had Pancho, the carpenter, make wooden rings which, floating in the pool, would hold glasses of tall drinks within easy reach while we swam.

He was not letting the dogs in the house "because Lem, the pointer, is too damned big and too affectionate, and Chickie and Negrita too fast and don't know the meaning of moderation. . . . Leaving the animals alone for a year, everything went to hell."

He was looking beyond our immediate life in Cuba. "With planes the way they'll be, it will be a nine or less hour flight from here to Paris. We can have a flat on the river in Paris, this place and a place in Kenya and nowhere will be any distance from anywhere else. . . . Now am working out a scheme whereby when we go to Paris and London and Africa, can keep this place sound on a minimum of people and dough. . . ."

His health was a question mark. His old friend Dr. José Luis Herrera, who had been chief surgeon for the 12th International Brigade in Spain, lunched with Ernest at the pool and told him that the first hemorrhage, from a motorcar's collision with a London water tank in the street, should have been opened and drained, with three months of convalescence afterward. Instead, in August 1944, Ernest, riding in a motorcycle's sidecar, with his driver and photographer Bob Capa, had rushed into the path of a German antitank gun. The three had jumped into ditches and Ernest had banged his broken head, hard, against a stone. But he now wrote: "Am so much better than have ever been since you've known me that please don't think of me as a hypochondrious."

Finally it was June. I flew to Miami, and Ernest got me a seat on a plane from Miami to Havana. My thick northern Europe army uniform was much too heavy for those latitudes; but I wore it to Havana as Ernest had instructed me to do.

Ernest was shaved, combed, and crisp in a white *guayabera,* the pleated shirt which the gentlemen of Havana had long before adopted from the *guajiros,* the farmland laborers. He got me and my few bags into the Lincoln convertible and introduced Juan, the chauffeur, all formal and correct, without any show of sentiment. As we inserted ourselves into the front seat, he said, "I hope you don't mind sitting next to a Negro."

"Don't be silly. You've got me mixed up with somebody else."

I remember the royal palms clustered in the valleys between the green hills through which we drove to the Finca Vigía, one block away from the town of San Francisco de Paula, which was on the main west-east road burrowing through the island, the Carretera Central. Of names, locations and the Spanish language I knew nothing. I thought it odd that Cubans should say good-bye with *"hasta mañana." Hasta* must have something to do with "haste," I guessed. Why should Cubans be so eager for the morrow?

Inside the Finca's wooden gate we drove through a bower of scarlet flowers, up a little rise and half around a circular driveway from which rose a prodigious tier of broad old stone steps, with an enormous tree growing out of one rise. The house seemed to have grown gradually out of its hilltop. Its roof and a projecting terrace were laden with flowers and the air smelled of plants growing. I thought of Jane Austen and Louisa May Alcott and country vicars' manses and fell instantly in love.

"A ruin," Ernest said.

"It's beautiful. It's wonderful." Afternoon sunlight was brightening the inside, making the house look hospitable through its open doors and windows. I wouldn't care what it was like inside, I thought going up the steps, which was lucky. The long, pink-ceilinged sitting room looked like the waiting room of a funeral parlor. Giving off it, the dining room was austere-bare except for a refectory table and its chairs.

Juan and the butler were bringing my bags into the sitting room.

"You can stay in the Little House if you like," said Ernest. "It's where the children stay, but it's ready for you." He was polite and distant.

"Wherever you prefer."

He opened the door to a big blue room filled with sunshine, an immense bed, an immense desk, an immense chest of drawers and a large dressing table. There were not many mementos of its previous inhabitant, Martha Gellhorn. It took me twenty minutes to finish preliminary unpacking and change from my woolen uniform to a cotton frock and sandals. Then Ernest showed me around, accompanied by his favorite cat, Boise, black and white, long and skinny, a native of Cojímar, the fishermen's port where Ernest kept the *Pilar*. Ernest introduced the cat and me and, to his surprise, we liked each other immediately, Boise rubbing against my legs as we went down the path to the pool.

"Strange," Ernest said. "He hates wimnies, really. It was a wommy who sent him to have his balls cut off."

The pool, big and deep, looked delicious and I remembered I hadn't swum outdoors since 1940 at the swimming club in the Bois de Boulogne, and at Roehampton near London.

Ernest was lamenting the previous fall's hurricane. "Everything looks so stripped now. Arid, with this drought. But it will grow back again. You'll like it." He sounded like a real estate agent, his voice and manner formal.

"It looks lush to me," I said.

As we walked up the path to the house with Boise springing at imagined ambushes around us, happy as a cat, Ernest pointed out a fragile-looking tree, stubs of green seed pods creeping out of its lacy branches.

"That's a tamarind," he said, beginning to relax. "Exotic tree. Romantic name, don't you think?"

But I was tense too. "We could use a little romance," said I brusquely. Ernest's face stiffened as though I had slapped it. I could have bitten off my tongue.

5

Cuba Bella

ERNEST AND THE Finca Vigía and Cuba Bella presented me a variety of challenges: a new language, a new climate, a world of blossoms on trees, vines, shrubs and stalks I didn't know, a large staff and so a new manner of living, new diversions requiring new skills—fishing and shooting—a one-leader boss of operations instead of the complex hierarchy of Time Inc., a new focus of interest and activity. No office. I had an entire new life to learn, and I was glad that I had decided, leaving Europe, that I would refrain from trying to keep close ties by regular correspondence with my friends there. A sharp break, but neat.

Ernest introduced me to the other servants and the gardeners, to Pancho the carpenter, and to the principal cats: Princesa, the fine-boned elegant gray Persian mother of the tribe, beautiful, and with her Persian secrets a bit too feminine for me; Uncle Willy, the children's favorite cat, a square, striped, businesslike male, who disdained cats but liked people; Bigotes, the big rough endearing fighting stud of the family; Uncle Wolfie, long-haired and silvery like his mother, debonair and timid; and that year's crop of young mothers with their children. They sunned in their respective favorite places along the terrace every morning, I noticed, and took to promenading it regularly, offering greetings and ears for scratching. Like its scarlet-flowered royal poinciana trees and pink-blooming frangipani, animals were the Finca's indigenous decoration.

We lost no time finding a Spanish teacher for me, a pleasant Spanish girl, Pilar, who came to the Finca three or four mornings a week. Her accent was Castilian, as Ernest required. If I learned Castilian, I could be understood in any Spanish-speaking country, he explained. Whereas, if I learned the Cuban accent, with its plethora of vowels and paucity of consonants, other Spanish-speaking lands would find me half incomprehensible. Meanwhile Ernest patiently attended to menus and supervised household chores.

His friends came out for lunch almost every day and spoke in English or French for my benefit. They were an assortment of Spanish grandees, Peps Merito, the Marqués de Valparaíso, and others, Mayito Menocal and Elicio Argüelles, giving Ernest their tacit approval of his nonconformist conduct. I was interested in the politics of this new country. But my questions elicited only mollifying phrases. Women were not supposed to know or care about government, I concluded in frustration. As we were finishing our luncheon wine on May 8, we heard an explosion of shouting and singing outside. Crowds of boys from the village were dancing in the driveway. "The war is over," Ernest said quietly. "They've just heard it on the radio." He went down the steps to hug the boys and sent back for money for beer for them. A sense of distance from everything I knew washed over me, a stranger there in the sunshine beneath the ceiba tree.

Ernest's friend and fellow fisherman, Dr. Cucu Kohly, brought his pretty blond U.S.A. wife, Joy, to lunch one day and, delighted to see her, I nonetheless realized without regret that I had seen no other woman except our Cuban maid since I arrived. For the sake of my parents' respectability, I was supposed to be staying with the Kohlys as their house guest ten miles away on the other side of Havana, and they were conscientiously forwarding my mail sent to their address. All during the affable easy conversation I wondered if and how I could retract the boundaries of my interests to simple stifling domesticity.

Came the day when we settled into the Lincoln convertible, drove along back country roads to Cojímar and Ernest, trying to be casual about it, introduced me to Gregorio Fuentes, his mate on *Pilar,* and to *Pilar* herself, black-hulled, green-decked, his dearest possession. They both gained an immediate new admirer. Gregorio's handsome weather-worn face showed the familiar kindness I had always found in outdoor faces. *Pilar* was shiny and clean, with all gear in its proper place. I knew nothing of fishing boats, but on first acquaintance this one looked like a wonderful boat. I would learn her measurements and biography later; but this day I explored, hunching along her scuppers to sit on the very tip of her prow, dangling my legs overboard and jubilating in the pearl and diamond necklaces she made nosing through the water, and finding my own route from the stern deck up to the flying bridge where Ernest was steering. He could vault from the fishing chair to the bridge, but his legs were five or six inches longer than mine. A horizontal strut stretched on the port side from the housing to a post of the afterdeck, and I found that by standing on it, I could hook a foot and knee onto the edge of the flying bridge. Neat, quick, and joyous.

"I found a way to get upstairs, I can't remember what you call it on boats," I fibbed, hugging the skipper.

"Upstairs, of course," he said. "And that's the front," pointing, "and back there is the back. And down there is downstairs." Thistledown jokes. I knew most nautical terms.

"And where's milady's chamber?"

"Everywhere. Anywhere you like."

"You're always welcome there," said I.

That May morning we had a light *brisa,* the northeast trade wind which crosses the Atlantic in a 3,000-mile fetch and tempers Cuba's warmth, its airs sweet from the flowering sea grapes on the eastward islands. The sun in Cuba's cobalt sky scattered sequins on the sea, and *Pilar*'s engine hummed comfortably. Ernest showed me his prewar rods and reels, irreplaceable because their makers were still producing war materials, and gave me a beginner's course which I promptly forgot on what size reel required what strength of line.

We zigzagged eastward with the Gulf Stream into the wind and pulled into Bacuranao, a small, snug bay with an empty golden beach, to anchor and swim off the boat and later to lunch on Gregorio's glorious fresh-caught tuna, simmered in sea water and herbs. From his little radio Cuban tangos and rhumbas emerged softly, and the waters of the bay slapped lazily against our hull. Lolling in the shade of *Pilar*'s afterdeck, I felt, after the gray years of Blitz in London and the frozen winter in Paris, that I had returned to the remembered paradise of childhood summers.

My comfortable euphoria lasted a couple of hours. As we trolled homeward that afternoon a small striped marlin took one of our baits and Ernest urged me into the fishing chair to reel in the fish. With Gregorio handling the boat and Ernest swinging the chair for me to keep the rod pointed at the fish, I pulled up slowly, as instructed, and reeled fast, lowering the rod, perhaps no more awkwardly than any greenhorn. The marlin was a stout-hearted, athletic fish. He jumped and tailwalked as I had never before seen a fish do, and I watched his performance in wonder, more than I watched my own business. When we got him to the boat and Ernest was reaching for the gaff, the fish swam under us. Snap, went the rod, only a foot above the reel. Snap, went the line without the rod to support it. Mere high school geometry should have told me that I should stand up and hold the rod, the old, laminated wooden rod, horizontal to the sea to prevent its breaking. Knowing I could not buy a replacement I sobbed in fury and frustration, while Ernest pretended the loss was unimportant. That was the first and last rod I broke in seventeen years.

Through the years we lived more halcyon and exuberant days aboard *Pilar* than in any other place except, possibly, East Africa, to which we clung only six months. By 1934, when Ernest knew he could afford his own fishing boat, he had ordered *Pilar* to be built by the Wheeler Brothers in Brooklyn. He had fished enough off Bimini, Key West and Havana and knew precisely what he wanted in his boat. She had to be sturdier than most craft both below and above the waterline. *Pilar,* with close-set ribs of steam-bent white oak, 1¼ by 1¾ inches, was as solid as Mt. Everest. She must have her flying bridge high enough for seeing fish within a quarter-mile radius and to give decent headroom from the lower deck. The bridge was seven feet above the afterdeck. The space above must be big enough to hold a half dozen friends. It was as big as a Hollywood bed inside its steel railings, and sometimes became one, with three or four people sleeping on a big air mattress behind the topside wheel and controls.

Pilar was 38 feet long with a 12-foot beam and drew 3½ feet of water—spacious and still maneuverable in the shallows where the tarpon live. Having no siding along her afterdeck, an innovation in those days, when most boast' cabins extended to their sterns, she stayed cool on the hottest days in her sub-tropic seas with the canvas curtains rolled up and the breeze rushing through. Her propeller was powered by a Chrysler marine 110-horsepower engine, providing enough cruising speed—eight to nine knots—since the Gulf Stream poured along Cuba's north coast usually only a few hundred yards off shore. Ernest had no need to run ten or fifteen miles to his fishing grounds as boatmen must do in many areas. *Pilar* also had a small Universal 35-horsepower auxiliary engine, which could provide strength enough to hold her way against heavy seas. She had no ship-to-shore telephone, no fathometer, no gadgets, although she carried two small boxes to hold old-fashioned fifty-pound blocks of ice, one in the galley and one on the afterdeck. Sunk in a cork-and-zinc-lined hole below the afterdeck was another box which held a ton of ice, essential for two-week cruises. Whenever we left harbor, we had our private world, isolated and self-contained.

Pilar was a seasoned ship when Ernest introduced me to her. In World War II she had been loaded with radio, high-explosive and sound-detection gear and had served as a Q-ship hunting German submarines which were torpedoing Allied tankers off Cuba and along the eastern coast of the United States. She had cruised the Gulf Stream and the islands off Cuba's north coast a month at a time for about a year and a half pretending to be a scientific expeditionary ship. With Gregorio Fuentes attending her, she had ridden out the vicious hurricane of the fall of 1944 which had put half the Cuban navy and merchant and private shipping into the streets of Havana or on the bottom of the harbor. In May 1945 she was still in the prime of life, and freed of her wartime gadgets.

In time I would understand the wild excitement stirred in us by the sighting of the erect curve of a marlin's slicing tail, and the delights of setting the hook in the mouth and of maneuvering and persuading the fish to the boat, even though it would be, as Ernest maintained, an unequal contest.

Straight from prison camp, Bumby arrived at the Finca in early June, a handsome, jolly young man who seemed to me marvelously undisturbed by his having been wounded and imprisoned. He won my allegiance at once by laughing at my quips and by his devout appreciation of our cuisine which I was beginning to supervise. The three of us swam, played desultory tennis and loafed about the Finca, and Bumby taught me his 3rd Division song—"They're tearing me down to build me over again. . . . Your dogfaced soldier boy's okay." Or we went to drink double frozen daiquiris and josh with friends at the Floridita Bar in Havana. We squandered a few days in delicious, contraband sloth before Ernest's two young sons, Patrick, nicknamed Mouse, and Gregory, nicknamed Gig, joined us and our living pace turned to a canter, sometimes a gallop.

Expanding and embroidering menus to accommodate healthy young appetites, Ramón, the Chinese cook, and I were developing our private esoteric language, he with his Chinese accent, I substituting *l* for *r* in my babytalk Spanish, words without sentences. Using the wicker baskets Ernest had brought from Hong Kong, Justo, the butler, and I packed picnic lunches to be celebrated beside a stream or on a hilltop farther down the island. In country sheds fitted with scaffolding benches we yelled at roosters and tried to see the injuries they were inflicting on each other in the pandemonium of cockfights. At the Club de Cazadores, just down the road toward Havana from the Finca, the boys shot live pigeons in private competitions Ernest arranged for them and a few friends. I was memorizing the names of plants and vines in Spanish and English: Mar Pacífico was Hibiscus, Coralillo was Coral Vine,

Adelfa was Oleander, Cola de Camarón was Shrimp Plant, Rosa de Madera, those flowers carved out of walnut veneer, were Wood Rose, or Honolulu Rose. They were all blooming and scenting our air. Because I had noticed a rotting window sill, I showed Pancho, the Spanish carpenter and conscientious craftsman, the multiple pieces of wood which needed replacing.

With hodgepodge success I was trying to memorize twenty new words of Spanish every day. One of the most elusive was *mantequilla,* for "butter." I finally managed it by two detours. The lace or veil with which a Spanish woman covered her head or high combs was a mantilla. The chiefs of Haile Selassie's Ethiopian tribesmen had rubbed their heads with grease when they attended the funeral of his oldest daughter in Addis Ababa in 1942. So I went from heads with lace to heads with grease to butter. From that it was easy to remember *manteca,* the less refined cooking fat. With everybody talking in concert, family luncheons went on from two o'clock until four or later, Bumby lilting and gay, Mousie thoughtful and bright, Gigi sardonic, muttering gleeful gibes, Justo pretending exhaustion as he brought in the final bottle of wine and the coffee. Dinners moved more quickly, partly perhaps because the dining room was then lit only by a single bare electric bulb hanging from the middle of the twenty-foot ceiling. No matter what welcoming aromas we had from the food, the bare white walls remained inhospitable.

In his private store of weaponry Ernest found Martha's Model-21, 20-gauge Winchester shotgun, and one evening urged me to try shooting it. Gigi volunteered to show me how to shoot. We went up the hill behind the dignified old ruin of an abandoned brick and plaster cowshed, the *vacaría,* to practice. Gigi found a big piece of a cardboard box and propped it against the broken stone of the *vacaría.* He loaded the gun for me and explained the trigger action, then walked me back about thirty yards from the piece of carton, and explained "bead on target, head down, stock firm at shoulder." As I saw, the shot was widely scattered in the cardboard, most of it too high. He moved me up much closer and I shot again and saw the pattern of the shot condensed.

In the province of Havana there then existed a phenomenon of bird flight which no one we knew could explain. From ten to fifteen miles outside the city small blackbirds—the size of thrushes, all black and called *negritos* in Cuba—migrated each evening from their daytime country habitat to the laurel trees of Havana's double-laned street, the Prado, in the city's center. There they roosted overnight and, mornings, returned to the farmlands and canefields surrounding the city. In the evenings they flew straight and level in flocks of thousands, and a few hundred winged above our heads on the rise behind the *vacaría*.

"Move with them and shoot," Gigi said, and demonstrated. *Pam, ping*—two little birds spun down, and that flock flared away. Another covey was approaching off to our left. *Pam, pong,* two more birds fell, so far away I thought they might have had heart attacks.

With Gigi coaching, I aimed and shot, aimed and shot, broke the gun, reloaded, aimed and shot, and finally, before all the shells were used, one little bird fell near my feet.

"How did you do?" Ernest asked, back in the sitting room.

"Okay," said Gigi, with a rising inflection. "Okay for a first go." He was protecting me and enrolling me among his admirers.

In spite of visiting children and the challenges of a whole new range of skills to learn, I sometimes sank into depressions of spirit, no deeper than gullies; I was probably longing for the concomitants of my old life. Instead of independence and my personally earned income, I was dependent on Ernest in all decisions about our living as well as economically. I didn't like my income appearing haphazardly as gifts. Economic slavery, I thought. No more shackling than that of Time Inc., but more personal. But Ernest was also steadily and without fuss or pretensions supplementing my parents' modest income. Enterprises I had thought worthwhile, such as collecting and sending news stories, were of no importance at the Finca Vigía. Talk of politics and the manner and stratagems of European and British recovery from the war interested nobody in Cuba. I had been an entity; now I was an appendage.

On June 7 I wrote: "Thrusty is here, clawing the sheet, asking affection. [Thrusty was one of the young mother cats.] Thrusty mistakes me. I am not hers, nor she mine. The man has his house, his writing, his children, his cats. Nothing is mine. . . . I can't fight for areas of personal domination . . . I feel very much alone, knowing nothing of the pursuit of fish, animals and birds. . . . Muscle may not be a bad god, nor the worship of same."

That Ernest was to blame for my troubles I never questioned. What made me pause and procrastinate about removing myself was the question of the gravity of my fits of dejection and revolt: Were they serious enough to warrant my busting up a generally good alliance? Before I could decide, there would be Ernest, gentle or thoughtful and loving, and a lilt in the breeze.

The younger boys had occasionally been aboard *Pilar* during the war when she was hunting German submarines, and now Ernest decided that they should make a sentimental journey with all of us to a tiny island flanked by huge coral reefs, Megano de Casigua, which Ernest had nicknamed Paraíso. He invited his Basque friend, the pelota player Paxtchi Ibarlucia, to come along, piloting the small work launch, the *Winston*. Aboard *Pilar* with Gregorio we were six, plus a ton of ice and copious food and liquids.

Gregorio brought *Pilar* to one of the Havana docks early that evening but, busy drinking daiquiris and dining at the Floridita, and winding up landlubber connections as though we would be gone for a year, we did not manage to get aboard until well after midnight. Then we headed out of the harbor past the Morro Castle, and set our course at about 270 degrees, due west. We had hardly cast off when the boys were making themselves beds below decks with blankets from the clothes locker, but Ernest was on the flying bridge, peering a bit fuzzily, maybe, into the darkness of the sea. It was a joyous starlit night, the sea only slightly ruffled, the east breeze cool and gentle.

204

I grabbed a blanket, dragged it up top, and held it there with my feet, standing with our skipper while he steered, softly whistling some of the songs the *conjunto* of guitars and maracas had been singing at the bar. Someone had been teaching me the words of one, and I tried it:

> *Soy como soy,*
> *Y no como Papa quiere,*
> *Qué culpa tengo yo*
> *De ser así?*

I even knew what it meant.

> I am as I am
> And not as Papa wishes,
> What fault have I
> To be like this?

"Is it the lament of a local whore?" I mused aloud.

"Just the invention of the *conjunto,* my Pickle," Papa said, putting his arm around me.

Gregorio bounced up onto the flying bridge asking something in rapid Spanish, and Papa replied.

"I told him I wasn't sleepy," he translated, "and to go to bed. It's good up here, isn't it, my Pickle?"

"It's wonderful." I hummed the little bar song, but I was drugged with daiquiris and weariness. "But, if you'll excuse me, I'll take a nap right here beside you." I was asleep on the deck in a minute.

Dawn was climbing up the eastern sky astern of us when I opened an eye, looked for Papa's legs slanting up to the steering wheel and couldn't find them. He was sleeping sweetly on a piece of my blanket. I bounced up, terrified we might run into something, but nothing was in sight, not even the coastline. *Pilar* was humming away on what looked to me like a northwest course; up top we had no compass. Ernest hadn't even tied the wheel when he left it. As I stood wondering whether or not to turn us more to the west—maybe there were reefs I didn't know of—Ernest woke up.

"You sure have confidence in these waters," I said irritably.

Ernest swung the wheel. "Not much shipping here."

"What about fishermen? We could have sunk them."

"We might have heard their greetings. We've lost an hour or two. That's all."

Eastern light was tinting the satiny waves lavender and pink. It was a morning too pure and beautiful for obloquy, and I went below to wash away my sour face. I never again saw Ernest abandon *Pilar*'s wheel while she was under way.

If I had dreamed of a tropical island with polished palm fronds protecting a huddle of thatched *bohíos,* a curve of empty beach, blond grasses nodding, Paraíso in her mounting of blue and turquoise waters was the dream *in situ.* Currents foamed against the long ridges of coral flanking the island, but inside the channel through which we had maneuvered, the lagoon was so calm that we could see pebbles on the sandy bottom four or five fathoms below the surface, and creatures new to me—a school of infant mullet flashing silver like a handful of flung sequins, and among them skinny green-blue needlefish, their long jaws snapping.

With the little .22 pump-action rifle Gigi shot one of the needlefish in the head as it surfaced and we watched as it lurched, stopped and slowly moved toward a small clump of weed growing on the bottom. It turned into the weed, head downward, tail projecting slightly above the tips of the grasses. A new actor appeared, a barracuda, almost as luminous as the water as he swung and hovered and side-slipped around the clump of weed. The needlefish had emitted only a tiny trickle of blood, but the 'cuda's smelling devices had found it. At two yards, and gradually, cautiously, one yard from the wounded needlefish, the 'cuda hovered and waited and watched, only the patches of black on his sides easily visible in the bright water. Then, quick as a snake, he dashed at the needlefish, sliced it in two and was away. Paxtchi went out and brought back the forward half of the victim, and we saw how efficiently a barracuda's teeth are designed. The sharpest butcher's knife could not have cut more cleanly.

Patrick and Gigi wanted to fish for tarpon among the

roots of the mangroves which made green islands between our lagoon and the mainland. Gregorio rigged baby rods and reels for them, and with Paxtchi steering the *Winston,* we set off. Bumby, immersed in the book he had brought along, Lloyd Douglas's *The Robe,* remained in his upper bunk in *Pilar*'s cabin. Paxtchi paused at the southeast tip of the island, and Papa and I dropped off to swim ashore and into a new world for me. That lovely, empty, remote beach was more crowded and busy, if less noisy, than the Place de la Concorde, and many of its occupants were menacing to a stranger.

As I was dribbling my toes in two inches of water along the beach, Ernest suddenly whisked me ashore and pointed downward. "Stingray," he said. "They don't like being stepped on." Just awash was a square pancake with a snout and two black eyes protruding from the inshore corner and a stringy tail pointing seaward, the whole thing delicately camouflaged by sand shifting over it. The tail was the tricky part, Ernest explained.

"You'd think they'd have the decency to honk."

The beach curved northward and two kinds of birds on stilts, some on wet sand, some in the water, moved ahead of us chattering softly to each other. "Wilson's plover," Ernest said, "and sandpipers. They're in the bird book at home." He whistled a high crescendo flute call and a few of the sandpipers took off and flew inland answering him with a single-noted long wail. Paraíso was a paradise for birds too. A fine thick tangled swamp cut the island nearly in two at high tide and provided a comfortable winter resort for loons, curlews, grebes, ibises, sometimes, and stilts and other birds who nested far to the north. That morning we swam long and lazily in the iridescent water and on the way back to be picked up by the *Winston* I decided to have some swimming suits made with pockets. Of the dozens of shells I wanted to take back to *Pilar,* I could carry only a few. One of the island fishermen had caught a small octopus and Gregorio, one of the best cooks in the western hemisphere, I was discovering, prepared it for our supper. *"Pulpo en su misma tinta,"* Gregorio announced, bringing it up from the galley, and Ernest and Paxtchi and the boys welcomed it like an old friend. The meat had the texture of an inner tube, and no discernible flavor, I thought, but the black, garlicky sauce was glorious.

My friend Sarah Brown of the Chicago *Daily News* days had long been married to a prominent lawyer, William Boyden, Jr., and in correspondence he indicated that my status as a resident of Chicago, even after eight years in foreign parts, might be viewed not inhospitably. So Ernest and I decided I might as well go up and arrange the legal formalities of a divorce from Noel. It rained for the first time in months on June 20, the day I was to fly north, and simultaneously the chauffeurs of Havana went on strike. Juan turned up on time, neat in his gray uniform and cap, but Ernest decided it would be prudent for Juan to refrain from driving me to the airport, and so got behind the wheel, me beside him and Juan in the back seat.

At the Club de Cazadores we turned off the main road to Havana and took the old high-crowned shortcut road to Rancho Boyeros, the airport. Trucks had been hauling clay, leaking hunks of it onto the old road, and with the new rain the surface had turned greasier than a pancake skillet. Topping a slight rise, we skidded downward and Ernest warned me, "This is bad, Pickle. We have to go off," and steered us into a high bank of earth. Ernest's forehead went into the rearview mirror, his ribs into the wheel and a knee into the dashboard. I went through the windshield, and was confused by the warmth of my blood running down my neck.

Only fifty yards back we had passed a roadside first-aid station, a panacea apparently preferable in Cuba to the more expensive business of leveling the roads and improving their surfaces. My face was bleeding so much that Ernest, with his multiple wounds, insisted on carrying me back to the little wooden house with its Red Cross insignia.

Inside, bleeding onto his shirt and refusing to sit down, he explained our accident and then they whisked me away from him, laid me out on a table and closed the door. A very large black woman, making pleasant conversation I did not understand, dipped a piece of cheesecloth in alcohol and began to clean the glass out of my cut left cheek. Then, without turning over the cloth or rinsing it, she began to scrub the dust from my forehead, cutting into the skin with the bits of glass she had picked up from my cheek. I could not remember the word for "stop." I could not remember the word for "cut." I screamed "No, no, no," and tried to get up. But she pushed me down. In her business she must have been accustomed to women screaming.

Cucu Kohly hurried out from Havana and took us home in his car, the Lincoln being unserviceable. Cucu put a few tentative bandages on each of us, found out that Cuba's best plastic surgeon was quail shooting five hundred miles down the island and would not be able to sew me up for a couple of days. "Don't cry, or smile or talk," Cucu ordered, putting me to bed in Martha's room, and I remember lying there watching the daylight fade to mauve among the trees outside, and listening to birds murmuring their good nights. Ernest came in, his face grave. His ribs and knee must be paining him, I knew, but he wanted to cheer me. He had been telephoning people in the United States, postponing my arrival.

"No bones broken. That's good."

"Scarface," I mumbled.

"Don't you worry, please, my beauty. We'll get you sewed up fine."

A couple of days later Juan drove me into a clinic in Vedado, one of the more elegant and expensive areas of Havana, and the following morning I was on the operating table with a local anesthetic blocking the nerves of my cheek and enormous fingers wielding a needle and thread in front of my eyes. The surgeon spoke English.

"Your hands look very big," I said. "But you seem to be taking fine stitches."

"I'm working on very fine fabric," he said cheerfully. The sewing seemed to me to take an inordinately long time and I was tired when they trundled me back to the high-ceilinged room with its big unscreened window. Tired, and yearning for a cigarette, I asked the nurse for one and gestured. *"No, no,"* she said. *"Sí, sí, sí,"* I yelled, at risk of pulling stitches. *"No, no, no cigarro, y no se mueve,"* she said, pushing my head flat against the mattress. *"Uno, un cigarro,"* I begged, hating her. *"No, no,"* she went on, the stuck record, arbitrary, mindless, without compassion. Tears for my helplessness slid out the sides of my eyes, and I was lying there, merely enduring, when Bumby, tall and cheerful, marched into the room.

"Gosh you look pretty," said he, his insouciance reviving me.

"Give me a cigarette, please."

Bumby lit one and put it gently between my half-numb lips, a gesture of kindness unparalleled in my lexicon. He found the cigarettes and lighter in my handbag across the room and tucked them under the mattress for me. "Cuba is a screwy country, anyway," he said, "and when they add slippery roads to it, it becomes unique."

Ernest, with his aches and pains and the bleeding from his forehead whenever he moved about, stayed home at the Finca but wrote me constantly, Juan delivering the letters together with magazines and sacks of fruit which I gave away since I couldn't chew. "Bad luck automobilistically evidently comes in bunches," he wrote. "You were so *brave* and good and sound and non-hysterical under the very worst circumstances. . . . I have slight hemorrhage in left knee. . . . Cucu says your cuts are nothing for a good surgeon to fix. . . . So sorry dearest kitten. . . ." "Brave," underlined, was lovely but too theatrical, I thought.

Lying still in the clinic I reflected on the irony, really comic in its dimensions, of a creature's having come to bleeding and disfigurement on a side road in Cuba after surviving unscathed a couple of years of Blitz, then buzz bombs and the hazards of military flying and icy French roads. When night came, I had a diversion. The Vedado mosquitoes bred and born around that clinic possessed not only immunity to mercurochrome with which my face was coated,

210

they had developed a positive taste for it. Through my open window they swarmed in hungry schools to feast on the antiseptic and me, and my concern over dislodging bandages partly prevented me from dislodging them.

At my insistence they brought me a mirror on the day before I left the clinic. There, reflected, were my eyes where they belonged, sunk in a bowl of raw hamburger with a small railway track running across one side and some black fences staked up and down above it. It was not, it could not, be me, I first thought. I handed the mirror away, and this time the nurse made croaks of apparent sympathy. There was no point in blubbering, I decided finally. That would not banish my horrible mask.

I'll frighten little children, I thought. I can never appear in public. How can I organize a life of solitude, permanent solitude? No one will be able to look at me, not even Ernest. He'll seek pleasanter faces, inevitably. What can I do in a lifetime in some cell by myself? The impact of that look at my face was less a blow to my vanity—I had never pretended to be a beauty—than to my being. From agreeable-looking to monster. How did one accommodate one's self to monstership? I remembered the young R.A.F. pilot, fiercely burned and much repaired but inhuman and still embarrassing to me, who had come to my flat in Grosvenor Street in London in 1942. I lay quiet, and waited for some wisp of resolution to come back to me.

"One more day and there will be all your pals to take care of you good," Ernest had written. How could I impose my disaster on them, I wondered.

At the Finca Vigía I stayed in my room a couple of days, pondering, not believing Ernest when he came in looking worried to say, "Please don't worry. Please."

One morning I awoke with my resolution firmly in place again. "Don't be a bloody fool," my resolution said. "Throw away the sorry-for-yourself nonsense. It won't do you any good. The sooner you forget how hideous you look, the sooner it won't be noticed by others." I had lots of work to do, and the first thing

211

was a conference with Pancho, who had set up his workshop in the garage. I went there and in my skimpy Spanish said, "Good day, Pancho. Excuse my face, but we have to arrange . . ."

Pancho looked down and a tear or two dripped from his eyelashes. *"Sí, sí, señora."* Then we got to work, I showing him more termite-ridden window and door sills needing to be replaced. A week later the plastic surgeon plucked out the stitches in my cheek and forehead, leaving fiery red gashes. "You have been very lucky," he said, wielding tweezers. "One millimeter closer to your nose, and the nerve would have been severed, the face paralyzed. We don't know yet how to repair that nerve." I followed his orders about greasing my face and went right on pretending there were no scars. In about a year the rewards began to reach me. If, by chance, I mentioned my scars to new acquaintances, they might ask, "What scars?"

On July 5 Ernest gave a pigeon-shooting party complete with luncheon for Bumby and his friends, everybody bursting with cheer and sky-high spirits. Everybody but me. "After luncheon, hideous in its disorder and raucous bad manners, I sat watching the shooting by myself," I wrote that night. "How could I ever sit on an endless succession of club verandas with those vacant-eyed cows? When Papa took me down to the bar for a drink and a little boy threw a firecracker, I started to bawl. Juan drove me home. Now at 9:20, since no one has come to inquire how I am, I've had several hours to think. I can only conclude I'd be an idiot to stay on here. I don't think I could ever work up any enthusiasm for an endless series of what seems to me not quite adult pastimes, good for holiday but not as a steady diet. Papa just came in and asked 'What's that? Your Horror Diary?' Yes, I'd better go."

Ennui enveloped me like fog whenever I had to watch pigeon shooting, but it never got as much as a toehold aboard *Pilar,* whether or not the fishing was good. And the fishing was wonderful that summer of 1945. Despite the gas shortage, we celebrated the Stream's bounty regularly, trailing baits over the best swirls and holes, keeping our excursions short, spending gas carefully.

With Ernest coaching, Patrick and Gigi and I learned to handle the auxiliary jobs while he worked on big fish. Usually we trolled downstream to Bacuranao, the lovely empty harbor to which Ernest had taken me my first day aboard *Pilar,* swam and lunched there, then trolled back against the current in the late afternoons when, Ernest and Gregorio had decided, the big fish came to the surface to feed. My favorite spot was the flying bridge, the better to see around, and usually we all stayed there until a tail or a dorsal fin appeared in our neighborhood. Then we burst apart, Ernest thumping down to the afterdeck to grab the most likely rod, Mouse and Gigi and I sliding down the port side to haul in the teaser and, when a beast was hooked, to reel in the other lines. Ernest taught me to handle the steering wheel and gears in the crucial moments when the fish was close and Gregorio in the stern ready to gaff. "Ease her forward—Easy—*Sauve.* Throw her out" (meaning into neutral). Gregorio would have the fish's bill in his left hand, the gaff in his right hand with Gigi deftly hitching the gaff's rope around the Sampson post on the stern. Then, pulling in unison the men would haul the prize over *Pilar*'s stern roller, onto the deck where we would admire it, gloat a little, and toast the trophy. Then we headed for Cojímar. The low-roofed town, strung out along two sides of its bay, was a simple settlement of men who fished for their livings in small boats with oars and sails, no engines. Everybody knew everybody, and if *Pilar* pulled in with a sizable fish, Gregorio's friends ashore would catch his signal and come out to help him unload our catch into our dinghy and then hoist it up to be weighed by the town's communal scale which hung from a scrawny, twisted laurel bent over by the east wind. The tree grew beside the village's only bar with restaurant, La Terraza, and while Gregorio butchered on the beach below, Ernest used to buy drinks for the locals and catch up on the fishing news of the day. Sometimes he asked for steaks from the fish, inch-thick slabs cut through the round back and spine, the only bone, to take home or to send to friends. The rest of the catch was Gregorio's to sell in the Havana market.

We caught six or eight large marlin that summer and

on August 8 Ernest hooked a small giant and brought him to gaff in fifty minutes. He weighed just under six hundred pounds on the Cojímar scale, but he did not provide Gregorio with that summer's fortune because a number of other fishermen had caught giants that day and the market price dived down.

As we were taking predinner drinks a few evenings later, Justo, the butler, whizzed into the sitting room announcing that Japan had capitulated. He had heard it on the servants' radio in the pantry. The next morning Juan, the chauffeur, arrived with a new song. Cuba, the nation of spontaneous songsmiths, celebrated the Japanese surrender with a typical carefree jingle:

> Ping, ping, cayó Berlin
> Pong, pong, cayó Japan

Cayó I discovered was the past tense (third person, singular) of the irregular verb *caer*, to fall.

Joy Kohly recommended a hairdresser in Havana and Ernest suggested that I might have my hair bleached, as a present to him. I had lived peaceably with the color of my hair, which admirers called Titian and I called peanut butter, but, a bit discountenanced by such a bow to the artificial, I submitted to the bleaching, and Ernest was entranced by the result. Deeply rooted in his field of esthetics was some mystical devotion to blondness, the blonder the lovelier, I never learned why. He would have been ecstatic in a world of women dandelions.

If it were to be Ernest's primary home, the Finca Vigía offered unending suggestions for improvements beyond the small problems of rotting window sills. The fences were rotted away or broken down, especially along the road to the big handsome place of our neighbor, Frank Steinhart, Jr., who owned the Havana Streetcar Company. The then twenty-some cats which had accrued to the household slept on the bare mattresses of twin beds in a room just off the sitting room and left behind their odors, no matter how well the room was washed each morning. During months of drought, we poured enough chlorine into the pool to murder the algae, but it also made our eyes smart and our skins dry. In the valleys between the Finca's three hills there was enough pasturage for two or three cows, but instead we were buying watery milk from the Steinharts. The old icebox in the pantry into which was fed fifty pounds of ice daily could not cool enough food for both family and servants. The rose garden on a far slope below the garage was a maze of brambles. In the 38-foot sitting room there were only five places to sit, and two ugly reading lamps. About my bedroom I offered a suggestion. "This could be a beautiful, open-air room, if we made some alterations," said I.

A squall threatened on Ernest's face. "What sort of alterations?"

"Oh, open up the windows. Make them larger and lower. Put a big window there at the end, letting on to the bamboo. Take away that useless bulky closet."

"You chip away too much brick, the house will collapse."

"Somebody can find where the main supports are."

For the time we left it at that. But we embarked on a decade's course of improvements which made the Finca Vigía comfortable and serviceable without impairing its original charm. We installed a few cows, made vegetable and flower gardens, built a filter for the swimming pool, put a deep freeze in the basement and an electric refrigerator and stove in the kitchen, built a tower—to accommodate the cats, and provide a storeroom and a quiet and airy workroom for Ernest —turned a worthless bedroom into a useful library, augmented the sitting room and dining room furniture, acquired such agreeable extras as Murano tableglasses designed by me, Burano lace and embroidered Venetian bedware. Year by year the place grew more endearing to its inhabitants, consoling, pleasing and delighting us.

On August 31, 1945, I flew to Miami and Chicago where I saw my parents and with Bill Boyden's deft assistance was processed in a ten-minute court hearing from Mrs. Monks back to Miss Welsh, thankful for no opposition, thankful for the simple mechanization. Legally—no emotions required—a free woman.

My cousins Homer and Beatrice Guck insisted upon celebrating with a trip to their beloved summertime retreat, a log cabin on a slight rise above Lake Superior in the village of Eagle Harbor, Michigan. The squirrel at my cousins' back doorstep elicited less enchantment than the birds and fruit rats outside my windows in Cuba. Still we moved through an unencumbered two or three days as in a dream, and my face scars continued to heal. Ernest wrote me prodigiously, as always when we were not together.

"There is no time, really, ever, but the present," he wrote. "We have really used it well. . . . We have had great and lovely happinesses together and that is the guarantee of what we can have. . . . Hope I don't sound like a Camp-Meeting Dr. Hemingstein and His Inspirational Prose . . . will work hard and happily to be a good husband to you all my life . . . and try to be a good and responsible citizen of the world. . . .

"If you take care of your old man and make it possible to race him instead of him having to sell the mutuel tickets and haul the vans with the other horses etc., as well as administer (badly) the hot dog concession we can win many races with him yet. . . .

"We are both big loafers but capable of working and overworking. . . . I just remember watching you work and remember me working too. . . . When we are so lazy that we STINK we can always take measures against it. . . .

"I think our one and only life is the best one I have ever known (as far as the absolute wonderfulness of happiness goes) and has the finest prospects any ever had. . . . You always say I write better letters than I talk or act, but that is because . . . my conduct always falls behind my intentions or between two stools."

One of the Finca's insufficiencies was its water supply, which Ernest proposed to improve by enlarging the gutters beneath the eaves around the house and sending rainwater down to a well near what would become the vegetable garden. He sent me daily, detailed reports on all aspects of the work in progress, and also speculated on new constructions.

On September 7 he "was up on the roof working at that rainwater catching problem [and] seeing that beautiful view thought how would it be to build a tower at one end of the house or one corner with a pleasant room you could have and a tiled and railed roof we could have chairs on and a table to look off over country from in the evenings. Both tower room and roof could be reached by an outside circular staircase. Could be lovely I think.

"Also we need another comfortable piece of furniture in the living room for when kids are here. . . . We have the Lincoln and it looks better than before accident. $567.75. Maybe I can write a helluva good short story and sell it for a large piece of dough. . . ."

On September 11 he had decided to install a new #24 zinc gutter nine inches deep and connect it to a tile pipe going directly to the well. "Maybe you can get a good portable battery radio. . . . We need it for the boat and is very good to have in room. . . . Haven't had a drink in the night yet and you've been gone now for eleven days."

On September 12, with plasterers, stonemasons, painters and Pancho to deal with and an introduction for somebody's book to write, he felt as churlish "as an old bear that used to kill cattle on the open range and now has to live off the garbage dump behind Old Faithful Inn in the Park . . . [but] am not cross against you, kitten. . . . Must stop and do the unpleasants."

On September 13 he had received a cable from Buck Lanham saying that he and his wife Pete would take an 8 a.m. plane from Miami to Havana on September 22 and was busily arranging with painters to repaint the big guest bedroom and the living room, and afterward the pantry and kitchen, all before Buck's arrival. Meanwhile he was indignant about the Allied treatment of the Germans. "Don't you think it is sort of cruel to cure Goering of his dope habit before they hang him? They'll probably hang Ribbentropp without champagne too. Do we have to cure Streicher of hating Jews before we hang him. . . . We kill 60,000 civilians with one bomb; hang sixty-year-old women for killing aviators. . . . I'm getting so I don't want any part of it. . . . War is completely and utterly barbarous, a crime against man and mankind, and it should be fought that way and people not be nice-Nelly or hypocritical about it. Who that has ever shot up civilians

217

from a plane has any right to think they are being mistreated if the civilians lynch them?"

He had bought a record of the opera *Boris Godunov,* sung partly in Russian and partly in German and on September 13 at 9 p.m. was playing it on the Capehart record changer. "All servants gone and have set up the write-typer in the living room where our friend is playing Boris Goudonov, a roughhouse thirteen foot high opera . . . with all of opera sentiment that is so facile and chickenshit and pleasant. It is so wonderful hearing this to hear the Russian (advertized) which I don't understand but which sounds logical and the other voice box maniacs singing in pure kraut which can just follow. . . . Have ditch dug for big flow-pipe. . . . Four more days will be completed and pipe laid and all sodded over. . . . They still won't send flowers from here by wire. Please accept the intention." He drew a tulip on the page.

He was concerned about my having abandoned my life of journalism—"I thought all that you had was wonderful"—and as consolation offered the reminder that it becomes more and more difficult to overwork as one grows older. "It is fine and it is fun and you can do more than anyone—and then one day you are through. Or you are through just a little bit more each day. . . . I know part of the life with me is dull for you. But it isn't all going to be. And we have really good and big and important work to do in this world and we will do it together as partners, and also let's be happy."

A big hurricane was approaching either Cuba's north coast or the Florida Keys and at 8:30 a.m., September 15, Ernest wrote he expected to know what the storm would do by two o'clock that afternoon. "We are not out of the woods until the first Norther of November. The worst danger is from the 18th of October until the 4th or 5th of November. . . . I wish you weren't having to come down before hurricane months over. . . . We are both sensitized as hell to weather from being brought up on boats and the water and living outside. But, if no hurricane, October can be a lovely month. High skies, cool on the water and all the migrating birds passing. Last night there were many flocks of ducks like smoke wisps and quick, shape changing dark clouds. I love to see their flight. And the poor warblers, making their first flight across the Gulf that light on the boat and rest and then set out for shore again. It must be a terrible flight to have to make the first time (or the last time).

"The leaves must be beautiful where you are today if the first storms haven't come yet. If you see a deer or a bear give him my love or a lovely skunk or a chipmunk or a mink or an otter, especially an otter.

"I'll lose this fall out of my life I guess unless we should get some good fall days on the water. But it is not the same as up north or out west. . . . I think you would love [out west] because it has such wonderful light and air and the people are young instead of old."

On September 17 he wrote: "We had no trouble from the hurricane at all and weather clear and a northwest breeze yesterday and clear today. . . . Sunday morning woke feeling really lousy . . . wanted a drink bad. . . . Then thought what the hell had gone all that time without taking a drink in the morning so didn't do it and wrote the damned Introduction instead. Finished it. But have to let it cool out to go over again and see what is wrong. . . ." He sent me a copy of it.*

On September 18 he was having a noisy, unpleasant day "with the hammerings, diggings, painting, cleaning and carpentering. . . . This letter whines like an air raid siren. Play it on your pianola and scare the inhabitants. . . . I was just saying I felt a little low today, chucking it off to you to get rid of it."

Later that morning he wrote again to report he had finished redoing the introduction. "Cut off last three pages and wrote seven new ones. Think have it good now. Anyway feel good. . . . This non-drinking thing is a bastard to have to do by yourself but it pays off terrifically in the writing thing."

On September 19 the tinsmiths were soldering, the pipelayers were finishing their work, the painter was repainting the Venetian-pink ceiling of the living room, Pancho was finishing the window screens and

* The introduction was for an anthology, *A Treasury for the Free World*, edited by Ben Raeburn (New York: Arco Publishing Co., 1946).

219

Ernest was worrying that Buck and Pete would not like the Finca. The next day he was feeling "absolutely wonderful and gay and full of love of life and you and everything." He had had two lovely dreams, and wrote three single-spaced pages about the repair work in progress, his plans for further improvements, the importance of planting the vegetable garden in November, the fish we would catch in the late fall, the prospects of duck shooting at Winston Guest's place, Gardiners Island, in November.

"The place has turned the corner really from the deadly problem and drudge stage into the fun stage. . . . If we can get North in November . . . I'll get some Perrier Jouet and we can have some in bed. We can really walk there and will be wonderful to be cold again.

"Kittner won't it be nice to have ham and eggs for breakfast too and in our own bed in N.Y. with no hangovers and a lovely crisp day ahead of us? Imagine seeing that great Brueghel of the harvest together and Greco's Toledo at the Metropolitan. Such lovely things to do in New York. And no war . . . Twenty-one days since saw . . . Long time . . . We are going to be so good and kind and jolly and have fun. Maybe I'll get a letter tonight."

In another three-page, single-spaced letter on September 21 he aided my education. "Ducks are flocks. Covies are the short winged, fast beating wing birds; quail, partridges, or grouse. . . . Nobody except book sportsmen use all those fancy terms like a gaggle of geese. You just say a flock of geese. Or even a god-damn big sonofabitching flock of more damn geese than you ever saw in your life. . . . Only rule is covies are quail and partridges. Big grouse are flocks or bunches. Ducks are flocks and so are geese and their movement is a flight. . . . An old bull can be a male buffalo, elk or elephant. But an old buck is a deer or any sort of antelope except a kudu, an eland or any of the spiral horned antelope. They are bulls. . . .

"Want to get good small house for the cotsies now [Oh, joy!] with easily cleaned arrangements and nice shelves to sleep on and places to have and raise their kittens. . . . It ought to be almost a part of house so cotsies do not feel sent to Siberia or abandoned and it should be close enough so that from house you can see whether it is well cared for and cotsies well and happy. . . . Will make a big scratching pole covered with carpet for them to use their claws on and have a catnip bin and ping-pong balls for kittneys to play with. Can even put in a Shakespeare First Folio for Friendless to spray on. It is unfair to keep cotsies, not feed them properly, and interpret their natural impulses and needs as sins."

On September 25 Ernest was nostalgic, missing his old friends. "Like Charley Sweeny, Evan Shipman, Koltsof, Werner Heilbrun, Jan Flanner, Dawn Powell, Max Perkins, John Bishop . . . But they are scattered all over the world, or in Siberia or dead and there isn't any use to miss them. . . . I am as lonesome without you as I've ever been in my life." The signature was a big line drawing of a bear.

"Had a lovely letter from your Dad," Ernest wrote, "wishing good luck with you. He sounds like awfully fine man and always did ever since you told me about him in Paris."

He was trying to be a good host but was uncertain about the balances between his being available and entertaining his guests and leaving them to themselves. "Leaving people alone (regarded as highest form of politeness with guests in circles I used [to] frequent) may be regarded as thoughtless or ungracious. Hope am doing it right."

On September 27 Ernest was unhappy because he had received no reaction from me about the introduction, of which he had sent me a copy. "Wish you could have let me know or just mentioned. . . . Worked on it sort of hard and quit drinking but was all alone with nobody to discuss with—and we are supposed to be sort of partners. . . . If it was rotten, appreciate hearing that just as much. . . ."

On Friday, September 28, Ernest could tell me that both he and Buck, who had never before shot a shotgun, had done well at a live pigeon shoot at the Club de Cazadores and "You wrote such a lovely letter and am so happy with all the house plans and so happy you liked the piece [introduction]. It wasn't I wanted praise. Was just to know what my partner thought.

"Wish had enough money so could write and never have to sell it," he continued. "Know that is what is cramping now; thinking must write story that will also bring dough. So will write fine and unsaleable story. Then afterwards we will write one that can sell. Have the think machine going fairly O.K. Now have to get the narrative and invention machine going. Been grinding the valves and putting new rings in it lately. . . . I wake up always happy you not married even in name to anybody else."

On September 29 he wrote: "Another lovely letter from you this morning. . . . Now you make me such a big praise [about the introduction] it makes me spooked. . . . Now you say is good am happy and don't need to show to anybody. I can tell myself about whether a description, or an action, or a conversation is good on acct. have a built in radar on that, but when it is a question of an idea or an opinion . . . always distrust what I think unless can get it all the way down to the bone. And then how do you know whether it is down to the bone when you are by yourself? Maybe you've just got sheepherders madness. . . ."

With flourishes and frozen daiquiris Ernest welcomed me back to what I was beginning to consider "home." Fishing with Paxtchi and Gregorio the next day, "a wonderful, happy, sound day," we also conducted a top-level conference on programs and projects. Ernest had an idea for a short story about A Man and His Letters which would be entertaining to amusing to hilarious, if he got it in type as he outlined and then embroidered it while we cruised the Gulf Stream. Something must have turned up to prevent or obstruct the story's being written, but that was standard operational procedure with us. We were not disciples of the wire or tape recorder and we had already decided that I would not be a Simone de Pouvoir (sic) maker-of-notes on Ernest's observations. Our principle was that the observations and gaiety of a day were sufficient unto it, and recording be damned. The local fund of wisdom and wit was rich enough to provide for tomorrow's or next year's needs.

From our project conference a few assignments emerged for me. I would type all but the final definitive versions of his work, and attend to whatever correspondence he chose not to handle. While the servants would do the marketing for their own table, I checking their receipts, I would take on the commissary job for us, going with Juan to the big markets in Havana to find goodies. I would supervise the gardeners and their plantings and waterings and prunings and harvestings. Most important, I would keep Ernest's privacy "absolutely intact" for whatever hours he might work each day "and let nobody get at him."

To my room at the Finca I brought back a few family photos, my parents in twin gold frames, and Homer and Beatrice Guck, and set them up on a corner of Martha's enormous desk. Inexplicably to me, they irritated Ernest who muttered something about my trying to "clip" him.

"Clip you? With four photographs?" I stared. "In that room which has nothing at all that belongs to me?"

In his study Ernest had a handsome framed photograph of Martha which I had noted with interest and some curiosity. He explained how much the children loved her and how hard she had worked to please them and make them happy there. I felt like an interloper. I left my photographs in their place and wrote him a note. "You speak of gaining confidence to write. What I need is confidence to live here. I put the pictures in what I thought an unobtrusive corner. . . . In all this place you are master. You are comfortable. It was made with your approval, or at your instigation. . . . I only wanted some small thing that could look like it was mine. . . . About your picture of Martha . . . I cannot help wondering whether or not you kept pictures of Pauline around for the sake of the children, when Mardy was here." Not long after that, Ernest, with an assist from me, decided that Martha would probably not approve of her furniture being used by a successor and authorized me to design and have made

223

by Pancho my own smaller and, I thought, much more beautiful and appropriate desk, chests, window seat, bookshelves, bedside shelves, a table made from a tole tray and an enormous round pouf, crisply slipcovered like the long window seat, and a low chair, an admirable place for people and cat lounging. Ernest sent Martha's furniture to storage in a Havana warehouse, notified her of its address, and paid storage rental on it for fifteen years.

One afternoon Ernest invited me to lunch at the Floridita behind the bank of palm trees which separated the bar from the restaurant with Leopoldina, the long-time occasional girlfriend of many of the bar's habitués, himself among them. Leopoldina claimed that she was a descendant of Maximilian, the Emperor of Mexico eighty years before, and she had the lovely green-tinted skin of Latins and the large lugubrious dark eyes of the offspring of deposed or murdered potentates. I found her conversation less alluring than her looks.

Having seated us, Ernest drifted back to the bar and Leopoldina said, "You can't appreciate what a wonderful man he is. *Simpático, y generoso.*"

"No, but I'll try."

"Everybody loves him. *Todo el mundo.*"

"That's a lot of people."

"Everybody hopes you will be good and sweet to him. Everybody."

"That's nice of them." I was learning that Spanish-speaking people love to repeat words for emphasis. I didn't know the word for "solicitous."

"Do you enjoy living in Havana?"

"No. It's an evil city. *Depravada.*"

"What a shame. I haven't yet seen that."

"It's evil, and it's too hot," Leopoldina declared.

"But not as hot as Paris."

"No. Not as hot as Paris," she agreed. Then she glowered at me, suspicion in her lovely eyes, and told me that her liver was bothering her.

With the summer's crop of kittens flourishing, we held baptismal ceremonies. Thrusty, Martha's favorite cat, as a first-time mother had produced two spirited sons, black with white markings like their grandfather,

Boise. Thrusty wasn't much of a cat or a mother, I felt, being too egocentric and careless in her manners, despite the teachings of Princesa, her noble and elegant mother. But the children showed promise and Ernest suggested we name them after poets. We agreed that cats like to have *s*'s in their names and decided that one of the boys should be Stephen Spender, which we switched to Spendthrift and Ernest promptly shortened to Spendy, who soon became my shadow and loving companion. Shakespeare, we felt, would be too great a burden for any Cuban cat to carry as a name. So we named Spendy's brother Barbershop, abbreviated to Shopsky, and beneath garlands of red bougainvillaea on the sunny front terrace we anointed them with catnip I'd brought from Miami and taught them their names.

In spite of his devotion to Ernest, Boise had developed a crush on me and before I had journeyed north had turned so possessive that he disapproved of Ernest's attentions to my person, and expressed his feelings with his claws on Ernest's most vulnerable parts. When I returned to the Finca, Boise's jealousy flared again so forcefully that after applying unguents we decided that we must attempt a cure. We were both distressed that Boise should be unhappy. "Let's just explain things to him," Ernest said, and that evening in the sitting room with Boise curled in his lap and I squatting beside his chair, touching Boise's head, he explained.

"I understand why you love her, Boy," he said, "and why you'd like her all for yourself. She loves you too. But wommies can't live on fruit rats. They can't truly." (For months Boise had been bringing half-dead rats to my bedroom windows in the night, his most precious tribute.) "She would like it so much if we could all be friends, and you not jealous and unhappy. You see, Boy, I can give her the things she needs to eat, things she likes better than fruit rats."

"It's darling of you to bring them, Boise," I said. "Please don't think I'm unappreciative. It's just unfortunate that I like other things more. You mustn't be offended, Boy." We went on in that vein, trying to dissolve the enmity.

225

Boise was mollified. He made no further attacks on Ernest, resumed his role as benign head of his family and a loving third of our triangle.

I noted at about that time that "Papa has been kind, thoughtful and loving and has said several times that he was happier than ever before in his life. . . . He has certainly been better for me than any man I ever knew. He refuses to fire Justo and is bad tempered about Julia [maid] and Juan. But he has been making life pleasant for me, taking me on a picnic to Rincón, taking me for an evening walk through the village, taking me to two movies and making me a present of two seats to the fortnightly Monday night concerts and taking me to two of them. . . . He tries to stay awake after dinner and I try to learn to go to bed early. . . .

"Last night with Bumby and Dick and Marjorie Cooper we went to hear Yehudi Menuhin, wonderful, rich, brilliant. Then to the International Club which turned out to be a little neighborhood pub and I had a great time singing with the orchestra. But as we left Papa intoned that we'd ruined his work. . . ."

We had a few cool words about it that evening and the next morning after I had rung for breakfast, Ernest padded into my room with a hand-delivered letter.

"Dearest Kitten. Here is the gen on night clubs," he had written in pencil in his round, sturdy hand, "I like them very much. I always have fun at them, but I never go to them when I am writing a book because cannot stay up late and drink and write well afterwards. . . . I have a lot of hell writing but it is my own personal hell and I do not usually try and inflict it on my partner. Also have much heaven, good rewards and try to share them. . . . What I mean is, I guess, that there is nothing *positive* that can make anyone write, surely, each day. But over an extended length of time a good writer will write ok if he takes care of his instrument . . ." and on for seven pages.

I typed a reply. "Gradually I've been learning how to stay home at night and enjoy it. I don't want you to write hangover prose. I want you to write like Yehudi plays."

Spindly, exhausted Christmas trees began to appear for sale in front of Havana shops, having been shipped all the way from the state of Washington. I took one home early to plant in a tub and ply with water and vitamins to encourage its revival, if not survival. The tree responded cheerfully, we installed it in a corner of the living room, and I planned exuberant festivities. It would be my first Christmas in six years free of anxieties for friends and of underlying sorrow over man's brutality to his kind. *Feliz* was the word in Spanish. Happy. We would have a *feliz* December 25.

We invited the Kohlys, also Don Andrés, Ernest's "black priest," a sweet, devout and innocent Basque who was also devoted to wine and food and came regularly to lunch from his parish some thirty miles eastward. Bumby, still on terminal leave from the army, was with us, emitting sparkles, and Roberto Herrera, the brother of Ernest's doctor, and now Ernest's sometime odd-job helper. Mousie and Gigi arrived from Key West the next day.

On New Year's Eve the boys and I walked the approximate block to the front gate and the block of slipshod wooden houses in the villages to its main street which was also the Carretera Central, the principal road running seven hundred miles between Cuba's west and east coasts. The streets were empty. Radios which screeched all day from most houses were silent or muted. The biggest, most popular *bodega*—beer, rum, canned food, sandwiches, coffee—showed only its clamped-down steel shutters. Light shone from a small *bodega* at the end of the village, and we went there. A single customer was sipping beer and chatting to the *patrón* who said, "All the lively ones have gone to Havana." We ordered bottles of the good Hatuey Cuban beer, drank them soberly, and walked home through the night's stillness. I imagined London and shining floors and enticing dance music and stylish conversation and pretty dresses again after so many years of austerity.

We bustled into the new year with a dozen projects demanding attention. Stonemasons, the carpenter, and painters were transferring my room from indoors to outdoors, sunshine and the east breeze, insect and bird

227

songs and the smells of greenery and flowers flooding into it through its big new windows. House guests were trickling in and out, Ernest was working steadily on a new novel set in the south of France, we had to set a date for the formalities of a marriage ceremony, not that that was urgent. A session of drought began and our water supply system balked and broke down. When Charlie Ritz arrived from Paris, his ride from the airport to the Finca was hot and dusty. "What mark of hospitality may we give you first?" I asked, hugging him on the front steps.

"A bath," said Charlie. All we could produce was one pail of water.

With the appearance of Nancy de Marigny we had new diversions. She was a graceful, dark girl whose father had been mysteriously murdered, and she was on her way to her family home in the Caribbean. She was flirty in a wistful, waiflike way and after dinner showed us ballet steps she had been learning, the Capehart producing accompaniment. We, and especially Bumby, were enchanted, and Ernest and I moved into his room so that she could have my room for the night. A day or so later Bumby, mesmerized by our young guest, announced he was going with her to Miami and on to her Caribbean island. He would return soon, he said. Ernest was enraged, and later, as he frequently did, poured his ire onto his typewriter. Bumby need never return to the Finca, he wrote with epithets, and further paragraphs of vehemence. He had not sealed the envelope when I heard him asking for Juan to take the letter to Havana for expeditious posting. I intercepted him, asked to read his letter, and we sat together on the front steps while I read it and then maneuvered myself into a task of mollifying: a word of sympathy, two words of regret, a quip which made him smile, a caution about man's pride, especially Bumby's. The typing had already dispersed some of Ernest's anger. When I finished my comments Ernest took the letter back to his room and rewrote it. The revised version left no doubt of father's disapproval and displeasure with son, but it did not break off diplomatic relations. It was the first of many such letters which by happenstance I was able to get amended.

Slim Hawks, the wife of the filmmaker Howard Hawks, came to stay in the Little House and went with us and our Cuban friend, Elicio Argüelles, on a three- or four-day cruise, fishing west to Paraíso, fishing the reefs there, and on the way back Slim in a flurry of giggles and protests brought a marlin to gaff. The Gulf Stream was on its best cobalt-blue mild-tempered behavior, Slim was decorative and gay, Elicio, one of Cuba's most skilled fishermen, contributed his oblique wit and impeccable manners. Slim was the girl, I remembered, whom Martha Gellhorn had recommended to Ernest in Paris more than a year before as her proper successor, and I did not care. Slim was one of his admired and admiring girlfriends who refrained from telling me how to care for him.

Ernest's men friends also appeared and turned the house into what seemed to me a raucous, rowdy, affectionate boys' dormitory. Tommy Shevlin, skinny and urbane, with whom Ernest had been fishing friends since long before in Bimini and who, later, had been in the navy section of the U.S. embassy in Havana. Winston Guest, immense and sweet and winning in his manner, whom Ernest had first met in East Africa in 1933 or '34, and who had hunted German submarines aboard *Pilar* a few years before. Tommy had been in the Pacific performances and Winston had been in China. They had both been liberated from their respective services and came down to Cuba to celebrate. They were so endearing that I, who was still balking at the prospect of a legal wedding, softened a bit, concluding that a man who had such devoted friends must be worth marrying.

They were a boys' club and they did not need me, and my Finca wardrobe of shirts and shorts and printed cotton frocks offered nothing sufficiently sober for the ceremonies of wedlock. I went up to Miami to sponge on Bill Lyons who ran the Miami office of Pan-Am, and red-headed Maruja, his wife, find a suitable dress and, free of pressures from Ernest, make a final decision on the move into marriage. When I mentioned this purpose, my hosts, whose judgments I admired, were appalled.

"You can't let Papa down now," Bill objected, lounging in his sitting room.

Maruja, fingering her copper-strand hair, giggled. "Wouldn't that be a surprise? I'll bet nobody has ever turned him down. Not on marriage," Maruja mused. "All you have to decide is whether or not you love him enough. Enough to stick with him. Even when he's beastly. . . . He's apt to be beastly sometimes. Everybody is." The daughter of Spruille Braden, who had been the U.S. ambassador in Havana, Maruja had known Ernest longer than I had.

For twenty months my first waking thoughts had flown to him, as a homing pigeon darts out of the opened door of a cage.

Ernest's personal radar must have picked up traces of my doubts. He wired flowers and sent loving letters and cables.

"Thank you for your lovely not to be opened until bedtime note . . . Juan brought your photos and they are absolutely *beautiful* . . . good enough for a Life piece." (I had been photographing wind at the Finca and Norther storms pounding over the Malecón, the drive along the ocean front, in Havana.) "I miss you, just so you know, to be just sick all the way through me. But can handle this job of lonely. . . . Kittner we don't have to wait until Mr. Bumby gets back (two weeks from yest) to get married. . . ."

No merger of commercial companies could be executed with more serious attention paid to property rights than the Cuban marriage contract which was straight out of the Napoleonic Code. So complicated were the depositions required that they took two long sessions in a somber lawyer's office, full of old-fashioned cane-backed Cuban furniture, voices funereal, I rocking gently, understanding almost nothing. Far from such sticky hypocrisies as "with all my worldly goods I thee endow," the agreement specified that any gift made by one party to the other must be returned if the merger ruptured. In Havana I had bought myself a little gold and diamond antique *novia* (fiancée) ring, a present from Ernest.

"Even my engagement ring?" I asked on hearing the translation of the property paragraph.

230

"Of course," he grinned.

"I can't take you for anything?"

"Just for everything I'll ever have, my Kitten." Perhaps that was too felicitous for rough jolly fun, for as we left the car for lunch at the Floridita, with Winston and two younger boys, who had come to Cuba on their spring vacation from Canterbury, he said, "Let's take the cup of hemlock now."

"You bastard. The condemned man will drink a hearty lunch."

"The bride wore a dark scowl."

"I feel more like a middle-aged sparring partner than a bride."

Winston was upset by the acrimony and gently maneuvered us into more amicable territory. Later with Dick and Marjorie Cooper he arranged to celebrate the final signing of the treaty on March 14 with champagne and fresh caviar at the Coopers' airy flat in Vedado. With some two dozen friends assembled for the toasts and countertoasts, we all enjoyed an increasingly spirited few hours, but on the way home Ernest and I got entangled in some misunderstanding of phrase, a sudden surfacing of underground tensions into a small, furious earthquake of incrimination and abuse from which Ernest retired with apparent ease into smooth sleep. I dug some luggage out of closets and started packing clothes, but the decisions—what I would need in New York, what I would leave behind —were too difficult to complete that night. I decided to finish in the morning and sloped softly into bed.

When he awoke the next morning, refreshed and cheerful as always, Ernest saw the half-packed bags and said, "Let's never get married again, Kitten."

"Certainly not to each other."

"Certainly not to anybody else." Skirmish terminated, truce, peace, if not permanent, declared.

A week later I wrote my family, "The house is full of children and plans and things happening, with me having to help them happen properly." If my parents were hurt I had not invited them down from Chicago for the formalities, they generously refrained from indicating so to me. Ernest was more thoughtful of them. He wrote a two-page, single-spaced letter explaining the "interminable judicial delay . . . survival of the Spanish regime. However we are well and soundly married with no debts, the March income tax installment paid and others provided for and us both healthy and happy. The boys love Mary very much and she is so good, thoughtful, friendly and wise with them. . . . Patrick and Gregory, the middle and youngest boy, were both here and delighted. . . .

"I know I have been very remiss about writing and can only plead that I write each day until I am too tired to write any more. It makes a man a miserable correspondent."

One evening before the advent of *cuaresma* (Lent) Ernest took me to dine at an upstairs French restaurant overlooking the Prado, the lovely wide avenue with spreading Spanish laurel trees lining a pedestrian walk down its center, which ran from the Capitol to the Malecón. As had been their custom for a century, neighborhood groups of *habañeros* and guilds of artisans—bakers, tailors, cigar rollers, saddlers—masked and brilliantly costumed, danced toward the Capitolio, pipes piping, flutes fluting, voices chanting, whirring African and Latin American rhythms beneath tall colored lanterns whirling. The *comparsas*. It was the nightlong or two- or three-night-long celebration with which the Cubans greeted Lent, and forty days of self-restraint in one manner or another.

For us it was an enchanting evening, especially for me since I had never seen such a public show of combined formality and spontaneity. The next day we settled into diligent self-discipline, Ernest at his typewriter, I into housekeeping and gardening, Spanish irregular verbs and a new project, learning navigation. Ernest had his international pilot's license as master of *Pilar,* and his nose, with which, he maintained, he could navigate all the Cuban coast and mangrove islands he knew; *Pilar* had her charts and sextant. If we organized voyages into farther distant waters, as we planned, it would be useful if I could pinpoint us on a chart. With our friend Carl Bottume, a gay companion who was just out of the U.S. Navy, as coach, I studied the necessary vertical geometry, drift, modifications, and practiced with the sextant which was stiff from disuse and the corrosion of seadamp. A stimulating enterprise while it lasted, which was until Carl had to leave sometime in May for New York and a job with the National Broadcasting Company. Gregorio wrapped the sextant in one of his old shirts and put it away in *Pilar*'s "Miscellaneous" locker, assuring me he could get it out and functioning in a minute. I never saw it again.

The searing spring sunshine was scorching the above-ground plants in our vegetable garden and I made notes to put in more yucca, malanga, sweet potatoes, beets and other underground goodies, and a bit less lettuce, chard, spinach, broccoli and tomatoes. A sunburned tomato was a sad tomato.

One afternoon Justo banged through the pantry door as Ernest and I were finishing lunch alone, banged through the door to my bedroom and came out waving the pistol Ernest kept beside the bed. From the pantry rushed Ramón, the Chinese cook, slicing the air with a two-foot-long knife, prancing and yelling and slashing with the knife, his old black eyes shifting wildly. Justo had cocked the pistol and pointed it at Ernest as he said, "Give it to me." I eluded the point of Ramón's knife and said, "Calm yourself, calm yourself" in as quiet a voice as I could manage. Ernest disarmed Justo with no shot fired, and with comic reluctance Ramón relinquished the knife to me. Ernest sent them both back to the kitchen to wait quietly for the inquiry. While we finished our wine we exchanged views.

"I love Cuba. Always the unexpected."

"That son-of-a-bitch," Ernest said.

"Entertainment in the home."

"I'll have to find out about this."

It turned out that Justo had cooked for himself and eaten that morning all of the twelve lamb chops Ramón had bought in the market for our next day's lunch. If he bought more chops Ramón would have been blamed for extravagance. After learning something of Justo's recent medical history, with his undertreated case of gonorrhea, Ernest sacked him that day. Poor old Ramón stayed quiet with repentance for days.

René Villarreal, the Negro boy whose family lived

233

in a small wooden house just outside our gate and who had been helping tend the cats and dogs for a year or more, looked at me with questions in his eyes when we mentioned Justo's dismissal. René was a quiet, intelligent, well-mannered young man of seventeen. Ernest was teaching him boxing, and he and I were tacit friends. He was gentle and kind with the animals.

"Be patient," I said. "I'll ask Papa to give you a chance. I'll teach you about the dishes and how to serve, and about Papa's clothes." Ernest agreed to the trial run and René learned so fast and worked with such devotion and goodwill toward all the Finca's people and projects that he became my *hijo Cubano* (Cuban son) and remained the farm's major-domo all the years we were there and long after, when the Finca became the Museo Hemingway in Fidel Castro's Cuba.

I had not yet forgotten London and one evening made a list of the friends there I missed and our mutual interests. Mark Abrams for talk of economics. He was on the staff of the London School of Economics. Michael Foot and James Fergusson for politics, with Harold Laski for everything. Alice Astor Harding for ballet. Somebody else for concerts and theater. But fishing and swimming and gardening and the wonderfully self-indulgent pursuit of the printed page only for pleasure instead of information were weakening my nostalgias. Moreover the little Winchester .22 pump rifle as well as Martha's shotgun were becoming more amusing toys the more I used them. Even though I hadn't learned much about rhythm, timing and swinging, shooting trap with Peggy Steinhart I was beginning to feel comfortable with the Winchester Model-21, 20-gauge, and on a bright windy afternoon I went along with Ernest to the Club de Cazadores, pleasantly old-fashioned under its towering laurel trees. He had got a shipment of *correos,* strong, fast-flying pigeons, down from the north and had organized a private shoot with some friends.

Ernest gallantly chose me for his team, and I discovered that day that pigeon shooting as a participating game was vastly more entertaining than it was as a spectacle. We had twenty pigeons apiece to shoot and each time I walked out the cement path to call *"listo"* and then *"pajarero"* my breath faded away. Most of the time after I had shot my two barrels, my hope faded away too. My total score was nine birds knocked down inside the fence. But Ernest had a near perfect score.

Nobody wanted to stop the competition. Iced champagne as well as the shooting had stirred our spirits. Ernest chose a big oyster and hurled it over the lawn. Dick Cooper hit it squarely. Peps Merito splintered an empty crab claw. Wolfie Guest hit a flung shotgun shell. I missed an empty paper cup. Only dusk moving in on us stopped the exercise.

The little .22 rifle was a simpler toy for me. It did not hurt my shoulder and all I had to do with it was hold my breath and squeeze the trigger. Novice though I was, since my father had never taught me the use of any weapon, I found it comparatively simple to hit targets set up on the steps of the *vacaría*. "Mary is getting to be . . . the terror of the dead light-bulb, the empty vitamin bottle, the used cocktail onion jar," Ernest wrote Buck Lanham.

For more than a year Ernest and I had been talking about a baby. "I'd like so much to have a daughter. With your legs," I said. We would be alone in the sitting room, taking a martini before lunch. "And your chest," said Ernest.

"Your eyes."

"No. Your eyes and hair. A light among the darks. But we ought to remember Mr. Shaw's reply to Isadora Duncan."

"Yes. But she must have your brain."

"And my always sunny temper," said Ernest.

"God save us from that. If she were bright, and also always sweet, she'd be a bore."

"Young babies are a bore. You have to wait until they're two."

"Two years old? I've never known any babies, really."

"Two, maybe three."

"My friends who were having babies in '39 or '40 took them out of London. I never saw them."

"You didn't miss much."

"But this child. Couldn't I fix a nursery in the Little

235

House? Put the kids somewhere else when they're here. That would be as far as possible from you."

"Mmmmmm. We could get a first-class nurse."

"And, darling. Don't fuss. Don't fuss right away anyhow. I'd like to name her Bridget. Short and non-fancy."

"Bridget Hemingway. B.H. They'll call her Bridie."

"I won't let them."

"You have some secret formula for that?" But Ernest decided he liked the name, and thereafter Bridget became part of our plans for the future. In July the plans became a program, an adjunct to a pro-jected journey in the Lincoln from Miami to Idaho. After mid-July when the gynecologist said "Certain" I ignored Cucu Kohly's advice to curtail my swimming —I felt so good and was so sure I needed that exer-cise—and prodded Josépha, my village dressmaker, to hurry up with the clothes I wanted to take to the beckoning new country, Out West.

From Miami we drove north to Palm Beach then angled west, watching young quail and their mother dusting themselves on a country dirt road, and along the old storm-battered Gulf Coast road of Louisiana to New Orleans. Staying at a hotel of frayed glories in Royal Street, we took a day's break there, wan-dered the French Quarter, lunched lavishly at Gala-toire's, loitered in bookshops and antique shops. In one of them I found a long-handled pair of English serving spoons, asked that one of them be cut to fork form and sent on to us. In another, Ernest noticed a square-cut yellow Brazilian diamond ring, bought it and slipped it on my finger. "With this ring I pledge my troth," said he. Hugs, kisses, and from behind the counter giggles.

From Baton Rouge we rolled westward on the long bridge across the Mississippi, then traveled up through forested hills in Arkansas to the flats of Missouri where we turned west. On an afternoon of furious south wind and a beating sun we headed due west through yellow waving grain for Kansas City, pulled off the road to put the Lincoln's top up against the sun, sipped water, sucked ice, and still my head felt dizzy. Maybe it was my baby protesting the heat, I thought happily. When we reached a gas station south of the city I hopped out into the shade murmuring, "How heavenly cool this is." The station man pointed to a thermometer hanging in the shade of the roof of the gas pumps, and I read it twice. It was registering 120°F.

On northwest through Nebraska we went and an evening or two later hunted all over Casper, Wyoming, for a place to stay since Ernest disliked small-town hotels, not only for their war-worn dilapidation but for the bother of hauling luggage up stairways and of garaging the car. In a gully near the railway station we finally found the ramshackle, linoleum-floored Mission Motor Court, no worse than the other night perches we had occupied, but worthy of inclusion in a book I was thinking of writing, to be titled *Slumming Across God's Country*. Ogallala, Nebraska, had provided for me the definitive signal that we had arrived Out West. There in a hotel coffee shop a waitress leaned on our table and asked, "What'll you have, dearie?" We had left behind us the world of waiters in jackets and black ties.

6

Out West

YEARS BEFORE IN England someone had told me about the glorious sport of pig-sticking in India in which horse riders with beribboned lances race through forests stabbing to death the native wild hogs. That night, August 18, in Casper I dreamed I had joined such a boisterous hunt and then one rider lanced and gored me and I lay writhing and screaming on the ground. My cries woke both Ernest and me and we knew I had been gored, but internally. Ernest went to call for a doctor and ambulance and came back to report that the only competent surgeon in town was on a fishing trip three or four hours away. But, after what seemed five or ten years to me, an ambulance arrived, someone gave me a shot of a pain softener and big hands lifted me gently onto a stretcher and into the ambulance. In my mental haze it seemed to me that the size of the pain was monstrously disproportionate to the size of me. But it did not occur to me that the happenings inside of me could be fatal, which is perhaps why my heart continued beating after my veins had collapsed and there was nothing but a trickle of blood for it to pump. Eight or ten hours after I had wakened screaming I heard Ernest's voice beside me on the operating table and saw his rubber-gloved hands milking plasma down into my left arm.

A week later he reported in a handwritten letter to Buck Lanham: "Tubular pregnancy and tube had burst. Very heavy internal hemmorhage. . . . While Dr. administrating spinal anesthetic (20:30 Monday night) Mary's veins collapsed, there was no pulse and he could not get a needle in to give plasma. Dr. told me was hopeless; impossible to operate, she couldn't stand shock, to tell her good-bye (useless manoeuver since she unconscious). I got assistant to cut for a vein and got plasma going. . . . I took over the plasma administration, cleared line, milking the tube down and raising and tilting until we got it flowing, and by the latter end of the first pint she was coming back enough so that insisted they operate.

"She took four bottles of plasma during operation, two blood transfusions after, been under oxygen tent ever since and now today is feeling fine, blood count okay, pulse and temperature normal. . . .

"But, Buck, it was closest one I've ever seen. Dr. had given her up and taken off his gloves. . . . Certainly shows never pays to quit. . . . Lucky it was in Casper instead of up in the hills."

When I woke up the next morning and looked out the little window of my oxygen tent, Ernest was sitting near the bed reading. I thanked the fates that he had been with me in my time of trouble. He alone had saved my life. If I didn't know it that first moment of consciousness, I soon learned it from the pretty nurse who had been the anesthetist and from the doctors.

Bumby, Patrick and Gigi waited for us in Idaho, as we had arranged to meet them there. Ernest had planned a couple of weeks of fishing and shooting for them around Sun Valley before they headed back east to school. Now they drove over to scout the local streams and hills and prairies with their father while I luxuriated in my little tent, as drowsy and contented as a lizard in the sun. Two or three of the nurses attending me had become such devoted disciples of Papa that they suggested, each in her respective inspiration, that they accompany us to Sun Valley. "To look after Miss Mary," each said. They would take a couple of weeks of sabbatical leave, they suggested privately, their eyes raining devotion on Ernest. That would be dandy with me, I said, admiring their performances. They would have looked after me well, I felt sure, while trying to look after themselves, but when the Lincoln pulled away from Memorial Hospital of Natrona County, Wyoming, three weeks after my blowup, only I accompanied the chauffeur. (The boys had gone back to Idaho.) In the day's drive to Cody, we passed miles and miles of cattle ranches, the ranch houses small and courageous in the distance, and miles and miles of empty sagebrush, and I was grateful again that my accident happened in Casper instead of "up in the hills."

Ernest had written an old friend, Lloyd "Pappy" Arnold, chief photographer of the Union Pacific at Sun Valley, asking that he find us a place to live in Ketchum, the once populous and prosperous mining town a mile from Sun Valley. Pappy had found a congregation of low-roofed rooms in the log cabin which extended from the side of the office of the MacDonald Cabins which overlooked the north/south road just south of Ketchum. We had a kitchen with a breakfast table, a sitting room with a dining table, two or three small bedrooms with double-deck beds, which the boys used, another small bedroom which was just big enough for me. The sitting room sofa opened into a bed for Ernest.

It was turning dusk when we arrived at the cabins,

my sitting muscles tired. We had driven from Cody through Yellowstone Park, pausing here and there to look at the lingering vacationers, Old Faithful and some colored bubbling pools, and had stayed that night at a ramshackle deep-freeze motel in West Yellowstone. The day's drive took us from there to Blackfoot and westward on a narrow road to Arco and Carey and up through Picabo and Hailey to Ketchum. From the folded golden hills of Carey on up to the rugged pine and sagebrush mountains of the Wood River valley, the country captured me as simply as a trout takes a May fly.

At our cabin door, on Friday, September 13, Ernest unloaded primary necessities from the Lincoln and then drove us across an ancient board bridge to a red-painted frame house where Pappy and his stub-nosed, cricket-cheery wife Tillie and his parents were waiting to share with us a marvelous dinner of roasted doves. They deposited me in a padded rocking chair within range of the old iron cookstove's warmth and bestowed on me such a generous blanket of kindly acceptance that I fell asleep in my chair as soon as dinner was finished. Ernest brought coffee to my bed the next morning and continued to do so for a week or two and I lay peacefully, rereading *War and Peace* while the household noises gathered momentum. Then my accumulating strength dictated that I help to get the days started and one morning assist with a breakfast of trout caught by Ernest's beloved friend, Taylor Williams, the "colonel" from Kentucky and Sun Valley's chief hunting guide. Ernest sautéed the trout in butter with squirts of lemon juice, and they were wonderfully sweet and hazel-nut-tasting. The kitchen afterward was a disaster area.

Ernest and the boys, and later Ernest and Taylor Williams and Pappy Arnold, and later Ernest and Pappy and Slim Hawks, who came up from Los Angeles, and I went regularly to hunt ducks and pheasants, mountain quail, Hungarian partridge and chukars, partridges which had been brought from the Himalayas and seeded in various mountain areas of the U.S. and had sustained themselves in the Idaho uplands. We hung our loot in a beautiful, weather-worn barn just behind the cabin to cool out and tenderize, and presently added a mature buck deer shot by Patrick who was taking a leave of absence from school. With our wild provisions hanging from its dim rafters, the old brown barn looked like the cave of a greedy medieval huntsman. But, being on slim rations of money, we wasted not a wing nor a liver. I learned fast how to broil, roast and stew wild creatures.

Ketchum was still a sentimentalist's dream of the Old West. Aged wooden boardwalks provided footpaths along the two blocks of Main Street which was U.S. Highway 93 heading toward Alaska. Most of the one-story brick or frame buildings held up innocently pretentious peaked false fronts another story high. The drafty red brick post office with its little frame windows was about Civil War vintage. There was no bank but all the bars cashed personal checks. Canned milk and pinto beans and homegrown cabbage were popular items in the assortment of the only grocery store, whose front window displayed not merchandise but a long row of slot machines consuming nickels, dimes and quarters.

The Alpine Restaurant, where we devoured "sizzling steaks," inch-thick sirloins served on fired metal platters, with potatoes and cole slaw "on the side" for $1.25, was the town's refuge for stomach hunger, and its adjoining bar and casino, where silver dollars clanked day and night at the poker and roulette tables, appeased other appetites. Ernest admired the Alpine especially for its rule that drinks were on the house from the morning opening, about six o'clock, until 7 or maybe 8 a.m., thus enabling the town's impecunious drunks to "get a hold on" themselves for the day. But he was also a faithful patron of the Tram, a long dank-smelling bar on one side of the Alpine, and its twin on the Alpine's other flank, the Sawtooth. Across the street was the Casino, also offering booze, games of chance and light conversation. Opposite on one corner was Bud Hegstrom's Drug Store where good-sized ice-cream sodas cost ten cents and their big brothers were fifteen cents, and on another corner was Jack Lane's store and warehouse, essentially a storage place for the requirements of his sheepherders, but anyone could buy heavy denim Levi's or Pendleton pants and shirts there and watch the world go by from a couple of long benches on the store's front porch.

Before the war Taylor Williams and Pappy and Papa had made friends with some of the potato farmers of the rolling fields east of Shoshone, our nearest stop on the east-west Union Pacific line. Prewar they had shot jackrabbits as a favor to one such farming family, the Freeses, of German origin, and now they invited our mob to shoot pheasants on their land the opening day of the season in mid-October. Their irrigation ditches provided good cover for the birds and so did a half-acre patch of corn behind their barnyard. On a brilliant breezy morning our convoy of cars left Ketchum loaded with guns, shells, bird carrier jackets, bottles of water and stronger liquids, extra sweaters, extra socks and high spirits. At Shoshone we turned east, passed the cluster of houses and post office proclaiming Dietrich, Idaho, and reached the Freeses' gate well before noon. Mrs. Frees and her daughters-in-law had hospitably prepared an opening-day feast for us, stewed chicken and dumplings, half a dozen vegetables from their garden, two or three different fluffy pies. While we adjusted our gear, and passed bottles, talking softly in the barnyard so as not to disturb nearby birds, the Frees girls handed heavy plates around the yard and we sat down in its sunshine, listening to the wind in the dry cornstalks and in the copse of golden cottonwoods and aspen across the road. As we were digging into chicken breasts, a shiny cock pheasant rose squawking from the copse, flying toward us. Ernest looked at his watch, put down his plate, picked up his gun, shucked a shell into its chamber and shot the bird which fell straight down to his feet. To our chorus of compliments and complaints he muttered, "It was one minute past twelve." Far away, across the fields we heard other guns popping.

We had a glorious afternoon tramping through the corn, tramping the plow-furrowed edges of ditches, hawing and hurrumphing to put birds up, making forays into acres of sagebrush surrounding the fields, breathing the pungent air of autumn earth and grasses.

Everybody got his limit of three, maybe five, cocks. By the time we got home the sun had gone down behind Baldy Mountain and crisp darkness enfolded the cabins. From the back of Dollar Mountain behind our barn came the sweet lonely calls of coyotes, dear to our ears.

Somewhere in the recesses of that barn a wild tiger cat had produced a family and one of her daughters joined up with us, adopting Patrick and Papa as bed-warmers and me as climbing trellis and commissary. She was striped, black and gray, with a face like a pansy, convinced that humans in all their parts were made for amusement and the exercise of her athletic skill, and she learned immediately that a change of her voice brought her loving attentions both in food and fondling. Papa named her Miss Kitty, and none of her wild brethren had so good a fall. One of her favorite ploys was that of climbing the back of my pants legs and shirt and sitting on my shoulder murmuring flattery in my ear as I cut up meat or birds for cooking. My left shoulder showed neat little claw scars all fall. She achieved her most renowned stunt one morning while I was away from the cabin.

I had found a little hairdressing shop, Marinello's, on a side street of the village and, having left Papa peacefully reading in his bathrobe at home, was having my hair dried and nails done when Slim Hawks rushed in, flushed and breathless.

"You've got to come quick. Hurry. It's Papa."

"What do you mean?"

"Miss Kitty's got Papa. He can't unhook her." I guessed Papa's predicament, with Miss Kitty dangling from an appendage. Painful, doubtless.

"Go back fast, you dope, and help Papa unhook her. I can't move now, as you see." Miss Kitty's nails must have been clean. The wounds healed quickly with no noticeable aftereffects.

For more than a year I had been suggesting to Ernest that he meet my parents, even though I felt the Finca Vigía was not yet in sufficiently smooth operation to invite them there. My mother disapproved unconditionally and vocally of alcohol consumption, of smoking and of blasphemy, which made me feel that prolonged association might not be pleasant for any of us. But for their pride's sake, I wanted Ernest to meet them; and our plans for the return journey to Cuba included that rendezvous. Moreover Ernest was plotting a reunion with Buck Lanham, arranging for Winston Guest to invite all four of us, Patrick, Buck, Ernest and me, for a few days shooting ducks and pheasant at Gardiners Island.

In order to avoid Chicago where it would be difficult to have a quiet family meeting in the midst of so many friends and acquaintances, we arranged for my parents to meet us for Thanksgiving in New Orleans, a place new to them and so a treat. We would drive the Lincoln there, get up to New York and Gardiners Island by some other wheels, and afterward ship the Lincoln with or without us back to Cuba. On the way south we would pause for a day or two at Didi Allen's wild, romantic place at Murray, south of Salt Lake City, and shoot ducks. On Sunday morning, November 10, we took off from the MacDonald Cabins, with Patrick and mounds of luggage in the back seat, Miss Kitty in my lap, cold roasted teal and a bottle of tequila in an ice chest at my feet. We couldn't bear to leave Miss Kitty to the hazards of a homeless winter in Ketchum, so at Didi's invitation, our cat would join her ménage.

About ten days later, at a railroad crossing town, the fellows put me aboard a Southern Pacific train which reached New Orleans in time for me to welcome my arriving parents. My ever-seeking father explored the wharves and ships and offices along the lowest port of the river whose headwaters he had known so long and delightedly stuffed a new drawer in his head with facts and figures of tonnages, tides, cargoes, destinations, costs and profits. We dined on an embarrassing plethora of local delicacies.

"You are so extravagant, Mary," my mother repeated as I picked up bills and left tips.

Ernest and Patrick reached New Orleans late on Wednesday, November 27, barely in time for a late light supper at the hotel with my parents.

When we met for lunch in my parents' sitting room, Thursday, Ernest was scrubbed, necktied and shined and he had a program for the day. We would go to the

244

big popular Thanksgiving race meeting at the local track. My mother was looking adorable in a soft blue suit with the customary touch of lace at her throat and a chic understated hat ready to put on her dandelion-gone-to-seed head. My father had ordered their unopened bottle of champagne re-iced and his cheeks glowed with excitement. With a childish sense of helplessness I had anticipated that this encounter would run its course with as little spirit as a British drawing room comedy, everybody speaking set lines in decently modulated voices. Not at all. In a few minutes we were on a spree, even Adeline sipping champagne and merely wrinkling her nose at it.

"My but you're big," she said in awe rather than disapproval, eyeing Ernest. He moved to her chair and kissed her on the top of her head saying, "It's just that you're not so big. Tom, I hope you don't mind horseracing." My father had not seen a horse-race for years but remembered vividly some he had seen in Chicago including the names of a couple of famous runners of those days. After a flurry of ordering, eating and more champagne, of which my mother took further sips, we were off to the races, Tom and Ernest and Patrick talking football.

Ernest had been given the names of a couple of gentlemen who were known to be especially well informed about stables and the horses therefrom which were performing that afternoon, and after we had been seated Ernest found them, conferred, marked his card, and made some investments at a wagering booth. Patrick appointed himself runner, and after nearly every race climbed up to us with fistfuls of money.

"Give it to Adeline," Ernest instructed, and since her small purse couldn't hold the paper, in wonderment she kept the treasury in her lap. As her pile grew, so did her delight and consternation.

"It's just wonderful, and it's really legal?" she asked.

"It's entirely legal, and it's yours," Ernest said.

"Oh, no. It's too much. I couldn't." She looked like a child seeing a Christmas tree.

"A Thanksgiving present." Ernest was exuding cheer like the sun's rays, and Adeline turned thoughtful.

245

"But if you can make all this money in one afternoon, why do you bother with writing?"

"We're lucky today. You've brought luck."

"It must be easier to bet on races than to write," Adeline decided. "I think you should just attend races."

"There might be a certain monotony."

On the way home Adeline counted her winnings, and announced with awe that they amounted to something over $400 and handed them to my father, murmuring she would trust him.

Waiters brought a whole roast turkey to their sitting room for dinner and we shared a tranquil evening of stories, Tom's and Ernest's impressions of the Chippewas, Ernest's flagrantly invented tales of the bear who shared his shack the winter he ran a trapline in Montana, Adeline's account of Gina, the Bemidji harlot she had innocently hired as a maid: on the afternoon the banker's wife came to call she had found Adeline washing windows while Gina swished out the front door in a pink taffeta dress and Adeline's best hat. As amateur naturalists they had dozens of observations to exchange—the eerie cry of a lynx, the blue jay's scatterbrained nest-building, the compounds elk build in northern Minnesota winters of heavy snow, the joyous toboggan slides otters make. My father never told his stories better, I thought, and Ernest paid them tribute by listening with total attention, a long-time habit of his whether or not the talk was interesting. I was enchanted with the evening and when we got back to our twin-bedded room, began so expressing myself.

"You think I'm made of asbestos?" my husband asked.

"A nice little fire on Thanksgiving."

"Mmmmmm. Like the early days in Paris." Woven together, we slept all night in his bed.

Back in Cuba, we had a very quiet Christmas, just the two of us alone. We had walked the small path under the satin-leafed avocado trees from the Finca Vigía to the Steinharts' farm, exchanged holiday wishes over dry martinis, walked home to share a small tough Cuban turkey. Patrick and Gregory arrived from Key

246

West the next day and a few days later Papa's big blond sister, Sunny, with her young son, Ernie, Papa's namesake, Sunny both shy and proprietary. We were back in the grind of entertaining six or eight guests at table twice a day. But the throngs soon dissipated except for Patrick who was at home with us for another semester quietly studying for Harvard College Board exams in the Little House. With relief and contentment the three of us moved into the tranquil routine—never so much routine as to become monotonous—of study, writing, reading, gardening, tennis, swimming, fishing. Bed by eleven o'clock, a new day opening for Papa at 7 a.m. or 8 for me.

For weeks I had been making casual references to our Cat House, Ernest's envisioned shelter complete with shelves for our cat family's beds and an inclined floor for easy hosing and cleaning each morning. Papa had been concerned that the cats might feel rejected and hurt if they were moved from the main house away from us and I sympathized. I had never seen him be mean, unkind or less than loving to any of his animals. Animals were love sponges, we knew, and wanted never to let the sponges go dry.

"Remember the tower you wrote me about?" I mentioned one day at lunch.

"We could see the sunsets better," Papa agreed.

"If I sunned on the roof, the gardeners couldn't see me." He liked me to look brown as Cuban mahogany. "I could be brown all over."

"Maybe I could work there."

"We could have a tower with a top room for you. Think of the peace and quiet, and the views. We could build it by the pool."

"Too far."

We decided to make the tower at one end of the red-tiled terrace behind the house, with a room for the cats at the terrace level, a carpentry shop built into the sloping hillside below the Cat House—carpentry would never cease—a storage room for luggage and hunting and fishing gear and Out West winter clothes above the cats, a many-windowed room for Ernest above that, and a low-walled deck for sunning on the top. The tower should not be so big or tall that it would overpower the house and belittle it, I felt. I took measurements and estimated the height of the royal palms bordering the old carriage driveway, and arbitrarily concluded that it should be about 4 meters 80 centimeters square and 12 meters (about 40 feet) high above the ground level. In Havana I found a beginner's book of architecture in English and translated its few technical terms into Spanish, did some comically amateur drawings and asked the principal building contractor of San Francisco de Paula, Eduardo Rivero, for a consultation. The eaves of Ernest's room must be double the normal length, to prevent all but early morning and late afternoon sunshine entering his big windows, I explained, and their concrete plaques must be doubly reinforced with steel rods to hold them steady in hurricanes. The staircase would run up the outside of the tower. Sr. Rivero went home to estimate costs. The tower would be a useful, happy addition to the Finca, I thought, and we started on it.

7

Unsettled Weather

WE WERE LUXURIATING in comparative freedom from intruders. But in April our lovely life fell apart. My father, who had been enduring rectal pains for some months from cancer in his prostate gland and "treating" them with Christian Science, fell unconscious in their flat and my frightened mother at long last called for a doctor and ambulance and wired me urgently to come north. Almost simultaneously, Patrick, with little warning, took leave of his senses. He had gone over to Key West to share Gregory's spring vacation from Canterbury School with Pauline, and on returning to the Finca mentioned that they had had a minor car crash in which he had bumped his head. After the crash he had slept all night out on the lawn of the house in Whitehead Street in Key West. His head still ached, he told us. He needed an extra desk in the Little House, he said, for his various papers and when I suggested that Pancho could make one, he brought me a design he had made between sedulous sessions of cramming for the college exams. It showed an average-sized desk topped by a dozen rows of tiny little drawers, with similar rows of drawers built in below the writing surface.

"But none of these is big enough to hold standard-sized letterpaper," I said.

"I know. I'll put that somewhere else." The ground floor of the Little House already contained two big office desks with large drawers.

"What will you put in these drawers? You know drawers take four or five times as much carpentry as shelves."

"Oh, lots of things. And lots of my ideas."

"Let's talk about it later." I thought the aberration a passing one and dismissed it.

Dinner that night was a disaster. Patrick talked irrationally of the next day's College Board examinations as though hobgoblins were conducting them. Ernest went on and on about concussions and how they need not interfere with the performance of duty and how aircraft pilots should be grounded for them but might nonetheless fly in an emergency. A mess of tosh and no help to Patrick, it seemed to me, and I made the silly mistake of interrupting.

"It will all be facts you know, Mouse. Don't be scared of it. . . . You know fear only paralyzes your thinking."

Ernest was infuriated, escorted Patrick to bed and took the trouble to write me a two-page letter explaining the situation.

On April 12, Ernest shepherded Patrick into Havana to deal with the exams and I booked passage on Delta Air Lines's new flight to New Orleans and Chicago. As I was packing in my room two days later I saw Ernest carrying Patrick into the Little House, ran down there and found Ernest tying his son into one of the upstairs beds with sheets from the other bed.

"Get my Seconal," he said, "and call José Luis. And Cucu Kohly." I fetched the Seconal and ran to work at the old wooden-box telephone on the pantry wall which sometimes got us onto our party line. By the time the two doctors arrived Patrick was sleeping restlessly under his father's eye. Ernest sent René to watch over Patrick and the men held a conference in the sitting room. José Luis knew a German psychiatrist who was highly regarded in Havana. They agreed that Patrick should be moved to his father's room in the big house for easier case.

I felt treacherous leaving the Finca in such trouble, but my mother had telephoned that the surgeons at St. Luke's Hospital in Chicago were making an exploratory operation on my father the next morning. They both needed me more than Ernest did.

My father was in a ward with other patients in the hospital and looked a gray and shaking wraith of himself.

"Mary, Mary, help me. They cut into me without any anesthetic," he said.

"Darling, they couldn't have. I'll check. Please rest. I'll get you something. You're going to feel better soon." I found a nurse and arranged for more sedatives, then petitioned the always overcrowded hospital for a private room.

It was a time requiring fortitude in us all. My parents and me in Chicago, and Ernest and his crowd in Cuba. As I sat beside my father's bed, first in a ward, later in a big high-ceilinged room, reading news, politics and poetry, I remembered from Casper, Wyoming, how, being tired from pain, one might find even loving voices an intrusion, and the effort to respond almost too great to attempt. For my father, who had been in sinewy good health all his life, pain and the indignities of illness were alarming new acquaintances, depleting his capacities for attention. So I sat many afternoons simply holding his hand.

For my mother I ran errands, did our modest marketing in the neighborhood, cooked her favorite dishes, refrained from arguing about Christian Science and some evenings sang hymns from her hymn book. It was her unswerving devotion to the religion, more than my father's, which had too long delayed his asking for medical help for his trouble, and I thought her attitude morally inexcusable. I wondered how a registered Christian Science practitioner, seeing my father's distress, could in decency offer him only the balm of words. But I held my tongue and wrote my disillusions to Ernest. Simple reason could not dispel my mother's thirty years of faith, and if I evoked a sense of guilt about my father in her, it would not help him in his dilemma. Millions had died for faiths no more obtuse than this one, I remembered.

Both Pauline, Patrick's mother, and Ernest wrote me letters on April 18. "I am over here in Cuba and staying at your house," wrote Pauline. "I hope you do not mind. . . . I was very worried about Patrick when he was in Key West. . . . This is the first real trouble I've ever had. We have a good doctor now who seems to think Patrick will get over his attack in about two weeks. . . ."

"News from here good," wrote Ernest, a euphemism for their drastic circumstances. "[Patrick] is much better. . . . I sleep just outside his door on a mattress, René and Sinbad in white room . . . a passing thing . . . a psychic state precipitated by the accident. . . . Hope your end doing o.k."

I wrote Pauline that my fresh shirts and shorts were in piles in the bottom drawer of the mahogany chest of drawers in my room and please to use them as she wished, not to take any guff from Ramón and recommended palliative books from the shelves in my room. I wrote Ernest sympathy and love.

Another day Pauline wrote: "Ernest has been marvelous, organizing everything and keeping the troops cheerful. Sinbad and Roberto have been on the job constantly and Ernest has seen to it that they get their sleep, altho he hasn't had much. . . ."

During my month's absence from the Finca Ernest sent me five or six cables and wrote me twenty letters, some in two parts, nearly all in his penciled round hand, most in the stillnesses of the very early mornings—0230 hours, 0320 hours—when his helpers,

Sinsky (our friend Juan Duñabeitia, a Basque captain of merchant ships plying between Cuban and U.S. ports, who had helped in *Pilar* in her Q-boat days, and was Sinbad the Sailor at our house) and Roberto, were sleeping and Patrick was quiet in Ernest's bed while he stretched out on the sitting room's woven grass mat, writing on his clipboard, his shoulders propped with pillows against a table leg.

The letters were essentially reports, five to fourteen pages long, on Patrick's ever-changing behavior, what nursing care they were giving him, how much sleep his team had achieved, how the weather was, with sympathy for my problems and my parents, and always warm endearments.

On April 19, he reassured me about finances. Speiser (his lawyer) had written that Mark Hellinger had bought the rights to film four short stories, at $75,000 each, plus a percentage of the film profits, the deal coming along, and there would be money from that. ". . . I can send you direct to your address, in the meantime, from Chicago bank whatever money you need for Papa's hospital and medical expenses and whatever he and your mother need."

On my father's typewriter I wrote long paragraphs of worry and affection. "Two special delivery letters in two days. . . . Wish the timing of these misfortunes had been a little less subtle. . . .

"About Dad, he improves very slowly, still taking no food but milk, and generally uncooperative with doctors and nurses, refusing to take pills and eat. Dr. said tests will show by next week whether or not it will be possible to operate on prostate now." For his reassurance I wrote a detailed account of my finances— a comfortable balance in my New York bank—and my family's resources.

"Longing for the day when we can get back to our own fine life. . . ."

On April 22 he wrote: "Just a line to let you know fight here very difficult but doctors say is a passing thing. . . . Sinbad wonderful. Takes it all just like a good guy in a fight. . . . René same and has fine control with Mouse. . . . Roberto couldn't be better but tires quicker. . . .

"During all this the long prong of our orchid has bloomed in a cluster of very dark and miniature orchids. Still about ten to come at the tip so will have for your return. [We had a dozen different orchid plants attached to the trunk of the ceiba tree outside my bedroom windows and this was the latest addition to our collection.] . . . All cotsies are well. . . . . Keep house clean as possible and good discipline with servants. . . . We are violating adage of not fight on two fronts but can't help it and will do best we can on both and then together. . . . Don't worry about cash. . . . These are the times that savings accounts were made for. . . ."

"I'm going to swim twenty laps, take some champagne and think about how much I love my kitten," he wrote on Saturday, April 26. "Our orchid is superb and looks like a series of very dark lady slippers. This trouble has made me appreciate what a lovely, wonderful place we have—seeing it all of the hours of the day—cool at night—fresh daytime breeze and all the different lovely skies. . . . Mousie talks wonderful poetry. . . . This just from lonesome partner."

At 4 a.m. May 2 he wrote: "This letter sounds like a circular from a complain house—also written in semi-darkness of the bedroom while sitting in chair within reach of bed. It adds up, in fatigue, like working on election day on a newspaper, only for eighteen days straight. . . . It's 1600 now and nothing is as bad once it's daylight and in two hours René can take over. It's a beautiful morning. There are still three unopened buds on the strong, long elk-prick orchid, so there will be orchids for when you come home. . . . You get long letters [this was fourteen pages] even if no good. But not as bad as being married to Thomas Wolfe . . . Am glad am just a good writer and my Kitten's husband and not a genius."

On May 5 he reviewed his finances, anticipating income from Mark Hellinger's films, and, "So now you have to stay in Chicago longer than you thought, *please* get some clothes. . . . I never figure on moneys until they are in the bag. . . . But your kitten will be good provider. . . . My preservation of savings and undesire to borrow on book . . . is almost completely psychological. But I have to have some psychological safeguards to write. . . . Through all this have kept work desk in white room unchanged and untouched so can go back to work just as was working, with no disorder. . . . When I get a letter from you it is just like having replacements, ammo and chow come up in a fight. I slept three hours last night and will get some more this morning. . . . Please keep on writing if you have time because it helps me so much. . . . Have told Pauline to teach Ramón how to make biscuits. . . . I love you. Big kiss. Smaller kisses [17]."

On May 7–8, Ernest wrote at 1145, 1350, 1840, 1900: "It has been a hard night. . . . But pretty soon we will have our lovely love and holding close and caring for each other (we don't owe any debts to each other—we always pay them each night). . . . Your duty in Chicago involves kindness and delicacy and patience and fortitude and I know you have them all. You must make your father happy in his great pain and trouble and I know you will. . . . Place lovelier and more beautiful every day."

"Wonderful news tonight," Ernest wrote on May 8. "I haven't wanted to write it—not to make horror stories. But we've had deadly drought ever since you left. Wells dried up. Been living out of cistern—drawing water in buckets for baths—garden drying up. . . . But this afternoon at 6:30 it started to rain—first lightly, then heavier, then really heavy for *five* full hours. Now cistern water replaced, all trees okay, no wells will fail, place will look wonderful for when you get back. . . . Pauline goes on Saturday. She has been splendid lately. . . . I've behaved in every way as you would want me to if you had been here to guide me. . . . it's 0015 now on a new day, May 9. . . . Past twelve months been a bad one for me on illness— Casper and now here. But truly believe have learned much from same and learned to be a better guy, I hope. Tired guy tonight and with big urge to be a completely worthless character with my kitten."

At 0340 on May 12 Ernest wrote: "The rain is over and the barometer is up and it's blowing half a gale out of the S.E. . . . I'm getting as beat up as a scarecrow and getting gray everywhere, didn't get gray at Casper. But we won at Casper and we'll win here. . . . Thank Christ we won at Casper . . . and am certainly glad I saw you in the White Tower restaurant and told you I loved you as soon as I did. . . . It's 0425 and Mousie just started talking . . . 0635 and it's raining like a bastard . . . this is the fifth day of rain . . . strange rain."

By mid-May I had my father comfortably settled in their Drexel Boulevard flat and a maid coming daily to help my mother and I flew back to Havana, my luggage brimming as usual with U.S.-created gewgaws for the Finca—a new battery-powered radio for Ernest to use at the pool, table mats, breakfast tray linens.

I also brought to Ernest a message from my father dated May 16, 1947: "Dear Ernest I wish I could express to you what Mary's coming to my bedside in the hospital brought to me. . . . It seemed as though the heavens had opened and sent an angel to me to lift me up. . . . God bless you for all of the goodness in your loving heart. . . ."

With Juan, in my stylish yellow convertible, Pauline came to meet me at the airport. She was crisp, cool, and chic in the best sub-tropics way and I was immediately her admirer.

At the Finca Ernest took me in to greet Patrick, established in his bedroom.

"Mouse, I'm Mary," I said approaching him. In the white sheets he looked skinny beyond belief and his brown eyes big as cow's eyes.

"Mary, Mary. You're not Mary. You're the Tin Kid." (Later, we baptized my small 20-foot, open-cockpit fishing launch with that name.)

Pauline had moved to the Little House, so that I could re-establish myself in my room, and between sessions of attending to Patrick we had a few pleasant hours of family life in the sitting room, Pauline complimenting Ernest on his choice of a new wife, most conversations superficial as they are apt to be in times of siege. We were alumnae of the same Alma Mater, Pauline and I agreed, giggling.

Due to a strike there was a desperate shortage of beef on the island and our supplies of fish were dwindling. When Ernest suggested I go fishing in *Pilar* with

Gregorio for food for the household, I was enchanted. Only fifteen or twenty minutes after we were in the Gulf Stream off Cojímar, our feathers picked up a pair of dolphin, slashing and swirling, iridescent and sparkling in the water. Soon one of the outriggers dipped and bent, the line pulled out of its clothespin, and I had the rod in my butt-rest and held the line tight while Gregorio reeled in the two feathers and the big white teaser. It was a small—eighty-pound—striped marlin who had sunk the hook firmly inside his cheek. He walked and danced and dived and jumped against my fetter and I hated and also exulted in the process of drawing him slowly and inevitably to the gaff. Gregorio was delighted, and we would have food for all the household for a week. Gregorio's household too. Like beef, marlin should be hung in a cold room for a fortnight or a month to become tender. We did not hang my small fish. With gusto we ate his tough fibers the next evening, and the next, and the next.

My father wrote of his recovery, "The thing that tells the story best is that my trousers belt which has nine holes was buckled up to the 9th hole the first day I wore my trousers, and today the 8th hole was as far as I could buckle." As always, we had too many letters to read, welcome news from friends and requests and demands from strangers and people with simmering ideas about projects for converting Ernest's work to something else for their benefit. We were receiving too many magazines without enough time to absorb their contents. Treasures, I used to think, seeing them in the magazine rack I had designed and Pancho had built, and never enough time to dig into them. Everywhere stacks of books were inviting us to pause and explore, and I could not manage to corral them into our library for several years.

I saw Pauline off at the local airport from which small airplanes went to Key West and a couple of mornings later woke up choked, breathless and inordinately hot. A thermometer pulled out of my mouth read 104. When José Luis came, probed, poked and questioned, he decided it must be undulant fever.

Maybe the milk from one of our cows was contaminated. But no one else at the Finca was affected. Lying weak and useless, requiring only slight attention from the already overworked servants, I felt like a fool, particularly because the fever refused to subside. Awakening at two or three o'clock June 4 I read my temperature as 105, remembered that I had no written will, and in the gentle predawn breeze wrote one at my desk, affirming my mind sound, leaving a few pieces of jewelry to daughters of my friends and everything else to Ernest. "Now I know what it means, 'My blood was boiling,' " I concluded.

José Luis had been feeding me sulfas and penicillin and hinting that, if I could make it, I should go to a Havana clinic for more elaborate tests than he could make at the Finca. When Ernest found the will on my desk the next morning, he decided that I must go into town for the laboratory tests. Juan, having managed to run all three cars to burning point without proper watering and oiling, was occupying the lowest rung of Ernest's esteem, but he looked after me with super solicitude, and this time, with my knees wobbling, sweat running and breath jerking, I was grateful for it. Three or four days later the findings of the tests indicated that my fever was not undulant but some vague cousin of it. Lying helpless in my bright, airy room I wondered if disgust with it could cure a fever. I wondered how I could compensate for the time I had lost working in the vegetable and rose gardens and the plantings around the pool, the abandoned kitchen, the neglected house, I wondered how many other fathers would rip apart their lives and their work to care for a sick child twenty-four hours a day, as Ernest was doing, when other facilities for caring, even though inferior, were available.

When my fever abated to 101 degrees and Pauline suggested on the telephone that the air of Key West might prove invigorating, I flew there, still groggy, weak, groping for exits from our problems.

Pauline, who was living in the main house in Key West's Whitehead Street, assigned me the big room above the Pool House which years before Ernest had used as his workroom, reaching it by an elevated catwalk from the main house. Gigi was there, his voice deeper than it had been the previous autumn, and Ada, the cook-maid, brought me breakfast in bed. I loved the house with its tall French doors, animal skins on the polished floor of the sitting room with its green light filtered through the bougainvillaea vines outside, and its seclusion behind the high ancient brick walls bordering the lawns. Pauline had acquired the brick when the town tore up an old street to replace the brick with asphalt.

On the scratchy telephone connection we talked to Ernest almost daily. Meanwhile we wrote letters. On June 28 he wrote Pauline and me jointly: "Today is Leopoldina's birthday and we all chipped in and sent her fifteen dollars. . . . The mangoes are all starting to ripen and Boise [who liked mangoes as well as fruit rats] is in his glory. He turned down an inferior Chino yest, but today ate an entire Filipino."

On June 30 he wrote that a new doctor was due at the Finca to examine Patrick. On July 1 he wrote: "Patrick slept all night and woke lucid." On July 2 he typed a one-page letter and on July 5 three pages single-spaced, devoting much of it to a defense of the current condition of the Finca which I must have criticized with asperity. "My own parents were scrupulously neat and foes of dirt. . . . I'm terribly sorry to have given such an impression of dirt, ill-kemptness and disorder. But try sleeping on the floor sometime for say, not to exaggerate, sixty days, with no room of your own, no bathroom or washbowl of your own . . . your toilet articles used by two and three other people. . . ." A heated rebuttal from a man tired beyond the boundaries of cool judgment and ending, "Much love dearest Kittner."

Having received a cheerful letter from me, Ernest wrote again on the fifth. "This is to tell you not to pay any attention to anything I wrote in the other letter. When people are awfully tired they get gloomy about small lacks of confidence. . . . Have a lot of good new books and we are all going to try to be very cheerful and handle things good. . . . Wizard ops in prospect."

Of Patrick's improvement Ernest wrote on July 8: "Just like coming out of the forest onto the high ground. . . ." Getting back a few days later I was relieved to find the household re-adapting itself to its pre-emergency routine, tile floors being polished, books and bookcases dusted, silver shined, gardens weeded.

We were relaxing in the sitting room one evening with José Luis who had come for dinner and to have a look at Patrick. José Luis mentioned a house call he had made on the way to the Finca. "His dog always tries to bite me, and he won't discipline the dog or himself," he complained in Spanish.

"What's his *problema?*" Sinsky asked.

"High blood pressure. Much too high."

"I'll bet you mine's higher," Sinsky said, grinning. José Luis went out to his car, came back with his pressure-measuring machine, wound its flaps around Sinsky's arm, pumped and snorted, *"Caramba!* This is no joke." Ernest, who had been reading in his chair, closed his book on one finger and listened to the doctor urging Sinsky to restrict his eating, smoking, and drinking, his flings with the girls in Havana, to swim and to rest even at the risk of boredom.

"What a *puta* shame, Sinsk," Ernest was saying as he stuck out his arm for the same test. "But stick around. We'll get you in shape." José Luis pumped his little rubber bulb, shook his head, took off the wrappings and then put them on again. Sinsky's blood pressure had read 180 over 120. The little dials reported Ernest's to be 215 over 125. A grave circumstance, they agreed.

To nobody's consolation, I tried for mild optimism. "The other pressures are off now. We'll all ration booze and I'll watch our food like a jailer." For a week or two the Finca pretended to be a Boy Scout camp, the boys competing not only about symptoms but in their exercises and restraints.

Sinsky: "Have you got a tight steel band around your head?"

Ernest: "Fairly tight. Can you hear a swarm of bees above the roof?"

Twenty laps in the pool before lunch became standard operational procedure.

Sinsky: "I had two drinks this morning."

Ernest: "That's cheating."

Sinsky: "Plain coconut water—no gin."

I had not bothered taking my temperature for a fortnight, but that evening I stuck a thermometer in my mouth. It came out almost normal.

The nursing team broke up, and Pauline returned to us to help around the house. Sinsky got a job as captain of a merchant ship, Panamanian register, carrying cargo between Havana and southern U.S. ports, principally Houston. Felix took off for Mexico City, following Ermua, both Basque pelota-playing friends. A brother of Roberto wrote from Santiago de Cuba at the eastern end of the island that a good job was available there and Roberto prepared to move. He was packing in the White Room off the sitting room when I chanced to hurry through and noticed Pauline and Patrick perched there with SOS expressions on their faces. "He's packing all of Patrick's clothes," Pauline whispered.

"What nonsense." And I went to check. Roberto was folding a pair of Patrick's trousers to fit his suitcase.

"Papa told me to take them," he said, his dignity unruffled. I looked around.

"But this is Patrick's entire wardrobe." Roberto continued his packing.

Ernest was working in his room and Pauline had hesitated to interrupt him. I did not hesitate and Patrick's clothes were restored to him. Roberto sometimes reminded me of tales I had heard of Spanish grandees of old and their retainers, their houses ever expanding to accommodate increasing families. The relationships were brotherly and in return for faithful and honest service the retainers often assumed that the property was communal. The Herrera brothers' father had been the court chamberlain to Alfonso XIII. Roberto had perhaps acquired his habits about property in his childhood.

In Cuba, as in Spain and other Latin countries, the anniversary of one's birth is less celebrated than the day of the birth of the saint with the same Christian name, and Ernest used to receive telegrams from near and abroad on his saint's day in October. But we also made small-to-elaborate celebrations of his birthday. This year I arranged a modest birthday lunch at the pool with miles of tinted tissue paper and bright ribbons holding surprise presents, music from Miami squeaking out of the birthday present battery-powered radio and a few friends stopping by for champagne and cold, juicy Morro crab and roasted ham. Cucu Kohly and José Luis came out and also Paco Garay, who did something in Immigration and Customs and knew many Cuban government officials.

Pauline and I had wrapped the presents elaborately and before luncheon trundled them all down in a gardener's wheelbarrow to the pool. Afterward René carried down two birthday cakes, one made of ice cream and another, from Havana's best cake-maker, topped with mountains of frosting and inscribed, *Salud, Mountain Man.* Ernest announced that it was the very best birthday he had ever had ever, and repeated himself for several days more. He was a man who did not shrink from superlatives. He embraced them.

The very next day was Pauline's birthday and I made her a cake myself, inscribing it, *We love Pauline.* Since I had no advance notice about it, even from the children, her celebration was modest, but cheerful.

During all the summer's struggle for Patrick's recovery, Ernest had been using his dream of autumn in the crisp clean bird-spangled air of Idaho as a sweet future haven. With Toby Bruce, his friend and aide-de-camp for many years in Key West, arranging details he bought a beautiful Buick Roadmaster convertible, royal blue with bright red-leather lining and seats, and in mid-September he flew to Miami to join Toby and the car for a leisurely detoured voyage to Sun Valley via his childhood haunts in northern Michigan. Pauline, Patrick (who was still recuperating) and I stayed behind, it having been decided that Pauline and Pat would move on to San Francisco for a month or so, for cooler weather and a rendezvous with her sister, Jinny, who lived in Los Angeles. As soon as Ernest reached Sun Valley I was to fly there, bringing with me a half dozen of our rifles and shotguns. Flying the artillery would be safer against thieving, Ernest thought, than carting it around the country in the car.

Pauline had never seen anything of Cuba except a few Havana streets and the Finca, so we organized a two- or three-day tour along the rickety north coast road westward. She set off accompanied by Patrick and his physician, Dr. Stetmeyer, in my yellow convertible.

They were still away, the servants were taking their siestas and I was puttering around in my room when our dogs burst into cadenzas of unwelcome. As I moved down the front steps, Cuban soldiers emerged from behind a dozen different trees and shrubs and a young lieutenant, very shaved and polished, approached me, his rifle in the over-the-top position. I pushed its barrel downward.

"Put that thing aside," said I in Spanish. "What kind of joke is this?"

"I'm sorry, señorita. . . ."

"Señora. Señora de Hemingway. And I am also a captain in the army of the United States."

"You're under arrest."

"By whose order? And tell your men to put down their guns. This is my husband's property. You were not invited."

"I'm sorry, señora. But I have my orders."

"This is idiotic. But show them to me."

Out of his breast pocket the lieutenant drew a piece of paper. Standing in the shade of our ceiba tree which grew out of our front steps, I took plenty of time to read it. Much of the paper's legal, formal phrasing I could not understand. But I saw the words *antipático* to the Cuban government, and the signature, that of the chief of the Department of Defense.

"What rubbish," I said, using the word for garbage —*basura*—for want of one more ladylike. "This *cabrón*, your minister. He has no right to search us. Only *antipático*. I ought to shoot you, and your loving troops too."

René, in his off-duty, short-sleeved shirt, came walking up the driveway and I yelled at him. He came up to the ceiba tree, listened to the lieutenant and me and read the piece of paper and concluded, "I'm very sorry, my señora. But this appears to be legal. They have the right to search the house."

"Please call Cucu," I said and ushered the lieutenant and a couple of his men into the house.

"We are searching only for guns and ammunition," said the lieutenant.

"You won't find anything," I prophesied, too soon. I had forgotten that the family custom was to dump unused shotgun shells, both .20s and .12s, into any convenient box, drawer or wastebasket after we shot live pigeons at the Club de Cazadores. Also that we practiced target shooting with .22 rifles and other calibers at bottles and tin cans set up on the cement steps of the collapsed and abandoned *vacaría* on the hill behind the driveway. To my dismay the lieutenant found some .30-06 bullets in the drawers beneath the window seat in my room. I couldn't remember how or why they lodged there.

A small truck had backed up the driveway and with surprising efficiency the little army unit filled it with rifles and shotguns, the Duke of Alba's shotgun which E. had somehow acquired during the Spanish Civil War and Ernest's favorite old Winchester pump gun among them, U.S. and German army pistols and hundreds, if not thousands, of shells and unopened boxes of rifle ammunition in various dimensions, our wicker wastebaskets of shotgun shells looking incongruous and cozy among the guns.

"You must come with us now," the lieutenant said.

"Muy bien. I'll come to see that you don't steal our guns. What a gallant army you are, to arrest a defenseless woman!" I added a few imprecations in English to lower my steam. I changed from my Finca shorts into long pants and off we went to the police station of Cotorro, the next village eastward, and its clean, whitewashed jail. There the police allowed me to use the telephone, and I called first the military attaché at the U.S. embassy, a man I knew slightly and to whom we had lent *Pilar* on occasion for fishing.

"Take down the numbers on your guns," he advised, snug in his naïveté.

"But can you do something to get me out of here?"

"It's so late . . . the government offices are closing. . . ."

"Thanks very much you slovenly bastard." I had

Paco Garay's telephone number, which René had given me, and I called him.

"Let me talk to the commandante," said Paco, and the police chief came to the telephone. When he finished the conversation, he said, "We did not intend to molest you, señora. You are free to leave."

"Then you may take me home," I said, having no other transport. A day or two later I discovered that a Miami paper had published a piece about the hijinks in Havana of some U.S. aircraft pilots who had been hired by a group of Cubans who were planning to "liberate" Santo Domingo. Their headquarters, the newspaper had printed, was a house owned by an American writer not far from Havana. The house, we learned later, was that of J. P. McEvoy, an editor of *Reader's Digest*.

Among the weapons the Cuban army had confiscated were five or six I had intended to fly to Idaho with me. I was booked to leave in a couple of days. Paco talked to his friends and miraculously I was allowed to call upon a judge in his chambers where he accepted my assurance that I would return to Cuba with the guns later that year, the date not specified. But first I must produce Ernest's arms license. I wired Sun Valley, and he wired back his license number, 4278, assuring me he would airmail the license, describing the pistols as war trophies never fired in Cuba.

When I disembarked with my battery of weapons at Twin Falls, Idaho, Ernest, who had said he would meet me there with the car, was nowhere visible. (Some car disorder had delayed him, I found out later.) I caught a ride, reached Sun Valley Lodge, where the desk clerk gave me the key to Suite 206. It was unmistakably Ernest's habitat. One of his green-and-white Suzanne Lenglen eyeshades hung from the back of a chair. A pair of still muddy boots were slowly drying, keeping their proper distance from the corner fireplace. Three or four books were doing the splits, face down, on chairs and tables and another table held an improvised bar with a few bottles and glasses on a waiter's tray. With French doors and a balcony overlooking well-groomed lawns and a bedroom and bath for each of us, the place suggested lingering lovely breakfasts, dilettante afternoons of reading, cozy quiet dinners by the fire. False dreams.

When the meeting came to order that night I learned that Ernest would not hunt deer that season. Our friend Dr. John Moritz thought the mountain climbing after animals too risky for one with such high blood pressure. But I could go deer hunting if I wished. Venison would be a welcome addition to the repasts we would provide for Sinsky and Roberto, whom Ernest had invited for a fortnight at Christmastime. Meanwhile we would hunt ducks, partridge, and pheasants whose pursuit entailed no climbing.

Idaho was providing us with one of its spectacular, beautiful autumns, its daytime air shimmering with undiluted sunshine, its nights cold enough to freeze the water in my bedside glass. With Taylor Williams and his Roberts rifle, I shot paper targets until he decided that I could hit a deer within the rifle's range. Then we started climbing mountains, Taylor swinging along as smoothly as a metronome, zigzagging up the inclines, I frequently puffing until we reached level going. Marvelous exercise but with no prizes to show for it. Three weeks later, hunting with Pappy Arnold, I got a young buck.

To share the fun of our duck season, two sets of Coopers arrived, Gary and Rocky (Veronica) from Los Angeles and our wedding reception hosts, Dick and Marjorie Cooper, from their place at Laramie, Wyoming. The weather hung on to its extraordinary iridescence and we hunted happily together, beating sagebrush for pheasants or climbing irrigation ditches to jump-shoot ducks.

Gliding softly around the curves and twists of Silver Creek, near the settlement of Picabo, was Ernest's and my favorite way of hunting duck. Not the most productive, perhaps, but the most beautiful with the satin river reflecting the sky, the rust, crimson, carmine stalks of willows stretching up to their clusters of tawny leaves and a surprise around every turn. A heron sometimes, or a duck family which would rise, not in panic, merely in precaution as we approached. Since our rule was that only the bow-sitter could shoot, the ducks were in small jeopardy when Ernest paddled in the stern and I had the bow seat. I was so absorbed each time just watching them, and so slow heeding Ernest's admonition, "Shoot!" that they were frequently out of range before I got my gun up.

When I paddled and Ernest had the bow seat the ducks fared almost as well since, with his weight lifting the canoe's stern comically almost out of the water, I had less than a foot of leverage on my paddle and could not put the canoe where we wanted it. Whatever the limit was that year, we seldom had it filled by the time we beached the canoe east of Picabo and started the thirty-mile cold drive home with the top down. Cold because Ernest refused to turn on the Buick's heating system. "Bad for lungs," he said.

Pauline, her sister Jinny and Patrick were nesting cozily in a sublet flat in San Francisco, with Bumby rooming nearby tying trout flies to make a living. I must go down there to do my Christmas shopping, Pauline wrote.

Ernest declared I would enjoy San Francisco, which I had never seen. He had several invitations for Thanksgiving dinner and would accept the one from Chuck and Flos Atkinson who owned the canoe we used duck hunting at Picabo. I assembled my paltry city wardrobe and some plucked ducks and boarded a train. It was heartening to see Patrick his original smart and gentle self, and Pauline's gaiety, as well as the forebearance with which Bumby was accepting his indifferent financial fortunes.

An aunt and uncle of Pauline's invited us to Thanksgiving dinner at their comfortable old house overhanging a wide valley, and as she parked the car sideways on a steep hill Pauline mentioned that our hosts were serious, practicing Catholics.

"What's 'practicing'?" I asked. "Just 'do unto others' stuff?"

"More than that. If I hadn't been such a bloody fool practicing Catholic, I wouldn't have lost my husband." Pauline sounded both vehement and convinced, and I wished we could go on a bit, but the timing was unseemly. Coitus interruptus? I wondered but never asked and never heard.

Ernest wrote to me in San Francisco reporting his

work accomplished, over eight hundred words each day, and that he had been scouting for ducks along Silver Creek. "There are simply hundreds of thousands on the upper creek, in the marsh and on the main creek and all the tributaries," and he welcomed me back with detailed plans for shooting expeditions for the second half of duck season, which was split that year.

In every department Sun Valley was industriously primping for the mid-December opening of its first winter season since the war. Workmen checked every hook, buckle and hinge on the chairlifts up Dollar Mountain and Baldy. New lamps appeared in the lobby of the Lodge and a little hill of four-foot logs grew in a corner by the big hospitable fireplace. Young helpers around the place turned into bellboys in new uniforms, and at the Ram, a restaurant about three lawns away, new napery appeared on old oak tables on which hundreds of customers had carved or burnt their initials. Johnny Lister, who played the piano during dinner at the Ram, posted a notice asking people to audition for the chorus which would sing carols on Christmas Eve and I got a place among the altos.

We had to move from the Lodge, but this year we couldn't get the rabbit warren apartment adjoining the office of the MacDonald Cabins, only standard cabins —living room with wall bed, minute bedroom, kitchen and bath—were available and of those we rented three, one for the children who were converging on us for Christmas, one for Ernest to work in, one for our living quarters, functionally the kitchen and mess room. We reserved a room for Sinsky and Roberto in the old farmhouse which was part of the complex. The appetites arriving in waves of exuberance caused Ernest and me to adopt one rule of procedure. The fellows could have morning coffee in our cabin, finishing off any leftover pie or cake, but not full-scale breakfast, and they would lunch at one or another of the village cafés. I would provide dinners, *chez nous*. The MacDonald barn was again festooned with ducks, pheasant and a few partridges, and roasts and steaks from my deer hanging in the Lodge cool room. Besides Roberto,

267

Sinsky, Ernest and our three boys, Taylor Williams usually dined with us, making us eight at table. I spent four or five hours every afternoon processing dinners and practicing one of my newer skills, the baking of pies full of apples, lemon custard, pumpkin or mincemeat redolent of brandy, or layer cakes, preferably chocolate nesting beneath inch-thick coats of frosting. "Sure smells good in here," Gary Cooper would say, sniffing my pastry as it lay on top of the refrigerator.

Further approval of my food came from our new dog. Making his accustomed rounds of his three or four favorite bars, as much for local news as for booze, Ernest noticed a black springer-looking dog faithfully following. When he walked back to our cabin, the dog followed and Ernest gave him something to eat. Late that night when I opened the back door, I found the dog there, huddled close to the cabin for warmth, and invited him inside. He slept beneath Ernest's bed. All around town and at the Valley we inquired if anyone had lost a black springer spaniel or knew anyone who had lost, etc. Nobody knew. Inadvertently or not, someone had left him friendless in Ketchum. Prosaically Ernest named him Blackie and the dog appeared to approve. He accepted me politely and with obedience. He was an Alaskan springer spaniel, Ernest decided.

When we heard of Mark Hellinger's death in Los Angeles, we were doubly grateful for our hoard of wildlife food, for Ernest told me that he had returned to Mrs. Hellinger the $25,000 which was the first payment under her husband's contract. "She'll need it if he always gambled as he did here," said my fellow. But it left us without reserves. Neither of us was concerned at being broke. We had both been poor before. But I was offended at Mrs. Hellinger's apparent failure to appreciate Ernest's gesture. She did not even acknowledge the receipt of the money. When we heard later that she had married a Canadian millionaire I resented her discourtesy more. But Ernest dismissed the neglect with only a few expletives.

With the candles lit on the tree we opened presents that Christmas morning and there was something for everybody including Sinsky and Roberto, the Arnolds and Taylor, who dropped in, and Lillian Ross of *The New Yorker,* who had appeared the day before to talk to Ernest about Sidney Franklin, the bullfighter from Brooklyn. The most endearing—and, it turned out, enduring—of all the gifts, I thought, was a Western leather belt with a chased silver and gold buckle which the three boys bought for me. It became a prized part of my wardrobe and continues so.

After a frigid night of carol singing with Johnny Lister's chorus while ski instructors snaked down Dollar Mountain making a river of light with their big torches, I was too tired to cook. But the children wanted pheasant for Christmas dinner and implemented their choice by plucking the birds. With accompanying fruits and vegetables we disposed of a gala, if crowded, dinner. (I was always appalled by the speed with which an entire afternoon's work disappeared.) Afterward I pressed Lillian into dish-wiping service, which she performed without complaint. No dishwasher graced my tiny kitchen and very rarely did it occur to any of my male guests that I could use help at clean-up time. I almost enjoyed transforming the kitchen from rubble to order.

It seemed a long time since Ernest and I had been alone together and I was beginning to feel merely a piece of his backdrop. Any fool could observe that this interval was not a matter of intentional neglect, I reflected. Whenever I was not handy, he wrote copiously how much he missed and needed me. With so many friends to entertain and amuse, he simply didn't see me in the landscape. I did not like it, but I could not invent a situation which would correct it. A paragraph in a letter from my father helped me. My mother must have perpetrated some local explosion, for my father wrote: "Sometimes I think that woman was not made out of a rib from Adam when he was asleep, that Darwin's idea is much more reasonable—that women came up out of the water— they are so closely related to the nature of water in so many ways. They can be so calm, so friendly, so attractive, so comforting to look upon in their quiet moods, but when a breeze comes up they change and when a storm rages within their depths, they can bring terror to the heart of a man."

If, after forty years of companionship, a misunderstanding between my parents could evoke such reflections, I had better keep my peace, I decided.

8

Changing Scenery

LATE JANUARY AND early February accorded south-central Idaho charming weather that year—bright skies, no storms—so pleasant that Sepp Froehlich had to dismiss his beginners' class, which I had joined, on the lower slopes of Dollar Mountain, there being nothing on which to ski except mud and sagebrush. I arranged with Les Outzs to practice privately from the top of Dollar where something resembling snow remained for a while on the ground. Leaving the liftchair, Les would find a few skeins of ice among the sagebrushes and shout, "This is dandy. Come on." I would follow doubtfully. Moving well away from the accustomed runs, Les would find patches of snow miraculously close enough together to propel skis, and thus lead me finally to the mud of the bottom of the hill. Until one morning I asserted, "It's amusing. It's comic. But it's not skiing." Wistfully, Les agreed. The top slopes of Baldy Mountain were still sufficiently padded with snow, but my untrained knee muscles—I did not think then about ankles—were still not strong enough to use them. I was ready to go home, and we prepared to return to Cuba. In late February or March I was supposed to stand trial in Cuba for possessing weapons of war. A week before we left, new snow whirled down.

When he saw luggage dragged out from closets and under beds, Blackie sensed change in the air, and established himself in the front seat of the Buick even before we started packing it and refused to move out, even for food. So I gave him food and affection and assurances in the car, and Ernest murmured, "Don't worry, old boy. You'll come with us."

Thirteen days later, walking Blackie in Daytona Beach, I reflected that we had traversed four different zones of place names. In the Northwest, shops and cafés, streets and motels were named Rocky Mountain, Alpine or Sage. In west Texas the names were Cortez, Coronado, Mexican or Gringo, while along the Gulf of Mexico everything was Magnolia, Southern, Live Oak or Delta. Now we had entered the Surf, Sun, Sea Breeze and Pelican zone. By the time we reached Pauline's house in Whitehead Street, Key West, we had driven 4,246 miles, and been contented and entertained every leisurely foot of the way.

Pauline and I made a cheerful girls reunion, but Ernest was uneasy as guest in the house where he had so long been master, and now that their mutual danger of Patrick's illness had passed Pauline could not resist pricking his self-esteem.

"Nice little place I have here, don't you think?"

Ernest's antennae reported the oncoming attack and he kept silent.

"Of course, you know a woman really can't run a place properly by herself. Needs that wonderful authority of a man. There's nothing in this world to match the male prerogative. His right to come and go . . . especially go. . . ."

I dropped a book on the floor and began apologies. Pauline did not hear me.

"These animals on the floor. They were my partner's idea. Lovely word, partners. Lovely idea . . . until it blows apart."

Charles and Lorine Thompson arrived for dinner and I greeted them with such effusion that they were embarrassed. Pauline's attack collapsed and she was instantly the winning, thoughtful hostess. Ernest uttered no syllable, his face only settling into a petroglyph.

"My poor lamb," I muttered as we were going to bed in his old workroom. "Tough going."

"My poor kitten," Ernest said.

Two long-ingrown convictions had stopped me from probing into Ernest's reasons for his "poor kitten." One was that, having heard my mother repeating herself on some subject from various points of the compass, I had, aged fourteen or fifteen, resolved never to be a nag, however deficient I might be in other manners. The other, developed in years of newspaper reporting with its delvings into people's privacies, was that people have a right to keep their inner sanctums secluded from public scrutiny.

Amidst the joys and surprises of homecoming I was concerned that our other dogs, the band of agreeable but nondescript characters who had gravitated to the Finca but lived outside the house, might upset Blackie's introduction to his new domain. Ernest had thought of that. While we were still unloading luggage and I was greeting servants and looking about, he introduced Blackie to the incumbent beasts. I noticed him following some of them around the corner of the garage, Blackie at his heels. Whatever the dog dialogue was, Blackie had to assert his authority only a couple of times before peace reigned. He was a bit bigger than any other dog, and the problem of territory never arose, since little Negrita never challenged his place at Papa's feet, his realm for some twelve years. To us peripheral characters of the household he was always polite, often enchanting.

Inspecting the Finca, I decided that there was truth in the ancient Spanish proverb, *"El ojo del dueño engorda el caballo"* (The eye of the owner fattens the horse). Our house servants and gardeners were not shiftless. Fico, René's young helper, had filled some bowls with assorted flowers to welcome us. They were willing workers and bright, lovable people. They simply did not notice dust, tarnish, stains, weeds, plants needing pruning. I got busy.

Our law case as suspected gun-suppliers to the now-aborted invasion of Santo Domingo was due in a provincial court and Bumby flew down to lend his prestige to our hearing, which was pre-fixed by Paco Garay

272

anyhow. We appeared on time in the little whitewashed frame courtroom, sat on wooden benches until we were called to testify to our innocence against the charge. The German pistols, Bumby testified, were souvenirs he had picked up from dead Wehrmacht officers, and since they were no use to him, he had left them among the general detritus of his father's house. When it was finished in about twenty minutes I asked our appointed lawyer why I shouldn't sue the Cuban government for arrest on false assumptions.

"Costará tiempo y dinero, y además, no vale la pena" (It will take time and money, and besides it's not worth the trouble). Suing governments was an exercise in futility, I knew, but I yearned for a demitasse of revenge.

Ernest was writing on something steadily every morning and I was getting the tower windows and staircase railing installed and designing the Spartan furniture—bookcases and a big table without drawers for Ernest's workroom there—the table of majagua, a beautiful, soft-toned Cuban indigenous hardwood which was streaked with gray, olive and lavender, and so would blend with the olive-green tiles of the floor. It would take Pancho a couple of hours to drill the holes for each of the table's few screws, but the majagua was impervious to the assaults of termites and I could feel assured that the table would last as long or longer than we would.

Ernest had mentioned several times during our journey from Ketchum to Key West that this year he would like to go somewhere other than Idaho for our hiatus from Cuba during the humid, heavy, hurricane weather of autumn. Sun Valley was becoming too popular, he felt, with too many newcoming jerks among the returning old-timers. Looking at a book of Cézanne reproductions one evening he suggested, "We could cruise the Cézanne country this fall."

"Why not? Let's take the Buick. And hire a chauffeur there, so you can look instead of always driving." Provence might be lovely in the autumn. The harbor of Havana was constantly studded with ships from European ports.

Driving home with Juan in my convertible one noontime after marketing in Havana, I noticed a smartly painted ship warped to a nearby wharf and stopped the car. Aboard the ship some kind fellow showed me the first-class staterooms (small), the salon (small) and the dining room (small) and told me the ship's schedule. She was off the next day for Genoa, but she would be back in Havana in June and again in September. Her scheduled stops on the northward route included the Madeira Islands, Lisbon, Cannes then Genoa. She could, maybe, lash an automobile to her forward deck. Her name was *Jagiello*. She had been built in Hamburg before the war for the Turks for passenger and cargo service in the Black Sea, had been awarded to the Poles as a war prize and was now earning her keep —perhaps—on this trans-Atlantic route. The officers were mostly Polish, the crew Italian. I got home bursting with the news and at lunch we got out charts and made plans. Ernest would like to try fishing in the Sargasso Sea.

With delight and dismay I became a capitalist on or about my birthday, April 5. Beatrice Guck sent me some common stock of a well-established U.S. company, the first such property I had ever owned. Sinsky, as always when his ship was in the port of Havana, was staying with us, and he and Ernest grinned when I pranced about the sitting room proclaiming my new status, waving my stock certificates.

"Not that I'm sure I approve of capitalism," I said after a pause. "Do you suppose this company is grinding its workers' bones to powder?"

Sinsky emitted one of his rumbling, ear-hurting laughs. "You shouldn't worry."

"You work harder, for nothing, than they do, my kittner," Ernest said.

"Ha. But I get special compensation," I said and pounced on him for a kiss.

As Ernest's forty-ninth birthday approached, he decided that he would like to observe it aboard *Pilar* rather than at the pool at home, as the year before, or at the Club de Cazadores, the day's disruptive setting years earlier. With Gregorio's cooperation I transferred caviar, champagne, food and birthday cake to *Pilar* and before boarding her for a short cruise to

Puerto Escondido, we dropped into the Floridita with Sinsky for a couple of Papa Dobles (double-sized daiquiris without sugar) before we went down to the city dock where Gregorio would take us across the bay to *Pilar*'s anchorage at Casa Blanca. The Floridita was demonstrating its usual conviviality. Cuban girls wearing bright dresses, bright smiles, with elaborate hairdos and ample posteriors, clung to the arms of men in *guayaberas* on their way through the bar to the dining room at the back. The sounds of laughter mingled with that of dice rattling in their cup, of the *conjunto*'s guitars humming, electric mixers whirring and the lottery-ticket man's hawking on the street outside. *"Gana un millón de pesos,"* he was yelling.

Ernest fished in his gray-flannel pocket and sent Sinsky outside to buy a ticket. "Let's buy Miss Mary a *millón de pesos*." Papa was a faithful patron of the national lottery, but he never won. Maybe he thought that a ticket designated for me would bring better luck. He handed me the bulky packet of thickly printed gray papers. "Here you are, heiress."

"I'm an heiress, already. I feel just like an heiress."

"You mean rich,—or poor?" Papa asked.

"Both, of course. I'm so rich, I'm stingy. Never tip more than seven or eight percent. But I'm so poor, I compare prices in three stalls in the market before I buy a tomato. I'm so rich I never pick up a tab. Give my friends the honor of buying me food and drink. I'm so rich I never carry that commonplace stuff, money. I'm so rich I'm afraid of strangers. And of being taken. Unlike you poors."

"The rich are different from us," Ernest muttered, paraphrasing Scott Fitzgerald. "They think money alone confers distinction."

"The poor slobs. I'm not that kind of heiress. I'm democratic. Not the fragile, untouchable kind of rich. You touch me any time you like, lamb." We had kept Gregorio waiting more than an hour. But we were amusing ourselves, it was already Ernest's birthday, and for once no tourists had come over to bother us. In the cool quiet of 2 a.m., we ambled down Obispo Street to the dock where a fish wholesaler, a lantern held high in front of his scale, was weighing the catches of Havana's commercial fishermen, great baskets of red snapper, mullet, kingfish and groupers, sweet-smelling with their eyes still bright from the sea. Star reflections glinted from the moving silky surface of the bay, the lights of Regla, far across the water, and Casa Blanca shone dim yellow, and the shaft of the Morro Castle's beacon swung smoothly in its arc. We lingered in the beauty and tranquility, watching the weighing, the lantern rays touching the patient faces of the fishermen reminding me of Goya drawings. But as I learned the wholesaler's weighing and paying system, I decided he was shortchanging some of his suppliers and said so. "That's closer to thirty-nine kilos. Not thirty-eight," I chirped.

"Pay her no attention," Sinsky said in quick harbor-accented Spanish. "She's just received a big inheritance." The fishermen grunted, and the wholesaler and his helper paid no attention, as suggested. He was weighing a gleaming 26-kilo wahoo.

"He is worth more than seventeen cents a pound," I protested. "He'll bring more than the others in the market."

"Eighteen cents," said the wholesaler.

"I'll give you thirty cents a pound for him, right here," said I grandly.

"We don't need him," Gregorio interrupted. "We haven't got much ice aboard." It was time for me to shut up, I realized, not a minute too soon. Gregorio rowed us across the bay in our skiff, caught Sinsky's arm to steady him as we climbed aboard *Pilar* and went immediately to his bunk in the fo'c's'le. He had waited three hours for us at the dock. Our three bunks were made up and waiting, but Papa and Sinsky decided they needed a morningcap and uncorked a bottle of champagne. Five hours later I did not hear us weigh anchor, or start the motor, or even the scratch of the outriggers as Gregorio swung them to their working angle after we left port. As we were angling across the Gulf Stream off Bacuranao about noon, Gregorio's shout, "Feeeesh! Feeesh!" finally woke me. The fish was a wahoo, smaller than the one we had admired on the dock.

"Birthday present. What a beauty birthday present,"

I shouted from below as Papa carefully reeled it in from up top.

"I accept him with pride, joy, and thanks," Papa said, still reeling.

"I was just stink happy all day," he wrote later to Lillian Ross with whom he was conducting a spirited correspondence.

Months later in Italy my husband sometimes whispered into various ears that he had married an heiress, and behind a curtain in a hairdressing shop I overheard one customer confiding to another that Signor Hemingway had married a childbride who was also an heiress.

"Remember he is a creator of fiction," I whispered to my friend, Isabella Angeloni, who ran the shop.

In June I had run over to Key West to escape hostessing duties at the Finca Vigía and swim quietly in Pauline's pool. Now in late July we agreed that I should make a short checking-up visit to my parents in Chicago before we took off for Europe. Ernest, who had encumbered himself with little more than a hip-pocket flask, an extra shirt and binoculars on his last tour of France, now tended to think of it as some sort of course for survival of the best-equipped. With dedicated devotion to his diet, both liquid and solid, he had got his weight down to about 210 pounds and his blood pressure almost to normal, and France would present problems to his keeping thus. José Luis with reason complained that many French medicines were not trustworthy. So we planned a sizable suitcase which would contain only vitamins and medicines made mostly in Switzerland, Germany and the U.S.A., and available in Havana. On such a long sea voyage we would need books. We planned a book bag. We would need both town and country, daytime and evening shoes, a shoe bag.

The *Jagiello* was to sail from Havana on September 7. A month earlier I flew to Chicago to visit my parents and my Guck cousins.

On August 3, Ernest wrote: "Last night when I woke in the night and you weren't there I thought I must have done something awful for my kitten to have left me for another bed. Then I knew you were just on a trip. . . .

"Cotsies Pride came. Lovely cow [Mayito Menocal had sent us a milk cow as a present], small, sort of Topi colored. Gives seven liters in the morning and seven at night. . . . Calved a month ago. . . . So she will save us 44.60 [$] a month on milk and give us double what we are getting plus a calf a year. . . . Draining pool today . . . there will be lovely clean water for you to swim. . . . Gigi sends his love too. . . . Try to go to Art Institute and see the Manets and the Winslow Homers for me. Also Inness's The Haunt of the Heron. . . ."

My father was job hunting. Since his recovery from his year-old ordeal in St. Luke's Hospital, he had felt well enough to work full-time in one or another office dealing in timber, although he was refusing to take the medication his doctors urged on him. He had sent me copies of several good, succinct letters outlining his experience, and now he was applying for a job to the commissioner of lands of Idaho. Which caused Ernest to ask me to reply: "Ernest feels very strongly that now is the time for you to rest, write if you like, read, and look after Mother. But not for rushing into strenuous outdoor work. He asked me to tell you so. You deserve a little leisure in your life, darling . . . why not take it now."

I was in the final throes of packing—early on, Ernest had discovered that if he neglected long enough to pack for himself, I would do it—when John Dos Passos called from Miami to suggest he come over for a few days. We would be leaving in three days, Ernest said, but Dos came anyway, a large, subdued-seeming man in our boisterous household, and chatted to Ernest while he wrote scores of predated checks for the Finca's weekly and monthly expenses. I had been so impressed with the research which had gone into Mr. Dos Passos's books and their sharp prose that I found him disappointing as a companion. But if little wit crackled, at least he and Ernest managed to repair some rifts in their friendship from long before.

9

The Italian Journey

AFTER A PROLONGED farewell party, we afloat in champagne in the ship's bar, the *Jagiello* pulled out of Havana's harbor, and by middinner, our Polish captain, Jon Godecki, and Ernest were addressing each other with Christian names. We made easy, immediate friends with Ben Lorini, the bartender, with Felix, our Genoese room steward with his ski-jump nose, and with Polish Rosa, our stewardess, Ernest advising me, "Always trust a woman with steel teeth," and with a few passengers. The *Jagiello* seemed almost our private yacht.

Until our Polish chief engineer approached me unsteadily in the bar one evening, obviously drunk, muttering, "What are you—what are you?" My husband introduced himself and asked how the engines were doing. The engineer demanded to know if the big blue car bolted to the forward deck was ours, and what right had we to such a big car. "Capitalist, bourgeois pig," he muttered, poking Ernest in the chest. With conspicuous constraint, Ernest wrote his name on a bar slip, handed it to the man and said, "I have never killed a chief engineer, but now I'd like to very much. And if you do that again, I'll surely kill you in the morning." He would send his second within half an hour, he said, then found Vittorio Maresca, the second purser, and sent him to challenge the engineer to a duel on the boat deck at seven o'clock the next morning.

Vittorio delivered the message, found pistols in the crew's quarters and brought Ernest an Italian officer's sidearm from World War II, with ammunition.

"I want to go with you in the morning," I said as we were going to bed.

"You can't do that, you might get hit. I'll shoot him low," Ernest said happily. "Just mess up one leg."

As I was breakfasting Ernest came into the cabin and reported that Vittorio and he had waited forty minutes on the boat deck, Vittorio had gone to the engineer's cabin, tried without success to rouse him and that some of the crew had overheard him shouting through the door.

Since Ernest had tried fishing off the stern of the engine room, its crew were his friends, and now a succession of envoys presented themselves surreptitiously with messages. They would be overjoyed to push the engineer overboard and save the Signor the trouble of shooting him. The ship's blacksmith would with pleasure do him in with one blow which all would swear was accidental. The engine room had several poorly protected moving parts into which the chief could drunkenly fall or be pushed. They would really be doing the ship a favor. When Ernest withheld approval of the death-dealing schemes, the crew's poet-in-residence sublimated them into a poem of some thirty four-line stanzas which with due ceremony and much wine was presented in the engine room, Ernest accepting it in an atrocious hilarious blend of Italian and Spanish. (The poem's fervor far outranked its quality, but Ernest kept it carefully in his bottle bag for months.)

When a dance was scheduled for first- and second-class passengers on the calm, warm afterdeck, I turned it into an all-ship party, bringing Cuban boys up from third class and priests and grandmothers to applaud them, and drastically depleted the ship's supply of champagne. At Funchal, Madeira, with Vittorio the purser, we zipped up the mountain from subtropical palms and bougainvillaea to temperate-zone pines, and toboganned down, Vittorio and I screaming between narrow walls, Ernest entranced. At Lisbon we toured the fish market and dug into the first newspapers we'd seen in two weeks. In the swirling currents beyond Gibraltar we saw huge schools of smiling porpoises and five sperm whales spouting plumes of water. At

Cannes, where we intended unloading the Buick for a tour of Provence, we found only a narrow wooden dock tilting in a storm, and decided to go on to Genoa. There the friendly sing-song language and cheerful welcomes so beguiled my friend that he decided that we must go on in Italy, at least to Stresa overlooking Lago Maggiore. People working in the fields hailed the blue car with its bright red-leather seats, *"Che bella macchina!"*

At Stresa the doorman of the hotel came out and said, "Welcome back, Signor Hemingway." After thirty years. Papa *très émotionné.* Our sophisticated, cheerful chauffeur, Ricardo, whom we had hired in Genoa, had indubitably telephoned ahead, identifying Ernest, I felt sure. We shelved our plans for touring Provence. The next day Ernest told a coterie of the Italian press that I was his "childbride." They took the joke as fact, and it accompanied us for months.

A week later at Cortina d'Ampezzo, a local sportsman, Count Federico Kechler, came to our hotel to invite us to fish at his favorite lake, just across the Austrian border, and a few days later with new Italian friends we set off. Up the valley from Cortina the fields were leaf-green, pine-green, olive-green and a dozen shades of mustard and gold. We fished the lake with Federico's spinning reels and from the shore Ernest caught one small salmon trout. It was a day of less achievement than expectation. But it led Federico, who had been big in the Italian navy and spoke English with a pure, unembroidered Mayfair accent, to adopt us as fledgling members of his and his brothers' families, and many other families of the Veneto and Venice subsequently gave us unexpected and unstinted hospitality.

At our Cortina hotel, Mizzi Springer, the hotel's secretary, told me her life story. Before the war she had lived in Australia, with her husband, and learned English. "But madam, it was so terrible—my heart nearly broke of loneliness." They came back here, her son went to Africa with the Italian army and when the Germans came to Italy she worked in an officer's mess. "That was better than being a translator." Then she heard that her son had been killed. Then

281

that her husband, in Sicily, had been killed by a bomb. Then, in 1944, when the Germans retreated, the local guerrillas clapped her in prison at Vicenza. When the Americans came to interview prisoners, some of the guerrillas accompanying them, she offered to translate. That night the guerrillas whisked her to another prison and there one midnight got the women out of their beds onto the stone floor and indiscriminately shot thirteen of them. Mizzi was so horrified at their shooting a sixteen-year-old girl near her that, trying to stop the holes in the girl's chest, she only realized later that she had a bullet in her thigh. That was June. Until December she had no medical attention. Then they finally released her and she came back alone to her mountain country. "But none of it that happened to me seemed so bad," she says, "because I had already lost my husband and my son. It was like walking out into the streets with no clothes—so unprotected."

Years later when she was hospitalized in Rome, Mizzi mentioned that Ernest had befriended her in Cortina (with a generous gift of money). She wrote us that the medicos did not believe her story. When Ernest replied, enclosing a check, the hospital moved her to better quarters and doubled its attentions to her.

That October of 1948 we chatted haphazardly of wintering in Portofino, pausing in Venice on the way. But Ernest was finding Cortina so enticing that I began house hunting there and soon found the right place for us, the Villa Aprile (endearing name) on the edge of town overlooking gentle green slopes which would give us front-yard skiing later. With renting formalities completed we turned the Buick southward and at San Martino found Federico Kechler hospitably waiting outside his house to welcome us. That night I wrote: "Lovely lunch, lovely people, and tonight, Venice, Venice, Venice—city of exquisite bridges, the moon just after full, coming up grandly over the Grand Canal, a wonder challenge in its 'mystère' but Papa falling asleep soon after dinner, 9:30. Night is the best time to approach an unknown city, so your first explorations are in semi-darkness and mysterious. But we dined in the room and went to bed.

"We are in the Palace of the Compte Gritti (1496) with an ebullient Venetian glass chandelier, a huge inconvenient room just opposite the Church of Santa Maria della Salute on the Grand Canal."

The next day, October 19, I wrote: "Venice is more beautiful, and more mixed up, than I could have imagined. There is not only the Café Florian, rather like Maxim's in Paris, where Casanova used to eat and drink. There are the 13th Century mosaics, Byzantine, in St. Mark's along with the mosaics copied from modern 18th Century painters showing all of Noah's story, the ark and afterwards, also the whole story, in precise lines, of Adam and Eve. There is the Palazzo Ducale one wall of which is 18th Century and very modern looking, and three walls of pre-Renaissance. The stairway of the giants, surmounted by statues of Mars and Neptune is a 'bijou.'

"I went in the morning with the sculptor Ennio Petenello covering my eyes just before we entered the Piazza San Marco, and he explained its properties and where the ancient church had been and all the changes to the tower, the campanile. Everywhere in the church garnets gleam, sapphires, rubies behind the looted screen and outside a tremendous variety of style, each column of the Doge's Palace distinctive, with cormorants and lions and fruits and senators and virgins. Century sifting down on century and each leaving its mark.

"The bells, beginning at daylight and continuing intermittently until well after dark seem more mellow and less clangy than in other towns. Water softened bells?

"Took photo of Papa beside Sansovino statue of Neptune above 'Heavenly' stairs at Palazzo Ducale. Neptune and he have the same structure, except that Neptune has narrower shoulders and more hair. Of course Neptune was nude and Papa was covered by his old flannel slacks and tweed jacket."

At the invitation of Nanyuki Franchetti, we went duck shooting at his big place edging the lagoon northeast of Venice. One of his men poled us in a skiff to our blind, a big barrel sunk far out in the lagoon, and we waited there for the sound of a horn signaling that shooting would begin, smelling the marsh, watching the sky change from orange-pink to silver and the reedy shores emerge from mauve to yellow and green and rust and later the mountains appear smoky blue in the north. We never heard the horn, but when ducks began coming over us in pairs, families and clouds, some so high they were fly-sized, we began shooting, Ernest knocking down eighteen with a new gun he had bought, I shooting horribly with a borrowed gun too heavy for me, hitting one. He must have been ashamed of my shooting but he said nothing.

That night we stayed at the country house of Federico's brother Titi Kechler and his wife, near Latisana, and the next day the three fellows walked the place and got fifteen pheasants and six hares. "We've been shooting in a Venetian blind," Ernest muttered happily.

On All Souls' Day we splashed across the lagoon, past Murano, the glass-blowing island, Burano, the lace island, to lunch at Torcello where we loved the inn—Cipriani of Harry's Bar was and is its owner—and Papa decided immediately after looking at the rooms, a little sitting room with a fireplace and French doors overlooking the garden and cathedral and a big enough bedroom with two big beds and a yellow bathroom, to move there instead of going to Portofino. Home in the dark by vaporetto, Ernest singing vigorously and slightly off-key to the gondolieri in the canals. Two days later we moved in a luggage-stuffed launch to the Locanda Cipriani, Torcello. I installed our books, rearranged furniture and reading lamps, and made a pile of sweet-smelling logs in front of our fireplace. As we lunched near the fireplace in the inn's empty dining room, Ernest entertained me with reminiscences of his boyhood.

When he was four, they told him that if he put salt on a bird's tail, he could catch it. He found a robin, stalked him carefully all over the lawn, waited for him to find a big worm and when the robin was occupied pulling all the long worm out of the earth, he put salt from his left hand on the tail and caught it with his right. He was an obedient boy, he reported, and thought his parents always right and their decisions unquestionable. But as he grew up he was increasingly disturbed by their quarrels when many nights his father revised his will, and they both charged him with family responsibilities beyond his capacity. In the mornings they were friends again and looked on him, as the only spectator of the quarrel, with hostility.

From about age nine to fourteen, E. used to make horseshoes at the forge of Mr. Jim Dilworth, forcing the fire with the bellows, in Horton Bay, Michigan, putting in the straight piece of iron, holding it with the pincers.

He would work heating the iron until it was incandescent-silver, then take it out, bend it over the nose of the anvil, then bring it down, put it back in the fire, and put it on the anvil once more and hammer down into the hot iron a spike to make the holes. They used to shoe the horses with big calks, he said, the shoes much heavier than the racing-type or those of Dan Patch in his pictures. (I was a Dan Patch fan.)

In Oak Park one day when he was about seven years old, there was a railway strike. It was 1905–06, and Marshall Field was making deliveries with armed vans. (M.F. delivery people had gone out in sympathy.) An M.F. van arrived with a hat for his mother. Ernest signed for the hat and noticed the price, $135, and he was horrified at his mother's extravagance. Also horrified, I doubted the figure but he maintained it was that much.

His happiest time in Oak Park was one fall when his mother had typhoid fever. "We had no discipline at all by that bitch. We took the driving horses and the girls used to ride behind in the buggies." Their mother was in the hospital. They never went to see her. "We had complete anarchism in the house. We used to go out to where the gypsy wagons were, twenty or thirty, in Thatcher's Woods." When Ernest killed his first pheasant, the pheasant went almost straight up. E. led a long way with his single-barreled 20-gauge shotgun. Ernest put him inside his shirt. "He was dead but he wouldn't recognize it," and he flopped and scratched Ernest's belly. "You had to get rid of them quick because they had just introduced them, and we had no permit to shoot them."

Over leisurely luncheons in the empty dining room at Torcello my husband gave me a series of autobiographical sketches, each in such precise detail that I could never detect when he skidded off fact into fiction.

Marcelline, his older sister by one gestation, he tried to like, but never did. (She was pretty "with a beauty Indian nose, but a crowder." He had to wait for every social date until she had been invited, and only the scum was left. "That's enough to embitter anybody.")

Then Ura, the nicest and the best, who used to sit on the stairs when he had returned from World War I and eat shrimp salad from the icebox so he wouldn't have to drink alone, which she thought especially evil.

Sunny (Madelaine), his third sister, was a great baseball player, also a pianist and harpist.

Carol was the most beautiful of the family. "She married Jack Gardner. I was always absolutely nuts about her. She looked as a girl exactly as I looked as a boy. No compromise, no change. We called her Beefy." It was a love name, had nothing to do with beef.

The Baron, his only brother, the girls called Dregs. He was born when Ernest was away on a trip his senior year in high school.

E. was the pride of the Petoskey baseball team, he averred. One winter he worked on the county road, shoveling gravel at $2.25 a day, and the same winter in the cement factory, shoveling as always. "I had the theory that if you shoveled good enough, you wouldn't have any trouble."

Ernest also worked in the pump factory—$4.65 a day—collaring pumps, but he was "a big *fracaso*"; then for George O'Neil, who ran the hotel in Petoskey, as doorman to throw out drunken lumberjacks.

Dutch Pailthorp (Edwin C.) was his best friend. His father was prosecuting attorney. "I thought maybe I ought to be a lawyer, as a recourse, a thing to fall back on, and I read law all winter in his office."

Ernest got engaged to two girls at one time. "I was twenty to twenty-one. Both of them were absolutely wonderful girls." Marjorie Bump and Grace Edith Quinlan, "the most beautiful girls I ever knew."

And then he found his true love, a Jewish girl, Irene

Goldstein. He had seen her just the year before on the drive to Sun Valley, the best-looking woman in the town. "She owns the ex-Hart Schaffner and Marx store."

He didn't go back to Chicago for two winters. He had had a break with his family after some Petoskey kids invited him to a night picnic and he went as chaperone. The next day the mothers of the children came to complain, so his mother accused him of molesting the children. Ernest left Windemere, the family cottage on Walloon Lake, and went first to see his friend Bill Smith and told him the accusations, then to A. B. Nickey, who was a member of a Memphis lumber family, because he was the only man around who'd been married twice.

A better chapter than this was when he was under indictment for killing a blue heron. "It happened at the upper end of Walloon Lake, just where it joins Little Traverse Bay." A family named Weyburn chartered Ernest to take them to the head of the lake, so they could walk over the hump of the land and see Little Traverse Bay. Ernest had a two-cylinder motorboat, the *Ursula,* the same he used for delivering the mail and selling the vegetables. "We reached the head of the lake and a blue heron got up, the biggest I ever saw. I picked up my rifle, a .22-caliber Marlin, lever-action, and I thought, just for fun. Try to shoot him in the head and if I don't hit the head, no harm done. Just shot in high spirits, showing off a little bit. Hit him just behind the eye.

"I'm fourteen, not more. Heron was flying with his long legs out and he fell down dead in the water. So I put him under stern seat of the launch, folding his neck around and making him comfortable. Then ran up to the end of the lake, anchored launch, put Weyburns ashore, took them across height of land to show them the bay, came back to the boat and my heron was gone. So then I knew there was trouble.

"What happened was, the game warden lived at the upper end of the lake and his son had seen me shoot. He took the name of the boat and the heron. I had a sinking feeling in my stomach."

He took his passengers back home calmly. "Next

thing I heard, I was working on the farm in Longfield [on the other side of Walloon Lake from Windemere], which I managed, worked and ran—beets, carrots, Swiss chard, lettuce, new potatoes, radishes, tomatoes, peas, beans, both snap and string—sister Ura comes over in a canoe and says 'We must get away right away because there are two game wardens at Windemere waiting for you to come back. They're going to arrest you and send you to the reform school.' " He left home, he said, and went to live with the Ojibways.

My enduring friends Alan and Lucy Moorehead had invited me to stay with them at their beautiful house at Fiesole, above Florence, and on November 17, I was off on the 8:50 vaporetto to the garage of Venice and Ricardo and I left in the Buick in the rain for Ferrara and Bologna.

On November 19 Lucy Moorehead met us at Fiesole, she looking every bit as fresh and pretty and alert as when we were girls in London. Her and Alan's house, which in the fifteenth century belonged to one Poliziano, family poet to Lorenzo "the Magnificent" of the Medici and his children's tutor, was rambling, drafty and lovely, filled with a handsome assortment of heavy furniture, huge tables, small tables, big divans, an enormous fireplace. We lunched with the children in the sunroom off the terrace, they both very sweet, Caroline a gay doll with big brown eyes, Johnny a thoughtful, undemonstrative, very adult boy with many of what I remembered as his father's mannerisms.

Lucy and I chatted breathlessly far into the night. Alan was in Beirut making speeches at a UNESCO meeting as one of the British delegation.

As usual Ernest wrote to me consistently. The day after I left Torcello he wrote: "Felt pretty damn lost and lonely when you left but got to work cleaning up the letters. . . . Today is sharp, cold and beautiful, the haze burning off the lagoon. . . .

"I'll bet even you get tired in the Uffizi. That was the gallery that really used to knock me out. I'd think, 'show me one more goddamn Madonna and see how you like it Gentlemen.' You'll love Siena. I expect to hear you went to Rome since it is so close. So don't mind doing it. That's what there's a car for. See some of the Etruscan stuff if you are in Umbria. They have me mystified still. Good around Orbetello if you go that way. I walked all over that country with Ezra. . . ."

On November 22, Lucy and I went to look at the Uffizi Palace and I liked best the Fra Angelico of the crowning of the Virgin, the angels tooting horns and trumpets so intently, the host of people lower down such individuals with faces as in portraits. Also, the various Virgins of Lippi, who fell in love with one girl when he was doing a fresco in the chapel of her convent, and carried her off.

Lionel Fielding and the J. B. Priestleys came to lunch at Lucy's one day and afterward we all went to Bernard Berenson's house for tea. Mr. Priestley didn't recognize me as the woman who had unintentionally libeled him "too big for his britches" years before or politely pretended he had forgotten it. But his ego continued fascinating. Driving to the Villa I Tatti of Berenson, he mentioned a cultural meeting of the United Nations in Mexico City last year and said in that deep Yorkshire drawl, "Mind you, I was the only one who could have put it through."

Lucy had lent me their copy of B.B.'s *Florentine Painters of the Renaissance* and I had skimmed it briefly on the way to sleep a couple of nights but still felt much too ignorant of the great critic's work to merit meeting him. Ricardo drove us all up to I Tatti, squeezed together in the Buick with its top down, the sight of us so alarming the household that the footman asked us to wait when we knocked at the door. Then Berenson's kind-faced secretary, Nicky, graciously invited us inside and onto a terrace which overlooked elegant formal gardens descending in giant steps with fountains into the distances below. After we had chatted a bit with her and a librarian of the household, she suggested that I find Mr. Berenson, who would be strolling beneath his tidy trees, to tell him that tea was being served. "Don't bump into him," she ordered, smiling. Mr. B. was then eighty-three, I knew.

I raced down the lawns, found our fragile host, a fashion plate in his citified, faultless blue suit, gray fedora and gray suede gloves, and breathlessly introduced myself. "Mary Hemingway, sir. I'm to tell you that tea is being served."

"What number are you?" asked Mr. B.

"Sir? Do you number your guests?"

"Wife," said he, excusing my density, and when I told him "number four" he asked how it was Ernest had managed to get through so many wives.

"I have no simple answer for that, sir," said I as we moved up toward the house. "Of course, Ernest is a man of tremendous energy and exuberance."

"Does he demonstrate those characteristics in bed?" the renowned art expert asked in the most casual tones, totally flummoxing me. I was relieved to turn him over to the other guests and Lucy, noticing my strawberry-red face, giggled knowingly.

My moments of worry about my limited education in art were time wasted, I realized as we arranged ourselves for tea in the rather cramped space before the living room's fireplace. Mr. Priestley took over. While we women sat silent, I marveling, Mr. Priestley told Mr. Berenson about the Renaissance art of Italy, expounding articulately, elucidating cogently, even, to my stunned admiration, explaining. Clearly, he had looked at the paintings in the Uffizi and Pitti palaces at least once. Mr. Berenson received this flow of information with the grace of a great host and I sat there amazed that nobody including Mrs. Priestley interrupted with some such admonition as "come off it." If the lecture, also including some philosophy, may have wearied Mr. Berenson, I saw no signal. But Nicki, rising behind the teapot, indicated that it was time for us to leave. As we were straggling toward the doorway, Mr. B. called me back. He was standing beside the fireplace and said with authority, "You may not leave until you have given me a kiss." There he stood awaiting my salutation, his eighty-three-year-old lips still full and sensuous. I gave him what I hoped was a generous kiss and muttered, "You and Mr. H. G. Wells." But did not linger to explain.

"His primitives are really something," I wrote in my

diary that night. Lucy and I talked long and late again, I suggesting the advantages of being simply a wife, and not a harried and competing career woman. "Such fun being a wife."

From Torcello later I wrote Mr. Berenson what I hoped was an amusing note of thanks for his hospitality. To my surprise he answered it. He had been entirely aware of Mr. Priestley's pretensions. Thus began a charming exchange of letters which so attracted Ernest that after we had returned to Cuba he edged me out of the correspondence, taking over most of our end of it, wherever we were through the years, until 1957, two years before Mr. Berenson died at the age of ninety-four.

Everybody in Fiesole had gravely warned me that the road from Florence to Nervi was constantly harassed by highway robbers, *banditi*. But we encountered no *banditi*.

There were very dark-looking characters in the La Spezia suburbs, with burning black eyes, and so many young boys standing around in the streets I imagined there was much unemployment. As we left La Spezia (badly bombed—it was a naval base) Ricardo said, "Now a little stairs," and we wound in quick turns up, up, up, the engine clattering. Poor gas. We passed wonderful wild mountains with a few broken houses, but the women, children and men smiling, lifting caps, saying *"Ciao"*—still no *banditi*.

In Genoa, Ricardo took me to look at the Christopher Columbus house, a dusty two-storied tiny place abutting a big noisy street. In bed that night I noticed that a week without Ernest was about all I could stand. Then my battery needed recharging and in the middle of attending to chores, I was devoting most of my attention to wishing for him and worrying about him.

On November 28, in Milan, I wrote an observation: "I am a bad traveler. My inclination is to acclimatize myself and feel at home and therefore to minimize or ignore the differences between what is new and what I am accustomed to. A better traveler, or one who sees himself as dramatic because he is moving through new places, is one who always retains his original values and habits and who, therefore, is constantly impressed,

291

awed, frightened, amazed, delighted, disappointed, excited, inspired, fascinated, disgusted, stimulated or appalled by his new sights. I don't like Milan much. It is too big, too impersonal, too hurried, too uncurious, too brick-faced and brisk-voiced. Too commercial. But, poor traveler I, I am not indignant about Milan, merely judging, maybe unjustly."

A few days after I returned to Torcello, Papa made a short trip to Mt. Grappa and the Piave to look at his old battlefields, negotiating in the Buick the old army road which, the local guards predicted, they'd never make. Up on top he had a gala encounter with girls who were carrying a stuffed fox, the girls beating him on his bosom, wanting to be taken to America.

From our first week at Torcello I made regular pilgrimages into Venice on the afternoon vaporetto to get my hair and nails done, learning my way through the tangle of streets from the Fondamenta Nuova to the hairdresser's place near the Piazza. On my journey homeward the first afternoon, the lagoon was bleak and cold. But when a crowd of glass-blowers came aboard at Murano, bringing with them the odor of their work at the furnaces, I moved to the fresh air of the open afterdeck and into a huddle of passengers who shifted over to make room for me. After suitable *grazies* I tried to remember the word for "cold" and couldn't. So, touching the gloved hands of a bulky fellow next to me, I sang Rodolfo's phrase in *La Bohème,* "Your tiny hand is frozen." In a minute the dozen of us were sending an a cappella concert of Puccini songs with lyrics intact out over the ruffled water. They all lived at Burano, the last island of the vaporetto's circuit. Our singing society flourished once a week all the autumn.

While I was away Tony Lucarda, Venetian sculptor, persuaded Ernest to sit for him and he went out several times to work at the clay, E. in the garden looking into the sun. Each time I had seen it, the head looked excellent to me in its general lines, sides, ears, back, top, forehead, eyebrows, but too pinched together from the nose to the chin. The mouth not wide enough, the cheeks too close to the mouth. With that sour puss he should wear a pince-nez and be a Republican banker.

Tony explained to me all the steps that have to be taken between the clay and the finished bronze. They were too many, it seemed to me. Unless the art were very great, it could not be worth the trouble.

With Ricardo, I went to Cortina December 13 and found the house *piccolissima* for having guests, but the *chauffage* was working well, fireplace not too smoky, views superb. Mme. Aprile was there to help install me and we did business with the inventory, and she got out extra towels, a sled and pans, put away her cherished bric-a-brac.

It was fun fixing the house, planning food again, thinking how Ernest would enjoy the fire, the view, his reading lamp. But in the evenings, I felt quite empty, and noted how quickly—four years seemed quick for this—he had become the most important part of me.

On Christmas Eve, Maria and Liza and I fixed the tree and the crèche below it, with real white candles on the tree.

Maria was the daughter of our Austrian neighbors at the top of our hill. She brought us milk from their cows imprisoned in their stable all winter and fresh unsalted butter and was knitting us glorious almost waterproof wool socks from their sheep's wool she had cut and carded and spun herself.

Darling Liza was Eliza di Grande who, when she heard we needed a maid, walked the twenty miles from her village to ask for the job. We hired her at once. She was unsophisticated, untrained, but sweet, gentle and ever willing to do our house chores eighteen hours a day with never a frown. We paid her more than the customary wage, as much for her kindness and smile as for her steady effort, but did not tell our friends her wages, which might have irritated them. Maria hung around a lot, helping Liza ostensibly, and escaping her perhaps dour family.

Soon after we arrived Ricardo was with the two girls in the kitchen while I was buzzing around there and stepped outside to get milk from the back doorstep. As I came in again I heard Ricardo asking, "Does the

Signora do the *cucina?" Cucina* (Italian) must equal *cocina* (Spanish for kitchen, cookery) I translated to myself.

"*Sì, sì, Ricardo, è molto bene,*" I answered him and whisked off. I was learning household Italian. I was also doing most of the cookery, but Liza was the artist with homemade pasta which she rolled out on the kitchen's marble table, adding an egg or two to make it richer, or spinach juice to make it green. It was the best pasta, cut thread-thin or an inch wide, we ever ate.

Now we were alone again, reading during lunch, relaxed and free. It might have been dull for Ernest, but we stayed up engulfed in talk until 2 a.m. Christmas morning discussing U.S. trees and bloodlines and China. When I was rushing to serve dinner one evening I asked our visitor, Nanda Pivano, who is a professor of philosophy as well as translator of E.'s books, to open the wine. To my amazement she burst into tears. Didn't know how.

Lucy and Alan Moorehead arrived the evening of January 17. I met them in front of the Hotel Posta with a sleigh and we got out to the Villa Aprile in time for dinner with Ernest, just back from Venice, and good table talk, mostly of books, went on and on.

On Thursday, January 20, having come most of the way down from Pocol then heading south down the valley to lunch at our house, Alan, Lucy and I were skiing fresh tracks through one foot of fresh snow, when, after a fast, lovely schuss, I fell head over heels, thereby snapping a V-crack in my right ankle. Dr. Zarote at the Istituto Codavilla set the bone and slapped on plaster, skillfully and cheerfully. I stayed in bed until Monday, when the Mooreheads left. The cast stayed on twenty-five days, but I clumped around gingerly, careful of my pains, using Maria's *bastone*. Then Dr. Domengo made me a black felt shoe with rubber sole, and I could negotiate the tiled kitchen floor, too slippery for the plaster alone.

For a break from slush in mid-March we went down to Venice and our old room at the Gritti with new white silk curtains, the sheets ironed rose-petal smooth, the pillows soft, and its effulgent chandelier.

I woke long before sunrise, perplexed for a minute at the whole new set of night noises—dip of oars, slap of wavelets. Then heard the lonely night cry of Venice —*Po-Pe*. The man called three times, the last loud and long and sad. But I could hear no gondola sounds in response. In the morning we had gulls instead of crows, the mouth of the canal shining in a golden haze, and the orchestra of bells with new tones, limpid as the pre-sunrise sky, less throaty than those of Cortina. Counting them, Ernest said, "This town was designed for a man without a watch."

Venice was a shimmer of light, sequins on the ceiling, flutings under the eaves.

The concierge at the Gritti had sent a newspaper to E. at Cortina saying Sinclair Lewis was at the hotel, which depressed him. He liked Venice the way it was.

Anyhow, we went up to Lewis's suite, a luxurious new one at the other end of the hotel and there ensued a brisk battle of roses, almost thornless. Lewis was traveling with Mrs. Powers, the mother of his ex-girl friend, Marcella, who had up and married somebody else. "Nice chap, too," Lewis said. Mrs. Powers appeared, a silent blinking little white-haired Trilby who, seeing Europe for the first time, Lewis said, was like the child pointing out, "But father, the king has no clothes." I found it just barely possible to look at Mr. Lewis. His face was a piece of old liver, shot squarely with #7 shot at twenty yards. His hands trembled when he ate, blobs of everything oozing out between his lips. His walk was more brittle, the hinges more rusty than those of G. B. Shaw, when I last saw him in Dean Street, London, aged eighty-seven. But his mind was still sharp and glib and slick and I could accept him because he loved Italy.

He went downstairs to sit with us while we ate dinner, told us of the eulogy he had made for Ernest when they awarded him some prize or other and how neither publisher, Charlie Scribner nor Bennett Cerf, had sent a stenographer to take it down. I could see E. growing weary of the overstuffed compliments, maybe also of looking at Mr. L., but we parted amiably. During the three hours, I watched Mr. Lewis grow older and feebler and shrink, and E. grow younger, boyishly more shy, more vigorous, letting out his wit and wisdom cautiously, rationing it.

Mr. L. was disillusioned at the reception of his later books after the Nobel Prize in 1930 and hopefully predicted the same thing could happen to Ernest. He had done a series of pieces for NANA (North American Newspaper Alliance) on his winter here and gave me the cuttings to read. A few of them were pleasant travel information, two on the importance of learning languages of which he arbitrarily insisted that an educated man must read, speak, and write at least eight. (But when our courteous Calsavara, the maître d'hôtel, asked me if I didn't want "*tout petit peu*" of dessert, Lewis remarked that my Italian was excellent.) Several of his pieces were short stories of Americans in Italy, artificial and fabricated, I thought. The series ended with a one-paragraph bow to American chauvinism saying how he truly preferred a tarpaper shack in the U.S. to all the castles of Italy.

When Ernest went shooting with Nanyuki Franchetti, I took Mr. Lewis and Mrs. Powers to dinner at Harry's, he making overlarge sympathy with me at the problems of being married to a genius. He recalled bitterly Dorothy Thompson's homecomings after lecture tours, the dramatically quiet voice saying "I *do* think someone might have come to meet me," laying down her gloves. He was tormented apparently by never having time for his own work, but I pointed out that I didn't have any personal and sacred work. Back at the hotel, I wanted to talk to the gondoliers and Lewis went into their hut for a bit to listen, but soon left. I got two bottles of wine, one after the other and talked until one-thirty. Ernest was back from shooting and dead asleep. He got the best bag of the day—sixty-five —but was exhausted, his fingers nipped by the triggers, and decided to go to bed without a bath.

On March 21, we renewed our passports, remembered, as usual, a week late, it was our wedding anniversary—lunched with Gianfranco Ivancich, the brother of Adriana, who had gone duck shooting with Ernest.

Back in Cortina we found the town empty of tourists, heather brightening the hillsides, crocuses peeping out near the house, and I could walk to and from town, triumphantly, not limping. The stream still murmured busy and friendly in the night and by day the town resounded with mattress beatings. From every house and hotel came the flat noises of the poundings of furniture with the woven wicker beaters. They beat everything, chairs, sofas, mattresses, rugs. Signora Rosa told me it was absolutely necessary to keep things clean, that a vacuum cleaner would not get them dustless.

One morning Ernest said his left eye felt funny at the corner where he had been hit by the end of an oar while going to the duck blind. Also we noticed a swelling of the left side of his cheek.

The swelling grew worse, and he felt miserable. Three days later a bulge appeared behind his ear, and we called Dr. Giovanni Apostoli, our friend. He thought the eye had conjunctivitis and declared the neck swellings of no consequence, ordered an eyewash and some dark brown salve for the swellings and went off leaving me doubtful. E. had supper in bed, roast duck, and woke up in the morning with a fever.

Apostoli came the next day, gave an oil-based penicillin shot and went off satisfied. But the fever continued and a slight rash began to appear on the face, and E. more miserable, eating almost nothing, his eye constantly sticking together with mucus and the light badly hurting him. Also he was missing his reading glasses, one lens of which was shattered when the bed broke down before we left for Venice.

Before dinner the next day, Dr. Apostoli returned, confided he was worried about Ernest's having erysipelas and went upstairs to persuade him to go to a clinic in Padova for treatment. E. squirmed, fussed, objected the trip would kill him, his fever having abated only slightly, but then, facing facts and seeing Apostoli truly worried, settled down calmly and made his plans for the morning and helped me remember things to take with us.

At the Padova clinic, the Casa di Cura Morgagni, I noticed thin coatings of dust covering all but the most obvious surfaces, and the chief of staff, Dr. Bastai, who arranged for penicillin shots every three hours, took E. off sulfa and his blood pressure pills, also ordered no liquor of any kind. The next day E.'s face looked worse than before and the eye as bad. Urine tests not good. No sugar, but too much albumin. He was bored, not being able to read, and miserable. While being constantly stabbed like St. Sebastian, with needles instead of arrows, Ernest grew slowly better. I was little use at alleviating his discomforts. I read him articles from *Holiday,* and *Treasure Island,* with Jim now seeming a horrible boy, wildly undisciplined and stupid. E. said of *Treasure Island,* "It disgusted me, an adventurous little jerk like that."

Numb with boredom, the clinic food and the fluttering attentions of the nuns, Ernest recovered from the erysipelas infection, firmly refused to talk to a meeting of local doctors and we returned to Cortina. We planned to sail again from Genoa aboard the *Jagiello* on April 27. The boat would pause at Algiers, South America, Mexico and Panama, then Havana.

The first Arab I saw in Algiers was sitting in an armchair in the tree shade of a square, chatting with a white-bearded friend. The Arab had a wide, pointed, clean-shaven face, straight fierce eyebrows, luminous laughing black eyes, an attractive fellow. The women's face coverings, E. thought, looked "ridiculous" and I wondered what they could do if they had a cold in the head. They appeared to wear little or no makeup.

But those faces wrapped in white were beautiful, with thin proud noses, sharply cut lips, pointed chins, alert eyes repeatedly photogenic. My chief memory of Algiers—how very French, even Parisian, it was, with its sunlight, not the blinding white I expected of Africa, but palest Vermeer yellow of a May morning in Paris.

After stops at Gibraltar and Funchal, we rolled contentedly the 2,982 miles to La Guaira, Venezuela, savoring our luxurious leisure—I was reading André Gide's diaries—using all the time we wanted for personal games. We had joyous late mornings in bed, making happy loving talk of friends, we unpressured, unselfconscious and in effortless harmony with each other. Small loving jokes, speculations on girl and boy love, with which E. was brimming those days. The Kinsey people would not have believed us, I noted.

Ernest taught me many new delights and I taught him some. I told him my old principle of never letting myself contribute to the breakdown of somebody else's marriage, no matter how shaky a man might describe it. We mentioned Teresa "putting all her cards on the table," offering to be his mistress, the shameless contessa. The Italians were such an ancient civilization, I thought, that they don't seem to have a sense of shame as Victoria imposed it on Anglo-Saxons.

Papa's theme song those days: "I'm headed towards my Black Dog."

We made minimum efforts to get acquainted with the other passengers or the new crew, but I talked one morning with a gray-haired woman from Venezuela and found her charming, though I was distracted from our topics by her lower teeth, which to my incidental glances were a short pink stubble. We chatted Paris and fashions and servants, of the Vatican's espionage system and how it had sent large sums of money to Argentina, and about the other passengers. I liked her tranquil tolerance and eagerness to see pleasantness in everybody and her admiration for Ernest—"Many women must fall in love with him because he is so good and sweet." So I told her of his Venetian admirers, aged seventeen to eighty-four. It was her ready willingness to admire others which had surrounded her with friends on the boat.

The *Jagiello*'s passengers arranged a big day of festival before we reached La Guaira. After morning mass, it began with a centennial tribute to Chopin in the bar, the Arabian consul explaining Chopin, the Pole, with brief biographical details and ending with the rococo pronouncement that he was sure his (Chopin's) spirit must be hovering over the *Jagiello* that day. Wasn't it a teeny bit egotistic of us to monopolize him thus, I wondered.

After dinner the program of entertainment in the bar went on endlessly, broken occasionally by dancing. The French buffoon, loud and sweating profusely and unfunny, who conducted matters at the microphone was, it turned out, fleeing France for Venezuela, in fear of another war. It was all too dreary to endure and we went to bed at 2 a.m.

Many of the passengers were going to Venezuela, knowing very little of it, because they were afraid to stay in Europe. The French buffoon was long in a concentration camp. The pale-eyed old man and his heavy-faced painted wife were refugees from Berlin. He was a great kidney surgeon and she was Lizzie Arno, old actress. They left their house in Berlin on two hours' notice and now would have to start anew in Venezuela. She gave a necklace to their table steward as tip. I felt sorry for them all in various degrees. What admixture of courage and misplaced hope, to move from France to South America, I noted. How sad and second-rate that all these migrations should be motivated by fear rather than enterprise. And how smug and superior it was of me to say so. What problems of adjustment for those who don't know the intricacies of Spanish influence in these countries, the Latin American version of Spanish life being a vulgarized dilution of the original, as is usual, I think, with colonies.

On Sunday, May 22, 1949, I noted that this had been the best vacation of my life in interest, what learned, friends made, general charm and delight. Italy had been a great discovery for me. And probaby the chief thing I learned or relearned was the untruth of the concept that the actions of governments represent the wishes of their people.

At about 9:15 on May 24, we saw Paraíso, our favorite anchorage, with its strip of beach, its few trees and its gap in the mountains inland.

Gregorio and a *Pilar*-full of Cuban friends coming to welcome the *Jagiello* into Havana's harbor, our homecoming felt auspicious. Our cases of Venetian glass, china, linens, laces and books, and the Buick, *"bella macchina,"* arrived safely at the Finca. The house looked spacious and cool and my own room fresh and pretty. The star jasmine vine growing up the gnarled trunk of our ancient ceiba tree had filled out so much it looked like Grecian draperies. Our cats and dogs remembered us, or pretended to. Our birds in residence and making nests included three families of mourning doves, one pair nesting in a tree near my rose garden, one near the path to the pool, one near the tennis court. Their wings whirring like eggbeaters, they would fly off their nests as we approached, but only for a moment, and they disdained our well-fed cats who were too lazy to climb as high as their nests for plunder. Our miniature Cuban owl retained his house near the garage, screaming *"shitty-shitty-shitty"* to encroachers into his territory. The air was bright with Cuban robins, swifts, the colony of little doves in our four-storied, colonial-style dovecote. Of the mockingbirds, Ernest said, "You can play Bach on the phonograph and they will give it right back to you, cadenzas and arias."

10

Back to Base

DURING THE WINTER in Cortina Ernest had started to write a story about duck shooting in the Veneto. When I had read the first few pages I said, "Please don't let it be just ducks and marshes. Please put in Venice too."

"Mmmmmmmmm," said the writer.

Now at the Finca, hardly waiting for his clothes to be unpacked, he dug out his manuscript and resumed working, the rest of our ménage moving full speed in his wake.

The Spanish verb *vigiar* derives from the Middle French verb *vigilare,* both meaning to "look out," to "watch," or "keep vigil," and while we were forever looking at the hills beyond our valleys, the concerns of home were that summer's big business. With the acquisition of a woven reed chaise longue for Papa's new workroom in the tower, I had the room ready for his inspection and occupancy. The reed was impervious to assaults by termites, I pointed out. There were his bookshelves ready for his favorite books, his big plain writing table uncluttered by drawers, and its leather chair open-sided to let air pass through, the long lowering eaves which protected the room from all but the cool early and late sunshine, an unobtrusive chest of drawers to hold paper and clutter. From all four sides the room's deep windows gave views of the hills and Havana and the sea. It would be a quiet refuge from our inevitable household noises. Ernest moved armloads of books up there and his typewriter, paper and hand-scribbled notes. A new thermos bottle of water sat on top of the chest and a bell to the pantry could summon René bringing supplementary liquids or solids. For the first time I had freedom from worry when the telephone rang, and stopped hushing the more strident conversations in the kitchen.

Only a week or so later, bustling into the house with a basketful of fresh-picked vegetables, I found Ernest standing in the sitting room looking apologetic, his little typewriter on the palm of one hand, papers in the other. "It's lovely up there," he said. "It's calm and beautiful, and thank you very much for it."

"Something must be wrong about it."

My husband looked sheepish and bemused. "It's too lonely. I'm used to the sounds of the house. Miss them —René sweeping the matting. You clicking around."

When tedious visitors stayed too long, he used to slip up to his tower room to read or snooze or think. It was also a cool and pleasant place from which to watch the sun set behind Havana and the quick violet twilight seep into the valleys between us and the profile of the town. But Ernest never used it again as a workroom.

Seeing the Finca with a fresh eye after eight months away from it, I found challenges to a summer-long program of repairs and rehabilitations. The ancient red tiles of the terrace were crumbling and calling for replacements. We needed more bookshelves and I perceived that the White Room, a sweetly proportioned, high-ceilinged area between the living room and the back terrace, was space wasted as a guest bedroom since it had no bath of its own and only an eight-foot-wide arch instead of a door for privacy. The hinged screen we used in the doorway failed to block out sitting room noises. The former Cat Room, now cleaned, repainted and refurnished would provide sufficient guest sleeping space when the Little House was occupied. We could make a wonderful library in the White Room, I persuaded Ernest, and drew plans for bookshelves, an enormous writing table, a sofa equally spacious, tables, clam-shell sconces for its wall lights, and clam-shell drawer pulls of cast bronze for the chests of drawers which would support our bookshelves rising all the way to the five- or six-meter ceiling.

Since the head of the house loathed the disruption of our life by workmen pounding or painting, I stayed home to supervise the work. Nanyuki Franchetti came to the Finca, together with Patrick and Gregory fresh from school, and General Lanham. After a crowded couple of days in our house and a cheerful pigeon shoot at the Club de Cazadores, the men took off on June 11 for the Bahamas. I gave myself a short holiday with Pauline in Key West. "I am enchanted at the possibility of a visit while the men are en voyage," Pauline had written. "How pleasant to hear about the Old Country and those sexy Italian women. I think it is the olive oil. Will you try to smuggle in a few mamey (calocarpum sapota) seeds? The two royals [palms] I smuggled over in my bag are now more than three feet high."

In the Bahamas Gigi was struck with fearsome pains in his stomach and the *Delicias* called for help from Key West, *Pilar* having no ship-to-shore radio-telephone. Gigi was picked up by a noisy U.S. Navy cutter. Key West surgeons found his inflamed appendix straggling haphazardly up his left interior, far from its correct location, and he was resting, wan and weak but cheerful, by the time Pauline took me to visit him in the local hospital. As soon as Gigi had recovered, Pauline took her two sons off for their introductory tour of Europe. With all guests dispatched, we settled into comparative tranquility, Ernest working beyond the noises of the installation in the kitchen of our first electric refrigerator and a new electric stove.

After a scrambled courtship in Sun Valley, where they first met, San Francisco and New York, John

Hadley Hemingway (Bumby) and Byra (Puck) Whitlock were married on June 25 at the American Church on the Quai d'Orsay in Paris, with the bridegroom's stepfather, Paul Scott Mowrer, protesting, "I don't want to give her away," and the Hon. David Bruce, our then ambassador to France, serving as best man. Jack was stationed in Berlin with the U.S. Army and the children made their first home in army quarters there.

Acknowledging wedding photographs they sent us, Ernest wrote: "We had them framed and they hang in the corner of the wall where the old picture was of you with the Croix de Guerre. . . . We never had a member of the family soldiering in peacetime but I suppose that now there is no peacetime. . . . Take care of yourself and of Puck. . . . Much love from all of us here."

With his half-a-hundred birthday approaching, Papa scouted through magazines for modest, amusing presents for himself and the house. To a company in Topeka, Kansas, he sent $15.95 for an assortment of twenty-six marine signal flags. From Hammacher Schlemmer, New York, he ordered eight Currier and Ives ten-inch dinner plates at $24.75. From our embassy in Havana he had acquired a pretty, pleasant, moonlighting secretary, Nita Jensen, who came to the Finca and took dictation on her days away from government business. To a variety of suppliers in the U.S. she wrote letters ordering cases of Mexican enchilada dinners, pinto beans in chili sauce, El Paso tortillas. She sent for a cheap sextant with a book of instruction on celestial navigation, two quarts of Mildew Stop, sponge-rubber ice buckets, a U.S. Navy ship's clock, which we immediately mounted on the sitting room wall, a safety-type, waterproof, floating flashlight (98¢). Most impressive of all the new toys which began arriving before July 21 was a pair of black-iron miniature cannon no more than twenty inches long which fired real shells with impressive sound effects and backfired a mist of black soot which nestled snugly for days in the ears, eyebrows and hair of the artillerymen. Although it terrified our cats, the shooting of the cannon became a ritual in the reception of honored and startled guests, and sometimes also what Papa might decide was a proper dispatch for them.

After eight months of paying homage to Italian pasta in its myriad forms, Ernest and I welcomed our return to the Chinese cuisine I had been learning before we left home. Ernest decided that his birthday lunch should be Chinese, and with the help of Fico, René's original helper with the animals, now volunteer cook, I produced a miniature feast of stir-fry dishes, winter melon soup, slippery chicken and almonds in champagne sauce and a Cuban ice-cream cake from Thorwald Sanchez's factory. Our favorite Cuban dessert was coconut ice cream frozen inside the brown and hairy half-shells of real coconuts, but they would not have supported an array of birthday candles. Otto and Betty Bruce were there, and four or five Cuban friends waving chopsticks and predicting future felicities, and when the lunch party broke up about 5 p.m. I made a body count of dead wine bottles standing in neat rows on the pantry floor, some fifteen. It was two or three bottles more than I had expected. Boise, our first and foremost cat, had attended the lunch and it was, the birthday boy proclaimed, his best present that Boise fell headlong in love with our Beansprouts Stir Shrimps dish. Nothing that they liked of our food was too good for our special feline friends, he always said, because they would not take the consolations and pleasures of alcohol. Brown and healthy from the sea, soft and sure of movement, confident in his work on his new book, Ernest on his fiftieth birthday seemed to me to show little of time's attrition.

From my diary, July 29, 1949, Finca Vigía:

"Lillian Ross has written Papa after five nights in the Algonquin—which is 'like being on the operating table with the ether mask over your face'—saying: 'Maybe I just ought to get married to one of the dull Joes hanging around with their mothers. . . . Just when they are beginning to get interesting they always spring a mother on me. . . . What is your opinion Mr. Hemingway, of the future of the career girl?'

"Must tell her standard procedures for career girls

305

over age 30. It is instructive, entertaining and sometimes satisfying to shift careers."

Friday, August 5, 1949, 15:50:
"Papa just came into my room, looking around, hunting. He said 'an accolade.' Because lunch was 'the best
meal I have ever eaten in my life.' It was chop-suey
made entirely by Fico, with ears, the new beansprouts
I found yesterday with bigger beans, onions, fresh
shrimp, hardly cooked celery, fried noodles from a
can, white rice, mushrooms and the sauces.

"Bright sunshine outside, temperature now 84. At
table Papa was ebullient, said he would marry me,
even if I didn't go to bed with him."

Sunday, August 7, 1949:
"Papa at the pool, saw eighteen different kinds of birds:

> Tobacco dove
> Mourning dove
> Kingbird
> 2 pairs of Orchard Orioles
> 4 types of Warblers
> 7 Mockingbirds—all in sight at one time
> 2 Woodpeckers
> Buzzard
> Sparrow Hawk
> Cuban Robin
> 3 kinds of Blackbirds—Grackles
> Every early morning we hear the Quail
> Grooved-bill Ani
> Cuban Blackbird"

Saturday, August 13, 1949:
"We are gliding from Havana to Bahía Honda in *Pilar*.
From the inner end of Papa's long bed I watch the tips
of the rods weaving in the sky, their motion caused by
a gentle sea. They do not saw through their arc. They
bow it with long-toned emphasis at the end of each
note, pointing up at faint ribbed clouds in the blue,
with the engine for tympani. . . .

"Anchored at Paraíso early in afternoon, swam
ashore, I marveling that it had frightened me, the star-

fish, crabs, stingrays, all being so new and their dangers undefined, four years ago."

Monday, August 15, 1949:
"This evening after a *chubasco* [thunderstorm] over the land, the sea is satiny, the sky mauve, silver and rose. We are anchored again off Paraíso and living inside a pearl. Papa and Gregorio are talking about mosquitoes, with Lilo, the boy helper, listening doubtfully.

"When he is good Papa is very, very good, and endearing. Today he reached into our Kleenex box, found only one last piece of tissue there and asked me, 'You need Kleenex?' He was prepared to tear his piece in half."

We were dreaming of returning to Italy in the fall.

On August 27 Jean-Paul Sartre and a girlfriend came to dinner. Sartre's girl was so freshly abloom and attentive and Sartre's looming intellect so masked by his slow-moving eyes and square contours of face that I wondered what forces had created their mutual attraction and concluded that the girl must be more profound with him privately than she was with us and somehow more beguiling. They praised our food and wine, but the evening was a disappointment for me. I had hoped for surveys and reviews and the "inside gen" of the French existentialist movement. But our two conversationalists, the men, passed it by lightly, Sartre saying only that the term was invented by his disciples, who pressed it upon him. Otherwise they talked like businessmen. Sartre's Paris publishers were not giving him large enough percentages of his royalties. He mentioned the companies. Ernest suggested counterthrusts and they talked percentages rising with so many thousands of books printed, agreeing that Sartre's esoteric readership was about as large in France as, translated, in the United States. Surely larger, Ernest suggested.

With dessert Sartre made a small poetic speech about his incapacity to make use of nature for his personal satisfactions as Ernest did with his fishing and bird and animal hunting. It was a loss—*"une privation de mon esprit"*—he said. *Esprit,* hell, I thought. More than *esprit.* Horizons and the sky and the bloody sea and being alive. That time, for once, Ernest made no offer to introduce Sartre to the sea, to my unconditioned relief.

Thursday, September 1, 1949—06:25, Finca Vigía:
"Papa says of the animal situation here at the Finca 'Dogs is trumps but cats is the longest suit we hold.'

"Papa also says, 'You're the rich man's Mary Martin.' "

With my luggage overweighted by chunks of frozen wahoo, I flew to Chicago in late September and our customary parabola of letters in the sky started moving again. On September 22 Ernest typed: "My dearest kitten: It is just starting to get light and I write you with love. Also with a cleaned typewriter and a new ribbon. [I had done the cleaning and re-ribboning.] After we left you in the big airplane (over sixty gadgets that I did not understand) . . . we came back home and met the lion tamer and two apprentice lion tamers."

A poor and brave little country circus had moved onto an empty lot outside our fence and Ernest made friends with the animal trainers and also with their beasts, and wrote in detail about their business and financial problems. Also, to my dismay, that the lion man, who starved himself in order to feed his two lions, allowed Ernest to play with them in their cage. "The lion tamer said the public likes only that which is false and is absolutely ignorant of that which is dangerous." He had shot pigeons at the Club de Cazadores, was keeping track of five different hurricanes budding or blooming in Cuba's latitudes. He enclosed three checks and urged, "Please get lovely coat. . . ."

In his down-slanting handwriting Ernest wrote aboard *Pilar* on September 24: "It turned out I had eight small chickenshit scratches from the lion incurred while we were not yet completely friends. Lion is fast. . . . Book, I think will be wonderful. . . . Here are many strings of ducks in the evenings but they all go through to the south coast where the rice is. So do the white herons. . . .Gregorio really loves you. So do I. . . . We sounded in the Tin Kid all the way up the river and know how to take her [*Pilar*] inside o.k. So no worry. Am over 4,000 [words of book] on the week and it is all good. So proceed with Operation Mink Coat." He was writing about an American Army officer in the Veneto.

I was buying surprise presents for him, catnip for our cats, presents for us to take to friends in Italy including a smart jacket for Teresa, the conscienceless countess.

"It's a whole week I've been away from you," I wrote on September 29. "Getting impatient to be home."

On September 29 Ernest did 705 words for his book, he wrote me, a slightly larger than average day's production for him, and also sent a letter about Teresa. "I am polite and loving to all these dames but who I love is you," he wrote. "You ought to begin to suspect that by now. It is just that they are fun, probably, like going in the cage with the big cotsies. . . . I only play for keeps with you. . . ."

Ernest wrote warning me, "Your [meaning his] head is full of nitric acid that you test everything to see if it is gold OR NOT. You are as nervous as a racehorse and you are like a matador doing it with no audience. Maybe I romanticize it. But lately it impressed the hell out of me just as a sporting event." The Hearst enterprises were going to buy his new book and serialize it in *Cosmopolitan* for a comfortable sum, he indicated.

On Thursday, October 6, I flew home to Cuba, my luggage bulging with presents, my new mink coat riding grandly on my arm. As always the sweet smell of warmth and damp earth and flowers enchanted me. So did my husband and the frozen daiquiris he had brought from the Floridita for us to sip on the road home.

From my notebook, Monday, October 24, 1949: "The before sunrise clamor intensifies with cooler mornings, all the cocks of the new houses of the *reparto,* the growing little settlement beyond our garden fence, giving voice, our own doves gurgling, the *shitty-shitty* owl denouncing the pigeons talking, and a couple of birds I don't know carrying on in the ceiba tree, but out of sight.

"Papa in final phases of *Across the River and into the Trees,* nervous and tired, but fine yesterday after four days in Rincón and Puerto Escondido. Huge *oleajes* [waves], the greens of Escondido bluer in fall. He slept well last night and went to work at 7:15, still at it now at 8:40. Temperature when we woke and took a half bottle of champagne, 70°."

I was unhappy about the middle and later parts of the manuscript I had read since my return from Chicago. But I had not figured out why and mentioned it to no one, not even my notebook. It made me feel disloyal, but I was finding Colonel Cantwell's and his girl's conversations banal beyond reason and their obsession with food and the ploy of the emeralds a mysterious lapse of judgment. I kept my mouth shut. Nobody had appointed me my husband's editor or the bombardier of his self-confidence. Someone at Scribner's would help him improve those passages, I hoped.

We were longing to return to Venice, and about a week before we were to leave Cuba a radiogram arrived from a ship approaching Havana saying that Gianfranco Ivancich was aboard, had no visa, could use help. Ernest got in touch with Paco Garay who attended to the immigration formalities, and went in to meet our unexpected guest. At our house Juan unloaded an old-fashioned steamer trunk from the car and put it in the Venetian Room, formerly the Cat Room, to which we assigned our guest.

At a luncheon in Venice the previous March Gianfranco as a person had been overshadowed by his sister Adriana and Ernest, who had met each other on a duck-shooting weekend and were busily launching a flirtation. Now we had a chance to know him and we both found him delightful. Slim as a cypress, and with the deep dark eyes of his sister, he had been wounded with an Italian cavalry unit—tanks—in North Africa, then bombed again as he lay with other stretcher cases waiting on a wharf to be evacuated home. Released from a military hospital in Italy he was convalescing at his family's country villa on the Tagliamento River near Latisana when Allied bombers attacked a bridge nearby. They missed the bridge but demolished the Ivancich house. Gianfranco had been lying under a tree on the lawn and got a few more wounds in his legs. *"Non tanto. Non tanti,"* he said. They had merely lost their beautiful country house and all it contained.

As the Allies were pushing the German forces northward, Mussolini's Fascist forces collapsing in 1945, both Gianfranco and his father, Carlo, had been working with the pro-Allied underground in the Veneto, taking grave risks to seek military information and relay it to Allied Intelligence. Both father and son had been captured by the Fascists and managed to escape, but in the spring of 1945, Carlo Ivancich had been caught and murdered in an alley of the village of San Michele, just outside his estate. Gianfranco had found his father's body.

Gianfranco offered us no account of his family's disastrous recent history. He answered our few questions laconically, did not wallow nor even drag his toes in resentment, made one-line jokes and, having no one to unpack his steamer trunk as meticulously as it had been packed, strewed his clothes all around his room or at the pool. He had come to stay a couple of weeks, he mentioned in his rich claret voice. None of us had any idea that his visit would stretch, with intervals, to seven years.

11

New York—Venice

WITH A MERE fourteen pieces of luggage we flew to Miami and on up to New York and a suite at the Sherry-Netherland Hotel on November 16 when we began a couple of days of open house with fresh large-caliber gray caviar and superior champagne as our staples of nutrition. In salute to my new freedom from kitchen and housekeeping I chose them one day for all three meals, caviar on buttered toast, coffee and champagne for breakfast, caviar, green salad and champagne for lunch, caviar, blinis and champagne for dinner.

Lillian Ross came to chat with Ernest. She planned to write a profile about him for *The New Yorker*. George Brown, loving and debonair, who ran a gym mostly for prize-fighters on West Fifty-seventh Street, came to drink and eat sparingly as always. Marlene Dietrich came over from the Plaza, neat and not gaudy in a simple black dress and a single strand of diamonds, and arranged for us to see a private showing of her newest picture, *Foreign Affair*. Jigee Viertel, Peter's wife, came to sit smiling and silent with her eyelashes curled. We had known them since Ketchum, 1947. Charles Scribner, Sr., an alluring, venerable gentleman, came for lunch and low-keyed jokes one day, Winston Guest and Alfred Rice, Ernest's lawyer, dropped in, and Patrick, now the self-contained Harvard man, came to spend a couple of days talking art and politics with his father in the marginal moments when Ernest was not occupied with other people. C. Z. Guest dropped by with a sackful of right-foot shoes from a shop in the rue Cambon with instructions to order each shoe made larger.

Toots Shor had sent a bucketful of beautiful bottles to our Senlis suite aboard the *Ile de France* and flowers from friends glowed everywhere in our swaying cubicles above the gray North Atlantic. We made our respective arrangements for exercise and massage in the big airy gym up top, Ernest persuaded the purser to make out a *laissez-passer* for Jigee Viertel, who was also sailing, so that she could come without embarrassment from tourist class to lunch and dine with us, and I organized walks on the cold but glass-enclosed promenade deck and congenial bar dates with old pal Sam Boal.

Ernest was tired from his long effort to finish his book. I had seen him tired and ill in Paris in the winter of 1944–45 and ill the past winter in Cortina

312

and Padova, and it seemed to me his weariness blurred his personality. He was making constant repetitions of his philosophies and catch-phrases and jokes, and omitting his customary beguiling grace notes, his featherweight wit or mimicry or bright flash of eye. I had heard him say "truly" in solemn voice too often, and "daughter," voice benign, and "when the chips are down" and "how do you like it now, gentlemen?" I was also bored with his war. But these were all new to Jigee, and she listened with devoted attention, rather like our Black Dog, I thought, while Ernest, wrapped in his voluminous red-and-white plaid bathrobe I'd had made for him in Cortina, his "king's robe," expounded. I found them thus in our sitting room every afternoon, recognized the risk I was taking and dismissed it.

Ernest was drinking too much and when at lunch he declared that he knew the French Line's wines and whiskeys so well that he could identify them blindfolded, Sammy arranged a tasting party in our cabin. Our steward brought in eight or nine bottles wrapped in napkins, their corks removed, their wrappings camouflaging their shapes. Since Jigee did not drink alcohol, our contest concerned only the three of us, and the fellows insisted I be the first sampler. From each bottle Sammy poured me sipping measures then wrote down my guesses. Blindfolded I confused a Scotch whiskey with Canadian, a Rhine wine with a French rosé and identified only the claret correctly. "The Palateless Ponderer," said I, nonplussed.

"Better than Panderer," said Ernest.

"I'm working up to that, haven't you noticed?"

To our surprise Ernest did little better, identifying only three beverages, and Sam won the contest, correctly naming four bottles. We accused him of munching longer than we had on the pieces of toast which were supposed to clean our tastebuds.

From my notebook: "Room 86, my old wartime room, Ritz Hotel, Paris December 1, 1949—23:45 hours.

"It is now one hour and a half since I left Jigee Viertel's room, #94, and Ernest said, 'I'll come in a minute.'"

313

"December 6, 1949 . . . Night—stormy weather.

"E. says 'It has been the most disappointing thing that has ever happened to me in my whole life—the way that you have behaved in this bed—under the circumstances of having just finished a book of which all proceeds were to go to you, under a will made and witnessed in New York.

" 'Further the deponent sayeth not.

" 'I've seen you get out, and pack your bags, rat out, whenever the going gets rough. I don't say rude things, I only state things which have happened.

" 'Can a man speak off the record? I don't mind speaking on an *accurate* record.' "

Ernest fell asleep and so did I after writing his speech in my notebook and ten minutes of wondering what could have provoked the explosion.

Knowing that Venetian women did not dress elaborately for restaurant dinners in the winter and that we were unlikely to be invited to any fancy private parties, I had brought only one evening frock, a creation by Josépha of black with a gray satin décolletage. When our ambassador to France and Evangeline Bruce invited us to dinner at the embassy residence, I had my San Francisco de Paula dress pressed and put it on, thinking, so what?

Our hosts had chosen the menu and guests with their usual expertise, partridge David Bruce had shot himself as the entree, and among the company, the Hon. Duff Cooper whose writing Ernest much admired, Christian Dior, who had come up for the dinner from a sailing holiday on the Côte d'Azur, and other decorative charmers. When they seated me next to M. Dior at dinner, my "danger-approaching" signal rumbled. I couldn't think of one sensible question, either philosophic or practical, I might ask him about haute couture. But we got on comfortably about Mediterranean sailing, its wind hazards, port accommodations, and the problems created by guests more enthusiastic than seaworthy. The evening swung gently and before it finished I couldn't resist whispering to M. Dior that for once he had been in the company of a woman cheaply dressed, my dress having cost about twenty dollars.

"Mais, vous avez raison," said the famous designer. *"Ça c'est pratique."*

Like minnows in a whirlpool we spun through the days. Ernest wrote and rewrote his book, but he was also allured by the committee meetings he arranged in the hotel bar to make book on the steeplechase races at Auteuil. Ed Hotchner flew over to collect the manuscript for *Cosmopolitan* and, at Ernest's hint, fell to editing the pages, Jigee assisting, both of them with what seemed to me a formidable inattention to style. Ernest sent me to the Left Bank offices of Gallimard, his French publishers, to collect hundreds of thousands of francs to spend at the races and to pay for hotel bills, my couturier, some clothes for Jigee and for a *prêt-à-porter* winter coat, a half circle of blue wool hung from the shoulders, with deep pockets, the best coat I ever had. Almost every day we taxied en masse to lunch at the glass-walled, tiered restaurant which hung beneath the roof of the Auteuil grandstand opposite the finish line. Its food and wine were good, its air of holiday excitement stimulating and its view across glowing green to the autumn russets of far tree-tops beguiling. Betting on behalf of Georges, chief of the Ritz's Big Bar, Bertin, who ran the Little Bar, and others, Ernest brought back modest winnings or nothing most evenings. But one morning Georges rang him from downstairs, so unusual a procedure that Ernest knew the tip he offered was much hotter and more genuine than simple horse talk. It was about a horse named Bataclan II, and, pushing his manuscript aside, Ernest spread racing forms and the past fortnight's sports pages all over our little writing table in front of the French doors, the same on which I had pecked with freezing fingers seven months of wartime cables.

Bataclan II was not the fabulous athlete Georges had predicted, but at the last hedge before the finish line bad luck befell the two horses by then far outdistancing him. The first horse stumbled on the hedge and fell over it and the second horse fell almost on top of the first. Bataclan's jockey moved him aside from the accident, he took the hedge in stride and crossed the finish line lengths ahead of the pack and paid 232 francs to 10. When Ernest unloaded the pockets of his new Abercrombie & Fitch raincoat onto one of our beds of Room 86, the pile was as voluminous as three of the Ritz's big pillows. He took a walking stick and slashed at the pile of notes. One huge covey fluttered to the floor on the right of the bed, that for me. A second flock fell to the left, Hotchner's. He would keep the third third which remained on the bed. He had already given a percentage to Don Andrés, our "Black priest" from Cuba, who had shown up unexpectedly that spectacular day and had insisted upon investing half his life savings in the race horse, in Basque bravado. For years Bataclan remained a famous name in the rue Cambon bars.

On one nonracing day Jigee and Hotchner were lunching with us at the Ritz and Ernest decided he should show Jigee something of his personal Paris, as he had shown me five years before. I had a date with Charles Sweeny who would show me his favorites among the Greek sculpture at the Louvre, an enchanting prospect.

"Great idea," said Hotchner, beaming, of Ernest's plans, "I'll buy that."

Ernest chewed his grilled liver thoughtfully. "You're welcome, Hotch," said he, "if you're invited."

With Georges Mabilat, our favorite chauffeur, driving his Packard, we planned to leave Paris for the Riviera and Italy on the morning of December 24, and Peter Viertel arrived in time to share the Christmas celebration we held in Room 86 on the eve of departure. With champagne toasts, songs, unwrappings of multitudinous, mostly silly gifts, our room reverberated with such good cheer that the neighbors rang the concierge and he restrained us. My favorite gift was one I had bought for myself, a paperweight which, when shaken, produced a small snowstorm falling on an inch-high fir tree, our only Christmas tree that year. It reminded me of Christmases in Bemidji, Minnesota.

Later than we had hoped but earlier than we had expected, we loaded the Packard, established ourselves in it, Ernest beside Georges in the front, Peter and Hotchner on the jump seats and Jigee and me

316

astern, and eased out of the Place Vendôme south-ward.

Through Villeneuve and Sens we went to Auxerre where we found warmth and marvelous food at the Café Cerf-Volant.

On Christmas Day we rambled southeastward through Bourgogne catching glimpses of snug villages and handsome villas through rifts in the fog, and reached better weather on the day after Christmas, with patches of blue in the sky, the country looking wilder, more broken and more beautiful, and Avignon creamy-beige in the sunshine, its plane trees taller than anywhere and more gnarled. We parked below the Château des Papes and climbed, prancing like ponies in the wind, to lovely gardens overlooking the two wide swift branches of the Rhône and enriched with memorable pines and holly bushes. We read the sundial, snapped photographs and posed on the bench where, Ernest said, he had written some parts of *In Our Time,* having come down from Paris with his bike on the train. How much harmless humbug might live in that tale, I wondered.

On we went from Avignon to Pont du Gard and Nîmes and then to Aigues-Mortes, abandoned by the sea. Papa and Jigee and I went into the church, which smelled of rotten cheese, and read about St. Louis on a plaque and saw a picture of his leaving for the Seventh Crusade in a small dinghy, as overloaded as our dinghy when we had guests. We also read about the supplies he required of his enlisting crusaders. They had to bring their own fresh water, also their personal piss-pots.

We went to the Tower of Constance, whose walls were fifteen feet thick. It could resist all modern assault except a direct hit, we agreed. On the second floor they kept prisoners, who must have had plenty of ventilation but not much else, without sanitary facilities of any sort.

After the revocation of the Edict of Nantes in 1685 the prisoners were mostly Protestants. One woman who was imprisoned there for thirty-eight years, scratched *Résistez* in the wall, an admonition which they now keep under glass.

317

That afternoon we pushed on through Van Gogh country, the grain waving in my imagination, and curling living cypresses in the hot sun. Then straight through Arles, looking for Cézanne landscapes until certain mountains which Cézanne never painted showed up on the left. But many of the pink-orange-roofed houses with pines and cypresses clustering around them looked Cézanne. It occurred to me that he didn't see much of these mountains. Perhaps he was limited by the distance his horse could go in a morning. Finally to Aix, and late the next day to Nice, where Peter and Hotchner arranged train tickets to Paris.

Quick farewells at the bar and I went to the train and more farewells. "Of the three people I like Jigee best," I noted that night. (About a month later my husband described to me in devastating detail Jigee's campaign to snare him. "She [me] obviously doesn't appreciate you. We'll have a ranch with horses in California and you can give up the heat of Cuba. I understand your wonderful sensibilities.") Jigee had been so sweet to me, the crook.

Through Monaco and Genoa we chugged to Nervi, where on New Year's Eve we dined early and glumly and went to bed. Ernest was miserable, missing his cortege. I exuberant, but it seemed merely polite to show sympathy.

Even after we explained Venice to him, our well-traveled Parisian chauffeur, Georges, couldn't believe the city rising from the lagoon. All the way to the Hotel Gritti he murmured, *"C'est un miracle. Incroyable,"* and we enjoyed his awe. The Gritti welcomed us with a big fire murmuring in the small winter dining room, the Gran Maestro beaming but looking grayer, Renato our room waiter loving, as ever, small boys grown taller; and new rooms, 115 and 116, the sitting room windows overlooking the traghetto dock and the little shack of the gondolieri, one bedroom facing the Grand Canal and the luxury of two bathrooms.

Her voice welcoming over the telephone, Bianca Franchetti invited us for lunch at San Trovaso, her elegant estate near Treviso, and there we found her looking handsome and chic in a nondescript brown woolen dress and woolen stockings, surrounded by her family. Nanyuki, the shy, soft-spoken son of the house, was limping. He had broken his right leg skiing four times altogether, recently had fallen badly at Cortina but had continued skiing until, said he, "It began to hurt a little." Now he had broken his ankle, and had allowed plaster to be wrapped on it, but had already ripped off the cast.

In a century of San Trovaso's guests, Lord Byron's visit had been memorable for his charm, Bianca said, and her mother-in-law had entertained Ruskin, "more serious, less winning." If we went to Africa I must take double hats, she advised, and clothing to cover me completely against the sun which quickly eats up one's red corpuscles. If he arranged a safari in East Africa, would she care to join us, Papa asked. "If I go, I would never come back," she said.

I slipped outside and found Nanyuki, Tiberto Brandolini and Simba Franchetti shooting a .22 rifle at the bronze bell above the carriage house door, each of them trying to hit the bell clapper. I asked a chance to shoot, overshot once and then hit the clapper resoundingly.

Simba had been talking about shooting statues, and presently there on the green lawn were the guns of Nanyuki's father from Africa including the heavy .477 with its twenty-five-year-old ammunition and Bianca urging Papa to shoot the almost life-size majestic statues which surmounted the back wing of the carriage house. "We're replacing them with better ones of marble," Bianca said. "Do shoot them. Bring them down. I don't know if the gun still functions."

"I'll shoot one stomach," said my husband; shot and missed, intentionally, I felt.

Italy was host to an international winter sports convention that winter with the ski jumps, bobsled and other competitions scheduled for the slopes around Cortina. With Ilerio, a new, endearing Italian chauffeur, we drove up there, Adriana Ivancich, who was becoming our constant companion, her friend Giovanna and I in the back seat, Ernest, as usual, beside the chauffeur.

We had a room at the Posta, the hub of the town's sporting life, and as we arrived I asked the concierge to telephone my friend Isabella Angeloni to come to give a manicure. But no name, only a room number. She arrived wearing her preoccupied business face which fragmented into grins, smiles and kisses. "Ah, Signora. Ah, Mrs. Hemingway," the *H* very guttural. I had brought her one of the new U.S. nylon uniforms which she greeted with joy. Ernest and his vestal virgins joined us to sip dry martinis in the room. Our reunion gaiety was faintly shadowed because, as she told me the next day, Isabella did not like Adriana, or approve of her interest in my husband.

That was the week I decided to avoid discussing the imbroglio with anyone including its protagonists. From his romanticized memories of Italy in his young manhood, from his concept of the girl Renata he had created to be the heroine of *Across the River and into the Trees* and the enticements of proximity to Adriana herself, aged nineteen, Ernest was weaving a mesh which might entangle and pain him, I felt. But I was sure that no cautionary phrases of mine could arrest the process. I held my tongue, even when Ernest quoted to me in tones of awe such commonplace young-woman ambitions as Adriana's wish to do good deeds for her family.

But once, getting dressed in the chill of 7 a.m., I moaned, "Nobody knows the trouble I've seen."

"Nobody knows but Gellhorn," Papa amended. Martha had published a book with that title.

We had gone back to Venice when a snowstorm that brought a one day's frosting to the city also brought jubilation to the ski slopes around Cortina and friends telephoned, "Come up, come up." Ilerio drove us north and Adriana, who had also come to Venice, accepted for herself and a girlfriend our invitation to join us. She was already invited by friends who had a villa in Cortina to stay with them for a spot of skiing.

Ensconced at the Hotel Posta we moved into mid-current of the winter season's busy leisure, Ernest revising and rewriting his book, mornings in bed for warmth, while I cautiously began to ski again, on the lower slopes of Mt. Faloria, the children's territory.

I was reading a Tauchnitz edition of *Untrodden Peaks and Unfrequented Valleys,* published in 1873 and written by Amelia B. Edwards of Westbury-on-Trym, England. Like subsequent observers, Amelia was entranced with the range of Antelao, "a near mass of clustered pinnacles, then the Pelmo on the opposite side of the valley, uplifted in the likeness of a mighty throne canopied by clouds and approached by a giant staircase . . . trodden only by the chamois hunter."

Practical as well as poetic, she noted that only one road, the Strada Regia, traversed the whole length of the Ampezzo thrall, that the district contained only one telegraph station, the one at Cortina, that the Dolomites were named after a French savant, M. Dolomieu, who traveled in the limestone mountains of the South Tyrol in 1789 or 1790, that the extensive timber industry of the area sent its stamped logs down the Beita River from Cortina to its confluence with the Piave at Perarolo, then down the Piave to the Val di Mel and the mills.

"It is as natural to the natives to be kind, helpful and disinterested as for the Swiss to be rapacious," she wrote. ". . . Food and cooking are indifferent but beds irreproachable. . . . A small store of tea, arrowroot and Liebig's extract, a bottle or two of wine, brandy, a flask of spirits and an extra one almost indispensable." A sensible traveler, Miss Edwards.

On February 18 I wrote: "We've been here more than two weeks, all the time in a haze of delight with the mountains, the air and these last days, magnificent sunshine." But Ernest decided to return to Venice. Since he was not skiing, he was finding his life indoors too constricted. We had left the typewriter in Venice, and our room at the Posta was too chilly for long hours of sitting at a desk. Adriana's mother had summoned her back to Venice and Ernest could give her a lift south in the car.

I took a smaller, warmer room at the Posta, and skied mornings and afternoons with Zardini, my *maestro,* until, Saturday morning, the twenty-fifth when, practicing right turns, my left ski failed to track, I fell forward, heard a crack as of a chicken wing, felt no pain but a spasm of nausea in my stomach and yelled at Zardini that my husband would be angry. I had cracked my left ankle—only a couple of hundred yards higher up the slope of Faloria than a year earlier I had cracked my right ankle, and it was then that I remembered that both ankles had always been weak with a tendency to turn inward when I skated as a child on frozen Lake Bemidji.

My left ankle was not as badly damaged as the right one had been a year before, the doctor told me after he had looked at the X-rays. But another bone man looked at the cast, decided the bone had been badly set and took me up to Codavilla to rebreak the bone and set it again. I wore the new cast until mid-March when it was removed at the American Hospital at Neuilly, outside Paris. The resetting had prevented my walking forever with a limp.

On Sunday, March 5, Ilerio took me down to Venice where I found our suite overlooking the Grand Canal in homelike disarray and my husband in a state of cheerful asperity. I had been reading Thornton Wilder's *The Ides of March* and remembered, "There is no drunkenness equal to the memory of whispers in the night," and the next morning set to work packing. I was finished for a while with whispers in the night. I learned the neat trick of bending down to bags on the floor, too heavy to lift to a settee, with the *gesso* (plaster) on my left leg reaching to my knee.

When Ernest announced that he thought he should invite Adriana and her mother to visit us in Cuba for a reunion with Gianfranco, I demurred.

"Invite them, by all means. But it should be both of us—me, too, as hostess—who do the inviting. For propriety."

"You're right, my kitten. You fix it up, then."

The idea of two Venetian ladies traipsing down to Cuba to visit us seemed utterly irrational to me. At nineteen or twenty Adriana could use more education on numerous subjects, and travel was educational. But she had the whole of Europe closer to hand and much less expensive. Except for some other Latin American countries and the wastelands of the Arctic, Cuba was the end of the line in culture, I thought, even

322

though I loved it and its people. Anyhow I invited Dora, Adriana's mother, to lunch with us at Harry's Bar and agreed to her suggestion that she bring a woman friend of hers.

When I arrived at Harry's and found the ladies seated at a side table, Dora appeared not to remember me and to be somehow startled at my appearance. Perhaps she had forgotten my existence, I surmised, and we spent most of the lunch jockeying for position, exchanging formal trivia about the weather, the food, the current mode, she in excellent and careful English. Obliquely she wondered how long I had been married to Ernest and seemed relieved—my imagination perhaps—when I mentioned it had not been "in the Church." Ernest lunched half at the bar with cronies, favoring us with his presence only occasionally. So it was my job to extol the charms of Cuba, its countryside, its native music and rhythms, its attractive young men, the sons of rich, rich sugar and tobacco growers.

Dora seemed not at all surprised when I spoke the formal words of invitation that she and her daughter visit us, but she also appeared not to find the suggestion ridiculous. She would consider the matter, she said cautiously. No hurry, said I. They were welcome any time.

That afternoon and later that year I tried and failed to understand Dora Ivancich. Unlike Gianfranco, Adriana and the younger son, Giacomo (Jackie), who inherited their father's dark coloring and pronounced face bones, Dora was small-featured and gray of hair, eyes, manner and wardrobe. Her family was of Mittel-European ancestry, she once mentioned, and the Ivanciches from an island, Mali Lošinj, off the Dalmatian coast. With her husband's murder, she had involuntarily become the authority acknowledged by her children, and she gave no evidence of needing or using the counsel of various scattered relatives of her generation. Since her elder daughter, Francesca, was already married to an Italian naval officer, Dora must have considered Adriana the last jewel of the family's depleted fortune and wished for her an alliance both economically and spiritually lustrous. Whenever I made any slight reference to such hopes or plans, she

323

deftly fielded it or cut short the chat by changing the subject.

Spring reached the Veneto turning the canals limpid green beneath a warm sun and unclouded skies before we left Venice on Thursday, March 9, a hill of luggage strapped to the top of the car. The next day, as we were passing Cap d'Antibes on our left, Ernest remembered the year 1926, he said, when he was revising *The Sun Also Rises*. He and Hadley first lived at the Hôtel du Cap, later in a villa where Pauline came to visit them. He was already in love with Pauline and used to bicycle one hundred kilometers a day, trying to sweat out his passion, he said. That was also the year he served as one of the crew of Gerald Murphy's sailboat, he told me.

"Sixty-two miles a day, cycling?" I asked.

"About that."

"That's most of a day. How often did you sail?"

"A couple times a week."

"You couldn't have had much time for revising."

"No. It was a worthless year for working."

"This time in Italy wasn't worthless, though."

"It wasn't too good."

"Baby, my faith in you is unshakable. I know you can work well if you want to."

"I want to be a good boy." He shook his head.

"You've got a wise head, quick to correct mistakes."

"But my heart is not subject to discipline."

"My poor big kitten."

"It's a target of opportunity."

"My poor big kitten with a fractured heart. I wish I could help you." I was not feeling ironic. He was trying to be honest and I felt sorry for him. I did not define "helping" as turning him over to a budding Venetian girl.

We were traveling through blooming bright acacia, pruned shrubs of it in cultivated gardens and great spreading trees of it, like lighted candelabra, in the pine forests of the Estérel Mountains which dropped sharply into the sea near St.-Raphaël, where we stopped for the night. The evening sea was stippled by breezes, breaking up the colors and forms of the dried-blood-and-rusty mountains. It was my favorite part of the coast. Any chunk of it you could enclose in a frame to make a Cézanne.

We reached Paris and the Ritz on Monday, March 13, were given Marlene Dietrich's old suite, 52-53, and had time for a drink in the bar, opening masses of accumulated mail, before lunch. Ernest's bronchial tubes had begun to strain and pain him so much that we remained upstairs to dine quietly during a couple of days in which he dealt with correspondence, sent off tax money, studied the racing forms, organized bets with Georges in the bar and worried that the new general strike in Italy—begun when soldiers shot some strikers at the Breda Works and supported by the Communist mayor of Venice—would prevent Adriana's and her mother's leaving. I busily explored the galleries of the Place Vendôme neighborhood and of Montparnasse, hunting for artists new to me and shopping for a mirror with an exuberant handcarved frame for the Finca.

Dick and Marjorie Cooper arrived from London and we held an extraordinarily long session in the bar before dinner in the corridor, which then was serving as the main dining room.

Dick and Ernest having first met in East Africa, their favorite talk was of adventures there and of mutual friends there, one of whom was Baron von Blixen, the irrepressible Danish explorer, daredevil and hunter. Dick and von Blixen had once made a memorable safari deep into then little-known parts of Kenya and Uganda, returning with tales of splendor which so enthralled us later listeners that, like children demanding repetitions of Peter Rabbit tales, we clamored for accounts of their exploits we had heard before. One I remembered was of the two Europeans coming upon a native girl staked in a stream docilely awaiting her fate which was that of being gutted and roasted for a tribal feast, there being a surplus of girl children her age that year. The river was supposed to make her young flesh tender. Baron von Blixen had paid the tribal elders the going rate for young females, attached her to his retinue and on their way back to western civilization had given her as a present to a native friend of another tribe.

325

Another Dick Cooper story I treasured was a one-liner about a morning of the safari when he was impatient to get started and von Blixen was tarrying over his breakfast. "Excuse me, Richard," said he. "But it is not easy to eat a dozen rotten eggs—quickly."

In Paris Dick told one of his repertoire new to me. Von Blixen had eaten some tinned fish and appeared to be dying. Dick could find no pulse at all and no flutter of a paper held in front of his friend's nose. He ordered the local natives to dig a grave but the digging was not finished by sunset after which they refused to work more. Dick laid out von Blixen on a cot in his own tent and covered the face with a sheet. In the night he heard the corpse gasp, "Water!" then saw the sheet move.

On Saturday Adriana presented herself, youthfully excited and vivacious, to shake up Ernest's heart a bit more. She had left her mother at home but was staying with the eminently impressive and respectable de Beaumont family whose marvelously beautiful daughter, Monique, with her masses of sparkling auburn hair, accompanied Adriana everywhere as a substitute chaperone. That day we lunched at the dear, now-departed La Rue in the rue Royale near the Madeleine, a restaurant that had attended to the taste-buds of Paris's gourmets for half a century before it was transformed into some kind of cafeteria. We were all happy listening to Ernest acclaim Adriana, who had been drawing sketches for the jacket of *Across the River and into the Trees,* as the girl wonder of the art world.

At seven o'clock the next morning Adriana and Monique were at the Ritz's Vendôme entrance waiting to drive with us through still wintry countryside to Le Havre.

Adriana had never seen the insides of a trans-Atlantic liner and had with her no passport or identity card. It became Ernest's project for the morning to get her aboard the *Ile de France* and shown all over the ship, before the "All Ashore." In our old familiar Senlis suite, we took siestas in the afternoon and dined there quietly.

It was a heaving, pounding, gray-skied, cold North

Atlantic we were crossing and we spent little effort buffeting about the outdoor decks, instead read in the cabin, chattered with our favorite barmen and each other.

In our cabin Ernest regaled me with stories of his cub-reporting days on the Kansas City *Star* when he covered the police station, city hospital and the railroad station beat. Once he saw a man collapsed on the floor of the station, he said; the little crowd and also the police backed away, terrified of smallpox. Ernest picked up the poor fellow, put him in a taxi and took him to the hospital.

Ernest used to sneak meals at the hospital and thus heard the cook complaining of pains in his kidney and sores on his back which failed to heal. He got a doctor from outside to examine the cook and the diagnosis was smallpox. Practicing in the hospital was a good doctor whose license had been revoked in California because he had prescribed some kind of dope for such people as Wallace Reid and Mary Miles Minter, the movie stars. This doctor used to go to the Kansas City jail to give daily dope injections to the hopheads there and Ernest accompanied him sometimes. The hopheads used to scream and plead for a shot in "the gut"—it lasted longer—and to jostle Ernest, holding the bowl of dope, to make him spill a little, he said, and then get down and lap it up with their tongues from the filthy floor. He remembered well their unearthly screams when the doctor refused them shots.

12

Fluctuating Tempers

WHEN THE *Ile de France* docked in the Hudson River at noon, March 27, we were elated to find Charlie Sweeny, my favorite general, awaiting us, together with Lillian Ross, Al Horowitz, Hotchner and some others, all of whom accompanied us to our suite at the Sherry-Netherland Hotel for booze and news exchanges. Thus began the usual merry-go-round of people, projects, problems, pretensions, pleasantries and pleasures which blocked all communications between husband and wife except an exhausted "Sleep well" or "Good morning." It reminded me of a military message center. The weather was cold and raw and the enemies inside Ernest's chest continued the attack. The telephone rang on what seemed to me an average of every five minutes, eighteen hours a day. Still it was stimulating.

Patrick came down from Harvard to announce he wanted to marry Henrietta Broyles from Baltimore and to ask his father's approval. Slim Hawks Hayward came to pay and receive compliments. Winston Guest and Tommy Shevlin came to talk about fishing off Florida and a joint return to Africa. Wallace Meyer came from Scribner's to talk details of the publication of *Across the River and into the Trees*. Harold Ross came to lampoon brilliantly in his Western accents the literary life of New York and its leaders. Marlene Dietrich came for dinner and to deliver a harangue against Ingrid Bergman and her latest film made in Italy.

Hoping to begin the production of a baby, I had gone that afternoon for an elaborate examination by Dr. Lester Spier and his associates on the Upper East Side, had passed with good marks all tests of blood, lungs, heart, blood pressure 128/80, and no signs of cancer or conditions favorable to same. But in a painful test they discovered that my remaining fallopian tube was so "occluded" that my chances of a normal pregnancy were zero. A complicated operation might improve the situation. They could not guarantee it. I went back to the hotel eager to share the gloomy news with Ernest and so shift part of its burden away. But there were the Vanderwickens, spirited and gay, showing us colored photos of their children. I kept my grief to myself. Some days later when I told it to Ernest, the cheer drained away from his face. But he rallied himself and me, saying, "That's our lousy luck, my kitten. But we'll share it. It will be our lousy, dark secret which we keep together. No. You won't have that 'maybe' operation. The hell with it. I wouldn't ask you to jump off a roof with an umbrella for support." Ernest never referred further to that incapacity of mine, but for years I felt myself a failed member of the human race, being unable to contribute a creature to it.

I flew to Chicago to see my parents and my cousin Bea—her wonderful husband Homer had died the year before—found them all well, my parents having decided they would like to move to Gulfport, Mississippi, because a Christian Science friend of theirs had recommended it. I was back in New York in a couple of days.

While we were dining with Harold Ross and his blond, giggly wife in the bar at "21," Irwin Shaw, my jovial friend who had been with me the day I met Ernest, came to the table and Ernest exploded. To my distress, he delivered himself of a violent, scarifying critique of Shaw, his character, his person, his writing, which caused Ross to wiggle on the seat and me to marvel that Shaw stood there failing to bleed from every pore. The performance installed a ridge of acrimony between us which Ernest breached the next morning with a note he had written on the ladylike Sherry-Netherland paper before going to bed.

"Please let us not fight about what I said to Irwin Shaw. I love you and I was so happy to have you home again and I thought I had never seen anyone more beautiful and I was so proud to be seen with you. . . . the Shaw thing had been an anger that I had like a boil or something for over a year. . . . I thought what he wrote about my poor bloody unfortunate brother, you, and me was quite despicable. . . . I had warned him to keep away from me. . . . If you want to see Shaw because he is an old friend, that is perfectly o.k. and I understand. . . ."

Twenty-two pieces of heavy preflying-type luggage precluded our going south by air. We took the train to Miami feasting on the caviar Lillian Ross had sent us, moved from the railway station to the wharf of the old Havana ferry, the *Florida*. At the Finca Vigía the next day we managed to unpack quickly and stow away our travel gear, greet the servants and cats and dogs, and accommodate ourselves to the warm Cuban springtime, in order to welcome the next day Pauline, Patrick and his pretty, vivacious fiancée, Henrietta Broyles.

Flirting in what I assumed was old southern belle fashion, flattering, appealing, cajoling, Henny entranced and won over her future father-in-law in a silky ten minutes as we sat around the sitting room with drinks before lunch. Ernest displayed some show of reluctance toward the prospective marriage, less for reason, perhaps, than for the fun of playing hard-to-persuade. Henny undid him with soulful eyes and such phrases as, "I'm going to be a happy, faithful and obedient wife."

Brimming with cheer, her luggage bulging with presents for the house, Bea Guck arrived in late April, charmed Ernest with her knowing talk of baseball, especially the Chicago Cubs, and declared immediate affection for the Finca, our animals and our ways of living. Having other women about so seldom, it was a joy for me to share breakfasts on trays in my room and plan the days. Except for a couple of sightseeing forays into Havana we stayed at home, leaving Ernest to work in peace, ourselves prowling the vegetable and rose gardens, sunning at the pool and swimming.

Two accidents marred Bea's visit. Our sea captain friend, Sinsky Duñabeitia, had a heart attack and was brought out to us, half dead, and installed in Ernest's room, using his pajamas, sweaters and bathroom, an inconvenience to the head of the house, and requiring special meals cooked and served him in bed. Then there was the day when Ernest invited us to lunch aboard *Pilar,* tied up at the little Club Náutico in the bay of Havana. To give Bea a small sample of our life on the Gulf Stream I arranged for us to go early to the boat, chuff out of the harbor into the Gulf Stream for an hour of fishing before lunch; to Bea's delight, I caught a dorado (dolphin).

Tied up at the club we waited lunch more than an hour before the captain appeared, brightly lit up with frozen daiquiris and with his faithful follower, Roberto

Herrera, and also Havana's youngest, prettiest whore, whom he had nicknamed Xenophobia. I couldn't blame the shy, ignorant girl for accepting his invitation to share our good food, but fury burst inside me at Ernest's insolence and arrogance in making Bea and me wait so long and at his shoddy manners toward Bea. She generously murmured she thought the ploy amusing. She had never seen a designated whore before, and Ernest had contributed to her education, she suggested. I was less amused. A couple of days later when I had regained some semblance of coherence I wrote him: "This is to let you know that I was both serious and truthful the morning after the luncheon you gave for me and Bea when I said I am planning to leave you. . . . As soon as it is possible for me to move out, I shall move.

"Maybe it is unnecessary for me to explain my reasons for leaving. But I write them because you should have the opportunity of knowing precisely how I feel about this marriage.

"In 1944 . . . I thought you were a straight and honorable and brave man and magnetically endearing to me . . . although I was suspicious of your overdrinking, you said so often that your chief desire was to be GOOD and adult, I believed you and in you. . . .

"About your work, you scoffed at others who couldn't go the distance on a book. You reiterated your phrase 'You hired out to be tough, didn't you?' You affirmed that you knew how to handle yourself in a long tough bout. And you said you loved to write and were never happier than when doing so. It was therefore not unnatural for me to assume that, working, you could, if you wanted to, be a companionable and considerate husband—as well as gay and charming and sturdy in spirit, which you are when you are not drunk.

"What I expected to contribute to the marriage were loyalty to you and devotion to your projects . . . your family and house and possessions . . . care of whatever things or jobs you entrusted to me and in daily living a certain good balance, alertness and tenderness towards you.

"With these mutual contributions it looked in 1944

331

as though we could achieve the fine life we both wanted and sometimes we have done so. But now in May, 1950, my view of this marriage is that we have both been failures. . . .

"My principal failure is that somehow I have lost your interest in me, your devotion and also your respect. . . .

"Your principal failure is that . . . you have been careless and increasingly unthinking of my feelings . . . undisciplined in your daily living. Both privately and in public you have insulted me and my dignity as a human being. . . .

"If there were any sign of remorse after such bouts of behavior on your part, I could believe we might try again and make things better. But for a long time now your only reaction to the possibility that you have been mistaken is a petulant irritability, protecting your steel-bound ego, that your rectitude or infallibility should be questioned. Please notice that I did not say 'apology' but remorse. See Mr. W. Shakespeare:

'Tis not enough that through the cloud thou break
To dry the rain on my storm-beaten face,
For no man well of such a salve can speak
That heals the wound and cures not the disgrace:
Nor can thy shame give physic to my grief;
Though thou repent, yet I have still the loss:
The offender's sorrow lends but weak relief
To him that bears the strong offence's cross.

"I think we must now both admit that this marriage is a failure. Therefore let us end it. And if we have not succeeded in conducting it gracefully, let us, please, try to finish it gracefully and without further violence. . . .

"Until I leave I will continue with all possible good temper to run your house. . . ."

Ernest's response to my letter produced as many edges as a cookie cutter. He came into my room and solemnly announced that he had read me. He thumbed through my book of sonnets, found the one I had quoted and without tears or show of sorrow read me the last redeeming couplet.

332

Ah, but those tears are pearl which thy love sheds,
And they are rich and ransom all ill deeds.

"Stick with me, kitten. I hope you will decide to stick with me." Then, baiting my zeal for improving the house and farm, he kept me so busy with so many projects, none of which I could drop in the middle, that I could scarcely snatch minutes to write my family, much less organize a job hunt by airmail.

Planning the first of what became Cuba's annual marlin-fishing tournament with a silver trophy cup provided by himself, Ernest revived his old R.A.F. phrase, "Wizard ops in prospect," and I could not restrain my anticipation of three days on the Gulf Stream.

I did not spend those days in *Pilar* with Ernest. Taylor Williams, our bird- and beast-hunting friend from Sun Valley on his annual vacation with us, and I decided to use the *Tin Kid,* my little launch, with the pennant of the Ketchum Rod and Gun Club flying from her mast. When we announced our intention one night at dinner, Sinsky roared, "No, no. You couldn't. You can't. You'll never stand it. I'll bet you ten dollars you'll ask to go aboard *Pilar* by noon."

"It's a bet," said I.

"Too much for a woman," said Sinsky. "I'll bet five to one she won't last out the first day."

"I'll take that," said Ernest.

When the Club Náutico held a Calcutta auctioning of boats the night before the tournament, sportsmen wagered $200 and $300 on each other's luck. Nobody showed any hopes for the *Tin Kid* except Ernest who bought us for a modest $35.

Later I wrote in *Cosmopolitan* magazine:

Only in her construction, which makes her slide like a buoyant leaf up and down the sides of the waves, her faithful little four cylinder engine and her well functioning bilge pump, can *Tin Kid* compete with the other boats, nearly all of them more than twice her size. Her cockpit, five by seven feet, is about as commodious as an executive's desk. For luxury she has an ice chest

333

the size of an orange crate and a gear box of the same proportions. These, with a couple of sofa cushions, are our seats, and we live on intimate terms with the elements. The sea, statistically, is a foot below us, but it seldom stays there. As soon as we leave the harbor, it comes in showers of spray upon us.

It was not until the second day of the tournament that our luck showed. We were a good five miles offshore and the gray and white hills inland stood high above the coastline when we saw our luck. It was Taylor's fish, since he was senior partner, and while he grabbed the rod, our fragile, old boatman and I danced up and down shouting at the width of our marlin's violent wings showing just below the surface and at what seemed the enormous length between his head and the purple scythe of his tail slicing the water.

As soon as Taylor, whipping his rod back sharply, had driven the hook into his fish's jaw, we discovered problems. This was a white marlin, a rough, tough fighter, extremely difficult to catch on the prescribed light fifteen-thread line. White, striped and blue marlin all count in the tournament; but the striped and the blue, usually more docile although heavier, are seldom seen in late May, the contest season.

Our brave ornery fish jumped thirty times before I stopped counting, lifting himself entirely out of water, vaulting fifteen or twenty feet before he settled down to his underwater fighting. Since *Tin Kid* has no fishing chair, Taylor's problem was to resist the lunges with nothing but our gunwale to brace against.

When the marlin went into a determined escape effort, diving three hundred yards as the line whirred off the reel, I had a new difficulty at the wheel. *Tin Kid,* light as a cork, provided no solid platform from which to resist the fish's pull, and our marlin could easily drag us all over the ocean, which is what he proceeded to do, I trying to follow his circles so that Taylor would not lose all the line on his reel. *Pilar* had seen our plight and edged near enough so that I could shout our news.

"Two hundred pounds," I yelled, not knowing that in these waters white marlin seldom run to half that much.

For an hour we weaved and turned across the sea, Taylor growing tired and I beginning to fear that this gallant fish would never submit to our light persuasion, when another problem arose. Our boatman, a tiny, normally cheerful Spaniard of seventy years, showed that he was over-awed by the fish and afraid to bring him aboard. Reeling skillfully Taylor managed to bring the fish near us. But the boatman declared the fish still too fresh and strong to gaff and Taylor had to postpone his final effort.

Then *Pilar* approached us again and I noticed Gregorio spring up onto the flying bridge where Ernest was steering. Gregorio was wearing his usual working clothes: no shoes, blue cotton trousers and shirt, Panama hat, a big black Cuban cigar in his mouth. He spoke to Ernest then, hat, cigar and all, he dived overboard. I remembered that sharks live and hunt there in the deep blue water.

Gregorio came to the surface beside us, his cigar missing but his hat, its brim ruffled around his brown face like a woman's cloche, still firmly in place. He climbed, dripping, aboard *Tin Kid,* put on our gaffing glove and told Taylor to bring his marlin alongside. Three minutes later Gregorio jabbed the gaff into the fish's shoulder, lifted him clear of the water and yanked him aboard so forcefully that they fell together into the cockpit and wrestled there a moment before Gregorio could extricate himself.

"Ya," he said grinning, meaning "Done now," jumped over the side and swam back to *Pilar*. Gregorio was fifty-two.

On the first night of the tournament *Tin Kid* had been the only boat which failed to tie up at the club's deck in the chic approved fashion, nose out, stern just missing the deck. Our little boatman had been afraid to back in. Now with our mighty fish aboard I felt we couldn't go in thus feebly. As we approached the club I took the wheel, turned us around, ordered our anchor tossed out in front of a berth between *Pilar* and *India III,* a big beautiful gleaming white boat. It was then that I discovered I did not know how to steer backwards.

From the club deck and surrounding boats streams of frantic Spanish poured down on me, instructions, imprecations, exhortations I couldn't understand in the din. I couldn't either stop or steer. So *Tin Kid* ran smartly into the polished white side of *India III* and scraped bare a good two square feet of her planking. They were wonderfully kind about it and I was very embarrassed and ashamed.

When they weighed our fish he was an even hundred pounds, and it was not until the end of the tournament that we discovered he was the single biggest fish of any class of marlin taken during the contest that year.

The Finca's cat family, which had begun felicitously with Boise and Princesa and continued with their children getting on more or less equably, that summer degenerated into a society of civil strife, anarchy and crime rampant among the crotons, ixora, philodendrons and ginger plants around the house. While Boise had never made much effort to teach his sons his own winning manners, Bigotes, our brave and cheerful principal stud cat, had behaved politely toward Fatso, his brother, the other functioning male, also toward his sisters, Friendless and Friendless's Brother, and the two bachelor boys, Uncle Willy, a conservative banker-type fellow who believed privately he was not a cat, and Uncle Wolfie, a fringed-gray esthete with the delicate sensibilities of his Persian mother.

For a year or two this family tolerated and supported the third generation. When Barbershop (Shopsky), one of the black-and-white youngsters, grew old enough to learn, Bigotes taught him how to hunt lizards and fruit rats. Uncle Willy took under his tutelage another youngster, Ecstasy, and taught him the joys of pigeon stalking so well that when a stalked pigeon in the grass took notice and wing, Ecstasy's expression of embarrassment matched Willy's. The third brother of the triplets was Spendthrift (Spendy), the love-sponge and purr-factory who preferred cuddling and typing with me to outdoor sports.

Perhaps it was Boise's lack of leadership in his frail old age which disrupted our cat colony. A big blond hoodlum tomcat from the village was the principal villain. Marauding the Finca's outer reaches, he found Bigotes defending them and taught him the joy of killing. One morning I found Spendy curled up, looking sweet and gentle as always, dead beneath the orejas palm near the garage. Ernest and I questioned the gardeners and learned that it was Bigotes and Shopsky who had been the murderers. Soon afterward we found Ecstasy so badly wounded that he soon died. This time the assassins were the strange cat from the village and Bigotes. We held a solemn conference about the police action required to restore order and decency to the family. In the CIA manner, we committed political murder. Ernest shot Fatso and Shopsky. He was irritable and mean-tempered for a couple of days after that, but the nasty stranger from the village disappeared and the murders within the cat family ceased. But not the sadness. Without Spendy draped over my books or across my breakfast table, my room looked heartless.

Princesa had long shown evidence of her aging. She no longer rolled ecstatically, beckoning a lover, in the catnip we put on the dining room floor. She allowed herself to be picked up rather than leaping to Ernest's knee. Beneath her silvery plumage she grew thin and fragile. She made herself a soft nest on top of Ernest's shorts in his cupboard one day. We found her dead there, ladylike and elegant.

Looking for ginger flowers (*Alpinia speciosa*) on the back terraces, I found Boise wandering mindlessly and spoke to him. He didn't recognize me. His heart was fluttering in uneven beats. I took him into Ernest's study, where for years he had been most at home, with apologies pushed vitamins down his throat, and

337

he revived from what I assumed was a heart attack. After that he had all the pleasures we could conjure for him—catnip for breakfast, along with a bit of Papa's marinated herring, lunch sitting on top of the table beside our plates, from which he accepted offerings including curried shrimp, and sweet-sour turkey, also mango slices. He took siestas with his head beside mine on my pillow and nights of sound sleep beneath the sheet on Ernest's stomach. He lived several years longer.

Black Dog and Negrita were, meanwhile, flourishing, together with the eight or ten dogs who lived behind the house and on the back staircase leading to the kitchen door. That summer Negrita, whom Ernest had thought well beyond the age of romance when he had taken her home from the Floridita years before, was attracting all the boy dogs from the neighborhood, frisky-happy with the attention she was receiving, and pretending annoyance when her best friend, Blackie, jealously tried to protect her from the visitors. They both had a dandy summer.

The children were far from home. Patrick and Henny were moseying around Italy and Greece. Bumby and Puck and their new baby, Joan, were in West Berlin. Gigi was working on what was supposed to be a new psychoanalytic science in New Jersey. We were having few visitors from the north, only Gianfranco Ivancich and Roberto Herrera being in residence with us, and our occasional local lunchtime guests. The relaxation from entertaining gave me time to attend to household accounts.

The better we knew where the household money was going, we decided, the better we might learn how to curb the flow of it. So I wrote down what I considered careful dated listings of expenditures from my house money.

The list went for three pages, including $258.90 for new shirts for Ernest and ending with six weeks' food for the servants, six of them lunching in the pantry, three dining there every day, at $29.00 weekly— $174.00.

Of course, our grand total for the six weeks,

338

$1,760.46, omitted almost as many expenditures as it included. I never knew how high my husband's monthly bills ran at the Floridita, or how much he gave away to its little squad of hard-luck hangers-on or other friends in need. Gregorio's $155.00 monthly wages were triple what we paid any of the Finca staff, and more than we paid the carpenter and the stonemason who worked for us six to ten months of most years. But *Pilar*'s care and feeding, her engine and structural repairs, gas, and her quarterly sessions in dry-dock to have her sides and bottom scraped and repainted, reached to about three times the maintenance costs of the Finca.

Except on days of fishing, the clicking of portable typewriters was as indigenous a sound as the clacking of palm fronds like dry sticks. In April Ernest had received a copy of "An Open Letter to the Writers of the West" by Ilya Ehrenburg quoting an address from the World Peace Congress held in Russia:

> We demand the unconditional prohibition of the atomic weapon. . . .
> We shall regard that government which is first to use the atomic weapon against any country as a war criminal. . . .
> We call upon all men and women of good will . . . to affix their signatures to this address. . . .
> I call upon the writers because each of their signatures will be followed by thousands of their readers' signatures. . . .
> Ernest Hemingway, I call upon you. You know my high esteem for your talent. . . . Almost all your books have been translated into Russian and are well known to Soviet readers. . . .

In May Ernest replied: ". . . For your information I not only oppose all atomic weapons but also all weapons above the potency of the .22 caliber sporting rifle and the shotgun. I am also opposed to all armies and navies and to all forms of aggression whether they be warlike, economic or religious. I am also opposed to all large police forces, all customs barriers, every form of censorship and all forms of propaganda or attempts to control the beliefs of peoples.

"I am also opposed to droughts, famines, disease, fear and despair. . . . I am opposed to war itself as a crime. But if my country were attacked . . . I would fight any aggressor."

He brought me the letter to read, he reading over my shoulder, pleased with my approval of it. I did not know until later that he stopped there and did not send the letter.

On July 1, we set out for a vacation at sea, Roberto Herrera piloting the *Tin Kid,* Papa, Gregorio and I in *Pilar,* Gianfranco having chosen to stay home. There was such a heavy sea from the east, an *oleaje grande,* that having fished without success we decided to put in for the night behind the reef at Rincón, some miles to the east of Bacuranao, our favorite lunchtime harbor. As we began to turn, Gregorio and I topside, Papa gave his usual jump-up from the fishing chair, aft on the lower deck, when a big swell caught us, rolled us sharply to starboard and caught Papa midway with his head hitting one of the hooks which held the big gaffs on the flying bridge. He stepped backward into the fishing chair, Gregorio motioned me to steer, and jumped below, and Papa came topside again, bright arterial blood streaming down from his head.

Papa was saying, *"Estoy bien,"* taking the steering wheel when Gregorio jumped topside again, saying to me, *"Yodo y vendajes"* (iodine and bandages). I couldn't find gauze in the first-aid kit in the head, so carried up a roll of toilet paper with the iodine and held wads of paper against the wound. In a minute I had been below and climbed up the side again, a quart of blood must have pumped from Ernest's head. It covered his chest and stomach, arms and legs and was making the green slats of the deck slippery. Gregorio told me to steer at slow speed and urged Papa to go below. He descended carefully for the only time by my side route, using its easy hand and foot holds. Gregorio threw out the anchor. I pushed hard aft to give the anchor good footing and Roberto came aboard. He found the bandage gauze, made a tourniquet to quiet the pumping blood and its flow slowed.

With salt water Gregorio washed Papa and the two decks and me and himself and we headed homeward. On the way I checked the wounded man's pupils. Normal. Concussion unlikely. I covered him in his afterdeck bunk with his favorite light cashmere blanket, and he dozed.

Having left other instructions to Juan, we took taxis to the house, found it in disarray, summoned servants and telephoned Roberto's surgeon-brother, José Luis. Ernest sat in my big leather desk-chair for the scalp-sewing, sipping a gin and tonic for anesthetic while José Luis cleaned the wound, slowly, patiently, hair by hair, and then made three stitches with silk thread. Clara, the maid, was holding a bowl of burning alcohol for antisepsis of the needle and thread and nervously spilled some on the patient's leg.

"No need for that, daughter," he said. "My feet are warm enough." He did not move his leg.

With the final galley proofs of *Across the River* corrected and sent north and the pressure of work lifted, Ernest floundered in the void and the need to wait for the arrival of Adriana and her mother. He was a simmering, restless stew of impatience. He yearned for approval of what he then considered his best novel. He wanted some big, important project on which to embark. He spoke of "attending" the Korean war. He was tired in spirit, and so sometimes ill-tempered, ill-mannered and nasty to me. He could barely stand the waiting for Adriana's bright, admiring glances. He was less than a good companion around the house. When in mid-July I read him Charlie Scribner's letter saying, "The novel is running on press and we should have bound copies about the end of the month," he was only slightly mollified.

Going to bed one night I said, "You know, lamb, each of us has a little sack of darkness smoldering down there inside of us. It sounds like a soap opera ... but ..."

"Mmmm. Pandora's box."

"When she opened it, she still had hope left. If I recall."

"Shit on hope."

"Oh baby, you should have hope. Think of all the people all around the world who love you. And admire you. You write wonderful things. You can write more of them."

"I'm just a desperate old man."

"You're not old. I wish I could help you cure the desperation."

"Wish you could."

"Maybe it's a tiny little bit of self-indulgence."

"Wish it were."

So we went fishing to lighten the desperation, also because the village stonemason was making extensive repairs to the house, reinforcing cross-beams, supporting columns, floors, ceilings, walls in an uproar of noise and dust.

We took a short jaunt westward, anchoring the first night in big, beautiful Bahía Honda with its forested islands and empty, uncluttered shores, the second and third nights behind our favorite reef at Paraíso. Early the next morning Gregorio hoisted our anchor and Ernest woke me and told me to go topside to steer. He had to finish some work before we reached Havana.

"Take her well out, Mary," Gregorio yelled from the galley as I climbed topside.

I put *Pilar*'s stern carefully out from the center of the saddle of the hills ashore, since we had no compass up top, and as we cleared the reefs and moved farther and farther into the Gulf Stream observed with mounting awe a condition of the ocean I had never seen before, not even in the wintertime North Atlantic.

The wind was moderate, only about Force 4 on the Beaufort Scale, I judged. But the gray sea was lifting up a square half-mile of itself into the sky, rising muted and inexorable against the horizon, so that we were chuffing over moving mountains of water with sizable, four-to-five-foot waves running helter-skelter down their sides as ridges clutter earth mountains. Behind each rolling water mountain another higher swell moved against us.

Increasing our power a fraction, I put our bow into a cautious, 90-degree turn so that we were plunging head-first onto the rollers on a course toward Goberna-dora Light which should soon appear as a toothpick on the horizon a bit to starboard. I had never seen such a display of power. For the first time I thought of *Pilar* as fragile and vulnerable against this force, and for the only time I could remember I felt unstable and uneasy in my stomach. The waves crisscrossing on top of the moving mountains were challenging me second by second and I needed some morning coffee or tea, some reassurance in my empty gut. The rolling mountains were endless.

I took a few deep breaths and gave myself a concert. "Onward Christian Soldiers," I shouted into the wind which whirled the notes away, "Swing Low, Sweet Chariot," "How Come You Do Me Like You Do, Do, Do?" As I went on hurling my songs at the sea, my queasiness departed but I was beginning to think that Gobernadora Light was retreating from us when Gregorio swung himself up like a monkey balancing a cup of hot coffee. His binocular eyes found the light just where it was supposed to be, so we were making headway against that strange tremendous sea and I could go below and find breakfast and my book. Gregorio had not put out baits, since fishing in that sea would be impossible. Listening to the radio from Miami that evening, we learned that an untimely storm of hurricane strength had battered the Bahamas and moved westward, battering Cuba's north coast.

After conferences with Ernest and by telephone with my parents in Chicago, we all agreed that I should go to Gulfport, Mississippi, find a comfortable place for my parents there, then fly to Chicago to escort them to their new roost. Advance copies of Ernest's new book reached us in time for me to take one with me to Gulfport, reading the final version on the plane to New Orleans and at the Hotel Markham in Gulfport, and it saddened me for what I felt were its artificialities. Also it struck me as comic that of all his dedications the only one he made "with love" was this one to me which I least admired. But this year my husband needed friendship, sympathy, and, if I could summon it, compassion, more than at any other time I'd known him. In the airlift of letters between Havana and Gulfport, then Chicago, and Gulfport again, I exaggerated my praises of his style, his selection of detail, his understanding of the military mind, even while suggesting areas in which he might improve his behavior.

To which he replied: "Remember all my sins and write me about them if you like. It's not a good time, though, really. This is the time when people close up and make the old perimeter defense." He was right, I decided, especially after I had seen some of the more ferocious reviews of the book. I stationed myself on the perimeter defense.

My mother had written from Chicago: "After anyone is eighty everyone expects them to be old and wrinkled and weak and die most any day, when we should be getting better understanding of eternal life." My project in Gulfport was to prevent any demands on either Tom's or Adeline's strength to overtax them. I found them half a small white-frame house on a tree-decorated street near a row of shops, with a tall crepe myrtle bush glowing outside the sitting room windows, and pear and pecan trees edging the big backyard where my father might wish to grow flowers or vegetables.

In Chicago we packed books, favorite cooking pans, grandmother's silver teaspoons, dishes, glassware, necessaries and sentimental keepsakes. A few days later we unpacked in Gulfport my mother's rose and dark red afghan, crocheted by her mother, Christian Science books, my father's favorite bean-baking pot, his history and philosophy books, and their accustomed napery. I returned to Cuba. I had not bothered Ernest with the details of the migration, but he had written me regularly about the U.S. reception of his book, the crisis with his leg (which from shrapnel still embedded from World War I had begun to pain him), the weather, the gossip.

August 9: "Your funny letter came from New Orleans. I had to explain what Shriners were to Gianfranco. . . . Everybody misses you and time does not race along when you're not here. . . . Eleanor Welch [our friend at Time Inc.] cabled apologizing for it [*Time's* nasty review of the book] saying quotes give my love to Mary and tell her eye hope as old *Time* hand she can explain to you group journalism some-

Top. *Thomas James Welsh in Hancock, Michigan, in 1889. He wrote, "In my first tailor made suit, strictly up to date in cut."*

Bottom. *Adeline Beehler in Lansing, Michigan, a modern girl of the 1890s who worked in a state senator's office.*

Top. The steamboat Northland *on an excursion on Leech Lake,
Minnesota, in the late teens of this century. The bloomer-suited
figure in the lower front doorway remembers it well.*

Bottom. *With my father and two chums in the front yard of our
house in Bemidji, Minnesota. I had the biggest hair bow.*

Top, left. *Mary Welsh, aged about two, in Bemidji, Minnesota, already showing a streak of stubbornness.*

Bottom, left. *Schoolgirl.*

Right. *The idea of wearing shorts for playing tennis had not yet reached northern Minnesota.*

Top. *My press pass for
Supreme Headquarters,
Allied Expeditionary
Forces in the European
theater of operations.*

Right. *In my Time Inc.
office in Soho, London.
After bomb explosions had
pulled out the office
windows a couple of times,
we installed windows
reinforced with steel
netting. They cracked but
stayed put. (Robert Capa)*

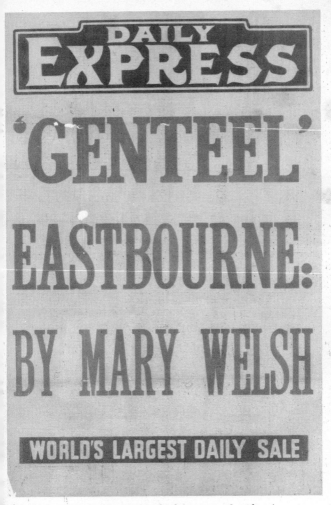

DAILY EXPRESS

'GENTEEL' EASTBOURNE:

BY MARY WELSH

WORLD'S LARGEST DAILY SALE

*Pleasant to see one's name in foot-high letters on the sides of
newspaper delivery vans in London.*

Cecil Beaton and I went down to the west of England to photograph the local Home Guard. They were not at all interested in the Blitz on London. (Cecil Beaton)

Top. *On the roof of our London office, the full Time-Life staff covering World War II before D-Day, June, 1944. Familiar faces: Bob Capa, lower left; David Scherman, behind my left shoulder—he set up his camera and ran around in time to be included in the shot; Bill Walton, third from right in the back. (David E. Scherman)*

Left. *Noel and I in our war correspondents uniforms, his British, mine American, both made by our mutual London tailor.*

Adeline and Thomas Welsh at their house in Gulfport, Mississippi, on July 9, 1952, their fiftieth wedding anniversary. (M. Hemingway)

Top. *Janet Flanner and Ernest in the bar of Les Deux Magots, Paris, 1944. (David E. Scherman)*

Bottom. *Puppy and kitten in Basque pelota players* cestas, *when I first arrived in Cuba, summer, 1945.*

The Smart Set

Top. *Even multiply wedded newlyweds have pretensions* From the *Chicago Herald-American, March 15, 1946.*

Bottom. *Ernest drew homemade birthday cards.*

Opposite, top. *Ernest called the house in Cuba "a charming ruin."*

Opposite, bottom. *When there was no big, exuberant bouquet of flowers on the living-room table at the Finca, I was not there.*

Top. *Adriana Ivancich and her brother, Gianfranco, at our pool in Cuba, 1951.*

Bottom. *I borrowed a guitar one evening at the Floridita. From left: Gianfranco Ivancich, Roberto Herrera, Taylor Williams, E. H.*

Opposite, top. *Lolling in* Pilar. *Few other people amused us more than we amused ourselves.*

Opposite, bottom. Pilar *heading toward the Gulf Stream past the Morro Castle guarding Havana's harbor. Felipe and I are in the Tin Kid.*

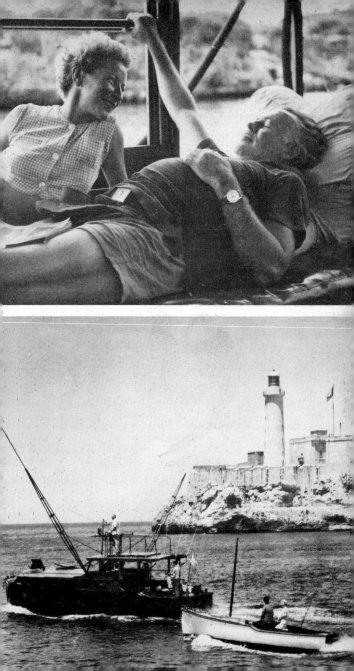

Top, left. *Taylor Williams and our prize-winning marlin.*

Top, right. *With the heavy tackle, it must have been a big fish I was working.*

Bottom, left. Pilar *was our happiest home away from home.*

Bottom, right. *E. H. and one of the near-thousand-pound marlin from the Humboldt Current off Peru. (M. Hemingway)*

Top. When Anastas Miko-yan came to see Fidel Castro in Cuba in 1960, the Russian Embassy telephoned to say he would like to come out for a visit. To my dismay he brought a dozen pals with him and a set of carved wooden dolls as a present. Having nothing better for snacks, I gave the crowd cold codfish stew on crackers. (G. Borovika, S. Sergeeva)

Left. In 1960, Fidel, follow-ing all the prescribed Big Game Fishing rules, won Ernest's prize for the heaviest weight of marlin taken during the Heming-way tournament. (UPI Photo)

Besides the ceiba tree on the front steps of the Finca Vigía, 1958.
One of Yousuf Karsh's few informal photographs.

Top. *Ernest and N'gui at Kimana Swamp, Kenya, with Kilimanjaro looming.* (Earl Theisen)

Bottom, left. *Our Cesna after the crash at Murchison Falls.* (M. Hemingway)

Bottom, right. *As we arrived at Entebbe after the two crashes. We did not know then how badly E's insides were damaged.* (Cifra Grafica)

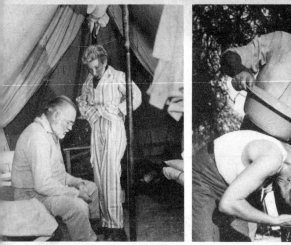

Opposite, top left. *Even though we were near the Equator, Kimana Swamp's 6,000-foot altitude made the nights chilly.*
(Earl Theisen)

Opposite, top right. *Days of cruising through fine red dust made shampoos a constant exercise. Finally Ernest shaved his head.*
(Earl Theisen)

Opposite, bottom. *"Bathi" with our tent's back flap open made a man feel dandy as well as clean.*

Top. *At the age of ten days Baa showed his character well developed.*
(Earl Theisen)

Bottom. *Even safari life presents problems to ponder.* (Earl Theisen)

Above. *At our rented house in Ketchum, Idaho, 1959, Big Boy Peterson was the most beguiling of the family (John Bryson)*

Right. *Photographer Bryson wanted an Action Picture in the winter of 1958–59.*

Top. *The first angel I made in the snow for Ernest was in the Tuileries of Paris in 1945. This was at Sun Valley fourteen years later.*

Left. *There is an elk standing on an island in the Big Wood River below my bedroom windows in Ketchum, and our gardener's Weimaraner, Lem, is being inhospitable.*
(M. Hemingway)

Top. *Nobel Prize winners looked solemn for the camera but I diverted the President's attention, at the White House in 1962. The lady at the left is Pearl Buck, and Mrs. George Marshall was on our host's left.*

Bottom, left. *Intrepid hunters, Clara Spiegel and I, joyous though badly wrinkled, with our safari guide, my stepson, Patrick, in Tanzania, June, 1962.*

Bottom, right. *A leopard in that area had eaten a baby alive, so without conscience problems I pulled a trigger on this beast of giant, pro-football size in Tanzania, 1962. (Clara Spiegel)*

Opposite. *Cesar Giron, a young matador from Venezuela, draped his embroidered cape over our barrera and dedicated a bull to Ernest at Logroño, Spain, on September 27, 1956. (Peter Buckley)*

Top. *The most glorious way to use an autumn afternoon in Idaho, tramping through sagebrush after doves or ducks or pheasants, who had no reason to be alarmed by me. I seldom hit anything. (Jack Ward)*

Right. *My triumph of a decade, a 130-pound broadbill swordfish, the only one I ever caught. Mr. William Shakespeare was the boat's captain, at Cabo San Lucas, Baja California. (Rogelio Covarrubias Wilkes)* times fouls things up unquote. . . . A letter from Lillian [Ross]. Book well liked on coast quotes wonderful and beautiful and almost weirdly marvelous book unquote."

August 14: "The counter-reaction to the reviews of the people who did not understand what the book is about are coming in. Later, of course, there will be the well prepared attempts to knock you off in the magazines. . . . You wrote a lovely loyal letter when the first attack came. I appreciated it and answered it the same day. . . . You remember Charley Curtis that wrote the *Practical Cogitator,* the book you liked? . . . He says I have magic, whatever that is. . . ."

September 11: "Please don't worry about the reviews of anything daughter and don't get any newspaper people to make you comment. . . . [Charlie Scribner] wrote he had ordered another printing of 25,000 the day of publication. . . . Finally had a letter from Venice. Afdera told everyone at the Lido last summer that I was desperately in love with her. . . . There was a picture in EUROPEO of Adriana and Afdera with this caption: Afdera and Adriana equal Renata. But the story was ok. . . . So no harm done. But what an Afdera . . . Nobody in Venice believes her but foreigners do . . . So when you hear she has been here with me and what a wonderful time we always have, just laugh. She's now made two trips to Cuba I think. In her dreams."

September 18: "José Luis has taken me off all medicines partly on account of a blood clot in right leg which caused the cramps and has been giving UHF Diathermy (15,000 volts) and various injections for last several days. . . . It interrupted circulation so feet ice cold. . . . Treatment goes on until September 27th. So please don't come home before then as everything is under control . . . and I want to be in such fine shape that you can say it must have been a hallucination. . . . I renewed the gun permits, both our carnets, and put Gianfranco's papers in order. They were far from same. . . . About book: It must have something to arouse such hysterical attack and defense. . . . The awful review you sent from N.O. was by a Literary Guild big shot. We did not submit it to them nor any other book club . . . so the reviewers have to try to kill it. . . ."

September 22: "My dearest kitten, not that you are any lower-case kitten. Hope you are settling your family well. . . . My leg and legs much better. . . . Am going to go out in the boat today and get a good salt-water swim and *aprovechar* [take advantage of] the beauty weather. . . . Had a four-page letter from Buck about the book. . . . He likes all of it . . . the military part magnificent. . . . On the other hand *Time* says I do not know how a Colonel talks. . . . I wish Max Perkins wasn't dead. He would have liked the book so much. . . . Well with him dead the only people that I cared about whether they liked it were you, Buck, Charley Sweeny, Gianfranco and Adriana. Have heard from three out of five precincts [meaning Buck, Gianfranco and me]. Charley Sweeny will probably say, 'Young fellow you may very well get to be able to write.' I can hear his lovely voice saying it. Some people might think it a little harsh for a lovely voice. [It sounded like a sour note on a cello to me, much as I loved him.] Always a lovely voice to me and making wonderful sense over half the time. . . ."

Fleur Cowles had asked me to do a piece about our Finca living for her gussied-up magazine, *Flair,* and we were politely disputing the price.

On September 26 Ernest wrote: "None of my business . . . but it is better to sell three pieces for $3,000 than not sell one for $1,500. If I can afford to sell two first class Venetian fables to HOLIDAY for $1,000, you can afford to accept something over $1,000 for a good, easily written price." [Indubitably, he was right.]

On a Sunday evening in Gulfport just before I flew back to Cuba we listened to Louella Parsons chanting Hollywood gossip over the radio and heard with interest that the Hemingways' marriage was splitting apart because of an Italian contessa with whom Ernest had fallen violently in love and who was at the moment visiting him in Cuba.

"I wonder if she is as inaccurate about other people, poor devils?" I said.

My mother was incensed. "What right has she to say such lies?"

My father was composed. "One of the prices of fame, I suppose. There must be many others."

My cousin Bea telephoned from Chicago to savor the nonsense and then there was Ernest's voice, agitated from Cuba.

"My kitten, my kitten. Did you hear that idiocy of Parsons?" He almost never listened to the radio except at sea.

"Yeah, by chance we heard it."

"That bitch. She's evil."

"Oh, lamb. Who cares?"

"I care. You know it isn't true."

"Of course. How are you otherwise?"

"Fine. Everybody here fine. But you don't believe that Parsons bitch?"

"Of course not. Look, lamb, we're not upset. Please don't you be."

"My good kitten. May I speak to your father?"

Ernest and my father chatted for several minutes before my father handed me the telephone.

"Kitten? We're all waiting for you. You'll be here Tuesday?"

"Hope so. That's what I'm planning."

"Kitten, don't let these lies bother you."

"Of course not."

"Sleep well."

"You too."

After the high-tension telephone call I poured myself a drink of whiskey, my father warmed some milk for my mother and took a modest sip of my drink.

"What did you two talk about at such length?" I inquired.

"Well, Dearidoo, it was confidential, I suppose."

"Oh, come now, Dad. What can be so secret from me?" A sharp breeze had begun to rustle the leaves of the pear tree outside our windows. I felt a bit ruffled too.

"Ernest seemed really embarrassed," my father said. "He wanted me to know that he was a responsible man and a serious husband. I think he said 'serious.' What a dear man he is."

I went to sleep wondering why Ernest had been so sensitive to the Parsons report, how close it might have

347

come to his daydreams about Adriana, but grateful that his money had provided my parents with this new cheerful nest. Ernest and I had never made any sort of formal economic contract, either oral or written, other than a phrase of his in Paris, in 1944, that he would undertake to look after my parents' well-being as well as I could.

No matter how firmly we ignored the bad book reviews or warmly welcomed the good ones, Ernest was restless and unhappy that October. I wished I could persuade him to talk to the psychiatrist who had helped Patrick, but decided the risk of his building up animosity against me was too great. The weather being too turbulent for fishing, he decided to go off on a journey alone in the car with Juan. Precisely where, he would not say, only "westwards, probably." He made the usual to-do about packing books, medicines, spectacles, landlubber *guayaberas*.

I wrote him a sort of poem, "For the Road, October 13, 1950":

> . . . You who understand me well by now,
> Must know what long ago I learned
> In love and loneliness,
> That there are secret places in a man
> A woman too
> Where no one for no reason
> Has right of entrance without invitation. . . .
> I love you poorly sometimes
> But would love better if I could,
> And maybe can.
> And on the road today and all your roads
> I wish you hope.

In midmorning the servants and I waved him off and I went eagerly to work catching up with long neglected household chores, also to swim my customary half mile, naked and happy in the pool before lunch. In mid-afternoon Ernest returned, well-filled with frozen daiquiris but apparently no less unhappy. A couple of days later in some dispute he said, "You camp-follower and scavenger." I never could remember what I did or said to elicit such a description, but I remembered the

348

phrase. A couple of days still later he said, "You have the face of Torquemada." I looked it up in the dictionary. My usual reaction to such pronouncements was to run down to the rose garden, sit under the lichee tree there to weep and coddle my hurt.

In the flickering shade of the lichee tree I held conversations with myself.

Wild Mary: "What about your pride? Haven't you any pride? You're too craven."

Mild Mary: "My pride? It's wounded. It stings."

W.M.: "Your pride should make you defend yourself."

M.M.: "Pride goeth before a fall. Mama's always saying that."

W.M.: "Fight back. Insult him. Leave him. That'll make him suffer."

M.M.: "That will make him suffer for ten minutes, maybe. He'd love it if I left him. Or he thinks he would."

W.M.: "You've lost your guts."

M.M.: "So I leave him, and I take my pride like a butterfly in a glass box. 'Here's my wounded pride. A nickel a look.' Where are the customers? It's embarrassing. Nobody cares about my wounded pride. I wish I had a big brother."

W.M.: "You're spineless. You should care about your pride."

M.M.: "I guess my pride is expendable. A luxury I can't afford. I've worked other places where the boss punctured, flattened and waltzed all over my pride. Leola Allard on the Chicago *Daily News*."

W.M.: "Hit him. Kill him."

M.M.: "Melodramatics. I can't afford them either. Kill him? I need him. Don't forget I love him. When he's good he's entrancing."

W.M.: "You're a spineless fool."

M.M.: "I'm where I want to be, at least."

The warm Cuban earth and the grasses beneath the lichee tree smelled good, and friendly. So did the air from the roses.

As the attacks continued sporadically, together with sudden outbursts of violence, I perceived that, rather than breaking into slobbering pieces of nervous break-

349

down as Ernest apparently expected me to do, I was building up some sort of resolve and resistance to the inanities. My husband might drive himself wild with his fluctuating tempers if he insisted on so doing, but he was not going to drag me with him, I determined. Too much of our life was too good to allow it to fall apart. We still shared too many times of friendship in solid footing, too many moments of airy wit playing with our languages, too many hours of sweet, if temporary, comfort together.

The seasonal hurricanes were receding and the air and the earth drying. The tiny rivulets of moisture which for weeks had been running down some of our indoor walls subsided. I got the gardeners to turn over and feed the soil of our big vegetable plot and also the rose garden where we would soon be planting half a hundred sturdy young tea rose plants. With luck they would be giving us blooms early in the new year as would the floribunda roses we would set into the back terrace to frame our view of Havana. Ernest's book was steadfastly ascending the bestseller lists and he endorsed my programs of embellishing the farm. "We don't need any extras," he might say, looking at the bougainvillaea, antigonon and thunbergia hugging the whitewashed walls of the house. "But they can't do any harm."

On October 27 I made an extra set of big cheerful flower arrangements and put them upstairs and downstairs in the Little House, checked that bed sheets were tight, pillows fluffed, light blankets, soap and towels more than sufficient, bed-reading lights in order, thermoses of iced water filled, ventilation modulated, pens, pencils, writing paper in good supply. Simple and unpretentious with its big western windows giving onto the whispering tops of the laurel trees behind it, our guest house looked welcoming to me. With Gregorio, Roberto and Gianfranco we swarmed aboard *Pilar* the next morning and moved down the bay to meet the incoming Italian passenger-cargo ship, *Luciano Manara*, on which Dora Ivancich and her daughter were arriving for their only visit to the western shores of the Atlantic Ocean.

For hours while the big ship got herself assigned to

a berth and tied up, we milled around the harbor, all hands on the flying bridge, trolled a feather outside in the Gulf Stream and caught one ceremonial dorado, waved and waved and waved to the figures on the *Manara*'s deck, Adriana in a lavender dress, Dora as usual in gray. We tied up finally at the Club Náutico, drove along the quai, went aboard the *Manara* ostensibly to help our guests through immigration, and took them back to the little club for a snack of Morro crab while Gianfranco and our old friend from customs, Paco Garay, dealt with their luggage, Gianfranco dizzy with happiness, grunting "*bene, bene, contento.*" If Ernest's eyes misted over with emotion, I did not see it. I was happy at the prospect of having women around the Finca for a change. Except for Pauline and Bea, we had had no women guests for more than a night or two.

I had planned lunch at the Finca but the debarkment of the luggage took such a long time that we opted to delay lunch, drove out to the Finca to introduce it to our guests, showed them their quarters which they declared "enchanting" and, after Gianfranco and Paco arrived with the luggage, lunched at suppertime. Gianfranco had lived both in the Venetian Room in the big house and occasionally in the Little House, and chose now to sleep on the wide, comfortable bunk on the ground floor there, with his mother and sister upstairs. From his choice of the new bed and their rapid Italian exchange of quips and endearments I realized how little he had indicated to us his loneliness for his family and country. The household embarked on a course of social festivities, both given and received, such as we never undertook before or since.

Ernest longed to show Adriana all his treasured aspects of Cuba, the view from the top of the tower across green valleys with their gray-trunked royal palms looking like exclamation points, the lively, aromatic narrow streets of the old city, not unlike Venice, the Club de Cazadores, the Floridita, the extravagant views from the road that ran westward along the north coast of the big, empty bays there. At home they made much of their partnership in their private, uncapitalized company, White Tower, Inc., and Adriana moved her drawing paper, pencils and paints to the tower's airy top floor, and there produced creditable drawings of local scenery. Gianfranco wanted his sister to meet the boys and girls he knew in Havana, and she used to climb to the top of the tower where I would be sunbathing to show me the charming frocks in which she was about to go, chauffeured by Juan, to luncheon parties at the Country Club on the other side of town or in the handsome houses of the local gentry. She was immediately liked and welcomed by the city's small Italian colony including their embassy crew.

Whenever I went to town to buy door hinges or varnish or window-screening or pillowcases or groceries Dora and Adriana came along to do "shopping," and there was the morning when Dora spent a long time in a bank. Just before lunch at home Juan sent word that he wished to see me. There in the pantry his usually black patent-leather face had turned lavender and I thought he was ill. With great effort he said in Spanish, "I have to tell you that I found this in the garage," and he handed me a bundle of bills the size of a quart bottle.

Mystified, I asked, "Where, precisely, did you find this?"

"On the garage floor, just near the door." Some of its customary color was returning to his face.

On our return from town, Juan had stopped the car as usual at the bottom of the wide stone steps in front of the house and we three women had scattered to wash our faces before eating. It occurred to me that someone might have stolen the money and, thinking himself detected, thrown it in the garage before being caught with it.

"I'm sorry that finders can't be keepers," said I, taking the bundle. The outside bill was a fifty, and I understood Juan's torment in making himself report his find. He could have supported himself and his family for the rest of his life with that cash. I put it on the sitting room table and told Ernest about it. When Dora and Adriana came in I told them, Dora went back to the Little House, returned and said that must be the sum which was missing from her purse—$27,000. She had taken it from the bank that morning to make a payment on a banana plantation Gianfranco was interested in. She handed me a $20 bill to give to Juan. I gave it to him later together with my check for $50.

Ernest's enthrallment with his house guests did not appear to redeem me from whatever sins I was supposed to be committing. His internal turbulence continued to explode, mostly in my direction, for unsuspected, unexpected reasons. Soon after the Ivancich mother and daughter arrived he disapproved of a dark dress I had chosen to wear for dinner at home and a film to which we all were going, a dress of which he had never before proclaimed dislike. Now he regarded it with distaste and commented, "Your hangman's suit. Your executioner's suit." As we were embarking in the car for the film, he announced, "You've sabotaged it."

Hunting for some papers in the drawers beneath my window seat, I noticed that his letters to me and mine to him had been removed, and asked him if he had taken them.

"I've put them in the bank," said he. I assumed he had destroyed them.

For years a well-designed lamp had from the front of the terrace lighted the way down our front steps and to the Little House. One night as the Ivanciches were preparing to retire, Ernest disappeared from the living room, returned, opened the front screen door and shot out the lamp. Luckily I had in my room a flashlight which could guide them home.

On another evening Dr. Herrera had dined with the Ivanciches and us, a serene evening, I thought. At dinner Gianfranco and I had agreed to fill out a U.S. government form with which he would apply for a visa to visit the United States, accompanying his mother and sister who would be returning a few months later to Italy via the U.S.A. I took my portable typewriter out to the living room table where we could work. From his room, Ernest walked in, took umbrage at the scene, picked up my typewriter and hurled it onto the floor. Amazingly, it was not much damaged. Later that evening as we all were sipping wine in the sitting room, something—some incautious word of mine—caused him to throw his wine in my face. It stained, irrevocably, the whitewashed wall behind me.

353

In semishock I headed for my room, then paused. "You must endear yourself to our guests, throwing things," I said and looked at them. José Luis, grim-faced, was walking back to the dining room, but Dora and Adriana Ivancich, like the monkeys on a branch, sat on our sofa, hearing no evil, seeing no evil. Gianfranco stood nearby looking nervous, keeping silent.

By mid-November I decided that I must attempt to construct some sort of order out of this intermittent chaos. Ernest was working placidly one morning at the typewriter on top of the bookcase in his room. I broke the rule that he must never be interrupted, no matter what.

"Will you please come to my room? I have some things to say to you." I had thought about this speech. It would be short and pointed. Dolefully but docilely, he padded across the living room to stand beside my desk.

"I will be brief, but you listen carefully," I said, looking straight into his gloomy brown eyes.

"I think I understand about your feeling for this girl." (I had edited out the word "infatuation.")

"As I told you long ago you have my sympathy." (I held back such words as "juvenile" and "fool.")

"Your insults and insolences to me hurt me, as you surely know.

"But in spite of them I love you, and I love this place, and I love *Pilar* and our life as we have it here normally.

"So, try as you may to goad me to leave it and you, you're not going to succeed. Are you hearing me? Because I think it would be bad and disorienting for you as well as me."

Ernest nodded. He was hearing me.

"Okay, that's it. No matter what you say or do—short of killing me, which would be messy—I'm going to stay here and run your house and your Finca until the day when you come here, sober, in the morning, and tell me truthfully and straight that you want me to leave.

"I hope you've heard me."

Ernest stood there a moment, his legs showing goose

354

pimples below his khaki shorts, his face thoughtful. It was a chilly morning.

"Yes, I heard you," he said and went out.

He never asked me to leave.

When I had last been in Gulfport, Ernest had written me about a young couple getting on well together partly because the husband was educating the wife in the nuances of how to live. "I don't know how long the fun of teaching a pupil with a definite *plafond* goes on," he said. "But maybe she gets a higher *plafond*."

Maybe it was sloth, maybe selfishness, which influenced my conviction that I was saving Ernest the trouble and trauma of finding out for himself how long the teacher-pupil combination might be fun.

Among Adriana's admirers was a young man of good family, Juan Verano, who had taken her dancing several evenings and on New Year's Eve invited her to join various festivities in Havana. After a long, late lunch that day Dora had retired for the night telling me she would not wish further food or drink. The servants having been dismissed for that big night of Cuban celebration, I made a light supper and took it with a bottle of wine on a tray to the sitting room and called "chow's ready" to Ernest, who came softly onto our Philippine matting.

"Where's Dora?"

"She said she wanted to rest. She doesn't want supper."

"You slut."

"I checked just now. She's reading in bed and says she's comfortable."

He picked up an ashtray I had brought in Venice and threw it out the door onto the red-tiled terrace where it shattered to pieces.

"You must know you're behaving like a pimply adolescent and a boor. Tell me, what do you feel you're achieving with it?"

No answer.

It was not the only grim New Year's Eve I'd ever known, I reflected. There had been the December 31 when one of my London friends, Philip Slessor, had invited me to something splendid the BBC was giving. But Mr. Wilson, the *Daily Express*'s benign-looking, devilish city editor had sent me up to the wilderness of Essex on some worthless story from which I could return only by a cold, clanking, slow milk train. From the London station I had taxied disconsolately to my chilly flat in Chelsea which contained nothing potable more cheering than tea. But I felt wonderful the next morning.

Before the holidays and again as we hurtled into 1951 none of us had time to squander brooding. We were forever going places.

We went to the old auditorium in Vedado to hear Arthur Rubinstein play Chopin and after that out to Montmartre, the nightclub with a palm tree growing up through the bandstand, found crowds of friends there and danced and caroused the night through. We went en masse to an evening at the cheerful one-and-a-half ring circus, which our friend John North of Barnum and Bailey used to send to Havana in the Christmas season, pausing as usual at the Floridita for a Papa Doble, the daiquiri without sugar, both going and returning. In *Pilar* we fished eastward to spend a night at Puerto Escondido and stayed aboard there two or three nights, food running low, while a violent storm from the north kept us at anchor. One morning Gregorio showed me a trail through muck and marsh to a tiny station on the Toonerville Trolley leading to Havana and the next morning I piloted Dora and Adriana there, all of us shivering in the north wind.

Never before and never afterward did we indulge in such social performances as that year, Ernest forbearing about it and I making the most of it. After days of preparation—Adriana painting posters and Spanish fans for the lamps, Gianfranco making signs, I arranging flowers, drinks at the pool, menus, music, extra servants—we invited all of Adriana's new Cuban friends as well as our old friends, Cuban, British and United Statesans, thirty-six people in all but about eighty came, confident of welcome. The night was cool but not cold. Drivers from the village under the supervision of our Juan parked cars after the guests alighted at our front steps. Double rows of little candles sparkling in the grass led our friends down the hill to the pool where lights gleamed among the leaves of the alamo trees and brightened the blue of the water, to the bar under the pergola at one end, with Havana shimmering beyond the valleys at the other end. Maracas and guitars of the *conjunto* of the Floridita thumped there while bartenders, also from the Floridita, filled glasses.

We served buffet dinner in the house where the furniture had been pushed to the outer edges of rooms, and low tables, cushions and foot-stools offered eating seating. The library was cleared for dancing by candlelight, the *brisa* being agreeably gentle that night. The French champagne held out all evening but at midnight we had to send to the village for more whiskey, having finished off some thirty bottles of it.

That was the coldest winter we ever passed in Cuba, and I wrote my parents hoping they, with their floor furnace, were not too uncomfortable. "My fingers are so stiff that I can't type; the servants stand around in their summer clothes shivering like droopy hens; Ernest has so many clothes on that it's hard to distinguish him from an overstuffed sofa; we don't even have enough blankets to keep warm in bed. . . . You know we have no heat of any sort in this house, except for cooking. I dug up one little electric heater and joyfully plugged it into the living room. But its effect is purely psychological—you can't feel anything from it at all until you stand right over it. The house with walls a foot thick in the old Spanish Colonial style is always a few degrees cooler than the outdoors, a fact we appreciate mightily in the summer. But now it is a refrigerator. . . . The thermometer in my room hasn't risen above sixty-four all day, even at noon when the sun was more or less shining . . . today's paper says it is the coldest December 19th in the history of Miami . . . [but] the air is fresh and clean . . . nearly all of the windows are open."

The cold wave had bypassed Gulfport. My father had sat reading Christmas Day in the old rocker on the back porch in his shirtsleeves. I did not feel too sorry that they were not among the crowded chilly mob at the Finca Vigía.

As the holidays ended Ernest set out by himself on a new adventure, a story about an old Cuban fisherman he had put on the tape recorder inside his head years before and had sketched in a piece *Esquire* published in April 1936. This was happy work. Every morning he unwound a bit of the tape, the words falling smoothly onto the paper in his battered Royal portable, with none of the problems of disciplining turbulent emotions, rephrasing meannesses, smoothing roughnesses that had so troubled him in the writing of *Across the River*. Every evening after supper when our guests had retired and the house was quiet I read the manuscript, beginning each time at the first page.

Those were sweet hours. Light from our reading lamps reflected down warmly from our pink-cinnamon ceiling, tinting the mahogany shine of tables and bookcases. Only the sighs of a breeze in the palms or the faraway chuff of a lorry on the main road came through the open windows. Ernest read silently in his chair, or, if I made some involuntary whisper of approval, came over to read, peering over my shoulder. This was simple line-drawing beauty, I thought. It reminded me of Bach fugues and Picasso drawings without clutter or frills. I could say truthfully after each evening's reading that I thought the work was wonderful. My cup kept running over.

For that last issue of *Flair* magazine, I wrote:

> I am constantly and unreasonably awed at Ernest's ability to work seriously in the midst of our perpetual weekend. Although he is not positively averse to tranquility and privacy, he moves amiably for months at the heart of a hubbub involving time, space, motion, noise, animals and personalities always approaching but seldom attaining complete uproar. Some people would call it chaos. We call it freedom. It is a manner of living about as formal and regulated as the wag of a dog's tail and Ernest seems to thrive in it. . . . I find it instructive, stimulating and busy. . . .

As February approached, Dora and Adriana began planning which museums, churches and Broadway productions they would fit into their first brief visit to the U.S.A. on their journey back to Venice. Gianfranco made a few more attempts, fully supported by Ernest and me, to extract from Washington a temporary visa with which he could accompany his family to their sailing exit from the Hudson River. To no avail. Some governmental red tape could not be unknotted. Then we all agreed it would be fun for the Venetian ladies to see a bit of Florida and New Orleans on their way north and I offered to drive them through those places in our Buick which we had left in Key West. Before leaving Cuba, we drove Dora and her daughter to the Hotel Ambos Mundos to spend a couple of nights so that Dora could truthfully report back in Venice that they had not spent *all* their time with us.

With Juan Verano, Adriana's suitor, we three women flew to Key West, then set off up the keys for Miami, Adriana beside Juan in the front seat, Dora and I sedately behind, Adriana and Juan in animated conversation, I trying unsuccessfully to direct their attention to the varying colors of the sea, the mangroves, the coconut palms, and the roadside grasses. Throughout that five- or six-day journey I noted that these people did not know how to travel observantly cross-country. They did not look out the windows at the countryside. Even with the windows rolled down, they did not smell the pine country of northern Florida, or the orange blossoms below it. They looked at the road and chatted the banalities of Havana's social structure. They mis-stowed their luggage in the car's trunk, so that half a dozen bags had to be removed before they could reach their overnight bags. They pondered, unnecessarily since I was hostess, over menu prices. I longed to be traveling instead with my husband, who was observant, forethinking and smooth about such details.

I had telephoned my parents that we would stop for tea with them and managed to get us almost on time to their house where Adeline had the tea things set out, her just-made baking-powder biscuits still warm and ready for butter and homemade strawberry jam. The Ivanciches and Juan went on to New Orleans for one night of its Mardi Gras, picked me up on their return eastward, were ushered onto a train at Jacksonville, and the following afternoon Juan and I caught the afternoon plane from Key West to Havana.

While we were on the journey to Gulfport, Ernest wrote me: "Couldn't work the first day and had black-ass the second but worked anyway and did 874. [Big for him.] Day before yesterday did 665 and yesterday 624. . . . Don Andrés came out to lunch Thursday and to spend the afternoon because he had black-ass and José Luis had it terribly last night. So maybe it is a seasonal complaint. I can cheer up everybody except me. You better come home and do that. . . .

"Am in the very toughest part of the story to write. He has the fish now and is on the way in and the first shark has shown up.

"Christ how I miss you being here to read it. Also miss you for several other reasons. . . . We went to the Floridita one evening . . . the day the old man caught the fish in the story. Have been a good boy all the time. No whores, fights, violence nor intemperance. Haven't spent any money except that one evening at the Floridita. . . . Maybe I'll work just a page. I love my sweet Kittner. Best to your family. . . ."

Conscientiously Adriana wrote thank-yous both from New York and their trans-Atlantic ship. On October 17 she wrote: "I have N.Y. now and it is so wonderful and exciting and new but my heart is still with my dear Finca and the little house and your flowers, fresh each morning and your pies and the yellow Buick. . . . I realize only now how much I am attracted to my second family. . . . Mary, you have been so nice to us during the whole time and on the trip too. . . ."

Almost immediately our departed guests were replaced by others, mostly in daytime visitations, except for Ernest's favorite sister, Ursula, a feminine modification of himself in stature, eyes, personality and wit so that we were instant old friends, and her husband, Jep Jepson. They were on their every-other-year holiday from Jep's bank in Honolulu and we made the most of it in *Pilar*, Havana, picnics, cockfights. Jep contentedly explored our library, saying, "No time for this at home." One day Charlie and Vera Scribner came fishing, a day of choppy, bucking seas through which Vera sat, solid and straight as a royal palm tree, on our unpadded bait box. Another day they came to lunch and read Ernest's first draft of his tale of the old fisherman, Charlie's verdict being, "Nice story. Interesting."

I had not found time before the Scribners arrived to tap out a neat copy and carbon of the old fisherman Santiago's story, but I had read it, as before the Florida interlude, every evening from the first sentence until the last of that day's work. Every night the simple story gave me goose pimples I could not control. Ernest would touch my arm and smile, murmuring, "I did okay today, mmmm?" To him the goose flesh was proof positive that the quality of his work was good. I could never have manufactured the little bumps.

But as the end of the story approached and Santiago had clubbed the sharks which had eaten half his great fish, I sensed something more than the tragedy of the fish.

"Darling, I feel something ominous. Something bad is going to happen."

"Maybe. I don't know."

"Oh, lamb, you're not," said I, divining. "You're not going to let this old man die. Please."

"Maybe better for him."

"How can you say that? He's old. But he's healthy, basically. He's brave and he's good. Please let him live."

Gianfranco came in softly from the library.

"Don't you agree, Gianfranco? This old man should live to fish again."

"Nice man," Gianfranco grunted. He was frequently monosyllabic, and clearly he felt this was not his business.

I tried another tack.

"You know I don't pretend to know about writing. You're the house writer, lamb. But it seems too easy to kill him off. Too facile. And nothing in this book so far reads facile or tricky."

"I'm glad you like him so much."

"I'll bet everybody would be happier if you let him live."

Ernest mumbled something.

361

A few nights later when I read the last lines of the story, my goose pimples sprouted again.

"Up the road, in his shack, the old man was sleeping again. He was still sleeping on his face and the boy was sitting by him watching him. The old man was dreaming about the lions."

13

Vicissitudes

IN THAT YEAR'S marlin-fishing tournament, Taylor Williams and I again fishing in *Tin Kid,* with strong young Felípe as our boatman, I hooked and, straining and puffing, brought to the gaff a husky white marlin. Half an hour later, Taylor got one, and we were pursuing a third, raging for another tournament prize, when a canopy of black cloud which we had scarcely noticed crashed down into the sea and in minutes churned it into soaring waves ten, to twenty, to thirty feet high, with the troughs between them merely slits and a barrage of cold rain beating through our shirts onto our skins. I had never seen *Tin Kid* in such danger, remembering that our nearest coast which would tear us apart if we had to swim. But steering with simple genius, Felípe maneuvered us into the little harbor of Cojímar where Ernest, straddling *Pilar* like a surfboard, brought his boat in and picked us up. (When I climbed aboard, his guests of that day were still on their knees, praying.) Hanging like a leech in the turbulence I climbed topside.

"You all right, my kitten?" he asked.

"*Cómo no?* But wasn't that something rough, how quick that storm hit?"

"I don't remember any *turbonada* coming so fast."

"Or with waves so tall and thin."

"A freak *turbonada*. We've been to the circus. But I don't think we've lost any boats."

Up there by himself he had taken a beating from exploding rain, cold and difficult steering, I saw. Beneath the buoyant cheer in his expression there was a layer of weariness. He had been concerned about *Pilar*'s ribs and planking, and a little bit disgusted with his terrified guests. Long before, I had learned that he felt the only acceptable response to danger was a sort of excited, exhilarated welcome. When people failed to show it, he was disappointed.

When they handed out the tournament prizes the next evening, Rafael Posso, the club commodore, gave Taylor and me one that had not been listed. "For valor," he said.

In July some seventy of us old Bemidji children shared a minor triumph, a reunion complete with a dinner-dance and a fish fry, in a web of recollections, to celebrate the twenty-fifth anniversary of our high school graduation. We found the town more changed than we were. The maples and lilacs and ivy our parents had planted on the edges of pine forests had grown beyond recognition, and my old twelve-room white clapboard house looked neglected and in need of paint. A boardinghouse now, somebody said. But as adults we classmates retained, reinforced, our youthful characters. Our beloved "Prof." Smith noted it. "Everybody fell right back into his old notch," he said.

Early in August my mother wrote that my father was not feeling well. He had entirely abandoned the medicines prescribed by his Chicago doctors to contain, we hoped, if not cure his cancer of the prostate. Then my mother telephoned to say that he had collapsed and been taken to the local hospital. I hurried to Gulfport, found my father comparatively comfortable in his hospital room but mistrustful of his doctor and all the medical procedures. I marketed and cooked for my mother and took her daily to the hospital to visit my father whom she chided for the "accident" as though it were his fault. Sleeping on my cot on my parents' back porch I took comfort in waking just before dawn to watch the trees in the back-yards taking shape against the sky.

As usual Ernest wrote almost daily. On August 14: "Don't worry or let your parents worry about expenses. They come to around what I had figured. . . . Had a wonderful kind affectionate and understanding note from Charlie Scribner. He wants to loan me, personally, any amount we need for this. I will write him and give a percentage of the eventual picture rights as security. . . . Sympathize *so* with your poor father. Give him my love. . . . You stay until things clarify or settle down. Don't have him think of leaving the hospital. We will get by fine here and I promise you to keep on a sound schedule and work as well as I can."

At the hospital I told my father that I must soon return to Cuba, since he was improving and no longer in pain. "You go along home. That dear man needs you and we will be all right. Your mother will be all right until I get back. You know she is not timid." I took a train for New Orleans to catch the evening plane for Havana. Ernest met me, complete with a jar of frozen daiquiris, at Rancho Boyeros at midnight. Slipping onto our cool six-foot-six-inch-square bed, I sent aloft signals of thanksgiving.

The Gulfport hospital let my father go home on August 28 and the doctor wrote me that the carcinoma was spreading locally but under control by hormone treatment. There was nothing more Ernest or I could do for my father except to persuade him to continue swallowing the hormones.

On September 7 Ernest wrote him: "I am prejudiced because my own life has been saved by physicians and surgeons many times. . . . Truly I do not think it would be too great a sacrifice for you to take the medicines prescribed for you by a conscientious and reputable doctor in order to avoid, if possible, an absolute and miserable end to your life. You feel better because you have had proper treatment and medication and then you stop that medication saying that you have been miraculously cured. . . .

"There are no miraculous cures at eighty and no man should be too proud to accept the aid of sci-

364

ence. . . . We must all die and it is better to die with the minimum of discomfort and true pain. . . ."

My father answered Ernest that his doctor had prescribed a new tablet. "Both bottles are here on the table and will be taken faithfully as long as he feels I should take them. I will call at his office next Thursday and as often thereafter as he thinks I should come. . . . I realize that there is about the same percentage of fanatics associated with the C.S. movement as with practically all other religions. . . ."

The heat of August ebbed and we were sleeping cool one night in mid-September when I woke up, touched Ernest softly and found he was also awake.

"Been dreaming about H.M. Tomlinson," I murmured. "He's replastering his dining room and he's mixing sliced peaches with the plaster. For the perfume." (I had been thumbing through *Gallions Reach* a few days earlier.)

"Been dreaming about Ford Madox Ford," E. said. "Him, the war."

"We're pretty literary tonight."

"Black Dog—he's been dreaming about Elizabeth Barrett Browning."

"Or about her little dog, what's its name—Ruff? Puff? Fluff?"

We dozed a few minutes. Then E. said, "Flush."

Two-thirds asleep, I tried to remember a famous Hollywood dog who might be the subject of Negrita's dreams, little Negrita sleeping softly on top of the bed between our feet, finally remembered and murmured, "Miss Negrita's dreaming too. Lassie? Negrita never saw a Lassie picture."

"No," said Ernest, muffled in sleep. "Rin Tin Tin."

On one of my last visits to Pauline, she had just returned from exhaustive examinations at the Mayo Clinic and hadn't found any definitive cause of the nasty headaches which had recently been bothering her or her newly discovered high blood pressure. She spoke casually of her ailments and so I regarded them as a sometime thing. Her downtown shop, Bahama House, which sold works by local craftsmen and objects for household use or decoration, was doing well, making a profit. She had seen a dress designed just for me, she said, and made me a present of it. On October 2, 1951, when a cable arrived from her sister, Jinny, in Los Angeles saying Pauline had died soon after debarking from a flight from San Francisco, I ran down to the rose garden to sit and try to find some sort of stability to contain this unexpected blow. Pauline, with her knowing eyes, was a high-spirited sharp-minded woman, an accidental friend to me, both generous and loving. I would miss her for a long time. The next few days Ernest was silent and depressed; they had got on cheerfully together for some years.

We read that Harold Ross of *The New Yorker* had died and Ernest said sadly, "People are dying that never died before," initiating a phrase he would repeat too often.

Anticipating Christmas, I wrote a letter to Santa in my diary. "Of course I don't expect to receive these things. . . . I put them down to take them out of my mind. So, I'd like:

"A new stainless steel sink for the kitchen and the pantry. [We installed them a couple of years later.] Replacements of our broken Venetian tableglass. [Yes.] A French clock to go beneath the mirror in my room. [Yes.] Rubber cushions with gay covers for the pool terrace. [No.] A new fishing chair for *Pilar*. [No.] Invitations to and happily going to chic parties. [No.] A ring with a marquise diamond surrounded by other diamonds. [No.] A silver platter, or two. [Yes.]

"Now, for balance, here are some of the gifts I already have:

"The gladioli, every one healthy this year and beautiful. So far we have white, pink, yellow and salmon.

"The war of the roses not yet won, but the attack well started.

"The vegetable garden full, full of rich and juicy fruits. Tomorrow I will stake and tie the tomatoes. The lettuce, radishes, chard, spring onions and carrots are all burgeoning and beautiful and bursting with fresh flavor.

"The sunrise happens straight out of my window

beyond the ceiba tree and is wildly glorious every morning.

"Last night we had the full moon in a sky of small sailing clouds.

"We have six freshly-blooming orchids on the ceiba tree, the first of the year, and the leaves of the rubber tree are shining from the morning's rain.

"Our miniature railway-train owl was tooting outside my window this morning.

"Another BIG reason to be happy is that we have a cook, Jacob Clement, a British West Indies Negro who, though not acquainted with our kind of food, appears to be clean, willing to learn, and good-tempered."

While the long short story about Santiago, the fisherman, reposed on a corner of the library table, correctly typed with a carbon by me and finally titled *The Old Man and the Sea,* Ernest noticed that our operating funds were low and we embarked on an austerity cycle. Austerity was a word of multiple translations. It would not have occurred to us to curtail the *biftec* which was the servants' favorite lunch food and the most expensive item in the village market. They did not stint themselves on *biftec,* I frequently noticed, seeing a platter heaped high with it, or on accompanying goodies such as a thick soup of pork and vegetables, black beans, rice and fried plantains.

At our table, we got on for a few weeks without the $2-a-pound U.S. beef we could get at Havana's Americanized grocery store, the Morro Castle, and ate fish or scrawny Cuban chicken. We made a show of going easy on the good but little-known French clarets we had in the basement. We could get fresh Iranian caviar for $35 the 14-ounce tin at Carmelo's, the elegant old *bodega* with its bar and café in Vedado; but we banned it temporarily. The roe of marlin we had taken sometimes in the spring while they were breeding off Cuba's north coast was equally rich and wonderful, even though we ate it fresh from our deep freeze and sautéed instead of salting and curing it.

We could live cheaper on the boat, Ernest said, forgetting the cost of gasoline. What did we consume there? Fish, rice, a few eggs, less booze and wine than we swallowed ashore, and nothing more than a bowl of soup for supper. Fewer guests.

Even though it was the height of the tourist season and we might miss seeing friends from the north and the Gulf Stream would not be offering any special prizes, we took off for a few days of cruising westward, anchoring the first night in the vast shallow harbor of Mariel. I had never seen the inside of that bay before and so cruised it in *Tin Kid* and discovered in some of its coves schools of sardines perhaps a mile wide. The commercial fishermen of Mariel would have bait for that summer's fishing.

When Juan met us on our return his face was solemn. Clara Paz, the maid, had taken a whole bottle of Seconal and died. Thoughtful of us, she had done her lonely, determined swallowing outside the Finca, so that the police would not molest Ernest. Gregorio, who had known her family in Casa Blanca and recommended her to us, wept in what looked to me like a combination of anger and incomprehension. Ernest's face was sealed up tight. I was stunned.

Clara and I had been friends, I thought, I always approving her astringent, impersonal attentions to our needs. She had never burdened me with the need to manufacture sympathy for her nerves, which so many Cuban women wanted, the delicacy of their nerves appearing to be in direct relation to the poundage of their bones. While I had never seen Clara, thin but vigorous, pirouetting with delight about anything, neither had she given me any hint of serious personal desolation. Later René wrote to me the account of his part in that unhappy Cuban night.

Having fed the cats and closed up the house against possible rain, René, Clara and her chubby, cheerful son, Arturo, and Fico had walked down from the house on the hill, through the little white people-gate at one side of the big auto gates, Clara mentioning that she was taking her son to Casa Blanca. Returning a little late from the movies, René and Fico decided not to go straight up to the Finca to sleep, as was their custom. Fico went to his family's house and René to his parents' shack. He was surprised to see its lights still burning and his mother standing in the doorway with

368

tears dripping from her eyes. Had they seen Clara? she asked.

René's mother, a handsome, vibrant woman, told her son that Clara, having left her son with her brother in Casa Blanca, had returned to San Francisco de Paula, dropped in on René's mother to announce her intentions for the night, saying she was *"aburrida de la vida."*

Like so many Spanish words, *aburrida* (fem.) has several meanings. It can mean "bored with" or "weary of," as in "I am *aburrida* with these road signs advertising toothpaste." It can also convey "uneasiness of mind and despondency."

René with his brother searched all around the Finca and its neighboring acres for Clara, went up to the house where she occupied one of the servants' rooms below the kitchen and found it locked, returned home at 2:30 a.m., answered the knock of one of the men who worked in the new bakery nearby. They had found Clara unconscious lying in the grass near the bakery door, very pale and, René noticed, not in the white uniform in which she had left the house earlier but in a bright flowered frock, her newest purchase. He spoke to her and shook her. No response. He held a blade of grass in front of her nose. It hardly moved at all. He could not hear a heartbeat. They borrowed the bakery's little delivery truck and carted Clara to the *casa de socorro,* the nearest first-aid station, eight kilometers away on the Hill of the Shoes. There the doctor on duty ordered out his ambulance and opened Clara's handbag where he found two bottles of Seconal, one empty, one half empty, and two open letters, one for her brothers and one saying she had taken this tragic decision because she found herself *"aburrida"* of life. René and his brother accompanied her in the ambulance to the old Carlixto García Hospital where they could not revive her.

14

Home on the Sea

WE GAVE OURSELVES two cruises to Paraíso
amounting to thirty days on the sea in February and
March and I preserved in writing every precious fish
we caught and every change of wind. With Gregorio,
Sinsky and Gianfranco, two cases of wine, a bulging
bag of books and minimum clothes, we left the Club
Náutico in a shiny spic-and-span *Pilar,* rejuvenated
with new Philippine mahogany planking, at 8:55 a.m.
on February 11 and hummed westward in light
weather, "not more than Force 2," with Felípe
chuffing along half a mile to port in *Tin Kid.* "A man
and his boat always catch my throat."

We passed a tranquil night (no mosquitoes) behind
the reef at the entrance of the great, deep bay, Bahía
Honda, caught a couple of fish on our way westward
the next morning and, rounding Gobernadora Light,
watched from topside a phenomenon new to me, a
loggerhead turtle eating a Portuguese man-of-war, the
iridescent bubble which floats on the surface trailing
yard-long, lavender-tipped fronds which are poisonous,
even killing, to both men and fish.

It was a great day for sightseeing. In lightly ruffled
water a bit farther on we came upon a family of
dolphin which looked like Papa, Mama and Child, lying
on their backs in a neat row, sunning their stomachs,
it seemed, as they floated on the surface. No more than
ten yards ahead of us, they heard us and in neat
unison flipped over and dived away.

The dozen or more Australian pines on Paraíso island had grown a couple of feet taller since our last
visit and a few local fishermen were encamped in the
bohíos (palm-frond shacks) near the freshwater well.

Without disturbing them I went shelling on the beach for a bit. We had our soup-supper watching the moon rise and were abed by nine o'clock. "Papa sweet and happy," I noted. So were all of us. But Sinsky and Gianfranco had to return to town the next morning. Felípe put them ashore and we took *Pilar* outside the reef and fished farther west toward the point, Purgatorio, which hits the Gulf Stream at the end of an immense, wide reef.

We were living in a world of twenty shades of blue, wind from some seventy different directions, sunlight and moonlight ever changing on the water, sounds varying from the gentlest slup of finger-sized wavelets against the hull to banging thunder of heavy seas against the outer reefs, the fishy smell of the beach at low tide and the lung-scouring cleanliness of the north wind to the sophisticated tastes of Gregorio's simple, exquisite food. We were caught in a web of endearments to our senses, from which no one wished to break away.

As I had noticed other times when we were alone together on the sea, my husband did not often invite me into his bigger bed, and I thought I understood why. In our mutual sensory delights we were smoothly interlocking parts of a single entity, the big cogwheel and the smaller cogwheel, I felt, with no need for asserting togetherness. Maybe we were androgynous. Anyway the challenges and physical exercise of fishing made us ready soon after sunset to sleep in peace.

But on the sixteenth, the outside world broke in upon us. After fishing in the morning I went with Gregorio through mangrove-bordered bays to the nearest village, La Mulata, and telephoned the Finca. All was well there, René said, but a telegram had arrived. Charlie Scribner had died unexpectedly of a heart attack the day we left home. Along with 1,500 pounds of ice and extra gas for *Tin Kid,* we took the unhappy news back to *Pilar.* Our lagoon with its evening light softening to violet and gray seemed a fitting place for remembering a friend and mourning. "We'll have to leave here," Ernest said, sounding sad. But the radio from Miami reported a Norther had struck there,

371

and we expected it to reach us in about twelve hours. It did, and it was not until the twentieth that we got back to the Finca. The house was neat, clean and in order and, as always after days in the confinements of *Pilar,* looked enormous, almost too big to control.

While Ernest attacked and demolished little hills of mail, I tried to dispose usefully of the greatest crop of tomatoes we had ever produced—sixty plants burgeoning with an embarrassment of riches. "I urge them on the servants," I wrote my parents. "I give them away to neighbors and friends—still there are too many. I clean them and cook them and strain them and make a rich tomato sauce which I quickly pop into the deep freeze, but now the deep freeze is becoming overcrowded with the cartons. What a shame our cats don't like them. . . . Meanwhile we seem to be having an extraordinary number of guests."

Gary Cooper came for a night in which we talked until near dawn mostly about his private problems, and went on talking about them the next day. Leland and Slim Hayward appeared the following day to stay in our Casita. We dined in town, we lunched and dined at home, Ernest took them fishing and one evening Leland took away *The Old Man and the Sea* manuscript to read in bed. When he brought it into the sitting room the next noon, he had decided its future.

"You've *got* to publish this, Papa. It's a terrible waste of time to let it lie around here."

We were standing by the front door of the living room and Leland patted the manuscript which he had put on the long mahogany table there.

"It's awfully short to be a book," Ernest murmured.

"What you've got here is quality. You couldn't put more in a thousand pages," Leland said. "It must go into a big magazine, *Life* or *Look.*"

"Scribner's wouldn't like that."

"Scribner's will get millions of dollars of free advertising. It should have a big spread in a big magazine. I'll handle it."

"You move fast, boy, Mister H." Ernest was visibly overwhelmed by Leland's enthusiasm. His voice was soft and his glance downward.

Leland, the Broadway producer—*South Pacific,*

Mr. Roberts, Call Me Madam—was now the super-salesman and thinking fast.

"We'll time the magazine piece just ahead of the book. Or simultaneously."

"A big circulation magazine? Scribner's won't sell a copy."

"Nonsense. People will read the magazine and rush out to buy the book. Who's your man at Scribner's? I'll talk to him. We ought to aim at publication this fall."

When they left a day or two later Leland carried with him a copy of the manuscript.

We had agreed to leave the house at 8:00 a.m. on Monday, March 10, and the car was loaded and we settled in the front seat by 7:59. As we drove down our hibiscus-splashed driveway Juan asked, *"Han oído qué pasa en la Habana?"* (Have you heard what's happening in Havana?) Papa switched on the car's radio. There was nothing from Radio Relox, the Havana station which ticked off time and news announcements twenty-four hours a day. There was no news, only ads, from the other stations. Juan had heard earlier on the radio that a company of infantry of the Cuban army had surrounded the Presidential Palace, he said, and that there was a great crowd there.

"Let us go as usual to the Club Náutico," said Ernest.

It was slow going. Our road to town was crowded with big, slow army trucks covered with gray-green canvas and crowded with drowsy-eyed soldiers, no shooting devices showing. Along the docks it was as empty as an early Sunday morning except for one ancient clanking tank and a few sailors with *armas largas* (Springfield rifles) standing at ease at the dock entrances. At the club a policeman told us the news: General Fulgencio Batista had successfully already completed a coup displacing President Prío, taking La Cabaña, Havana's downtown fortress, the naval and air centers, also Campo Colombia, the army headquarters, with only token shooting and nobody hurt. We would learn more about it later.

This was the finishing day of the international sailing race, St. Petersburg–Havana, some forty sleek craft having left their home port Saturday noon, the winner, *Ticonderoga*, reaching our club dock at 7:30 Sunday evening, an hour before the reception committee had assembled itself. Crossing the finish line, one of the yachts had seen shots crossing her bows and had put about and out to sea again. It was the only known discourtesy of Batista's revolution.

To make room for the racing yachts Gregorio had taken *Pilar* away from the club and anchored in the bay. So we went aboard from *Tin Kid*, left the harbor at 9:40 a.m., rolled all day in a heavy south wind (Force 6), Papa taking a couple of barracudas on the wire and also something which pulled so sluggishly we could not identify it. A big palm branch, we finally found out. "A sailfish *fracasado* [failed]," said our fisherman. We plowed against the wind into Bahía Honda, anchored well inside the channel near the first light to port and got Batista on the radio.

He had put on his old general's uniform over his civilian *guayabera*, he said, and now would bring order out of the chaos and gangsterism which prevailed in the country. He had by decree dissolved the Confederación Nacional de Trabajadores, Prío's powerful labor support, and had suspended constitutional rights. We had martial law. "It is my destiny to make bloodless revolutions," he announced, adding instinctively, "the only blood spilled will be that of those who oppose us. We are the law." If his words carried conviction, his voice did not. It was the thin voice of a fat man who had climbed too high too fast.

We could not imagine any reason why the new military dictatorship would molest the Finca, so early the next morning we lifted anchor and churned into the peaceful bay behind the island of Paraíso with its flanking high coral reefs.

On March 21 I noted: "For variety of fish these reefs are unexcelled. We have taken with Japanese feathers and a strip of pork rind twelve different species, all but one, the barracuda, edible and saleable. Besides the 'cuda they are: Cero Mackerel, Horse-eyed Jack, Red Hind, Speckled Hind, Red Snapper, Red Grouper, Yellowtail, Mangrove Snapper, Amberjack, Lane Snapper, Ocean Runner, Needlefish. On the *palangre*, the long line with multiple hooks, we have taken besides some of the fish who snapped at our trolled baits, Gray Snapper, Grunts and Parrot Fish. The Grunts, hoarse-voiced, really grunted when we got them in the boat, I noticed. For students of marine life there are also around the island and its reefs big Rays, various sharks, Puffer Fish, Crawfish (spring lobster) and Land Crabs."

One night we set the bright gas lantern on the stern fishbox, watched sardines in droves congregate toward it just below the surface and persuaded Gregorio to cast his net to them. His was the classic net of the Canary Islands which emigrated westward with the fishermen. Half-moon-shaped, six feet wide and at least twenty yards long, it was weighted on its lower edge with hundreds of small leads and threaded through with a drawstring which, on the net thrower's impulse, abruptly gathered in his small captives.

At the top center of the net was a small piece of leather which Gregorio held in his teeth as he folded its side flanges in his arms. Swaying like a ballet dancer, giving movement to the heavy folds, he flung them out and the net hit the water in an almost perfect circle. Then he quickly pulled the drawstring. On the first cast he brought up thirty-four sardines and also a long-billed balao, which looked like a baby marlin except that its little beak, half as long as its body, protruded from its lower rather than its upper jaw. Just after daybreak the next morning Gregorio and Felípe took the sardines out to use them as bait and in a couple of hours brought back twenty-five fish, a gorgeous collection of rock hind and Nassau grouper and also three turbot.

For six days we were stormbound with a Force 6 south wind pounding down on our bay and us, *Pilar* with two anchors forward and one aft riding more on her stout anchor lines, which held her pinioned like a bird in a trap, than on the waves slapping her hull.

On our last evening the wind fell off so much that we decided not to light the big gas lamp, and sipped our drinks in the twilight watching a soft tinted sunset, pillared, sculptured and festooned with clouds, and talked softly of our sadness in ending this vacation.

"Our voices sounding like children," I noted. "We ate our soup in the light of a slim, new moon."

The next morning, March 29, we weighed anchor and moved through a disturbed, crisscrossing sea to the Club Náutico. In the clumps of accumulated mail at home was a letter from Marjorie Cooper in Tanganyika, explaining how her husband Dick, Ernest's friend from East Africa, 1933, had drowned while bird shooting on a lake on their estate. They had buried him in the rose garden near the house. Ernest murmured his phrase about people dying who never died before.

But good news was arriving too. Scribner's had telegraphed and written their enthusiasm for *The Old Man and the Sea*. *Life* was going to break its habit and publish it entire in one single issue. The Book-of-the Month Club was interested, and Jonathan Cape in London wanted to publish simultaneously with Scribner's. Adriana sent a talented, impressionistic watercolor of a Cuban fishing village to be used as the book's dustcover.

In this year of a U.S. presidential election, Ernest wrote to Buck Lanham: ". . . disregard all my political gen since I know nothing about politics that penicillin won't cure. . . . I never thought Dr. E. was a very good general. But I did think he was a hell of a fine politician and in his job it was more important most of the time to be a politician. But if Dr. Taft gets to be president of this country we fight in Asia where you can't win and can be bankrupted so you just fall of your own weight. The haul is so long and they fight you with local troops that live on home grown rice, don't mind dying, and make their own mortars. . . . Have never seen things look worse ever and they've been bad somewhere ever since I could read and write."

Various aspects of the publication of *The Old Man and the Sea* were pre-empting more and more of the man's attention, the marginal details—particularly correspondence from everywhere—intruding on his working time. On May 16 he wrote Jonathan Cape: "I have no English edition of *Across the River and into the Trees* but I have been told there were a number of deletions and some changes. In this book I want there to be no changes at all. . . . Every word depends on every other word. . . . I rely on you to see that prose is neither changed nor improved. . . . Am most anxious to hear what you think about the book. . . . I hope you will like it. Have plenty more coming."

Harvey Breit had written suggesting an interview for his column in *The New York Times Book Review* and Ernest replied: ". . . with Cowley, Ross, Sammy Boal I had too damned much personal publicity. I ought to keep my damned mouth shut for a while. If the book is any good they won't forget you. If it isn't why should you want people to remember you for your extra-curricular activities?"

As earlier he had been upset and disturbed by Philip Young's psychoanalytic hypothesis that his work had been influenced by his leg wounds in July 1918, he was now being bothered and bedeviled by an instructor or professor from Yale, Charles Fenton, who had chosen to write his doctoral dissertation about Ernest's early writing at Oak Park High School and on the Kansas City *Star*. Fenton had sent a piece he had done about the Kansas City work, its inaccuracies of reporting clearly visible to Ernest. In a two-page single-spaced letter dated June 22, Ernest tried to explain.

". . . Did anyone in the old days have any right to work on a man's past and publish findings while the man was alive unless he was running for public office or was a criminal? . . . Don't you think there is some legal way, such as an injunction, that invasion of privacy can be restrained. If you do not, let me know why without getting sore. . . .

"I don't know whether you went to Oak Park or just wrote out there. But I do know that the impression you would get from it is quite false.

"It used to have a North Prairie and a South Prairie. The North Prairie ran from a block beyond your (our) house as far out as the Des Plaines River which then had plenty of pickerel in it up to Wallace Evan's game farm where we used to poach. Where you see an apartment building now there was usually a big old house with a lawn. Where you see subdivisions and row after row of identical houses there used to be the gypsy camps in the fall with their wagons and horses.

"Oak Park had its own artesian water supply and some of us kids used to bring pickerel from the Des Plaines River and put them in the reservoir at night and we watched them grow big for years and never told anybody. We caught goldfish out of the creek and breeding ponds in the game farm and brought them back in minnow buckets and stocked the reservoir to make feed for the pickerel. In the deep water the goldfish all turned silver or silver and black mottled. In Oak Park there was a Christer element which you have contacted. There were also a lot of fine people. Any picture you would get of Oak Park now would be false. . . .

"The point I am trying to make by talking all around it is that when you come into something thirty-five years late, you do not get the true gen. You get Survivors' gen. You can get statistics and badly remembered memories and much slanted stuff. But it is a long way from the true gen and I do not see what makes it scholarship. . . .

"From my own house here I could walk six miles across country five years ago and hunt snipe on the creek and quail on the upper country. Now the creek and the bogs are gone and there are subdivisions over all of that and real estate developments all the way through the country that we used to shoot over because Havana has expanded so. So if I had written of the country as it was then, anyone could come down now and see it and prove I must be crazy or a phony."

While we were lunching peacefully on June 23 a boy from the village knocked on the front screen door with a cable from Harvey Breit sparkling with approval of the new book. Ernest was so touched that he wrote back that afternoon: "I had my stuff in this one. . . . Don't you think if you have your stuff you can last as long as you live and live as long as you should? . . .

"On this everyone worked together like a good double play combination and an outfield. Mary stuck with me all through and nothing else in the world meant a damn to her. She typed and retyped too. I had sent off the Ms. just before the 10th March Revolution here and Mary and I gone to sea. . . . Gianfranco, Adriana's brother, brought me the galleys to correct down the coast and took them back corrected and mailed to Scribner's. I got the unusable jacket sketches from Scribner's and cabled Adriana who is playing a deep leftfield in Venice. It seems impossible that she could do them. But in comes that wonderful throw. We all felt happy and proud and good. . . . Anyway, it will be nice to win after the shit I had to eat about the last book. . . . Tonight was bank night."

In March my father had stopped taking the cancer-restraining drugs his doctor had prescribed and claimed that he was feeling much better without them. But now my mother was ill, the only (self-) diagnosis being some obstruction to her digestion. As she lay on the cot on their back porch she asked my father to summon me.

"Science treatment from several C.S. practitioners has not cured her," he wrote. "It grieves me deeply to have to write you in this way. . . . I feel quite sure she will rise again, but this is the first time she has requested me to write you. . . ."

I got them on the telephone and we agreed that, unless a new crisis arose, I would join them to observe their fiftieth wedding anniversary on July 9.

By July 6 when I reached Gulfport bearing gifts of wahoo and cartons of frozen mangoes, my mother's health had improved so much that she was sitting up, shortening a lilac-colored frock she had bought. But they vetoed my various suggestions for celebrations. Instead we would invite their friends and neighbors in for tea on Saturday afternoon. Adeline would make her famous ginger cookies and I would make a fruit tart.

Their celebration began the moment I opened my eyes mornings and sometimes my mother assisted the process in her sweet fluty voice. "Mary, it's nine o'clock already." After the evening radio news I gave a cappella recitals of Christian Science hymns, French, Italian, Spanish and Cuban folk songs, Army and Navy and WAC ditties and an improvised tribute to each of them. For their anniversary lunch I baked a thick wahoo steak seasoned with laurel and lime and also a deep raspberry pie, served with lighted candles, a loving speech, and clicks of my Rolleiflex shutter. I had brought George Orwell's *1984* on that visit and it was a lucky choice. A dozen pages in his mechanized, dehumanized world provided any necessary antidote to my sense of being trapped in my parents' small world.

Ernest wrote me four times in the week I was away listing his purchases from the Morro Castle grocery store, their menus at home including corn from the garden and fresh mangoes from our trees, and one day sending painstaking suggestions for my parents' ailments. "I think you ought to find out all you can about her condition and then talk confidentially to the doctor about it so that he will have a truthful account of what you know in case your father has to call him in to relieve pain. . . . I agree with you that given her mental attitude and religious beliefs, medication and hospitalization would probably do more harm than good unless it is a question of alleviating pain. . . . As I see it your mission is to attempt to arrange things so that neither of your parents shall suffer unnecessarily. . . . Mouse and Henny are going out to Africa on a boat which leaves August 20th which will bring them there with a week or so, possibly, to spare before the small rainy season. I wrote and explained this. They had to leave Piggott [Arkansas] on June 20th because it got too hot for Henny. . . .

"They say a young man married is a young man marred. But I know I wasted a lot of time not being married to my kitten. But then I couldn't have married you when I was Mouse's age without getting mixed up in statutory rape, I guess."

Ernest habitually drew illustrated kisses at letters' ends. This time I got an Empty Bed kiss, an Apple (given by Eve to Adam) kiss and an arrow-pierced heart.

I had written Ernest not to bother meeting me at the airport, but there he was with Gianfranco at midnight, helping his friends in the Cuban customs to whisk me through their barriers, and we rode with the car's top down through the caressing Cuban night. At home I dug out from my bags some, but not all, of the small cheerful presents I had found in Gulfport—new hair shampoos, new suntan lotions, a couple of adventurous shirts. Most of the presents would stay incognito until July 21. With presents-opening and homecoming celebrations we didn't get to bed until 4 a.m., and when Ernest got up in the morning he found that we had again been invaded by thieves who had in silence come through his bathroom window, taken some $12 from the pocket of his gray flannel slacks in his room and a pair of Gianfranco's pants and two pairs of his shoes. They had not touched our pictures, or, as far as I could discover, any of our bibelots—old English and French silver jugs, Venetian figurines, first editions, the flat silver in the pantry. While we voiced thanks for their ignorance, Ernest set up a series of booby-traps involving a bell, a Mauser pistol and a stack of shotguns which should both surprise intruders and alert us. But for weeks afterward I slept more lightly than usual and got up in the nights to investigate noises. Having heard unlikely sounds from the direction of the pool, I was padding down the front steps in my nightie one 2 a.m. when Ernest yelled at me from my bedroom window. He had me covered with the revolver from his night table.

"Come back here."

"I thought I heard something."

"Come in here, you crazy kitten. You're not even armed." I had thought that a short conversation was the only weapon I needed. But the Boss of our place was now prepared to shoot in the general direction of any sound he did not like. He advised me to keep out of his possible lines of fire and thereafter I did.

When Earl Wilson of the New York *Post* wrote reporting that someone considered that Ernest was shirking his duties as a U.S. citizen by living outside the country, he replied to Earl: "I always had good luck working in Cuba. . . . I moved from Key West over here in 1938 and rented this farm and finally bought it when For Whom The Bell Tolls came out. . . . It is a good place to work because it is out of town and on a hill so that it is cool at night. I wake up when the sun rises and go to work and when I finish I get a swim and have a drink and read the New York and Miami papers. After work you can fish or go shooting and in the evening Mary and I read and listen to music and go to bed. Sometimes we go into town or go to a concert. Sometimes we go to a fight or see a picture and go to La Floridita afterwards. Winter we can go to the Jai Alai.

"Mary loves to garden and has a good flower and vegetable garden and fine roses. . . . I lost about five years work out of my life during the war and I am trying to make up for it now. I can't work and hang around New York because I never learned how to do it. When I hit New York it is like somebody coming off a long cattle drive hitting Dodge City in the old days. Right now I'm driving cattle and it is a long tough drive. But this fall when The Old Man and The Sea comes out you'll see some of the result of the last five years work.

"You find me a place in Ohio where I can live on top of a hill and be fifteen minutes away from the Gulf Stream and have my own fruit and vegetables the year around and raise and fight game chickens without breaking the law and I'll go live in Ohio if Miss Mary and my cats and dogs agree."

Ernest was beating out his furies against Mr. Fenton of Yale on the typewriter instead of the household, several of the letters serving their purpose of cooling off their author even though they were not sent. In one he invited Fenton down to "say to me the sort of stuff you write in your letters. It would be a pleasure to hear it and give you an answer face to face. . . . [I] ask you again to cease and desist in this project of yours which, starting as a study in the apprenticeship of a writer for the use and information of university students, had reached such proportions that you wrote me you were receiving an offer or offers to write about my wives, etc. I doubt if your university would approve. . . ."

More abrasive to our peace of mind was the short visit of Alfred Eisenstadt, the photographer *Life* had sent down to photograph the village of Cojímar, *Pilar*'s old harbor town, similar to the Old Man's town. Eisie turned his various lenses onto the town, its people and the simple skiffs of the local fishermen loitering above their anchors in the bay. When we pointed out man-o'-war hawks (frigate birds), all sail and no ballast with

382

the greatest wing area in proportion to their body weight, the swiftest flyers of all sea birds, Eisie took their portraits in twenty or thirty different positions, the sharp dihedral angles of their seven-foot wings showing. Like all fishermen on the Gulf Stream, Santiago had watched and admired them. Eisie's photographs would provide the images from which Noel Sickles would make drawings to accompany Santiago's story in *Life*.

On a June afternoon of tormenting sun, Eisie, small, intent and quick-moving, walked Ernest all around Cojímar for a couple of hours, stationing him in front of various façades and views of the bay. Ernest muttered protests, wishing not to be obstructive, since he had agreed to work at this chore, but growing restive in the downbeating heat. Finally he said slowly to Eisie behind the cameras, "Eisie, you have competence. But you have no compassion."

Standing on the sun-blasted road overlooking the bay, Eisie heard it. "I never thought of it that way," he said. That wrapped up the filming session. On the way home with the car's top up, Eisie, the dedicated pro photographer, said he had not really noticed the heat.

Mother Nature turned particularly hostile toward Cuba that summer, with thunderbolts, spears and balls of fire and waterfalls of rain beating down upon the north coast. For two or three weeks big black clouds began mounting the sky about noon and the storms hurled down upon us as we began to lunch at two o'clock. Standing at the front door, which we could leave open with its protecting cement canopy outside, I noticed for the first time a difference between these rains and those of temperate zones. "I can't see any spaces between the raindrops," I said between thunderclaps. "It's solid water. No spaces."

"A fifty-square-mile raindrop," Ernest said.

With lightning cracking everywhere I kept my sandaled feet on the rung of my chair a few inches above the dining room floor, across which years before a ball of fire had rolled toward the pantry, Ernest said.

"How big? Pea-sized? Golf-ball?"

"Cantaloupe-sized," said my husband complacently, his feet at ease on the floor. "No, honeydew melon."

"It didn't burn the floor?"

"This tile floor?"

"It didn't hit people?"

"No one."

"So what happened?'

"It rolled into the pantry."

"And it didn't burn anything there?"

"I believe they let it out the back door."

"I see. Just like one of our sweet, friendly cotsies." Lightning barked outside and the dogs huddled closer under the table.

"That was nineteen forty-three, August, the big one. We had a few others," Ernest said.

"Smaller ones? Strange, there's none since I've been here." A huge crash rattled our foundations and there were protests from the kitchen.

"These modern storms are just small, chickenshit imitations."

"Like in *Faust,* the old ones?"

"Sure, Mephistopheles with Kraut fireworks."

We were trolling in *Pilar* a couple of times when the electric storms hit, and they frightened me. Not that the sea grew too violent. It was beaten down by the rain. But that the moving tips of our outriggers might attract the lightning bursting around us. Our outriggers were footed in *Pilar*'s sidedecks and directly below were her high-octane gas tanks.

We had occasional sharp seasoning in our social life at the Floridita. At the bar one evening, an American female tourist interrupted to remind Ernest what good, close friends they had been there in 1944 and how about resuming their romance. The muscles in Ernest's neck began to jerk. He had just got rid of her when a big square fat man pushed in, another tourist, put his arm around Ernest's shoulders and began to sing a dirty song. "Made it up all by myself for you," he said, and began the song again.

Ernest hated dirty jokes and dirty songs and would not tolerate them anywhere, no matter what their subject. This song was about him. He pushed away the fellow's arm and said, "Come on back here with me," moving toward the men's room beyond the far end of the bar. Our friend Dick Hill, who was with us, went too and emerged only minutes later looking like a triumphant, ecstatic angel. Ernest followed him looking woebegone. "Two quick left hooks and that was it," Dick murmured happily to me. "And a little chop wtih the right," Ernest added for accuracy's sake, having overheard. He still looked sad. Our evening of friendship and exchanged sympathy was spoiled. We left the bar without seeing the dirty-song man again.

In honor of a steak from the U.S. we dined at the big table, Gianfranco, Ernest and I, on Monday evening, August 25, savoring the receptions from the north of *The Old Man* as well as rare steak juices, chawing on the meat fibers in subdued candlelight and also on the first edition of Carlos Baker's book, *Hemingway: The Writer as Artist*. In a quick skimming Ernest had found the book pretty good and most of its interpretations reasonable, but a number of errors of fact. Baker had him living in the Place du Tertre (one of our favorite pieces of Paris), but he had never lived in Montmartre. Of his own writing Ernest said, "Nobody really knows or understands and nobody has ever said the secret. The secret is that it is poetry written into prose and it is the hardest of all things to do." Later the phrases sounded hackneyed. But that evening in our dim quiet dining room the definition seemed new and precise.

We got onto Santiago's Catholic prayers, which I thought good in the book.

"You don't give them any credence, though," Ernest said.

"No. But they can't hurt him."

"My kitten is a nonbeliever."

I sang, "I put my faith in yoooooou."

"Religion is superstition," said he, "and I believe in superstition." He had often shown the usual signs of superstition, knocking on wood, saying "bread and butter" when we parted to pass around a tree or a rock. If something menaced us, man, beast or nature, he was apt to say, "Don't put your mouth on it," which sounded Key West to me and implied that identifying the force somehow strengthened its power.

"I like that stuff, those old folkways," said I. "Even though I don't believe in them, I'll practice them."

385

"Tribal heritage," Ernest said. He would do what he could to preserve them.

Everybody we knew in New York was reading galley proofs of *The Old Man* either from *Life* or Scribner's and the mail René brought up from the village grew bulkier by the morning. Scribner's official publication date was August 28 and *Life*'s publication with Noel Sickles's strong sympathetic drawings was in the issue of September 1. But *Life*'s promotion department had slipped out six hundred pre-publication sets of its galley proofs around the country, thus instigating a breeze of whispers and for a week, we heard, the chic thing in the trade was to have read the galleys. The bookshops were equally foresighted and around the country wrapped thousands of pre-publication copies for their favorite customers.

From London Jonathan Cape sent a couple of advance copies of their edition which upset us all. The quality of the paper and niggardly use of space in the typesetting had improved a bit since World War II, but the dustcover—a figure with a Mexican wide-brimmed hat fishing backward, the mast of his skiff stepped, and a childish silly fish—affronted us and the book. Ernest wrote a stricken cable: I FEEL SICK OVER MY BOOK BEING DESTROYED BY THIS MISERABLE AND RIDICULOUS PRESENTATION. It was too late, momentarily. The book was already selling swiftly in England. But Cape conscientiously dumped the unfortunate cover quite soon, substituting a plain cover quoting flattering phrases from the British critics.

The mail had always been more than half discomforting—"Help!" "Give!" "Read and tell me," "We need"—hundreds of demands we could not meet. Now nearly all of it, thirty to forty letters a day, brought such bright cheer that if I happened into the sitting room at mail-reading time Ernest might pop out of his chair to give me a hug-a-lug (a super-hug) and show me a letter from Italy, France, Montana or Bimini, from Berenson or Bob Sherwood or Cyril Connolly or Quent Reynolds, all of them kind and appreciative or enthusiastic and loving. There came also scores of letters from G.I.'s, high school kids, housewives and fishermen in Montauk and Norfolk.

In two weeks the little book, priced at $3.00, had sold some 50,000 copies with reorders reaching Scribner's at a rate of 1,500 or more a day, one day reaching 2,400.

"We ought to do something to celebrate," I said, stretched out one evening on the living room sofa. "Oh, I don't forget, 'Director, Internal Revenue Service, Baltimore, Maryland.' But you should have some little extra fun, my lamb."

"Plenty good big fish in the Stream now," Ernest said.

"We could run over to Paris. Get our old Senlis suite on the *Ile*." Ernest looked composed, comfortable in his chair and immoveable for any distance. "They'll be jumping at Auteuil. We could run down to Paraíso. So what if it's hurricane season?"

"Catch big fish there, you can't get him to market."

I was reading the Sunday *New York Times*. Balinese dancers were performing on Broadway and *The King and I* was a smash hit. New York would be stimulating with the upcoming elections, fall and football season approaching, Broadway burgeoning.

"New York could be wonderful for a little while."

"Why don't you go, my kitten?"

"Without you? No."

On September 14 Ernest wrote Malcolm Cowley: "The current is still wonderful in the Stream . . . but the big fish, the biggest, must have some great quantity of squid down deep because they show up behind the baits, honest to Christ two as big as gondolas, and then go down. . . . Gregorio says they've seen the illustrations in *Life* and won't fuck with us. . . . But the current runs around 4 knots true, heavier than I've ever known it. I'm going to keep on it until it quits. . . .

"Mary is going up to town. I'm going to stay down here to fish this run and also my temper is short and it is no good for me to go to town after a book is published. Too much publicity etc."

Besides his heavy correspondence, Ernest's business reading was augmented by sheafs of clippings, literary critics' comments which Scribner's kept sending us. He read them with attention even though he insisted he disapproved of so doing and wrote Berenson: ". . . one

387

does not care about the reviews. I cared about yours. But reading the others is just a vice. It is very destructive to publish a book and then read the reviews. When they do not understand it you get angry; if they do understand it you only read what you already know and it is no good for you. It is not as bad as drinking Strega but it is a little like it."

Lee Samuels, who had snapped dozens of photos for the back of *The Old Man*'s dustcover—Ernest muttering, "Even you and your magic box can't make a pig look like a poet"—mentioned one lunchtime that he was going north again to help Cecile, his wife, finish settling into their new apartment.

"I'd like Mary to go up for a little holiday," Ernest said. "Somebody should *aprovechar* this book's reception."

I started to say, "You too, please, lamb," but held it. Years before I had vowed never to be a repetitious nag.

"She can stay with us," Lee said. "Freddy's room is furnished, in order, vacant and has its own telephone."

"House guests are such a bore," I protested.

Lee laughed. "Baby, you already know how much you bore us." We decided that I might go up on September 25 for a week. I had not seen the big town in two and a half years.

The Havana papers had printed squibs about the success of *The Old Man* in the north and once again it prompted local thieves to break into the house. (Our dogs were sleeping as soundly as we were.) Avoiding our fine new booby-traps, they broke open a lock on one of our six doors and savaged the house, tearing open desk and library drawers, scattering clothes and papers around, dropping tobacco ashes and matches, spitting on the furniture. They took four of Ernest's knives, war trophies, and his gold cufflinks, ties and silver picture frames and almost all of Gianfranco's extensive, excellent wardrobe, and we observed the next morning that one of the gang had stood guard at the door to my bedroom, grinding his cigarette butts into the floor there. All of us, Ernest and I and Blackie and Negrita, had slept peacefully through the raid, to our morning-after mystification. We told the local police about it and asked them not to publicize it. We did not want the government posting guards around the Finca, especially since they might well have been in league with the thieves. We continued to sleep with pistols on our night tables, Ernest's loaded, mine empty with the cartridge clip at hand.

Signs of autumn were beginning to appear. With no hurricanes hovering nearby the air was so bright and clear we could see palm fronds a mile away and the intervening atmosphere was a deeper blue than summer air in the oblique sun rays. The plumes of the high grass on our hillsides were turning silver. Birds traveling from the north paused for a night in our trees and gave us new morning songs before they departed. The cats were beginning to show thick wintertime coats.

Having finished at Harvard *magna cum laude* and done a stint at Pauline's ancestral cotton plantation in Arkansas, Patrick was now on his way to East Africa with the idea of finding a property and settling there, to be followed by his Baltimore-belle wife, Henrietta.

Ernest wrote a long letter of introduction to his old friend, Philip Percival, the white hunter of his and Pauline's 1933–34 safari and of *Green Hills of Africa,* defining Patrick's prowess as a shooter and his character: "He is not a boy that you have to kick his ass if he is wrong. If he is wrong just tell him. He is brave, like Pauline, and he has other of her good qualities.

"If you think it is a sound idea and if Patrick likes it I would love to come out too. Mary, my wife, is a good rifle shot [sic] and loves to shoot and can travel wonderfully. We got pretty involved in skiing but she breaks a leg at it every year so I've been keeping her on the ocean. . . . We've caught twenty-nine good marlin this season. . . ."

Thus he began preparations for the most exciting, instructive and prolonged holiday of my life and at least the second-best of his.

From Freddy Samuels's room in his parents' apartment in New York, I wrote my husband on September 27: "A hundred times today I've wished I had your arm to squeeze and say, 'look, look.' The town had one of those perfect autumn days, the sunshine soft and

389

golden, the breeze light, the river shining, the noise not overwhelming. . . . The flat is in a new building across the East River from Welfare Island which has lots of trees and the sitting-room and my room hang right over the river—lovely. Hot water. American milk. This is not merely another place, I'm squarely inside another civilization—easy telephoning, shopping know-how, integration with the city, luxury. Wanted to tell you about the big city faces—so closed and preoccupied and dour. The Kleenex here would astound you, it's so crisp."

On the same Saturday, Ernest wrote me the home news: Marlin appearing behind the baits but not biting, Sinsky home from Lake Charles, Louisiana, with two fine steaks, small bookstores which originally ordered fifteen copies of *The Old Man* now reordering fifty—"If this keeps up everything will be fine."

My father welcomed me back to Cuba with a letter of advice: "Nothing that you could give us or do for us would bring to us the deep joyous feeling that would come with the knowledge that you had given up smoking cigarettes. . . . Ernest would appreciate . . . The next important consideration is your enjoyment of a longer life . . . this evidence of strength of character on your part will not take from you the slightest particle of real delight or satisfaction in your family life. . . ."

I showed Ernest the letter and relayed his reply which was: "I didn't know there were women who didn't smoke/chew tobacco, although the pipe-smoking women sometimes make difficulties." My father was quite right, of course, but I continued smoking.

More than a thousand letters, each day's bundle held together by a rubber band, spread across the counterpane of Ernest's bed, and when it grew over-crowded, they strayed like refugees onto the big curved library table, an untidy mess. I wrote dozens of acknowledgments with thanks and Ernest managed to answer some, but it was a task impossible to accomplish, particularly because our Writer, finding a letter stimulating, would answer it so comprehensively that it would cost him a morning. He was also using up time trying to correct mistaken conclusions of Mr. Fenton at Yale, writing him: "In the first page or pages of your Ms. I found so many errors of fact that I could spend the rest of the winter rewriting and giving you the true gen. . . . You have me tutoring the two Connable children. . . . Dorothy Connable had graduated from Wellesley. . . . I certainly was not hired as her tutor."

He wrote to Carlos Baker mentioning the Nobel Prize: "That is the fourth time I had the same hot tip but I have not bought any tailcoats yet. . . . I had to accept this Cuban medal of honor because I live here and it would be discourteous not to. Also it is non-political." He spent another page of single-spaced typing to rebut Philip Young's "traumatic neuroses" theory of his work having been influenced by his World War I wounds.

He had given the original manuscript of *The Old Man* to Gianfranco, and when Hans Heinrich, a New York businessman, wrote asking if he would care to sell it and for how much, Ernest explained the gift and his ties with Gianfranco and the Ivancich family. He wrote Carlos Baker again sympathizing with him about the poor reviews his book was getting: "You must remember that your book and my last book came out at a time when most of the critics were committed to the idea that I was through as a writer" and "I can leave here now after November 1st when hurricane months are over if we have getaway money. Want to catch the end of the obstacle racing in Paris and then join Patrick who is now in East Africa. Have been here too long and need a change of altitude. Patrick loves Africa and I'm sure Mary will like it. . . ." He wrote George Brown a long letter about Kid Gavilan, the boxer, and about the technicalities of bar fighting. "In the old days I would touch a guy lightly on his left shoulder with my left hand and then throw with my right against that measurement. Now I have found that from bad eyesight I can miss clean with a right hand. So now I put my right hand on the guy dropping it inside his elbow to cut off his left and then hit him twice with a left hook, once up once down. . . . Naturally I step on his feet first to make sure he is there. . . ."

Patrick had been writing us delightful letters about the parts of East Africa he was exploring, his observations about its people and beasts and the Percivals' kindnesses. Ernest wrote Philip Percival a letter thanking him and saying: "I hope Mary and I will be able to get out after the first of the year. We can look around then and see if it would be good to come out for keeps. I would like it very much. It is getting fairly impossible here and what was our farm is now surrounded by urban and suburban development. Where I could walk all day with a gun and have snipe, guinea, doves and quail is now just spreading shacks and you must defend your property against thieves at night where once you never locked a door. I'll let you know our plans in ample time. They all depend on what the taxes leave me to maneuver with."

I had time to put some reflections in my notebook: "I never liked anyone because he was titled or socially important or rich or famous," I wrote in September. "It's only wit and charm which entice me, and hang the social status. Old men are the most attractive with their wit and wisdom, and I can think it because I have E. in bed for young men's games. Berenson is the single most attractive creature and still sensuous. Also there are Charlie Sweeney, Lloyd George, whom I don't consider dead, Taylor Williams and Beaverbrook, the devil. . . .

"Every day or week, having found some grain of what seems like a truth, I think 'But I will be smarter or know it better tomorrow or next week' and so postpone writing it. . . .

"New Spanish proverb—new to me—*Anuque la mona se vista de seda, mona se queda.* (Although the monkey—female—appears made of silk, monkey it remains.) Their version of our sow's ear."

On October 8 I rejoiced over Boise's good health: "Gay and healthy after his heart attack last year from which he nearly died, Boise has been lunching with us. He is probably one of the world's most sophisticated cats in his food preferences—no mere carnivore. Lately, joining us at the table he has eaten fresh mangoes, cantaloupe and honeydew melons, chop suey, Mexican tacos with burning hot sauce, potato salad including the raw onion, leeks, cole slaw, and today sauerkraut and potatoes and raw celery. He likes sun-

392

flower seeds, all pies and cakes, fresh apples although he prefers them in a pie, chili con carne and cucumbers raw with salad dressing. He still jumps like a feather in a breeze."

Edmund Wilson sent Ernest his latest book, *The Shores of Light,* generously inscribed, and Ernest thanked him at length, describing associations with the Russians in Spain, very different from Wilson's observations of them in their homeland, and "I read in the 'Times' a good piece about you by Harvey Breit. He wrote something about wishing to learn Spanish and know Spanish literature. The language is easy to learn superficially. But there are so many meanings to each word that, spoken, it is almost double talk. In addition to the known meanings of a word there are many secret meanings from the talk of thieves, pickpockets, pimps, whores, etc. This occurs in all languages and most of the secret language is very ancient."

The *Porana paniculata* (white ipomoea) was cascading white blooms over the front terrace of the house and the loggia at the pool, its fragrance almost too delicate for sated human noses to notice. "Like the lace on an old-fashioned Valentine," Ernest said. After weeks of drenching rains brought our way by hurricanes, seedlings were again in place in the vegetable garden and we were relishing the first of the year's yucca, the tuber which sustains tropical farmers around the world. The thin, light soil of our hillside provided yucca especially white, subtly flavored and without fibers, and we served it whenever we entertained Cuban friends. Cool north winds were drying the house. The salt in the salt dishes on the table was again salt instead of baby lakes. Doors were beginning to move without sticking, also drawers. By October 31 I could write my parents: "We are finally finished with another hurricane season. . . ." Our hurricane book, a history and analysis of the storms in the Caribbean since the late nineteenth century, showed there had never been a bad hurricane attacking Cuba after October 27.

Both *Look* and *Life* were trying to persuade Ernest that one of their photographers should accompany us on our prospective safari in East Africa, and Ernest was resisting the idea. He wrote Sidney James at *Life:* "I like to hunt by myself or I would enjoy backing up Mary with a big gun. But to hunt according to the ideas of a photographer is hard work rather than fun or a vacation. . . . This is another angle: If I went out for you and wrote as good journalism as I could . . . I would use up what I might write in three stories. The last time I was in Africa I wrote only two short stories, The Snows of Kilimanjaro and The Short Happy Life of Francis Macomber. I cabled some very basic journalism to Esquire."

Alfred Rice flew down for a day to discuss with Ernest foreign rights, TV rights, movie rights and what reservations and protections should be specified in any contracts concerning *The Old Man.* Leland and Slim Hayward flew down to sell Ernest on his various projects, especially that of fishing off the Cuban coast in order to photograph the Old Man's giant marlin. To save us bother, they stayed at the Hotel Nacional in Havana and we dined at the Floridita. Going home in the car Ernest muttered that he felt like a juggler with one hand palsied, and glumly concluded, "We'll never make it to Africa before the long rains."

15

Prizes, Surprises, Projects

AT MIDNIGHT OF January 1, 1953, I wondered if we could make the year outshine '52 in achievements or delights. Now we were beginning to deal with facts concerning the safari in East Africa. A Spanish friend with whom Ernest had worked on the Loyalist side of the Civil War came to call and to mention that in the fifteen years since Ernest had left Spain, all of his friends who had been imprisoned there had been freed, the last couple in the past year.

Ernest had told me a dozen times about the military actions he had seen in the rugged mountains of the Guadarrama northwest of Madrid toward Segovia and of the frantic fighting in the arid country south of the capital toward Aranjuez where the only cover the infantry could find were six-inch stones. He had told me about the varied and delightful cafés in the Puerta del Sol in Madrid, and of the Retiro Park and especially of the treasures to be seen in the Prado, not only the Goyas and El Grecos, but Velázquez and the wild men Bosch and Brueghel, whom I did not know, Rubens, and his favorite portrait painter, Andrea del Sarto.

He had vowed never to return to Spain while any of his old friends were still in jail there. Now he had the alluring possibility of revisiting one of his favorite countries, unencumbered by remorse, and I would be able to speak and understand the language.

"You ought to learn Swahili," said Ernest.

"Of course," I said in total ignorance. It was months before I learned that Swahili has eight cases of nouns.

In preparation for both Spain and Africa my husband selected a dozen books for me to read. Among them were two books by Philip Percival's brother, Blayney; the two-volume edition of Sir Samuel Baker's *Albert N'Yanza, Great Basin of the Nile* published in 1867; a slightly worm-eaten first edition of Isak Dinesen's *Out of Africa;* Lord Lonsdale's *Shooting Big Game in Africa,* Volume XIV of his sports library, with his preface—"Kill fairly and sparingly that the Big Game of the world may survive to give sport to those who come after." It was all marvelous reading, including the fairy tale prices those early hunters paid, such as a total outlay of £40 (about $200) for complete safari equipment including a tent, bed and bedding, table chair, water bottle, shooting clothes, plus £2 per month for safari servants. But that was in the teens or twenties of the century. Lonsdale's compilation was entirely bereft of dates.

Gerald Brenan's books on Spain swept up my time and attention as a vacuum cleaner does dust. My interest in the causes and developments of Spanish workers' syndicalism and the skulduggeries of the capitalists grew steadily from the first pages of *The Spanish Labyrinth* and I took the book fishing to read to Ernest. As we customarily fished in the winter "to get in shape" for the big fish of spring, now we tramped the hills around the Finca, and went shooting, the fast-breaking *correo* pigeons we got down from Philadelphia at the Club de Cazadores and quail and doves at friends' cattle ranches.

In mid-January, for the third time since July, thieves broke into the house at night. The first time they had entered through Ernest's bathroom window, only a few feet above the outside terrace. The second time they had pried open the door from the terrace to the Venetian Room, which was unoccupied. This time they came through the bathroom window again, carefully removing the bottles on top of the chest beneath the window and covering its glass with a towel, and this time Ernest heard them, slipped out of my room naked with his .22 rifle and shot the last one escaping through the window. We found blood on the terrace tiles and the next morning traced their escape route down the hill toward the village, through our hedge of prickly henequen plants and over the fence. They got away with the chrome fittings of a leather bar case Leland Hayward had given Ernest and some other gewgaws. Nothing much except another sizable bite out of our tranquility.

On January 31 I noted: "Papa frequently asks Black Dog now, 'Do you think man will survive?' Blackie looks serious. Says Papa, 'He always ponders that question.'"

With a temporary easing in the flow of guests, we had the pleasures of paying more attention to our beasts, making simple jokes to them, who were often more responsive than human beings. Ernest was sitting in the flickering shade of the loggia at the pool one day when Negrita and I went down for my pre-luncheon swim. He called out, "Have I met your friend?" and Negrita giggled audibly, her tail a-wag. She was a typical bright-spirited Cuban female, affectionate and as in love with Papa as was I, her 2′ × 1′ × 1′ size permitting.

Waking up at night he said, after all our robberies, "I could get a job as a sound-sorter."

While Africa beckoned, we had a week or two of rough going in the foreground. Leland was sharing with Ernest most of the pains of his decision making and breaking about the uses to which he would put *The Old Man*. He was booking a reading tour of it across the country. No, Spencer Tracy was tied to Metro for the year. He would buy the picture rights to the book and pay Ernest an extra fee to be technical adviser about the film. They would be right down to discuss it. No. Somebody on the Coast had devised a new gadget which would make developed film more three-dimensional. The industry was in crisis. Nobody would buy anything. They would not come down. I remember saying, "If we have to have tenterhooks around here, do you think we could park them outside the house?"

"We'll keep them outside the gate," Ernest said. His irritation was rising, and it was not ameliorated by the conundrums of financing our journey. He wanted to finance it by himself, to be free of any commitments, and he expected to do so, having the successful book and having paid off most personal debts. But *Life* and especially *Look* were offering tantalizing assistance to the treasury with few restricting conditions.

With atrocious timing my neck turned suddenly rigid and painful, its muscles so contracted that they impeded breathing. The malady, whatever it was, stuck with me faithfully four or five days, inconveniencing Ernest, who had to do my house chores, almost as much as me. One morning he came in to see me after having inspected the vegetable garden.

"Lots of stuff there we ought to be using," he said. "Carrots, onions, beets. We ought to eat the Swiss chard now."

"Why didn't you pull them and pick them?"

"We all know you hurt worse than anyone, ever."

"That has nothing to do with the vegetables."

"You and your ridiculous stiff neck."

"You're too important to pick vegetables."

"You coward."

397

"You spoiled slob. If you won't pick vegetables yourself, why don't you order Pichilo?"

"Coward."

"You grew vegetables and picked them when you were a kid at Walloon Lake."

"Coward. Coward . . . coward."

"Go ahead. Waste your substance here, with your overgrown, over-bloated importance."

Ernest rushed off, maybe suppressing the impulse to strangle me, and I fell back on my pillow, dribbling tears. But the anger somehow loosened some of my neck muscles, and in a day or two my husband brought me a small radio with which I could hear local stations, particularly that of a country nightclub a few miles away which broadcast imitations of old American jazz and such Cuban favorites as "Soong-Soong-Soong, Soong-Soong Babai-E." The music did more than anything else to loosen the stubborn muscles.

It was a timely recovery because we would need some of our reserve supplies of fortitude in the next few weeks. Gianfranco had decided he must return to Venice to attend both to family business and that of his employers' shipping company, and his departure seemed to us both almost a physical amputation. In four years he had merged into the Finca life so completely that his leaving was as difficult as disentangling the entwined roots of flowers. We three were political allies. We shared tastes in books, music, pictures, the sea as entertainment, wit as lubrication for the daily grind. Our slender friend from Venice knew how to be quiet in spirit and flesh. Ernest said, "If you can hear it, it's not Gianfranco." He was a younger brother to Ernest, and—twelve years younger—a younger brother to me. In disputes between the man of the house and the woman, his capacity for neutrality reached genius. He left a large empty space behind him.

Leland Hayward and Spencer Tracy continued setting dates for conferences in Cuba and then breaking off, and the constant readjustments of our own plans made us feel like puppets on strings. Ernest wrote to

Harvey Breit, "They are all in the third-dimensional high jerkoff notch now and little sense is made."

Harvey was having romantic troubles and Ernest sent a verse of one of his favorite women-defying songs:

> If you don't love me, Mama
> Then I don't care at all
> Cause I can get more womens
> Then a passenger train can haul.

As I came down from the tower after sunning on February 20, I found our cat Willie hunching himself forward along the terrace, all tilted to starboard. Willie was smiling and purring and his gray-and-black striped coat looked still shiny from his morning lick-bath. But his right forepaw was doubled under. He was crawling on the knee. Then I saw with horror that his back hip was broken, a bit of bone protruding through the fur. "Willie, Willie, wait," I moaned, stroking his head. He was heading for the Cat House, our cats' sanctum. I ran to Ernest in his room and panted, "Something terrible has happened to Willie. He's all broken apart." Ernest came back unbelieving from wherever he was in his manuscript. We went out and there was Willie near the Cat House door, purring, no blood showing. Tears were making rivulets down my cheeks as Ernest examined him.

"You think he's hurt internally? Could we make splints for him?"

"His whole hip is smashed," Ernest said softly, while he felt the bones with care. I knelt to pick him up.

"Don't handle him. Don't let him see you cry. Splints no good."

"A plaster cast?" René had joined us, and Roberto.

"Get me the .22," Ernest said.

"No. No. No. Why can't we try a plaster cast? Why can't we get a vet? Why does this have to be so quick?" I was blubbering.

"He's too smashed up. He'll begin to feel it soon."

I ran to my refuge, my bed.

The happenings of that day gave us no chance to try to assimilate our grief. While René held Willie gently in his arms and Ernest shot him in the head, a Cadillac stopped at the front steps, having ignored the signs on the gate, and a young man and his white-coated attendant emerged. Before anybody could stop them they were inside the house, the attendant saying their clinic for the mentally deranged had given them permission to come to Cuba to visit Ernest, as I heard it through the door as I dressed for lunch. The young man spoke cruel phrases. "An interesting time to arrive. . . . Hemingway crying because he has shot a cat. . . . He loves cats . . . so he shoots them." I waited for the sounds of a shot and a body collapsing but heard only conversation and the front screen door announcing their departure.

When the boys had been children, Willie had been Patrick's and Gregory's favorite cat and had elected himself a non-cat people's chum except when the lure of bird hunting overtook him. To strangers he presented a conservative banker's mien, aloof and businesslike. But with friends he allowed himself to be picked up, cradled, his stomach stroked, or he would dance across the floor chasing a wiggling string, or lying on a table in the lamplight would nuzzle into a pal's hair, teasing, pretending to eat it. Remembering Willie, Ernest and I held each other close for a long time that night.

Like San Vicente, our favorite hotel in Pinar del Río, Cuba's western-most province, we were booked solid for the later spring. Gilbert Miller, the famous Broadway producer, complaining about the bursitis in his arm, nonetheless shot very well at buzzards from the top of the tower—our newest Finca sport—and we managed to observe our seventh wedding anniversary, a week late, March 21, with no one but Roberto and José Luis with us—a relaxed evening with big-grained gray caviar and martinis in the sitting room before dinner and the simpleminded invention of a few more verses honoring our local hero, the Snicketysnee. Ernest started:

> Honest Mister Papa
> And *The Old Man and the Sea*
> Were given novice rating
> By the Snick-ety-snee.

I suggested:

> Albert Einstein's theory
> Of relativity
> Was merely mental pushups
> For the Snick-ety-snee.

Having given up hope for the Hayward-Tracy-Ernest conference, we organized a voyage to Paraíso for the last week of Lent, as was our custom. We had just settled into our tranquil happy life of fishing, shelling, swimming off the beach, and a couple of days later were reading after lunch when a sailboat approached bearing Roberto and Paco Garay and bad news, a cable from Hayward saying they were coming down the next Sunday. Ernest had written them that we were going for a short vacation and it had only begun. The news sent me into a personal fluster, so with Felípe in the rowboat I went to fish for balao, a marlin's favorite snack. I chummed them with bits of bread in the lagoon in front of the island's swamp and Felípe caught them with a hook no bigger than a watch hand which he tied to six feet of line on the end of a stick. In an hour we caught twenty-seven slender little beauties, with their translucent green backs and their golden lower caudal fins, each less than a foot long including their long lower beak tipped with red. They made excellent eating, Felípe said. But we already had plenty of food fish. We would save these for marlin.

By trolling, Saturday, March 28, in *Tin Kid,* I had taken more fish than Ernest, my score reaching thirty-six to his twenty-eight. I scribbled: "Here in *Pilar* now before lunch it is charming. Papa made super-dry martinis, the radio is playing waltzes, Gregorio is cooking something with wonderful smells (rice and *cherna*—grouper). We have plenty of shade with the side canvases stretched out like long eaves and the canvas at the stern let down and tied to the two outside stanchions, the breeze quite cool from the north, but light. Sun hot. We have no thermometer aboard but I imagine the difference between the stern in the sun and here in the shade is ten degrees, it being about seventy-two in here."

When I woke up the next morning, grinned and asked if I could sleep a little longer, Ernest looked me over benignly and said, "Yes, pretty kitten—all the wrinkles are gone from your face. . . . I was thinking, you keep yourself in good shape."

Two days later Gregorio and I went into La Mulata for news and letters brought by Roberto. A letter from Patrick included photos of the 2,300-acre farm he had bought in the inaccessible highlands of Tanganyika, the place accommodating the graves of two British generals, some planting of pyrethrum, some in coffee and a twelve-room house. They had that *sine qua non* for Africa as for Cuba, an unending supply of fresh water, he wrote. The inescapable news was that the Haywards and Mr. Tracy now would arrive on the afternoon plane from Miami on Friday, April 3. Bumby and Puck and their baby were arriving on Saturday to stay with us. We would have to get home by Thursday.

About sunset, trolling toward Havana, our skipper and Gregorio and I were all on the afterdeck, where its hatch, being open, impeded movement. Ernest was bringing in a barracuda on the port side feather and we all saw the heavy old Hardy rod with its monometal wire bending sharply. Gregorio leaped across the open hatch to grab it, when the rod broke off at its base and plunged overboard. Ernest had used it for twenty-two years and with it caught most of his record-breaking fish including the giant tuna off Bimini. Gregorio cut the monometal wire to save what little bit was left on the reel. It must have been an enormous fish.

By Thursday morning the Gulf Stream, which had been running backward (i.e., westward) and impeding our progress to the east, had reversed itself and we had a bright blue lively breezy morning on the flying bridge, pausing in our forward march only three times to bring in shining blue, green, gold dorado.

M. "I thought of having shark-fin soup for them tomorrow night."

E. "The fucking hypochondriacs would be suspicious. They're hypochondriac anachronisms."

M. "Out of this period?"

E. "They can't tell the time."

M. "So shark-fin soup would be the best thing for them."

Reaching Havana late Friday, the Haywards and Tracy came for lunch Saturday and we were eight at table consuming Roberto's Morro crab, *jambon à la crème,* sautéed sweet bananas and a big chocolate ice-cream cake from Thorwald Sanchez's ice-cream factory. That evening Bumby, Puck and their cherubic daughter Muffet arrived, and the next morning, Easter, Ernest, Bumby and Sinsky came trooping into my room to wake me up chorusing "Happy Birthday," my husband presenting me with a loving note and a check more than ample for a clock I had decided my room needed. Ernest took the movie people, with Sinsky and Roberto, fishing and when Bumby and Puck decided to meet them on their return to the Club Náutico I tried babysitting for the first time in memory and found it delightful. I took Miss Muffet down to the pool, played in the water and taught her a song, "What a pretty day, what a nice cool breeze," her baby voice repeating my tune precisely. Sunday being the servants' day of rest, I made her supper and read her verses from my childhood book *Mother Earth's Children.* We had a minute's screaming opposition to the approach of sleep, then sweet silence.

One advantage of the Hayward invasion was that it was short-lived. Another was that Mr. Tracy and Ernest got on cordially together from their first handshake. Mr. T. had declared a personal embargo on alcohol and he willingly left his bed early in the mornings as Ernest did. They went to Cojímar one morning, got a glimpse of old Anselmo, one of the village's senior fishermen, asleep in his shack after a night's work. Anselmo and Santiago, of the book, shared many characteristics and much philosophy, and Tracy was impressed by the look of him. He talked to Gregorio and Felípe about some of the technicalities of one-man fishing in a skiff, and they looked around the town.

"A fine man," Ernest wrote Gianfranco, "he is modest and intelligent and very delicate and fino."

On April 25 the elegant, snooty Vedado Tennis

Club ran a one-day fishing tournament for women only, all the other contestants going out in their husbands' luxurious boats but Gregorio and I in *Tin Kid* for a day of constant spray and teasing marlin which surfaced to inspect the baits, then sounded, surfaced and sounded. It was too early in the season for the big migration of marlin along Cuba's north coast, but we managed to pick up a couple of the young thirty-to-forty-five-pound early scouting fish. Among the thirty other boats, six took one fish each. We in the smallest boat were the winners.

At Paraíso again in *Pilar* and *Tin Kid* we were cadets under the command of the weather and students of wind, current, fish and stars, our major concerns the sharpness of a hook, the set of a bait in the water. On May 4, E. and I fished outside the reefs in the *Tin Kid* and found big schools of flying fish in the Gulf Stream there. "Flush like a covey of quail," Ernest said, delighted, "and so big at this low level." That evening in *Pilar,* half listening to the evening news on the radio from Miami, waiting for the weather report, we heard that Ernest had won the Pulitzer Prize for Literature. Oxtail soup from a can was our supper, but we celebrated the prize with an extra course, a piece of cheese for each of us.

In the night a sprinkle of rain on my face woke me. I dug a beer out of the icebox directly behind Ernest's head and went with it and a cigarette to the stern from which I found Cassiopeia and the Twins and the Huntsman and Pegasus and near him a small constellation I couldn't identify. Jupiter was blazing in the west and before I fell asleep again Venus was rising like a silver grapefruit in the eastern sky. Ernest's breathing continued slow and even throughout my studies.

On May 5 I wrote, "He has been happy to have the news here without the fuss and falsities and telephonings and Cubanos making their oversized compliments. . . . It is very nice to have a husband who takes his honors so lightly."

On May 12, Bill Lowe, an editor of *Look* magazine, and his wife came to lunch at the Finca. Lowe's assignment was to persuade Ernest that a *Look* photographer could accompany us on the first two or three weeks of safari without obstructing or even hindering our pursuit of the game, and I thought he handled it very well. He listened attentively to Ernest's objections: too many people, too much noise, too much space usurped in hunting cars and camp; too little light for photography when the hunting is good early mornings and late evenings. When all the objections had been stated and restated, Bill Lowe replied with simple arithmetic, to discuss which they strolled to the pool, leaving the rest of us in the sitting room. *Look*'s contribution to the expenses of the safari, as Lowe proposed it, was more than my husband could afford to reject. For a picture story about the safari, picture captions written by Ernest, *Look* would pay $15,000 of our expenses. For a story of 3,500 words or more, for which *Look* would receive world magazine rights, they would pay a further $10,000, Ernest told me that night. The photographer they had chosen for this job was an outdoors guy, Lowe said, who understood fishing and hunting and knew the tricks of walking softly and photographing in the early morning. He was from California and his name was Earl Theisen. He would be subject to Ernest's direction on the safari. With Philip Percival, Earl Theisen and perhaps Mayito Menocal we would set out from Nairobi on or about September 1.

Our blood coursing faster than usual, we began assigning dates to all the other projects we had dreamed of for that winter. A few days in New York to verify shipments of rifles, shotguns and ammunition from Abercrombie's to Africa. Pamplona for the beginning of the fiesta of San Fermín on July 7, then Madrid and Valencia. We would have hunting boots and mosquito boots made by Ernest's favorite bootmaker in Madrid and bush jackets and pants by one of the Indian overnight tailors in Nairobi. When we read that the French Line's new passenger ship the S.S. *Flandre* because of labor troubles had stalled a hundred miles or more out of port on her maiden voyage to New York, Ernest sympathized with the company and the ship's captain. "A shenzy thing to do, the poor, nice ship. We should go on her, if she's got a sailing in time for us."

Our plans were to fly to Key West to check on Pauline's property there which both Patrick and Gregory were ignoring, Henny having written that the Pool House was in such disrepair that it was not rentable. Then the Miami train for New York. And finally the *Flandre* sailing for France on June 24.

On Sunday the fourteenth, on the way to the airport, we all detoured to the Floridita for a final daiquiri over which Papa decided not to pay his big bill there, but gave the boys of the bar handsome tips. In return they gave us a gallon of handmade daiquiris which Ernest distributed on the road to the airport, and also on the windy runway. We had twenty-four pieces of luggage, which weighed 593 pounds, not counting paper-wrapped farewell presents. That day we did not guess it, but we would not touch down in Cuba again for thirteen months.

16

En Voyage

CONTRARY TO HENNY'S assessment, we found Pauline's Pool House, the lime-tinted pool and the flowering garden a doll-sized paradise. Some rotted floorboards sagged in the bedroom off the kitchen, and rain had leaked through a hole in its roof, but these required only minor repairs. It cost me ten minutes to clean away the discarded chop bones, a tattered sandal and other debris I noticed under the kitchen stove. Ernest rejoiced that the foot-high Madeira tree he had transplanted from a soup can in 1928 now towered fifty feet behind the old powder house. After the expanses of the Finca Vigía, this garden with its concentration of treasures seemed a jewel case.

Although the children had removed their favorite things among Pauline's possessions and all of the table silver, her sitting room looked intact with its small antique furniture, the floor tiles with pink roses which years before I had helped her find in Cuba, a few good oil paintings and prints, sculpture and lamps that were both pretty and functional. But except for sleeping we lived on the spacious secluded terrace which stretched from the doorstep to the rim of the pool. Pauline had left two or three thousand books on the shelves which lined the staircase of the main house facing Whitehead Street. We had one big canvas bag bulging with books among our luggage. Only inertia restrained me from filling another one.

The bedroom at the top of the narrow circular staircase, which had been Ernest's workroom—*Death in the Afternoon, Green Hills of Africa, To Have and Have Not*—and where I had luxuriated as Pauline's guest on various visits was holding together well with no serious threats to its comfort, even though woodworms and dry rot worked away silently on the bedstead and on the big elaborately carved Spanish desk there.

"It would be recklessly wasteful to let it fall into further disrepair," I noted, "or to sell it for less than its value just to be rid of the responsibility."

From the moment we stepped off the airplane we lived, moved, breathed, ate, drank, worked, gossiped, reminisced, expounded, joked in a nucleus of old friends. All the one-time servant girls came around to greet Ernest and he hugged each one, remembering they had been pretty twenty years before, overlooking their missing teeth and wrinkles. We got the car packed with twenty-three pieces of luggage and four guns, and with Toby Bruce driving, headed up over the keys for Miami.

Rolling between ranks of mangroves and sea grapes, Ernest remembered inevitably that Indian Key had been the "metropolis" with noisy bars and gambling shacks before the 1935 hurricane, how he and Mr.

Sully on the first emergency boat with medical supplies had found nobody alive after they passed Lower Matecumbe Key, and at Indian Key had watched moray eels crawling in and out of the slot machines. Warned of the hurricane, the World War I Veterans' Administration had sent down a train from Miami, Ernest recalled, intending to evacuate the veterans who were constructing a highway along the keys paralleling the railway, shepherding them to the safety of the mainland. "But the train was blown off the track at Homestead," he remembered.

Aboard the train from Miami we ran northward through wild swamp of scrub pine, palmettos and scrub palms, with zebu cattle in pastureland, and we squandered the morning bird-watching, discovering flights of great white herons, two sandhill cranes, two snakebirds, an everglades kite, a huge blue heron who was sliding down to land feet first, showing his lovely blue-and-gray wing pattern, white wood ibis. The rivers were choked with water hyacinth in bloom, we noticed, and flowering wild iris and water lilies. As the train was halted not far out of Miami a mockingbird flew toward our windows and swerved up to the car's roof. Ernest murmured, "Maybe he sneaks a free ride every day, if he can get a toehold on this roof."

We were in a menu-reading epoch, I realized with glee, rather than a menu-creating one.

Near Savannah we passed a pleasant brick Georgian-style house set far back from the railway behind green fields with live oak and sycamore trees towering around it and a TV aerial sprouting from its roof.

"Television aerials remove all the dignity from a house," I said.

"Inside and out," said Ernest.

Slim Hayward and her daughter Kitty Hawks met us at Penn Station in 92-degree heat and took us out to their pretty house in Manhasset for a few days of Long Island highlife. Then, aboard the *Flandre*, we suffered the ritual of the usual boring send-off. Our guests stood around stiff as poles, looking beyond help, which arrived only with the "all ashore" announcement. Alexander Calder and his wife were in the crowd on a forward deck and Ernest hailed him, "Sandy, you crook." It was the beginning of the most felicitous of a couple of dozen crossings I made by ship. At Plymouth we hid from the shipboard reporters and then there was Gianfranco waving and grinning from the dock at Le Havre. Gianfranco had brought along his friend Adamo de Simon, an undertaker from Udine, to chauffeur us, and Adriana had sent along little handmade cushions to comfort our spines. Adamo with his fierce black eyes and huge smile, lively as a puppet on strings, tied a mountain of bags almost as big as the little Lancia on top of it, and for the first time since June 1944 we took a look at Normandy. The smells of apples growing and new-mown hay replaced the old smell of cordite in the air and Rosa Bonheur horses and fat white Charolais cattle superseded the roaring military traffic we had endured under its curtains of dust. "Artichokes as big as cabbages, a nun on a motorbike, Marcel Proust country," I noted. "The new tower of the cathedral at Rouen is being made of steel. Papa says, rousing from nap, 'Wake me if they start to burn Jeanne.'"

At the Ritz the doorman peered into the car, exclaimed, *"Monsieur 'Emingway, bienvenu."* Miraculously they had a room available, Number 36 overlooking the Place Vendôme, and there followed exuberant hand-shakings and compliments with the reception clerks, the theater ticket man behind his pulpit at the foot of the stairs, the baggagemen, Georges, Bertin and Claude in the bars and Michael in the dining room. Charlie Ritz came down to meet us in the lobby, looking more chipper than ever, and later with Gianfranco we all convened at our old corner table in the dining room, embellishing salmon and later veal with a wonderful Montrachet 1943 and a spectacular Haut-Brion 1937.

Among the best local news was that Charlie had gained control of the hotel as chairman of the board of directors and was instituting a slightly more modern regime. None of those old high stiff collars on the staff. The same courteous attention to guests, naturally, but less pomposity. He had been ranging around the hotel from cellar to roof, sleeping whenever possible in different rooms to discover any individual inadequacies. When staff members addressed him as Monsieur President, he was instructing them, "None of that. We shall continue as always." Recently he had slept in a suite overlooking the Place Vendôme, as we would, and was awakened *"trop tôt"* by the doorman whistling for a taxi. That morning he informed the doorman that his whistle "resounds around the Place." The doorman produced the whistle, a variety used by the Swiss police, and explained that taxi men could hear it a mile away, "very good for rainy days."

"You'll have to find a whistle that can be heard only by taxi drivers," I suggested. "Like those inaudible dog whistles."

For a couple of days we luxuriated in Paris. Then, leaving a dozen lumps of luggage at the Ritz, we departed from the Place Vendôme before noon on July 3 with a chilly mist enclosing the windows, the still heavily burdened little Lancia carrying Ernest in the front seat beside Adamo, Gianfranco and me behind, upholstered in bags and bundles. Approaching Chartres Ernest remembered how he and Archie MacLeish used to pedal that road on bicycles, each of them working hard on the long flat stretch, but with himself winning on the last half mile of downgrade before the town because his extra weight carried him faster. We marveled at the gardens, at the ancient rose window of the façade and especially at the pagan figures in the bottom row of the high-relief frieze in the southeast porch. As I was photographing a *porte-bouteilles* at a town café where we lunched, I explained to the *patronne* that we did not have them in the United States. "You'll find them in Bloomingdale's," said she. On south we rolled. Ernest had long been worried that the officials of Franco's Spain would consider his re-entry there with hostility. It turned out that none of his apprehension was necessary.

Monday morning brought dark soggy clouds pushing down on the hills and collapsing into rain and an unseasonable, unreasonable cold dredging into our marrow. Sitting in front, Ernest was quiet. In the back Gianfranco and I were troglodytes, having burrowed down among our chaos of coats, sweaters, cameras, maps, guidebooks, the radio, bottles of water and wine, newspapers and magazines in four languages.

The French waved us across the Bidassoa River and at Irún we climbed doubtfully out of the car for immigration and customs ceremonies in a new building with the legend FRANCO—FRANCO—FRANCO on a wall above a stained-glass window. The immigration officer, seeing Ernest's passport, asked, preoccupied, "Relation?" Then he looked again at the passport picture and its subject. "Could it really be?" he asked and stood up and shook hands, welcoming him with emotion. We had no customs problems with car, radio, cameras or our prodigious luggage.

We climbed in the car into the Pyrenees, their heads and shoulders draped in clouds, on our way to the fiesta of San Fermín, following the same road that Ernest used to take thirty and twenty-five years earlier. The weather was beginning to brighten and the vegetation quickly changed from France and sea level. Here were trees with long white spiky blossoms, purple heather clinging to the granite cliffs, a wild lavender pea, luxuriant underbrush. Ernest said, "The country hasn't changed, and there's plenty of it too."

In the first six kilometers inside Navarre, we passed only two grinning soldiers in a horsedrawn cart. In the distance we saw a brown stone farmhouse, square and solid, with the tiny high windows of the Middle Ages. We paused at the ancient village of Sumbilla with its vine-clad bridge, and inside a house I noticed dark wide-planked shiny floors. They must have been polished for three hundred years, one hundred thousand mornings.

Talking about how Wellington fought through these dense forests, coming up from the south, taking all the small passes and finally reaching San Sebastián, we pushed up obliquely to the Punto de Velate pass, 947 meters high, through the same forests of beech trees Papa wrote about in *The Sun Also Rises*. On the bare brown slopes above the timber line Basque shepherds were tending their flocks. As in Idaho. From the top of the pass we saw a new range of mountains, blue, brown and barren, and Papa said happily, "Now there. That's Spain."

411

We descended in long loops through thick forest which, lower down, opened out into green fields and apple orchards. In *The Sun Also Rises,* Ernest wrote it: "There were trees along both sides of the road, and a stream and ripe fields of grain, and the road went on, very white and straight ahead. . . . Then we crossed a wide plain, and there was a big river off on the right shining in the sun from between the line of trees, and away off you could see the plateau of Pamplona rising out of the plain, and the walls of the city, and the great brown cathedral, and the broken skyline of the other churches." Then the road was gravel. Now it was paved. Otherwise we were riding through Ernest's first novel, with the colors changed. "When I wrote about it," Papa said, "the grain was further advanced, this year they've had so much rain."

"They still have bears, European brown bears in the forests here," he was saying. "They come out sometimes and kill the sheep. I remember during the war I saw a bear's paw nailed to the door of a church. That was in Barco de Avila in the Sierra de Gredos. That's outside Madrid, near the country of 'the Bells.' "

We reached Pamplona about one o'clock, Papa saying, "I wouldn't recognize it. These apartment buildings." But the old central square and the fiesta, which had started officially an hour before, had not changed. The streets were bright with scarlet and yellow banners, with the blue shirts of the country boys, and the small red kerchiefs tied around every neck. The main square was jammed with the before-lunch *paseo,* the girls fresh and pretty in their demure summer dresses, the boys in bands with arms around shoulders, always looking, always talking, some *grandes dames* with elegant pointed slippers, sleek coiffures, gloves. No hats. All the faces were alight with anticipation.

We lunched briefly, saying constant no's to the boys who wished to sell us black market pens and watches and to the bootblacks who not only wanted to shine our shoes but also to tear off perfectly good heels and replace them with rubber ones. Papa said they were doing it twenty-five years ago. The same fellows, maybe, or their sons.

There being no rooms available in Pamplona, we went out of town twenty miles to the village of Lecumberri with its big new hotel. On July 7 I wrote: "The fiesta of San Fermín began auspiciously this morning at seven o'clock with the *encierro,* the running of the young men and the bulls from the corrals near the railway station through the old streets of the town to the bullring. Only one boy was gored, not seriously.

"We got up at 4:30 a.m., hurried over the lovely golden road in misty dawn, excitement blooming in the car. We reached the town square as they were giving it its morning sprinkling, met Papa's old friend, Juanito Quintana who, Papa says, knows as much about bulls and the whole complex of bullfighting as any man in Spain. We gulped down strong black coffee, tied red kerchiefs around our necks, and hurried in the crowd, Rupert Bellville [an English friend, ever the British gentleman] running interference for me, Papa warning Rupert to watch his wallet, and made the arena in time to watch the boys and the bulls come racing in, to chase each other about for a bit before steers were sent into the ring to jockey the bulls into their darkened stalls beneath the stands.

"What I remember best: The crestfallen face of Papa when, as we left the bullring, he discovered his own wallet had been stolen, his fine new wallet I had just bought him in New York. 'The best pickpockets in Spain come to this fiesta,' he murmured sadly. 'They all work the first day then get out of town.' The brilliant colors of the crowd in the sharp morning light and the prevalence of red. The spontaneous gaiety, unforced and unfalse. The man who thrust a sprig of parsley at me outside the central produce market, saying, 'If you have a roast chicken.' The swallows whirling above the bullring and around the cathedral towers, their wings looking more sharply pointed than those of American swallows. The Goya faces, harsh-boned and unsoftened beneath the *boinas* (berets), in the workingmen's tavern where we broke fast with codfish and fresh lobster stew, washing it down with red wine at nine U.S. cents a quart. Gianfranco, tying on his red scarf, singing *'Avanti il Popolo,'* in this

413

fortress of anticommunism. San Fermín, shining in the candlelight of his chapel, his robe soft rose-colored and gold, and how full of worshippers the cathedral was at morning mass, with many army uniforms among them. Papa taught me the song the boys sing after the cathedral services on the last day of the festival:

Pobre de mí	Poor old me
Pobre de mí	Poor old me
Acabo la fiesta	It's finished—the fiesta
De San Fermín.	Of San Fermín.

"After our walk around town, Papa and I came back here to sleep until time to go to the *corrida.*"

July 7, Lecumberri
"Peter Viertel, Bob and Kathy Parrish, Lord Dudley and his brother, Eddie Ward and his blond bride, also Tommy Shevlin and Durie have all arrived and we move now in a mob. We lunched in cheerful confusion about four o'clock this afternoon then went to the principal square, the Plaza de Castillo, to watch the seven different local bands with their seven bright banners piping their thin mountain airs and dancing around the square on their way to the bullring, we following, I hanging firmly onto Papa's arm. The old amphitheater with its fretwork trellises, the lombardy poplars towering behind it and banners streaming from its rim was gay, the sun warm and there was almost no wind to distort the movements of the matadors' capes and muletas. Our seats right above the matadors in the *callejón* were excellent and today's bulls, from the ranch of Salvador Guardiola, were handsome, noble beasts. I was enchanted by their faces. They had no expression of menace or of a wish to destroy anything. They looked eager, excited, confused but wanting to learn this strange new game into which they had been thrust.

"But every bull this afternoon was wet from his shoulder to his feet, the blood bubbling like a spring from the wounds of the pics. Papa was furious and so was the crowd." [Later Ernest added his own notes: "We have started a movement against the way the

414

picadors are destroying the bulls. . . . None of the matadors was really good enough to get the best out of such simple and noble bulls, but Isidro Marin worked closer and had more command with the muleta."]

July 8, Lecumberri, noon
"Going into town this morning for the *encierro,* we noticed the end hotel of the village, its sign giving no name, saying only: HOTEL—ON PARLE FRANÇAIS. Papa says, 'Imagine. "Where are you staying?" *"Oh, moi? J'ai descendu à On Parle Français."* '

"Instead of going to the arena we went to take pictures of the boys and the bulls running in front of the cheerful old baroque town hall with its festoons of cherubs. Seeing me squeezing between taller heads and shoulders, a housewife with an apartment on the corner across from the town hall kindly invited me to use her balcony, which I did with plentiful thanks. Gianfranco with his new red cummerbund had intended to run in the *encierro,* but having danced all night long all over town, he said, and also at a club on the riverside, he fell asleep near the corrals about 6:30 and was wakened by the last bull thudding past him.

"After the *encierro* our mob walked around the town then down, below the ancient brown ramparts built by the Roman, Pompeius, to the horse and mule fair by the river where the farmers of Navarre do their annual bargaining. It was lovely there with the early morning light filtering like soft green rain through the leaves of the plane trees onto the shiny brown rumps of the horses, and the black hair of the gypsy women in their bright skirts moving around their cooking pots which gave out fine, garlicky smells. The mules were very talkative and the strong little mountain ponies were milling and moving about. After the noise and excitement of the *encierro,* the fair with its soft voices seemed a harbor of tranquility. Here at the hotel, all seems quiet too. It is the quiet of *excesos."*

July 8, Lecumberri, midnight
"It was a great bullfight today, stirring and exciting and emotional, because we had fine bulls, and espe-

cially because we had Antonio Ordóñez as one of the matadors. He is the son of Niño de la Palma, who was the bullfighter in *The Sun Also Rises,* and he was so skillful, valiant and melodic that he lifted the afternoon from sport to poetry. He is a dark slim boy with a sweet smooth young face, his expression in the ring grave, but not tense. He did the most brilliant passes, slow and sure, patted the bull respectfully on the forehead, and did the *cuadra* pass which puts the bull's feet in a neat rectangle and his head straight out. Then he was luminous between the great horns, and the bull died bravely.

"On his second bull, Ordóñez cut his hand. The chamois which covers the sword handle slipped off and the force of the blow carried his hand down along the sharp blade. With the bleeding hand he put the next sword well in. Papa said the brilliance of his performance grows from how closely to the animal he works, from how slowly he moved the muleta, how he dominates, almost hypnotizes the bulls.

"Knowing that the bulls have had a fine, free life with no chores and no burdens their full four years, thinking how lucky they are to have it finished in excitement in no more than fifteen minutes, I am not upset by the killing of them."

July 9, Lecumberri, midnight
"We have admired the charming behavior of the town these days. There is a good deal of wine-drinking but no ugliness, no fights. It is essentially a fiesta for boys and young men who have the privilege this one week in the year of drinking all the wine they can hold. Papa said, 'You see a boy walking with his mother and his sister, the boy glassy-eyed, barely able to walk, and the mother and the sister helping him and smiling composedly and bowing to their friends.'

"Everybody knew my folk song, 'Los borachos en el cementerio' and each of the seven different bands played it."

July 10, Lecumberri, midnight
"Looking on the way to town at the big scooped-out valleys on either side of the road with their bands of

green and lime and beige and gold and blond and rust-colored various crops, Papa said, 'It's a shame they didn't get Van Gogh to paint Navarre.' Lombardy poplars, dark and slim, break the sloping horizontal colors like exclamation points. Gianfranco said, 'Like asparagus.'

"In town at what had become our headquarters, the terrace outside Kutz's cafe in a corner of the square, our social life became a marathon of reunions with old friends, drinks, rendezvous, snacks, more drinks, more friends. There were the Robert Ruarks, Peter Taylor from New York with his own crowd, Aymar, the Marquess of Agudin, dear fellow, and his crowd of Spanish bull-owners, playboys and drinkers, the Wertenbakers down from Ciboure, the Bob Trouts, everybody in tremendous fettle. When I wondered aloud how the human constitution could support such a life, Juanito Quintana said, 'If you don't move with the indiscipline of the fiesta, eating and drinking and sleeping at any hour, it kills you.'

"Gianfranco ran with the bulls this morning and says it woke him up. After the *encierro* Eddie Ward was waiting at Kutz's when the rubber-heel specialist got hold of him and, deaf to Eddie's protests, was pounding on a flimsy rubber heel when Papa turned up. Papa threatened in strong Spanish. The bootblack reached for Eddie's other shoe. Papa shouted for a policeman. Then Gianfranco arrived. He and the rubber-heel man are dearest friends, having danced together all one night and shared a girl. The bootblack burst into apologies, almost into tears, carefully replaced Eddie's good heel and gave him a triple shoeshine, then stayed around to have a beer with us. He had worked the Pamplona fiesta for twenty-three years, he told me, travels to fiestas all over Spain in the summers and winters in Barcelona. He's our man now, and, because of the dust, shines us all two or three times a day.

"Yesterday the matador, Córdoba, dedicated his first bull to Papa and sent his beautiful dress cape to our *barrera*. It was a terrible bull, the horns wide set but curving inwards, a fly-brained beast and unreliable, and Papa pointed out that he could not turn fast or short, as a good bull does. Córdoba did everything possible with him, but the bull gave him a bad time.

"This afternoon's bullfight, with Ordóñez, was the best we've seen. He is beautiful to watch in the ring, the slim young legs quick but unhurried. He worked his first bull brilliantly, killed well with the bandaged hand and was awarded an ear. His second bull was huge-horned, fast, very spirited, turned well, and Ordóñez took the beast's first rush, resting on his knees near the *barrera*. When the bull upset the picador's horse, Ordóñez was instantly there, where he should be, deft and controlled, to take the bull away from the horse. He gave us easily forty passes with the muleta and then, in the center of the ring, dropped the red serge cloth and his sword, the bull standing quiet, and knelt on both knees facing the bull for what seemed a full minute. Watching it, I was feeling that there still remains in Spain some shred of ancient pre-history concordance between man and animals, a mystery we have not yet attempted to probe. Then Ordóñez killed the bull, gracefully, and after it was dragged out of the ring, the ovation ringing in violent approval, went to the spot on the stand where his noble beast had died, and saluted it."

Sunday, July 12, Lecumberri, 11:00 p.m.
"Another Pamplona song, with a cheerful tune:

Un' d' Enero	One of January
Dos de Febrero	Two of February
Tres de Marzo	Three of March
Cuatro de Abril	Four of April
Cinco de Mayo	Five of May
Seis de Junio	Six of June
Siete de Julio, San Fermín	Seven of July, San Fermín
Hemos de ir ahí.	We must go there."

Monday, July 13, brought the breakup of the San Fermín fiesta, and everybody rushed off, back to work or to new fiestas, in all directions. Ernest and I (Adamo driving) took Juanito Quintana home to San Sebastián, and Rupert Bellville drove Gianfranco to miss his train for Venice and continue on to France with Rupert. Heading back to Lecumberri again we passed a team of oxen pulling a two-wheeled cart, the wheels great high heavy disks of solid wood, the kind of wheels I imagined had been abandoned with the arrival of the Renaissance. People were working late in the fields, scything their small patches of yellow grain, which reminded me of Virgil:

> But the red-gold corn should always be cut in
>   noonday heat,
> In noonday heat the baked grain beat out on
>   threshing-floor.

The hoe and the scythe were the only farm implements we'd seen in use until then, and oxen the only work animals.

Approaching Burgos I asked Ernest about it and he said, "Rough town. Cold in winter. Wonderful cathedral. Ancient capital of Old Castile. It was from there that the Spanish, led by the Cid, started to drive the Moors out of Spain, in the eleventh century, I think. It had the greatest brutalities during the Civil War. Excellent cheese." I checked in the guidebook, found the Cid lived between 1040 and 1099, the cathedral built between 1221 and 1250.

Ernest had been looking along the road all morning for a bird he particularly associated with Spain, the hoopoe bird with its long curved bill and big crest. "They're rare," he said. "But they weren't extinct during the war here." We stopped at a government-run restaurant, The Cid, to lunch in the garden, and counted eight different hoopoes flitting about, thrusting their cinnamon-colored heads into bright blossoms.

On a whim we turned off the main road and followed a secondary gravel road through fields, then climbed a mesa to a town on the top, Sepúlveda, where we found a busy bar, refilled the *bota* and got acquainted with the regular customers, hospitable, sardonic people. They told us about their annual bullfight on August 30, a *capea*, when they barricade the little plaza in front of the ancient castillo with its tower. They let in one bull, which the town has bought by subscription, and, as in the old days, the brave boys of the neighborhood, and those who wish to appear brave, all go into the ring together to fight the bull. The bar customers showed us their one photograph of last year's bullfight and invited us to this year's fiesta.

Afterward I noted: "In small, lighthearted ways Ernest quickly discovers who in any crowd were on his side in the Civil War. In Sepúlveda it was with a small joke about slang names for paper money. He makes no politics. But he knows people who fought on both sides. They all welcome him."

That day we saw rooks, starlings, swallows, storks, a flock of some forty partridges which flushed from a field of cut grain, a hawk and two beautiful big silver-blue pigeons. Then we came upon a young wolf cub, trotting slowly away from us beside the road, his ears very pointed, his jaw much wider than a dog's jaw. In his excitement Adamo nearly put us in the ditch.

"Papa has been talking about Rafael Hernández, the bullfight critic and his old friend whom we met at Pamplona," I wrote. "Of Madrid on its high, dry plateau in the center of Spain, Hernández once said complacently to Ernest, 'The only thing Madrid lacks is the sea.'

"When Papa asked him what was his favorite winter sport, Hernández replied, 'The stove.'"

The Lancia climbed almost to the top of another mountain range, a wild country of granite rock and thick pine and hardwood forest, with underbrush and high bracken hiding unexpected caves. Below the road on our right a clear, fast stream, the Río Eresma, rushed under a small stone bridge. It was the forest of *For Whom the Bell Tolls*. Through the treetops we could glimpse a high barren hilltop, where Sordo had his fight, and we saw that new stones in the bridge filled the apex of the arch. Ernest murmured, "Now I am glad to see it is like how I wrote it," happy if ungrammatical. "We held the tops of all this along here. They were about three-quarters of the way down on the road you see to the right. In some places the two lines were less than ten meters apart."

Descending from the Guadarrama we went through barren gray hills with scraggly patches of gorse as their only decoration and Ernest excused the country. "Thankless looking mountains but lots of partridge here." Then we had at our right the great Escorial, and beyond a strip of dark green forest, Madrid luminous in the distance. As we approached the city, steadily descending as from the rim of a saucer to its center, Ernest reminisced, "The Nationalists held this road during the war. The Republicans had to go far around and get into Madrid from the north." As at Pamplona, he was dismayed at the new construction at Madrid's outskirts. "It has grown twice as much as Paris."

We buzzed through a flowering park, found the Gran Vía and settled into Room 109 at the Hotel Florida, a big cool-looking room with a small sitting room. Ernest turned on his portable radio and there was Tony Martin singing "Begin the Beguine."

Despite the new construction, there was still a severe shortage of housing for middle- and lower-income people, I was told by a young manicurist. I had asked her what I should see as a newcomer to Madrid and this modern *madrileña* said *Gone With the Wind* (*Fuera con el viento*). It had been running there two years and she had not yet seen it.

"You must be friends with a boy who would take you, a pretty girl like you."

"But, señora, to go with a boy, I must first be promised to him."

"You have twenty years? Yes, perhaps that is young to marry."

"It is not the marriage, señora, here no one well educated marries before two years after the engagement. Five or six years is usual."

"A waste of good time."

"It takes time to assemble the furnishings of the house and the linens. And it is very difficult to find a place to live, the quarters are so dear."

"What a pity."

"I have some friends who have been affianced for more than five years. They have their household things bought and paid for now but they cannot find a place to live."

"But there are many buildings."

421

"Yes, but people are always coming to Madrid from Galicia and Estremadura and from all the provinces."

It was my first excursion in years back among the last century's customs.

That evening Ernest and I went out to explore the Puerta del Sol, Madrid's Times Square, and his old haunts. His favorite bar had been torn down, but his bootmaker was still in business at the same spot. We came back along the Gran Vía which I thought not nearly as handsome as the Champs-Elysées or the Piazza San Marco or Regent Street or Fifth Avenue. But Ernest said he thought Madrid is "the best city in the world."

Ernest kept his room in that hotel for two years of the war, I noted, during which time it was hit 156 times by enemy shells or parts of them. At the Hotel Florida we had no shells in 1953. What we had was streetcars running all night.

When Ernest lived there, in Rooms 112 and 113, on the side of the hotel away from the front which was only 1,000 yards away, he told me, the chambermaids sometimes used to come into his room in the mornings carrying 155 millimeter shells, unexploded, exclaiming, "Look, look what we found."

On July 17 I wrote: "Today the concierge said as we were leaving the hotel, 'A thousand apologies, Don Ernesto. I didn't recognize you yesterday.' (The beard.) It was this same concierge who was hit in the hip with a machine-gun bullet as he opened the door of a car for John Dos Passos in front of the hotel. Ernest had carried him indoors."

That morning we made our initial visit to the Prado, Ernest joyous to find all his favorite pictures in their accustomed places, except for the Goyas which were temporarily in another room. On his visits to Madrid before the Civil War he used to go to the Prado every morning to revel in its treasures.

To compose ourselves afterward we walked up to the Plaza Santa Ana and a small dark pub, a favorite among bull-ranchers, entrepreneurs and bullfighters, where Ernest felt at home and we drank absinthe and munched cold, boiled shrimp. Later he found his old liquor store, and the ancient woman proprietor remembered him and did him the favor of digging out of her stock a bottle of legitimate Gordon's gin and some honest Scotch whiskey. The Spanish whiskey looked genuine, but most of it was doped with cognac. To me it tasted like deodorized ether.

Whatever else we did on that first visit to Madrid, we went each morning to the Prado for an hour, and I noted that in any gallery my eyes become surfeited in an hour. "Even though I have the most comfortable shoes and my feet are perfectly happy," I wrote, "after an hour I can look more, but I cannot see and assimilate."

From our first day in Madrid, the Cervecería Alemána, the bullfighters' bar in the Plaza Santa Ana, became our rendezvous place before lunch at four in the afternoon, and we made friends there. One of its regular patrons was Domingo Ortega who dominated bullfighting from 1931 to 1945 and although retired, still moved, spoke and smiled with the deliberation of a Personage. His hair was white, his skin very tanned, and his body moved resiliently beneath his handsome white linen clothes.

Another patron was the important bullfighter manager and entrepreneur Dominguín (real name, Domingo González Mateos), the father of the brilliant matador Luis Miguel Dominguín, with whom we talked bullfights and fighters, especially of Antonio Ordóñez, who, Doninguín told us, was a fine boy and would marry his daughter Carmen that year. Hunting around for presents for Ernest's birthday on July 21, I had found an antique bracelet made of gold and jade medallions strung together. Two of the medallions, exquisitely carved heads of a lion and lioness in gold with ruby eyes, would make a pleasant pair of cufflinks, I thought, and Sr. Dominguín helped me persuade the shopkeeper to that end. Another gift would be a replacement of the wallet which had been stolen in Pamplona.

The night of Ernest's birthday (which we celebrated with a quiet lunch), having tried to go to sleep in the din of the streetcars, I crept out of bed and in our sitting room wrote out of my system my opinions of them.

"This is the first time in my life I have ever lived close to streetcars and I am probably being stuffy and ungracious in resenting this new intimacy suddenly thrust upon me. There may be people who, deprived of the sounds of their local streetcars would feel cheated, who would find comfort in the noises these Madrid machines send up to us here on the first floor of this hotel. I am not so metropolitan.

"By day the racket of the streetcars dominates the sounds of motorcars, or horns, of paperboys yelling, of slamming doors, police whistles, and the midcity hum of crowds. By one or two o'clock in the morning we still have those sounds, but people are beginning to go home and the sounds subside. Except for the streetcars.

"Deep into my sleep comes the long, rising groan of a streetcar approaching our corner, a crescendo of sound and tone as the car climbs the slight rise in the street, its basic voice a deep growl, with arpeggios of screeches, screams and yells in higher tones giving emphasis to its complaints at working in the night. At the top of the rise, which sounds a mountain in my ears, there is a painful pause. We both wait, the car and I, breathing heavily. Then comes a crash of iron against iron, the bump. (There must be some small rift in the track.) I shake in my smooth bed and would be consoled by the tinkling of the conductor's little bell if he would only use it sparingly to notify the motorman that all is well back there. Two taps would clearly be sufficient. But no. He gives not two, not a dozen, at least twenty before the motorman revs up the power, the wheels grind into the tracks, the tracks groan, the car protests in all its joints as it heads toward the next bump, half a block away perhaps, but boisterously audible."

When I slid back into bed that morning, Ernest wakened and asked what I had been doing. When I told him he said, composedly, of the streetcars, "They're noisy. They're not dangerous." In his view, Madrid, or any of its component parts, could do no wrong.

That day, on our last visit to the Prado before taking off in the Lancia for Valencia and its annual week of festivity, Ernest found a hoopoe bird in Hieronymus Bosch's *Garden of Eden* painting. No discovery in Madrid pleased him more.

Juanito Quintana came from his home in San Sebastián to join us and Adamo for the fiesta at Valencia, and once out of town we had a morning of history, geography, agriculture and poetry.

But bad news arrived as we were leaving. Our fine chic French boat to Mombassa had canceled its sailing from Marseilles because of a smallpox epidemic. The only available ship was of the British Union-Castle Line which would give us a middle-of-the-ship cabin. It would sail August 6, a week earlier than we had planned.

My little thermometer showed the temperature in the car to be 88, the sky was cloudless and blazing, and the country dun-colored and desolate. "A bitter country to fight in," Ernest said. "The American battalion was a hundred and six days in country like this, along the Jarama [River], to our right. Not a piece of shade in the whole country." The desolation reminded Adamo of Calabria and Juanito of the hard life of the peasants. "Poors," he said. "They eat very little."

Presently we passed a grove of olive trees and rejoiced in the relief they gave our eyes. They prompted me to dig around in our multitudinous array of books, magazines and newspapers to find the C. Day-Lewis translation of the *Georgics* and read aloud one of our favorite passages.

> Olives are just the opposite: they require no cultivation
> And have no use for the sickle knife or the stiff-tooth rake
> Once they've dug themselves in on the fields and stood up to winds,
> Earth herself, by the crooked plough laid bare, provides
> Moisture enough for the plants and a heavy crop from the ploughshare.

Luis Miguel Domínguín, Spain's top bullfighter until he retired briefly in 1953 after a severe goring in

425

Venezuela, had at his father's suggestion invited us to stop at his farm near the road to Valencia for lunch and shade during the heat of the day. So we turned onto a country road at the village of Saelices, chuffed past stone ruins, copses of pines, streams edged with greenery and at the top of a hill pulled up at the entrance of a long low white house. A great carved door twenty feet high opened and we drove into the cobbled courtyard of the Villa Paz.

In the dim sitting room, its shutters closed against the heat, the round fireplace, a hole sunk into the floor with a white-plastered conical chimney sweeping far down to it from the ceiling, was still smoking. Luis Miguel, a millionaire at twenty-five, classically handsome with his straight nose, high cheekbones, straight brows above intelligent dark eyes, greeted us in swimming trunks and sandals and I noted the long scars of horn wounds on both legs. With the help of an uncle and aunt he ran a big establishment.

Among the company that day were Antonio Ordóñez with his lively gypsy face and gentle manners; his beautiful fiancée, Carmen, Luis Miguel's sister; another bullfighter, Rafael Ortega, a quiet blond man with cold blue eyes and stilted conversation. There were also a young French count in excellent tailoring; a pretty young girl, friend of Carmen and granddaughter of the Conde de Romanones (an important old man in Spain and Spanish rightist politics); as well as half a dozen of Luis Miguel's sisters, cousins and nieces. A dwarf, Marcellino, whom we had seen in Madrid, arrived before lunch. As were dwarfs in the days of Velázquez, he was entertained widely because of his wit which derived from a realistic rather than sentimental point of view, all of his pronouncements spoken in a flat, uninterested voice. With the light laughter, the momentary sitting on laps, the mild jokes, the touching of young hands and arms, the restrained gaiety in a faint haze of boredom, the household that day seemed to me a last European refuge of nineteenth-century *jeunesse dorée*.

I noted: "I think Luis Miguel's manner of relentlessness, hauteur and boredom grows not only from his having been so successful—rich, famous and pampered—so young, but also because he has these benefits without the educational background to sustain them and use them to best advantage. It might be good for him if someone could stimulate him to expand his intellectual interests."

The sky still blazing, the temperature in the car 92, heat-haze dancing above the yellow fields on both sides of the road, we swung up over the eastern ridges of the Sierra Martés, over the pass 890 meters high, I reading again from the *Georgics* as we passed vineyards growing in the rust-red earth of the eastern hillsides.

As long as your vines are growing in first and infant
    leaf,
They're delicate, need indulgence. And while the
    gay shoots venture
Heavenward, given their head and allowed to roam
    the sky,
Don't use a knife upon them yet—a fingernail
Is enough for pruning their leaves and thinning them
    out in places,
But when they've shot up and are holding the elms
    in strong embrace,
Dock the leaves, lop the branches.

The vineyards we passed had survived their first pruning and we could see that the vintners were keeping their soil busy by cultivating, as Virgil recommended. In the dusk we swung down to Valencia, all four of us hot and dry, the dust of Spain in our eyes, mouths, noses and hair, and—bonanza—we found a bar right near the front door of the Hotel Excelsior. When we gasped our requests for drinks, the bar had only one occupant, an immense young American, Peter Buckley.

On Sunday, July 26, in Valencia I wrote: "Papa comes in happy with the morning papers. They've signed the Korean armistice. Batista has suppressed a small military revolt, and Spanish bandits had killed a couple of English tourists in their car. 'Not good for tourismo,' says Ernest. His association with the Spanish press has been skillful throughout. With patience and diplomacy he has parried questions and lured discussion away from the delicate subject of the reporters' disapproval of *For Whom the Bell Tolls* and his other writings about the Civil War (disapproval being the official position). He never retreats from his original and subsequent support of the Spanish Republic, but manages to retain his probity and dignity without antagonizing anyone. It is a chore for him, but seeing Spain again is worth it, he says."

Directly after the bullfight that day we boarded the Lancia and hurried on the open road toward Madrid. We had less than a week to get to Paris, pick up our luggage for Africa and voyage down to Marseilles to catch the boat for Mombassa. Juanito, sad at our parting two days later, drove with us beyond San Sebastián to Irún on the French border, to bid us good-bye, his face gravely restraining a show of emotion. It had been twenty-three days of shared excitement, enlightenment and gaiety for all of us.

At our usual noontime rendezvous in the Ritz Bar we found Charlie Ritz eager to drive us to the national medical institute for our yellow fever shots and to lunch at one of his favorite places, Relais de Porquerolles, a triumphant lunch after which we cruised around the quarter pausing to admire Talleyrand's house in the rue Férou, to buy gin and whiskey, detective stories for Charlie and, my last purchase in Europe, two big black bookkeeper's ledgers, which would both be filled with notes when we left Africa. That night my husband and I kept ourselves so pleasurably occupied in bed for so long that I did not awaken until ten o'clock the next morning.

We dined delightedly the next day with Charlie Ritz who was dispensing juicy tidbits about the quixoticisms of his hotel's distinguished clientele—a Hohenlohe prince tossing lighted firecrackers into the garden, the Maharaja of Karpathula and the ambassador from the Argentine squaring off for blows over the precedence of their respective flags over the front entrance —and he told us how he had once snuggled into the lap of the great Sarah Bernhardt, one of the first but not the last of the actresses who commanded his esteem. He gave me his personal recipe for cheese fondue which he sometimes made for us in the small private dining room off the rue Cambon lobby:

Freshly grated Fribourg or Emmenthal cheese, 6 ounces per serving
One small glass of strong dry white wine
One tooth of garlic finely chopped
Grated nutmeg, pepper, cornstarch
One or two glasses of kirsch

In a heavy pan let the wine heat almost to boiling, add the cornstarch and cheese gradually, then the seasonings, the kirsch last. Keep warm over an alcohol lamp. The correct dipping thing was, of course, bits of crusty French bread.

At noon on August 4, Ernest and Adamo in the Lancia, my friend Georges Mabilat and I in a Ritz Packard stuffed to the roof with luggage, we headed south out of the Place Vendôme. Two days later when we got to Marseilles, the lavender-hulled ship was just tying up at the wharf. A couple of stewards and Adamo helped us maneuver our forty-six pieces of luggage, including two bags of books, three guns, our typewriter, a Spanish wineskin, and two cameras, into Cabin 34 with its linoleum floor and barrackslike furniture and we left the whole lot piled in the middle of the floor to go have a final drink with Adamo before the "all ashore" announcement. Adamo's fierce black eyes were awash with tears as we squeezed hands in *arrivederci*. "This voyage," I advised myself, "will either prove or disprove my theory that the British regard unnecessary discomfort—Oh, the fortitude!—as next to Godliness." With every nautical mile over thirteen days, through the Mediterranean, the Red Sea and the Indian Ocean, the theory grew truer for me.

Ernest was loving the voyage, making friends unhurriedly, feeling rich in leisure for reading, and I was busy typing my notes on Spain, studying Swahili and writing exercises in it for our morning classes. With the sweat rolling off him one morning Ernest said, "I wish I had a can of Budweiser right off the ice." By the time the bartenders poured their cooled but not cold beer into a hot glass, even the British could not describe it as cool. "This ship's ice has the unique quality of heating and at the same time watering a drink," I complained.

The captain had lent Ernest a U.S. military handbook of French phrases and pronunciations, and as we lolled in our cabin after lunch, he instructed me.

"Your canteen, madam, is your *bee-dawng.*"

"Not *my* canteen. Never."

"Yes, *Bee-dawng.*"

"Could you possibly mean *bidon?*"

"That's what I've been telling you. You remember what you paid for it? *Kawn-b-yang?*"

"What have the Chinese got to do with this?"

"Something, maybe. How much?"

"Those poor G.I.'s, if *kawn-b-yang* means *combien.*"

"French with a south China accent," he decided. After years in Cuba our accents in French carried a hint of Iberian airs.

Something reminded him of Mary Beck, his parents' Irish maid who used to smuggle forbidden whiskey into her room in the summer house at Horton Bay. "Have a nip, sport," he mimicked. "Good for ye." When she needed a push on her ample behind from a rowboat to the dock: "Just help me up the landing, sport."

She used to sing the Bathhouse John song:

> After the ball was over,
> Lizzy took out her glass eye,
> Put her peg-leg in the corner,
> And uncorked a bottle of rye.

As the captain had predicted, on reaching the Indian Ocean we plowed into the southwest monsoon. It was Wednesday, August 19, a 3-knot wind hitting our starboard quarter and everybody on the heaving decks a bit less sportive, more subdued. "A gentle, soothing, rocking motion," said the captain, "such as to remind one of cradle days." He did not expect to reach Mombassa until after 4 p.m. on Saturday, in which situation he would not dock because, "The immigration and customs people are civil servants and nevah work after six o'clock."

430

The captain recited a farewell present to Ernest and me, a composition by Bishop Waltham Howe.

> The traveller o'er the desert wide
> Should ne'er let want confound him,
> When he at any time may eat
> The sand which is around him.
> If it seems strange that he should find
> Such palatable fare,
> Remember that the sons of Ham
> Were bred and mustered there.

We crossed the equator on Friday, August 21, and with civil servants cooperating got into Mombassa and the ancient, charming Manor Hotel on Saturday evening, feeling welcomed by familiar tropical trees and shrubs, casuarina pine, purple bougainvillaea, antigonon, croton. On the streets I observed with admiration black maidens balancing five-gallon petrol tins on their heads—no hands.

Square, solid Philip Percival with his sea-blue eyes and sunburned jowls met us at the docks with a hunting car, miraculously big enough to hold all our luggage, and a couple of smiling black men to handle it. A big, back-slapping reunion with loving insults erupted between Ernest and Philip, who had been white hunter for Ernest and Pauline in the fall and winter of 1933-34, and we dined joyously on a fine spicy curry and slept under mosquito nets which enclosed our entire beds in the hotel—a first for me—before arranging ourselves in the hunting car the next day.

17

East Africa

As WE RATTLED from Mombassa inland and upward onto Kenya's 6,000-foot-high central plateau, we entered a life entirely new to me, with the herds of wild animals stretching across the yellow plains evoking happy memories for Ernest who had hunted there twenty years before. After two days of driving in the windowless, doorless hunting car, the gravel road giving us a backlash of red dust whenever we paused, we drew up to our boot camp on a hillside of Philip Percival's farm, Kitanga. Never before or since did we receive such an enthusiastic welcome.

Nine tents were already set up around a sort of village triangle, both the cookfire and our campfire were brightly blazing, and we shook hands with each of the twenty-two safari servants who would accompany us. These were not the flaccid handshakes of Europeans, but the much more welcoming African handshake, one hand in your hand and the other one on your wrist.

Mr. Percival, dean of Kenya's white hunters, had helped hunt Teddy Roosevelt in 1909 and 1910, before the profession of white hunter had established itself, had hunted both the Duke of Windsor when he was Prince Edward and his brother the Duke of Gloucester, had hunted many of America's and Europe's big-game hunters. He had agreed to emerge from his retirement of cattle- and horse-raising to hunt with us that fall and winter of 1953 and 1954. Now, in the firelight his blue eyes shone happily under his wide-brimmed, square-crowned felt hat as he introduced his "boys" to us. We were going to have a great time. The safari crew knew it too. They were all of the Wakamba tribe who lived in that area and they were delighted to be employed again by Mr. Percival. Whatever accidents or problems this safari might encounter, cheerful, even entertaining, solutions would be found for them, these men knew, knowing Bwana Percival.

We started right off with a cheerful gesture. The first case to be unloaded from our hunting car was a case of liquor, and for the first time in memory we had dry martinis without ice. Somebody went to Philip's house, high on the top of a neighboring hill, and brought back Mrs. Percival, baptized Mary but known for miles around as Mama. I found her at first awesome with her beautiful bony face, her acute intelligence and her unshakable character which had carried her, undiminished, through forty-four years of pioneering and farming in the harsh and inhospitable airs of Kenya, usually on her own since Philip was so much away on safaris.

Philip had first gone to Kenya from Scotland in September 1905, when he was a lad of seventeen. Three years later he journeyed back to England to marry his childhood sweetheart and bring her to this barely explored country, to live at first in a mud-and-wattle hut. I remember her telling me that first evening, on a foot safari in 1909 the cook had stirred and kneaded his bread before they set out in the morning, then carried it in a tub on his head, the African sun gently raising the dough until that night it could be baked in a tin oven surrounded by hot embers.

In Mombassa and on the road to Kitanga Farm Ernest and I became acquainted with Keiti, Philip Percival's friend since before the First World War, an elder of the Wakamba tribe and now executive officer and straw boss of the safari crew. We liked Keiti not only for set of his mouth beneath his stub nose, which made him look always amused, but also because he was a no-boss boss, his voice so soft, his gestures so slight that we never heard or saw him bossing, only his men bounding to do his bidding. "It's an excellent system Keiti has," Philip once said to me. "Nobody has a special job. They all just do what they're told to." Philip was referring especially to camp-moving days when everybody worked together pulling tent stakes, folding tents, loading furniture and our gear onto the big wobbly lorry.

Once *campi* was re-established, each man got busy with his own special job. (No matter what their ages, safari crews were all called "boys" in 1953, a patronizing term, I thought.) We were quickly friends. Under Keiti, wiry lean N'bedia was chief cook, his voice girlish, although he had fathered some dozen children, welcome when it drifted from his big round cookfire to our small campfire.

We both admired M'kao who was chief skinner and who, we later learned, tracked as fast as a trotting horse, seeing a drop of blood or a smudged pug-mark in the earth twenty yards ahead of us. We both loved bony old M'windi, our personal servant, with his green Kanza toga-type robe flapping about his thinness, his lined chocolate poker face, his soft voice, his attitude of patience although, as we found, he was inside a most impatient man. He washed and ironed our clothes and made our beds and cleaned our tent and brought us hot *bathi* water in the evenings. And we knew him only briefly before Ernest appointed him treasurer of the safari, turning over to his safekeeping a roll of Kenya banknotes the size of a breadbox.

Ernest immediately liked his gun boy, N'gui, no taller than I, for his solemn smile and later—when he discovered that N'gui was a son of M'cola with whom he had hunted in 1933—Ernest's approval moved into geometric progression.

One of Keiti's sons, M'thoka, was the driver of our hunting car and we wondered at his silence until we found out that he was deaf. His other distinction was the intricate and attractive arrangement of tribal scars which had been etched into his face years before.

"How can I remember our driver's name?" Ernest asked one morning.

"M'thoka," I said.

"Mathematics and okra," he said, and went over to the driver to explain in his hilarious combination of Spanish, Italian and Swahili that his, M'thoka's, tribal scars were very similar to those of the Memsa'ab's tribe in America, the Memsa'ab being me. He did not explain that my tribe was the auto-accident tribe.

Both of our mess-tent boys, M'sembi and N'guli, were big, young, handsome, cheerful men, who served us with the polite deference of good European waiters and who, when they were off duty, romanced the local girls in every district, danced all night at local dances and when there was nothing more exciting to do played a sort of African checkers, using stones for chips and for a board an upended box on which they drew the pattern with a burnt stick.

We liked both my gun-bearers, first N'zia with his jaunty smile, and later ancient, tireless Charo with his head as round and almost as big as a basketball on a frame shorter than my five feet two inches.

In the beginning there were others, assistant skinners and tent boys and gun boys assigned to attend the friends who would join us for the first part of this safari, but these and a few more were our constant companions for nearly six months. We felt that we had never encountered better ones. We bought snuff and sugar for them, and the best knives we could find, and eventually wristwatches, and when we left them six months after we first met, our faces were solemn with the gravity of the parting. Their faces were solemn too, and I wondered whether they had set them that way in western-style sentiment or African decorum.

Our friend from Cuba, Mayito Menocal, a marvelous wing and rifle shot and omnivorous reader, was to join the safari for its first six weeks of hunting, and Earl Theisen of *Look* who was coming along to make photographs had become a new friend. The day after they arrived we had a visit which was the beginning of a long and affectionate friendship. Denis Zaphiro, game warden of the Kajiado District, which included the first and second camps Philip Percival had arranged for us, came to our Kitanga hillside to give us maps of the country and handdrawn maps of the road there, miles and miles of national game reserve which the Kenya Game Department had generously opened up to us alone for a month.

We sighted in our rifles, large bore, medium and .22's, did some target shooting, learned where the shotgun ammo would ride in the hunting car and, right on the dot on September 1, with our village of tents struck

435

and loaded early in the morning, we set off from Kitanga Farm to our first camp on a bank of the broad yellow almost-dry Salengai River. It was a journey not so long as slow, on the narrow back-country roads, the lorry with our village and a month's food and drink packed into it puffing on small inclines, and many pauses for glassing the country with our binoculars.

After we had turned off the road and were following a dim trail toward our campsite, we came upon Denis Zaphiro, waiting for us with some of his native scouts in his Land-Rover.

"Do you want to shoot a rhino?" he asked Ernest. "Some bastard has wounded him. He's dragging one foot. I tracked him three hours. He's just by the road, back here a bit." Ernest got his big gun, the Westley Richards .577, out of its case, slipped in a few shells. Mayito Menocal, Earl Theisen, Ernest and I crowded into Denis's Land-Rover, named Lili, and hurtled down the road while Philip Percival took our hunting car and the lorry on to the river. We found the rhino standing beside a thorn bush and while I kept behind the men, as ordered, they went directly toward him in the lowering dusk, until, twelve paces from him, Ernest fired. Standing on a slight rise, I could see the action. The rhino spun completely around, raising a cloud of dust. Ernest fired into the dust and we saw the beast burst out of it to our left. Hunting for him we found blood spoor but no beast. Darkness quickly filled the forest of high thorn trees and thick underbrush, and Denis called off the search. We went on into camp, Ernest cheerful but, I sensed, privately concerned that by some accident of light or timing, he had failed to kill cleanly. (Early the next morning he and Denis went out and found the rhino dead twenty feet nearer the shooting than we had guessed. An auspicious start for a safari.)

When we reached camp we found the sleeping tents already up, Ernest's and mine opening onto the roots of an acacia tree fifteen feet in diameter, the bar and dinner tables in place by the campfire. Under the immense spread of the branches of our acacia tree we lived closer to the animals, I felt, than one could do anywhere outside an African national park. Almost every night, if we were awakened by some other noise and lay listening we could hear the swansdown-soft sound of elephants moving, like fishermen in waders, between our tents on their way to the waterhole in the river, forty yards beyond us. They must have smelled us, but in the darkness they disturbed not so much as one tent stake. One night one of Denis Zaphiro's favorite female rhinos, Suzie, came, apparently unexpectedly, upon the embers of our campfire, which infuriated her. She gored it and stamped on it and scattered it about before she went off, huffing. Denis and his scouts identified her footprints the next morning. Our toilet tent, a square yard of green canvas surrounding a stool which stood above a hole in the ground, was pitched behind the sleeping tents, close to the riverbank and facing the river. Emerging from it just at dusk, I saw with delight a mother rhino and her child trotting directly toward me, only about forty yards away. Standing there buckling my belt, I figured that they would slow down enough climbing the bank to give me time to run to the safety of the campfire. Then the mother noticed me, spoke to her child and they slowed down. Unlike most rhinos, this female was perhaps not born bad-tempered. While I stood there motionless, the pair of beasts came to a stop, slowly turned around, then trotted back across the dry riverbed to the forest on the other bank. It was the first but not the only time I had a rhino in my bathroom.

One of our spectator sports at Salengai was watching elephants amble single file down the bright riverbed in the dusk or the moonlight, and almost every morning we found both elephant and lion tracks in camp. In the early mornings too, they sometimes delayed us in making our appointed rounds. Our appointed rounds began with a journey down a forest track toward a tree where we had hung lion-bait, part of a zebra or wildebeest carcass, on which we hoped we might find a lion breakfasting. This because people of the Masai tribe who were living in our area had complained to Denis that lions were killing their cattle and, incidentally, that the hyenas were "as thick as grass." So we established the lion-control program and each morning before dawn piled into Lili the Land-

Rover and drove out the lion-bait track. A quarter of a mile short, we would disembark, softly move shells from the magazines to the chambers of our rifles, and, trying not to step on noisy dry sticks, walk Indian-file to the bait.

One morning we heard the sharp quick breaking of a branch. Theisen whispered, "There's something big over there." Then in the dusk of predawn we saw them in thin brush about thirty yards to our left and up the trail. They were moving slowly, browsing, a big bull elephant in the lead with half a dozen others behind him. Since we were downwind from them—their faint smell rather like that of mice reaching us—we quietly passed them and went to the bait which that morning had completely disappeared. The lion had left not a hoof or a piece of skin. Poking around his feasting place, we found one small piece of rib and then saw not twenty feet away three more elephants, still on their side of the path.

"We can't move on until they cross," Denis said. So we waited in the long shadows of some trees. A young bull saw Denis and then the whole tribe started across the track in a fast shambling trot, tails up, one back leg at a time almost touching the stomach, great red-tinted bulks against the earth and the pink sky, and we saw that many were cows with small children. Ernest counted fifty-two of them and a few minutes later, three more crossed. In his last census before we moved in, Denis had found some four hundred elephants in the area. The census would not be altered by us. Ernest had no wish to shoot an elephant. "Too big, too important, too noble," he said.

On the morning we were to strike camp and move from Salengai River to Kimana Swamp we went as usual to the lion-bait, excitement rising like a flood tide in the car, which Denis stopped far down the track. Excitement eddied around us as we walked in a faint drizzle, Denis in the lead, Ernest behind him, then Ernest's gun-bearer N'gui, Memsa'ab and Ty (Theisen). From behind cover, Denis spotted two lions feeding at the kill. We crept forward. At about two hundred yards from the beasts Ernest slipped around a tree and shot. We heard the *whock* of the bullet hitting and then both lions were gone, the wounded one failing to roar, as lions are supposed to do when they are hit. Making me stay behind in the car, where I kept my rifle ready, the men went into the thick bush, searching. In half an hour they found him, finished him off, loaded him in Lili and brought him back to camp where the skinning proceeded while *campi* came down and was loaded onto our lorry.

On hunting wounded lion in the forest, Philip Percival commented, "It's always a bit of a chance, you know." I remembered what I had heard and read of the many skillful hunters, including the great Frederick Selous, who were mauled and killed by lions.

Ernest's lion was a young male in his prime, four or five years old, with immense fore- and hind-leg muscles and thick bones and muscles in his paws. Watching the skinning, Ernest bent down and with his pocketknife cut out a bit of the tenderloin beside the spine, chewed some and offered me a tidbit. We both thought the clean pink flesh delicious, steak tartare without the capers. Denis scoffed that it would make us sick and Philip politely declined a taste. In Kenya neither the natives nor the whites ate lion, having against it some taboo which they would never define for me. Thereafter, Ernest and I had the lion marinated in sherry with some herbs and grilled over N'bebia's cookfire. It was firmer than Italian veal, but not tough, and as bland in flavor without a hint of the wilderness. Later we dressed it up with garlic and onion and various tomato and cheese sauces, as we had done with *vitello* in Italy.

"Swamp" is a misnomer for most of the area in which we were given the exclusive right to hunt. It is a mile-high tableland bounded on its south, Kilimanjaro, end by a clean shallow river hurrying through an escort of "fever trees"—*Acacia xanthophloea*—one hundred feet high, their smooth lime-colored trunks looking gilded in the morning and evening light. "We've got an orchard," Ernest said when he first saw the flat thorn-punctuated plain stretching out for miles northwest of the river. We had to go three or four miles north from camp, turn left and drive westward before we came upon the true swamp where the waterbirds lived. (The hippos had their own smaller swamp behind camp near the river.) Egyptian geese and elegant cranes *(Balearica gibbericeps Reichenow),* brown eagles with yellow pantaloons, and fish eagles lived there. So did Hottentot teal, black-winged stilt, the blacksmith plover, snipe, godwits and lily-trotters. The swamp with its papyrus and other grasses provided all the seeds and insects those birds required in their economy, and us with constant entertainment.

Far to the northeast our orchard erupted into kopjes and hills of lava rock and farther beyond rose the high Chyulu Hills, blue and inaccessible, protected by surrounding marshes. Both eastward and southeast we ran into flats, lava rock and copses of thorn, and everywhere, every day, we roamed among the game, everything from little bush babies and bat-eared foxes, through all the antelope to lion, buffalo, rhino and elephant. In the sixty-six days we lived there, in two separate interludes, we had the luck to see three different seasons, dry winter, the short rains of late November and, immediately following them, spring.

Waves of rust-colored dust were swirling across our plain, some of it lodging in our eyebrows and lashes, our ears and down our shirts when we arrived at Kimana Swamp on September 10, 1953. It did not appear to bother the herds of Grant's and Thomson's gazelle, wildebeest and zebra which grazed on the short dry golden grass fifty yards from where the hunting car stopped and as far as we could see in three directions. It did not deter Keiti and his crew from setting up our sleeping tents, five in a row, neatly spaced apart, with their sterns staked toward the river and Kilimanjaro, their triangular front flaps opening onto the vista of the gold and silver plain with its exclamation points of thorn trees and the myriad beasts. In front of the sleeping tents the big mess tent went up, its table long enough to accommodate eight or ten people, canvas camp chairs, the safari's green wooden "chop" boxes stowed in corners, and our improvised bookshelves, formerly wine boxes, installed at one end. Ernest was reading a lot of Simenon in French that fall. I was reading the *Georgics* and Polly Adler and *Jock of the Bushveld,* and there was a catholic assortment of other books. Fifty yards behind the sleeping tents, the safari crew installed our toilet tent, facing it toward the river and tribes of black-faced grivet monkeys which inhabited the stately fever trees.

Denis Zaphiro decided that we Babes in the Bush, Philip Percival's attentions notwithstanding, really required his chaperonage and so moved with us from Salengai to Kimana, together with five or six of his native scouts, and his police dog puppy Kibo. Ernest was delighted, having adopted Denis as a younger brother. I was delighted because I adored Denis and could expend floods of affection on Kibo, a self-propelled ball of fuzz with tireless teeth and an appetite for everything including tent poles. Also I was devoted to Kyungu, Denis's African friend and chief scout. I admired him for his knowing, after ten or twenty miles of contorted, heedless driving while we looked at animals, every mound and kopje and tree we had passed and where to turn to reach home again, for his good manners when we tracked in heavy bush, holding back a thorn branch so it would not slap me in the face, for his hard, cool handshake, for his self-confidence so solid inside of him that he never needed to display it, for his loving smile under his thin-line mustache which on another man in another country might have seemed foppish, for the cheerful ease with which he walked, springs in his legs, through thick high bush in country which was the homeland of rhino, elephant and lion, chewing a blade of grass as jauntily as a Frenchman swinging down the Champs-Elysées with his cane. (He now has a couple of wives, I'm told, and several children. I hope they all cherish him.)

It was Kyungu who found a newly born Grant's gazelle still wet in the Kimana grass near a dead zebra Ernest had shot for camp food. Fearing that his mother would be unable to find him after the shuttling across and around various herds of animals that morning, we took him back to camp and Earl Theisen, got tinned milk from N'bebia, constructed a make-do nipple of cotton-batten and gauze, and persuaded the small beast to eat. Finally the baby stood itself on its unsure legs and walked, trembling, ten paces off to a well-hidden nook by our smoldering campfire. We christened him "Baa" which was the sound he made in a small whisper, and he became the darling of the family and my constant concern. Two days later, when Kibo the puppy rushed up to him to investigate, our stout-hearted little goat butted the puppy, who thereafter kept his distance.

Ty fed the Granti for a day or two, dribbling milk down his finger. Then we acquired a baby's bottle and nipple from Laitokitok, our nearest village, which was a conglomeration of shops run by Indians, a sawmill, a hotel with earthen floors and a British police station, a lovely place on the lower slopes of Kilimanjaro burgeoning with rose gardens, bougainvillaea vines and wild pink antigonon beneath towering spires of cod blue jacaranda trees. We made Baa a soft harness from strips of cloth, and left him alone except to feed him. Three times a day he came eagerly for his bottle of tinned milk mixed with water and a little sugar and salt, and after each feeding I greased his behind with my face cream. The first time I took him into our tent for the night he pee-peed on our canvas floor covering, dropped a few black beans, mostly into my shoes, licked me generously and fell asleep under my bed.

When we moved camp I wrote: "I am concerned about what will happen to our baby Granti. He has taken breakfast, with some butter in his milk, lunch, tea and dinner, all with good appetite. He has grown accustomed to my smell and now identifies the shape of the bottle. For our three-hour journey I put him in a cardboard box next to me on the seat of the hunting car and he stayed there quietly the whole time. He is already interested in bits of dry leaves and he chews enthusiastically on my scarf, collar, pants. But everyone says that the other Grantis won't accept him, smelling of us, and if we let him loose, any of the predators—jackals, hyenas or leopards—will destroy him. Mayito Menocal says we should have left him where we found him, in spite of the zebra blood."

At Kimana Swamp we were in full winter, the night and early morning temperatures in the fifties at our elevation, even though we were only two degrees south of the equator, and we marveled that the antelope stayed as plump as footballs on what looked to us like the most meager dried-up forage. With their favorite food so plentiful, lions would also be about, we guessed, and on our first exploratory drive around the plain, a big old lion and two females, lying together in the pale shade of a clump of thorn, confirmed the guess.

The pattern of our days was simple: hot tea while we dressed by lantern light before dawn, off from camp afoot or in Lili or the hunting car as soon as it was light enough to see a beast, an apple or a tin of sardines tucked somewhere in case we went too far to return for breakfast, lunch in the mess tent and a siesta in camp while the animals were taking their naps in the shade, out to explore again in the late afternoon and at dusk back to the campfire and its nearby table of bottles and glasses. I never understood how I thought those 5 a.m. risings were halcyon, or even supportable. Unchanging though the routine, every day brought us some unexpected surprise, and early on I wrote that we were so busy I had been neglecting to clean my teeth. "I still haven't found a system," I wrote. "This recording of our days, learning to shoot better, identifying trees and birds and moths and dragonflies and flies, learning Swahili, learning to see the beasts and pick out the best head in a herd, learning the geology and history of this country, learning about the diverse tribes. A forty-eight-hour day with concomitant energy might suffice."

The excitement of the days carried on into the nights. Ernest and I had always made happy use of whatever beds we had, including the double bed Marlene Dietrich gave us as a Christmas present at the Hôtel Ritz in Paris in 1944, and our huge favorite bed at home in Cuba. Now with work and mundane responsibilities put behind us, we conducted in one or another of our narrow camp cots, little private carnivals, carefree and also with a sort of innocence, like puppies playing in the grass. We made up games and secret names and joyous jokes, as only lucky people who are friends do.

Although I gradually improved my Swahili, identified more and more fauna and flora, walked comfortably ten or fifteen miles a day, I could not, for some arcane reason, improve my rifle shooting. I practiced daily without effect. Kyungu tried to teach me to shoot sitting down with my arm braced against my knee. The tactic failed. Occasionally I dropped an animal properly with one shot. Usually I shot holes in the air all around the beasts. After Mayito acquired a lion and it was my turn for one, my failure to shoot efficiently became the safari's bugaboo, for everyone wished me or pretended to wish me success.

There came the day when some of the local Masai arrived at camp at noon to announce they knew where there was a big lion, a cattle-killer. (They always insisted the lion was a cattle-killer.) I checked my ammo, we crowded into the hunting car and drove eastward. After a few miles, Philip Percival decided we should continue the track on foot and we did so, the sun banging down on our heads through our felt hats, sweat sliding down my face and spine even in that high dry climate as I tried to keep up with M'kao, the skinner, and Kyungu, who were miraculously finding the pug-marks on the dry barren earth, moving, it seemed to me, as fast as race horses. Ernest was with them, and Philip and I were doing our utmost to keep up. After about an hour in the roasting sun we came to a copse of thorn trees, everybody halted in front of it, motionless with their noses pointed forward. It must have been thirty seconds before I saw the lion, lying facing us twenty yards away in the camouflage of the thorn trees. Hoping to miss his face, I shot for his shoulder. He stood up in deliberation rather than haste, turned around and disappeared in the copse of thorn. Nobody laughed. I had hit the earth a yard in front of him. It was such a giant mistake after so much effort exerted by so many people that overtones of comedy lurked around the edges of disaster.

All of our other days at Kimana Swamp during our first sojourn there were arduous but less disappointing and more fun. We learned that it was the custom of the buffalo herd which lived nearby to move in the early mornings from the shelter of the thick forest south of the upper swamp across the flats to the jagged kopjes, thorn-and-vine-covered, north of the flats. We learned that the herds of wildebeest, impala, Grant's and Thomson's gazelle, hartebeest, zebra and others moved rather widely from day to day, grazing, and that the eland and oryx preferred the pasture farther eastward, toward the Chyulu Hills, while the others regarded Kimana Swamp with its water always available as their headquarters. We found and admired a smallish family of waterbuck, one heroic and handsome male with perhaps ten wives and children, who lived in a thick growth of thorn trees near the corner where we turned westward to the swamp. He was a great slender-legged brown beast with a regal arch of lyre-shaped horns, standing in the thorn-dappled sunlight to face us, morning after morning, while his family silently melted from sight. We photographed him, with his expression of gentle interest and dignity, and vowed never to molest him.

We used to visit the hippos too. In their pool below the fever trees they had an enchanting place to live, well sheltered by pompom-topped papyrus grass through which darted brilliant golden weaverbirds, their red whiskers making them look like bright smiling flowers. The hippos were never noticeably hospitable. They retreated, huffing complaints, behind their reeds and grasses where we could not follow, camera-shy perhaps. But the antelopes of the plain and the grivet monkeys in the fever trees near camp soon grew accustomed to us and the sound of our motor and paused to watch us pass instead of stampeding away. One morning I found a grivet monkey sitting on a camp chair by the fire, shivering, his heart thumping, but eating a toffee. One of the boys had brought him from the fever trees as a joke. Earl Theisen took him home.

On safari I reveled in the personal pleasure of my simplified wardrobe. On September 11 at Kimana Swamp I wrote: "Just like the army in its freedom from concern about chic and colors matching and such nincompoop's chores. Plain cotton knitted underwear, easily washable, plenty of socks of various weights, a couple of pairs of warm pajamas, bathrobe, coat, three pairs of pants, three shirts, bush jacket, a couple of

445

sweaters. I change only to keep clean. So simple, so efficient."

On September 13 I wrote: "Although the Masai and the Wakamba tribes have resisted adopting nearly all the habits, foibles, gadgets, mores and customs of the white settlers and British government people they encounter, they seem to have acquired great faith in the white man's medicines, especially injections. We have already had numerous proofs. The other day there was the old woman we encountered with a group of Masai *morani* [warriors]. She had a chest cough and happily swallowed the aspirin Papa gave her. On our way here to Kimana from Salengai we stopped at the Masai village to show them proof of Denis Zaphiro's interest in the protection of their oh-so-precious-to-them (but really worthless) cattle—the skin of Papa's lion. An old man who had something wrong with him asked for an injection. When some Masai brought us corn last evening they also brought a boy who had skin trouble, his face swollen and covered with what looked like small boils. He wanted an injection, but instead Papa gave him eyedrops and some pills—Dipenicillin-6. This morning a man came into *campi* feverish and shivering in his blanket, and we quickly diagnosed his trouble as pneumonia, hoping we were right. He lay on the cold ground while one of our mob gave him a couple of small shots of penicillin. He moaned contentedly at the feel of the needle. This noon Papa treated another man who had a bad throat, septic glands and quinsy. We are becoming the only medical dispensary in this huge area and I wonder if psychosomatic illnesses can reverse themselves, if the old Masai woman's faith in Papa's pill could cure her cough. I wonder too how it is that they are not all exploited and victimized by quacks. Not long ago one of Denis's scouts fell from a bridge into a rocky gulch, bruising himself but with no bones broken. Denis wanted him to rest in bed a few days. The scout said, 'No bed. Please give me an injection.'"

One afternoon in the strange wooded desert country to the east of camp we saw a gerenuk which ran and hid in the thorn bush. But Ernest could see his head, and he shot. We found him dead, his head a really fine specimen of his kind but the poor old thing wrecked with some skin disease and something else which was tormenting his eyes, so that we did not feel too conscience-stricken at having killed him.

Wandering farther we came upon a class of half a dozen Tommy bucks, the small gazelles with the ever-wagging tails. Ernest handed me his old Springfield .30-06, the same gun with which he had killed buffalo, three lions, and twenty-seven other animals—one shot each—on his first safari twenty years before. "Shoot him with this," he said. I got him in the sights and dropped him with one shot, but he was still alive when we reached him, 142 paces from where I'd shot. I finished him quickly with the little .22 rifle, feeling sorry and ashamed but also pleased that I had finally hit something.

Late that afternoon we drove to Laitokitok to celebrate, and I photographed the clusters of Masai lounging about the village. Some of them came over to us to protest that we had no right to photograph them, having failed to ask their permission. "If you want pictures, we will come properly to pose for you," said one in a Cambridge accent. All the time they were protesting I was admiring them, with their great smoldering eyes, their aristocratic Nilotic high cheekbones, straight thin noses, thin lips, long necks, lean hips, the young warriors with their spears and intricately braided hair, done up from head to toe, hair, skin and side-ventilated shukas in the rusty ocher color they make from rubbing Kenya's red earth into grease. The girls with their handsome shaved heads wear the same color and as many bright bead necklaces, a dozen to twenty, as the young men, and weigh down their ears with heavy slabs of leather earrings.

We knew some of the local Masai legends—how they were descendants of kings, how a great king of scores of generations ago had ordered his people to move south, how they had made the trek, fighting many battles and moving their cattle and families with them—and we were prepared and eager to admire their prowess as warriors and spearsmen.

The very next day we had to face unwelcome doubts about them. They came to our camp, stood in

447

a straight line beneath a thorn tree, told us that they knew where there were four lions, that they meant to do a lion hunt (the lions had killed two of their donkeys) and would like assistance. After lunch we set out, Ernest and Denis running on foot with the yelling *morani,* Philip and I covering the right flank in the hunting car and yelling like hyenas too. We saw a lion and lioness, saw Ernest shoot, saw the lioness continue running, saw the crowd of Masai rapidly diminishing and finally only Denis and two *morani* closing in on the lioness. Afterward Denis told us sadly that when they got close enough to the lioness, he had said, "All right, spear her." But the warriors faded into the bushes, saying, "You shoot, Bwana," and Denis shot in irritation and disappointment. With the lioness safely dead, the Masai reassembled, brought their trophy triumphantly into our camp and then put on for their chief and for us a long, loud dance of victory. "Bubblegum Masai," Ernest muttered.

It had been a noisy, dusty day, but it had started out beautifully. I wrote: "We woke up with the opalescent morning showing in the wide triangle made by the open tent flaps, the early sky pale amber-pink with our thorn trees, *Acacia lahai,* etched in sepia against it, and the sharp slope of the white mess tent looking beige. It is like no other waking-up I've known, never such a wave of anticipation rolling in on me with the return of consciousness. I've seldom had quite so much delight as this at the recognition of a new day." (Unfair, unfair to *Pilar,* and the delight of waking up aboard her.)

While Mayito Menocal and Denis hunted buffalo near the upper swamp, Philip, Ernest and I looked for eland, the largest of the antelope, the males weighing up to 2,000 pounds, and the most delicious eating. We found two different herds one afternoon and, walking toward the first herd, followed them for a couple of miles, found them all to be females with calves, not an easy identification since the female eland's horns are as big and impressive as those of the males. When we found another herd the light had dimmed so much that none of us could be certain we saw a bull in the crowd. But when we came upon a lesser bustard, a russet-and-gray bird standing two feet high in the grass, I shot him with the .22 rifle. Then we ran into a flock of speckled gray guineas, and I shot one. They moved off, we followed them and I shot another. They moved again, I shot at one and killed two. For once I was provider of our next day's food.

Although shop talk about the respective merits and defects of hard-nosed bullets, softnosed bullets, solids, which grain bullets for which beasts, trajectories and other fascinations never ceased among the hunting friends, Philip, Denis, Mayito and Ernest, at our campfire, we got into all the other storytelling that had been going on around East African campfires for half a century.

Denis gave us native legends about the animals, one about the elephant, walking on a game track and coming upon an enormous leaving. The elephant said to himself, "I am the only animal that can make such a large thing." Then he met a rhino and asked him about the large thing, and the rhino admitted with false humility that it was his. This annoyed the elephant, who said, "No animal can make these things as big as I can, and I will not permit you to foul the path in this way. Go back and break it up and scatter it and tell all your tribe they must always do the same." Then the elephant went off and broke down a couple of big trees, to prove that he meant what he said. Ever since then the rhino has scattered or covered his dung.

N'bebia, our cook, had once cooked at the Governor's house, and, squatting beside his battered pots around the edge of his fire, big as a Hollywood bed, he provided us with food good enough for governors or gourmets. Lunch was usually cold roast of game we had shot, with hot baked potatoes, salad, fruit and cheese. Dinner began with a rich strained soup enlivened by onion or barley and continued with such main dishes as oxtail stew, roast Tommy, roast eland, curries of birds we'd shot, with such extras as grated fresh coconut, bananas, chutney and Bombay duck, saffron rice with sautéed guinea hen, or deepdish eland pie, the pie crust, rolled out on a wine box with a wine bottle, light as feathers. With our appetites constantly whetted by excitement and by walking in the fresh air, we all ate too much and my pants accordingly shrank.

One of Denis Zaphiro's scouts, Felipo, had brought his B-string guitar and on several evenings the scouts invited me over to their compound for a songfest which they performed in the classical African manner, Felipo singing verse after verse of long storytelling songs, the others repeating short choruses after each verse. There were war songs, songs of tribal history, songs about boys looking at girls, all in minor tones and sevenths, difficult for me to remember, but lovely. My contributions to the festivities were a few a cappella songs in Italian, Spanish and the only one I know in Basque. The scouts had all heard European and Indian music before. Nonetheless, their mouth muscles rippled with their courteous efforts not to laugh at my concert.

On September 19 we struck camp and moved past the Salengai River on our way farther south, and it was pleasant to encounter again the memory-evoking familiar hills we had used for landmarks, the dead tree near which we parked Lili on our dawn lion hunting, the draw with the black cotton soil where the lion-bait hung, the turnoff to the river where Suzie the bad-tempered rhino lives and the guinea fowl go down to drink.

We motored on, stopping for the night at Olorgasalie Camp on the eastern edge of the Great Rift Valley, which had been a factory in the early Pleistocene age, a million or so years ago. Stone axes and arrows had been found in quantities there, stone-cutting tools and the bones of prehistoric elephant, baboon, horse and hippo, also the femur of an elephant which had been broken. An African of those early days liked the flavor of elephant marrow.

On through the ugly, treeless town of Magadi, where the Imperial Chemical Industries Company runs a soda factory, to our new campsite beneath towering fig trees and a happy absence of flies, dust and mosquitoes. Denis had camped there frequently and baptized the place Fig Tree Camp, high on a bank above a tinkling little stream.

Fig Tree Camp was an adventure center for Denis. One night as he slept soundly there, the flaps of his tent open for coolness in the languid warmth, a smell awakened him. It was a leopard which had walked right up to his cot, hungry no doubt. Denis reached down to his gun beneath the cot and blasted off, dismissing the leopard. He was swimming alone and naked in the warm coffee-colored water of the Uaso Nyiro River when a buffalo came down to the river to drink, objected to Denis's presence in the water, snorted and started into the river after him. Denis swam mightily for the other bank and hid behind a tree, and the buffalo, seeing him no more, turned around and went back into the forest. While we all lived beneath the fig trees and wild cousins of frangipani, oleander and tamarind, Denis's morning bathing in our stream was twice interrupted by a rhino or rhinos. Each time they came chuffing down upon him, the whole camp shouting warnings and instructions, he leapt barefooted across rocks and driftwood out of the rhino's sight. I did my morning bathing in the safety of the front of our tent.

That camp was a paradise for naturalists but not for would-be lion-killers such as I was. The lion population of our area was standard for Africa, we could tell from the pug-marks around the waterholes, and on our second or third morning of hunting we heard a couple of them chatting in the thick underbrush but could get no glimpse of tawny hide. As we had done at Salengai and Kimana Swamp, we set up a bait-tree, kept it supplied with quarters of zebra, wildebeest or impala, and early every morning went hopefully to visit it.

On October 1, Mayito Menocal, Ernest and I and our gun-bearers were climbing the last hill before the bait-tree when Mayito, two paces ahead of me, shot to our right. Ernest shot and N'zia my gun boy grinned. *"Chui, Chui."* Twenty paces away a leopard lay dead.

It was a gift from On High for Earl Theisen who, for a long time, had been hoping for the chance to photograph Ernest with dangerous animals for *Look*. While I muttered protests—"We don't know whose bullet finished him. . . . This might be Mayito's leopard, exclusively. . . . I don't think you have the moral right, lamb"—Ernest submitted to Ty's arguments

451

and sat on the ground for portraits of himself and the leopard.

Mayito, if he knew whose slug had killed the young leopard, gave no sign that he cared for any dialectics about it. But the affair became one of the few disputes between Ernest and me during those months. "It's wrong," I contended. "It is moral disintegration and desuetude," I maintained with bombast. Ernest paid little attention to me. "I'll get a leopard to salve your conscience," he said.

"Before *Look* publishes the picture?"

"Sure."

Late in December of 1953, Ernest killed a leopard entirely on his own. *Look* published the picture of the leopard at which he and Mayito Menocal had both shot in its issue of January 26, 1954.

No lion was on the bait the next morning, so we bumped over the lava rock northward toward camp, haphazardly sightseeing until Ernest's gunbearer N'gui said, "Kudu," and pointed toward a kopje half a mile ahead. Silhouetted on the top of the hill were a handsome young male lesser kudu and two pretty does. Ernest said, "You take it." I shucked a shell into the chamber of my Mannlicher-Schoenauer 6.5 and we started off fast through thin pale-gold grass and rough red lava rock, keeping cover between us and the beasts, I puffing and sweating up the hills, N'zia climbing as light as a zephyr. At the top of a draw we found an anthill about my size, an excellent support for my gun. I found the patch of white on the kudu's neck, held my breath and squeezed. The young buck disappeared. We found him dead ten yards from where he had stood with his girls, the bullet apparently having opened his jugular vein. Ernest paced the distance of the single shot, found it to be 240 yards. All the gun boys and Mayito and Earl Theisen poured out compliments and when we got back to camp the whole safari crew produced a jamboree, shouting, singing, beating on tin pans and shaking my hand. But I felt bad, privately. The lovely young buck had been too handsome and too innocent to die by a lucky shot by a tourist in his country. I had shot badly and missed animals time after time, I decided, because privately I couldn't bear to kill them.

Again the next morning no lion was on our bait but we found tracks and hunted in all directions from the waterhole, in tall trees, thick brush, then through brush too thick for safety, then through sparse under-brush. We heard a grunt, cough, hurrumph and, ten to twelve yards away, no more, the biggest lion we had ever seen poured out of a bush, another younger male behind him, and in one second had disappeared. Ernest and I both shot into the air behind them.

We thought perhaps these two beasts had only gone a few yards into other patches of thick bush and we fumbled around, throwing stones into the thicker clumps of thorns. Then the boys found the track of the great beast and, warning that we must go softly and slowly, went fast and noisily up the west wall of the Rift, scrambling over lava rock, dried shrub and grass, like a pack of shod bloodhounds. Mayito wisely decided not to join in this hunt, and rested in the shade of a tree at the foot of the escarpment. When for the fifth or sixth time I had to put down my rifle in order to hoist myself over a rock and stop to wipe the sweat from my eyes, I called off the climb. Ernest was in-credulous and unhappy and so were the gun-bearers, but I felt sure we would never find this great beast that day, and if we had done so, I would not have been able to hit him neatly after the hot breathless climb. We named him Old Imperial, and we never saw him again, but that night I dreamt about him, him with his long thick black mane, his beautiful build and sure muscles and his ability to go quite noiselessly through thick bush. I dreamt that we saw him across a small draw in the lava rock covered with low shrub and green vines. He was standing there, immense in the sunlight, watching us, and before we could shoot, he said, "How do you do?" in the most cultivated Oxford accent. Ernest and I were so astonished we lowered our guns, and across the little gully, about six paces, we chatted.

Old Imperial told us that he had been sleeping in his thorny bower when we came upon him yesterday, and for a moment he had been nervous. Then he watched us clambering up the rocky precipice after him, making so much noise that even when he couldn't see us, he knew precisely where we were. "It's your wearing shoes, of course," he said.

We discussed his life in this area. "Most pleasant country," he said, "although not the abundance of food of some other places where I've lived." He had to work for food here, but of course that kept him in good condition. An agreeable thing about living here—very few people.

I asked him how he had learned the English language so well. He said, "Oh, I just picked it up."

He explained the pleasures of eating in the dark—"Like candlelight at your dinner tables."

He and we had unconsciously edged closer together and then he leapt on us and knocked us down. I heard Ernest protesting—"bad sportsmanship"—and he was eating me but I felt no pain. The last thing he said before I woke up was, "But, really, you are so salty."

Hunting out of Fig Tree Camp we never found a lion I could get properly in my rifle sights, but we had compensations. Having checked the lion-bait one early morning, we walked back to the hunting car, drove south over the valley floor then turned eastward following a faint track in the high yellow grass, which was like a big field of ripe wheat, bounded by forest half a mile away from us on our right and ending in thick dark forest through which the sun's horizontal rays were beginning to filter a mile ahead of us. Except for birdcalls and the chugging of our motor, there was no sound under the arching pearly sky.

N'gui pointed into the field and there fifty yards away a cheetah lay watching us from the top of a big round boulder. Cheetah were royal game and protected by law from hunters, but Ernest stopped the car, got out and walked toward this beast and just to watch him move sent one shot high over his head.

In a flash the cheetah was flowing like a swift stream across the track and into underbrush on our left, and a tidal wave was surging in the golden field to our right. Gazing in awe, I said, "Horses." Their coats gilded by the early sunshine, four lionesses, a young lion and five cubs rose from the grass and undulated smoothly and silently toward the security of the eastern forest. The five-minute performance was one of our two biggest surprises in the Rift Valley. We were so grateful that later in the day when we found the lionesses and their children resting by the forest's edge we threw them a haunch of buffalo meat from a beast Ernest had shot.

At Fig Tree Camp I wrote: "Baa is two weeks and two days old today and today for the first time I saw him actually nibble and swallow forage, a small green poinsettia-shaped leaf, a thick weedy green leaf and a dry brown fig leaf. He took one bottle of rich milk and a bottle of milk and water for lunch—double his usual ration, and the same amount for his tea. He knows his name and will stand up and come to me if he is hungry, otherwise he just waits prettily for me to go to him. He nibbles my arms and legs, and always my chin after bottles. He now stands half again as tall as when he was born and half again as long. . . .

"He has a definite sense of place. Whenever he is not feeding or romping with me he always goes now to his bent tree in the leafy shade without hesitation. He likes being held and stroked while he eats, hates having his face washed, is terrified of Shuka-wearing, spear-carrying natives but not of our domestic-smelling boys. He loves going for his walk and to eat from the bush, but takes no interest in food of the same sort when I pluck it for him. He is stubborn when he wants to move, but often obedient and loving and forgives me when I pick him up."

There was the afternoon when, returning from a hunt, we found Baa's leash broken and no sign of him. The camp boys said some visiting Masai had frightened him away. For hours I walked our various paths out of camp and through rhino-sheltering bush, calling his name. Night fell and no Baa and, my spirits entombed, I decided we had seen the last of him. Philip and Ernest and I were sitting subdued around the fire having our drinks before dinner when he approached us, a delicate golden silhouette in the firelight walking daintily toward me. We had a thundershower of affection all around.

But I had to face the circumstance that Baa could not live in a hotel room in Nairobi nor in a series of hotel rooms through Europe, and that the low altitude and humid climate of Cuba would probably be antipathetic to him. Mrs. Laurie Aitkin of Magadi, the soda town, came with her husband to call on us at camp and told me she would be delighted to take Baa and would faithfully care for him. I told her all I'd learned about him, and when we broke camp and went through the town I took him to her house, my spirits plunging at the sight of hot bright brick and cement, without trees, without foliage or camouflage. That night I wrote: "What he doesn't need and will be bad for him is domestication. What he won't be able to support is too many people and yelping children. He is accustomed to solitude and one voice, but he is going to get no peace and many voices. I feel terrible and wicked at having left him there."

In Nairobi, Carr-Hartley, the animal-farm man, told me that Grant's gazelle are among the most difficult of all animals to raise in captivity or semicaptivity. They get some digestive trouble, probably from nervous upset, and die. Baa's digestive apparatus had been operating with visible efficiency while he was with us. But a month later Mrs. Aitkin wrote me that he was dead.

There were other partings at Fig Tree Camp. Mayito Menocal left us to hunt in Tanganyika, and Earl Theisen with his cameras and hundreds of rolls of exposed film took off for Nairobi and New York. Philip Percival went home to Kitanga Farm for a brief rest, and Ernest and I and the camp crew were on our own in that thick forest among the buffalo, elephant, leopards and hyena, with no transportation. We loved the freedom of it, the hunting on foot, never more than eight or nine miles from camp, learned the fun of crossing rivers with our boots on, learned much better than we had known before the birds and beasts of our local glades and thickets. "Bloody dangerous place," Philip had warned us. "I never saw a more chancy camp." We could smell hyenas going through camp at night and almost every morning we found signs that leopards had been about, but no harm came to us.

When Philip returned with the hunting car and the lumbering old lorry we declared the first part of our safari formally ended. But we had not had nearly enough of hunting and living outdoors and seeing Africa, and I still had no lion. We struck camp, went through Nairobi to Kitanga Farm where Mama Percival hospitably invited us to camp right in her front yard. Where to go next was the question and Ernest's son Patrick helped us answer it. He and his wife Henrietta, farming, raising pyrethrum in the lovely green and rolling highlands dedicated mostly to tea-raising near a crossroad named John's Corner south of Iringa in Tanganyika, now wired that they had heard that there was good hunting south of them on a branch of the Great Ruaha River in the Usangu District. Ernest flew to Iringa, found transport, found that Patrick was suddenly ill and in hospital and his house locked shut. He found a window that could be pried open, found a bed in the dark and went to sleep. He wakened with a start when something soft plopped onto his stomach from the open window, thought "snake" and lay quiet with no muscle twitching, being a man who was not in favor of antagonizing snakes in the dark. Soon he thought he felt a small warmth emitting from the snake. Then it began to purr.

A few days later Ernest sent Philip a telegram: BRING SAFARI AS SOON AS POSSIBLE, and we went back to the business of assembling cooking supplies, ammunition and personal aids and comforts. In pursuit of some of these, Mama Percival took me up to Machakos where we did sightseeing as well as shopping and I was able to decipher the Swahili legend above the pulpit of the local church. It said "The Lord is my Shepherd. I shall not want."

Going through every kind of country from thick green forest to cut-over barren desert, Philip and I made the two-and-one-half-day drive in the open hunting car, camping twice along the roadside at night, and I noted that the country south of Dodoma was "dry, dead purgatory, the temperature in the car at least 120 degrees [I was guessing] with a 40-mile wind. My eyes burned through the sunglasses in the glare. If I were a loaf of bread, I'd be not merely

457

baked but burnt." But when Philip, listening to the boys pound tent stakes, would say, "Lovely sound," I agreed.

After a couple of exuberant days of reunion with Patrick, recovered from malaria, and Henrietta, we went, a three-car caravan with Patrick driving his Land-Rover, to the poetic sepia country of the Bahora Flats of the Ruaha River. A gray-flannel sky lowered onto us in pelting rain and Philip Percival's customary look of a cherub with a secret joke turned to one of concern as we neared our wet campsite. Keiti, supervising the construction of our damp camp, was grave-faced too. The short rains of winter were arriving and if we were careless we might get stuck in them, the wheels of our transport spinning helplessly in mud thirty or forty miles from anywhere. Patrick and I went on farther south through the tall-treed impenetrable jungle of true rain forest to M'beya, the provincial capital, to buy hundreds of shillings worth of shooting permits. But except for crocodile in the rivers, a few topi and odds and ends of other gazelles, the population of beasts was small in that area that year. To the relief of Philip, Keiti and all the safari crew, Ernest decided after only a few days of hunting out of the Bahora Flats camp to trek back north while the roads were still passable.

We stayed a week with Denis Zaphiro in his cheerful bachelor's house at Kajiado, then continued blithely on to Kimana Swamp, the Kenya Game Department hospitably allowing us to go back, and found that the short rains were starting a whole new cycle of life for our high plateau's myriad inhabitants. In the fifty days of our second stay there we watched its winter wane and full-blossomed spring take charge. Our plain, which had been so sere and dusty, in a week burst into knee-high greenery.

At the mud flats up near the swamp we watched ants wiggle out of tiny holes in the soil. They would rest a moment on a blade of grass letting their transparent wings dry in the sun. Then they would make a jubilant-looking first solo flight up into the sunlight. In the air they provided a couple of weeks of banqueting for the various eagles of the area, but the many that escaped the eagles came back to earth, lost their wings and set seriously to work digging new subterranean shelters and lining them with grass.

We saw dozens of other species of insects starting their new year, organizing their food, shelter and reproduction, among them the amusing bright-red fuzzy cochineal beetle which went strutting about on the warm ground long before getting down to business. Watching them, Ernest said, "These characters can swagger sitting down."

We found the "turd" beetle fascinating. From buffalo dung, everywhere available, they made round balls as big as Concord grapes and then appeared to engage in the solemn sport of pushing the balls with their hind feet, moving backward across the surface of the flats with no more visible objective than the human race has seemed to pursue through the centuries. A variety of the scarab beetle, they were rolling the dung to a hole in the ground where the female had deposited an egg. The larvae, when they developed, would have the dung as food.

Back in September, as we were making a morning patrol around Kimana Swamp, we had seen a tremendous black-maned lion and his girlfriend lying in the lacy shade of a thorn bush within easy range. I had begged to shoot him and Denis had vetoed the idea, theorizing that he seemed so tame he must be one of the picture lions from Amboseli, the game reserve nearby.

Late in November the fellows decided that I should do away with the old boy who, the Masai insisted, was killing their cattle. Now he was living with a couple of friendly females in a jumble of lava rock, thick thorn bush and vines four or five miles north of *campi*.

Our tactics consisted of providing food not far from the lion lair and chaining it to a tree so that the two lionesses could feast freely but could not drag the meat into cover for the Boss. Since the larger lioness was pregnant and temporarily unable to kill for her meals, the two females breakfasted daily on the baits we provided, apparently unconcerned that their male was growing thin and probably bad-tempered. For ten days of guile, trickery and deceit we tried to lure him from his den, and finally he came out himself to dine. In the late afternoon of December 5, we found him at the bait and watched him break for cover. With the Land-Rover Denis blocked his exit toward his lair, and the old boy lit out for a thin patch of thorn trees a quarter mile to the west, we chuffing after him. When Denis stopped the car there was the beast standing, watching us, twenty-five to thirty yards directly in front of us. Ernest jumped out and raced to our left. I hopped down, steadied myself against the front fender and got the lion's left shoulder in my sights; but Denis dancing to the right kept yelling, "Wait, wait!" so, uncomprehending, I waited, praying I would hit him squarely if he came at me.

Instead of coming, he turned and ran obliquely south. I ran to the right, got his moving hip in my sights, took a deep breath, squeezed the trigger, heard Ernest shoot, heard Denis shoot. We found him 350 yards away, dead with the small hole of my bullet in his right hip and the larger hole made by Denis's .470. (Next day when we skinned and probed, we found that the little bullet of my Mannlicher-Schoenauer 6.5 had cracked his right hind leg and Denis's big bullet had broken his spine and spinal cord.) He measured nine feet from tail-tip to nose, and after elaborate further measuring the skinner and our gun-bearers announced he had weighed 384 pounds.

Back in camp they had heard our ruckus. The truck drove up to us; full of people yelling, singing, beating on tin pans. The safari crew had waited a long time to celebrate this lion and now there was no shushing them. We did the double handshake all around, took photos in the lowering dusk, went home with the boys singing a new song of triumph about the small Memsa'ab killing the great menacing beast. The whole camp and Denis's scouts came to our fire, singing and banging tins, made me sit on a chair then picked it up and danced me round and round over their heads, round and round between the fire and the mess tent, swirling and milling and singing and shouting. I loved it but was embarrassed, not knowing then whether or not my bullet had even hit the beast, but remembering

460

that Charo, my ancient gun-bearer, had murmured, *"Piga"* (hit), when I shot.

"I haven't seen such a celebration as this in twenty years," Philip Percival said over our delayed dinner. After it we went over to the scout camp where they were dancing wildly and wonderfully around their fire, an African discothèque, one voice chanting a newly improvised song about the *simba* and the Memsa'ab, the khaki shorts glowing bright in the firelight, the firelight running in shining rivers down the long brown backs and the long-muscled legs, white ostrich feathers bobbing over their heads, whites of black eyes shining. The next day Ernest and I ate the lion's loin, marinated in sherry and grilled. Even though he was an old boy, his loin was tender and delicious. But for a day or two we felt empty and purposeless after the long campaign.

After a busy day on December 10, I wrote: "Rain all night and about 2 a.m. the hyenas came by in full concert. They were very close and giving out the high arpeggios, like a fire-boat siren, also the girlish laughter, the low cooing, the staccato chuckle and the hysterical, 'Don't do that.' They woke Papa too and we lay there laughing with them in the dark.

"There was the sound of something scratching beside my bed and Papa said, 'If it's a cobra, don't spit at him. He won't spit unless you do.' Papa had a 'May I come in?' beast on his side. Patter of rain on the tent very soothing and we drifted to sleep again. In the morning Papa said, 'Don't forget about the birds spreading themselves out in the treetops to dry out— for your diary.' There are sometimes six to ten in one tree.

"Coming back at dawn from the *cho* [toilet] tent, I was astonished to see a new formation on our front lawn, big square boulders piled irregularly together, where no boulders had been before. It was a platoon of zebras standing, regarding me curiously, no more than forty yards in front of the mess tent and the smouldering embers of our campfire. Excellent camouflage. N'gui, Papa's gun-bearer, came with the news that the pregnant lioness had killed a wildebeest right behind camp. She had passed between Denis's tent and ours. I imagine the hyena hijinks took place at her kill after she had abandoned it."

Some weeks earlier we had met Roy Marsh, a cheery spic-and-span young man who flew charter flights out of Nairobi in small planes, and with Roy discovered a new luxury, that of hedge-hopping, sightseeing Kenya's beasts. In 1953 animals still lived in large numbers ten minutes by air from the little airstrip we had constructed—by running a car back and forth over our flat 1,000-acre front yard. On December 12 Roy came out from Nairobi in the *n'dege* (bird) and we did an hour's sightseeing first over our swamp and then toward the Chyulu Hills and back and forth.

One day Ernest saw the old lioness heavy and inert with babies and two days later, hunting wildebeest which were flowing past us like a river, we came upon the lioness and her smaller younger friend sheltering under the brush at the edge of the upper flats and with the binoculars discovered that with them were two tiny fuzzy cubs. We shot a wildebeest and dragged him back to the neighborhood of the new mother and her companion, then watched them drag him toward the brush, the younger female gripping him with her teeth up near his neck and pulling him about twenty yards. Then the old lioness came out and together they pulled him into the camouflage of the shade beneath the thorn trees.

We called on the lionesses almost every day, not always finding them at home but knowing they could not have gone far with the cubs still very wobbly, as we could see from their tracks, and then, with guests coming to stay for Christmas and New Year's and a hullabaloo of hunting going on, we left the lion nursery to its own devices. On January 5, 1954, when we went to the upper swamp to check on them we found the tracks of the old lioness going toward her old home and carrying one cub and then the other in her mouth. Beyond, in a forest room walled with thorn trees we found and sadly identified the head of the gallant and beautiful old waterbuck with which we had been friends for what seemed a long time.

"He had always stood guard to protect the retreat of his cows into the woods," I wrote. "Nothing left of him now but his head bones and horns, the kill two or three days old. The lioness took advantage of his bravery and murdered him—handy food. Five cow waterbucks are still living nearby with no protector."

Going to sleep at Kimana Swamp was like going to the movies, our dreams were so vivid. I dreamt of a warthog which was impervious to bullets, of chasing him up the steps of the cathedral at Bruges and of his making speeches to me, dressed in a top hat and tail-coat, about peace on earth.

Ernest dreamt of a lioness who fell in love with him and insisted on preparing his meals, cooking his meat for him and explaining that cooked meat was better for his digestive tract than the raw meat which suited her. He did not suggest vegetables as accompaniment to the meat, wishing not to offend her.

On moonlit nights at Kimana Swamp Ernest used to go out for walks among the animals in our meadow and interviews with them, carrying only one of the spears the Masai people had given him. After such a walk, he slipped into bed and dreamt that, strolling near the fever trees along the river, he noticed with a spasm of delight that his Black Dog, whom we had left at home in Cuba, was trotting beside him. He was explaining the tantalizing new smells of Africa to Blackie, when Blackie, who never for a moment had attempted the role of brave, heroic, super-dog, let out a savage growl. "Really menacing," Ernest said proudly. A young impala doe slid out of the shadows of the trees and bounced determinedly across the plain. Ernest told Blackie about impalas, that they are gentle and gay and not dangerous, unless attacked, but Black Dog continued his ferocious growl, directing it toward the trees. With his spear poised, Ernest started probing the shadows and in a moment Senator Joe McCarthy emerged into the moonlight.

"Why, Senator, fancy meeting you here," Ernest said, amazed. The Senator appeared both embarrassed and disheveled. "What are you doing here?"

"I'm conducting an investigation," McCarthy said.

"Of the animals?"

"I have it from indisputable sources that very

463

serious subversion is going on over here," said the Senator, "and you may be contributing to it."

"We have pretty good communication with the animals around here," Ernest said. "But we don't talk politics much."

"I have proof that they are getting communist indoctrination from the Masai," said the Senator.

"That's strange," Ernest said. "The Masai are more conservative than the old-line Republicans or the Tories in England. And the animals, except possibly the bat-eared foxes, are anarchic syndicalists. Theoretically. They're not yet in practice."

Just then Ernest heard a pounding of hooves, which quickly grew louder, approaching them. He thought, buffalo, looked for Black Dog, and started for the protection of the fever trees. It was not buffalo, but impala. McCarthy started running down the plain. Then Ernest woke up.

"I wonder how far he got before they caught him," Ernest said when he had finished telling me the dream.

Roy Marsh flew me into Nairobi for a short interlude of Christmas shopping and when I got back to Kimana Swamp I found some changes, some good news, some welcome samenesses. New was Ernest's head, shaved to the scalp, like a Masai girl's, shiny and showing all its scars.

He had killed a leopard. He was cruising in the hunting car with the boys when his gun boy N'gui grabbed his arm and pointed. A leopard was sleeping on a branch of a thorn tree with many small branches and vines partly hiding him—not a good shot. Having walked toward him from the car, Ernest shot at his head and missed. The leopard put his head flat along the branch like a snake and Ernest shot at his shoulder. He fell like a bag of meal with his tail high and hit on his back, unlike a live cat. Joy prevailed, also congratulations and hugs. Then they went in to find him. No leopard was there in the undergrowth.

They started cautious tracking and came upon the first blood, one small drop, fifty feet from the spot where the leopard had hit the ground. Ten feet further on there was a big splash of blood and a piece of shoulder blade. Ernest was remembering that my gun-bearer Charo, who was in the mob that day, had been mauled three different times by a wounded leopard.

They tracked another eighty or one hundred yards in very thick close-growing thorn and found that the blood stopped at a dense rough clump of thorn covered with vine. The boys were all keen to pull it apart and Ernest, worried, admonished them in his mixed tongues. *"Chui molto periculoso. Yo responsable. Tu kuenda para atras. Dejami solo."* He fired seven shotgun shells into the bush, got no response.

They circled the bush, found no tracks or blood, and everybody but Charo agreed the leopard must be dead in there. On his belly Ernest crawled into the underbrush, shot again, and the leopard answered with a roar. Ernest shot at the roar, and when the leopard roared again he shot again, and there was no more roar. They circled the bush again and found the beastie dead. "The terrain was difficult," Ernest said, concluding the story.

Then they could celebrate wholeheartedly and Ernest handed out beer, a custom of which most white hunters used to disapprove. The festivities continued when they returned to camp and the local Wakamba girls, including Debba, Ernest's favorite whom he designated his fiancée, came over to join them. Ernest took a carload of girls to our village, Laitokitok, and bought them dresses for Christmas and when they got back to camp took them into our tent for further celebration so energetic that they broke the wooden frame of my cot. Keiti finally sent word that there would be trouble if the girls were not sent home. When I arrived the next day, my cot had tactfully been replaced by an undamaged one (Keiti may not have felt certain that Ernest would tell me the story) and Ernest gave no indication that either the leopard hunt or the celebrations had fatigued him. He welcomed me back with warm enthusiasm and we had a typical happy night.

Saturday, December 19, from my diary: *"Chai* today at 6 a.m. and we soon got off into the thick

thorn and Lion and Rhino country looking for Gerenuk. . . . No trophies today, only an impala for
meat. . . .

"Papa clowning an interview before lunch with an
imaginary reporter from an imaginary magazine, 'Re-
condite.'

"Reporter: 'Mr. Hemingway, is it true that your wife
is a lesbian?'

"Papa: 'Of course not. Mrs. Hemingway is a boy.'

"Reporter: 'What are your favorite sports, sir?'

"Papa: 'Shooting, fishing, reading and sodomy.'

"Reporter: 'Does Mrs. Hemingway participate in
these sports?'

"Papa: 'She participates in all of them.'

"Reporter: 'Sir, can you compare fishing, shooting
and cricket, perhaps with the other sports you practice?'

"Papa: 'Young man, you must distinguish between
the diurnal and the nocturnal sports. In this latter category sodomy is definitely superior to fishing.'

"Reporter: 'Sir, I've heard much of this sport.'

"Papa: 'Let us speak no further of it.'

"Then he had an afterthought. 'What about gomor-
rah?'

" 'You mean what we say to each other mornings?'
I asked.

" 'End of interview.' "

"Tonight we have Jupiter bright, bright near the
moon," I wrote, "Orion with Betelgeuse and the others
and Sirius blazing a little to the south, and in the night
air the sweet perfume of the white-flowered weeds."

Ernest added a handwritten insert that evening:
"Signing off happy about last night and every night."

On Sunday, December 20, Ernest wrote the diary
entry for me, a far departure from my recordings:
"We decided last night to lay off all huntings and shoot-
ings today because meat in camp by 18:00 last
night [1 Impala shot by Papa] and devote the day to
rest and Miss Mary's Christmas haircut, to look especially beautiful for all visiting guests. Her hair is
naturally blonde to reddish golden blonde to sandy
blonde. Papa loved it the way it looked naturally, but
Miss Mary had made him a present of saying to make

466

her hair really blonde a couple of weeks ago, and this made him want to have her as a platinum blonde, as she was at Torcello where we lived one fall and part of a winter, burnt the Beech logs in the fireplace and made love at least every morning, noon and night and had the loveliest time Papa ever knew of. Better than any, although many very good. But loving Mary has been such a complicated and wonderful thing for over nine years (sometimes fights and mutual wickedness (my fault) and sometimes hers too but always made up always made presents to each other). Mary is an espece (sort of) prince of devils . . . and almost any place you touch her it can kill both you and her. She has always wanted to be a boy and thinks as a boy without ever losing any femininity. If you should become confused on this you should retire. She loves me to be her girls, which I love to be, not being absolutely stupid. . . . In return she makes me awards and at night we do every sort of thing which pleases her and which pleases me. . . . Mary has never had one lesbian impulse but has always wanted to be a boy. Since I have never cared for any man and dislike any tactile contact with men except the normal Spanish abrazo or embrace which precedes a departure or welcomes a return from a voyage or a more or less dangerous mission or attack, I loved feeling the embrace of Mary which came to me as something quite new and outside all tribal law. On the night of December 19th we worked out these things and I have never been happier. EH 20/12/53."

On Monday, December 21, I saw for the first time a pack of Kenya's wild dogs, scruffy-looking mottled-yellow, rusty-and-brown animals the size of police dogs with longer legs and bigger ears, and Ernest covering me with his rifle in the background nearly exploded with concern that they would tear Charo and me apart.

We had gone softly in the car toward the swamp hoping to photograph buffalo. Charo, carrying my gun with solid bullets, and I left the car and crept through bush to a fallen tree at the edge of the swamp, only one hundred fifty yards from the nearest buffalo in a herd of eighty-six. I was balancing the camera on the fallen tree when there was a rustle and complaint almost under my feet and, annoyed that my pictures might be spoiled, I kicked at an animal. There was a sharp barking and a yard in front of us a dozen dogs rose from the grass. One of them stood undecided for a moment watching us, his white-tipped tail rising. Then he yelped to the others. They milled around, barking in tenor voice and, finally recognizing them from what I'd read, I decided that if they came at us I would kick the first one *hard* then jump aside so that Ernest could shoot. (Some books I'd read gave accounts of packs of wild dogs pursuing men, attacking ensemble, and finishing off their victims in a few minutes.)

The dogs, which had probably been waiting to separate a baby buffalo from its mother and have it for breakfast, decided against Charo and me and loped off eastward. I took a roll of black-and-white pictures of the buffalo, went back to the car for color film and only then discovered that Ernest had been bursting out all over with his anxiety about the wild dogs. He wanted madly to rush to protect Charo and me, but was held back by the consideration that his big silhouette would disturb the buffalo.

That evening we went looking for the wild dog pack. Zero luck. So we went to visit briefly in the Wakamba village where Ernest's fiancée lived. She was indisposed and out of sight, but we chatted with an old man, Abdullah, who spoke English—he had been among Lord Delamere's retinue—and reminded Ernest, "Don't forget my Christmas present." It was some sort of a revitalizing potion Ernest had invented for him, Ernest elaborating on its miraculous qualities. Ernest mentioned that he would like to go live in the Wakamba village for a week or two, and I agreed there would be no better way to learn about them. But he had better take some books along, since he might find it dull, not speaking their language.

On the evening of December 22 I quoted Ernest: "This week has been the happiest in my life." In Africa and aboard *Pilar* he was often given to superlatives.

William Hale, then chief of the Game Department

of Kenya, and our friend Denis Zaphiro had sent word they would join us for a few days at Christmastime, and we made fancy preparations. Twice Keiti and some of the boys and I went to the upper swamp, dug up and transplanted a thorn tree (*Acacia drepanolobium*) with such long white thorns that it looked as though it had decorated itself with tinsel. (From its bark the Masai brewed a potion which they claimed made them brave but which seemed to me to make them merely careless and drunk.) Each time our tree folded its small green leaves and expired. When it did so the second time after generous dousings of water, I decided to use it as our Christmas tree anyhow and planted it outdoors in front of the mess tent in the center of *campi*. N'gui helped me trim the tree with trinkets I'd brought from Nairobi.

On Christmas Eve Mr. Hale and Denis and Ernest and I went out sightseeing and hoping to find Christmas meat for the camp. We saw plenty of animals and one sizable tribe of zebra. Ernest got out of the car, walked toward them, sat down and shot. At about one hundred fifty yards away one male zebra did not stagger or stumble. He went down like a stone and rolled onto his back. The shot was in the shoulder, low, and the beast was quite dead when we reached him.

When we got back to camp and bathed and changed, our mess boys, N'guli and M'sembi, lit the candles on the tree, we put our assortment of brightly wrapped presents beneath it in the American manner, and assembled all the boys, Denis's crew and our thirteen. With Mr. Hale translating, I made them a little speech explaining that this was a part of one festival of the Christian religion, and while we had no wish to convert them to any religion, we wanted them to share in the rejoicing, the giving of presents and the feasting. If they had heard the speech before our African friends showed no sign of it.

We had already given Keiti seventy-five pounds of sugar, to be distributed equally, and a pound for each man of lard, tea, rice and dried milk. There were also skinning knives and jackknives and flashlights with extra batteries and envelopes with money. Ernest got a specially made carrier for birds, sweaters, socks and new shirts. The shirts he promptly gave to N'gui, his gun-bearer.

"Our thorn tree with its candles looked misty-white, lovely and mysterious—a part of some ancient pagan rite—in the starlight," I wrote. "Our dinner was spaghetti and cherry pie, and the talk was not of Christmas but of beasts and people. E.H., speaking of a one-time Casanova: 'He went down on everything except the *Lusitania.*'"

My special Christmas present in 1953 was to be a journey with Ernest and Roy Marsh across the Serengeti Plain and Lake Victoria and down the Congo River to Stanleyville, an air safari which we would make in January.

Before he left on December 30, Mr. Hale, who had already closed the Nyrok area to hunters, told us that we might not shoot any more Thomson's or Grant's gazelles, impala, eland, gerenuk, wildebeest, no trophies of any sort, but he also appointed Ernest honorary game warden, a valued title. I thought Ernest would be upset by the orders, but he said, "Imagine if we were out west and could shoot leopard, hyena, jackal, wild dog, warthog and baboon." The very next day we were presented a problem by elephants.

Nine of the great beasts had broken through the thorn fence of a farm in the foothills of Kilimanjaro and trampled down three or four acres of fifteen-foot-high corn. We found the farm, inspected the damage, and discussed means of preventing further invasions. The farmer's wife, her baby wrapped tightly against her back, was working there, trying to replant the broken stalks.

"You should build the boma higher and thicker," I said arbitrarily and stupidly. The woman laughed and said, "If an elephant wishes to go through a boma, he reaches out with his trunk and easily pulls it apart." Of course. I had seen big trees pulled down.

One of our boys mentioned that a good protective measure is the hanging in a tree of some object of unnatural outline, a square box, perhaps, with pieces of tin attached which clank noisily in the wind. The woman laughed again and said the elephants had ripped just such devices from the tree nearby. I asked if the elephants came every year when the corn was high, and the woman said, "Usually." We knew that the local game control officer had killed an elephant near there a couple of years before, leaving its carcass as a warning to intruders. The woman's and our boys' solution: kill the leader of the pack, skin him and burn the skin near the corn. Said one of our boys, "The elephants smell the burnt skin. They say, 'Oh, here is dead elephant. Here is bad for elephants,' and they do not come near any more." But Ernest had never wished to kill an elephant and had bought no license to shoot one. He gave the woman money to reimburse her for the lost corn, about ten times its value.

Friday, January 1, 1954. Kimana Swamp. From my diary: "The New Year started with a wonderful morning here, the mountain in rosy majesty, the sky high, high, and cloudless. We went up to the swamp and on the way home saw at least 100 zebra. . . . Abdullah, the old Wakamba who speaks English, has given Papa a beautiful King's stick, the wood a smooth blend of blond and black, as though someone had slightly stirred Guinness stout into honey. It is carved from the Altiasiga tree—the Masai name, Abdullah having sent a Masai for it far into the Chyulu hills. The elders of the local tribes carry such sticks as emblems of their authority. Abdullah said that Papa, as the leader of our tribe, should have his stick."

January 2, 1954: "Now at the fire we're happy, thinking what a marvelous year it has been, how very much we've learned, me especially. Papa says, 'I'm not a phony but I'm a terrible braggart.' No. Not really braggart. Just full of joy. He has been shooting doubles on the sandgrouse, no paltry trick, and he has a right to be pleased about it. He says, 'We were smart kittens to come to Africa.'

"Fisi [Hyena] is going Wuuuuu, Wuuuu, Wuuuuu in the middle distance."

January 3, from my diary: "Papa has been saying too many nice things, 'My kitten-brother is the —est, —est, most, best kitten' . . . Then he says, 'A slow shooter, apt to be impatient, and intolerant of fools and drunks [all true], but the best companion in the field when things are difficult that I have ever known,

471

bar none.' A modest woman wouldn't write this down. I do it to look at if I should feel low sometime."

With Roy Marsh we worked out our schedule for the next couple of weeks. We anticipated returning from the Belgian Congo between January 26 and February 1, after my *n'dege* Christmas-present trip, when we would move with all our safari boys to the coast for fishing below Mombassa, the boys having had ten days' vacation with pay, their first days home with their families since late August. It was sad to realize that our safari life—more free and exciting, more gay, more beautiful, more sybaritic than any I could have invented—was ending.

Friday, January 8, Kimana Swamp: "Campi at 6:15 p.m. Papa and I are comfortable by our campfire, he reading, I listening. N'guli and M'sembie are talking in their soft light voices against a background rattle of silver and plates in the mess tent. . . .

"From the cookfire comes laughter, the voices of M'windi (matter-of-fact, unemotional) of N'bebia (frivolous and young-sounding; he never loses his gay-fellow air). Keiti is speaking, light and soft but sedate and authoritative, and there are deep soft rumbles from Charo's throat, and rich, round-toned and respectful murmurs from the kitchen helper. Silence in the tent of M'thoka and the gun boys. It must be that we are so very attached to these individuals for two reasons: before we came to Kenya we had not anticipated—I certainly hadn't—that they would be so lively, intelligent, witty and kind; our isolation and sometimes danger with them only as companions has knitted a bond between us—they show they feel it a little bit—rather as bloody wartime operations made friends of groups of strangers.

"Papa in his Masai-red jacket is sitting sidewise to the fire, stroking his shaved head. The usual bottles are set out on the bar table nearby. Against the blue-gray of the Chyulu hills, Lion Mountain is showing pink in the late sun, its rim of trees still strong green, the plain between us still golden. Our fire with long slow flames is burning quietly on its mound of white ashes, its smoke going westward, away from us. The sky is the pale smoky shade of moonstones and the evening silence is punctuated by eight or nine different birdcalls, and a biggish bird, black and white with a tall thin crest, is molesting the doves who have their nest in our thorn tree. . . .

"Last evening we heard a car coming and sighed, sorry to lose our solitude. But it was Denis, always welcome, who stopped by to thank Papa for his birthday present, the airplane Papa had given to the Game Department. He says it will help him immeasurably to watch over the beasts in the huge territory of which he is Game Warden and also to detect and catch poachers, who are the game's worst enemies. We opened champagne and after dinner Denis took Papa on one final steeplechase in the Land-Rover during which Papa shot a hyena and again got tumbled out of the car.

"Papa is fascinated by the mixture of races and religions in even such a small town as Laitokitok. The man who owns the Adams Hotel, with its dirt floor there, is a Christian although an Indian. Singh, of the bar and sawmill, is Hindu and his God on the poster on the wall grasps one lion by the neck and has his foot on a lioness. G. H. Bhanji, who owns the general store is Mohammedan with appropriate posters and a lithograph of the Aga Khan. Some of the Masai who buy their spears from Bhanji have attended the Episcopalian missionary school and pay lip service to Christian dogma but most Masai and most of the Wakamba in our nearest shamba live by their respective tribal commandments. So do many of our boys, although Keiti, M'windi, Charo and some of the others are Muslims and will not eat meat which has not been halalled, the throat cut while the animal is alive."

Friday, January 15: "While the other boys struck our tent and the mess tent and did final loading onto the truck, our hunting mob went off in the car to the upper flats and there Kimana Swamp gave us a parting present—good closeup views of three lionesses lying near clumps of grass at the edge of the thorn forest, the two baby cubs playing near their mother, a huge dark lioness, new to us, and the young pale gold one, the mother's friend. They moved about a little,

473

but we got close enough to take pictures, and afterward Papa said, 'Goddamn, that mother was cocked like a gun, with the ears back and the tail up and down. I never saw anything more dangerous than this morning.' "

We got off from Kimana Swamp that morning, Ernest driving Patrick's Land-Rover which he had left with us after driving up from Tanganyika, having flown back there, I going with M'thoka in the hunting car until we reached a cottage, Ol Tukai Lodge, in the Amboseli National Reserve, and were astounded to discover that we had electricity, a toilet that functioned, and a bath. Before dinner on the front veranda that evening we both took big hot baths, mourning only slightly the absence of dead bugs in the water.

In the silvery-gray of predawn the next morning we went sightseeing, our guns empty, as required by the park, found lions and antelope, none of which were more impressive than ours at Kimana, we decided, and, turning a bend, saw what I first thought was a rhino with two calves nursing. I was standing on the back seat of the hunting car with head, shoulders and camera stuck through the open hatch in the car's roof, taking photographs in the dim light. As we drew closer to the rhino we saw him step forward limping and that the two animals were not nursing infants but two hyenas who were nipping and gouging the living meat from a bleeding hole in his buttock. The hyenas were devouring the rhino's genitals. (I had forgotten that rhinos have only one calf at a time.)

Ernest was rigid and pale because he could not with one well-placed shot forestall the rhino's further suffering, but the Amboseli regulation is that no visitors may shoot for any reason. While we watched and I photographed, the rhino, moaning and sounding like a domesticated cow, went down on his knees. Our approach did not disturb the hyenas. They turned to look at us, their muzzles dripping blood, then turned back to tear more chunks of meat from the widening hole in the buttock, and the rhino rolled all the way down.

Since we could do nothing to help the rhino, we hurried back to the office of Major Taberer, manager of the reserve, to report the slow slaughter. The major, who had some guests, seemed to us strangely unhurried about going to put the rhino out of its misery.

Not waiting for the major we drove the couple miles back to the place of the dying. At our approach this time the hyenas moved off, their glutted bellies almost touching the ground. The rhino lay unmoving in his blood but breathing, and Ernest and the gun boys got busy tracking and in a quarter of an hour found out the whole story. The rhino had gone, even-footed, in apparent health and complacency, to drink at the edge of a nearby swamp. In the tall grass he had run into and perhaps surprised a cow elephant and her small child which were also drinking there. The mother elephant had gored him and injured, if not broken, his spine. He had made it back to dry ground before the hyenas smelled his blood and attacked. By the time Major Taberer arrived with his guests the rhino was dead, a thousand shiny ticks boring into his carcass.

Following our plan we moved on from Amboseli to stay with Denis at Kajiado and crossing a vast yellow sand flat on the way saw the most convincing mirage of our lives. The sun was in the zenith, and about a mile to our left stretched a calm pale-blue lake, its surface shimmering in the sunshine, a peninsula with trees and soft green bush protruding from its far left bank, the greenery all perfectly reflected in the water, with gentle green hills and high grassy banks to the right sharply repeating themselves on the blue surface. We stopped and as I was photographing, a big dust devil formed and whirled toward us from the "lake."

After three days in Nairobi, repacking, eating and drinking too much and seeing too many people, we set off with Roy Marsh in the Cessna 180, on the first leg of my Christmas-present journey. Our stop the first night was at Bukavu on Lake Kivu, and the next day, Friday, January 22, we left Bukavu airport and flew north up Lake Kivu. We skirted the sides of volcanoes spewing sulphurous-smelling steam, with Mt. Ruwenzori a bank of dark cloud to our left, almost bumping into hippos, buffalos and elephants who had come to the shore to bathe and drink. We followed the marshy natural channel between Lake Edward and little Lake George counting six big herds of buffalo, with elephant living among them, scores of warthog and waterbuck, and hippos in families, communities and nations. White egrets perched on the hippo noses protruding from the water.

After a stop overnight at Entebbe, we cruised west above burnt-over country, slid above a high ridge bordering the lowlands at the south end of Lake Albert and chuffed up the west shore of the lake passing pleasant thatched fishing villages, whose men, women and children were working in the water around their dugout canoes. As we continued north, the mountains gradually crowded out the foreshore, dropping sheer into the lake with no beaches. We saw one fisherman with a Nile perch we estimated to weigh at least one hundred pounds, boated in the bow of his dugout canoe, and watched the mountains retreat at the north end of the lake where we had marshes below us again and the beginning of the White Nile meandering slowly through them northward. We turned east and another slow river beneath us was the Victoria Nile, with elephant, buffalo and hippo thick along both banks.

Gradually the shores defined themselves and we flew over low bushy country which rose into hills with thin-to-moderate-sized timber and so reached Murchison Falls where we circled while I took pictures, circled again, Roy tilting the plane so that I could photograph the falls, circled a third time and ran into the remains of an ancient telegraph wire which shaved off our radio antenna and rudder. Roy tugged and juggled controls and maneuvered the Cessna away from the sharp cliffs close to the falls. But the Cessna kept losing altitude, and Roy said, "We'll have to set down."

He pulled the plane over some low trees then between some high trees, saying, "Sorry, we're coming down now: Get ready, get ready, get ready!" I turned my face away from the windshield and covered my eyes with my arms. In rending, crashing, smashing noises we came to a stop among low trees and bushes. My feeling that last moment was irritation—*shit!*—

at being so unexpectedly dead or broken to bits. Ernest said later he had the same feeling and thought the same expletive.

Roy said, "Let's get out quickly," and we did. But the Cessna behaved with commendable decorum, restraining any tendency to explode or catch fire. Roy ran around outside checking the damage to the plane, having ascertained that neither of us was apparently seriously damaged. I started gathering up the mess inside the cabin, one camera caked with dust and twisted out of shape, the other, which had been in my lap, with no noticeable bruises. No lenses were broken in either camera, and the camera bag with light meters, lenses, filters was intact, but the contents of my straw handbag—passports, purses and such—were strewn all over. It was one o'clock in the afternoon about two degrees above the equator and the sun pounded on our bare heads like a pile driver.

In the shade of the port wing, Ernest and Roy studied the map. It clearly showed the span of telegraph wire crossing the river. (Natives had cut up the rest of the line for their personal uses, including the making of ample earrings.) The map showed that it was about forty miles to the nearest village, with no indication whether or not the village had a telephone. We could not be sure that animal and native trails in the actual walking would be less than sixty miles. I looked at my shoes with their fragile soft kid soles.

In the excitement of the crash and of having survived it without bleeding, none of us had paid attention to his physical condition. Then I noticed Ernest putting his hand to his back, and that my heart was pounding unusually fast and that I had a sharp pain in my left chest. From throat to feet I felt queasy. Roy suggested that I lie down in the wing shade, and Ernest came to take my pulse and his mouth turned straight. "I can't get any pulse on her," he said to Roy. But I felt better, lying down, and watched in a fog of withdrawal from reality, as Ernest, looking not at all well, and Roy worked with the radio antenna, trying to straighten it. Roy went into his seat in the plane to talk into his microphone. *"M'aidez, m'aidez, m'aidez.* Victor Love Item [the Cessna's initials] down approximately three miles south southeast Murchison Falls. Nobody hurt, nobody hurt [sic], awaiting overland rescue." Then again, and again. No reply.

The bushes around us looked thin but grew so close together that we could not see more than a few yards in any direction. We began to hear movements and noises of animals and Ernest decided that we should move up the hill away from the river toward a ridge with the telegraph poles silhouetted on it. We picked up some of our gear and slowly climbed, Ernest carrying a box of bottles and tinned food, I toting cameras and camera equipment. We paused to rest and opened one of our now precious bottles of beer. When Ernest handed it to me I dropped it and lost half its contents. Terrible to see the bottle with the precious beer flowing out and in my fog being unable quickly to bend down and retrieve it. Ernest withheld a burst of anger but I knew what exasperation he must have felt.

A quarter of a mile uphill from the ruined little plane we found a level spot of hardened sand which appeared to have been scooped out from the lower side of a small knoll topped by a single thorn tree. A good place to camp, we decided. The crocodiles and hippos would not move that far from water to feed. Ernest listened to my heart, tried again to take my pulse and couldn't find it, and told me to lie down, which I did, on top of my raincoat on the hard sand. All of us were unduly thirsty we confessed to each other, partly, probably, from excitement, partly from the climb up the hill in the heat and sun, and partly, no doubt, because we knew we had so little water. We handed around Roy's beat-up old Italian army canteen and moistened our tongues.

Roy picked his way among the rocks and thorn trees and the neighborhood elephant a dozen times to the plane and back up the hill, Ernest standing on top of our knoll and calling the locations of elephants to him. Each time he reached the plane we could hear his voice, very faintly calling, "M'aidez, m'aidez, m'aidez. Aircraft force-landed, awaiting arrival of search parties." Each time he came up the hill he brought something more to make us comfortable, the gallon tin of water with its faint taste and smell of gas and a few glossy spots of gas in it, but welcome. (We had the river water, but it would have to be boiled for safety. Tomorrow we could find something in which to boil water.) Roy brought up whiskey we had forgotten about, firewood, and finally the Cessna's plastic-fiber seatcovers.

Each time I moved to help gather firewood my heart thumped so violently that, craven, I slumped back again to the horizontal. Ernest scoured the area for wood—we would need a big pile of it to last out the night—but I had never seen him bend down so slowly or a woodpile of his grow so feebly. Not that we were gloomy.

"Unscheduled chance to camp out," Ernest said, grinning.

"What dopes we were, to sleep under canvas," I said.

"We'll have an Indian fire, like in upper Michigan," Ernest said.

"And in northern Minnesota," I said.

When I bemoaned having no face cream for bed-time cleansing, Roy offered to go back once more to the plane to get me engine oil, saying, "It's a lovely, clean engine."

Ernest was delighted with our view of the hippos and the elephants bathing in the evening on the opposite bank of the river and longed for his binoculars. We could hear them on our side too, but trees and underbrush blocked our view of them.

"I remember how the river turned color from bright, strong blue," I wrote a couple days later, "with the hippo constantly huffing and puffing, to light blue, then to silver with the sky pearly after the sunset, then to steely-gray. The last touches of light caught in the yellow grass on the high ridge to our right. Jupiter rising. Then Orion, brilliant in this high clear air."

Roy gathered great armfuls of tall grasses for us to use as mattresses, and with Ernest's knife dug and smoothed a bed for him in the hard sand next to me. We drank whiskey with the slightly-petrolled water and Roy served dinner, pieces of corned beef on the remains of sandwiches, I dining in bed.

"I remember my drifting to sleep, seeing Ernest's

and Roy's two silhouettes against our Indian fire," I wrote, "I comfortable with my blue cardigan for warmth above and my raincoat below, and thankful that my Belgian shoes are soft enough to sleep in, giving extra warmth, but worried about Roy in his shorts and shirt only, having nothing for warmth and the night growing colder and colder. And how hard and cold my bed grew, despite the thick grass under me.

"Papa patted his hand on my stomach saying, 'Better not to snore if you can help it. It's attracting the elephants.' I was incredulous and went heavily back to sleep, with Papa's voice whispering that we had elephants twelve paces away on one side and twenty paces on the other."

Cold and general ache woke me to see Roy moving about, hunting more firewood, about 5 a.m., Ernest hesitantly, heavily moving too, whispering with Roy and rebuilding the fire. I had slept straight north and south, for the early morning sky showed the Big Dipper with its cup turned downward directly above my feet. I had a sip of water and a cigarette and went back to sleep, happy that my heart had not pounded so wildly when I had moved.

When I woke up again Roy was taking off, softly carrying torn-up seat covers with which he would make an arrow at Murchison Falls pointing to our camp. Ernest gave me a little piece of cheese and two small bananas for breakfast and I also drank two thermos tops of long-soured coffee with milk, but most welcome that morning, from one of the Cessna's flasks. One cup should have been for me and one for Ernest, but he gave me his ration as a present.

While I breakfasted in bed Ernest scouted for firewood close to camp, he in obvious pain especially in his right arm and shoulder. Coming back to the fire with some sticks, he said, "There's a boat coming up the river." Impossible. We knew there was no regular navigation around Lake Albert. Ten minutes later I saw it too, white and incredible. But it was real. We waved. Then Ernest waved his raincoat, I mine. From the boat came no sign of recognition. We agreed that we could not both be seeing a phantom.

I wanted to run to the boat landing, a couple of old

480

planks nailed together at the bottom of the falls, where the boat had tied up. Ernest started down, then came back up and mentioned that we would be to windward of the elephants between us and the river. Without a rifle or any sort of weapon he felt vulnerable among the beasts. In near despair I watched people, small blobs, move away from the boat and disappear in the trees, and wondered how we could get down there, avoiding elephants, before the people returned and the boat steamed away. But Ernest had told Roy that he would stay at camp to await Roy's return from the signal placing, and urged me not to try to go down to the boat by myself.

Then we saw some Africans moving slowly up toward us, north of us and on the far side of a sharp-walled ravine. We waved to them and they managed to cross the ravine to us. They were doubtful about our story of the fallen *n'dege* and I was never more grateful for the imperfect Swahili I had learned. I offered to show them the plane and they cheerfully offered to escort me to the boat, assuring Ernest that they would protect me from the elephants.

Ernest stayed behind at camp and watched for elephants, to warn us in our descent, and with the four or five Africans, crew of the boat, whose curiosity had drawn them up to investigate us, I went slowly down, seeing no beasts, and found that the boat had been privately chartered by Mr. Ian McAdam, a surgeon from Kampala, next door to Entebbe, who had made the sightseeing voyage to Murchison Falls with his wife and son and his wife's parents who were celebrating their fiftieth wedding anniversary. Mr. and Mrs. McAdam and their son had gone walking on a path to the top of the falls, so I explained our predicament to the Indian skipper of the boat. He doubted seriously that we could come aboard. It was against the regulations. This was a private charter. We had not bought tickets at the shipping office at Butiaba, the boat's home port halfway down the eastern shoreline of Lake Albert. He had not replied to our signaling from the hill because he thought we were a bunch of drunken campers. He was not authorized to allow passengers aboard who had not been properly booked.

481

Back in Butiaba there might be some question about his judgment, even about his job, if he allowed us aboard. I yearned for my shotgun or even a hatpin.

Mrs. McAdam's parents were courteous and said they hoped a solution could be found. She was painting the landscape in pale English water-colors, which I admired vocally after having apologized for my intrusion on their privacy.

The doctor and his wife were not expected back for half an hour or more, so I went to take pictures of the plane with its bent propeller and broken rudder. Some of the boat crew accompanied me and I offered five shillings to any boy who would find my brown leather purse in the wreckage. One boy reached under the Cessna, pulled out my purse and said, "M'ungu [God] saved your life and now he gives me five shillings."

Roy came down to the boat with the McAdams and we sent some boys up the hill to get Ernest. It turned out that my trip down the hill had moved the elephants back up to him and they were disputing his knoll with him when the boys moved them off. Elephants understand the smell of Africans, we had been told, and are less antagonized by it than they are by the scent of white people. The Indian skipper carefully collected payment of our passage from Ernest before he shoved away from the landing. Mrs. McAdam showed me the bathroom and lent me talcum powder. I showered and before lunch Mr. McAdam examined me and found only a couple of cracked ribs. The heart-pounding, he thought, had been nothing more than evidence of shock. Ernest asked for no examination, simply sitting huddled and quiet in a chair, and the surgeon did not offer any assistance.

I found the trip downriver fascinating, since we were on a level with families and communities and colonies of elephants, crocodiles and hippos who yawned at us, opening up wide their cavernous Schiaparelli-pink mouths. The boat, the *Murchison,* which did not much disturb the beasts, was the one which John Huston and his film crew used when they made *The African Queen.* The film people lived aboard another boat, a paddle-wheeler, but the *Murchison* ran errands for them between location on the river and Butiaba. The *Murchison* chartered for 500 shillings ($71) a day, I learned from the Indian, and could be chartered for any sort of lake expedition and it might be fun to charter her for fishing. There was enough room, aft, for trolling baits, I noticed.

The weather had been tranquil that January day with little movement on the surface of Lake Albert, and as we approached Butiaba in the late afternoon a plane flew over us. We waved from the top deck and the plane circled several times. When we reached the dock at Butiaba the plane's pilot, Reggie Cartwright, and Mr. Williams, the police officer from Masindi, a town on the railway and the administrative center of the area, were waiting. Mr. Cartwright was impatient to get us aboard his plane and leave immediately for Entebbe, that airport having plenty of lights to allow us to land after dark. I thought how pleasant it would be to sleep in any rentable bed right there in little Butiaba and postpone rejoining civilization until the morning. But Mr. Cartwright was eager to deliver us to the press, waiting at Entebbe. Mr. Williams mentioned that Butiaba had no hotel.

Mr. Williams drove us to a field beyond the town, which had been used as an airstrip during the filming of *The African Queen*. Later it had been cross-plowed and then abandoned. In the failing light we could see the undulations of the old furrows. An old-fashioned De Havilland Rapide biplane, its canvas fuselage stretched over a wooden frame, stood at the field's edge. Rapides were still popular planes in East Africa because they required so little space for takeoff and landing.

Using the police truck, Mr. Cartwright cruised down the field and returned, asserting that we could easily get off it, although darkness was fast seeping down. We loaded quickly while a crowd of native villagers watched and gave advice, Roy going forward on the starboard side with me behind him, Ernest across the aisle and our gear dumped in three empty seats astern. Mr. Cartwright started the motor, did not bother gunning it, and we taxied off, the tail bumping over the furrows. We lifted slightly, set down, lifted again like a grasshopper, set down again, continued hopping, the tail bumping. I was listlessly chewing a dried-up ham sandwich. Then came the wrenching, creaking, crashing, breaking and we were stopped and flames were leaping outside my window. It took what seemed an age for me to get my unfamiliar seatbelt unbuckled.

Ernest said, "Open the door," and I found it in the firelight on the port side but could not budge it. The door was made of solid metal but the door frame had buckled. I heaved my weight against it, my ribs protesting, and kicked with my soft shoes. No result.

Roy had gone forward and broken a window and called to me to hurry there, and Ernest, now working on the door himself, yelled, "Follow Roy." I hesitated. Roy called again and I ran up the aisle and pushed him through the open window head first. Cartwright was still in his seat and flames were licking at the inside of the cabin, aft. I heaved myself up and through the window, feet first, observing that it was much too small to allow the passage of Ernest's bulk. Roy helped me down to the ground and walked me rapidly windward, ahead of the plane, I thinking, explosions.

Twenty paces in front of the plane we looked back and saw Ernest walking on the lower port wing, so we walked another thirty yards away from what was now a bonfire, with Cartwright emerging from it and Ernest in the firelight at the edge of the field to our right. Unable to open the door with any combination of his already damaged bones and muscles, Ernest had used his head as a battering-ram, butted the door open, given himself a concussion, and saved himself from burning to death. Now he came over to me and solemnly kissed me on the forehead.

The locals, who had clustered around our starting point, burst into a cheering section, delivering up a jubilant-sounding dirge, then came running across the field, yelling and shouting and hedging us in, insisting on shaking hands, hollering, "M'ungu, M'ungu. M'kono." (God, God, in the hand of God.) In the flickering light of the fire Roy eased me out of the crowd and to the police truck, which had driven up. When Ernest joined us we drove back to the starting place of the takeoff where Mr. Williams's car waited and pretty Mrs. Williams gave us strong hot black coffee. Ernest wanted to hear our beer and gin bottles explode inside the fire, but there were no explosions, or they were inaudible. We got into the back seat of the Williamses' car and set off for Masindi, Ernest and I holding hands tightly, I feeling very subdued, Ernest talking politics and tribal affairs and crops with Mrs. Williams, as though we were having a tea party. What we both wanted most was a drink, a big strong assist of alcohol. But there was no drink.

At the slovenly bar of the Railway Hotel in Masindi we got a noisy welcome from pilots who had been hunting for us all day, local barflies and Mr. McAdam, who bought drinks for everyone and a package of cigarettes for me. No word had been picked up from Roy's radio after the first crash, we learned, but a BOAC Argonaut pilot flying from Entebbe to Rome had spotted the Cessna and reported its position. Mr. McAdam looked at the hole in Ernest's head and after a cursory glance, said, "Nothing to it, old boy. Let's pour some gin in it," and did so.

The hotel's dining room having closed, we went without dinner, ate sandwiches with Roy in our room and appraised the situation. (Cartwright had faded into the background.) All of Roy's papers including his pilot's license and the Cessna's papers were ashes. All of our papers including passports, money, and bank drafts were ashes, and two cameras were burned. We were too tired to wash away more than the worst of the blood and the dirt before we went painfully to sleep, Ernest frequently coughing. When I started to get up in the night I screamed from an unexpected pain in my knee and woke him. Hyenas were howling right outside our window, smelling our caked blood perhaps. In the morning we found that Ernest's pillow was soaked with cerebral fluid.

Later that morning the African doctor of Masindi came with a nurse and cleaned us up a bit. He bandaged Ernest's head where it was suppurating above his left ear, perfunctorily cleaned the wounds on his knees and legs and the knee I must have cut open when the Rapide made its last jolt to full stop. The town's telegrapher would not open his office in the railway station the previous evening, a Sunday, January 24.

Regulations. But on Monday morning he accepted a wire to my parents, reassuring them.

The Indian manager of the Railway Hotel cashed a check for me, and Roy, who himself was going to fly to Entebbe, arranged for a railway company car and chauffeur to drive us there. We went in comparative comfort through country of small farms growing cotton and yucca, and admired the natives we passed on the road, tall, handsome people, stately in their carriage. When we swerved unexpectedly to avoid hitting a cart which came out from a side road, Ernest murmured, "I'm sick of the sound of rending metal."

Members of Kenya's civil aviation board and a crowd of newspaper people were waiting to interview Ernest at the hotel at Entebbe and while I climbed upstairs and went to bed he talked with precision and care first with the officials and then with the press, explaining for Roy's defense that a flock of egrets had rushed into the Cessna and battered it out of control, also the complications of the takeoff in the Rapide. When he finally made it up to our room, he looked exhausted and said he was thirsty. A few drinks revived us both enough to go downstairs to dine.

Entebbe, Tuesday, January 26, 1954: "I stayed in bed all morning but Papa was up and about, busy opening masses of cables from everywhere. . . . There are also many requests for stories, one London editor announcing he had deposited £300 with the local government. Governor Cohn sent kind messages, one saying if it were not convenient to dine at Government House as we had planned, we must not feel obliged to.

"Having chartered a plane from Dar es Salaam, Patrick arrived about noon with fat wads of money which, said Papa, 'is the most chic way of all for a son to arrive.'

"We both rested in the afternoon, uncomfortable with nothing to read except my book on the Belgian Congo, which I'd left behind. Papa is obviously not in good shape. He stayed awake and softly moved about half the night." Two days after the second plane crash we were both still too exhilarated simply at being alive to set out on the sensible processes of discovering how much was wrong with us and beginning to put it right.

I hadn't the faintest idea how grievous were Ernest's internal injuries and, never a complainer about his bad luck, he said almost nothing about how he felt. Although we had indications of the various wounds, it was not until months later in Venice that we learned the entire list: two disks of his spine cracked and impacted, his liver and one kidney both ruptured, a paralysis of the sphincter, his right arm and shoulder dislocated, his skull broken open.

While Roy Marsh got off on the regular East African Airways flight from Entebbe to Nairobi to bring back another plane for us, Ernest rested and read cables and with Patrick and his money I shopped at the Indian *dukas* between Entebbe and Kampala, found a blue sweater for Ernest and a basket which could serve as a handbag for me. Ernest's discomfort seemed to have abated not at all.

To indicate his faith in Roy's reliability as a pilot, Ernest flew from Entebbe back to Nairobi on January 28 with Roy in a new Cessna. There was space enough for me and Patrick in the airplane and I tried but could not build up courage enough to join in the graceful gesture. Having both confidence in Roy and affection for him, I nonetheless would have chosen to walk the three hundred miles to Nairobi if that were the only alternative that day to boarding a plane. But by the next day I was sufficiently reintegrated to fly over to Nairobi with Patrick on the regular flight of East African Airways. Only a few other hours in all the years were more difficult to endure. "Your fear won't hold this plane up, you idiot," I kept repeating in my head, and I pretended to read Osbert Sitwell. But I was not a woman tourist flying over Africa. I was a sackful of terror. There arose no other occasion requiring me to fly that year until mid-April when I booked passage from Paris to London. Getting dressed at the Hôtel Ritz in Paris, I had an unexpected seizure of fear so acute that I danced around my bathroom yelling, "I can't. I can't." Then I saw myself in the mirror, looking utterly ridiculous, and laughter dispelled the attack.

Denis Zaphiro brought his entire troop of game scouts, smiling Kyungu heading them in their smart starched khaki uniforms, from Kajiado up to Nairobi airport to welcome Patrick and me, and our reunion festivities stretched late into the night.

Before I left Entebbe I listed our losses in the two crashes and the fire.

Passports and International Medical Certificates
Ernest's Rolex watch and gold bracelet
Hasselblad camera with two magazines and four filters
Rolleiflex camera with two filters and magnifying lens
Light meter
30 rolls of exposed film, black-and-white and color, some of Lake Natron, magenta, silver and blue, with its huge flocks of flamingoes; of game in the Ngorongoro Crater and on the Serengeti Plain; of buffalo and elephant grazing together in the marshes between Lake Edward and Lake George, of elephant and hippo together, of waterbuck and warthog together, of hippo families in and out of the water
22 rolls of unexposed color film, 10 rolls of black-and-white
Hunting licenses, gun permits, receipts
Two pairs of Ernest's prescription glasses, his tweed jacket and raincoat
All keys to luggage
My gold cigarette holder, French powder case, pearl earrings, cigarette lighter, Venetian wallet, raincoat, cashmere cardigan

In physical terms Ernest had lost more than a year's freedom from pain. But we had not lost each other.

At the New Stanley Hotel in Nairobi Ernest was reading telegrams from everywhere while conducting *levées* in our room overlooking Lord Delamere's statue, the room a disconcerting mess of cigarettes stamped out on the floor, overflowing ashtrays, empty bottles, dirty glasses, lumps of discarded clothing. An M.D. had come to examine Ernest, recommended X-rays, which Ernest refused, felt his liver and ordered a drastic reduction of his alcoholic intake, total rest and no visitors. Ernest continued his drinking and entertaining, leaving his *levées* only to go to an oculist who would prescribe new spectacles.

I was touched by the very first telegram to arrive in Nairobi. It was from Noel Monks. Then the obituaries began arriving, first from London and Europe, then from the western hemisphere and India and Hong Kong, two- and three-column stories many of them, reviewing Ernest's life and appraising his work. He read and reread them enthralled and gave no attention when I objected that the everlasting reading suggested unseemly egotism. After our day's and evening's guests had departed, he read in bed. Then, heeding my objections to the light, he read in the bathroom. I understood that one reason why he read so long was that the reading deflected his attention from his pain.

Visitors and well-wishers were arriving sometimes before I awoke in the mornings. S. J. Perelman came in one evening in a benign mood. He had just finished attending what was billed as an "All-Girl Safari" and was delighted to be finished with it. A young man, Hal Oliver, brought us mangoes from his mother's garden, and the wife of a former R.A.F. pilot, Mrs. Figgis, sat silently hour after hour waiting for Ernest to dictate his story of our recent adventures for a piece in *Look* magazine.

"His kidneys were seriously damaged," I wrote on Sunday, February 7. "The urine samples he keeps in glasses in the bathroom are bright, dark red with an inch of sediment, the wound on the leg not good, hearing bad in the burned ear, eyes bad, the new glasses uncomfortable because of the broken or bruised bone at the bridge of the nose."

Since my fractured ribs continued hurting, I decided I might as well hurt a bit more and went to have my ears pierced, the prettiest earrings in Nairobi being only for ears with holes in them. I arranged new passports, visas, health certificates, banking facilities and for evening snacks in our room since my husband shunned the idea of formally served meals. Altogether it was a hideous, disheveled week, miserable for me but painful to a point near desperation for Ernest. (Years later I discovered that strong unalleviated pain can break down self-discipline, curtail thinking capacity, even disrupt the personality.)

Five days later it looked to me that his injuries, inside and out, were healing much more slowly than we had at first anticipated. His right shoulder and elbow continued sharply painful when he moved, the wounds on his left leg were crusting too slowly. But each morning he was dictating to Mrs. Figgis, and he was cutting shorter his night sessions of reading in the bathroom and writing less in the nights at the room's table.

To give him privacy for dictating or at other times to escape the pounding monotony of everlasting conversations, I began to slip out to dawdle in the bookshop of the *East African Standard,* or simply to walk around the town, or to drive out to the Coryndon Museum to wonder at the spectacular animal heads in its crowded collection or the exquisite flower drawings by Joy Adamson in its basement.

Patrick and Henny drove up from John's Corner, Tanganyika, and on February 13 we set out for the coast to get under way our long-made plans for a fishing holiday on the Indian Ocean from a base Philip Percival had recommended, a cluster of fishermen's huts and a few rentable shore cottages called Shimoni (Hole in the Ground), south of Mombassa. Its principal asset was a fish-packing plant which would sell us ice.

Weeks before we had found in Mombassa a boat for charter which presumably could accommodate the fishing gear we had brought from Cuba. Now Philip Percival and I inspected the boat, I signed the charter papers and Patrick and Henny installed themselves aboard to bring the boat to Shimoni while the Percivals, Pat's Land-Rover with a hired driver and our hunting car with our reassembled safari crew drove in convoy to our new camp, a *banda* a few yards inland from a warm sandy beach.

The *banda* was a new kind of architecture to me, a cement floor supporting pillars which upheld a thatched roof and a few half-walls four feet high which divided the floor into approximations of rooms. There were no outside walls. Sea breezes whispered through the interior from all directions. As Philip walked me there,

490

he opined, "Five pounds a week. But worth it, unless it rains, the roof is so broken. But it won't rain. Never does until March."

Dear slant-eyed M'windi, our old tent servant, had set up my bed in a back corner of one of the half-walls, with my sharkskin bottle-bag and green tin clothes-locker nearby, and I had started unpacking when a flash storm moved in from the sea, heavy rain coming under the thatched eaves. In five minutes half a dozen little waterfalls were cascading around my bed and onto the luggage. When two inches of water placidly blanketed the floor with no visible runoff, I hoisted myself to the top of a wall and read Bemelmans until Philip rescued me to take me to supper in a soggy mess tent, much smaller than our old one of the high Kenya plateaus.

Patrick and Henny brought our boat, the *Lady Faye*, down from Mombassa, with its Arab pilot, Athmani, maneuvering correctly through the improbable storm and they found safe anchorage near the *banda*. When I went aboard for a second inspection, I found no rod-holders, no outriggers, and shading the afterdeck a canvas canopy supported by numerous chromium poles which would entirely impede swinging rods with any fish we might hook. Athmani and his young Arab helper removed and stowed the canopy.

On Wednesday, February 17, Philip and Mama Percival, Patrick, Henny and I with a couple of our safari crew took out the *Lady Faye* for a trial run, took her over the 100-fathom drop leading eastward from our coast to the Pemba Channel and, a day's voyage eastward, fabled Zanzibar. Using the butt-rests we had brought from Cuba, we trolled Japanese feathers and pork rind, most effective in the Gulf Stream, but the day's only catch was that of a small female dorado by M'kao, our safari skinner, who was trolling a hand line. I was not surprised when Mrs. Percival declined my invitation to fish the next day.

Denis Zaphiro with his chief scout, my hero Kyungu, came to camp and fished with us, but did not bring us appreciably better luck. Fishing every morning both over reefs and in deep clear navy-blue water, we discovered that the current there runs from south to north at about three knots that time of year. But we found no sailfish, which were supposed to be as thick as sardines, nor any schools of sardines. We did bring in half a dozen different bottom fish of splendorous designs and colors which looked to me like members of the mackerel family but which we could not identify, even with the help of the government's fish directory. That week Denis took one kingfish of about twelve pounds and Patrick caught a sizable bonito. But Athmani's charts could not reveal the bottom holes and canyons where fish convened. The new local commercial native fishermen, who each day brought back loads of sparkling bottom fish in their dugout canoes to sell to the dealer from Mombassa, pretended they had no special knowledge of the areas of fish congregations. It was a dull week on the water and mostly my fault, I reflected, for having failed to learn more about the area.

On February 21, Denis, Patrick, Henny and I drove up the coast road to Jardinia Beach, a luxurious wide stretch of bright sand, to watch a little plane come in, circle and set down light as a sparrow—Roy Marsh bringing Ernest to join us. I was startled by the total absence of his usual ebullience in our greetings and his silence, sitting next to Denis who was driving, on our way south. He was still in obvious distress. But once he was established in his cot at the *banda,* and then in a couple of chairs on its side veranda, he resumed the continuous conversations with whoever was around, repeating oft-told jokes, proud/humble heroics, homemade philosophies. As in Nairobi, the declamations seemed to divert his attention from his aching back, his injured kidney and liver, his broken skull, bruised shoulder and leg and all his other pains—"Semi-unbearable suffering"—as he wrote in my diary. He fished with us only once or twice.

In variable winds we fished, swam, watched and photographed Arab dhows and an English yacht resting in our harbor, watched our native neighbor women carry clay jugs of water homeward, dined at length each night on the veranda corner opposite Ernest's command post. In the *Lady Faye* we were learning something of the local fish resorts, bringing in one red snapper, an Arctic bonito and some jacks, and another

492

day Denis took a 14-pound (biggish) red snapper. When Denis, Patrick and Henny fished northward toward Jardinia on February 25, they had their best day, taking aboard one 33-pound yellow-fin tuna, a 20-pound wahoo, two dolphin and a barracuda.

In camp we spent lazy hours in the 80-degree heat, watching small green lizards maneuver upside down on the inside of our thatched roof, watching families of little brown Rhesus monkeys swing and loll in our surrounding greenery, groom each other and frolic, always with an eye on us, ready to duck behind a branch if we moved. We watched the baobab tree, fifty feet in circumference (I estimated) in front of the *banda,* drop its brown-skinned cream-of-tartar seeds at the urging of the wind. When a boy from the small island across the channel from us brought me micromark cowrie shells as a present, I told him I would pay for any more he found and he brought me enough to fill a suitcase. Henny wrote in my diary the music of her Ben Jonson song.

> Have you seen but a bright lily grow
> Before rude hands have touched it?
> Ha' you marked but the fall o' the snow
> Before the soil hath smutched it?
> Ha' you felt the wool of beaver,
> Or swan's down ever?
> Or have smelt o' the bud o' the briar?
> Or the nard in the fire? . . .

Some of those delights we were having, and also the pleasure of hearing Philip dealing with his "boys":

To young M'sembi (both grinning), *"Kwenda M'bali.* Get out of here. I'll skin you alive." Turning to me, "He's a sweet boy."

To N'guli, *"Kuja,* you bahstahd." To me, "Good boy, that one. Good tracker."

On Sunday, February 28, we bid a sad farewell to the Percivals, homeward bound, and thereupon a plague began to descend upon us, an evil miasma, a foul-smelling deafening raucous bird of destruction and disaster enfolding us. Denis began to feel bad and feared that his old enemy malaria was arriving for yet another visit. The hot wind until nine o'clock at night became a torment. After swimming with me on March 2, Ernest took an unreasonable dislike to the dugout canoe of a neighboring native and banged away at it with a piece of driftwood, breaking a seat and a paddle. I sent the man apologies and payment.

As Patrick, Henny and I breakfasted on March 3, planning to go fishing, Ernest called an inquiry about what bait we had. Patrick replied that we had squid "more or less in order," a phrase he may have picked up at Harvard.

"I don't permit 'more or less in order,' " Ernest yelled from his end of the veranda.

He went on making a speech about responsibility and accuracy and the lack of them, a harangue so unfair and undeserved that I quaked. Tears filled Henny's eyes. At the end of the speech Patrick made a short reply. "I'm leaving," he said and left the table to give orders for the packing of their things and loading of them into his Land-Rover. In our hunting car I accompanied them to Mombassa to take luggage needing repairs and to buy food for camp. Henny sat with me on the journey north and we agreed that Ernest had not yet recovered noticeably from his concussion. For days he had been talking about becoming "blood brothers" with his Wakamba friends among our safari servants. That night I noted cryptically: "We got home before six. Papa had started ceremonies for face-cutting and ear-piercing."

A day or two later Denis and I came in from fishing to find Ernest sitting in his favorite chair on the veranda, a mass of raw, burnt, burnt-smelling flesh. I had never been trained in nursing or even in first aid, but I did what he told me to do, read instructions on boxes and bottles of burn-relieving chemicals and with Keiti and M'windi helping bandaged the parts of him that were bandageable. A bushfire had started south of the *banda* and in the wild wind had rushed toward us and our nearest native neighbors. All our boys had gone out to beat it down and in spite of Keiti's admonitions, Ernest insisted on joining them in the fire-fighting, fell down and was aflame himself before the boys could rescue him. Both his legs, his stomach and

chest and chin looked like raw steak, and his hands
and arms like hamburger.

Denis helped in everything, especially in the morale-
boosting department. I brought liquids, greased bandages, brought booze and Seconal, brought food and
sympathy. Ernest would not budge from his canvas
camp chair until a couple of days later when the boys
removed it to put it in our truck of camp furniture. I
had to trust Athmani to take the *Lady Faye* safely
back to Mombassa and Denis and Ernest elected to
voyage in the *Lady Faye* while I went in the hunting
car on our safari's last journey, and Kyungu drove Lili,
Denis's Land-Rover.

Ernest slept aboard the *Lady Faye* while I slept hot
and breathless in our cabin, No. 63, at the dock at
Kilindini aboard the beautiful white *Africa,* of the
Lloyd Triestino Line based in Trieste. While Ernest
made friends with the ship's crew the next noon, I
made the double handshake with M'thoka, our hunting-
car driver, and, to M'windi's consternation, kissed him
good-bye on his sere, lined cheek. As soon as we were
under way, Ernest took to his bunk beneath the portholes and thereafter on the ten-day voyage seldom left
it. The ship's doctor, a cheerful, witty, sympathetic,
cautious Italian, came to visit two or three times a
day and bring whatever palliatives he could find for
Ernest's pain. But his ship's surgery room was not
equipped for major operations, nor was his X-ray machinery suitable, he said. Better to wait for Venice, he
advised.

Whatever painkillers Ernest took could not long or
entirely disperse the nightmare of his discomfort or
the accompanying raveling of his nerves. He tried to
ease his situation by being abusive to me. I ached with
sympathy but promptly arranged a schedule of escaping soon after breakfast to the decks, the cheerful outdoor swimming pool with its children's slide down into
the water, or the air-conditioned public rooms and several bars, each one installed exactly where a passenger
might feel pangs of thirst.

Evan Shipman, Ernest's beloved friend from his
early days in Paris, a poet as well as a devotee and reporter of sulky racing, had sent him long galley proofs

of a new book of poems he was about to publish. Ernest was reading the proofs when I dozed off in afterlunch siesta in the bed opposite him. I awoke to see a ribbon of galley proof streaking out the open porthole, but, sleep-bound, I couldn't make it across the stateroom to catch the last of the paper before it escaped. For a couple of days Ernest upbraided me for incompetence. I found relief listening to Lord Portsmouth who for a dozen years had operated a big ranch near Kitale, Kenya, and who had studied in depth the colony's economy and political and racial problems. On his own ranch he had worked out sound solutions to many of the difficulties, and I hoped the British government would have enough sense to pay attention to his formulas. A refreshing man, and I refreshed myself by remembering the loving, friendly phrases Ernest had been making throughout Africa before the crashes and the fire.

On the port side of the *Africa* we passed miles and miles of broad empty golden beaches backed by visible expanses of desert. In Europe, or the United States, the beaches would be worth $100 a square foot, I imagined, if fresh water could be found. But there, worth zero.

When the *Africa* docked at Suez at the southern end of the Canal, Ernest stayed in his bed, but scores of us passengers debarked into a fleet of American motorcars to drive across the desert, which looked to my domesticated eye like the brown-tinted folds of the meringue on top of a lemon pie, to Cairo, colored pink, white and blue in the heat haze. We were herded to a Coptic church, a synagogue, the Mohammed Ali Pasha Mosque, and after lunch to the National Museum with its wonderful pieces of alabaster, the statues from Luxor, the thin beaten-gold sandals and necklaces and delicate gold gloves of pharaohs. As thousands of day-trippers before us had done, we went to the Mena House, mounted camels and rode bumpily to the pyramids, I on a beast named "Sugar-Honey" apparently no more ill-tempered than her sisters or brethren, the camel-man yelling repeatedly, "I hope you're enjying yurself," in a version of the Dublin accent.

"Did you ever work for an Irishman?" I yelled down.

"For what? I hope you're enjyin'."

"Never mind. Forget it."

At Giza the pyramids and the Sphinx were nothing less nor more than we had anticipated, but the Muslim bazaar back in Cairo offered temptations to some of which I succumbed, acquiring a camel saddle, an inlaid leather pouf, a round, air-inflated stool which became useful as a sit-on thing in the library at the Finca Vigía. After dinner we drove back in bright moonlight along the Nile delta and the Canal, I nipping at Lord Portsmouth's whiskey, to our ship tied up to a wharf at Port Said.

18

Springtime in Europe

AT VENICE ON March 23 the immigration and customs welcomed us so hospitably that they forgot to paste their "Inspected" stickers on our eighty-seven bags. Ernest put on a show of well-being for the port officials and local newsmen, but went to bed as soon as we got into our suite at the Gritti Palace Hotel. Carlo Kechler and his brother Federico, our first friend in the Veneto, and Maria Luisa, his sweet-spirited wife, came to call and insisted that we stay with them at their spacious, beautiful country place, Percotto. There could not be more thoughtful hosts. In our big room we had bed coverlets for varying degrees of warmth, good lights for supine reading, opened and recorked champagne in an ice bucket and other drinks and mixes, a tiny unobtrusive light in the bathroom.

Still, my heart's excessive pounding awoke me in the early morning and since Ernest was lying wide awake, I told him.

"It's going to shake the house apart."

"Breathe deep," he said. "Take some champagne." I followed both suggestions and soon felt better. Years earlier I had discovered that telling my troubles to Ernest, instantly, miraculously half dispersed them.

"You must be feeling pretty bad, baby?" I said.

"Yes."

"Is there anything—nothing—I can do?"

"Yes. Nothing."

With Federico acting as executive officer, Venice's best doctors and internists and brain and spine men were brought in to inspect Ernest back at the Gritti Palace, and X-rays and new assortments of pain-relievers were prescribed.

Meanwhile Ernest decided that I should have a break from my job as bumbling nurse and whipping boy for his frayed nerves, and on the telephone to Paris, London and Madrid, arranged a holiday for me from his bedside. I would see my London friends for Easter, I would join Rupert Bellville in Paris to drive south for the spring *ferias* in Sevilla and Ronda, then to Madrid where we would rendezvous with him. Walking to a semifarewell lunch at Harry's Bar, Ernest noticed something special in his favorite jewelry shop, an antique necklace and bracelet of black and white and gold enamel and garnets delicately designed as blackamoor heads, and promptly bought them for me.

We booked me to Paris on the Simplon-Orient Express and I went aboard alight with anticipations of seeing, maybe overhearing, beautiful girl spies, Bond Street chic counterespionage fellows, dope-smuggling duchesses, girl-smuggling Turks. Only part of the dining car was first class and its inhabitants were stubble-chinned, spotted-tied businessmen with briefcases. I decided that the big international crooks must travel incognito. The wine list was short and deplorable.

But in Paris my old friend the Ritz chauffeur Georges Mabilat shepherded me cheerfully to the hotel where they gave me a room under the eaves with a bathroom thrice its size. The light in the Place Vendôme below my windows was bleak, dark gray. The telephones of my friends *ne répondaient pas*. At his pretty, feminine desk below the curve of the marble staircase Henry Galopin, who had worked there so long as ticket agent that he seemed rooted to the carpet, told me there was nothing much interesting in theater or music. "Holy week, you know. Unless you like masses." Charlie Ritz was off somewhere. I booked a plane to London and after my few minutes of dancing around in my vast bathroom, terrified at the thought of flying again, organized my luggage and went off.

From Paris I wrote Ernest: "All the boys, Georges, Bertin, young Claude and all the others are so sad that you haven't come . . . because, as Bertin says, 'We do not only like him, we love him.' He described with emotion the news of our crashed airplane, how he found every face long and triste. They showed him the newspaper and he said, 'Impossible. Pas vrai,' and never believed we were kwisha [finished]. One of the other boys has saved all the Paris cuttings and I'll bring them. . . . Evangeline Bruce, whom I telephoned, said they were in Berlin at the big conference, but no conference took place that morning, only speeches—informal—about you. . . . They are going to Sevilla and I'm sad that you will miss them. . . . Can you imagine how much nicer it is with you than without you?"

A call was waiting for me at the Dorchester Hotel. Rupert Bellville was in the country and urged me to join the weekend house party there. I did not know the host or hostess and declined the invitation.

"But Mary, dear, everybody is out of town. Everybody."

"Rupert, do you mean to say that seven million people are leaving London?"

"Oh no," said Rupert. "But everybody is leaving."

Apart from everybody I found my old friend Joy Milne from the early Chelsea days, also Jacquie Kennish from the old days at *Time* and her beautiful nine-year-old red-haired daughter, who ordered raw liver for her lunch, also Alan and Lucy Moorehead who elected to spend the four-day weekend in town.

"Alan was at a dinner in honor of S. Maugham at the Garrick Club when news of your crash came through," I wrote my husband, "says it was only at the end of the party when everybody including Maugham remembered that the dinner was in honor of him, not you. . . .

"Today, April 18th, Easter Sunday, I went for a drive in the country, found everything in bud despite the cold—remember how lovely birch trees are in early bud, the white bark shining? The British leave many bits of their small, precious woodland untouched and I saw a man at the far edge of a field with his dog and his gun. Wonderful looking grouse country only twenty miles from London."

Back in Paris, Pamela Churchill gave me tea that Tuesday in her sumptuous flat near the Seine, Loel and Gloria Guinness gave me dinner that night at Maxim's and Rupert picked me up with my luggage on Wednesday morning in his rattling little car, heading south.

Rupert, once-blond, six-foot-two and baby-shaped, had after prep school been packed off by his family to the southwest sherry-producing provinces of Spain, had moved into the intimate circles of the dons of the sherry business and for diversion had accumulated a knowledge of fighting bulls, their breeders, bullfighters and the lore of Spain's bullrings, probably unexcelled by any other Britisher. Back home he joined the peace-time R.A.F., earned its highest marks as pilot and in World War II served as a test pilot in the unglamorous job of taking up plane after plane as they came off the assembly lines somewhere in the north country. He had married a girl of good family who then produced a son whom Rupert had the audacity to name Hercules, after an Irish friend of his father, he told me, had been divorced and acquired a string of girlfriends throughout France and Spain, had drunk too much alcohol for too long and was now rather precariously astride "the wagon." Our current itinerary would give Rupert the chance to visit several of his girls, a circumstance which cheered us both.

But grinding down and wearing away my private

cheer with every turn of our wheels was Rupert's driving. Skillful he was, indubitably, and in total command of his small car. But, as I wrote Ernest bitterly, "He drives like a maniac, passes on the curves of these narrow roads, passes going up hills. . . . Rupert is not drinking, but this business of hurtling through space—really rough."

At Biarritz Rupert picked up a Bellville nephew, Jeremy, a handsome sweet-mannered young man who, I noticed later, sat rigidly tense in the back seat when Rupert drove and who, when Rupert let him drive, took us to our destinations just as quickly as his uncle without the nerve-wrenching. At Biarritz we made a rendezvous with Adamo, our chauffeur from Udine, whom Ernest had sent ahead with a Lancia full of luggage. Since he would be returning to Venice via Madrid, I offered to go with him on that lap, leaving more room for the Bellvilles. No, no, no, they insisted and off we rushed, and reached the Palace Hotel in Madrid—from Aranda de Duero—in time to settle in rooms, lunch at Púlpito, and reach the bullring for a *novillada*.

The next day Rupert and I set off, Jeremy having jumped ship, on a bizarre race around southwest Spain, our mutual purpose being to see as many *corridas* as possible, and Rupert's being to make reunions with as many as possible of his old friends.

I made a final effort to put some kind of bridle on Rupert's whimsical driving. I tried importuning, which slowed us down for perhaps five minutes. I tried reason, as we zoomed up a hill in the wrong lane. I tried derision, without success. So I reminded myself that my worrying would save us nothing and settled back to develop an immunity to my fears. Within a few days I was finding it almost exhilarating to whiz around trucks and buses into oncoming traffic, as if on a roller-coaster gone berserk. In that fortnight Rupert's little car sustained not so much as a pebble scratch.

After Córdoba our program began with the *feria* and three days of bullfights at Sevilla and continued in Jerez de la Frontera, Algeciras, Jerez again, Ronda, then eastward to Málaga and Granada and north to Madrid, every road winding through grain fields ablaze with poppies and mountain pastures like vast bouquets of wildflowers.

In Sevilla, the important families of the area—sherry producers, olive-and cattle-growers for generations—each year erect *casetas,* one- or two-room pavilions of wood skeletons, gaily panoplied in swaths of flowered silks, the whole displays standing on stilts two or three feet off the ground. There the families receive their friends for a glass of sherry, a biscuit perhaps, and exchange of news and compliments. Several of Rupert's friends had invited us to their *casetas* during the hour or two of promenade at the fairgrounds preceding midafternoon luncheon, and I discovered why the little houses were elevated. It was the ladies of Sevilla who made the promenade on horseback. Seated in gleaming side-saddles in black habits, black hats and face veils, with a single red carnation pinned to the back of their heads, they were the epitome of chic, and so were their long-legged horses. Since the *casetas* were raised above ground, Sevilla's horsed ladies were not obliged to undo the meticulous folds of their long skirts and dismount for their sherry and chatter.

At one of our stops, our host mentioned the day's beautiful sunrise.

"You mean to say you were up before sunrise?" I asked, incredulous.

"Certainly not, señora. I haven't yet gone to bed." I had forgotten that in the summer heat of Andalucía the Spanish upper classes still followed the custom of the Moors from five or six hundred years earlier, that of sleeping in the day's heat and reveling at night.

After the first day's bullfights, back at my hotel, Rupert and I met Juan Belmonte, a small dark saturnine man, one of Spain's and my heroes of the bullring, who had survived twenty years of bullfighting, whose wit was as sharp as the blades he had plunged into more than a thousand bulls, and who was said to have made one of my favorite replies to stupid questions:

"What exercise do you take to prepare yourself for bullfighting?"

"Exercise?" Belmonte repeated. "The bull weighs a ton and I weigh fifty kilograms. What exercise do you recommend?"

We drove country roads watching fighting bulls grazing. At Jerez we saw Antonio Ordóñez both outside the ring—cheerful, gay and pouring out questions about Ernest—and performing with singular style and grace, giving the crowd the full repertoire of classical movements, both with the cape and with the muleta, and at the end being hoisted to the shoulders of eager young men who carried him out of the ring in triumph.

We stopped a night and a morning in Granada so that I could explore all too quickly the Alhambra and the glorious gardens of the Generalife, then we raced through flowering fields to the Palace Hotel, Madrid, and an excited brouhaha of reunion with Ernest, with waiters bustling in with drinks and snacks and buckets of ice, questions spilling out, answers unheeded. I was entranced to be with my husband again, but his face showed new lines of weariness. He did not look or act as much improved as I had hoped.

After the usual tumultuous luncheon, with ten or twelve at table, we moved in caravan on May 15 to Madrid's larger of two bullrings for the opening bullfight of the fiesta of San Isidro, Madrid's patron saint. In cold rain we stood outside the doors in a growing crowd for fifteen minutes before it was announced that the fight was canceled. Ernest and I had a couple of hours in our room without visitors and, although we had written back and forth, I finally heard something of the conscienceless treatment he had suffered from the doctors in Venice, how he had been made to wait, stripped, on an icy table in the hospital's X-ray room half an hour before the technician arrived to take pictures, how some heavy-handed doctor bruised his bladder while making a kidney test, how nobody professed any interest in prescribing a regimen to reduce his blood pressure which was 180 over 120. But Federico Kechler had kindly stayed with him through all the rough time at the hospital, a prop for his morale. He had wired me at Sevilla that his liver, internal injuries and spine were

503

all curing, but that had been less fact than morale-booster for me.

As we reached our door that afternoon we found a folded newspaper lying in front of it. On it, our next door neighbor, the genius Dali, had drawn bulls, picadors and capes, using the black letters of headlines as parts of his design, with a written phrase, "Welcome to San Isidro"—a treasure. I sent appropriate thanks, wrapped the prize in tissue paper and buried it in a bag beneath my best dresses where it voyaged to Cuba. (The Finca Vigía's household servants worked several days when we arrived in late June to unpack and put where they belonged the contents of our eighty-seven pieces of luggage—we had been away from home thirteen months, Ernest had acquired in Venice a plaid and leather bag seven feet long to hold his *m'zee* spears and we bought extra bags for sea shells, guns, more books, a few African animals' skins. One day I noticed that my best dresses had been hung up and ran to the pantry asking what happened to the newspapers rolled in tissue paper beneath my dresses. Lola, the housemaid, said she had thrown away the bundle. "I thought you put it there by mistake." I raged, I wept. We went out to the hillside where Pichilo, the head gardener, burned the flammable refuse. It was a day without rain. Dali's witty gift, which I had planned to frame and hang in a place of honor in the house, was ashes.)

At the rest of the San Isidro bullfights we all clung to the *barrera* in front of us, encouraging the cuadrillas, cajoling, warning, deploring, as though we knew as much about the strange sport-art as Ernest and Rupert, but none of the performances was exceptionally good. One evening Ernest and I went to dine with Victor and Maria Urrutia in their elegant flat in the Castellana. Ernest wanted to give some small for-old-time's-sake present to Maria, who had been such a pleasant shipboard companion twenty years earlier. His expression turned thoughtful as he looked at their library, their pictures, their porcelains. Then he smiled and asked if she could use a lion skin anywhere among their treasures. She could, and a few months later we sent one to them.

504

Ava Gardner was in a local clinic run by nuns, suffering terribly, trying to pass a gallstone, with minimum pain-relievers permitted by the doctors and maximum prayers offered by the nuns. Urged by her admirer, Luis Miguel Dominguín, Spain's supreme matador, we went to visit her in the small bare austere room at the clinic, and privately I cursed the Spanish medical profession with its dogma that pain helps the body cure itself. (They gave bullfighters none or minimum pain-relievers, no matter how gravely wounded, in the conviction that the drugs would retard their nervous reactions to danger when again they were in action.) Even in her misery, Ava looked lovely, and somehow tranquil—no knit brows, no puckered mouth.

A few days later she had passed the stone and joined us at a *tienta,* a testing of bull calves, at the ranch of one of Luis Miguel's friends near El Escorial. Miguel's latest wound, acquired in Latin America, was still a wide red trough running down the back of one leg from hip to calf. Partly because of the ineptitude of the local doctors, the wound had been a long time healing, and so our matador friend was testing his own reflexes and muscles, as well as the youngster bulls. While the genes of the stud bull determine the child's bone and muscle structure, it is from his mother that the animal inherits courage and the combative instinct, Luis Miguel told me.

In frisky May sunshine we watched Luis Miguel, smooth and as apparently effortless as a deep-flowing river, move interested young beasts around one side of himself and then the other side, his red muleta urging them and coercing them. Then he took Ava into the middle of the little ring to make a few passes with him. She may have been impelled to step back from an onrushing calf, but she kept her feet as solidly planted as were Miguel's. A happy morning, especially because Luis Miguel proved to himself that he could again be agile and graceful in the ring.

On June 6, with a handful of photographers clicking away in the rain, we went aboard the *Francesco Morosini* at Genoa, to settle into two separate cabins

—since Ernest was still staying awake to read half the night, and the best cabins were very small—for what turned out to be the only ocean crossing I ever made that seemed more dull than shiny. At Naples Ernest lazed at a table in the Galleria talking to reporters while I buzzed out to Pompeii to marvel at its brilliantly designed water supply system, at the comfortably declined floor of the dining room in the Vetti brothers' house, so that reclining on their couches while dining they could enjoy the spaces and flowers of their patio, and at the "forbidden" room with its carved male figures with penises as big as modern kitchen water faucets. The murals in the room showing three different positions of love-making were disillusioning. The expressions on the faces of the women were pleasant, but not eager, excited, desperate, yearning, nor even contentedly satisfied.

As we plowed through moderate seas toward Funchal in the Madeira Islands, I finally took note of the ship. There were fifteen passengers in first class, pleasant, but none stimulating. The captain, Ruggiero, did all he could to make us comfortable, and talked well of tides, currents and navigation, his only other subject being the joys of copulation and his triumphs thereabouts. An Italian man and his Brazilian wife who had lived for years in the East Indies played bridge every night with the purser and a young man from Rome. A young Mexican boy was falling in love with a chubby Venezuelan girl whose parents watchdogged her from breakfast until bedtime. In the dining salon they showed an ancient Italian movie almost every night.

Perhaps because of boredom Ernest nagged me at lunch one day because I had failed to get repaired in Paris a pocketknife he had entrusted to me for that purpose. Because of the Easter weekend moratorium on repair work, the Paris knife people had been unable to do the job, had returned the knife to me, and I had packed it away, but where among our eighty-seven pieces of luggage I couldn't remember. A tide of fury engulfed my husband at my memory failure, and he yelled, "You thief," instantly creating a hush in the small dining room. Perhaps I should have stood up

506

and addressed the company, explaining that I had not stolen his pocketknife but only mislaid it. Instead I finished my coffee quietly. That afternoon I wrote him a note: "Dear Big Kitten—Your books, *Green Hills* and *Death in the Afternoon* show that you used to understand justice and that other people also had feelings and truthfulness. . . . I hope for your sake especially, and for all us friends and lovers of yours that you have not completely lost those qualities."

At Funchal where the ship had stopped forty times in its voyages and he had never gone ashore, Ruggiero this time decided to look at the town. He took me in a car to a café where we sipped sweet Madeira wine, then to the chapel on the mountaintop where Carlos I, last Emperor of Austria, is buried, his life much less violent comic-opera than those of his granddads, his uncles, and his cousins and his aunts. What I had not noticed during earlier visits were the porcelain plaques of Saint Fátima with her sweet, young face and elegant blue and white dress. Down the mountain we skidded in the basket sled, the runners being wood, not steel as I had earlier recorded, to the fish market where we found big fresh 60- to 70-pound tuna and also bright-eyed fresh dorado. Back on the *Francesco Morosini,* the captain decided to send for some fish, and that evening the chef did well by them.

From Gregorio Fuentes, *Pilar*'s mate, we had heard for years of the glories of Tenerife in the Canary Islands, his homeland. After the orange-roofed good cheer of Funchal and the clean Portuguese-governed islands of Madeira we expected something maybe not cleaner, but more dramatic. Ashore at Tenerife we walked through hodgepodge of undistinguished architecture to Gregorio's prided market and found it dirty and crowded, fruits, vegetables and fish looking old and tired and poorly displayed, too many flies and a prevalence of skin diseases among the market vendors. Jacaranda trees, flowering lavender against the blue sky, and waves of bougainvillaea and hibiscus along the principal boulevard of the town gave us some consolation.

At the wharf in the arbor of Havana, old friends'

smiles welcomed us. Somebody had thoughtfully hired a small truck to take home most of our mountain of luggage. Evelio (Kid Tunero) Mustelier, Cuba's famous middleweight champion, and his wife, Yolette, had left the house, which we had lent them, shining clean and ordered, and on the front steps our sweet friend and butler, René Villarreal, greeted us with his smile and a banner: WELCOME. After thirteen months of living from suitcases, I sang praises to being home, and thanks for closets where clothes could be left tranquil without disturbance. But René and I had scarcely unpacked before bad news came from my parents in Gulfport. Again my father was in serious pain—he had long been refusing to take the medicines which would control his cancer of the prostate gland—and my mother was too tired, too discouraged and too weak to look after him and the house. I must come at once.

19

Problems and the Nobel Prize

I WANTED TO perk up the servants and the gardeners and speed up our house-running machinery. Yolette had been a bit too indulgent with them. Both around the house and at the pool the shrubs and vines needed pruning, which should be supervised by me. A score of minor repair jobs needed attention from Cecilio, the carpenter, with help from me. I wanted to loll naked and swim in the cool privacy of our pool, and to deck the house with flowers in my exuberant arrangements, to go fishing as soon as Ernest's back permitted, to savor our big airy spaces after the confinement of the ship, and, working in my own big bright kitchen, to dress up our menus with a few new recipes I'd learned.

With a board under our mattress and a big hardcover book beneath the cushion of his chair Ernest was feeling better and his sense of humor reviving. On July 11, a Sunday, I noted in my diary: "Papa, waking from nap—'Oh, I'se just a depleted area . . . I'se a insalubrious project. People say I don't know any words. I'se a good-humor man. The good-humor man will get you if you don't watch out. My motto is My Dog Was My Garden. I favor the return of the aborigines.'" I wanted more of such cheerful nonsense.

Instead I repacked, hopped a plane to New Orleans and bussed on to Gulfport.

In a heat wave of spectacular intensity my parents were struggling to keep alive in their once-happy little house. They had not told me, but before we reached Cuba my father had again checked into the Gulfport hospital, suffering from extreme uremia. Since he refused to take the streptomycin, penicillin and other drugs the doctors prescribed to ameliorate, if not cure, the uremia, the hospital had reopened a drainage system and sent him home. He had reached there only a few hours before I arrived and, as I wrote Ernest, was stretched out on the sofa in the sitting room, a true subject for El Greco, "the long bony fingers extended on the sheet, the sharp, bright eyes focused in the distance, the inattention to immediate concerns, the saint-like acceptance of ministrations.

"He lies flat on his back, the fine forehead and long Celtic nose in outline against the pillows like the bronze figures of dead knights at Salisbury Cathedral or the Escorial or Burgos; and beneath the sheets, attached to one leg is one of those rubber sacks, something like what the RAF used to wear, with a tube leading to it from his abdomen. It has to be emptied frequently. . . . He says he has no pain. . . . He has put his faith in another Christian Science practitioner. 'She will save me.' . . . Last night at 11:00 I emptied the rubber bladder. At 12:30 he called, wanted water. At 4:00 a.m. called, wanted the substitute bladder emptied. At 5:30 called, wanted blanket and juice and extra light turned on. Mother, who has been wonderful and nearly dauntless, took over in the morning and I slept from six until nine in the airless bedroom, but tonight I have my cot on the back porch."

Ernest answered me with sympathy and love, saying, "Honestly Kittner, he should go to the hospital. Cost means nothing. He can have what I have. But he is going to die and he should die with some dignity and some regard for other people."

On the telephone we agreed that I should find a nursing home for them, and after a brief search I found a good place, a big high-ceilinged airy old house set far back in a lawn overlooking the highway that runs along the Gulf Coast, with the Gulf of Mexico shimmering in the distance. The nursing home and its appointments were sparkling clean, the menus varied, the meals served either on pretty trays in the rooms or at the dining table which seated twelve guests. The rates were higher than I had anticipated. On the telephone Ernest hesitated not a moment.

"Go ahead and book them in," said he. "Do whatever you want with their stuff, and stay as long as you have to. Not too long. All us cotsies miss you." The next morning, July 15, he wrote another letter.

"I pity your poor father so much and dying is such a worthless business. . . . It was so sad about him not wanting his books. . . . For a long time I was bothered by the sudden flash and tearing of you apart of the big shell or oversize mortar burst. A big cotsie if he decided to come instead of go could make quite a thing if you hitted him wrong. But all these things are interesting at least and your poor father's isn't anything but awful. . . . My poor kitten. Please believe I understand and I feel so sorry for you in the heat and the loneliness. . . .

"Unlike the others I suggest you drink all you want and cushion it as much as you can with that. We can sweat the alcohol out afterwards and you will get in lovely shape with the pool and the ocean. We haven't

510

even had the ocean yet. . . . The pool is clear as Gordon's Gin and always cool. . . .

"Kittner we had such a lovely time in Africa and you remember the noises of the beasts in the night and how we would sleep in the tiny cot quite comfortably and really love each other . . . and the lovely days and how well we hunted together and how much fun it was when we would go partners on the meat animals. Remember the mountain in the moonlight and the early mornings and all our lovely life and times. With our Academy money [The American Academy of Arts and Letters had in May bestowed on him its Award of Merit, with some money attached] we'll get you a beautiful gun that really fits and cannot miss. I always thought the eccentricities of your 6.5 [the Mannlicher-Schoenauer lent by Philip Percival] were from being long-stocked. Also it was held together with Scotch tape. But I shooted a lion with it and so did you. Every night I look at the picture of you and your oryx and am so happy and proud of you. . . ."

From the moment of my arrival, my father affirmed to my chagrin, he had felt better, his pain had eased, his nerves eased, his appetite quickened, and my mother echoed him, smiling. Reasonably or not the sweet phrases tightened the sense of guilt with which they were unintentionally enmeshing me. I felt that they felt without saying so that I had neglected them, that I should somehow have managed to make a household for them near or with us in Cuba, that I should be more frequently, or constantly, on hand as aide, handmaiden, housekeeper, cook and companion. Since in Paris in 1944 he had undertaken responsibility for my parents' financial support, Ernest had never murmured questions or objections to their generally modest requirements. Year after year I considered the feasibility of moving them to Cuba, each time rejecting it as subjecting them either to cruel loneliness among aliens whose language they would never learn, or imposing them on our life at the Finca Vigía into which they could never fit without attempts at impossible adjustments by all of us. I was, in my view, generally happily and successfully working for

Ernest, and I could not also work steadily for them.

Still the sense of guilt shadowed me. It was not until several years later that I gradually learned from friends that they also had suffered the same doubts, tribulations and the feelings of guilt while they looked after parents or a parent in some place comfortable but removed an hour or a day from their own households. There must have been a sensible solution to such *en famille* problems, but I didn't know it.

The people who ran the nursing home welcomed my parents with gentle kindness, and I helped them settle, unpacking my mother's fresh cotton frocks and housecoats and my father's small wardrobe and his typewriter. They were both pleased with a bouquet of flowers I'd sent. The other guests, all ladies (except for one widower) who had doubtless once been southern belles, looked pleasant and covertly curious. If he had been feeling better, my father would surely have flirted with them. Discreetly, of course.

I gave the town library my father's books, sold a few pieces of their furniture and gave away most of it, and hurried back to Cuba where Ernest was waiting, a daiquiri in hand, at the airport. The next day, July 21, was Ernest's birthday and we went into town early, so that he could accept a unique birthday present, the beautiful gold and enamel medal of the Order of Carlos Manuel de Céspedes, Cuba's highest award for civilians.

Batista's government had wanted to hold the award ceremony at the Presidential Palace, but my husband, never wishing to appear to support the dictatorship, had politely vetoed the idea. The compromise site was our little yacht club on the bay. An undersecretary of state made a pleasant, not-too-pretentious speech with a dozen of our best friends standing in the bar. In his short acceptance speech, Ernest mentioned his admiration for the Cuban *pueblo*—the common people—and his best wishes for their welfare. Afterward we celebrated with a big boisterous lunch at the Floridita.

Partly to compensate me for the bad days and nights at Gulfport Ernest waived his rule of avoiding the festivities of Havana's Anglo-American colony and, dressed in our best, we went to a dinner party at the house of Harry and Greta Scott, the Canadian ambassador and his wife. It turned out to be an evening of spirited reunions with friends we hadn't seen for more than a year.

Accepting an invitation for a few nights later, I went alone with Juan, the chauffeur, to a party given by the British ambassador, Adrian Holman, and his wife Betty in their spacious old house overlooking the undulating green of the Biltmore golf course. Again I had happy reunions with friends of Havana, but my wagging tongue provoked the silliest contretemps of that year or any other. Discussing Africa with a man named Scott, a New Zealander who was then a columnist for the Havana *Post,* the local English-language paper, I mentioned that we had eaten the loins of the lions we'd killed and how good that meat was. Mr. Scott was visibly shocked.

"Barbaric. A barbaric thing to do."

"The meat is clean as a whistle."

"Barbarous. I can't imagine a civilized person eating lion."

"It tastes like veal. It's white when it's cooked."

"I can't imagine any Briton eating lion."

"They don't have wild lions in Great Britain, as you know."

"I mean members of the British Commonwealth."

"Our friends in Kenya ate it. But, of course, they're colonials." (I'd been reading some sociologist, probably my hero, Marston Bates.) "You know what the sociologists say, that colonies import material things from the mother countries and physical habits but only the cruder mores and baser philosophies."

I thought it was a joke, but Mr. Scott looked about to explode. I moved away.

A few days later Mr. Scott's column in the Havana *Post* expressed dismay, disillusion, disapproval and disappointment either about my eating lion or my cavalier attitude toward colonials, or perhaps it was both. Ernest was irritated by the column until I murmured such words as "childish" and "tempest in a thimble."

Still later, Mr. Scott returned to his disenchantments and in his column discredited me, repeating his displeasure and distaste and in a miracle of reversals

513

both blamed Ernest for my faulty behavior and suggested that either he defend my honor with the sword or lose his own good name, for appearing to agree with me. Something like that. (It was the best possible season for anyone with grudges to challenge Ernest, with all his injuries, to any sort of combat.)

After the publication of the first column Ernest wrote Mr. Scott an instructive little essay on the edibility of wild animals, both African and North American, adding, "I looked with very little favor on your attempting to make her speak badly of all of our friends in Kenya and other colonies because she hurt your feelings. . . . The piece, it is my duty to tell you, read quite screwy. In the first place I do not fight at Diplomatic parties, no matter what the provocation. I dislike very much being pulled in on a controversy at which I was not present. But don't write columns about what you would have done to me if I had been present and if I had said something I did not say. That is very many ifs. . . ."

Later he wrote: "For the second time in a month you have written dirtily, snidely, and insulting about my wife. . . . If you want to make a name for yourself, finally, and not reread your yellowing clippings, this is the best time of your life to get a decision over me. You'll be able to get a job anywhere. All my good friends in the newspaper business will write you up as you deserve. . . . At present I have one smashed vertebra. . . . Two others are pressed quite tightly together and hamper my movements somewhat. . . .

"If you are going to give people pokes in the mouth, as you have now written twice, I suggest you buy a child's baseball bat and saw it off. . . ."

With fisticuffs vetoed by Ernest in his sensible restraint, Mr. Scott enlisted the assistance of the husband of Mrs. Clara Park Pessino, the Havana *Post*'s owner. Dr. Pedro Pessino, a radiologist, came to call at the Finca in his capacity as a second for Mr. Scott to present a formal challenge to Ernest to a duel. A small, solemn man, he listened carefully while Ernest explained that he would make no apologies on my behalf and that he did not consider Mr. Scott a suitable opponent for a duel.

514

In a letter to Dr. Pessino he said: "I am not a publicity seeker and I will not be provoked into something which can only lead to the worst form of publicity.

"Aside from other considerations my obligation at this time is to continue my writing and regain my health. . . . If any friends of Mr. Scott consider that to be an act of cowardice they are at liberty to think so. . . ."

Ernest was beginning to write again in the mornings, standing up to the little portable typewriter on top of the bookcase beside his bed, and he did not allow the Scott nuisance to deter either his work or his health rehabilitation. The first time we went fishing my throat tightened while my husband slowly, determinedly let himself over *Pilar*'s side into her cockpit. Although the day was warm, he wore a safari jacket in the breeze of the Gulf Stream instead of going topless, as was his custom. Whatever we caught was of no great importance or great strain and for once I was thankful for little success. That evening Ernest read peacefully in his chair. It had been a day of true triumph.

Life at the Finca was regaining its customary momentum. Ava Gardner came to town, came to lunch at home with us, came fishing with us on a happy day, Ernest moving about the boat with noticeably greater ease and Gregorio sloshing pails of sea water onto our nymph, approval bursting from his eyes. We took her to dine at the Floridita where Ernest's old nodding acquaintances, rich, paunchy sugar-growers, politicians and simple men of business, became instant intimates enchanted to meet the señorita, even inviting themselves to join us for coffee or a liqueur. Ava was politely, picturesquely not interested in them.

Luis Miguel Domínguín appeared and slept a few mornings in our Little House, having prowled Havana each night until dawn with Juan chauffeuring, impressing even Juan, who considered himself a knowledgeable man about town. "Señora, he knew places I never even heard of. And such beautiful girls. So friendly."

Our friend Willie Hale, head of the Kenya Game Department, wrote that he had deposited Ernest's guns in the bank, where they would be safe from thieves, and asked us to send fees we owed for animals we killed in Masai-controlled areas, which included Kimana Swamp, and Ernest sent him a list:

 2 lions at 20 shillings each
 2 oryx beisa callotis at 15 shillings each
 1 leopard at 20 shillings
 1 buffalo at 15 shillings
 2 Grant's gazelle at 20 shillings
 1 Lesser Kudu at 10 shillings
 6 Wildebeest at 5 shillings
 8 Common (Granti) zebra at 5 shillings
11 Thomson's gazelle at 5 shillings
 2 Gerenuk at 10 shillings
 7 Impala at 5 shillings
 3 Coke's Hartebeest at 5 shillings

"I am very sorry that the two crashes kept me from tidying up properly at the end," Ernest wrote. "It turned out when the x-ray people got to work that the skull injury was quite a bad one. . . . [But] All this is clearing up very well and I hope to be back and at your orders if I can be of any use to you some time in 1955."

Anticipating forgotten debts or future presents we might wish to make, I had retained my checking account at a Nairobi bank and sent my check for 410 shillings. The East African shilling was then valued at about seven to the U.S. dollar. We were paying $58.57 for having killed fifty-one animals, including some shot by Patrick and Bill Lowe, of *Look* magazine. Nobody valued their lives very highly, I thought, as I wrote the check; but we had not consulted the animals.

My parents' letters were good-tempered. My father wrote: "I need not tell you of the wonders of this home. . . . Mother needs and enjoys it as much as I do."

"Tom is more interested in things in general," my mother wrote. "He walks all around the house."

Ernest was working contentedly mornings on his memories of Africa and their elaborations, and we were lavishing afternoons on frivolities. Of the thousands of shells I had collected, I took a couple dozen of my shiniest, whitest bivalves—cancellate semeles, cross-hatched lucinas and granular poromyas as I identified them—to a fashionable jeweler in Havana, who made me a golden fishnet necklace holding them.

My parents were turning restless again and nipping at the proprietors of the nursing home to lower their rent in the disarrayed assumption that they would be doing Ernest a favor. I learned about it in a short restrained note from Mr. Schustedt and promptly wrote my parents with unusual severity: ". . . Ernest does not wish you to make any effort of any sort to get the fees at that Rest Home reduced. He does not want you to cause bad feeling between you and the Schustedts. . . . The rate we are paying is not excessive for what you are getting—a big, comfortable room, private bath, good food, electricity, telephone, laundry and complete service. . . . Since Ernest is willing to pay for this, you should be willing to let him do so and not make trouble. . . . If Ernest thinks you are scheming to get away or making trouble there, it is that much more difficult for me here. . . ."

At lunch one day in early October, our dear little Negrita on the floor beside me made a frightened yelp and slumped sideways. I held her in my lap there on the red-tiled floor for an hour before her heart felt steadier and I moved her to a towel-padded box beside my desk. I nursed her devotedly and Ernest paid her a dozen loving, encouraging visits, but a few nights later her heart stopped.

I had finished and sent off to William Nichols at *This Week* the second of two short "inspirational" pieces I had promised him for his series "Words to Live By." The first one had been a quick toboggan ride. I had remembered Ole Helgerson, friend of my father and of my childhood, and engineer on *Northland,* my father's stern-wheeler. "Never worry. If it is something that you can fix, fix it. If it is something impossible to fix, all your worrying won't help it."

The small Bible my parents had given me some thirty years before in Bemidji, Minnesota, provided an idea for the other miniature sermon. On its flyleaf I had noted First Corinthians, Chapter 13—"Charity suffereth long, and is kind; charity envieth not; charity vaunteth not itself, is not puffed up"—and based my

517

homily on that, much aware that I frequently failed to practice what I was recommending.

These tiny pluses were smaller than eggplant seeds compared to the big illustrious bundle of satisfaction some of our friends were murmuring Ernest might receive. There were special requests from his publishers in Sweden. Harvey Breit wrote from New York a prediction which my husband showed me. "Let's wait and see," said I. Lee Samuels, who was again coming out to the Finca with armloads of books for Ernest to sign amid rounds of levity and lunch or supper, had heard rumors in New York. "They must figure it's now or never," Ernest said, his voice cold. I couldn't remember his having deplored the award to William Faulkner five years earlier. But now he sounded uninterested.

While I was sleeping late on the morning of October 28, Ernest, who slid away about dawn, came softly to my bedroom and tapped my arm. "My kitten, my kitten, I've got that thing. Maybe you better get up." A soft, happy voice. A hesitant smile.

"Huh?"

"You know. The Swedish thing."

"Hell's bells. You mean the Prize, the Nobel Prize?" I was all over him clinging and hugging and smooching.

"The U.P. rang."

"Hey, lamb. Hooray. May I be the first to congratulate you?" More kisses. Hospitality chores running through my head.

"U.P. was first."

"Well damn them, and thank them. We've got to get going."

"Somebody may be coming out."

"Sure, sure, sure. Coffee first. I'll get lots of stuff laid on." I was jumping into shorts and a shirt. Somehow I had overlooked the possibilities of our giving a flash-flood party. But my crew in the kitchen could move fast and suavely. Warned by René, Sonia was already brewing two big pots of coffee, the "black goats" on the back of the stove. Fico, René's helper, was polishing silver trays in the pantry and said the news of the Prize had just been repeated on the ser-

518

vants' radio there. The old-fashioned wall telephone in the pantry began ringing. The three U.S. wire services, correspondents from Stockholm papers in New York, and several of Havana's afternoon newspapers wanted to come out for interviews, and so did still and movie photographers and U.S. and Cuban TV people (and friendly spongers).

In a rather long citation, they told us, the Swedish Academy had called Ernest "a pioneer who started a new technique of fiction . . . and *The Old Man and the Sea* a true masterpiece." Later somebody brought out the full text.

The standard Cuban breakfast of those days was a cup of strong black coffee laced with hot milk and perhaps a piece of Cuban bread, a foam of arrested air and flavor entirely surrounded by crisp but fragile crust. But I thought we must not on this day appear to be skimpy. So we arranged platters of the makings of *bocaditos*—mouthfuls—of Spanish and English ham, cheeses and sliced fresh pineapple, onions, and opened a few bottles of Spanish wine, the red well-rounded, light Marqués de Riscal. No other month of October had brought us such tiresome weather as that one of 1954. Hurricanes with their harsh winds had loitered for weeks, moving east from the Gulf of Mexico or westward from the Caribbean, flooding Havana and washing away the seeds of our vegetable garden. The terrible hurricane Hazel head wrecked much of Haiti, the Carolinas and Toronto. But this day was calm and dry, with sunshine seeping through the open windows.

All over the house, on the broad front steps and outside on the terraces Ernest spent hours talking to one or more of the press, we had a dozen people for lunch, and at about three o'clock in the afternoon he settled in the crowded sitting room to say into a microphone for local consumption a wry little speech he had scrawled, with scant attention to grammar, in pencil that morning. "*Señoras y Señores (Dar las gracias,* etc.)," he had written. Then, in my translation: "As you know there are many Cubas. But like Gaul it can be divided in three parts. Those who have hunger, those who endure and those who eat too much. After this *suburbio* [bourgeois] luncheon we are all in the third category, at least for the moment.

"I am a man without politics. This is a great defect but it is preferable to arteriosclerosis. With this defect of being apolitical, one can appreciate the problems of the Palmolivero [the fellow who sniffs canned heat] and the triumphs of my friend Alfonsito Gomez Mena. I was friend of Manolo Guas who was the uncle of Felo Guas and also the friend of Manolo Castro [gamblers].

"I like the [fighting] cocks and the Philharmonic Orchestra. I was a friend of Emilio Lorents and this has not hurt my friendship with Mayito Menocal who with Elicio Argüelles are my best friends in this country. God grant that it is not a mortal sin to consider Antonio Maceo a better general than Bernard Law Montgomery and to hope for the death of Trujillo, that he dies in his bed, naturally. [He] is the only person whom I would like to see finished before I finish.

"Now excuse some jokes and a legitimate admonition which follows and which one sees every morning in the mirror. Lacking are those types by which one can see the good which is humanity and those who manage to eat their failures.

"So, these are many words. I don't wish to abuse the word and let us now go to acts. I wish to give this Swedish medal to Our Señora the Virgen de Cobre. . . ."

He added a few unwritten quips to the effect that the prize money ($35,000) had not yet arrived, so there was no point in anybody's breaking into the house to hunt for it, that he wished he could share it with his friends (panhandlers) in the streets of Havana, especially outside the Floridita, but that he must pay off debts with it, unfortunately. We had already been burgled enough times for one house. In any case, the money would not be in the house but in the bank.

He told the local press that day that he doubted that he would be able to go to Stockholm to accept the prize in person. He did not think his injured spine could sustain the journey without further damage. He also named three other writers who he thought, with possible false modesty, deserved the prize as much or more than he—Carl Sandburg for his six-volume biography of Lincoln, Isak Dinesen, and Bernard Berenson. By six o'clock I could no longer graciously endure the tumult and so slipped away, down to the pool to swim thirty laps in lovely silence punctuated only by bird murmurings and the distant grunts of lorries chuffing up the hill.

Somebody snapped, and later distributed, an unfriendly photo of me sneaking into the house in my scruffy terrycloth bathrobe, but the crowds departed soon after that and when, having dressed, I went out to the sitting room, Ernest was sitting tranquilly in his chair, reading telegrams and sipping a gin with coconut water, René softly removing the dining room debris.

"I have a two-minute performance to do," said I, kissing my exhausted husband on his nose, and began singing the old Gershwin song, "Somebody loves me, I wonder who. . . ." Gliding, arms and legs swinging around our grass carpet, I danced a parody, singing . . .

Somebody loves you
I wonder who,
I wonder who it can be;
Somebody loves you
I wonder who . . .
The Swede Academy . . .

I collapsed in his lap. It had been a tough day.

"I hope I didn't talk too corny to Harvey." Harvey Breit had telephoned for an interview for *The New York Times*, and I had stood beside him in the pantry listening to his replies—"To write as truly as one can . . . To invent out of what he knows . . . something which will be entirely new . . . something which will become part of the experience of those who read him. . . ."

"I heard you," I said, removing myself from his knees. "That was perfectly good, straight stuff."

"I hate that stuff. Like Bible-thumping."

"Honey, you couldn't clown around on this one. Poor form. Impudent."

"A whole day gone from my life."

"Oh, stop griping. You should complain. Your Day of the Annunciation, with the U.P. performing as the Angel Gabriel."

We were both ill-tempered because we were exhausted. We were not accustomed to so many hours with so many people, especially at the Finca.

"I don't feel pregnant," Ernest said.

The next day, the Swedish consul in Havana, Per Gunnar Vilhelm Aurell, and his pretty wife came out to lunch, together with a couple of the Swedish journalists who had come down from New York, and we stood about in the library while Mr. Aurell made a small, simple speech formally telling us the news we already knew. Ernest was the forty-seventh winner of the Award for Literature, he said. Alfred Bernhard Nobel, the Swedish chemist who invented dynamite and therefrom amassed a fortune, had directed in his will that the prizes be given for achievements in the sciences, literature and peace. He had died in San Remo, Italy, in 1896, and his executors working with Swedish authorities had begun to give his generous cash awards in 1901.

We moved to the sitting room for martinis before lunch and over them, with unabashed candor, my husband murmured that the Swedish Academy perhaps had decided to make the award now, mindful of our two aircraft mishaps, before he ran into further misfortunes, when it might be too late. Merry laughter. Then discussions of his professional concern with violence, which was mentioned in the official citation. I ran to get his preface to *Men at War* and quoted from it, and we arrived at loose agreement that Ernest's books implied a disapproval of war, if only in a backhand manner.

Since Cuba was a Catholic country, we ate only fish on Fridays. Our luncheon that day began with shrimp in the Hawaiian manner with a spicy sauce which Ernest's sister Ura had taught me, and went on to roast swordfish and vegetables and finished with cake and fresh pineapple and lingonberries from Sweden, the lot accompanied by champagne with bonhomie rising like mist from the table. After we bid our guests *adiós* at the front steps, I counted the empty wine bottles on the floor of the pantry. Eight bottles were there. We had been eight at table, from 2:30 p.m. until six o'clock. We worked steadily for more than a week, tapping out thanks letters to friends everywhere who had written Ernest congratulations. But we failed to acknowledge half the messages.

Naively Ernest and I had assumed that the few days of entertaining and brouhaha at the end of October would terminate the attentions from outsiders initiated by the Nobel Prize award. We were mistaken. Although a sign on our big gate at the entrance to the Finca said in definitive Spanish, UNINVITED VISITORS WILL NOT BE RECEIVED, limousine drivers from Havana's then best hotel, the Nacional, somehow persuaded René's mother that their carloads of tourists were invited friends, and she unlocked the gate for them. If I was working in my room, I might see the unfamiliar faces, race down the front steps and persuade the intruders to leave without disturbing Ernest. Too frequently the sightseers were out of their cars and ringing the big old bell at the front door, interrupting Ernest's work or destroying it for the day before I could intercept them.

With minimum advance notice, a journalist and photographer appeared, having flown from Stockholm, and because of such bravura felt entitled to a share of Ernest's time. Time—hours, days—which had been awarded us, a special dividend after the two aircraft crashes in Africa, was the most precious of the attributes of our lives, we felt, and should be used with the best discretion we could manage. But Ernest gave eight hours of his time, that November, to the Swedish journalists.

Ernest decided that we must escape further invasions of the Finca with a week or two incommunicado aboard *Pilar* at Paraíso. He sent Gregorio ahead in *Pilar* and, Felípe being otherwise occupied, a new young man, Oscar, accompanied him in the *Tin Kid*. In my little yellow Plymouth convertible we drove to La Mulata along the high coast road skirting the sea, and lunched under a tree overlooking the enormous deep-blue bay of Bahía Honda. Gregorio was waiting for us at the fishing village and we were unpacked and settled aboard the boat before dark and Ernest was asleep by eight-thirty. He described our holiday in a letter to Bob Manning of *Time:* ". . . there was one heavy Northwester after another. But we lay in a well-sheltered anchorage and went to bed at dark and heard the surf on the reef. It was cold enough for two blankets and a sweater. Gregorio was cooking wonderfully and we got young Green Turtle and African Pompano and brought back plenty so the deep freeze is full."

I couldn't be so condensed after more than a year's absence from our favorite anchorage. I drew a sketch for my parents of the island with its coconut palms and casuarina pines and thatched fishermen's huts, the sun beaming above La Mulata Mountain to the south, white horses dancing on the reefs to the north, Ernest stretched out on his bed reading *The Eddie Chapman Story,* I sitting on the stern with the writing board, the *Tin Kid* bobbing astern of us and two anchors hitched to our bows.

When Gregorio and I fished the coral heads toward Levisa Island to the west we found the water wonderfully clear navy blue, bright electric blue and green above the brown and gilded reefs, the bigger waves throwing white plumes a dozen feet into the sky. "A couple of boats with outriggers are anchored in the bay," I noted. "But this is the weekend. Nothing else has changed. The children's voices shouting in the distance are the same, the same dogs' barks. At night we have only the wind and the buzz of my cigarette end as it hits the water."

Since the first couple of nights of going to bed at dusk, we were reading in the evenings by the strong white light of our new air-pumped gas lamp, the light blazing through little knitted white sacks, and we were also adventuring into a new indulgence, listening to radio broadcasts from New Orleans (WWL) or Miami. In the comparatively cold weather, the strong light lured no mosquitoes. In the full moonlight of early mornings we had Orion and Sirius glimmering and Venus blazing huge in the eastern sky.

On Thursday, December 9, I wrote: "Papa and Gregorio went to La Mulata to meet Juan, bringing

524

supplies, mail and periodicals including *Time* with Papa on the cover. . . . Bob Manning's story is very friendly, pleasant and accurate and Papa in the interview did a good deed for Ezra Pound, suggesting this is a good year to release poets and that they should let Ezra go back to Italy where he is appreciated. Manning mentioned that I am 46, so I've decided not to equivocate about it any more. One more conceit overboard . . . Good news from Scribner's. They found Papa's lost Warner Company stocks, worth about $10,000."

On Saturday, December 11, I wrote: "Last night we listened to reports of the Nobel Prize proceedings in Stockholm, our reception poor and wavering, but we caught some phrases." The U.S. ambassador in Stockholm had read the short speech Ernest sent to the ceremonies. ". . . I wish to thank the administrators of the generosity of Alfred Nobel for this prize. No writer who knows the great writers who did not receive the prize can accept it other than with humility. . . . [The writer] should always try for something that has never been done or that others have tried and failed. Then sometimes, with great luck, he will succeed."

20

Bad News

FROM KIMANA SWAMP, Kenya, in January 1955, Denis Zaphiro wrote with nostalgia: "How strange that you and Ernest want quietness all to yourselves and I, who have more of it than I need, brood at night for the sound of people laughing, for music

525

and the charm of inconsequential small-talk. At the moment life seems to be drifting past me with the strains of gaiety in the distance while I move through the bush dreaming of wallowing rapturously in sin and inventing joys which would make Dorian Gray look like a schoolboy. . . . Remembrance makes a bad bed-mate. . . . The elephant skull and the dried out Christmas tree are symbols of my dejection. . . . I can still see you dancing in the carpet of white flowers, whirling round and round while Papa looked on with an enigmatic smile. You were laughing happily like a small child surrounding itself with make-believe, wrapping the moment up forever in joy. . . . Kyungu has come silently to the table . . . taking off his watch asks me to set it. I give it back to him and he fingers it gently. Missy Mary gave me this in Mombassa, he says. Could anything be more subtle?"

By mid-January we were planting floribunda roses along the terrace behind the house and marveling at their persevering to survive. They had somehow been detained thirteen days in Miami from the growers in Pennsylvania, but now were miraculously flourishing, with Ernest solemnly noting each day that they had grown half an inch since yesterday's inspection. At the pool, beds of nasturtiums were capturing sunshine, and a newly planted African tulip tree was flaunting bright scarlet flowers against our blue sky. From our vegetable garden I was delightedly gathering baby heads of broccoli, to arrange in my Cuban wicker basket with radishes, onions, string beans, beets, Swiss chard, a still-life picture to show Ernest on my way to the kitchen. It was a little interlude of peace and pleasurable work and we made the most of it.

About noon on Sunday, January 30, Mr. Schustedt telephoned to say that my father had collapsed with a "cerebral accident," and would I authorize their taking him to the hospital. Certainly and please summon all possible care. I couldn't get a seat on Delta's flight to New Orleans that afternoon, tried and failed to get a connection via Tampa, and instead wrote my father a letter, hoping my mother would read it to him and that he would understand it: "Just a year after Old Man Luck gave Ernest and me a nasty whack with the two airplane crashes, he has come back and given you a cruel blow in the head. . . . But people do recover from this thing. . . . Your great friend and aid in this battle is the wonderful constitution you inherited from your parents. . . ." Later I read him parts of the letter, but he did not understand me.

Two days later, I flew to New Orleans and reached the hospital where my father was asleep in apparent comfort and the nurses reported he had already regained the use of his right arm but was not lucid in his head.

The next day I wrote Ernest: "Report from hospital this morning, Tom had a quiet night, ate porridge and an egg for breakfast, is calmer this morning and slightly more lucid. . . . No sign of pain, no more paralysis. He is still a living organism, breath moving in and out . . . a faint, sad resemblance to my father. . . ."

That same day Ernest wrote me: "I feel awful to be here with such a perfect day for my kitten to sunbathe; bright and clear and a very light SE breeze. Everything beautiful about the place. . . . The roses lovely with 97 good buds in the upper set. . . . Many people trying to crash the place all the time."

My mother dressed in her prettiest clothes and hats and I took her to visit my father in the hospital where she read him passages from *Science and Health*, he comprehending nothing. Or I sat beside his bed, announcing myself at intervals, hoping he might recognize my voice. He talked about the freight rates to Duluth and the estimated board feet in unknown stands of pine.

On the telephone Ernest made one of the most helpful suggestions he had ever given me. Pretend it is all something you're just covering as a reporter. Be objective about it, to save your nerves. On February 8, I wrote him: "Your suggestion is precisely the therapy I need. Listen to this, which was over the phone just a few minutes ago.

" 'Now, Mary, when you go to the hospital, I want you to take a *Science and Health*.'

" 'What for?'

" 'Because the nurse must read it to him. You know

Mrs. Eddy says so. If you're having treatments, you must read *Science and Health*.'

" 'But he doesn't understand anything.'

" 'That doesn't matter. She must read it to him,' said my mother.

". . . Don't think I've gone crazy yet, but it may be a better investment all around for me to come home, if only for a week, than to stay on here." The next morning I flew back to Cuba. Ernest sent a welcoming note with Juan. "I woke up feeling lousy and thought maybe not better take a chance of presenting you with another sick. You must be sick of sicks. . . . Preliminary kiss . . . Looks like a super aphid but it's not."

On February 17, Mr. Schustedt telephoned to say my father was failing fast. I reserved a seat on the Friday plane, and that evening Mr. Schustedt called again to report that my father had died peacefully and without pain, also without regaining his mental equilibrium. He was eighty-five years old. My father had once told the Schustedts that he would like to be cremated, and we agreed that the funeral service should be held on Saturday.

The Schustedts kindly met me at the New Orleans airport, and the next morning in Gulfport took me to the undertaker's establishment. During the twenty-minute service there that afternoon, my mother kept herself calm. But all my muscles shook like aspen leaves in a breeze, uncontrollably. Afterward I noted: "I cannot talk to her about how I feel about my father . . . so whatever mourning I do must be private. She and I talk Christian Science platitudes."

Alone I remembered how Tom Welsh and his daughter had tooled along northern Minnesota's narrow gravel roads, singing together in his one-seater Model-T Ford with the gas tank underneath the seat, how they had bumped and splashed across Leech Lake with an outboard motor pushing the rowboat, how, coming upon a clump of white birches on hikes through pine forests, they had paused in shared delight. From our days together he created a gift for me, a sense of assurance that men and women can be friends without antagonisms based in sex. My father had been a man of innocence

528

who believed mankind could reclaim its savageries, a man of enterprise and hope, diligence and kindness, a gay and handsome companion. I have loved him more than forty years.

My mother was turning restive and wrote that she was looking for a less expensive place to live and that the rest home wasn't like her own home. I replied, admonishing and entreating, "Please try to be contented there." In lieu of a home with us in Cuba, I could give my mother the poor substitute of frequent letters and telephone calls and of presents, particularly dresses. I sent for her measurements and set Josépha, the Christian Dior of San Francisco de Paula, to stitching on creations with lace-edged collars.

A series of letters began to arrive from my mother.

April 7: "I must find a home soon. . . . This is not a rest home but a hospital where I have to see and hear sickness day and night. . . . The food is the cheapest they can get. . . . I hesitated to tell you this but the time has come and I refuse to go on here any longer. . . . A view of the water and a good room is not what I need. I'm able to eat better but get very little sleep. There must be a better place for me somewhere. . . . I could go to the Crosby hotel for the time being. It is not a place where I would like to stay." (It was a third-rate hotel.)

April 10: "I've just written to [a friend] in Chicago asking her if she would get an apartment there and live with me at least for a while. I cannot stay here. Any place I've ever lived would be more harmonious. I cannot sleep day or night. . . . The telephone here is not working since the rain started so I'm cut off from my friends." (There was a telephone strike throughout the South.)

I wrote back: "I know you miss Tom, who was a good friend to you and helped to keep you cheerful. . . . I know you must be lonely. But loneliness is a minor ailment which is suffered by almost everyone on earth." I checked by telephone with the Schustedts about my mother's health and general welfare. She had friends visiting her almost every day, including a Christian Science practitioner whom she paid to chat with her about the religion or to read aloud from

529

Science and Health, or was being taken out by friends to visit them. They were having roast turkey and stuffing for dinner that night.

Ernest and I took off for Paraíso in *Pilar* for another fortnight of fishing, reading, swimming, exploring the beach which every day produced new displays of shells, crabs, starfish and sand patterns for us. As always, Gregorio worked from dawn until dark and later, keeping *Pilar* and her motor and our fishing gear immaculate, reels oiled, any linen lines washed in fresh water after a day in the sea, shifting anchorages as shifting winds required, fishing with us or maneuvering the *Tin Kid* over reefs while we fished, acquiring and preparing our favorite meals, foresighted in behalf of our felicity, good-tempered, sharp-witted, tireless. On that trip I realized what close friends we three were and how little I knew of Gregorio's personal history. He outlined it for me one evening while he peeled and minced, chopped and sliced in the galley.

Gregorio's father, who was a fisherman at La Palma in the Canaries, first took him to sea when he was four years old to work as mess boy on a commercial fishing boat, a two-masted sailing ship which fished between the Canaries and Río de Oro, a Spanish colony on the west coast of Africa. Spanish law did not allow youngsters to work officially as able seamen, but Gregorio was a crew helper, aged ten, when his father was hit by a swinging boom and so badly wounded that he died. Gregorio's duty became that of supporting his mother and sisters. Along the docks at La Palma he got a job on a Spanish-speaking cargo ship making voyages to South American ports, and to Sevilla and Valencia. He worked on a Portuguese ship on voyages to Puerto Rico and Trinidad, sailed home again and, aged eleven, came to Havana and decided to stay there and work out of there.

When Gregorio was eighteen his older brother sent him money for his passage back home to La Palma, but Gregorio returned the money. When he was twenty-one he worked his way home, stayed there two months, bought his mother a house and returned to Havana. He no longer knew people there in La Palma whereas he had many friends in Cuba, and could get increasingly better-paying jobs on ships out of Havana. For a time he abandoned work on cargo and fishing boats and took a job caring for nets on the *Atlantic,* a research vessel sailing from Woods Hole, Massachusetts. An achievement there he remembered with satisfaction was the making of a big net which the ship needed urgently. He worked four days without stopping and finished the net ahead of deadline.

Sometime before World War II the Cuban fishing smack of which he was captain was stormbound at Dry Tortugas and *Pilar,* also anchored there, ran out of salt. To borrow some, Ernest went aboard the smack, the two captains chatted and Ernest observed the boat. It was the cleanest and best run of such boats Ernest had ever seen and that day he invited Gregorio Fuentes to become mate of *Pilar.* He stayed with her for the rest of her and his seagoing life.

When we had first met ten years earlier, Gregorio had been teaching himself to read the newspapers in Spanish with coaching at home by one of his five schoolgirl daughters. ("Five daughters," Ernest used to say. "Fisherman's luck." "Fisherman's luck," our phrase ran, "a wet ass and a hungry gut.") Now Gregorio consistently read one or another of the daily papers and also Havana's popular weekly picture magazine *Bohemia,* and one of his daughters had acquired a *novio* (fiancé). Among Cuban working people the parents of brides seldom hesitated to spend half a year's income on weddings, and the festivities at the marriage of Gregorio's and his wife's first bride were elaborate to sumptuous, the ceremony complete with organ music and lighted candles, the bride and bridesmaids in homemade, hand-stitched gowns, taking place in the big cathedral at Guanabacoa and afterward hundreds of guests sipping wine in the tiny garden of Gregorio's thatch-roofed cottage at Cojímar.

As he told me about himself that evening in the galley, Gregorio was making us beef stew for supper. As with nearly all his other dishes, we thought it the best in the world of its genre, and I asked him its secrets. You do the sauce first, he said, with plenty of garlic, onion, tomato purée, a can of pimiento chopped fine, lard, sherry, oregano and laurel. No water. You cook

531

the sauce for fifteen minutes, stirring and improving seasonings, then add the beef in one- or two-bite sizes, turn the fire low and let it simmer slowly for an hour. Add raw potatoes in small chunks and cook another half hour. He usually served his stew with white rice. He never appeared either to measure his rice and water or to time its cooking. We might be lounging and talking on the afterdeck when Gregorio would spring down to the galley to yank the rice off the fire. He could tell by the smell when it was cooked, he said. It should begin to smell faintly, barely noticeably, of mothballs. That was when it was sufficiently cooked and that was proof of its goodness.

He gave me tips on his red snapper stew which guests aboard *Pilar* from far and wide had hailed as sensational. An hour before beginning to cook, you score the fish diagonally and rub salt into the cuts. The dish is best if your pan and fire are big enough to hold the entire fish with head and tail. (His two kerosene burners in *Pilar* were too small for that). As with the beef, he made the sauce first, with garlic, onion, fresh chopped red peppers, purée of tomato, bay leaf and oregano, cooking and stirring for half an hour. Next he added a tin of pimiento chopped very fine, capers, raisins, green olives, Manzanilla sherry, salt and finally the fish to simmer slowly just until its opalescent flesh turned white. He never liked fish to be too fresh, he mentioned, because the skin shrinks in the cooking.

"How fresh is too fresh, Gregorio?" We were slupping up beef-stew juice from our plates on the generator box aft, while Ernest ate, plate in hand, cross-legged on his bunk.

"Oh, under an hour, depending on size, depending on the fish. Two hours maybe."

"Not a universal dilemma," murmured Ernest.

On our way home from that holiday we had a heavy wind from the north which kept *Pilar* rolling from side to side all the ninety miles, but we had spectacular fishing. Ernest mentioned it in a letter to Bob Manning: "Mary is very well and fine. . . . I'm so much better that it's comic. Took off twelve pounds and have kept it off three weeks. Will be down to my very best weight

532

in another month. Light on feet again. Blood pressure 140 over 68 (was 180 over 100 a year ago). Steered 7 hours 50 minutes on the flying bridge . . . running up from westward and six at the wheel below with a big beam sea and Mary and I caught 24 dolphin, a lot of barracuda and I got one nice marlin. We had been down the coast for two weeks anchored and I would run every day on the beach and swim and that was what took the weight off."

A couple of letters from Fred Schustedt were awaiting me at the Finca. On April 21 he had written: "To answer your inquiry about your mother is difficult to do in a few words. She is typically senile—forgetful —contrary to extremes—going to die if she must stay here—radio is too loud in the morning—radio not working right in the evening—her room is too cold at 74°—too hot at 80°—she will report the phone company when the girls do not answer promptly. We are used to this, but sometimes it is annoying. . . . Don't let your mother's troubles trouble you too much."

On April 30 he wrote: "We are not permitted the advice of any medical men and Christian Scientist faith admits no physical ailments. So we have to judge by appearances only. We do not know your mother's pulse rate, her blood pressure or her temperature. We do know that she is very weak, that she is failing rapidly, which fact will not be admitted to by her or any of her intimates. . . . Even though your mother may drive us all nuts, don't let her get you down. We have lived through many similar cases."

Our house was full of people: Sinsky, home from the sea for a week and sharing Ernest's bathroom; Roberto Herrera, importantly filing papers and eating prodigiously; Alfred Rice, Ernest's lawyer, down for a few days of consultations concerning Leland Hayward and the contract for the film of *The Old Man and the Sea,* in which Ernest was supposed to get an extra fee for acting as technical adviser; Taylor Williams, our old friend from Sun Valley, who came every year for a couple of weeks of springtime fishing for young white marlin. Having climbed half the mountains of Idaho hunting deer or elk, Taylor in his sixty-sixth year had stepped off a curb in Miami and broken a bone in his ankle. He arrived in Cuba, cheerful, uncomplaining, cackling his dry laugh, cleverly maneuvering his crutches, both around the Finca and aboard *Pilar*.

Ernest had written to Harvey Breit about males and females (*Homo sapiens*) and showed it to me for my approval. Later Harvey sent me a copy. An excerpt: "Certainly man is not made to live alone and neither is women or woman . . . certainly not me. But I know that a woman forgives a man nearly everything if he is a man (not he-man; just man) or she has some sort of respect for him maybe. Maybe is the strongest word of security we have in these times. . . . It is simpler in Africa, maybe. . . . It doesn't seem so stupid to me to have five wives if you can afford them . . . instead of having one wife at a time and paying them alimony when you need another wife. . . . I am very faithful. But I can be faithful easier to four good wives than to one. . . . The only advice I can give now is that you can get an awfully good wife for forty goats if she loves you. When you're married you can't afford champagne and brandy and anyway sooner or later the champagne will make your stomach sour and the brandy will make you mean. So take it from here Ecclesiasties (misspelled).

"I am not against american womens because Miss Mary and I were just on a fine long trip and went to bed every night by ten o'clock at the latest and slept well every night and drank good gin and coco-nut water . . . and were happy as before we were ever married and drank champagne and brandy always . . . and that's been eleven years and it was as lovely as always . . . !"

In mid-May my mother forwarded a letter from our mutual long-time friend Rose Winter, a piano teacher who had lived in our block in Bemidji forty years before, telling of a "one of the family" home, run by a Christian Scientist in Minneapolis, to which she wished to move immediately. I replied asking her to be patient and to postpone any move. "We should consider seriously the longness and coldness of the winters there, which might keep you cooped up for months, also how far it is from here. . . . You have no cold-weather wardrobe now and would need new woolen dresses, shoes, a fur coat—remember how the floors get cold everywhere when it is 30 degrees below zero...."

Our part of Cuba had endured a drought that spring longer and more vicious than any we had seen, with our lawns turning brown, shrubs and vines sickening from thirst and my vegetables and flowers ruined. Concomitantly some mishap befell our aqueduct and we had not a drop of water in the house except what we could haul up in pails out of our old cistern below the front veranda, a situation not conducive to easy entertaining. But only a day or two before Leland Hayward and Peter Viertel arrived, the rains came and the aqueduct got repaired. They planned the making of the movie, fished and one day caught three marlin and returned to the Finca so late that dinner began at 9:30 and lasted until midnight. Having decided with Ernest to bring down a Hollywood crew to begin in September hunting a giant marlin and filming him, if they found one, Leland took off for New York, and Peter, who would write the script, stayed on in our guest house to learn the ways in thought and action of Cuban commercial fishermen, with me as interpreter on visits to Cojímar.

Determined to move to Minneapolis, my mother was alerting her many old friends there of her imminent arrival, while so behaving in Gulfport that the Schustedts would be happy to see her departure. Ernest patiently agreed that I take her north and also, accepting my cousin Bea Guck's invitation, relax a few days in the cool of Lake Superior's shore at her cabin at Eagle Harbor. From Abercrombie & Fitch, I had ordered $512.88 worth of birthday presents for Ernest, including a miniature radio, a windspeed meter, slacks, shorts, cotton T-shirts, pullovers, yachting caps, polo shirts, checked Aertex shirts in all available colors and a few shirts for me. I had Abercrombie's send everything to Key West where we found them when we went over for a few days to check on Pauline's property.

On July 10 Willie Walton had sent us a headline from a Washington paper to brighten our day: ARCH-

BISHOP TURNS SOD FOR SCHOOL. "Anything for the old school tie," Willie had written, and wondered if he might come down to visit. "I have a burning hope that I might be able to see you two, eat mangoes, swim, paint some bamboo, and talk endlessly." A gift of the Magi for us, since Ernest would have Willie as companion, fellow joke-maker, thinker, appreciator of sights, sounds, tastes, fellow sybarite, in each of which processes none of our friends excelled him. The color scheme of Ernest's birthday party that year was to be saffron and violet, the colors of the two sides of Spanish matadors' big fighting capes, and Willie was scarcely unpacked in our Little House before I had him wrapping and making bows, all the time pretending to grumble at such foolishness. With Gianfranco Ivancich, Paco Garay and some other local friends converging for it, we had the birthday luncheon that year at the pool, René installing a tubful of iced champagne under the shade from our vines at the pool's loggia, most of us using chopsticks for the sweetsour shrimp and other Chinese dishes which were favorites of the birthday boy. It was a cheerful celebration, and more relaxed than usual. A few days later I took off for Gulfport.

Once there, my irritation with the chores of getting my mother packed and ready to travel spilled over to cover the whole area, and I wrote Ernest: "Let's not move to the lovely, romantic ol' Deep South with its picturesque Spanish Moss hangin' in shadowy mystery from the Live Oaks, and its beautiful, fragrant Magnolia trees and its luscious pecan trees and its historical accumulated centuries of chickenshit. . . ."

"It begins to seem possible that loneliness was driving mother crazy. . . . Mother says, 'Infinite Mind directs each day, All we should know, do or say.' Mumbo-Jumbo, God of the Congo couldn't do better. . . . The Romans arranging chicken entrails for divination were a cut above mother's practitioner, divining the cause of mother's constipation, 'It's a thought of resistance. We must work on that.' "

Ernest wrote me that Alfred Rice and Hayward had finally worked out and signed the agreement concerning *The Old Man* film. "Leland full of good will but very tricky and tighter than a hog's ass in fly time," and that, having promised not to interrupt Ernest's work from June 15 until September 1, Leland was "crowding" him with letters and telephone calls during his working hours, and sending down a special super-photographer who would study the possibilities of photographing the fishing from a submerged raft. And: "Don't worry about anything! Do you need any monies? We are o.k. on monies. . . ."

Once again I got my mother's possessions put in order, giving to her vulture friends most of the old junk —towels, napkins, lengths of material that used to match her curtains, an ancient electric plate—that she had been lugging around for forty years, and at noon, July 28, we settled in to a "bedroom" on a train to Chicago and the next morning transferred to a train for Minneapolis. A further journey north to Eagle Harbor would be too fatiguing for her, Mother decided, so I took her directly to the home of Mrs. Kerr, the Christian Scientist who would be so happy to look after her. Having bought her a winter wardrobe and stocks of all the small comforts we could anticipate she might need, I flew to the Upper Peninsula of Michigan. From her first day with Mrs. Kerr my mother declared she felt much better. Many of her old friends, widows all, telephoned they were coming to visit, and the home in Groveland Terrace near the center of the city was more easily accessible than the home outside Gulfport had been. Even in the 100-degree heat wave, little Adeline was beginning to smile, and I left her with both of us more hopeful than despairing. A few days after my return to Cuba came a letter from Mrs. Kerr: "I am beginning to understand that having your Mother will be more of a problem than I had realized and that my original price will not cover my expenses." An additional $75.00 a month would provide her with extra help in the house, and an electric heater for my mother's room.

At 5 a.m. September 1 eight of Cojímar's foremost commercial fishermen left the bay in four old-fashioned seagoing skiffs such as they had used for generations and old Santiago had used. In the last few years most of them had added outboard or inboard motors to their boats, but this morning they rowed eastward with the Gulf Stream, their sails stepped and furled, each craft loaded with a marlin's idea of tasty morsels which would drift at varying depths in the moving Stream. At six o'clock Ernest and Gregorio would turn *Pilar*'s beautiful black nose seaward, five technicians from Hollywood — cameramen, assistants and grips — aboard, to ride herd on the fishing boats and photograph any action they encountered. Likewise, our friend Mayito Menocal's fishing boat *Tensi* put to sea with Mayito's cousin Elicio Argüelles in command and four camera crew aboard. At ten o'clock, Juan drove me to La Terraza restaurant at Cojímar, where with Felípe, my boatman, I collected hot lunches in neat, tightly covered metal canteens, twenty-seven every day, and in *Tin Kid* delivered them to each of the six boats of our fleet, usually eight to twelve miles offshore by that hour. La Terraza produced noble fare for the sea picnics—fried chicken or steaks or grilled lobster with rice and black beans, big salads, fruits and cakes—and the fishermen and their herders, working assiduously twelve hours a day, welcomed it.

September was the month when the great blue marlin cruised past Cuba, and every year a few fishermen took fish weighing up to a thousand pounds. When hurricanes bypassed the area, September was a month of lovely, luminous weather on the Gulf Stream. This year the weather opposed and nearly defeated us. A couple of hurricanes hovered in the vicinity, high winds battered the boats, exhausting everybody, especially the men in the four fishing skiffs. With cloudy skies and intermittent rain showers, the light was often worthless for photography. In two weeks of unremitting effort, the cameras got pictures of two marlin hooked by the little boats, neither of them big enough to serve as models for Santiago's giant fish, and of three sharks. In conference at the Cojímar dock on September 14, the fellows decided that they might as well pack up the project, for the moment at least, and the Hollywood crowd took off for home. It had all been so busy every day on the ocean that the two weeks disappeared in a minute.

While I was working at my desk the next afternoon,

Ernest came padding in on bare feet and murmured, "You'll look after the kids, won't you?"

"Natch. What do you mean?"

"I'm making a new will."

He had made several wills that I knew of. This one was no surprise.

"I'll do whatever I can," said I and forgot about it. Six years later I learned that this afternoon's holograph will left me "all of the property . . . to which I may be entitled at the time of my decease, of whatever kind and nature, and wheresoever it may be situated, be it real, personal, literary or mixed, absolutely" and that I had been nominated, constituted and appointed executrix. George Brown, René Villarreal and Lola Richards, our maid, were the witnesses.

We were just beginning to settle back into the Finca rhythms of work, read, swim, garden, when Slim Hayward flew down from New York to stay with us and consult Ernest about her various personal problems and what she called "miseries." We took her fishing and to dinner in town, and invited half a dozen of her Cuban friends for dinner at home another evening. George Brown and Peter Viertel stayed on after the fishing stint, and Freddy Zinnemann, whom Leland Hayward fancied as director of the film, came down with his sweet soft-voiced wife Renée to get acquainted with Cuba and Ernest. Fred Zinnemann was a darling man, I soon decided, sharply aware of people and nuances, and gentle-mannered.

Writing every morning about Africa and his native friends there, Ernest had developed a fever for some outward sign of his kinship with the Wakamba. He wanted to have his ears pierced and wear gold earrings in them, as I did. Wouldn't I do the piercing for him, with a sterilized needle and a cork? For a few days I put him off. Then I wrote a note for him to read in the early morning when his spirit was fresh and his head cool:

"For the well-being of both of us, I ask you please to reconsider having your ears pierced . . . it would be flouting the mores of western civilization. I do not defend the idea that men, except for some sailors, rakish fellows, do not wear earrings—but I think we should recognize that it exists.

"Everything you do sooner or later gets into print . . . and your wearing earrings will have a deleterious effect on your reputation . . . for seeing reality and truth. . . . The fiction that having your ears pierced will make you a Kamba is an evasion of reality . . . the attempt to convert fantasy into actuality can only result, I think, in distortion and failure. There are other ways of proving brotherhood between you and the Kamba. I do hope you will find them, my Big Sweetheart."

My note seemed to ease the earring crisis, and it was dispelled by the arrival of Bumby, Number One son, who came down, this time without wife and children, to jolly his father, talk a little bit of business, shoot buzzards from the top of the tower, praise our cuisine and coat our days with cheer. For further homemade delight that autumn we had new kittens born in the Venetian Room who, aged one month, joined us in the sitting room. Curled around each other they slept in Ernest's chair or, as in twin beds, one in each of his moccasins. Among the big, dangerous, leather-clad feet moving about they danced and wrestled and rolled, hitting each other with all the force of a dove feather, or raced up trouser legs without fear or even discretion. In tribute to their adventurous natures we named them Cristóbal Colón (Christopher Columbus) and Isabella la Católica (the queen) which Ernest shortened to Izzy the Cat. For more tranquil viewing we watched the *Porana paniculata* above the front terrace and at the pool unfold its billions of fragrant, fragile white flowers in lilac-like clusters to look like drifts of snowflakes on their green leaves.

Eager to latch on to Ernest's spreading recognition, the Batista government insisted on presenting him with yet another medal, that of the Order of San Cristóbal, and friends persuaded him to attend a long, loquacious ceremony in the glare of television lights at the Sports Palace in Havana. In Key West, where I went to supervise repairs to Pauline's Pool House, I set quickly to work getting water pipes, electric wiring and broken shutters repaired, and the chic little house properly cleaned. When I got back home the following Sunday afternoon I found Ernest ill in my bed with a kidney infection—probably from the chilly ride home after the heat of the Sports Palace performance—and miserable with fever, swollen glands, and malfunctioning liver. "Hepatitis," said José Luis.

My principle of conduct concerning Ernest's infirmities was to refrain from bothering him with my worries. But one night in bed, each of us rolled like cigars in light blankets, I blurted something such as, "This seems like an unduly long siege, unduly long for you. You've always been so resilient."

A pause, and he said thoughtfully, "I've never given my body any quarter."

"No. Not since I've known you."

"No quarter, ever."

"Maybe now is a good time to adopt a new program. Give yourself some quarter."

"Well, maybe fifteen cents."

More to give me freedom from his clutter and to use my desk than because his own bed was more comfortable, he moved to his room after our quiet Thanksgiving, taking with him half a dozen mounds of newspapers, magazines and books. Checking one day I noted that he had several Cuban newspapers in Spanish, *The Times* and the *Herald Tribune* from New York and the two Miami papers in one pile. That was his morning reading. His hump of magazines included *Time* and *Newsweek* and *Collier's* and *The Saturday Evening Post,* also *The Saturday Review, U.S. News and World Report* and a couple of weeklies each from London, Paris and Italy. A half dozen books were scattered over the counterpane. When printed pages tired his eyes, he sometimes switched on his birthday-present radio or watched Cuban baseball on a new TV set. I bought a reading lamp to put behind the chair at the foot of his bed and many evenings read aloud all sorts of people, from Shakespeare (the sonnets) to T. E. Lawrence to Jim Corbett to Anne Morrow Lindbergh to *The Oxford Book of English Verse*.

With the Head of the House still more in bed than out of it, I planned a low-keyed if not Spartan Christmas. By early December Christmas trees from Idaho, Montana and Colorado, miraculously retaining their sweet smell of northern forests, were stacked on Havana's hot pavements in front of the Sears, Roebuck store and our grocery store, the Morro Castle, and I brought one home in the back of my convertible for Pichilo the gardener to plant in a washtub of earth and water where it revived and survived beyond all expectations. That year's tree even kept its fragrance, endearing itself so much to Ernest that for weeks he vetoed suggestions concerning its removal and on St. Valentine's Day produced his homemade valentine with verse:

> If my Valentine you won't be,
> I'll hang myself on your Christmas tree.

21

Motion and Action

FOR A COUPLE of months assorted visitors kept appearing, requiring hospitality and providing us with diversions. Mike Burke, our wartime pal of the OSS, with his pretty wife Timmy; Fred Zinnemann, to scout locations for the film; one-of-a-kind Jimmy Robinson, scouter of Canadian provinces for Ducks Unlimited; Charlie MacArthur and Helen Hayes, with Anita Loos; Bernard and Alva Gimbel; George Plimpton; a girl from *Sports Illustrated* and half a dozen other people came to the Finca for extra-dry martinis made by the host or gin in iced coconut water and chitchat accompanied by three or four courses of the most interesting food I could dream up, and ample pourings of Spanish or Italian wines.

Finally left to ourselves, we felt more privileged than deprived, particularly because of Feather Kitty and her growing twins. A pale-gray-and-white striped cat, Feather Kitty was secretive, impatient, preoccupied and ill-tempered in the least endearing ways. But nearly every day she put on a performance of speed and daring unsurpassed in circuses. As we sat at table she would lie on the dining room floor in apparent utter relaxation until René pushed through the heavy swinging door to the pantry. Watching the door swing, Feather Kitty on lightning impulse would streak through the fast-closing gap without a hair's width to spare while we watched, gasping. "If we could only teach her to shoot," Ernest used to murmur, or "Talk about a death wish."

But she was a good mother, feeding her children regularly, bathing them thoroughly every day, cuffing them when they seemed impertinent, teaching them the arts of self-defense and later of offense and bullying them into working up speed from a prone start that might eventually put them somewhere near her own class. By themselves Cristóbal and Izzy discovered the techniques of ambush, secret maneuver, the advantages of attack from high ground, and it gradually became evident to us that Izzy was a beast much bolder, more aggressive and faster than her brother. She was also mean, like her mother, and greedy, and that was her undoing. After lunch one day we tossed a juicy steak bone to our Black Dog on the front terrace. Izzy streaked out for it and Blackie bit her head off.

Neither Feather Kitty nor Cristóbal saw the accident or the funeral rites and for a week they hunted for Izzy under chairs and beds, behind books, in the linen shelves and among pantry dishes, slowly losing interest in the search, and Feather Kitty grew more irritable. She had never wasted civil words on the other cats and now disdainfully abandoned her old occasional civilities with us, ignored Cristóbal and after a while walked off and moved in with a family on the other side of our garden fence.

543

Cristóbal began hunting among the other cats for a playmate to share his built-in gaiety and ebullience, but none of them seemed fully satisfactory in that capacity. Ambrose, the black-and-white short-haired teenager, had no sense of humor and tended to be offended at Cristóbal's good-natured attacks. Stranger, the soft brown-haired descendant of our beautiful Persian queen, had fragile bird bones and fled, terrified, from Cristóbal's hearty overtures toward palship. Most of the other cats Cristóbal didn't speak to, having been spoiled by us into regarding himself as the household princeling. He had to resign himself to accepting us as providers of entertainment, and he did so with imagination and zest, showing us new uses for our ordinary tools and thereby generating a new vivacity in their uses. He learned to climb up Ernest's pants and shirt to sit on a shoulder watching a pencil skitter across a page until the movement and scuffing grew too entrancing to resist and he joyfully pounced on it. He loved riding around the house on my shoulder, practicing his balancing skills as I bent and turned, hooking his nails through my shirt to the skin for a good grip.

If the black *M* on his face represented Mesopotamia, the storied homeland of domestic tiger cats, some of Cristóbal's ancestors must have stopped over in Venice on their trek to the western hemisphere, for the little tiger cat who was immortalized by Veronese in his huge glowing canvas *Cena chez Levi* in the Accademia must have been one of our tiger's grandmothers.

Cristóbal loved tape measures. Wiggling around the house to measure furniture for slipcovers or people for shirts or shorts, they were something to chase, nuzzle, bite or fight, catch and chew. When they were rolled up and hidden in a drawer, he did not sulk. He was not a brooder. Like Sir Winston Churchill, Cristóbal spurned milk and cream. But unlike Churchill, he took no interest in alcohol, no matter how cleverly we thought we had disguised it in meat or fish trappings. His nose knew immediately. But he was always on hand when we opened a tin of fresh Russian caviar for celebrations, and he graciously accepted cooked shrimp—no sauce, please—or freshly cooked fish or lean meats. He was keeping his cholesterol count down. His favorite among all foods was a cob of corn, half chewed by Ernest, the soft paw stretched out, pulling the corn toward him. He taught us gradually that he most enjoyed the cob without kernels to be held steady for him to chew on.

One day we missed him. He did not come trotting into my room under my breakfast tray to share my egg. He was not lounging on any window sill with his DON'T DISTURB sign nearly visible. Ernest could not recall having let him outdoors after dinner for an hour or two of helling around, pretending to frighten lizards in the dark, and we had heard no vigorous climb up a window screen, meaning "Let me in."

I put the whole household on search detail, hunting the thick shrubbery outside, calling, checking the gutters of the roof and, most unlikely, the corners of the Cat House. We hunted under chairs and beds, in linen shelves and closets. We suspected the ice man might have run over him with his rickety truck, but there were no traces of slaughter on the road. We interviewed the dogs, but none of them looked guilty. I wondered if we had been hexed.

On the third morning I pulled open my big bottom drawer for clean shorts and a shirt, and out jumped Cristóbal eluding my arms and heading, composed but determined, for the pantry where the food was. He spurned our effusive welcomes, ate a snack of ground beef and went to loll and bathe himself on his favorite window sill. He had been most respectful of my clothes, sullying only one pair of shorts. His three-day imprisonment lessened only slightly his interest in the contents of drawers, but ever afterward we left them open a couple of inches.

In early March 1956, the movie entered our lives again, and brought us an explosion of people—Spencer Tracy was delayed in New York with a cold—but Leland Hayward and the Zinnemanns and the whole Hollywood company which was to film the land parts of *The Old Man and the Sea,* including Santiago in his shack, the village awakening before dawn and the fishermen rowing out to sea, Santiago carrying his mast and sail up from the bay after his long struggle.

In a small viewing room at the Warner Brothers office in Havana the next day we saw four hundred feet of the best of the film taken on the Gulf Stream off Cuba in the strenuous fortnight of the previous September—not very good footage. We also saw the film taken by a fisherman from Texas of an enormous fish he had caught off Peru. Its disadvantage for our purposes was that the thin sports fishing line showed inexpungeably, whereas Santiago's hand lines were thick and heavy. I wanted to suggest that we consign the fish part of the film to the Walt Disney studios which had produced so many patient, accurate wildlife films. But I kept quiet. Ernest persuaded Leland and the others that he should try to catch and photograph a really big fish off Cabo Blanco, Peru, and they agreed that he should spend a month there, if necessary, with fishing and camera crews.

The Cabo Blanco Fishing Club was so expensive —$100 a day for each guest or thereabouts—that I hesitated to accept Ernest's invitation to join the expedition. Then over lunch he said, "You better come, my kitten. I may really need you."

"If I turn out to be only excess baggage, I'll come home," I suggested.

With Elicio Argüelles and Gregorio we flew to Miami and down to Panama and Talara then motored through equatorial desert to the rectangular club huddled on a sandy ledge only a hundred yards back from thudding Pacific breakers, and we promptly discovered the expedition had a good use for me, as translator. Leland had chartered the club's only three fishing boats, on one of which, *Miss Texas,* Elicio and Ernest would fish and Gregorio would supervise tackle and baits. A smaller boat, *Petrel,* carrying only its native crew, would scout for fish and signal any sightings of marlin. The third boat, *Pescador Dos,* would carry a big Cunningham camera and its operator Lou Jennings and grips Stew Higgs and Bill Classen, with the native crew of three. The Hollywood photographers spoke no Spanish. The Indian boatmen, segment of the Sachura tribe, they later told me, spoke no English. I would serve aboard *Pescador Dos* as translator.

The plan of operations was simple. We would patrol the Humboldt Current in the cold south wind with its six-thousand-mile fetch from the Antarctic ice cap abreast in twenty-foot waves until someone sighted a marlin fin. Then the two or three boats would converge, keeping *Pescador Dos* within lens range of a surfacing fish but out of interference with fish and fishing line.

We ended the month with indifferent success, the biggest of eighteen fish we had seen, and the fourth caught, weighing 915 pounds on the dock's scale, which had been adjusted downward. From his measurements, we estimated he weighed 1,035 pounds. But we couldn't get a decent picture of him jumping from the sea. The sluggard beast wouldn't jump.

The film budget dictated the ending of our sea hunt. The Peruvian expedition disbanded. Back at the Finca Vigía we learned with sorrow that Boise, Ernest's dearest cat friend, grandfather of the family and my one-time suitor, had died. "Peacefully," René consoled us.

In June Earl Theisen, our photographer friend from *Look* who had been with us in Africa, called to say they would like to do a follow-up piece on how we were getting along some thirty months after the airplane crashes. Ernest froze in our 90-degree heat at the thought of another abandonment of his manuscript, but we both loved Ty and his good comradeship and knew him to be unobtrusive with his cameras. Also the $5,000 *Look* would pay for a short piece and picture captions would come in handy on a trip to Spain we were considering.

Simultaneously, Alan Moorehead came down for a few days of our homemade festivities. On a day of fishing we cheered a little striped marlin Ernest hooked. Unlike the huge lethargic beasts of the Humboldt Current, this gallant fish, hooked on light limber tackle, jumped all over the ocean, thirty-seven times before I stopped counting. After Gregorio had boated him we were sorry we had kept him aboard. He deserved to return to his natural habitat.

When something else took a bait, it was Alan's turn at the reel. Protesting the assignment, asserting his inexperience, he nonetheless following my instructions sat himself on the generator box astern, braced his feet against the gunwale, lowered the rod and began to reel. "Now—steady—don't jerk, lift a little."

Alan, no mean athlete, tried lifting, his arm muscles bulging. "I must be hooked into the bottom, or a sunken ship."

"Keep the tip up, and now pull, pull back."

None of us knew what monster this might be. Gregorio checked the rod and decided it could hold the weight. Alan groaned and laughed and cussed and apologized.

"It can't be a marlin," Ernest said.

"But it has to be something marvelous," I opined. "It could be a wahoo. Don't let the line slack."

Alan worked and sweated. His hand holding the reel was getting tired, but his blue eyes continued merry. At last his intervals of reeling grew more frequent, and finally there appeared near the surface a mottled silver rectangle. Gregorio harpooned it.

"What is it?" the weary Alan asked.

"A horse-eyed jack," we boomed in dismay.

"He felt like a horse pulling."

"But he's a really big one," said Ernest, trying to be consoling.

"A sort of booby-prize, though?"

"Well, sort of. You might eat one if you'd had nothing for a week. But that was a good show. And he *is* very big, in his league," Ernest said.

"If this is deep-sea fishing, you make the most of it," Alan said. "Here and now I retire."

"You mean you didn't love it, every minute?" I asked.

In July Ernest's sister Ursula and her husband Jasper Jepson came over again from Honolulu to stay for a bit on their tour of South America, and the head of the house could not have had a happier fifty-seventh birthday present. We lavished the birthday morning fishing eastward in *Pilar,* almost caught a sizable marlin which threw the hook a minute before Gregorio would have gaffed him.

548

"That's good luck for next time," said Ura.

"I had the pleasure of bringing him in," said Ernest. "We didn't need him anyway."

Hours in the pool were refreshing and a series of blood transfusions alleviated temporarily my long-enduring, too-faithful anemia. But even with the *brisa* fresh off the Atlantic sweeping over us, the heat and 90 percent humidity that summer kept us in a state of dripping perspiration whatever we did. Ernest decided we must get out of it. We had been thinking about the tranquil hills of Spain in the autumn and Ernest had written Harvey Breit our intentions. Harvey replied with an invitation for us to use his and Patricia's house in New York. They would be going to the country but their cook and maid would stay on and look after us. We accepted with joy and Ernest made reservations on our friendly old ship, the *Ile de France*.

One of my obligations before leaving the United States was somehow to restrain my mother from depriving Mrs. May Kerr, who was looking after her at Groveland Terrace, Minneapolis, of rest and tranquility. While she continued to write me of her pleasure in seeing local friends and of the Kerr family's kindness to her, my mother spent the nights telephoning Christian Science practitioners asking them to come to treat her at 2 a.m. or awaking Mrs. Kerr to ask that she come to sit with her. I wrote a strong letter urging my willful mother to consider other people, and to take a sleeping pill Mrs. Kerr would get for her. Telling her of our plans for Europe, I said that on the way back to Cuba I would arrange to visit her. "I haven't the strength or energy to do it now."

In New York I tried to learn from Ernest how to be graceful with people who rushed toward us with kindly impulses. Walking alone one noontime I turned toward a car screeching to a stop. A couple of pretty girls jumped out hollering, "Miss Mary, Miss Mary." They had perhaps read Ernest's piece in *Look*. There was no place to hide, so I managed somehow to be polite, in a country bumpkin manner. The lovely anonymity of the streets of New York had forsaken us, but only temporarily.

In our usual suite, Senlis, on the *Ile de France* we

549

had time to read and rest after morning workouts in the gym, Ernest exercising much more strenuously than I. The passenger list was such that we felt little obligation to accept invitations to cocktail parties, but we had amusing verbal games with Irving Stone and his wife Jean, who came to our small table at one side of the dining salon for after-lunch or after-dinner coffee. I was struck by Mr. Stone's account of his constructing small models of rooms he had in his writing. "So that I don't have a character entering from the wrong side." He was a precise craftsman, I thought, and reflecting on Ernest's work I decided that he would not have needed such model rooms because most of his people lived their lives outdoors. Certainly one of the best presents he had ever given me was the opportunity to live under skies instead of ceilings, after my years of confinement in cubicles.

His "Situation Report" in *Look* that autumn had read too flattering for comfort when I had retyped it for him.

"It's too much, lamb," I had protested. "People will think I'm an heiress again, or some such rot."

"Couldn't you just type it like that?"

"I don't want to look like a bloody saint."

"You don't."

In this piece, after complaining about the wastefulness of writing journalism, Ernest continued: "Down in Peru, 420 miles south of the equator, where she was working as interpreter on the main camera boat between the Spanish-speaking, Indian-blooded captain and crew and the United States-speaking cameramen, putting in a full day under arduous conditions, Miss Mary announced one evening that the first thing her husband needed in a wife was that she be durable. Miss Mary is durable."

After a few more extravagant compliments, he added: "Miss Mary can also sing in Basque and is a brilliant and erratic rifle shot. She has been known to be irascible and can say in her own perfect Swahili, 'Tupa ile chupa tupu' which means take away that empty bottle. . . . She does not suffer fools gladly. She does not suffer them at all."

He also wrote about an evening at the Floridita.

Several U.S. fleet units had anchored in Havana harbor and some midshipmen had gone to call at the Finca. Ernest was telling them that Ezra Pound should be released from St. Elizabeth's Hospital and be allowed to practice poetry without let or hindrance.

At this point a group of Navy CPO's, all with the several long hash marks of their re-enlistments, turned up to see old Ernie. They tolerated the midshipmen but were suspicious that by these queries about Pound and other subjects alien to them, they might be preventing old Ernie from writing; a thing they themselves would never do.

"Give me the word," one of the chiefs said, "and they're out of here before they know it. Who the hell is going to bother you while I'm alive?"

I suggested we all go to the Floridita because Miss Mary doesn't like things broken in the house.

"Ernie," the chief said to me, "you got to have somebody steer people away from you. . . . I will be your A.d.C. I will be your personal aide. I will be the man that wears the chicken guts on his shoulders for you and I will handle all your public relations."

"Chief," I said. "You are my pal and now you are my personal aide. Handle my public relations."

"Sir," he said, "let there be no familiarity between us even though I may sometimes speak as man to man under stress. Sir, this is the chance I have prepared myself for during long years."

"The Floridita," I said. . . .

The Floridita was quite crowded, but my public relations officer evicted a number of characters from the stools in the corner in which we usually sat.

We sat and ordered and various people approached, some seeking autographs, others wishing to shake hands.

"Do you know Ernie?" asked my public relations officer. "No? You don't come from his home town or anything? Scram. He's thinking."

551

We were all engaged in serious literary discussion and had gone very deeply into things. Another chief joined us and he said, "The two books I like the best were . . . No, three . . . were *When the Rains Came, The Mooney Sixpence* and *The Towers of Babel.*"

"Mac," I said, "I didn't write one of them!"

"He probably means *The Torrents of Spring,*" one of our chiefs said. "I liked where that no-armed Indian shot that wonderful stick of pool . . ."

"Ernie wrote them all," my aide said. "Only he's too modest. He wrote them under a synonym. But every one of them has got the old touch." . . .

Around then I got the eye from the naval attaché who was sitting at a table with the admiral and a couple of other people, all in civilian clothes.

I refused the eye once, but I got it again and I said, "Excuse me, gentlemen, but I have to go over and speak to a man I know pretty well who would feel I was rude if I did not come over." . . .

So I went over and sat down with my good friend and found the visiting admiral to be cordial, extremely intelligent, pleasant and good company.

We had talked for some little time when I heard a voice at shoulder height, "Ernie, what are you doing here, wasting your time with a bunch of civilians?" It was my aide and public relations officer.

The admiral stood up and said, "I'm sorry, son, but I am your admiral."

"Admiral, sir, excuse me, sir. I have never seen you before, sir, so I did not recognize you in civilian clothes."

"I understand that perfectly," the admiral said.

"Admiral, sir, may I respectfully request, sir, that Ernie be allowed to return to our group?"

"It's not necessary to make the request," the admiral said. "Mr. Hemingway had said he was overdue to return."

"Thank you, sir."

It was a very good evening. At the end the

chief said, "Ernie, I hate to relinquish this job I have worked for so hard and so well over so many years."

"I feel bad too, chief," I said. "I'll never have another personal aide and public relations officer if it isn't you."

"Stand back there, you guys," the chief said. "Let Ernie get in the car. He's got to get home so he can sleep and think right and work good tomorrow."

With the new restrictions on auto-honking, one could hear distant church bells and Paris in September 1956 was blissful with the light shimmering pale gold in the plane trees. At the Orangerie the French government was displaying a collection of seldom-seen pictures by some of the Impressionists. There were Monets, Manets, Seurats and others assembled from private collections, so many of them with such impact and appeal that I went back to spend a second hour studying them. I also took a look at the Balenciaga collection. On Monday, September 17, we took off with Mario Casamassima, a dark, devilish-looking friend of Gianfranco's from Udine, chauffeuring this time, leaving five bags for Rupert Bellville to bring to Spain for us.

We crossed the Spanish border at Beobia on the twenty-first, climbed through pines, purple heather and poplars, with sheep still grazing on the higher slopes, slid down to Pamplona for a hectic lunch then rushed pell-mell to Logroño to unload luggage at the Gran Hotel and push on in the *feria* crowds to the Plaza de Toros.

Our friend Antonio Ordóñez was one of the matadors on the program and to our relief and the crowd's indignation quickly dispatched his first bull which was a worthless beast, and with his second animal gave the whole repertoire of movements, the bull cooperative, Antonio grave-faced, suave, poetic. Another matador, Giron, dedicated his second bull to Ernest and then worked with it extensively and beautifully. We returned emotionally exhausted to the hotel with its floors bare to save the carpets from the crowds.

Ernest gave Giron his new wallet in appreciation. The next day Joselito Huerta, a young little-known Mexican matador, dedicated a bull to Ernest and thereupon executed a succession of passes of a virtuosity that awed us—*reboleras,* two passes on his knees, *cambios* with the cape, a *veronica* of absolute purity, four passes as he sat on the *estribo, naturales, redondos* with the bull circling his figure one-quarter inch away. To kill he went right in between the horns and sank the sword to the hilt. He was awarded both ears, the tail and a leg, and in his room later Ernest noticed the leg beneath his washbowl. It was a once or twice in a lifetime triumph. Ernest had found another wallet to give him, and Huerta like some chipper high school basketball player came to sit with us in the hotel's bar. He was scheduled to fight at Arles the next day, about 1,000 kilometers to the north, and Ernest shooed him off.

The *feria* a few blocks away continued well into the morning, its din pervading every corner of our room. Later, I asked from a fog of fatigue, "Isn't there a button you can push to make the maids come?" My husband considered. Finally he said, "It's called a clitoris."

Peter Buckley, our dear semi-giant friend, had joined our outfit from the beginning of the festivities, and on Monday, the twenty-fourth, offered to drive me to Madrid and on to San Lorenzo del Escorial where we H.'s had rooms reserved at the Hotel Felipe II. Ernest, who had arrived earlier with Rupert, had allowed his luggage to be put in a double room, pleasant enough but less than my idea of home base for a couple of months. I had us moved to a suite he dubbed Club 215 with a sitting room overlooking the monastery with reading lamps near sofa and chairs, and the bar installed on a marble-topped table, my pink and ivory bedroom on one side and Ernest's crimson snuggery on the other. It was the beginning of an interlude of rest and leisure such as we had not known even on our old-time holidays in *Pilar.* Indulging in my favorite luxury, I lolled in bed and breakfasted there. In crisp autumn air we walked a dozen paths among the pine-clad slopes above the village. I found a guide willing to show me at leisurely pace the wonders of the

Escorial—the Salas de Claustro, the library, the apartment used by the friars in Felipe II's time and later occupied by Carlo IV and Maria Luisa of Parma, the crypt, the magnificent tapestries, stitch by patient stitch following the designs of Goya and Velásquez. I was beginning to feel less comatose, and my appetite was stirring.

On a Sunday we joined Antonio Ordóñez at a village outside Madrid, Las Cubas de Sagua, for a benefit bullfight which would raise funds for a new roof for the village church. With Antonio were the good matadors Aparicio, Litri, Pedrez and a gay young Mexican, all of them in their chic *trajes cortos* dealing with young calves, playing with them gaily in the small ring surrounded by temporary wooden bleachers. Other Sundays we went with Peter Buckley to Aranjuez and to Madrid for afternoons of bullfights ranging from marvelous to worthless.

For the five-day *feria* at Zaragoza beginning October 13, our little band of *aficionados* made a rendezvous in the provincial capital. Rupert Bellville and Polly Peabody, and Ralph and Baby Henderson came down from London, Hotchner flew over from Rome, and Peter Buckley took the train northeast from Madrid. Mornings we went to the *apartado,* the sorting and pairing of the bulls for the afternoon's *corrida.* The bulls were uniformly poor. Ernest thought their blood strain had run out. Peter Buckley thought they were doped. Their spirits looked good. They seemed eager. But they kept falling on their knees for no apparent reason, and could not turn fast as cats, as healthy Spanish fighting bulls do. Our matador friends, Antonio, Jaime Ostos, Joselito Huerta, Giron and Litri, did their respective best possible work with the underprivileged beasts, but the afternoons were a bust. Bhaiya, the Maharaja of Cooch Behar, came from London to join in the festivities and Ernest invited him to dine with our mob one night. With a combination of disappointment in the bullfights and indigestion, I excused myself. It was at the dinner that Cooch Behar invited Ernest and Antonio and us campfollowers to a tiger-shoot in India, a project which supplanted earlier chitchat about a safari in East

Africa and kept the men in stimulated rosy anticipation and travel bookings for weeks.

Ernest had been drinking too much and his blood pressure and liver were rebelling. In Madrid we both went to see his old friend from Civil War days, Dr. Juan Manuel Madinaveitia, who gave me barium tests and put my husband on a regimen of six ounces of whiskey a day and no more than two glasses of wine. Ernest followed his orders faithfully and I caught a violent cold. Together we entered a period of passivity, if not doldrums, nobody creating anything except letters. But we had the stimulation of each other's company and almost daily of friends.

In our sheltered nook remote from world aggressions, we read about them with some envy. It seemed odd to me that I should be so far away from the centers of world actions—Poland, Hungary and the Sinai Peninsula, which the Israelis were invading. By early November Ernest was getting his blood pressure under control. By strict discipline he had reduced it in three weeks from 200/100 to 120/80, and we gradually re-entered the world of fiestas, dominating personalities and the autumn bird shooting.

On November 17 we left Escorial in the car with Mario, slid along the Guadarrama road between poplars burning like candles among the pines, the snow-capped mountains ahead slashing the blue sky like quick-frozen waves. We stayed at the Plaza Hotel in Biarritz the first night and eased through luminous autumn days and familiar towns—Bayonne, Dax, Cadillac and Mont-de-Marsan where the red oaks in front of the old bullring were, I decided, the biggest and most beautiful trees of anywhere, anytime—to Angoulême for a night, Chartres another night and then, at the Ritz, into quarters new to us, rooms 56 and 57, a tiny little salon which Charlie Ritz had thought would serve as Ernest's workroom but in fact served as little more than a luggage closet, and a spacious bedroom, both overlooking the hotel's small inside garden. "Same side as *Il Barbiere di Siviglia*," said Charlie.

When our old friends *les bagagistes* deposited the last of our current luggage in the sitting room they made a speech to Ernest, its tone so formal they had obviously rehearsed it. It was now thirty years or more since monsieur had left with them two pieces of luggage, one rather large, one smaller, enjoining them to care for them well since they contained important papers. In their opinion, it was now time for monsieur to relieve them of the responsibility . . . the baggage room was overcrowded. Ernest asked them to bring up the cases and they proved to be really old-fashioned, the larger one lined in patterned silk in the mode of the twenties. Their contents gave Ernest a couple of weeks of intermittent excursions back into his early days in Paris via a dozen or more blue and yellow notebooks handwritten mostly in pencil and hundreds of fragile pages of typed stories and sketches, as well as some ancient sweatshirts and sandals and oddments. For hours on end he sat on the floor beside the trunks reading his early efforts, discovering with delight that it had been just as difficult to write in those days as it had been lately.

Disquieting news was coming from Minneapolis. Mrs. Kerr had sold her boardinghouse and my mother was denouncing as inedible the meals provided by the new landlady. She was also harassing the woman to the point where they said she must leave. My mother wanted to go to a hospital and loving friends there, Bee Burris and Rose Winter, scurried around, got her into a hospital and then to a Christian Science home, The Star of Bethlehem. On November 27 the matron of the home wrote that she did not know how long they could keep my mother. On November 28 Rose Winter wrote that the matron had telephoned to say that they could not keep my mother after the month ended. I wrote a stern letter to my mother and a placating letter to the matron. In mid-December Rose managed to get my mother into a private sanatorium at St. Croixdale, Wisconsin. Dear Rose Winter had given me and other neighborhood children happy lessons on playing the piano. I should not have been burdening her with the chores of looking after little Adeline and brooded about it to Ernest. His reaction was specific and convincing.

"If it's going to keep you miserable, staying here

until we both leave, go over there now," he said. "But she'll be reasonable only as long as you're there. Then the miseries again. You know that."

"I don't want to go now."

"Then forget it." I didn't forget it but I stopped nagging myself about it. Other unhappy news came from Cuba. Ernest's devoted Black Dog had died.

Except that we were surrounded by the joys and treasures of Paris and with friends floating in, Ernest had little cause for jubilation. With the Suez Canal closed, we had canceled our bookings for Africa. The doctor had put my husband on a diet restricting the intake of almost everything interesting, a regimen designed to lower his much too high blood pressure and much too high cholesterol count. We had anticipated quick results, and the blood pressure had dropped dramatically for a while. But the diet was a bore—five ounces of meat a day with no fats, no eggs, none-to-minimum alcohol and wine, some vegetables—and the blood pressure crept up again.

Thinking about Christmas I wandered up to the Avenue Montaigne and the Christian Dior boutique where I found a present for Ernest I couldn't possibly afford, and bought it, a pullover consisting of two soft, heavy slabs of brown suede, back and front, held together by huge-coiled knitted sides, sleeves, shoulders and a thick turtleneck. We noticed our bartender friends shivering in the rue Cambon side of the Ritz, especially in the Big Bar with its high ceiling, full winter having dropped down on us. I wanted to buy decent woolen sweaters for all the bartenders to wear under their white coats.

London friends were urging us to visit there and share their salubrities.

"You go, kitten. You have so many friends there," Ernest said.

"Without you? Without you, nobody will want me."

"Don't be so bloody modest. You go. I'll stay here and vegetate."

Come to think of it, I had a £500 war bond moldering away in my London bank. On December 2 Ernest took me to the night train for London. The next evening I wrote him from Claridge's, "If you haven't done the journey except by air in sixteen years, you can't believe how far it is between Paris and London." For a week I buzzed around London lunching and dining with old friends. My best find of the week was a small silver flask for Ernest. Along with half a bagful of Scotch woolen sweaters, I took the flask to Paris, rushed it around the corner to Cartier's begging them to finish the engraving before Christmas and, especially, to bill me, Mme. Hemingway, at the Ritz rather than my husband. "A surprise, you know, for my husband."

Cartier's sent the considerable bill to Ernest who opened it while I was contentedly reading the Paris *Herald Tribune* over breakfast in bed.

"You've bought something in Cartier's?"

"Huh? No, lamb."

"You *had* your holiday in London." His tone was doubtful.

"What's that thing?"

"It's a bill from Cartier's."

"Those bastards." Without upsetting the breakfast tray, I was out of bed to see the bill in Ernest's hand. Luckily the French script was illegible. "It's my bill. I told them to send it to me. Please, lamb, this is not a deception. It's just a momentary secret." Ernest gave me the bill and that morning I went around to Cartier's to upbraid them. Their "thousand pardons, madame" could not assuage my consternation that Ernest might be thinking I was dishonest with him. But when he opened his package Christmas morning the flask with his facsimile signature and a cat's face resolved the matter.

Free and easy Ernest and I walked favorite old streets, the Boulevard St.-Michel, St.-Germain, the rue de Seine, the rue Bonaparte, and from behind the Panthéon up to the Place de la Contrescarpe where Ernest and Hadley had lived when they were young and poor. One day Ernest announced he was taking to lunch at the fashionable Berkeley a beautiful girl who had crossed with us from New York that last September. I had noticed her in the ship's gym and recommended her to my husband as a possible diversion. She had been the mistress of some impressive industrialist or wine baron. I was busy at the typewriter when he returned.

"How was it, lamb?"

"*On s'ennuyait è mourir,*" said Ernest, resignation in his voice.

"You didn't even take her home?"

"I took her to the door. The street door of her building."

"Poor lamb. Anyhow you're on a love-making diet. Or supposed to be."

"Like 1944 here in this hotel."

On January 22 we left Paris with Georges Mabilat and our thirty-three bags in his Cadillac to settle next day aboard the *Ile de France*. Bucking powerful winds the dear old *Ile* creaked and groaned in every timber, shuddered on the tops of the mountainous waves and leap-frogged into the troughs with thunder crashing along her keel. Neither the bars, with our friends Gaston and Adolf in attendance, nor the dining room were ever crowded. We loved it. In the six-day crossing Ernest further reduced his alcohol intake, began to sleep better and got his blood pressure down to 140/80, the lowest in months.

From New York the *Ile* would be making a cruise of the West Indies—Martinique, Trinidad, Grenada, ending at Matnazas, Cuba—and Ernest decided to continue aboard, herding our luggage with him while I headed for Minnesota on filial duty. Except for a few small inside cabins the *Ile* was totally booked for the cruise, but Jean Monnier, the *Ile*'s doctor, offered Ernest the use of his *femmes isolées* quarters in the ship's hospital. Ernest took a small cabin for the luggage and by ship-to-shore telephone persuaded George Brown to accompany him on the cruise.

On Sunday afternoon, February 3, aboard the train Hiawatha, I watched Midwest towns slide by with fascination growing from long-lost acquaintance. The cities, Albany, Chicago, Milwaukee, had been unredeemed dirty dark brick, but the small towns with their gabled, gingerbreaded houses set in neat squares were picture-book scenery, the front yards uniformly neat, the back yards uniformly cluttered with the snow-draped relics of summer living, barbecue racks, canoes, wheelbarrows. No European villages that I could remember displayed half as many accouterments of family fun-making. Middle America looked rich to me.

A friend drove me from Minneapolis to Prescott, Wisconsin, and the St. Croixdale clinic, where in her bright, clean room, its window overlooking lawn and trees, little Adeline received us formally as though we were new acquaintances. For hours Adeline told me about the "trying" conditions in which she was living. I bought and brought her comfortable, pleasing new clothes. Along with her nurses, I gave all I could imagine for several days to console her in her lonely realms of senility. She continued to be dissatisfied, miserable and pitiful. Maybe she needed entertainment. I read aloud some *Just So* stories and *New Yorker* pieces, which amused her. As I was leaving after a week I said, "I'll try to get back here in June or July, Mummy dear, and read you some more good stories."

"You won't come back," she said. "You don't care anything about me."

22

Sweet Home

ONLY A FEW days after Ernest and George Brown and Dr. Jean Monnier disembarked from the *Ile de France*, Jean to stay with us for a couple of days ashore, we relaxed into an epoch of near tranquility. There were fewer than the usual number of people down from the U.S. wishing to come out for lunch. There was ceaseless rain with thunderstorms. *Pilar* was undergoing drastic basic repairs as well as face-lifting, so we busied ourselves at home.

Rather than risk damage to his windfall of old notes and manuscripts in their dilapidated trunks from the Ritz basement, Ernest had gone up to Louis Vuitton's shop in Paris and splurged on a battery of luggage big and varied enough for a troupe of chorus girls. Now he was spending mornings picking gingerly through his records of his early Paris days, making little piles of papers on the library floor, and in his head correlating the memories they evoked. He continued missing the company of his faithful Black Dog, but elfin Cristóbal, the love sponge, was always available for pampering. All spring the weather stayed fretful and hostile with storms, but our lawns and trees and vines and flowers flourished. Abstaining from alcohol except for a couple of glasses of wine a day put a serious strain on the man's nerves (I didn't even try to match his discipline) but the Paris notes stimulated his spirits.

By mid-March *Pilar* could ease off her rehabilitation stilts and we took her eastward from the little Club Náutico in Havana's harbor for a trial run in choppy seas, the Gulf Stream running strongly backward, *abajo* as the local fishermen said. (The oceanographers in Miami and New York politely doubted our word that the Stream reversed itself, sometimes for several days. But there it was, thrusting westward instead of on its usual course eastward along the north coast of Cuba.) We saw a whale shark cruising below the surface with his mouth open with bait fish splashing all around him, a good omen for the future. Ernest took two female dolphin and I brought in a big male dolphin and an Arctic bonito. But in May the current turned more sluggish and patchy more frequently than we had ever seen it, and our marlin catches declined by more than half those of other years. By May 27 we had taken only nine marlin aboard *Pilar,* four by Ernest, three by me, two by Taylor Williams. None of the fishermen, sports or commercial, suggested sensible causes for the Gulf Stream phenomenon. Atom bomb tests, said some. Could Mars be attacking us? asked others. In the known history of the Stream's performance, there had never been such deviations.

A girl in a flirtatious, floppy red straw hat came to call, Miss Phoebe Adams of *Atlantic Monthly* magazine, who wanted from Ernest some contribution to their hundredth-anniversary issue. She reminded him that the magazine had been among the first to publish his stuff in the United States, but it was hardly necessary. The hat and her charm impelled Ernest to promise a pair of stories which would reach Boston well before deadline. Both stories concerned blindness, one, "Get Yourself a Seeing-Eyed Dog," about an American losing his sight and nobly, maybe a bit too nobly, sending his wife away on a holiday, the other about a disgusting old blind man brawling outside a Western village bar, "A Man of the World." Typing them I was confused by the disparity between the genial, jolly temper of my housemate those days and the turmoil he could stir up inside his head.

Denis Zaphiro came from Kenya, bringing us in Cuba all the charms we remembered from Africa, his sharp wit, his warm affections, his tough-minded judgment, his large capacities for both thought and frivolity. He settled smoothly into our Finca habits. Day after day he fished with one or both of us or alone with Gregorio, and even after a month he had caught no marlin. We had never before seen the Gulf Stream and the fish so curiously haphazard. After all our talk in Africa of the glories of the Stream, we felt like phony promoters and liars.

Fidel Castro's clandestine supporters were harassing Batista's dictatorship with unexpected bombings around Havana and one in our village which did little harm except to our sense of security. Jack (Bumby) and Puck and their two pretty daughters moved down to Havana, he to work for a brokerage firm, and unintentionally we gave them much less help and hospitality than we had planned. Acute hepatitis attacked Jack and kept him helpless in their small apartment, and as I occasionally looked after their spritely children, as well as our local beasts and plants, I reached a couple of new hypotheses concerning human behavior. One was that people grow to love living creatures

563

from taking care of them. It is not necessarily love first impelling the care. As Ernest worked at the typewriter atop his bookcase in comparative comfort and I sweated through four or five changes of shirts and shorts doing house, garden and kitchen chores, I reflected that males of our species make the best music, pictures, sculpture, dams, ships, corporations, books partly perhaps because they never question the superior importance of their endeavors over the mechanics of living, the cleaning, grooming, feeding. When I mentioned these considerations to my lovable males, Ernest's reaction was practical. Seldom one to juggle philosophical theses, his refrain as long as I had known him had been, "If you have a message, call Western Union."

"It's a bitch of a summer," he said now. "Gulf Stream worthless. Everybody sweating too much. We ought to get away." I had been concerned that Denis's holiday with us was proving much less festive than I'd hoped. Since Ernest was sipping only his two glasses of wine with dinner, we seldom went in to the Floridita to absorb its cheer, liquid or oral. Also, of the few unattached girls to whom we could introduce Denis, none held his eye and none was enthralled by fishing.

Ernest read in the papers that middleweight Sugar Ray Robinson would be boxing Carmen Basilio in New York, and with the fight as a good reason for getting away we flew up with Denis and installed ourselves in the Westbury Hotel. In a big, pretentious black Cadillac Toots Shor took us out to the fight and I found it wonderful to sit so close to the ring that we could see the fighters smack the sweat off each other, and although the *aficionados* may have been disappointed that they did not murder or badly maim each other, the fight delighted me.

While Ernest kept appointments with Scribner's and Alfred Rice, I showed Denis my favorite galleries at the Metropolitan and Modern Art museums. While Ernest took Marlene Dietrich and her full-length mink wrap to "21" for a sentimental dinner, Denis and I dined cheerfully with Dr. Jean Monnier aboard the *Ile de France*. The men went to big-league baseball games and we saw some easily forgettable Broadway plays. So that Denis could see something of Washington we arranged with Bill Walton to stay overnight with him and on Thursday, October 3, moved down on the train. Ernest would join us the next day. In Washington we wondered at the news that the Russians had sent into space the first satellite ever to circle the earth. Jim Hagerty, the Preident's press secretary, reported the White House reaction was something such as "interest but not alarm." But we were stunned. It was as important as the Wright brothers' first flight, Bill suggested. Maybe as the invention of gunpowder, I thought.

Ernest was unperturbed by the Russian exhibition when we met him at the train. It should help our space people to get further funds for research, he said. "Foxy, those Rooskies."

A young professor of English from Norfolk, Virginia, William W. Seward, Jr., who for several years had been letter-writing with Ernest, joined us at the railway station to ride back with us to Norfolk. After Mr. Seward had left us Ernest declared, "Bill's a fine-textured guy. A legitimate gent."

Back at the Finca rehashing our jaunt, we concluded it had been one of mixed assets. We had all gained weight and doubtless additional cholesterol, but we had enjoyed the recess from sweating and the weather was turning cooler. I bemoaned the circumstance that Denis hadn't found any girls.

"Pooh," said he. "Don't worry about me. I go without girls in Kenya for months on end."

"But being a monk is bad for you."

"Supposed to unbalance the judgment, I know."

"You look fairly normal to me," Ernest said.

"Oh, I like vice—several vices," Denis said.

"Me too, I like vice," said I. "We ought to make a song: 'I like vice/its charms/More than suffice/To quell the inner/Protests of a voice/Saying, No!' "

When Denis had to leave us after nearly four months, nothing filled the spaces in the house for us.

"Empty as a discarded cocoon," Ernest muttered.

"Worthless as a spent shotgun shell," I said.

On Thanksgiving Day I wrote: "We have good reason for observing the day with thanks, most important the regeneration of Papa's liver and kidneys and the reduction of his blood cholesterol and my reduction of anemia, our deliverance this year from a close hurricane, our harmony and happiness and companionship together. . . .

"It hasn't all been rosy. . . . There is the unhappy situation of my mother and of Gigi, ill in Miami, Bumby's problems with finances, the fishless Gulf Stream and bombings and new poverty in Cuba and someone shooting our dog, Machakos, in the night. But the negatives are overbalanced for me by the good things."

We were staying home as usual on New Year's Eve and I was making a lime pie for lunch the next day when Western Union telephoned and read a cable from St. Croixdale: YOUR MOTHER EXPIRED 2:35 P.M. FOLLOWING 24 HOURS ILLNESS AWAIT INSTRUCTIONS.

I telephoned the sanatorium and ordered flowers, a singer, a Christian Science reader, then reserved airplane seats to Minneapolis, left Havana the following evening, got to bed at the Curtis Hotel in Minneapolis about 5 a.m. and was up again at 8:30 for more telephoning. At the funeral service at the "Temple" in Prescott, Wisconsin, my mother rested among flowers in one of her favorite rose-red dresses, her skin made up unobtrusively with rouge, her thin old hands crossed on her stomach. But no artistry could erase the look of permanent distress on her features. Pretty nurses from St. Croixdale joined some of my mother's old friends who came down from Minneapolis to hear hymns, "Oh, Gentle Presence" and "Abide with Me."

On the train ride back to Chicago, I was comforted by the pastel landscapes, whole towns of one-story houses with Christmas wreaths on the doors, lighted trees gleaming behind windows, bright sunshine melting not a drop of snow on the roofs, people preceded by plumes of white mist. Back home again I found that a branch of the ceiba tree had broken through the roof of my room and rain had poured in. Rather ineffectually Ernest and René were trying to dry out my mattress in our feeble winter sunshine.

566

23

Cuba in Crisis

HAVING ENDURED THE summer of 1957—
the hottest, most humid summer in memory—Cubans
were now assaulted not only by the heaviest ever, coldest and most frequent storms from the north but also
explosions of human violence and covert brutalities.
Between October 1 and May 1, an unprecedented
twenty-five Northers struck the island, and on one
February night the two thermometers in our house
registered 46° F. I had never before seen the red
streak below 58° in my room.

Rumors, half-verified reports and facts whirled
across our luncheon table and trickled in each morning from our Finca employees. Fidel Castro's underground forces daily displayed more and more violence
against Batista's secret police, S.I.M., and the army.
Batista forces retaliated. Our Cuban friends had not
seen or heard of such atrocities since the old macabre
days of the dictator Gerardo Machado, twenty-five
years earlier.

Some young men from our village had been arrested
by the Batista police or the army, imprisoned and tor-
tured, and one of them left dead in a ditch down the
main road. In mid-March Batista reinstated news censorship and we had little information beyond crop
reports, shipping, weather and pictures of girls engaged to be married. The Miami papers were slashed
into ribbons before they reached the newsstands. The
rumors were that men were being found head-down in
wells, their bodies mutilated, their faces unrecognizable
from beatings, others hanged, women beaten and tor-

tured, canefields and tobacco-drying sheds burned, live phosphorus thrown into busloads of passengers, particularly one on the Number 7 route which went through our village to Cotorro, because its driver was said to have informed against the villagers who were trying to help Fidel.

Cardinal Arteaga, head of the Havana diocese, tried to set up a commission which would bring the opposing forces to a talk table, but Fidel, who wore a religious medal on a chain around his neck, refused the invitation and warned that a general strike, a powerful weapon of workers against Batista, might occur. Going for what seemed necessary shopping in Havana, I found tension everywhere in the streets, eyes darting suspiciously, no more than a dozen customers in Havana's most elegant women's clothes store, El Encanto, or even in Woolworth's, and few pedestrians anywhere.

With the collector of internal revenue in Baltimore, Maryland, demanding whopping sums of income taxes from us, about $20,000 each quarter, I undertook to find out where our cash was going, noted every expenditure down to a new broom and paper napkins, and made charts from which we easily saw that our liquor consumption and that of our guests in March 1957 amounted to $250.64, more than half the total money spent, excluding salaries. Again in April, our bills for Chianti, gin, tonic, Campari, Pinch Bottle, Marqués de Riscal, La Ina, White Horse, Tío Pepe, vodka, and vermouth totaled $240.94, more than half our expenses, since our bounteous garden was giving us more vegetables than we and the servants and the deep freeze could hold, making us marvel at the miracles performed by seeds stuck in our thin topsoil.

"We had *filete* four times," I read from the chart. "$26.62. We had chicken three times, only $6.97."

"I like your Chicken Tarragon the best," my husband said. "Maybe we should cut down on the paper towels."

A new phrase, *treinta-tres* (thirty-three), caught our attention. It was a reference to informers (*chibators*) because they were said to be paid $33.33 a month, and Fidel's Revolutionary Council announced it would "liquidate" all known informers. While the Council continued propagandizing for a national strike, Batista officially authorized workers to shoot employers or anyone else urging them to strike.

One morning Ernest said, "It's quite possible looters will come here when there is no law. We will try to shoot them." But despite unpleasant weather, we went fishing a few days later, Gregorio surprisingly putting not quite fresh bait on the hooks, with the outriggers trailing their Japanese feathers and pork rind, customary for spring trolling.

Although there was a fair current offshore, Ernest took us farther and farther out, saying, "We have a little business to do," and about ten miles out, with no other craft in sight, slowed the motor, gave me the wheel topside with instructions to keep in that course, roughly 45 degrees, and went below. Down there Gregorio was opening drawers and tearing bunks apart, unearthing heavy rifles, sawed-off shotguns, hand grenades and canisters and belts of ammunition for automatic rifles I had never known existed aboard *Pilar*, and he and Ernest were throwing them into the sea. It took them half an hour or more to dispose of the arsenal.

"Stuff left over from the old days," said Ernest, when he returned topside. "Nobody's going to use it now."

"So many weapons. They must be worth a couple of grand." I had been watching from above.

"My contribution to the revolution. Maybe we've saved a few lives. And please remember, kitten, you haven't seen or heard anything."

"I'll remember. I haven't even seen a flilie." The subject was closed.

Coming into the kitchen with supplies for the servants' table, René mentioned that for the first time in his memory our village housewives were buying tinned food, hedging against a general strike and the possibility of shortages. Their custom had been to buy only each day's needs each day. Lili de la Fuentes, who came out every week from Havana to wash my hair and fix my nails, reported that police had invaded

569

her building the night before and without explanation taken away a man from the apartment below her.

That Good Friday the Revolutionary Council announced that the general strike would begin at midnight. But we heard traffic on the central highway moving as usual. A United Stateser, who was supervising a group of cartographers who were surveying the countryside in jeeps to make a contour map of Cuba, telephoned to ask Ernest's advice on how to insure the safety of his crews. Ernest suggested that he bring them into Havana from the province of Camagüey where they were working, billet them in the Hotel Nacional, equip them with portable radios from which they could hear the news from Miami and set them to work in Havana province, which then seemed comparatively safe for foreigners.

Ernest came into my room the next morning bearing gay homemade presents including a fat check for my fiftieth birthday, I refusing to believe and repudiating the "50," and after lunch we happily blasted away at bottles on the steps of the ruins of the cow barn. But about five o'clock three goons identifying themselves as Wall Street biggies installed themselves in the sitting room, immoveable lumps drinking our whiskey, their empty guffaws ringing out whenever Ernest said anything. They had seen our signs on the gate, but couldn't believe the KEEP OUT referred to them. I wished I could horsewhip every one of them. When I saw their chauffeur from the Hotel Nacional he apologized to me, and I solemnly promised him I would shoot him the next time he brought out a load of sightseers.

By April 7 the general strike still had not been activated, and nobody seemed to know when it would begin. None of our people was in favor of it, or of any other violence. Not Arnoldo, the village plumber, who was repairing the servants' bedroom. Not Cecilio, the carpenter, who was making a big new window for the kitchen. *"Son los políticos,"* he sighed. *"Quieren poder y dinero."* (It's the politicians. They want power and money). Not Pichilo, the head gardener, who cared not a fig for politics and was worried about three dogs of the village who had been bitten by another dog with rabies. Not our fat Yugoslavian laundress, Ana, although she tended to grow excited about politics, perhaps because she had few other outlets for her emotions. Not our dear René who simply wanted peace and contentment for everyone. Not Sonia, the cook, who had no room in her consciousness for affairs beyond her own, or her sister, Lola, the maid, who was too relaxed and comfortable to disturb herself with vague issues.

The morning news of April 10 included the item that the police sergeant of the Cotorro station down the road from us, the same who, they said, had shot our dog Machakos, had been killed during the night along with several other people. Roberto Herrera, who came out in the afternoon, reported he had heard shooting in all directions in Havana all night, and left again without supper, to reach home before dark. We reflected that our arsenal of weapons in the house consisted of nothing more for protecting us than Ernest's small Wehrmacht pistol and our .22 caliber bottle-shooting rifle. The rumors and alarms did not deter us from attending the opening of the new Trader Vic's restaurant in the Havana Hilton Hotel.

A few days later we heard the tale that Fidel had ordered the chiefs of his revolutionary groups all over the island to report to him in the Sierra Maestra to explain why they had failed to execute the general strike, and to be excused or punished. Punishment, so they said, was supposed to be assassination by their sub-chiefs. I could not imagine how this strategy would endear him or his cause to his compatriots.

Except for my lingering anemia, we were flourishing personally. Ernest, whose blood pressure was behaving well (136/66) was contentedly working mornings from about 8:30 until we went down to swim twenty-seven round trips, a half mile, before lunch, and afternoons and evenings I was typing his recollective essays about his early days in Paris and his friends there, Ford Madox Ford, Gertrude Stein, Scott Fitzgerald, Sylvia Beach and Ezra Pound, who that April 19 was released from St. Elizabeth's Hospital in Washington, a joyous day. Ernest had written the Attorney General that he would like to send Pound

$1,500 to help him return to Italy and that day wired Washington for an address to which he might send the check. Years later Olga Rudge, Mr. Pound's devoted friend, told me they had never cashed the check, instead had it encased in Lucite to use as a bibelot/paperweight. But too many visitors, especially strangers, fingered it. They had to hide it away.

The population of the Gulf Stream having apparently migrated to distant, unknown waters, we gave *Pilar* long vacations that summer and more and more splashed up and down the pool, listening to the news from Miami on the portable radio. One evening when Ernest had made forty-five round trips for the day, I swam the fifty-two trips lengthwise and a double crosswise for an even mile, and continued with that pleasant diversion until I had swum twenty miles in twenty days.

Having finished work, at least temporarily, with his Paris reminiscences, which, typed in triple space by me, reached about three hundred pages, Ernest was devoting himself to a book of fiction he had started ten years earlier and worked at intermittently. It began as a short story set first in the pretty French fishing village of Le Grau de Roi, where we had lunched on detour to Nice years before, and later at Aigues-Mortes a bit inland, both of them northwest of Marseilles, the time being in the nostalgic midtwenties. He did not invite me to read this new work each evening, as I had done with other books, and I did not press him about it. Eventually the book, titled *The Garden of Eden,* grew very long and, when finally I typed it, seemed to me repetitious and sometimes supercilious, and also containing some spots of excellent narrative.

When a new Spencer Tracy film, *Bad Day at Black Rock,* appeared in Havana cinemas, I went in to see it and was enthralled not so much by the action or acting as by the settings, vast sweeps of sagebrush with violet mountains in the distances, cottonwoods shining in the sun and bending in the wind, high, clear skies. At lunch the next day I told Ernest about it.

"Montana, maybe, or Wyoming, or Idaho. That

wonderful, empty space out there. You loved it, didn't you?"

"I always worked well there."

A week or so later Ernest suggested a plan for the autumn. "Let's go up to Ketchum. Do a little bird hunting."

"It's a long, tiring drive."

"Not necessarily. Toby Bruce likes to do it."

"The Finca seems safe enough now for us to leave it. We've had no night intruders."

"I'll get on to Toby."

The telephoning produced plans for travel beginning in late September. Betty Bruce and I would fly separate routes to Chicago and on October 4 be collected by our husbands and we four would drive west in the Bruces' big comfortable station wagon.

24

Joys in Idaho

RIGHT ON SCHEDULE, Saturday morning, October 4, the Bruces and the H.'s slid out of Chicago, Toby driving, beside him Ernest navigating, bird-spotting, commenting, Betty administering food and drinks in the car, cocktail hour beginning about six o'clock, Toby sipping rum on ice, Ernest Pinch Bottle and fresh lime juice, Betty and I dry martinis, the speedometer ticking off the miles, easing speed near Casper to watch antelope grazing or lazily resting only a hundred yards from the road, Ernest saying, "We should see pheasant now" and five minutes later spotting a cock pheasant in the roadside ditch. In Yellowstone we stopped to chat with a boneless-looking, rubberized-looking black bear and later a brown bear who sat up on puffy soft haunches to chat back. Bear-talk was one of Ernest's specialties.

"How you doin', boy? They treatin' you right?"

Six or seven yards from us the bear looked away.

"All that posing for pictures. Gets to be a bore, eh boy?"

The bear looked back at us, his eyes sleepy in the sunshine.

"With no compensation. That's tough. You fellows ought to get together, like the Masai. Charge ten shillings a shot. Or a goat's leg."

The bear ambled off.

"Very uncommunicative bear," said Ernest. "Montana bears are loquacious." He was referring to a storied winter years before when, he claimed, a bear shared his cabin while he trapped fur-coated animals for a living.

Just at dusk we slid up Ketchum's two-block main street and maneuvered directly to Pappy and Tillie Arnold's house, to receive a bone-bruising welcome from them and Taylor Williams, their consistent dinner guest. The comfortable smell of frying chicken pervaded the house. I ran kitty-corner across the street to the door of Clara Spiegel's new house to shout, *"Jambo Memsa'ab."* In the indoors twilight she and Don Anderson, who ten years before had hunted deer with Taylor and me, welcomed me with surprise. Ernest had asked Pappy Arnold to keep quiet about our arrival and about our renting the Clark Heisses' house, a log cabin just across an empty lot from the crystal-chandeliered Christiania bar. Day after day, we went chuffing down U.S. Route 93 in an ancient station wagon to walk up chukars, Hungarian partridge, sage hens, pheasants or ducks in the fields of cattle-rancher friends, in glorious crisp sage-scented air. After years of neglecting my Winchester Model-21, 20-gauge shotgun, except for a few quail hunts in Cuba, I expected to shoot poorly to terribly, and I was right. Early in the season when we were working over Bud Purdy's big spread near Picabo, thirty miles down the road, Ernest set up a beautiful shoot for me alone, having

574

spied mallards on a small slough in one of Bud's north pastures. We crept softly through dry grass, carefully up the rise above the slough. As we stood up, four handsome drakes took off, wings creaking. I shot both barrels and failed to drop even a feather. "Behind and below," I muttered before Ernest could say it. There wasn't any excuse for such slatternly shooting. I had pulled back the safe on my gun in the last step of climbing. I had had solid footing. I had simply failed to put the bead on the bird. Ernest kindly refrained from describing my failure to the others, and gradually I moved into the pleasant circle of shooting better and so enjoying the hunting more, and so shooting better.

One day, hunting ducks along his drainage canals with us, Bud Purdy, a slight, slim one hundred forty pounds of muscle and intelligence, put his hand on a fence post and vaulted the four-foot-high, tightly meshed wire. Never to be outdone, Ernest with his seventy-some extra pounds, tried the same maneuver and on landing sprained a heel tendon. When we got back to the Heiss cabin that evening, Pappy telephoned young Dr. George Saviers, of the Sun Valley Hospital staff, who came to the cabin, bandaged, recommended rest for the tendon and subsequently became one of our most valued friends, as well as an instant member of our hunting mob.

On opening day for pheasants, October 15, a whole army of us deployed ourselves in hot sunshine around a friend's stubble field, waited, moved forward, waited. There were supposed to be pheasants among the weeds of a ditch ahead of us; we must not put them up until noon. But on the tick of noon we moved. One, two, three cocks and some hens got up and we let off a blast like a salute to the Queen, with one shell of mine dropping a bird crossing to my right. We beat a half-dozen other fields of Hagerman Valley, our feet hot in hunting boots, found a few more birds, lunched from the tailgate of our station wagon, and in the late afternoon pulled into Tom Gooding's backyard to reorganize for the 100-mile drive back home.

All the way south that morning Ernest had clowned, giving us impersonations of a British admiral, a tart, a general, a duchess in his most outrageous accents. On the way home we were not so amused. Our leader had the *idée fixe* that car heaters were a lethal weapon which poisoned the lungs and that, even with the heater shut off, a closed car menaced one's health. Ernest had rolled down his front window all the way, and as we gained altitude and a bitter wind whirled around us in the back, he failed to hear our protests. The front trio were nipping whiskey and passing the bottle back to Taylor. Rummaging in our gear I found a plastic bottle I'd filled with 100-proof vodka and took a sip. The flavor was pure plastic, but the effect was vodka. I handed the thing to Pappy. "Forget your tastebuds. It's central heating." When we reached home, the bottle was almost empty, and I gave it to Ernest. "See what you've done to us." He took a sip and hurled the bottle into the darkness.

On Halloween we found on our doorstep a present from neighbor children—two gray-and-white striped kittens, brother and sister, weaned but still wobbly. We welcomed them with warm cream and more sophisticated tidbits, nests by the fire and floods of affection, and after they had explored all our corners and smells and settled in comfortably, we found the boy cat, Big Boy Peterson, to be one of the great charmers of his tribe, sweet-natured, witty, stout-hearted, loving, trustful, entranced with the movement of water running from a faucet. The girl cat, Sister Kitty, proved to be Big Boy's opposite. She was self-centered, suspicious, mean-tempered and a bore, but we put up with her because we felt Big Boy might like a companion in the hours we were away, prowling around in sagebrush.

One afternoon on John Powell's ranch I managed a minor triumph. Ernest assigned me to scramble along an abandoned ditch some fifteen or twenty yards above a field where he and some others moved northward in line abreast. There was some shooting and retrieving in the field and when a bird flew up from my ditch I hit him and was watching Don Anderson's dog retrieve him when ten yards behind me another bird whirred up and I caught him with my second shell. It was my only double of the year made at 180 degrees.

On a bleak December morning of whirling clouds and roads so coated with menacing black ice that we could drive only at twenty miles an hour, and should have known better, Pappy Arnold and I slid down to Hailey and climbed aboard one of Larry Johnson's airplanes, already inhabited by a couple of burly silent fellows with rifles. We were flying, we thought, into the Middle Fork of the Salmon River where deer-hunting season was still open. Larry ordered me to the co-pilot's seat beside him, and before takeoff gunned the motors more than plenty. Twenty minutes later we were bobbing around like a cork in a choppy sea, a howling blizzard from the north pounding at us and absolutely no hole visible in the Boulder Mountains through which we could slip to their northern foothills and our tiny landing strip. Larry made a couple of tries for the pass he wanted and I wondered, as I had wondered often before, why aircraft builders thought it unnecessary to put wipers on their windshields. Snow was heaping on ours.

"Turning back," Larry said. I never ever heard more welcome words.

The next morning turned up bright and clear. Pappy and I climbed down from Larry's airplane on the landing strip of Mahoney Creek, a horse camp, no machines being allowed in that area, and moved into saddles atop horses. I had Blondie, a huge mare blind in one eye, sure-footed and mean, whose notion of good fun was banging her rider's legs into the pine trees along our steep and narrow path. She desisted only when I learned to punch her with a spur a minute before impact and she turned surprisingly willing and persistent when we got into snowdrifts up to her belly. We saw three bunches of does, each half a mile or more away, watched them move off as they saw or smelled us, then within range a couple of does and a young buck. Pappy and I and our guide all shot and the deer fell instantly. That night we hung him in the Heiss garage to marinate for a month in the cold air.

With Pappy Arnold acting as stand-in for Ernest, to keep the price fair, we had bought four adjoining lots on a hillside across from the Arnolds' house and I had sketched what seemed to me the perfect house to sit crosswise on them, big windows and doors facing south-southwest to collect winter sunshine, Ernest's quarters at the east end to hold the morning light, mine at the west to avoid it, a guest room or two and the garage below. But Ernest felt no rush to grapple with the problems of construction, and when the Heisses reminded us that they needed their house for their customary Christmas family reunion, we looked around the village for FOR RENT signs. After a day or two of fussing about with a balky heating system and supplementing the furnishings, we moved into the Whicher house with Big Boy Peterson and his sister, leaving our autumn's harvest of birds and beast in custody of the Heisses together with Owlny, a small brown owl Ernest had earlier winged to use as a decoy for blackbird shooting and then rescued and installed in a cardboard box in the Heiss garage. He had poked a walking stick through the box to serve as perch, and daily carried juicy mice or other goodies to his slowly mending patient.

While the autumn had brought us occasional cloudfuls of snow, the sun had burned it off all but the tops of our local mountains. Since most of the Big Wood River valley's population depended for livelihood either on Sun Valley's operations or on village motels and related services, tension rose like a fever as December unwound without snowstorms. We watched the skies, hoped, welcomed every errant flake, gave thanks that reservations at the Valley were not being canceled and rehearsed carols. It was not until mid-Christmas Eve that businesslike swirls of white appeared outside our windows. By midnight we noticed there were two or three inches of the precious fluff nestled onto the car parked outside. By December 27, the Forest Service could record five inches of snow on the Valley floors.

With hospitality spreading rampant through the valleys, people jumping out of ski clothes into glitter, gloss and dancing pumps, I had snagged Trail Creek Cabin, Sun Valley's informal log house with its blazing fireplaces, for a dinner-dance on Saturday night, the 27th, and transformed it into a bower of spicy pine with branches protruding from walls and ceilings to embrace us. We dined at tables in a hollow square with Herman Primus playing Austrian mountain songs on his zither in the middle and later wore out our shoes dancing the "Jelly Roll Blues." On New Year's Eve we went to bed early, but Ernest awakened cheerfully at midnight for a kiss, to eat grapes and think good, secret wishes for far-flung friends.

From Cuba came the news that Batista had fled from Havana and Fidel Castro and his cohorts had taken over the capital. The news services were telephoning Ernest for comment and he wrote on the back of a postcard: "I believe in the historical necessity for the Cuban revolution and I believe in its long range aims. I do not wish to discuss personalities or day to day problems."

As we were finishing a big lunch on New Year's Day and watching the Rose Bowl game, *The New York Times* telephoned about Cuban events. This time Ernest said he was "delighted" with the news and I felt instant disapproval of the word.

"It's too strong. You don't know what excesses they may commit."

"Nobody cares what I think."

"They called you. Please call them back and modify the word."

"Newspapers hate people's making retractions."

"You don't want that on the record, baby. It's not like you. Too hasty. You're much too responsible a man."

"Oh hell, you just want me to be wrong."

"Precisely not. I want you to be right."

"If you're going to make a correction," I said a few minutes later, "you should phone soon. They'll be going to press. Castro may be lining up his firing squads already."

"One bloody word."

"You're a man of words. You know their power."

Eventually Ernest picked up the telephone. His revised comment reached *The Times* City Room moments before copy went to the composing room for the first edition. His revised word was "hopeful."

During the Christmas holidays some stranger had

purported to envy me the wonderfully rewarding life of the intellect I led and our "inspiring literary discussions." Later I made a few notes on one such discussion: Watching our kittens chasing their cork, Ernest said, "The thundering herd."

"Yes. Thomas Hardy."

"Who?"

"You know. Thomas Hardy. *Far from the Thundering Herd.*"

"You mean, Zane Grey."

"I'm sorry."

"Hardy wrote *Far from the Madding Crowd.*"

"Well, was it General Lew Wallace who wrote *The Wandering Jew?*"

"No. He wrote *Quo Vadis.*"

"Well then, who wrote *Ramona?*"

"Gene Stratton Porter, of course."

"Oh yes, she was some relation to Jude the Obscure."

It was our crackpot version of cork chasing.

On Sunday, January 18, we tooled down 93 with Chuck and Flos Atkinson, shotguns, shells, four and a half gallons of wine and a huge salad to shoot magpies and eat roast duck on the happiest, most sunlit day thus far of 1959. Bud and Ruth Purdy were giving the first magpie shoot of the year at the Silver Creek Rod and Gun Club close by the shining river. A hundred and four magpies had been lured into unharming traps on their ranches, and gunnysacks full of them sat on the lawn outdoors while we organized the shoot and the betting odds around the humming fireplace inside. A thirty- to forty-mile wind was blowing from the west, leaving us no doubts that the fastest trigger-pullers would win the biggest shares of the betting pool.

With ruffles of laughter accompanying our blasting, sunlight changing the white etchings of brown mountains and each of us relishing the little ping of pleasure one gets from a shot well taken, we were a jolly crowd, almost too busy to notice our joys. When I downed a couple of fast birds neatly, Ernest said, "Like a razor blade cutting," flattering me. So ended the first of sev-

580

eral of that winter's magpie shooting sessions, happy afternoons for everybody except the magpies.

After two more months of quiet work and noisy winter sports, we were joined by A. E. Hotchner who came out to chauffeur us on the journey homeward. We left Ketchum on March 16.

At a motel in Phoenix we watched the second half of Hotchner's adaptation for TV of *For Whom the Bell Tolls* and I thought Jason Robards, Jr., and Maria Schell good in their roles and Maureen Stapleton excellent. Ernest reserved his approval. He disliked the uneven implications of guilt, having tried in the book to show that both sides had been corrupt or evil in one way or another. He was disappointed that Jordan failed to "light up" when he was hit and the enemy was approaching.

Rolling southeast we reached Tucson and telephoned Ernest's friend of thirty years, Waldo Peirce the artist, who seemed a flowing fountain of volubility, a cigar-ash dropper with an entrancing childlike delight in ideas, jokes, words, and a true modesty about his excellent work and an overwhelming generosity. An enchanting man.

Most of his pictures were then in New York on exhibition but he brought out some to show us: *The Silver Slipper,* of a Key West nightclub, full of dizzy movement with Ernest in the background; one of the *encierro* in Pamplona with bulls piling up over fallen boys in the early morning light; a tender, lovely portrait of his daughter Karen standing fresh and innocent in her ballet costume; a wonderful unfinished design of monks sweeping the floor of the Pamplona cathedral with ballet movements.

Playing with words much as he played with paint, Waldo mentioned, "I'm an invertebrate letter-writer," and for years after our visit he proved it, sending us reportage, notes, comments and a vigorous flow of wit, his envelopes always adorned with amusing sketches. He also sent us the canvas of monks, floor-sweeping, still on my wall and a daily present to my eyes.

We celebrated Palm Sunday, March 22, with a taxi

ride from El Paso across the Rio Grande to Juárez where crowds of townspeople moved from mass and a religious procession directly to stalls selling pottery, basketry and typical ridged blue glassware in the bustling market. After Ernest said a prayer in the cathedral we bought a chunk of ham, on which we lunched a hundred fifty miles later, welcome sustenance for our passage through the Judge Roy (The Law West of the Pecos) Bean's country, a fatiguing piece of Texas, rolling, treeless, empty, dry. Diminished in the distances, ranch houses looked so forlorn I wondered what motivations prompted men and women to such lonely enterprises, what sustained their determination. That fragile component, hope?

Farther southeast in Texas the roadsides were flowering like a medieval tapestry, even the ubiquitous low cacti flaunting huge pearly-white blossoms, and after Corpus Christi we had birds for sightseeing—curlews, ducks, boat-tailed grackles, gallinules, and in the marshes along the old coast road sandhill cranes feeding. When we left Texas just beyond Orange, our speedometer showed we had driven 1,156.6 miles from its northwest corner.

After we dropped Hotchner at New Orleans, Ernest drove us along the coast road through miles of front yards that were compositions in pinks, fuchsias and reds—azaleas in full bloom—and beside country ponds whistled at white ibis standing, fishing. As we approached Fort Myers Ernest remembered that his Hemingway grandparents used to spend winter vacations at Sanibel Island off the coast there when he was a child and, considering inviting him to join them, had invited him to lunch to observe his behavior and had decided against him.

"But nobody warned me," he said. "Didn't tell me I was on trial."

When we reached Key West on Saturday, March 28, the speedometer showed we had driven 6,284.9 miles from Ketchum.

The next afternoon we flew to Havana, found Juan's welcoming face behind the immigration barrier, paused at the Floridita for reunions with our bartender-friends, and hugged René, Lola and Ana, the laundress, on the front steps of the house beneath the ceiba tree.

25

A Disturbing Summer

IN KETCHUM THAT winter Ernest had been considering the job of updating his book *Death in the Afternoon* and had corresponded with an old friend whom he had never before mentioned to me, a man who had been a taxi driver in Mexico City, he said, one Bill Davis. Mr. Davis had invited us to stay with him and his wife at their house, La Consula, near Málaga so that Ernest might watch that season's bullfights and perhaps see a succession of *mano a mano* contests—only two matadors with six bulls, the most difficult and dangerous of games—between his pet, Antonio Ordóñez, and Antonio's brother-in-law, the cool, sharp, intelligent Luis Miguel Dominguín. Ernest had accepted Mr. Davis's invitation, he informed me soon after we arrived home. I felt doubtful. We had never been house guests anywhere for more than a weekend. In hotels we could order food, liquids and services whenever we wished, without consulting anybody. As house guests we would be at the mercy of our host's living habits, I feared, and said so.

"Can't we afford to stay at a hotel?"

"We'll be moving all over the country."

"But couldn't we keep one room in Madrid? It's almost in the middle of the country."

"You may love it near Málaga."

"And I may hate it. I don't even know these people. And you've never met the wife, have you?"

"No."

"I don't like this plan, lamb," said I. "We may be imposing on these people. I don't like us committing ourselves to a program we know nothing about."

"Don't be a spoilsport. We have a very kind invitation."

Mr. Davis had written Ernest a hospitable note assuring him that his house and staff were ample enough to take care of us. He had not mentioned his wife's views of the arrangement and I wondered whether she felt doubtful about it as I did, and then decided that my caviling would achieve nothing.

For once, no drastic deterioration had happened to the Finca while we were absent, our people were sweet and cheerful, the pool deliciously clean and cool, the house fresh and airy, beasts healthy, vines, shrubs, flowers and trees flourishing. The ocean fish we dug out of the deep freeze enchanted our palates after the fishless Idaho winter. Mayito Menocal and Elicio Argüelles and other friends converged on the Finca, each with a personal interpretation of the Castro revolution, Mayito and most of the others feeling hopeful. But in the month we were at home we noticed too many signs that the economy was sliding downward. Private construction had halted, suggesting that investors were doubtful if not scared. But the new police displayed a new courtesy in all directions and, as people repeated proudly, there were as yet no signs of corruption in the new government.

On Wednesday, April 22, in New York we entered an uproar of people, business, entertaining, last-minute shopping, before installing ourselves in Stateroom U 143 of the S.S. *Constitution,* bound for Algeciras. Neither of us had traveled aboard either a U.S. ship or such a modern conveyance, and much of its hotel manner was new. One did not ring for a steward or stewardess. Bellboys did the errands. The portholes were sealed tight, but the air conditioning functioned quietly. I was appalled at the number of female bosoms sprouting orchids as we left the pier, but we soon

584

discovered that many of the passengers were making their first Atlantic crossing.

"Nice but unexceptional people," I informed Ernest as we were breakfasting the next morning.

"I'll miss the gym," he said, remembering the *Ile de France*. The *Constitution* carried a small pool, aft, but only a few warm yelling children were using it in the chill April airs, and we admired their fortitude from a small bar nearby. At a larger bar behind the principal lounge Ernest made friends with the bartenders.

Mr. Davis, a tall, grave-faced, balding man, was waiting when we finally docked at Algeciras. He helped us transfer our twenty-one pieces of luggage into a pink Ford sedan he had chartered from a garage in Gibraltar. Mrs. Davis had sent turkey sandwiches to sustain us on the drive and we munched them and sipped wine as we moved through squares and rectangles of fields in varying greens in the dusk to the village of Churriana and beyond it to the private road and tall iron gates of the Davises' house.

As in other Spanish houses of the 1830s, La Consula's doors, fifteen feet high or more, were of heavy carved oak. Its walls and slipcovers were all pristine white, its furniture simple and straight-lined with vases of flowers everywhere. We felt at home with the vegetation outside, the pines, palms and acacia trees, the alpinia, the *Russelia equisetiformis*, lilies and vines, brothers or cousins of ours in Cuba. Somehow the Davises had learned that Ernest preferred standing while writing and they had provided a chest-high slanted writing table for him.

While we unpacked and settled in with the help of smiling servants who addressed me as "Doña Maria," we and the Davises indulged in a talk-jag about people on two or three continents, painting, prize-fighting, books and bulls, food and flowers, drink and dieting, health and disease, work and plans for the summer. Annie Davis seemed a generous hostess, an American who had lived abroad so long she seemed to us European.

On Sunday, May 10, we went in the pink Ford to the bullring at Málaga to watch a *novillada*—young bulls and not-yet-accredited matadors—which, as Bill Davis noted afterward, would remain memorable because it was surely the worst any of us had ever seen. The three first bulls looked to us as worthless as the three aspiring young matadors, but the three last bulls showed some quality and dignity. Having been ineffectively stabbed a dozen times, bulls 5 and 6 left the ring upright, dying from loss of blood, number 5 trailing his blood across the yellow sand, simply walking back by himself to the stables beneath the stands. We were so disgusted that we drank an extra martini before dinner about 11 p.m. and too much wine with dinner, and Ernest brooded that the rest of the season might continue on such a low, disgraceful level.

Gerald Brenan lived nearby and with his wife came to lunch on the wide upstairs veranda at La Consula, never obtruding his scholarship on us, talking about Beatniks and their language. " 'He made it,' " said Mr. B., "means a fellow got the girl to bed." " 'Dig' means 'to like,' as in 'I dig this music. I dig that chick.' 'Chick' means 'girl.' " I felt embarrassingly démodé. The phrases were entirely new to me. The Brenans had a rule about traveling. They refused to pay for it. On roads they hitchhiked, they said. "Bill Davis and I, we don't live in Spain," Mr. Brenan said. "We live in freedom, using the Spanish earth and climate as conveniences."

On May 13 we drove in the pink Ford through Granada, through a corner of La Mancha with its windmills, and on the next day to Madrid, its profile much enlarged with new buildings, to attend the fiesta of San Isidro.

For eleven days the bullfights dominated our Madrid stay, our emotions at the *barrera* bounded by festive luncheons and dinner parties which lasted until 2 a.m., completely exhausting me.

Antonio Ordóñez's wife Carmen invited us to a small family supper, "early," she said, since Antonio was fighting the next day. "Early" meant that we sat two hours chatting and some twenty people arrived before the dining room doors were opened to an enormous buffet at 11:45. At the restaurant Valentín, a thunderous place, we ran into the famous matador

Juan Belmonte. The summer heat of Sevilla did not bother him, Belmonte said, because, "I do nothing. It's the work which heats one." He was planning a year of Sundays, he said, with no work at all. When I asked his Sevilla address, he said, "Belmonte, Sevilla, or Belmonte, España."

At dinner in his luxurious apartment a few nights later, Victor Urrutia, the husband of Ernest's friend Maria, told me about Belmonte while across the room Belmonte, the sculptor Sebastiano Miranda and Ernest charmed each other. Belmonte, Victor said, must be keeping sixty former mistresses all over Spain, and did nicely for them. Belmonte had denied to Victor that he had any financial interest in the Maestranza, the bullring at Sevilla. But after one *corrida* he and Victor waited until the plaza was empty, then went to the office where Belmonte scooped up all the cash and took it away. On a journey to Portugal with Sebastiano Miranda, Victor paid for everything including a taxi which Miranda hired by the day. Returning to Spain they stopped in Sevilla and went to a café where they found Belmonte. From habit, Victor reached into his pocket to pay the bill, but Miranda held up his hand, protesting. "Now we are in Sevilla, you may not pay," said Miranda. "Here Juan pays." Miranda and Belmonte had been friends for forty-six years, and during each of those forty-six years Juan had complained vocally because Miranda told Juan's admirers who wished to send him presents that the great matador admired the hams or sausages or whatever of the admirer's province, whereas Belmonte, a slight, delicate eater, admired only the women. Miranda ate the ham and sausages.

Whenever we weren't out for drinks until about 11:30 p.m., we had clusters of people perched around the tiny salon of our suite at the Suecia Hotel, Antonio and Carmen singing folksongs, Noel Coward regretting that his arranger had cut some of the ballet music he had written for the London Philharmonic and expounding on his feud with Lord Beaverbrook, saying about Ernest's hairy chest, "We're so very different. What we have in common is we're both great artists."

In the Plaza de Toros the matadors flattered Ernest.

On May 16 Antonio dedicated his second huge, heavy, Pablo Romero bull to "Ernesto" and nursed along the beast which was good-hearted but weak in the knees and killed it in front of us. On May 24, Segura in his sparkling suit of lights dedicated a bull to Ernest and performed with a doubtful, difficult animal a wonderful *faena* with long, careful, slow passes in generous repertoire and was awarded two ears.

Half dead with exhaustion as I was from the *madrileños'* crazy time inversions—luncheon at 4 p.m., dinner at midnight—I managed to get to the Prado museum for a couple of peaceful mornings renewing acquaintances with its Patinirs, Brueghels, Hieronymus Bosches, Titians, Tintorettos and Veroneses.

On Tuesday, May 26, at Córdoba we went to the small, pretty bullring with its unusual iron balconies and lacy, painted woodwork, where Pepe Luis Vázquez, displaying his fear, and Jaime Ostos, wild and reckless and brave, were performing with Antonio who made a gesture I had never before seen. His second bull was a baby with minimum horns. Wild protests from the crowd. Stamping and roars. Antonio signaled the president he would kill this baby and himself pay for another, bigger bull. The baby had been picked, and Antonio ordered away the banderillas, made a few passes with the muleta and then a quick, straight kill. Antonio's new bull came pouring out of the chute wearing the biggest horns I had ever seen, thick, long and balanced, followed by a big, sturdy body. He looked difficult at first, banging at the *burladeros,* thrusting a horn over the *barrera.* But his eye followed the cape, and Antonio made a series of majestic passes. A motion picture would have shown thirty frames of the bulk of the bull passing close to the man's body, the cape slowly, gently, suavely changing position. Only one pick from the man on horseback, the banderillas, then the *faena,* the small red cloth bringing the enormous beast to one side of Antonio's waist, to the other side, some high *pasos de pecho* with the bull passing his head across Antonio's chest, the *naturales,* the full circles slow and sure, around the man's body, the big beast more and more convinced or hypnotized or enthralled by this game. For a full ten minutes Antonio must have played at maneuvering his huge, dangerous toy, before he placed him in position for the kill, the heavy rectangle steady on straight legs going down into the sand fore and aft, and went in between the huge horns to thrust the *espada* down to its hilt into the bull's lungs. In a minute he was dead, and Antonio was awarded two ears, and accepted the traditional tribute of being carried around the ring.

After his triumph and a shower, Antonio joined us at the Palace bar for a few minutes, reported he had paid 40,000 pesetas, then about $727.00, for his extra bull, drank a beer, stamped out a cigarette and departed.

On Thursday, May 28, we drove to Sevilla and the Alfonso XIII Hotel, saw a boring, shapeless *corrida* with dumb, unmanageable bulls. Bill asked Ernest about them. "Their meat is tender," Ernest said. Slim Hayward had written Ernest asking him to take her to the bullfight at Aranjuez on May 30, and the men left Sevilla early on May 29 to reach Madrid by bedtime and the rendezvous with Slim, while Annie and I drove southern roads back to La Consula.

Since the Davises did not permit a telephone or radios in their house, our only communication with the outside world was by post and telegram. Late on Saturday, May 30, the telegram man arrived at La Consula with a message saying Antonio had been gored at Aranjuez, dangerously but not critically. It was foul luck for Antonio, grim news for the dozen and more bullfight impresarios around the country who had counted on filling up their stadia with Antonio *aficionados* and a cause of sadness and lamentation among millions of Spaniards, including our bootblack in Málaga who followed the news of *tauromachia*.

Later Ernest explained to me. "Antonio was fighting in the part of the ring where the picadors had worked, and the bull's hoof slipped in the sand disturbed by the horses. It was like a bad bounce in baseball. Ordinarily the ring would have been smoothed and watered after the third bull—and before this one, Antonio's second of the day. But in that ancient little ring, there were no watering facilities."

If the wound had been one-quarter inch higher or one-quarter inch to the right, it could have crippled him permanently, or killed him. Unlike bullet or knife wounds, Ernest said, a horn wound is sharp-pointed but widens to the size of a baseball bat and tears and destroys many muscles. The surgeon must open and clean them all. The mishap would cost Antonio at least twenty-five days of convalescence and loss of income during the height of the season.

Having stayed in Madrid to attend Antonio, although he was already overattended as is the Spanish custom, the men returned to La Consula with news from the *clínica*. From Granada came a telegram announcing that Slim Hayward and Lauren Bacall were awaiting an invitation to lunch, dinner or anything else from Ernest, and a day or two later they came to lunch. They both greeted Ernest as a long-lost friend, ignored Annie and me, and for Bill and Ernest produced their man-capturing show.

"Darling, you're so thin and beautiful," said Slim.

"You're even bigger than I imagined," said Miss Bacall, and Ernest puffed up.

"It's so long. Papa, you never pay any attention to me," said Slim. Ernest looked contrite. "One bullfight isn't much of a reunion."

"Not much for Antonio," said Ernest.

"Couldn't you teach me about bullfights?" asked Miss B., moving in very close, smiling up at Ernest.

"The essence of Spanish *tauromachia* is not the *clínica*," said Bill.

"If we could go to just a few, just a few," said Miss B. ignoring Bill also.

When we reminisced about Noel Coward she quoted her husband Humphrey Bogart as saying to Coward, "I think you are wonderful and charming and if I should ever change from liking girls better, you would be my first thought." We were at the luncheon table that day from 3:30 until 6:30.

On Wednesday evening, June 10, Antonio and Carmen arrived by plane from Madrid, Antonio leaning heavily on a cane, looking exhausted, his face drawn and bony, but he smiled and said, "I'm splendidly well. But the doctor says I must throw away this cane soon." Together Ernest and Carmen helped him up the marble staircase to the second-floor dining room, and he went to bed immediately after dinner. Carmen's ankles were swollen. For nearly two weeks she had stood twelve hours daily on the marble floor of the clinic receiving her husband's hordes of visitors.

The next morning Antonio put aside his cane and with Ernest holding an arm walked slowly and painfully around the Davises' big bright rose garden, then made a second tour slowly by himself. In only a few days of splashing in the pool, sunning, lazing and swimming at the long empty beaches nearby, Antonio improved visibly, one evening jumping up from the dinner table to bounce on his knees with Carmen, thrusting one foot then the other toward her in a classic folk dance of Navarre.

A few days later, after seeing the bullfight at Algeciras in which Carmen's brother, Luis Miguel Domínguin, made a classically beautiful fight, the Davises, Rupert Bellville (who had come from London), Ernest and I went on to Valcargado, Antonio's new bull ranch. When Antonio came out of his house to greet us at midnight, we saw him and his welcoming smile already less thin and weary than it had been ten days earlier.

"Come in, come in, my stomach tells me it is well beyond suppertime," he said, and, "Now I have only slight pain from the wound."

Being in love with her husband, Carmen had the toughest job of any wife I knew, I thought, and also as devoted younger sister of Luis Miguel. Miguel was only ten years old when he began to play and then work with the bulls in Portugal. "His first fighting suits were like doll clothes," Carmen remembered. Then after fourteen, he sprouted up much taller than she was. By the end of that strange summer of 1959, her handsome, glamorous, top-ranking brother had been gored twice, and her husband of six years, somehow elfin in the ring and beautiful and skillful, was also twice caught by the horns. All together, she had endured the vicarious suffering of twenty-nine gorings of her husband and brother. Carmen had not imagined that so much misfortune could strike one family—four

591

gorings in one summer—she told me later. The odds were against it. "But I have revised my estimates."

The daughter of Domingo González Mateos, a bull-fighter and impresario, Carmen had some sort of intuition about bulls, some laser-beam-swift comprehension of their respective dangers, so that Luis Miguel once said, "A good thing Carmen was not born a boy. She would have outshone us all." She hated bulls. If she could have, she would have dissuaded her husband and her brother from their bullfighting fever. Since she couldn't do that, she spent most summer afternoons alone with her children in the Madrid apartment, waiting for telephone calls and praying, her fingernails cleaned of polish, because, she said, it seemed to her impertinent for praying hands.

On fighting days Antonio telephoned her from wherever he was before he dressed for the ring, and again when he returned to the hotel. If there was bad news, Antonio's devoted sword-handler, Miguelillo Moraleda, told it without camouflage.

"When people try to soften the report, I never believe them," she once said. "Trying to be kind, they are cruel. Antonio always tells me the truth, but often they won't let him telephone." Dr. Manolo Tamames, surgeon to Luis Miguel and Antonio and then considered the best man in Spain for bull wounds, never tried grief-postponing trickeries on Carmen. Said he, "She's a woman you can't fool anyhow."

Imperceptively I once suggested that it must have been more difficult to hear of the woundings when she was a younger sister and wife. "Now you are so experienced with it all."

"No, it is the reverse," Carmen said. "Each year it is more difficult because each year the nerves are more punished, more worn down. Their elasticity has gone. They respond less readily."

Like a matinee idol with the added attraction of visible bravery, Antonio impelled women everywhere to desperate, silly measures to gain his favor. Once in Peru, Antonio and Carmen found a woman fan in their bed in their hotel room. Antonio wasted no time evicting her. In San Sebastián, Spain, a girl pulled Antonio away from Carmen and pressed on him a photo of herself complete with name and telephone number. Antonio tore it up then and there. Carmen regarded such creatures with patience. "They're crazy about his suit of lights and his grace. They don't really care about him," she said.

She also viewed with composure the discrepancies, still noticeable in 1959, between other countries and her own in their attitudes toward women. "The Spanish woman of today is not as before. Not quite," she said. "She goes out with her husband or with married friends, always depending on the approval of her husband. It is an arrangement I like. It makes me feel more protected. It may seem stupid to others, or not very free. But it enchants me. When Antonio is away I stay in my house, and I am never bored." When I saw Carmen in Madrid several years ago she was driving her own car and, Antonio being out of town, took me without other chaperonage to a neighborhood restaurant for dinner. Through some twenty years of persistent, persevering, unpretentious bravery confronting the vicissitudes of Spanish *tauromachia,* Antonio and Carmen Ordóñez have won.

Almost. Their two daughters, whom I first knew as flowerlike, yard-high sprites, are both married to serious young matadors, and their three-year-old grandson is the most beautiful of all the family. So said Carmen, lovely and serene as always when they were in New York last winter. Among his myriad Christmas presents, the first he chose to play with was a miniature muleta. But Antonio will fight again twice this autumn of 1976 at Ronda and at Málaga.

From our first few days with the Davises, Ernest had been working, whenever he wasn't traveling, on an introduction to a new edition of his short stories, an essay that grew longer than his customary introductions and, when he gave it to me for retyping, dismayed me. It seemed to me tendentious, truculent and smug. It contained brutal, irrelevant references to a friend of ours. It ended boastfully.

I wrote my husband a short note, specifying the paragraphs I felt should be cut out or rewritten and my reasons for thinking so. "You're a loving generous

593

man," I wrote. "This is not like you." Ernest cut out the malicious sentences about our friend and modified some words, but, frozen-faced, without any offer of discussion, told me to retype the manuscript as amended. I retyped, sniffling and hacking with a long faithful cold.

Later Ernest received a letter from Charles Scribner, Jr., whose opinions coincided with mine about the introduction. Mr. Scribner wrote about revising the book's table of contents, and, "You do not want to sound pompous and hit upon a kind of jocular informality. But I am afraid that in so far as readers will not be expecting this, they may misunderstand it as condescension, and that would not be right either. . . ."

On June 25 the men took off at what Ernest liked to call "first light" but was really sometime after 8 a.m. for a strenuous round of Antonio's bullfights beginning at Zaragoza. Annie and I waved them off in our dressing gowns and I went to work on a story I was doing for *Sports Illustrated* which was published in August under the title "Holiday for a Wounded Torero." I was glad to relieve Annie, at least for a few days, of any chores of entertaining me. I had time then to begin to understand how widely we differed in character, she a cultivated woman, gentle, passive and unpunctual, I aggressive, impatient and unsympathetic to feminine niceties. I wished I could escape. I wished for a room of my own for which I would not be beholden to anyone. I realized that for the first time in our lives, Ernest had not invited me to join him on a journey. With my colds and aches I could not debit him. Still, it was a strange departure from our habits.

It had been decided that we would celebrate Ernest's and Carmen's birthdays on July 21 at La Consula and, knowing something of the lethargic attitudes of southern Spanish workmen, I began consultations with electricians for outdoor lighting, carpenters for building booths for play-target-shooting as in carnivals, and with the gray little impresario of Málaga who controlled the local musicians. I wanted a six-piece orchestra. He wanted to send out a piano to sit on the lawn in the nighttime dew. We agreed to eliminate the piano. I wrote and posted some thirty invitations in Spanish and Italian and English, and the very first to accept were David and Evangeline Bruce from the American embassy in Bonn. Carmen would attend to the invitations for her friends.

On July 2 Annie and I drove to Madrid in one day, our journey lightened and brightened by ever-changing vistas of gold, tawny and russet grainfields, the wind weaving patterns in them on the mountain slopes. We made a rendezvous with our husbands in Madrid where, to Ernest's annoyance, I excused myself from our group's three-to-four-hour lunches and dinners, needing to finish my story about Antonio. We moved and ate always in a crowd, now augmented by an Irish girl, Valerie Danby-Smith, who came to the Suecia Hotel purportedly to interview Ernest for the Irish press. The prolonged meals were becoming tedious for me, as were Ernest's performances at the head of the table as jolly host and raconteur.

On we went in cavalcade to Burgos for a Sunday afternoon bullfight, the Miura bulls performing better than the matadors. In Pamplona the next day Annie and I failed to find the small house in a row of middle-class duplicates, No. 7 calle San Fermín, where rooms had been rented for us. We went back to the central square and there found our friends outside a café, three or four tables having been slid together to accommodate our crowd which now included Peter Buckley and his bride, Dr. George and Pat Saviers, fresh from Sun Valley, A. E. Hotchner, Juanito Quintana and his son, Valerie Danby-Smith, who had made it up there on her own, and José Luis Castillo-Puche, a Spanish journalist, everybody in soaring spirits and Ernest devotedly signing autographs for every-one who came along and asked for one. We dined ensemble at the restaurant, Las Pochólas, and made it to bed about 2 a.m., to sleep until 5:30 a.m. when the drill was that we be bathed, dressed and assembled at the Choko Bar in the square for coffee before the beginning of the *encierro,* the bulls running through the boarded-up streets from the corrals to the bull-ring, where we went to await their entrance and the succeeding hijinks among the beasts and the young men of the town. Antonio was cavorting among them, his left leg bleeding. In the rush through the streets, he had been pushed onto a horn which had hit an inch into his left calf. Ernest was deeply concerned about the wound, but Antonio said, "Nothing. A Band-aid will do." But he prudently got George Saviers to wash it with antiseptic. We were fifteen or twenty at lunch and dinner.

One noontime we got off in the various cars to the village of Aoiz and beyond it along the Irati River for swimming and a picnic, the Irish girl Valerie now installed in the front seat between Bill and Ernest. Scrambling over rocks to get to the deep water, I stepped on a stone that tilted, heard two bone cracks. Petty tragedy, the third toe of my right foot was broken in two places, and there was nothing to do about it—no splints or bandaging—except to put it in a hard-nosed shoe. I swam anyway with the wobbling toe giving me the impression that I was trailing a long waving plume behind me in the river. Sitting under a shrub ashore Ernest said politely as I passed, "I'm sorry you broke your toe."

Apart from my reduced mobility with the painful toe and Ernest's increased consumption of vodka and wine, something was changing in him or me or both of us. He was averaging three or four hours of sleep in twenty-four, leaving our little house in Pamplona before 7 a.m. to walk around the town, chatting and drinking four or five hours at a stretch at his long table in the Plaza del Castillo, getting to bed about 3 a.m. I was increasingly repelled by the dirty tables, the sour smell of spilled wine, the stupid chitchat with strangers who moved in for autographs and free drinks, and Ernest's endlessly repeated aphorisms, and I could not endure four hours of it before dinner at midnight. I went back alone to the house in San Fermín street to read and rest and dine on a piece of fruit.

Back at La Consula scores of final arrangements for the birthday party absorbed my attention. What Ernest was calling a "little country fiesta" would be lighted by scores of Japanese lanterns in the gardens, at the pool and along the upper terrace of the house where most of the guests would sit at one long table. The fiesta would have a burro for people to ride on, a stack of silly hats for them to wear being photographed. It would have a target-shooting booth for the delectation of guests who enjoyed pulling triggers. It would have a little band of Flamenco dancers swaying to guitar music on a softly lighted lawn, and toward the end of festivities just before dawn a mighty barrage of fireworks zooming into the local sky. I had ordered Chinese vegetables from London, champagne from France, and the menu's principal dish would be Chinese sweet-sour turkey, the sauce made by me, with one of Ernest's favorite dishes, codfish stew and garbanzos, roast ham, salads, a joint birthday cake and ice cream accompanying it. With Annie Davis fully occupied entertaining a houseful of guests, my responsibility was to provide with proper timing the components of these diversions down to the last servant, salt shaker, and a bowl for the burro's drinking water.

Guests began arriving a couple of days early and we put them up at one of the pretentious, Las Vegasy new hotels along the beach where Ernest entertained them at pre-party luncheons and dinners. General Buck Lanham came over from Washington and at the party endeared himself to me, complimenting me on the decorations and diversions, the only guest to do so. Gianfranco Ivancich and his wife came from Venice, driving over in a Lancia Ernest had bought to replace the pink Ford. Harris Williams and Ricardo Sícre and the photographer Cano came from Madrid, together with Peter and Connie Buckley and Bhaiya Cooch Behar and his English girl, Gina Egan, and his in-laws, the Maharaja of Jaipur and Ayesha of Jaipur and their son. In Pamplona our fellows had picked up a couple of pretty American girls who were sightseeing Europe in a little French car, and we added them, Teddy Jo Paulson from North Dakota and Mary Schoonmaker, to the guest list together with Beverly Bentley, who was making a movie in Spain, and Hugh and Suzy Millais, traveling Britishers and troubadours we had met somewhere, and Valerie Danby-Smith who now became Ernest's secretary-handmaiden and a temporary appendage to the outfit. Among the thirty-four guests, only four were Carmen's and Antonio's personal friends.

At dinner David Bruce made a gracious toast to Ernest—"warmth, manliness, generosity"—and Ernest toasted Carmen's valor and beauty. The birthday boy displayed his virtuosity with the .22 rifle, shooting the tips off cigarettes held in the mouths of Cooch Behar and Antonio. The women in their long summery dresses looked lovely, and almost everybody danced around the young Flamenco dancers and then moved en masse into the kitchen where Pepa, the cook, danced exuberantly on the big wooden table to wild applause. The fireworks roared up splendidly and when a spark set afire the top of a summer-dried palm tree near the house there was a great rush for ladders —too short—and hoses—too feeble—until the local fire department arrived in a red truck with red helmets and tooting sirens and pumped out the flare in minutes. We brought them drinks and borrowed their comic-opera helmets, to dance improvisations of a new fire-extinguishing dance. Nothing I could have planned would have been a more suitable climax for the evening, but it failed to end when the firemen rolled away. When I went to bed at 6:30 a.m., the guitarists and dancers and shooting-booth men having long departed, some people were still sitting around the house and the pool, and they were there when I awoke, sodden with exhaustion, at 9:30. Annie's people were serving them eggs and coffee. With champagne Ernest toasted the Bruces onto their returning airplane.

A few days later the remaining mob took off more or less in cavalcade eastward along the wild empty coast road, its mountains rushing sharply down to blue sea and many tiny half-moon coves with beaches, through Almería and Murcia to Alicante with its broad checker-paved promenades overlooking its harbor on Spain's east coast of the Mediterranean. Still using the pink Ford, Bill Davis drove with Valerie and Ernest in the front seat and Hotchner and General Lanham in the back, Buck Lanham throughout the expedition seeming to me to look mystified by the whole business of the nonstop circus in which we were, willy-nilly, performing. George and Pat Saviers drove their rented car with Juanito Quintana as passenger and Annie and I were in Rupert Bellville's Volkswagen.

July 30, in Valencia, was the first day in which the brothers-in-law, the two top matadors of Spain, would perform *mano a mano,* each man dealing with three bulls instead of the usual two. The day was one of sad and menacing weather, clouds gray and lowering, wind gusting and blowing little dust devils in the sand of the ring, and we disliked the bulls from a ranch near Salamanca. They were lethargic, unresponsive, and frequently immoveable. Working with his third bull of the day, an erratic beast, Luis Miguel took him to the center of the ring where the bull bumped him and dashed his muleta to the ground then lowered its head and gored him in the right groin. His elder brother, Domingo, was in the ring in a flash, with no cape or protection, and immediately after him went Antonio to lure the bull away. They carried Luis Miguel out of the ring and along the *callejón* in front of us, his small hand covering his wound, his pants ripped wide apart, his face pale, but not contorted. Within a few minutes Antonio, his face stony, had maneuvered to one side of the ring, squared the bull and with one stab of the sword dispatched him. With his own final bull he presented under poor electric lighting the whole repertoire of passes both with the cape and the muleta, and killed, receiving, as the bull lunged at him. Thunderous *olés* and two ears. That evening we heard that Luis Miguel's wound was deep and high, the horn penetrating to within millimeters of the peritoneum, and I began to appreciate and share Carmen's dislike of the beasts and their domination of her family's fortunes.

From Valencia the Pamplona birthday-party crowd dispersed in all directions.

Ernest had brought to Spain with him that year the idea of garnering information new to *tauromachia* since *Death in the Afternoon* had been published and updating the 1932 book with a prologue or a post-script. But word of his activities seeped outward and Will Lang came down from the Paris bureau of *Life* and persuaded Ernest to give them a crack at his proposed manuscript before it would come out in hardcover. Ernest had not put a word of it on paper, but he agreed to our old friend Will's proposal, and consequently felt more than ever obliged to finish out the summer's program of *corridas*.

While Luis Miguel was still recovering from his wound in Valencia, Antonio was gored again in the ring at Palma de Majorca, and as the brothers-in-law recovered together in the Sanatorio Ruber in Madrid, they agreed that if they could manage to walk, they would continue their *mano a mano* performance at Málaga where they had been scheduled to appear on August 14.

A few days earlier Antonio talked his way out of the hospital and came down to rest and recover at La Consula, the wound in his right thigh still emitting an occasional drip, to which he paid no attention. The men played baseball with a tennis ball, Antonio's greatest hit propelling him into the pool and sending the tennis ball to the far bottom of the rose garden. Then and there they decided that since Hotchner had taught him how to hit a ball with a bat, Antonio would annex Hotchner to his *cuadrilla* as a *sobresaliente* (substitute, understudy) and a few days later Antonio took Hotchner into the ring with him but required nothing of him other than to carry out the personal possessions raining down on them after Antonio's triumph.

On August 14 Luis Miguel and Antonio, neither of them completely recovered from horn wounds, resumed their *mano a mano* competition in the smallish baking-oven ring at Málaga and between them produced a *corrida,* together with respected Pedro Domecq bulls, of gallantry, skill and grace unparalleled that year, or perhaps in many years. From his three fights, Luis Miguel, looking thin and exhausted, won four ears, two tails and one foot. Antonio was awarded six ears, two tails and two feet.

Off they flew, the two champions with Ernest accompanying them, to Biarritz for an engagement in Bayonne. In yet another *mano a mano* a few days later in Bilbao, the cruel town of the Civil War, a horn caught Luis Miguel so badly that it finished the competition. Still later in Dax, a bull stepped on Antonio's foot and he went into a hospital at San Sebastián. With Bill Davis driving Ernest to Madrid and Valerie accompanying, the Lancia burst a front tire and the car busted into concrete road guards, ruining its hood and parts of the engine. The three of them managed to get to Madrid and flew down to Málaga. For ten days Annie and I had pursued the domestic life, I still choked in nose and throat and breathing menthol vapors.

Ernest had written me a couple of sweet notes during his absence, but in a few days' reunion at La Consula and on a journey to Linares for another Antonio bullfight, I noticed that I seemed to have become inaudible to him. After the fight we drove back to Córdoba and a flashy hotel for the night and the next morning wound through four separate harvests, foot-high acres of cotton blooming in unirrigated fields, melons ripening with families camping in the patches to ward off thieves, white grapes sweetening in the sun on disks of *esparto* (feather) grass, olives being plucked from ancient groves with some trunks two feet in diameter.

The plan for Sunday, August 30, was an early take-off from the Davises' house so that the party could reach the town of Calahorra, far to the north near Logroño, in time for Antonio's *corrida* there on Monday, and I excused myself. I wanted a day or two of shopping in Madrid for furniture for the square, poured-cement house in Ketchum, Idaho, Ernest had bought from Bob Topping instead of building on our lots there, and took a bedroom on the ancient, rickety night train from Málaga.

In the wee hours two nights later the voyaging trio, Bill, Annie and Ernest, arrived at the Hotel Suecia and slept briefly before we all took off again in the pink Ford to watch Antonio's fight at Cuenca. After the bullfight we drove to a new government *parador* (rest house) near the village of Motilla del Palancar, slept and moved on to Almansa for lunch and to now familiar Alicante to spend the night. As we were going to bed I asked for more water, Ernest having

601

poured me only a few tots, and thereby unintentionally set off a torrent of harangue. I had refused to buy Listerine for him in Madrid. (I had bought it and given it to him.) My demands for water were excessive. I was just like my mother, or his mother, who drove his father to suicide. He went on until 4 a.m.

For another fortnight we hurtled around the country, attending the bullfights and Ernest signing endless autographs, in Murcia, back to Alicante to sleep, again to Murcia with a strong wind in the ring, twisted southwest over narrow mountain roads to Ronda where Antonio fought beautifully, winning four ears and two tails, off at 8 a.m. the next morning without breakfast for Sevilla then north to Mérida and north again to Béjar, almost due west of Madrid. At Salamanca a message was waiting from Carmen. Antonio and his picadors had been jailed in Albacete for some minor, perhaps false, infraction of bullfight rules. Would Ernest come quickly to Madrid? We re-embarked and reached the Ordóñez flat in Madrid that evening. A congeries of Dominguíns and supporters palavered without action in Carmen's sitting room until 2 a.m. or later when we went on to the Suecia. About noon that day we heard that Antonio had been released and escorted by the police to the border of the province of Albacete, now a dirty word with us. We stayed a couple of days in Madrid before rolling down to Málaga and La Consula, with its bright sunshine, plenty of dawdling in the swimming pool and interesting food. But, whereas I had been inaudible to my husband, I now seemed also to be invisible, a worthless quality in a wife, I thought.

Ernest announced that he had invited Antonio and Carmen to visit us in Cuba and Idaho, and since I was of no use to him in Spain, I decided that I should get back to the Finca Vigía to put it in working order for their arrival. I saw no future in this job as ghost wife, but I would not allow hurt or pique to propel me into hasty, hysterical action, I resolved, remembering that I loved Ernest in spite of himself and also our life in Cuba and also in Idaho. While the others chose to drive to Paris, I took a train, and after a couple of days at the Ritz, Ernest conscientiously accompanying me to an exhibit at the Jeu de Paume, he saw me off on one of the new jet planes at Orly on October 4. It was my first crossing by jet and it entranced me.

The Toppings had removed from the Ketchum house everything but the furniture listed in an inventory Chuck Atkinson had sent us, and I reported to Ernest my arrangements for acquiring linens, kitchen utensils, china and such. And, "The letter you asked me to write about our personal relations, I find very difficult to do. Too clogged up with emotion and loneliness and heartbreak. The essence of it is that all evidence, as I see it, shows that you have no further use for me in your life. I am therefore beginning to arrange my removal from it, and hope to establish a new life for myself. . . . Love and devotion, just the same as always, and good luck to you and to all at La Consula."

Hoping not to worry us, the servants always wrote that everything at the Finca was doing fine. But in half a morning I discovered, and so wrote Ernest, that not one single machine there except for my typewriter was in proper operating order. The lighting system in Ernest's big Chrysler was not functioning and its muffler was polka-dotted with holes. My little Plymouth's battery was dead or dormant, and so was that of the station wagon, which was essential for hauling luggage. The pool pump was not functioning. When Schmidt, the pump man, took the motor to town to clean it, he found a family of dead rats inside. The record changer in the living room was not working. Neither of the two radios was functioning. The latest kitchen stove produced some light, but little heat. From Gregorio I learned that *Pilar* had not been up on the ways in seven months for a cleaning of her hull, which he normally managed three times a year. The liquid in the fire extinguishers around the house had not been drained and replaced. The front gate looked weatherbeaten and dirty. Broken window panes in the Little House, from a big explosion in Guanabacoa nearby, had not been replaced, and some of its furniture needed repainting or revarnishing. Hurricane Judith had passed close to our part of Cuba, and we had heavy rains, with water dripping through the roof of my room as through a sieve, and hitting my bed and desk.

In contrast to my expectations from having read Spanish, French and United States newspapers, the atmosphere of Cuba was happy. People were proud of the new government's honesty, proud of their new home-building program, proud of Fidel's tree-planting, which was everywhere visible. "The people seem to breathe confidence and hope," I wrote.

Since Ernest had asked for it, I also wrote him my view of his behavior toward me that summer, three and a half single-spaced pages itemizing instances of his neglect, rudeness, thoughtlessness, abusive language, unjust criticism, false accusations, failures of courtesy and friendliness. I would take a small flat in New York, I wrote, and after getting the household in Ketchum in operation would install myself in the big city.

Ernest's cabled reply from Paris said: THANKS LETTERS AND TREMENDOUS WORK DONE. SORRY CAN'T AGREE ITEMS AND CONCLUSIONS PERSONAL LETTER BUT RESPECT YOUR VIEWS ALTOGETHER DISAGREE PROFOUNDLY. . . . GLAD GOOD NEWS ABOUT CUBA, SORRY SO MUCH WORK AND NUISANCE. . . . STILL LOVE YOU. Reading it I thought, let's see a bit of evidence.

Fidel was conducting rallies in Havana, summoning people from all over the island to stand and listen, and on several days I gave our people half-holidays so that they could catch a crowded bus to Havana to join the multitudes. On October 26 I went down the hill for a drink with the Steinharts, among whose guests were a couple of Fidel's bearded soldiers. When our hostess, Olga Steinhart, mentioned that the revolution was Communist-inspired, one of the bearded soldiers laughed. "Better to be charged with that than with capitalism."

I had installed a television set in the pantry of our house so that the servants and gardeners could keep abreast of the news. Sitting on a stool out there that evening I watched and heard Che Guevara exhorting the crowd to support the new regime. Then Fidel's brother appeared behind the microphones, dedicated to the revolution but hardly articulate. For the finale we had Fidel excoriating the United States and its government and capitalist economics, flourishing phrases, repeating those he found stimulating, in love with the sound of his voice and with the microphones —he who so long had remained silent, building his revolution in the eastern mountains of the island, spellbinding and hypnotizing the people. Lola, the maid, had gone to the rally but came home early, while I was still listening to Fidel in the pantry. "Too many people," she said. "Tiring."

On November 4 I sent Juan in the reconditioned Chrysler to meet Ernest, Antonio and Carmen at the airport where, whether or not by design, a crowd of Cubans welcomed him with cheers and the traditional hugs, also cameramen. The Finca was finally in working order and I had decked the Little House with bouquets for Carmen and hired an extra girl from the village to look after the Ordóñezes and their wardrobes. Antonio being less than entranced with the idea of bouncing around in *Pilar* in rough seas, they lolled around the farm, sunning and swimming a few days, and explored a couple of Havana's nightclubs, which for the moment were not thriving, nobody having then decided whether or not they were good for the revolution.

To put the Ketchum house in operation, Lola and I flew to Chicago for a couple of days of intensive shopping, sending china and glassware, pots and pans high speed to Idaho. Chuck Atkinson had already begun the improvements to the Ketchum house I had requested. Lola and I ate from picnic paper plates and shifted furniture to make the sitting room less like a furniture showroom, washed windows, housecleaned and unpacked and installed the shipments from Chicago which mercifully arrived a day or two before Ernest blew in with Antonio. Carmen and Roberto Herrera, old friend and secretary, who had spelled Antonio at the wheel of a new station wagon. They had driven all the way from the south side of the Grand Canyon that day.

Pheasant season was almost finished, but duck season was still open and the next day Ernest telephoned Bud Purdy at Picabo to learn how his winged transient guests were behaving, Bud reporting something such as "We have a few." Tomorrow we would go duck hunting along Bud Purdy's numerous irrigation ditches, Antonio happy with one of Ernest's 12-gauge shotguns, Carmen sharp with one of my pair of Winchester Model-21, 20-gauge guns.

From Mexico a telephone call came which destroyed our plans. One of Antonio's sisters wanted to leave her husband there, and nothing would do but that Antonio get down there and help her depart. Ernest spent two days at the telephone talking to Washington and the Mexican consulate in Los Angeles arranging visas and transportation for Antonio and Carmen and off they went.

In Spain Ernest had been working rather haphazardly on the book of memoirs about his youthful days in Paris and had temporarily abandoned it to do the photo-bullfight story for *Life*. Now he returned to work on the Paris book, duck hunting that year being indifferent, while I followed my program of civilizing the house, finding acceptable reading lamps and slipcovers, papering shelves.

26

A Time Benumbed

ONE AFTERNOON WE went after ducks with George Saviers and his brother in one of George's favorite places, a frozen swamp with thin timber leading to a piece of open water. The ground was so ironhard that even walking carefully in soft old boots we made crunching noises and put up from the water a few ducks, one of which, a high-flying female pintail, I brought down precisely with one shot. She fell right behind me and I gave her to Ernest to carry. A few steps later as we headed toward the water I caught a stick between my boots and knew I was going over. George and Ernest were about twenty paces directly in front of me. As usual, I was carrying my loaded gun, with the safe catch locked, in my right hand. My concern was to hold the barrels high, and the gun did not go off as my left elbow hit the frozen ground, shattering the elbow, not denting the ground. It was not until some minutes later when we were settling into the car to drive to the Sun Valley hospital that pain surged over me like heavy surf, producing low, quite uncontrollable groans. Ernest in the front seat voiced his disapproval.

"You could keep it quiet."

"I'm trying."

"Soldiers don't do that."

"I'm not a soldier." Long, drawn-out, unanticipated, irrepressible groan.

"You're making us all uncomfortable."

"I'm sorry and poop on you."

At the hospital George got some pain-quelling drug into me quickly and, having summoned a colleague, put me onto the operating table, a local anesthetic effectively cutting off the pain messages from my arm to my brain. They stretched a little white canvas fence across my chest so that I could not see what they were doing to my distal humerus, which was fractured, the proximal radius and the proximal ulna, which George later described as the shell of a turkey egg hit by a mallet. Much to my husband's displeasure the doctors decided I should stay in the hospital for a night or two where I could summon help when the pain grew too severe. I had broken bones in both ankles, cracked a couple of ribs and there was the toe of that summer, and the distress from the injuries had been supportable. But this was a pain of a different caliber, a kind of fury which moved into the center of me usurping my attention so that for a few days I could not even read. While he made a few tries at showing me sympathy, Ernest behaved in the ensuing weeks as though I had broken the elbow with the explicit purpose of interrupting his work on his Paris book and the piece he had agreed to do for *Life* on the past summer's *mano a mano* bullfights. He grouched about having to do the marketing, although he was the only one in the household who could drive. He grumbled about my one-armed cooking, although Lola was helping with both hands. When late one evening I asked him to help me take off my pants, he mumbled that he was being asked to do the work of servants. After that I undressed with Lola's help before she retired for the night.

A week or so before Christmas Ernest drove me to the hospital one night and early the next morning at the operating table the doctors re-broke my elbow, which had been healing straight up and down, and bent the arm to a 90-degree angle, applying plaster from my upper arm to my hand, the resulting pain being as ferocious as with the original break. Giving me a bottle of morphine tablets to take when necessary, George Saviers said, "Cut down on them and cut them out as quickly as you can." A few days later I handed him back the bottle, still half full.

Without pals to accompany him duck hunting in the snow, Ernest took to giving clay-target shooting parties at the edge of our parking lot, the blasting going on long into the winter dusk when the targets became finally invisible and the guns spouted licks of red flame. Then into the kitchen with its fireplace glowing for a quick snort, the shooters standing around the kitchen table, before they headed for home.

Early in the new year, Pappy and Tillie Arnold invited us for roast beef at their house and, since Ernest hesitated to drive at night on the slippery roads, came out to pick us up. Snow was drifting down without wind, huge quarter-sized flakes, and in the eave lights outside their big dining room window it was a fairy-tale spectacle. But looking out Ernest noticed lights in our local bank down the hill a couple of blocks away.

"They're checking our accounts," said Ernest.

"What nonsense. Who?" said I.

"R.G. works late sometimes," Lloyd said. R. G.

608

Price was the bank manager and a genial friend of all of his clients.

"That's just the usual cleaning women," Tillie said.

"They're trying to catch us," said Ernest. "They want to get something on us."

"Who's they?" I asked.

"The F.B.I.," said Ernest flatly.

"Maybe you're tired, honey," said I. I had never seen my husband so disturbed about an imagined, illusory threat. I tried to remember ever having seen him fearful and couldn't recall any instance. When the lights were turned off in the bank he began to worry that the snowstorm would hinder our getting home, a mile away, and kept glancing so balefully at the lovely, waltzing flakes that Lloyd put chains over his snow-tires, and we made it to our house in five minutes.

After the snowstorm we had days of brilliant sunshine and bright blue skies, cold but cheerful, which seemed to dispel Ernest's worries. But he was restless around the house and decided he could work better in his old familiar place, standing at the bookcase in his bedroom at the Finca. He had no time for the leisurely cross-country motor trip of other years and the possible problems of getting our black Lola into Southern motels. We would go by train.

On our return to the Finca Vigía I found it wonderful to be back among our caladiums, satiny frangipani, white ixoras and pink antigonon, but one north storm after another dumped cold rain on us, transforming the house, with its one tiny electric heater, into a giant refrigerator, and a lump of ice nestled into my aching elbow and stayed there, helping out the pain. José Herrera recommended massage and exercise for my smashed joint and Ernest, although he was working steadily and longer hours each day than had ever been his custom, devoted a half hour of every day to massaging my arm with an electric vibrator. I spent another hour swinging and pushing and pulling heavy weights and at the rate of a few millimeters a month the bent elbow straightened itself.

None of our seasons at the Finca had been so quiet as that winter, with Ernest preoccupied with his work and worried about what he thought was failing eyesight but refusing to go to an oculist for examinations, I unable to use my typewriter, the weather too cold for swimming. When he suggested that we invite Valerie to come and help him with his manuscript, I quickly agreed. She might not be much help or any, with the manuscript, which had mushroomed far beyond the 10,000 words *Life* wanted, but her gentle Irish wit and candor might brighten his nonworking hours. Ernest sent her flying money to Monkstown, near Dublin, where she had been spending Christmas with her mother; she reached Havana about the end of January, and we installed her in the chilly Little House.

Of his previous work, put on paper while I was around, Ernest had usually offered me first-reading privileges, which I had happily accepted. Now no such offers were forthcoming. As he was massaging my elbow in the sitting room one afternoon, I asked, "How's it going?"

"It's hell. I can't get it all down."

"Could you summarize, or digest, or something?"

"I don't see how I can do it."

"You've always had a built-in editor in your head."

Ernest brought me a sheaf of his typical, haphazardly spaced manuscript which I read in bewilderment. The fifteen or twenty pages included graceful or striking passages about the Spanish countryside, the exuberant crowds, the spirit of fiesta in its varied phases in the different provinces. But his accounts of the bullfights with their passes with the capes and the muletas became a catalogue and, I thought, repetitious.

"Maybe you could cut some of those passes in the *corridas*," I suggested, handing back the manuscript.

"That's how they happened. They belong there," said Ernest.

"But honey, *Life*'s readers, most Americans, don't care all that much about some gestures in a Spanish bullring."

" 'Gestures'? You are demeaning an art. Not to mention courage."

"I'm sorry. I was being commercial, I guess, considering what *Life*'s editors would think publishable."

He offered me no further batches of manuscript to read.

For recreation, we read. For exercise the three of us walked to the top of the hill behind the ruined cowshed to watch the sun set behind the profile of Havana and admire the progress of our flowering fence post trees, *Gliricidia sepium*. On occasional Saturday nights we went to the Floridita for a drink. Except for a luncheon or dinner shared with the Herrera brothers, Lee Samuels or Mayito Menocal, we gave only one party, and that one unplanned. The Russian delegation to the new Cuban government had telephoned to say that Anastas Mikoyan, in Havana to sweeten relations with Moscow, would like to come out. We set an hour the following afternoon and I was appalled when half a dozen carfuls of people stopped at the front steps. The few snacks I had set out were ridiculously insufficient. I ran to the refrigerator and there found a big bowl of codfish stew left over from lunch, which quickly disappeared, and the party moved onto the back terrace, up to the top of the tower, back to the library, back to the sitting room, everybody including the host in animated good spirits.

Ernest's spirits revived again in April when George Saviers came down for a few days of our vaunted fishing, of which we managed less than we had hoped, the weather being peevish, and the fish skittish. Most of the time Ernest kept pounding away at his bullfight story, and, contrary to his customary stoicism amid difficulties, complaining. "Sixty-eight thousand, three hundred," he would say. "It's beating the pith out of me."

"It can't go on forever," I would tell him.

Gardening or arranging flowers or sunning on the top of the tower, I had tried to find a key to his dilemma, without success. If some way could be found to help him stand back and look at the story objectively, he might see how overblown it was and quickly finish it. But our carefree days on the Gulf Stream had failed to provide him with a new perspective about his work. I was no helpmate because I could not find a formula for helping.

We had a welcome respite from the solemnities of

work and worries at the end of May when Ernest entered *Pilar* in the annual Hemingway marlin-fishing tournament. A number of our fishing friends had already moved away from Cuba, leaving behind their boats, which the new government allocated to representatives of groups of workers, and one of which Fidel appropriated for himself and a few friends. Those of us who were still on hand eschewed the evening of pre-tournament festivities with their high-powered Calcutta auctioning of boats at the Club Náutico in the bay. Something sybaritic in the air, of men of means frolicking with their expensive playthings, was missing. With my ineffective arm I had chosen not to fish in the *Tin Kid*. But aboard *Pilar* we were cheerful. Toby and Betty Bruce had come over from Key West for the holiday and as usual Gregorio had the best bait anyone could net or buy.

But the Gulf Stream which had been behaving erratically all spring continued so for the two days of the tournament. Instead of coursing along for eighty to a hundred miles just off Cuba's north coast, it presented itself on the surface only for some fifteen miles running eastward from Havana. Since there was no point in fishing beyond the Stream, the tournament, with about forty boats entered, was confined to that small patch of water with everybody fishing in each other's wakes. With plenty of eyes to watch our baits, one or another of us kept our big old U.S. Navy binoculars on Fidel's boat and watched him hook and bring to the gaff two marlin. He was no deep-sea fisherman, as far as we knew. But he followed precisely the big-game fishing rules, hooking the fish and playing them, and his boatman made no attempt to gaff before he could grasp the leader, rather than the line. The second day he caught another marlin, and the combined weight of his fish earned him Ernest's silver trophy cup, which he presented that evening at the dock. On the way home in the car Ernest murmured, "He said he'd read *The Bell* in Spanish and used its ideas in the Sierra Maestra."

While in his marathon speeches at televised political rallies Fidel said repeatedly that those United Statesers who had not exploited the Cuban people would never be molested by his regime, squads of bearded revolutionary soldiers were moving without notice into the homes and businesses of North Americans, rich Spaniards and rich Cubans, appropriating everything. One Spanish countess whose gold dinner plates and flatware were famous in Havana society had it all stacked in a cupboard and then plastered over and painted to match the adjoining walls. The day after she departed for Spain, the army moved in and broke open the wall, so people said.

Old hangers-on, long-time recipients of Ernest's largesse, still hailed me when Juan took me shopping in Havana in my yellow convertible, and in our village people still yelled, "Mismary." But signs daubed on walls everywhere proclaimed, CUBA SÍ! YAQUI NO! By simple consumer-product buying and the payment of wages and services, Ernest in some twenty years of residence there had fed into the Cuban economy about three-quarters of a million dollars, if not more, I estimated. But we were beginning to feel unwelcome.

By the end of May, having spun out his manuscript to twelve times what he had contracted for with *Life,* he felt obliged to cut the story drastically, but also felt unable to do it. Another problem was that the piece had no succinct ending, and there now arose the possibility that Luis Miguel and Antonio might resume their *mano a mano* competition in the coming summer. By June the weather had turned oppressively hot with heavy rains and high humidity. And always there was the problem of our remaining as foreign residents in Cuba. Ernest would not entertain the idea that we should abandon the Finca and our people there, removing some easily portable possessions. (By chance, his best painting, Miró's *The Farm,* had already departed. After months of correspondence, the Museum of Modern Art had persuaded him to lend it to an exhibition in New York.) For seven months I had been considering some manner by which, with the least trauma for each of us, I could retire from what seemed to me his new style of living. But I shelved the idea. He seemed to have so many grave problems confronting him that I could not increase them. Again he was addressing me as "My dear kittner."

By the end of June he had still failed to make much headway with the cutting of his manuscript, as he reported daily, and asked Ed Hotchner to come down and help him. In a few days together they whittled out about a quarter of the excess words and Hotchner took the manuscript, finally titled *The Dangerous Summer,* back to New York. With the help of our New York friends Hotchner had found a modest half-furnished apartment at 1 East Sixty-second Street which he had rented for us.

Even after he had relinquished it, Ernest continued to worry about his bullfight story and concluded that he must return to Spain that summer to make ultimate assessments on the whole world of *tauromachia* and its practitioners. With so many of our friends leaving Cuba, I chose sadly not to stay on there by myself and opted for New York.

Ernest wanted no birthday festivities this year. "Can't use a birthday," said he, "or a birthday party."

On July 25, Ernest, Valerie and I boarded the ferry from Havana to Key West, leaving our house fully staffed, expecting to return in the autumn or winter. We had left at the Finca all its silver, Venetian glassware, eight thousand books, a number of them autographed first editions, and Ernest's small collection of paintings, one Paul Klee, two Juan Gris, five André Masson, one Braque and several good, lively paintings of bulls by Roberto Domingo. At my bank in Havana we had left reams of unpublished manuscript.

At Key West the immigration officer noticed that Valerie's visitor's visa for the U.S.A. had not been renewed, and sent Ernest into a disproportionately large tizzy. He muttered about the dire consequences of law-breaking, our Key West friends the Bruces and the Thompsons paying him little heed. Toby helped us ship cases of papers and hundreds of bullfight photographs to Ketchum, Ernest flew off to New York and I reserved three bedrooms on the train from Miami, one for Valerie, one for me and one for our luggage.

27

Hope Reviving

THE FLAT IN Sixty-second Street exceeded my expectations. It was in a handsome, once-elegant town house with a marble foyer, a grandiose marble staircase sweeping upward from it. Once again my nest-building instincts aroused themselves. For very little outlay I could make the place comfortable, I assured Ernest. Valerie moved into the Barbizon hotel for women, not her idea of a scintillating roost, but she tolerated it.

On August 4 Ernest took off by jet for Lisbon and Madrid, and the next day a cable arrived saying, GOOD TRIP WRITE SUECIA LOVE. After the violent, fatiguing heat and humidity of Cuba, New York's temperatures seemed positively refreshing. Old friends were inviting me to pleasant doings or inviting themselves to picnic dinners in the nest. There were centuries and miles of treasures awaiting appreciation all over town, and my interlude of single life looked promising.

Until Monday, August 8. A friend of Valerie's on Long Island had invited us both to a hen luncheon out there which would launch a local charity campaign, and using my grade-D judgment I had accepted. We were seated at lunch among the pleasant, rich, harmless women when a call came from Greta, the maid at the flat, saying that Hotchner had called from Maine where he was vacationing to say that Ernest had collapsed in the bullring at Málaga and was very ill. He had heard it on the radio and had instructed Greta to wire Málaga asking for details. She had sent the wire. I told her I would get back to New York as

615

soon as possible, and decided not to tell the luncheon ladies, all strangers, with a reporter from a Long Island paper there to make publicity for the charity. I must get back to New York by four-thirty to take a telephone call from Spain, I mentioned. Nobody paid any attention. "No fuss," said I. "I'll get a cab."

"No, no. We'll drive you in. The Cadillac is air conditioned."

"I don't want to impose. Or hurry you."

"Oh, no hurry. Plenty of time." I contained my anxiety, planning to catch the 7 p.m. plane for Madrid. The twittering luncheon went on and on, sparkling with inanities. The photographer arrived, the ladies had their coffee and he had a discreet glass of ginger ale, and the picture-taking began, everybody arch and girlish, first indoors and then on the lawn. I took Valerie aside and told her of Hotchner's message. She helped me emphasize the phone call from Spain, and a lifetime later we got into the air-conditioned Cadillac which moved at a leisurely pace to Sixty-second Street.

I called the A.P. cable desk. Sure, they had heard the report. They had two stringers in Málaga, both unable to confirm the news. It was late there now. I remembered that Ernest had been feeling poor-to-terrible before he left New York.

I called Alfred Rice, Ernest's lawyer and our friend. Yes, he had heard the report. He gave me the telephone number of an all-night travel agent. He could get me traveling money.

The Davises had never allowed a telephone in their house. Neither had Gerald Brenan, the only neighbor I knew in nearby Churriana.

I called the U.P.I. cable desk. Yes, they had heard. The report originated in Stockholm. By 10:23 Spanish time they had had no confirmation. They were unable to locate Ernest. They had heard he was not attending that day's bullfight.

I called the travel man. He would make me one reservation on an 8 p.m. plane to Paris and one on a 10 p.m. plane to Lisbon and Barcelona.

Toby Bruce called. He had heard the radio news. Could he help?

Greta had left a message in the flat saying that Hotchner would call again, and her telephone number. I called Greta. Had Hotchner heard only the radio, or had he a special message from Spain. Greta didn't know.

I called Hotchner's house in Connecticut and his mother answered. He had left no forwarding address or telephone number. "He's far away, in the woods like."

Greta phoned to ask if there was any reply yet to her cable. No, she had not sent it Urgent, just a straight message.

The travel man called. Would I make the eight o'clock plane or cancel? I would cancel the 8 p.m. and hold the 10 p.m. reservation.

Awaiting the Hotchner call, I started packing my bottle bag. I was shaking and smoking. Valerie was pacing the floor.

I called the CBS news desk. All inside lines were occupied.

I wrote and telephoned three cables, one to Apartado 67, Málaga, the Davises' post office box, one to the Hotel Felípe II at Escorial, one to the Hotel Suecia in Madrid.

I called the CBS news desk again. They had received a flash, "Hemingway stricken," from Cifra, the Spanish news agency. So far no denial. They would recheck and I would call back. It was now about 8:45. I was hanging up when Ned Calmer got on the line. "I'll check everything possible, Mary. Will call you right back."

Had Ernest given Bill Davis our telephone number in New York, Val and I wondered. Since Bill had not telephoned, maybe that was good. Maybe not.

The travel man called. Yes, please hold the reservation.

I called U.P.I. again. They had a report that Ernest had left Málaga for Madrid. They thought it was reliable. I made myself a drink. We had been served La Ina sherry before lunch.

Hotchner called from Maine. No, he'd had no special message, just heard the radio.

617

Western Union called. "Your cablegram to E.H. forwarded to Málaga."

Ned Calmer called. They had a new A.P. dispatch filed at Churriana. "E.H. took time to deny," etc. I wept, Val danced around the room. I called the travel man, canceled flight. Got another drink, made a drink for Valerie. Called Alfred. No need for money. Called Toby Bruce. Called Greta. Called Hotch in Maine. RCA delivered a cable from Granada. REPORTS FALSE ENROUTE MADRID LOVE PAPA.

Valerie and I found we couldn't unwind quickly, even with the help of alcohol. She wanted to go to the Stork Club to celebrate, but we lacked an escort. Instead we telephoned Charlie Sweeny and Dorothy Allen in Salt Lake. They had heard the news and understood our madness.

I had been planning a short journey to Cuba, to check on the Finca and our people there, as soon as I finished making the Sixty-second Street nest livable. But the New York newspapers of Saturday, August 13, reported that the Cuban government had imposed new travel restrictions requiring Cuban nationals and "foreign residents regardless of nationality" to secure military permits for departures. Correspondents reported long lines of people waiting for permits outside the principal Havana police station. The Russians were establishing a full-fledged embassy there, with twenty-two new arrivals in the first batch of staff. I wrote Ernest that I was reconsidering my journey.

Valerie had been feeling at loose ends in New York, with nothing special to do, and late in August she took off for Paris, agreeing to send her Paris address, when she had one, to Ernest in Spain. She had been there only a few days when he summoned her south to help with his apparently complicated problems of selecting photographs for his *Life* story.

Before we left Cuba I had arranged to telephone René once a week for news of the Finca which I consistently forwarded to Ernest in my letters. In late August thieves had broken into the gardeners' tool house and stolen machetes, hoses, rakes and other tools. The pool needed attention. Cecilio, the carpenter, had discontinued his repair work around the place for lack of money to buy materials. All letters arriving at the local post office for us were being opened and resealed. When I asked René what he thought about my flying down for a week or two he said, "No, no, Miss Mary. Much better to stay there. Much."

From the day he arrived in Spain, Ernest sent me once a week or more often long handwritten letters, the sentences frequently running up the margins and upside down across the tops of the pages, his customary manner. On August 15 he wrote: "You had an awfully good reason for hating Spain in the dust. I wrote you how it blew in solid clouds in Escorial— pack way back up into your sinuses so you would sneeze mud and I sneezed all the way down on the road like one of those click-click cameras. . . . Couldn't sleep at the wonderful motel nor here [at La Consula] cramps and nightmares, but got first good sleep last night, swam a lot to get tired that way, not just the head. . . . Kittner I don't know how I can stick this summer out. Am so damned lonesome and the whole bullfight business is now so corrupt and seems so unimportant and I have so much good work to do. . . . If there was any way to do it would take the next plane. But every time I've ever been this bad have pulled out of it into a belle epoque and will try to do it again. . . . Here endless all day going over of pictures (always the missing picture). We arrived night before last but yest seemed 72 hours long—your 2 letters came—the one about the ghostly illness and death report (faked to sell a piece by some Torremolinas Swede as near as we can figure it). If I lie down and try to rest somebody calls me dead and there have not been enough hours in the day to do the things *Life* has been asking me to do. You wrote such a lovely and sweet letter. . . . Only thing I am afraid of, no, not only thing, is complete physical and nervous crack-up from deadly over-work. . . . Today is another killer. . . . Please excuse this type of letter. But am not in good shape my blessed. Feel much worse than in N.Y. although have tried to rest every chance there has been. Have drunk no hard liquor. Even good wine seems bad for me although it makes me more cheerful and get awfully nervous without it. . . . Would have given anything to have pulled out of here as soon as I saw how things were. Honey I miss you so and our old lovely life. You made me so homesick about Africa. I loathe this whole damned bull business now and I want to clean my work up and get the hell out. Would *not* go to Cuba in Sept. . . ."

I reread the seven-page letter several times, concluded only that my husband was overtired, assumed that he would quickly recover when the *Life* job was finished and wrote him urging rest and relaxation. On August 24 in Bilbao a bull dumped Antonio on his head causing what appeared to be a concussion and Ernest wrote he had stayed up all night in the hospital attending his young hero and awaiting X-rays the next morning. "Wasn't the blind leading the blind," Ernest wrote on September 3, "but the brain fogged shepherding the concussed."

On Friday, September 2, I cabled Ernest that everybody in New York was enthusiastic and delighted with his first installment of the *Life* piece, *The Dangerous Summer*. I happened to go to Scribner's bookstore that day to pick up an atlas, and found the bookshop buzzing with approval. They had made a window display of *Life* and some blowups of *Life*'s pictures surrounded by their various editions, of all of Ernest's books. Miss Grace Johnson, a long-time saleswoman in the shop, said, "Oh, please tell him we want the book for the Christmas trade. Couldn't he get it ready in time? Hundreds of people are asking when they can buy the book."

"Hundreds?" I asked. "In so short a time?"

"Oh, yes, hundreds," she said. "Well, a great many. And it's heart-breaking to tell them they have to wait so long—1961. Doesn't he care about money?"

"I'm sorry. I'll tell him. He doesn't dislike money, I guess. But he doesn't love it."

On September 7 Ernest wrote from Málaga that my letter about the first *Life* installment made him feel fine but the magazine "made me sick . . . the horrible face on the cover . . . the comparing journalism with 'The Old Man.' . . . Just feel ashamed and sick to have done such a job. . . . Am much better than when I hit here. Have slept and swam up to 30 round trips—still not good in the head but am working to get that back."

On September 8 I wrote Ernest: "I wish I could give you something wonderful and refreshing and renewing—3 weeks of our old-style holidays at Paraíso in an air-mailable capsule—but containing all of it— the changing winds, the long view across the violet satiny water towards the sunset, the gay fun fishing in the mornings and then the welcome shade of *Pilar* at noon, and the long, cool starlit nights with us kittens sleeping as softly as Cristóbal."

On September 23 Ernest wrote from Madrid at length about Antonio's arm swollen from a bump by a bull and, "I wish you were here to look after me and help me out and keep from cracking up. Feel terrible and am just going to lie quiet now and try to rest. . . ." I failed totally to evaluate the importance of these successive warning signals. Ernest had always recovered both from his physical hurts and mental aberrations, I thought. If this behavior the previous summer, which wounded me, had grown from some kind of abnormality, the condition seemed to me to have disappeared during the winter. His letters were coherent. His fears and nightmares and excessive fatigue would recede and depart when the whole *Life* ordeal was finished, I concluded.

"Must get out of this and back to you and healthy life in Ketchum and get head in shape to write well," Ernest wrote me on September 25. He had gone to the Prado museum (encouraging news), found the museum in disorder with its wooden floors being replaced with marble and many of the pictures removed from their customary places. "But as wonderful as ever when you found them. Light perfect. . . . As soon as I know what date in October (early) can leave will cable. Lots of problems but we will solve them all."

George Brown drove me out to meet him at Idlewild and he waved cheerily to us on the balcony of the arrivals building when we spotted him going through customs and yelled. After the welcoming embraces, he paused, pulled his silver flask from a pocket and tipped it up jauntily for a swig. My hope sank. The gesture was an anachronism, a reversion to his early days in Paris when a single-engine plane journey suggested panache. How unrealistic might he be about other activities, I wondered, and in the ensuing weeks began to learn.

28

Hope Receding

IN THE LITTLE flat in Sixty-second Street Ernest acted as though he were a stranger, courteous but unfamiliar with the rooms, quiet, inattentive to the news issuing from the radio, preoccupied with problems he seemed not to wish to communicate. Standing at the door of the small kitchen, watching me prepare dinner, he murmured, "My, how dextrous you are with those things," as though he had never seen me cooking before. I lured him outdoors to take comfort from the animals in the Central Park zoo, but he hesitated to leave the flat. "Somebody waiting out there," he would say, and when I lost patience and asked him to quit acting like a fugitive from justice, he retreated into silence.

George Brown put us on the afternoon train for Chicago and the next day Bea Guck met us at the railway station to take Ernest to her apartment for a quiet lunch while I transferred luggage to the Union Station for the trip westward. An afternoon, night and a full day later George Saviers helped us carry luggage from the Shoshone station platform to his car parked across the street. As we were arranging ourselves in his car, a couple of men in topcoats—not the usual Western dress of parkas or ranchers' garb —emerged from a restaurant nearby and got into a car. "They're tailing me out here already," Ernest said.

"Don't be silly, Papa," George said. "They're a couple of traveling salesmen." On the road north Ernest explained his kidney infection to our doctor, and also his impression that his blood pressure was rising dangerously high. George promised to arrange for tests at the Sun Valley hospital.

Re-established at his stand-up writing table behind a big window looking up the Big Wood River valley, Ernest's spirits seemed to rally. He was remembering more and more of Paris when he was an ebullient young man there, and getting words on paper, and our friend Betty Bell, champion skier and efficient secretary, came regularly to collect manuscript for copying and also take down the occasional letters he wanted to dictate. But doubts, suspicions, and unreasonable fears hounded him. A windstorm had blown down a tall cottonwood tree which now spanned the Big Wood River below the house, and it caused Ernest undue anxiety. "Anybody could get over here from there," he said.

"Nobody would have to do that," I said. "They could just come up our road. But, honey, we're surrounded by friends and goodwill." He didn't hear that.

He was obsessed by what he considered his implication with Valerie's having failed to renew her tourist visa to the U.S.A., but even more worried about his finances which, he was convinced, were in desperate straits. Trying to ease his anxieties, one day I telephoned Joseph Lord, a vice president of the Morgan Guaranty Trust Company in New York, whom Ernest knew, and asked him to call us back to report the balances in Ernest's various accounts, one for taxes, one for savings, one for current checks. We had a telephone in the kitchen and another one thirty feet away in the sitting room and I suggested that Ernest, with pencil and notepad, listen in the sitting room while I would listen at the kitchen counter, also with pencil and pad. When Mr. Lord called back within half an hour, I wrote down the three or four balances he told us. They amounted to more than we could conceivably need in the next year or two. I thanked Mr. Lord. Ernest had uttered no syllable.

"Now, lamb, see. You're not all that hard-pressed," I said, relieved. I had never known or cared about his financial holdings, concerning myself only with the modest sums entrusted to me for household expenses.

Ernest's face showed no relief. "He's confusing us," he said. "He's covering up something. . . ."

"Why should he? You're a valued customer of his bank. He hasn't any possible reason to deceive you."

"Yes he has. He has."

"Well, such as what reason?"

"I don't know," Ernest said. "But I know."

Ernest's preoccupations with his poverty, his health —his blood pressure was fluctuating unreasonably— and his guilt about the legality of Valerie's visitor's visa, especially since she had now returned to New York considering a course of studies at a dramatics school, seemed to enclose him as the tentacles of an octopus envelop a mollusk. Ed Hotchner came out for a couple of days and suggested that he consult some New York psychiatrist about Ernest. I was in favor of anything which might alleviate my husband's distress. Gradually, subtly, George convinced his patient that consultation with specialists on the treatment of worries could cure him. But Ernest would not tolerate the idea of going to the Menninger Clinic in Topeka. "They'll say I'm losing my marbles," he said. George telephoned the Mayo Clinic in Rochester, Minnesota, and arranged that Ernest go there, officially for treatment of his high blood pressure, unofficially for treatment by a psychiatrist. At Rochester they bedded Ernest, under the name of Mr. Saviers, in a bright corner room in the medical patients' wing of St. Mary's hospital and Dr. Hugh Butt, a genius and angel of character, as compact as a baseball, took charge of the blood pressure. Dr. Howard Rome, of Mayo's psychiatry department, would deal with the psychotherapeutic treatments.

A few days later I flew to Minneapolis, bussed down to Rochester, took a room (as Mrs. Saviers) at the

Kahler Hotel, which was inhabited almost entirely by Mayo patients and their relatives, and embarked on the bleak routine of two and three daily visits to Ernest's bedside, walking the mile and a half from and to the hotel whenever the temperature climbed to a warm 15 degrees below zero, lunching and dining alone in the hotel's coffee shop or its more impressive and expensive roof garden.

Already Ernest was bewitching both the nuns who ran St. Mary's and the medical nurses who were competing with each other to do him extra favors, finding tempting tidbits in the kitchen or amusing reading. From the Mayo laboratory Dr. Butt knew almost everything measurable about the organs and their functionings under his patient's skin. Apart from a mild form of diabetes, the organic tests were mostly negative. However, the blood pressure was still sailing up to 220 over 150 some days, and Dr. Rome in his consultations with Ernest was finding no appreciable decline in his guilt feelings or his delusions of persecution and poverty. In the assumption that the medication he had been taking for the hypertension could be increasing his depression, they cut off the blood pressure pills, and Dr. Rome ordered a series of electric shock treatments, thereby shifting Ernest's worries a bit away from his persecutions and toward his predictable loss of memory from the treatments.

Dr. Rome may have concluded that the shock treatments were more effective than they actually were. On December 4, 1960, Ernest wrote a statement on a diet order sheet of the hospital: "To Whom it may concern: My wife Mary at no time believed or considered that I had ever committed any illegal act of any kind. She had no guilty knowledge of any of my finances nor relations with anyone and was assured by Dr. George Saviers that I was suffering from high blood pressure of a dangerous kind and degree and that she was being booked under his name to avoid being bothered by the press. She knew nothing of any misdeeds nor illegal acts and had only the sketchiest outline of my finances and only helped me in preparing my returns on material I furnished her. The bags that I carried had her labels on them but she always believed from the time I met her in New York that the only reason I traveled as I did was to avoid the press a practice I had followed for years.

"She was never an accomplice nor in any sense a fugitive and only followed the advice of a doctor friend that she trusted." He had signed the paper with his formal signature, Ernest M. Hemingway. I found the paper later.

We had kept our Saviers camouflage intact for six weeks, but the local press was sniffing around both the hospital and the hotel, and early in 1961 as I was lunching in the hotel's coffee shop, a memory-evoking face approached me. It was Dorothy Kjerner, a grade school chum from Bemidji, now married to a man who worked in the administrative department of the Mayo Clinic. We had scores of long-ago classmates to remember, along with ancient adventures, and soon thereafter the story of Ernest's being a patient at the clinic was published around the country. Dozens of letters with good wishes began arriving daily at the hospital and from his bed Ernest dictated happy replies to a secretary his devoted nurses had found and who could be spared from her regular job for an hour or so. Dr. Rome thought it was good therapy.

Another big prop for Ernest's self-confidence came along, an invitation to the inauguration festivities of President-elect John Kennedy. It was at Willie Walton's suggestion, I suspected, Willie having worked for Kennedy's election both in Wisconsin and New York. Ernest sent regrets, a bit too fulsome for my taste, and the televised broadcast of the inauguration prompted him to send another message: "Watching the inauguration . . . there was happiness and hope and pride. . . . It is a good thing to have a brave man as our President in times as tough as these. . . ." Ernest was also displaying good cheer and hope to Dr. Rome and so frankly that the psychiatrist decided the cure was complete. I sent for Larry Johnson and on January 22 off we flew on a shiny bright day, stopping to refuel at Rapid City, then climbing above the sparkling Tetons, spotting a herd of does in the snow-fields below us, an ermine with everything about him camouflaged except his tracks, and a couple of elks.

626

At home again, with Kate Brown helping me around the house and driving me in her ancient jalopy to do the marketing and other chores, Ernest was free to get at his Paris book again, rewriting, revising and reorganizing the chapters. I was working at my typewriter too on an off-beat piece of fiction, but only fitfully. Since he was drinking only a bit of California claret, I wanted our meals to be surprises, if possible, and made them the most delectable I could concoct.

Ernest didn't want to jeopardize the peace and quiet which favored his working, so we accepted no invitations to friends' festivities and asked only a few friends to dine with us. He must get outdoor exercise, he felt, so I bought us snowshoes and for a time we padded after lunch across the hills north of the house, finding gophers' tunnels or fox footprints for treats. But the empty white hills became too remote and lonely for him. He wanted some sign of civilization. The village streets, mostly without sidewalks, were too crowded with cars for comfortable walking, and I suggested we try going up old Route 93, which ended in Alaska, and along which the traffic was sparse. Day after day in our woolies and parkas Ernest drove us to a milepost sign and parked the car on the shoulder. Then we walked at the old army pace of four miles an hour, two miles up the road and back, timing ourselves. Each day we drove another two miles north before parking and in a couple of weeks we had walked back and forth almost to the base of Galena Summit, about twenty-five miles.

A woman in Washington was assembling a book of handwritten, individual tributes to the Kennedys and sent Ernest a request for one, together with a specific kind of paper and the required size. In the village I found the paper and had several sheets cut to the specifications. After lunch Ernest sat down behind the desk in the corner of the living room to write the tribute, practicing first on ordinary paper. In the adjoining kitchen I cleaned up our lunch things and fussed around with early preparations for dinner, thinking he would be finished any minute. At the desk Ernest was still bent intently over his writing. I stretched out

627

on the sofa to read, and after an hour said, "Could I be of any help, lamb?"

"No, no. I have to do this."

"It only needs to be a few sentences, you know."

"I know. I know." But his pen hovered with nervous uncertainty. A sense of urgency, futility, almost a smell of desperation oozed out of him until, I felt, it clouded the big room. Finally I could not withstand the pervading tension, excused myself and went for a long walk, down our road, up past the Siegels' house on the narrow, slippery road, past the Greuners' house and horse pasture, breathing deeply, down the quarter-mile to the Warm Springs road, east and then north to our house.

In the sitting room Ernest was still hunched over the desk. A week later he finished the three or four simple sentences of tribute.

Throughout the month of March he turned more and more silent, his eyes more vacant, concerned now that our staying in Idaho would make us taxable there. After a late-night pointless discussion about his blood pressure and possible other diseases, I slept one Sunday morning until the delicious hour of 9 a.m. and down in the kitchen found a note on the table marked: "8:45 a.m. Have gone for milk and juice. . . . Careful not to disturb you. . . . But the day is ruined." One evening our cable TV set presented a remarkably good production of *Macbeth*. As I sat watching, I felt Ernest hovering behind me, his attention riveted on the tragedy, his hands twitching.

"It's terrible, terrible. Cruel," he was muttering.

"It's a great play."

"It's terrible," Ernest said. "Terrifying. I can't stand it."

I turned off the TV set.

The highlight of Ernest's days now was George Saviers's visit on his way back to the hospital after lunch at home. Sitting on the living room sofa together, George reading the blood pressure dial, he was father-confessor and consoler, giving his patient whatever philosophical panaceas he could find. Other than George, Ernest wanted no visitors, spent his mornings mute and brooding at his writing table, his afternoons wandering aimlessly around the house or resting without reading in his room. Kate Brown, cheerful and good-hearted, tried to amuse him with local gossip and jokes when she arrived as he was breakfasting. I read aloud any diverting paragraphs I found in newspapers or magazines. But it was a vegetable life, with our spirits half atrophied. I remembered my father's frequent recommendations when I was a child that I cultivate fortitude as a useful characteristic, and the importance of giving love and understanding. "To live is not enough."

The only time of day Ernest turned talkative was when I had turned off my light to go to sleep at night. Then he would stand beside the open door of my room and at length upbraid me. I did not appreciate the dangers of living in Idaho, where we would be taxed if we remained more than one hundred days. I was not helping him find someplace safe from taxes. I was spending too much money on groceries. I had neglected him throughout his stay at St. Mary's hospital. How could I have enjoyed a TV program that evening when we were in such great danger? I was betraying our well-being.

I made few efforts at self-defense and in the mornings Ernest appeared to have forgotten his bedtime performances. After one night's tirade I slept fitfully and awoke in the dark with a sense of foreboding, padded into Ernest's room, found him sleeping peacefully, and at the top of the stairs missed my footing and fell headlong downward. An edge of the stairs cut my head open and after Ernest and I tried and failed to stanch the bleeding, I telephoned George Saviers who arrived in a wink, carted me over to the hospital, sewed me up and took me home again. I had also sprained my right foot, which kept me hobbling with a cane for a few weeks.

To our mutual pleasure, Ernest remembered my birthday and at the Sun Valley drugstore bought generous bottles of toilet water, but could not bring himself to acquire one named "My Sin." With Kate Brown's help he wrapped the boxes in pretty paper and without her help wrote loving messages accompanying each package.

On Friday, April 21, I clomped downstairs to find Ernest, still in his plaid Italian bathrobe, standing in the front vestibule of the sitting room, one of his favorite shotguns in his hand and two shells standing upright on the window sill in front of him.

"I was thinking we might go to Mexico," I said softly. "Gregorio might be able to get *Pilar* over there." Ernest turned and looked at me, but my message didn't connect. "I read somewhere that there's marvelous fishing off the Yucatán peninsula. We really haven't discussed Paris, either. We could sublet a little flat there. We've been awfully happy in Paris, lamb." Ernest stepped down from the vestibule to look out the big south window from which he could see the road from our gate to the house. George Saviers was about due then. But George did not come. Still holding his shotgun Ernest returned to the vestibule. I sat on a small sofa nearby thinking it would be useless, my trying to take the gun from him, thinking that he could blast my head off at this short distance, about four feet, and all the while talking quietly. "Honey, you wouldn't do anything harmful to me as well as you," and about courage and his bravery in the war and at sea and in Africa, reminding him that he wanted to return to Africa, reminding him how many people loved him and needed his strength, his wisdom, his counsel. About fifty minutes later than usual George tramped from the back door through the kitchen, followed my motion toward Ernest in the vestibule, said, "Hang on, Papa, I want to talk to you," then telephoned Dr. John Moritz, who joined us quickly. Together they persuaded Ernest that he needed rest and took him with them to the hospital. They gave him sedation and he slept most of that afternoon and night, but when I went to see him the following morning he was awake and wanted to go home, saying, "There are some things I want to do there." Couldn't I do them for him? "No."

Years later, reconsidering, I wondered if we had not been more cruel than kind in preventing his suicide then and there. But now only bad weather detained George from flying Ernest again to Rochester. A few days later when Ernest insisted on coming to the house to get some things he needed, George sent our friend, big, husky Don Anderson, and Joan Higgons, one of the nurses, back with him in the car. At the back door Ernest was out of it a minute ahead of them, rushed through the kitchen where Kate was working and had a shell in his shotgun before Don could reach him. Don managed to open the breach and Joan picked out the shell before they got the gun away from Ernest and shoved him onto the little sofa. Upstairs I barely heard the almost soundless scuffle, and it was over, all three of them puffing, before I got down. Back at the hospital they locked Ernest's clothes away when they put him to bed. The weather turned benign the next day, April 25, and from the Hailey airfield George and Don flew with Ernest to Rochester, Larry Johnson piloting. I tapped out a report of events to Ernest's favorite sister, Ursula, in Honolulu. "He is immoveably convinced that he cannot be healed," I wrote Ura. I had already written both Jack and Patrick Hemingway the bad news. At St. Mary's hospital Dr. Rome assigned Ernest a room in the closed wing with its entry double locked and constantly guarded, no latches on the individual room doors and heavily barred windows.

Both from the radio and from TV broadcasts, we had been hearing of the invasion of Cuba's Bay of Pigs by a task force mounted in the U.S.A. and had been appalled by the choice of the landing site. Many of our Cuban friends had shot ducks in that area and could have told the invasion planners that the swamps behind the beach left no room for maneuvering vehicles, which would be, and proved to be, easy targets for air attack. But our private preoccupations blurred our concerns with the distant fiasco.

On the day Ernest left I wrote him a note reporting I had forwarded the two messages he had sent back from Hailey, one to Mr. Lord at the Morgan bank, one to Charlie Scribner, and sent "Rivers of love from here to there." It was the beginning of a two-way stream of correspondence between us, Ernest's letters full of concern about our finances and of his loneliness, mine with daily trivia. I had taken his manuscript to a safe-deposit box in the bank at

Hailey, a mallard drake was sliding down the rapids in the river in front of the house, Rocky Cooper had called to thank me for my letter to Gary who was having a rough time with his cancer but "gallant as springtime," she said. I was planting flowering plum and mountain ash trees on our hillside and seeds of annual flowers beneath the pines, after dark the house got bigger and emptier and more silent and, "I hope you will stay there until it is absolutely positive that you are wholly recovered. Please, Lamb, don't con them into sending you home until they are sure you are ready for it." That is precisely what he managed to do five weeks later.

Late in May I flew to Minneapolis, and at St. Mary's hospital in Rochester the nuns and nurses generously arranged to give us a little dinner alone together outside the barred wing where he lived. As we dined he grew restive and resentful. "You had things set up there [Idaho] so that I'd go to jail. . . . You think as long as you can keep me getting electric shocks, I'd be happy." I flew on to New York. From a big old trunkful of receipts I had brought up from Cuba, I would dig out those which might be deductible from our expenditures to alleviate Ernest's menacing income tax payments. All these clarifications of Ernest's finances would help his recovery, I was told. But I did not believe it. His finances had been shown to him, crystal clear and more than adequate, half a dozen times and the statements had not reduced his unnatural worrying about them.

Many months earlier, Ed Hotchner had consulted an eminent New York psychiatrist, Dr. James Cottell, about Ernest's problems and he had recommended his fellow practitioners at the Mayo Clinic, since Ernest refused to go to the Menninger hospital. Now I arranged for another interview. Never having seen the patient, Dr. Cottell could make only the most generalized recommendations, but he intimated that, with Dr. Rome's approval, Ernest might do well to go to an institution near Hartford, Connecticut, to convalesce, and suggested I look it over. I flew up, was hospitably shown around, noting people reading peaceably in a library and others playing softball outdoors, and concluded that our only problem was that Ernest would never consent to go there. It was a known mental rehabilitation center, and he would deny that he needed that. All he needed really was some miraculous relief from illusory financial strictures, from persecution by the Internal Revenue Service or the F.B.I., and sometimes from an imagined dread disease.

In New York I received an urgent call from Dr. Rome. Ernest was feeling so good that his sexual impulses were reviving. An interlude of privacy with me might do him inestimable good. Embarrassed, I flew to Minneapolis and bussed as usual down to Rochester. Our interlude of privacy would take place in my room at the Kahler Hotel, where I was a familiar face, I assumed. No, no, said Dr. Rome, it would have to be in the locked, barred wing of the hospital. I had never been in a place like that before, and I mourned at Ernest's pitifully small collection of comforts, a few books, a few magazines, a few letters. No typewriter, no telephone, no pictures, no flowers.

As we lay comforting each other and friendly together in his single bed—"Like Africa," I said—other inmates pushed through the door, hollow-eyed men looking for something we could not give them. Ernest seemed to accept them as part of his incarceration, but they unnerved me. Our "solitude" together was not entirely satisfactory to either of us, and I was, maybe cravenly, relieved to be let out of the locked ward. It was no place for my husband, either, I reflected. But I had no solutions for his problems.

An evening or two later Dr. Rome telephoned me at the hotel. Could I be at his office at eight-thirty the next morning? He had good news for me.

Dr. Rome's office at St. Mary's was a small rectangle with one window and as I entered it on time, I was dumbfounded to see Ernest there, dressed in street clothes, grinning like a Cheshire cat. "Ernest is ready to go home," said Dr. Rome. I knew that Ernest was not cured, that he entertained the same delusions and fears with which he had entered the clinic, and I realized in despair that he had charmed and deceived Dr. Rome to the conclusion that he was sane. With Ernest there in the small office, I could make no protest or rebuttal. There might still be some therapy which could cure my husband. But this was no time or place for such discussion.

From the hotel I called our old friend in New York, George Brown, to ask if he would fly out and drive us home from Rochester. He would. Ernest slept at the hospital for a night or two. I rented a two-door, hardtop Buick, and early on June 26 we pulled away from St. Mary's and headed west on U.S. Route 63. I made detailed notes on the journey, recording each day's mileage, the receding landscapes, temperatures. In the flat fields of southwest Minnesota the corn spread out about a foot high for miles, we had wild roses and kinnikinnick, which as children we thought to be Indian tobacco, among the grasses of the roadside and the perfume of new-mown hay sweeping into the car. A thermometer in Mitchell, South Dakota, showed 92 degrees when George and I went shopping for the next day's lunch, but our motel was air conditioned and we slept well. It had been a pleasant day with each of us in good temper.

On Tuesday, June 27, we rolled through blue greens, yellow greens, gold greens, black greens with the aluminum domes of white silos shining in the sun, to stop for lunch at a roadside table near the town of Spearfish. Ernest wanted to stay there for the night, predicted we would find nothing farther along and that state troopers finding us sleeping beside the road would arrest us for carrying wine in the car. We had a couple of bottles in the trunk and I put them in the ditch before we drove on through round mountains feathery with forests to Moorcroft, Wyoming, where we dined at a greasy café which served us indubitably the worst coffee I had tasted since World War II. Wednesday morning's country was a panorama of big skies, gray-green hills and the sweet smell of sage, and as we went through the town of Spotted Horse, with its painted, cut-out sign, its single gas station and post office, Ernest said, "Spotted Horse. Kind of limited." At Lodge Grass in the Crow Indian Reservation we refueled the car and ourselves with a delayed breakfast, and farther up the road we paused but did not stop to look at the hillside of Custer's Last Stand with its white triangular teepee. Having covered 409 miles, we stopped at 4 p.m. at the Island Resort Motel in Livingston, Montana, where the faint song of the Yellowstone River climbed through our open windows.

On Thursday, June 29, we saw an antelope family, one big buck, a young buck and five does grazing beside the Canyon Ferry Reservoir and George, the city man, asked, "Where can they go for shelter when it rains?" We turned south onto our familiar, twisty U.S. 93 and stopped at 5:45, late for us, at the Herndon New Courts at Salmon City, Idaho, and the next after-noon, after picnicking beside the Salmon River pulled up at our house in Ketchum, George having driven beautifully and amiably the 1,786 miles from Roches-ter, I having unpacked my husband's few things each night and repacked in the mornings, and along the road leaned forward to sing into his ear many of our old Spanish, French and Italian folksongs and a then favorite American tune, "Love Makes the World Go Round, Love Makes the World Go Round." We un-packed in leisure and I rustled up dinner from supplies stored in the refrigerator. Before I had left Ketchum I had locked all the guns in a storeroom in the base-ment, leaving the keys among those on the kitchen window sill. I thought of hiding the keys, and decided that no one had a right to deny a man access to his possessions, and I also assumed that Ernest would not remember the storeroom.

On Saturday, July 1, Ernest dragged George Brown out to walk in the hills north of the house—George's low New York shoes were no protection against our local nettles—and later they drove up to see George Saviers at the hospital, who was in his office, and Don Anderson who was not in his office at the Sports Department. Chuck Atkinson came over for a chat in the sunshine outdoors and that evening Ernest enter-tained George Brown and me at dinner at the Christ-iania Restaurant, just across the street from Chuck's motel and grocery store.

As we wedged into the small far-corner table, Ernest noticed a couple of men seating themselves at a small table farther inside and asked Suzie, our waitress and the long-ago object of Sinsky Duñabeitia's infatuation,

635

who those men were. "Oh, they're a couple of salesmen from Twin Falls, I think," said Suzie. The town was brimming with tourists.

"Not on Saturday night," said Ernest. "They'd be home."

Suzie shrugged.

"They're F.B.I.," Ernest mutttered.

"Oh, come on, baby," said I. "They're showing no interest in us. How about a bottle of wine?"

George, who did not drink wine, drove us carefully home and as I was undressing in the big front room upstairs, I sang out the old Italian folksong, *"Tutti mi chiamano bionda. Ma bionda io non sono."* Ernest in his room joined me in the next phrase. *"Porto capelli neri,"* and I huddled into my big sweet-smelling bed. Ernest knew he was always welcome under my pink, perforated blankets. "Good night, my lamb," I called. "Sleep well."

"Good night, my kitten," he said. His voice was warm and friendly.

The next morning the sounds of a couple of drawers banging shut awakened me and, dazed, I went downstairs, saw a crumpled heap of bathrobe and blood, the shotgun lying in the disintegrated flesh, in the front vestibule of the sitting room.

I ran for George. While he called the doctors, I went upstairs, called our friends the Atkinsons to ask if I might stay with them for the day. They came to collect me and at their flat above the grocery store, gave me a tranquilizing pill and put me to bed again. For an hour I shook, unable to control my muscles. Then in a flash of sanity I wondered why I should be so destroyed by the sudden violence I had long but too vaguely anticipated. It might be partially shock at Ernest's deception, I thought, and dismissed the notion. He knew he could not confide in me.

As the Atkinsons' telephone was ringing incessantly, we decided that I should move up to the Sun Valley hospital, and there the dear nurses left me tranquil until the next afternoon when Colonel Charles Sweeny, who had flown up from Salt Lake, came in to chat and gave me the courage to rejoin the living. Patrick was coming from East Africa, Ernest's brother, Leicester, from Miami, and his other sons, sisters and friends from everywhere. We had a day or two of what seemed to me an allegory with people speaking their assigned lines, but these speeches and gestures seemed somehow peripheral and irrelevant to the black hole in the middle of the scene.

After the funeral ceremony in Ketchum's peaceful, pretty cemetery, Alfred Rice, Ernest's lawyer, read his will to his sons and me, assembled in our sitting room. It was the holograph document dated September 1955, bequeathing to me all his estate. Now Alfred proposed that he create a trust fund into which would be paid the royalties from foreign publications of Ernest's books and that the sums accruing be divided equally between Ernest's three sons and me.

Not consciously lying, I told the press that the shooting had been accidental. It was months before I could face the reality.

29

Reconstruction Operations

VALERIE DANBY-SMITH had been accompanying the Irish poet Brendan Behan and his wife on a poetry-reading tour around the United States. The tour had ended and although Ernest had sent her funds for her tuition at an academy of dramatic arts in New York, Val was not burning to get started there. She would be glad to stay on with me for a while in Ketchum to help with my still formless plans for putting Ernest's papers in order, and for company in the house.

Only a few days after the funeral, Cuba's Minister of Foreign Affairs telephoned to say the Cuban government wished to acquire the Finca to be used as a *monumento* to Ernest, and with whom should they negotiate?

"With me, I am the inheritor of all my husband's estate," I said in Spanish.

Could they send me a contract by which, signed by me, the property could become that of the Cuban government?

"Hold on," said I. "As you doubtless know my husband and I left the house with every intention to return to it and live there. We left thousands of papers and personal things there which have no significance for the Cuban government or people, but are important to me. We left manuscripts of my husband in my bank. . . . I'm not sure if I wish to give you our Finca. [They could appropriate it, of course, as they had done to so much U.S. property there.] Perhaps your government would give me permission to go down to remove our personal papers. Would you find out and call me back tomorrow? This same hour? *Muy bien*." By telephone I consulted Alfred Rice and Lee Samuels, both advising me to take the chance of recovering Ernest's manuscripts, if nothing more.

By this time United States citizens were prohibited journeys to Cuba. I got on the telephone to Willie Walton. Would he ask his friend, the President, or somebody on his staff, to provide me and Valerie permissions for a return trip to Havana? Within a few hours Willie reported that the U.S. immigration authorities in Miami would give me the exit and re-entry permits. With her Irish passport Valerie did not require them.

Juan met us at Rancho Boyeros, the Havana airport, with my bright yellow convertible, our loving butler René embraced me tearfully on the front steps, and the next day Roberto Herrera, Ernest's long-time, part-time secretary, came out to the farm with the key to our three-tiered steel file in the library. Apart from odds and ends of letters and a few notes for stories in Ernest's handwriting, it contained one envelope on which was typed: "IMPORTANT To Be Opened in Case of My Death Ernest Hemingway May 24, 1958." Inside it was a typed note dated May 20, 1958. "To my Executors: It is my wish that none of the letters written by me during my lifetime shall be published. Accordingly, I hereby request and direct you not to publish or consent to the publication by others, of any such letters. Very truly yours, Ernest M. Hemingway." I noted the four-day lapse between the date of the note and that of the envelope, and wondered whether Ernest had pushed the instructions aside for due consideration or whether he had simply been interrupted and for a bit had overlooked his note among the cluster of papers on the top of his bookcase where his typewriter lived.

Except for a few nicks in the white plaster outside the house, from Castro's militia mistaking each other for enemies and banging away, the Finca retained for me its timeless quality of muted tranquility and hospitality. The bougainvillaea vines, orange, red and purple, climbed the walls and clustered on the roof. So did the *Porana paniculata* with its soft gray leaves, and *Antigonon leptopus* with its showers of Schiaparelli-pink bloom and half a dozen others. I had assumed somehow they would be wilted, but they were flourishing. Cristóbal, who had been my day and night constant companion, had developed a new life in the pantry and among the servants downstairs, greeted me politely as a visitor but rebuffed my gushing advances. The little ceremonies of sympathies given by our gardeners and friends in the village were a strain, with the gentle Spanish phrase "I accompany you in your sorrow" echoing around my head.

Months earlier, the Cuban government had opened all safe-deposit boxes in the island's banks and confiscated whatever valuables it found. Now my branch of Havana's First National Bank of Boston assured me that Ernest's manuscripts were safe in the Banco Nacional de Cuba, and Juan drove me in to collect them. The government agents had wrapped and sealed with red wax all thirty or forty pounds of Ernest's manuscripts and after some signing of papers handed them to me. I kept them in my locked luggage in my bedroom.

One of our treasures was missing. In his early days in Paris Ernest had bought a Braque still-life, one of his series of mostly tan, brown and black paintings, showing a covered table, a scrap of newspaper, some dice and a wine jug. Sorting papers in Ernest's study adjoining his bedroom, I suddenly noticed the vacancy on the wall. It had always stood, unframed, on top of the bookcases behind his desk. I asked René about it. He didn't remember it until I described it at length. Sometime earlier Roberto Herrera had taken twelve of our pictures into his flat in Vedado for what he considered safer keeping and later had returned all twelve of them, René remembered, when the Castro revolution simmered down. Together they had rehung the canvases in their accustomed places and set the Braque on its shelf. Nobody had broken into the house in our absence. Nothing else had been taken.

Then René recalled that only a couple of weeks earlier two men professing to be art surveyors for the new government persuaded him that they should make an inventory of our pictures and presented some sort of identification. He accompanied them around the house and when one of them asked for a glass of water went out through the living room and dining room into the pantry and chipped ice from the big block in the pantry icebox for a glass before he filled it with tap water. It could have taken him three or four minutes before he returned with the glass on a tray and found the visitors where he had left them. In that time the pair could have slipped the Braque out the screen door onto the front terrace and dropped it into the flower bed below the balustrade. I made no protests to the Cuban police or to the newly established Council of Culture. Communications between Cuba and the U.S.A. were dwindling daily and I would have a fairly large shipment of boxes for some ship's hull, if any ship were available. Galerie Maeght in Paris were Braque's agents. When I looked through their photographs of his paintings a year later, I could not find a reproduction of Ernest's painting.

In twenty-two years of accumulating correspondence

and printed materials, Ernest, who never discarded anything but magazine wrappers and three-year-old newspapers, had managed to stuff to its brim almost every drawer of the Finca. The two big desks on the ground floor of the Little House were crammed with papers and grocery lists and charts of the Gulf Stream, many of them concerning his months of German submarine-chasing off Cuba's north coast. Twelve big drawers beneath the bookcases in the library were stuffed with ancient, mostly unanswered correspondence and thousands of photographs. His bedroom and study held piles and drawerfuls of papers. So did our storeroom, intended chiefly for luggage, in the tower and his four-viewed workroom and retreat on the tower's top floor.

As René and the gardeners were wheelbarrowing load after load of five- and ten-year-old copies of *Ruedo,* the Spanish bullfight magazine, of the London *Economist* and other British weeklies, of French and a dozen United States publications to a bonfire below the tennis court, I received a copy of *The New York Times* letters page. They had published a letter from the writer Glenway Wescott urging that I be deterred from destroying Ernest's work, or something of the sort. We were dealing with bookworms and mildew-infested layers of the old magazines. Valerie and sometimes Roberto Herrera and once or twice Mayito Menocal and Elicio Argüelles, for whom I scraped together meager lunches, came out to help sort the worthy from the worthless in the immense reserve of paper, testimony perhaps that a man had hoped to return to those old fonts of information.

Five André Masson paintings, one Paul Klee and two Juan Gris paintings hung on the walls, and since Ernest had given most of them to me one by one in various years when I surprised him with acknowledgments that the day was my birthday, I felt entitled to take them with me to the United States. I decided to leave in the house the Roberto Domingo bull paintings and several other semi-treasures. Cecilio took measurements and made a box in which to ship them. On the telephone I got on to somebody at the Council of Culture to explain the box.

"We don't allow any paintings to be exported," said the Council of Culture voice.

I telephoned the Minister of Foreign Affairs, with whom I had chatted about the Cuban government's acquisition of our house. Twice, three times. His secretary said he would call back. The Minister did not return my call.

Our doctor, José Luis Herrera, an ardent revolutionist and now chief of the medical section of Fidel's army, came out to one of my austerity dinners—there were only a few packages left in the deep freeze—and helped resolve the impasse. He telephoned one of Fidel's aides saying I needed help with a problem. Half an hour later the aide called to say that the Prime Minister would be at the Finca the following afternoon. "Afternoon" translated as any minute from 12:01 p.m. to midnight. In a flush of whimsey I opted for giving Fidel the old-fashioned welcome of Spain in which all the household lines up outside the entrance to greet a visitor. I alerted the gardeners and old, deaf, sweet Mundo, the cows' caretaker, as well as Ana, Juan, and the house servants. They were all in a place, double row of welcomers, about eight o'clock when the Prime Minister arrived in his jeep, accompanied only by one nondescript car.

In the sitting room he headed for Ernest's chair and was seating himself when I murmured that it was my husband's favorite. The Prime Minister raised himself up, slightly abashed.

"No, no, señor, please be seated there."

I explained that some paintings my husband had given me were being refused an exit permit from the Council of Culture. "They are part of his bequest to me, and I feel I cannot leave Cuba without them."

"Why don't you stay here with us in Cuba?"

"Oh, señor, that would be interesting. But there is much work to be done about the estate, and it cannot be done here." If he would care to look around the house, the Prime Minister would observe that the removal of my few pictures was not noticeable. After cups of strong Cuban coffee, which should have been whiskey, I later heard, we toured the house, my guest particularly interested in the animal heads, and when

642

I mentioned that the eland was the best meat producer among Africa's wild beasts, he wondered if they could not be imported to Cuba and domesticated.

"Who knows? It could be possible. But their natural habit is at an altitude of two thousand meters."

He inspected Ernest's bedroom and climbed to the top of the tower to look out over the hills toward Havana and the valleys with their groves of slim white-trunked royal palms. "I imagine Señor Hemingway enjoyed this view," he said.

"It's the truth. Every day."

"I will help you with your pictures," said the Prime Minister at the front door. Outside it he noticed our Little House snuggled near the broad front steps.

"That is your guest house?"

"Yes, Señor."

"We will leave that untouched, for your use when you may return."

"Very many thanks, señor." For what, I wondered. For appropriating Ernest's valuable property? At least they had preserved his manuscripts.

Two days later Fidel's aide telephoned instructing me to have my boxes at a pier in Havana bay at 8 a.m. the following morning. In a battered old truck from the village we made the appointment and in a few minutes I understood why the aide had been so prompt with his arrangements. Tied up at the pier was a shrimp boat from Tampa, one of the fleets which had plied between Cuba and Florida carrying shrimp and other fish from Cuban waters in refrigerated bottoms back to U.S. markets. This boat's refrigerating machinery had failed and the spare parts necessary for its repair were unavailable in Havana. "This is the last ship from the U.S. which has clearance papers from the port authority," the aide said. I looked inside the little hull, found it dry, thanked the aide and told him I would send him some explanatory notes about our house and Ernest's life there. They would perhaps deter the Council of Culture from inventing gaudy tales about the place. There were no passenger accommodations aboard the shrimp boat, which was about the size of *Pilar,* and I arranged with the captain to pick up my cargo from his company's warehouse in Tampa whenever I could get there.

A few more duties required attention. Gregorio Fuentes came to the house to discuss the fate of *Pilar*. Some twenty-five years earlier Ernest had brought her down the inland waterway from the Carolinas to Key West, so he had told me, and with several extensive repairs and replacements including a new teak deck she had remained a lively seaworthy vessel, a one-man boat all her life. I loved her.

"Could you step her engines and her outriggers, and take her out into the Gulf Stream and sink her?" I asked Gregorio.

Gregorio's loving, furrowed face furrowed further. "You have to abandon her, Mary?"

I didn't know the word for "relinquish" in Spanish. "Everything has changed, you know, Gregorio, not only because of Papa's death. Things have changed here. There isn't gas for sports fishing. Even if you could get her to Key West . . ."

"That's a better idea."

"I don't know if I could maintain her there, with or without you. I don't know if I'll have any funds."

"I couldn't leave my family for long."

"The death taxes in the North are very heavy. Anyhow, Gregorio, as soon as you can, will you take all our fishing gear, rods, reels, line, everything, to use yourself or sell or as you wish, before the government claims *Pilar*. But if possible, please take her out and sink her in the current."

"That would be a decent and dignified termination for her," Gregorio said. "I will try to do it. . . . And you will abandon the sea?"

"I must, for now." I still couldn't remember the word for "relinquish" with its implied reluctance. As it turned out, the Cubans used *Pilar* as a workboat for a while, and then installed her (poor thing) as an exhibit on the Finca lawn, so I was told.

In my Havana bank I deposited a check for $3,000 drawn on my New York bank, and then drew local checks dated August 25 against it, gifts from Ernest to his long-time employees, the largest sum going to René, and lesser amounts to Gregorio, Pichilo our head gardener (it was equivalent to his year's wages), Roberto Herrera, the chauffeur Juan, the laundress Ana, the maid Lola, René's helper Pedro, the carpenter Cecilio, the Gallego and Mundo gardeners, the masseur Mario Sanchez, and Lili, who for years had come once a week to wash my hair and manicure my nails. With eloquent gestures and protestations of the revolution's good faith a man from the Council of Culture assured me that all our staff would be kept on and paid by the Council until such time, remote of course, when they would no longer be needed. Then the Council would help them find other employment. René had already found himself a job in an ironworks in a nearby valley, but the Council soon summoned him back to the Finca to work as curator there. Late in August Valerie and I boarded a plane for Miami, its passenger compartment filled to the ceiling with Cuban families sitting on each other's laps, frightened children at the tops of the pyramids. In my handbag was a small envelope circled with a rubber band, a little cache of, I estimated, about half a million dollars worth of jewels, family heirlooms, that I was conveying from a Cuban friend of ours to relatives in Miami. It was the only day in my life when, if I remember accurately, I transgressed a law, and my sneaky little pleasure in the deceit was balanced by guilt.

Valerie and I extricated my boxes from the warehouse in Tampa, flew to Chicago and took the comfortable old train from there to Shoshone, Idaho—the long, pleasurable rumble through the Midwest to the Rocky Mountains, the dining car steward rushing out at stops to find California wines which were listed on the menus but missing in the galley. In Idaho for the opening of dove season, I went tooling down Route 93 with Dave Roberts, Don Anderson and other friends to blast away from various corners of several fields at the pink-footed, pretty little birds and, shooting more than a box of shells, downed a couple. I had all the coordination of a cornstalk in the wind, but it was a warm-hearted, healing day.

In correspondence from the East, business concerning Ernest's life and work now revived. Dr. Carlos Baker at Princeton University would like to write a biography of Ernest. Would I give him access to letters and other papers. Yes. Malcolm Cowley wrote suggesting that a committee of responsible writers and critics could relieve me of the onerous job of reviewing Ernest's manuscripts and deciding which of them should be published. No. A more careless or conscientious widow might have said yes. He had said nothing in his will about committees. I approved the democratic principle of decisions made among peers, I replied to Malcolm. In practice I thought it worthless. One individual had to make the decisions, and take the risks and consequences. But I could not yet summon the strength to confront Ernest's manuscripts. Charles Scribner's Sons and interested bystanders would simply have to wait.

After a lifetime of being chauffeured by others, I rented a car from Sun Valley, tried a few driving lessons and in the hot sunshine and bright skies of Indian summer drove Valerie and Tillie Arnold on a couple of picnics a few miles out of town. On October 16 I noted: "I continue functioning like a wheel that has lost its hub."

Alan Moorehead had flown from London to consult New York editors and publishers about his second book concerning the Nile River and telephoned me in mid-November, inviting himself out for the weekend. He and Val and I picnicked on hot dogs by the river, jumping up and down to keep warm. In spite of the cold we went down to Bud Purdy's ranch with the Arnolds to tramp over frozen stubble looking for ducks on Bud's canals which were still partially open with their swift currents. As we approached one stretch of water three mallards got up in front of Pappy Arnold and he knocked down all three with a wizard triple shot. As we walked on after he had retrieved his birds, a pain sharp as a dagger-thrust hit me in the middle of my chest. A heart attack, I assumed. George Saviers came to see me back at home in bed and contradicted my diagnosis. "Probably an ulcer," he said. "They're apt to develop from excessive tension, and you've had plenty of that."

In spite of my discomforts I assembled the usual Thanksgiving dinner for my friends and having fasted since midnight went the next morning to the hospital for X-rays. There it was: an ulcer in the upper stomach. They put me to bed, dosed me with tranquilizers and healing potions and for a week I dozed, swallowed and dozed again. When they let me stay awake for a couple of consecutive hours they gave me a fascinating book, a one-volume education on the digestive system, *Experiments and Observations on the Gastric Juice and the Physiology of Digestion* by William Beaumont, M.D. (Nov. 21st, 1785–April 25th, 1853). A Canadian Frenchman had been wounded by a gunshot blast in his stomach and had survived although the hole never healed over. In months of observations through the hole Dr. Beaumont discovered for the first time in medical history how the stomach functions. Three weeks after I bedded down in the hospital, I went home feeling dandy and a couple of days later X-rays showed the ulcer to be healed. With the good news George Saviers gave me some good advice. "You haven't got Papa to handle your health problems. You must learn to deal with them yourself."

For the first time since Ernest's death I discovered, both in the hospital and in the humdrum days at home before Christmas, that I had time for reflection on the year's happenings, and perhaps for some reassessments, and, remembering my mother's admonitions throughout my childhood, "count your blessings," I tried to do so. I gave thanks that the Cuban government with its demands for quick action had forced me to deal with the tactical problems of arranging the whereabouts of material things. I was grateful to be in Ketchum where I had more friends per square mile than anywhere else, people with no need for reaffirming their dismays and sympathies. I repeated my thanks to my ancestors that they had kept themselves in good physical health and thus bequeathed to me a constitution usually capable of surviving storms.

But I starved for the smell of Ernest's chest, where my nose always nuzzled. I ached to touch his skin, which was smoother than any other, I thought. Having no creature to absorb and appreciate pats, hugs, kisses, I floundered in a void of unexpressed affections, and I missed my husband's daily offerings of endearments and flattery. I also missed his discipline, his counseling of restraint when I veered into erratic enthusiasms or fears.

A minor difficulty was that I could not imagine giving a party without Ernest there to do the hosting. Don Anderson found a sagebrush six feet high for a new version of a Christmas tree. I sprayed it with silver paint and hung it with tiny ornaments which would not overpower its spangle-sized leaves, and on Christmas Eve Val and I entertained a crowd of friends with minimum difficulties.

On her first African safari with my stepson Patrick, my friend Clara Spiegel had collected a fine array of antelope heads and a couple of imposing buffaloes but no lion. Now she wanted to go back for the biggest lion with the blackest mane in all of Tanganyika and invited me to accompany her, the month's safari beginning on June 1. The idea of shooting further beasts to hang on my walls did not allure me. I had shipped three handsome heads from Cuba to Ketchum. I would go along, however, "for the ride," I decided. But first I must sort through the thousands of papers Ernest had, way back in 1938, stuffed into their boxes in the storeroom behind Sloppy Joe's Bar in Key West. On January 18 I left Idaho for Chicago and Key West. Having borrowed big white bartender's aprons from the barmen, to keep the dust off our clothes, Betty Bruce and I worked six or seven hours a day for a month, sifting papers, coming upon the skeletons of mice, rats and many cockroaches which had apparently died from starvation, their flesh having been nibbled away by ants. We also found scores of family letters, perhaps worth saving we agreed, original drafts of Ernest's early short stories, and an early draft of *A Farewell to Arms,* together with his hand-corrected galley proofs of the glossary of *Death in the Afternoon.* At the end of it I shipped a half-dozen numbered boxes of papers to New York, and put in my purse lists of their respective contents.

To settle another bit of business, Toby and Betty Bruce flew with me to Bimini, where I ascertained that the vacant lot overlooking the Gulf Stream, which Michael Lerner had given Ernest in the thirties, was still listed as his property. It was a clear title without any legal questions appending, and since it had never been developed, with any facilities piped in, no taxes had been levied on it. (Later, I gave the lot, one of the few open spaces on that crowded island, to the American Museum of Natural History, for the use of the Lerner Marine Laboratory people.) As Toby and Betty and I wandered along the main street fronting the bay one night, we looked into several nightclub hovels where calypso music blared in deep dusk and plump, middle-aged women, obviously United Statesers, bounced around the dance floor in the arms of native blacks. "We're widows from Iowa," one of them told me happily. "My husband died last year. A farmer. He left me a little something."

"Now, missy, you wouldn't spoil our fun, would you?" her big escort asked.

"What's a better way for a man to earn his living in these islands?"

"Certainly not." I was sorry I couldn't join them; Ernest hated dancing.

Back in Ketchum I tried and failed to grapple with the chore of looking over the manuscript of Ernest's book about Paris, possible editing in mind. His words, especially his handwritten corrections, blurred and distorted my judgment. I wrote Harry Brague, Ernest's editor at Scribner's, that I would have to postpone the work. After only two weeks of work and loneliness in Ketchum I lit out again, manuscripts in my luggage, for the little flat in New York.

There was work to be done on two years of Ernest's and my joint income tax, my chore being to find and list receipts for all expenditures possibly, if not probably, deductible. But Alfred Rice's paperwork, required for the determination of the inheritance tax, was both more detailed and cumbersome. His job was to discover the earnings during the past five years of every single piece of Ernest's copyrighted writing so that the Internal Revenue people could estimate their future earnings. His worksheet was a piece of brown wrapping paper about eight feet square covering his office floor, the whole embellished with hieroglyphics and figures thickly enough to impress any Internal Revenue man.

Even so the I.R.S. eventually collected nearly all of Ernest's cash savings unto itself.

From Cuba and Key West I had assembled hundreds of letters from Ernest's friends to him, and Charles Scribner, Jr., generously lent me an empty room in his building where Valerie could sort them and, if they seemed pertinent, could write their senders asking for copies of Ernest's letters to them. Unknowingly I had shipped with the letters little colonies of bookworms or minuscule paper-eaters. When Valerie noticed them, she gave an alert, a minor flap ensued, and a bug exterminator was summoned, who stopped the beasts in their tracks. But I shivered, imagining what the minute hungry hordes might have done to a building full of books, especially Scribner's rare book room which was on the floor below, and gave thanks for Val's sharp eyes.

Late in April an invitation came from the White House to a Sunday night dinner for United States winners of the Nobel Prize, together with a note from Miss Letitia Baldridge saying that Fredric March would read Ernest's "The Killers" to the company after dinner. I had, I thought, a better idea, which was that Mr. March might read an excerpt from the unpublished book I called "The Sea Chase," something new. I found the manuscript in Alfred Rice's office, cut out a readable piece of it and sent copies to Mr. March and Miss Baldridge. President Kirk of Columbia had earlier come to call on me in Sixty-second Street to propose that I give Ernest's manuscripts to the university's library, and now in Washington I made a Sunday morning high-spots tour of the Library of Congress with its directors. Down in its basement depths they showed me some of George Washington's and Clare Boothe Luce's papers, and upstairs we looked at a neat, bright room where at rather dinky little desks scholars might study their choice of the library's treasures. As I had said to Dr. Kirk, I told the Washington librarians I would think about it.

Circulating among the White House guests as we drank cocktails before dinner, I found some of the Nobel Prize winners shy but kindly, Mrs. J. Robert Oppenheimer being the liveliest and prettiest of the few wives the Prize winners had brought along. I noticed Miss Pearl Buck surreptitiously scratching notes on a pad half hidden by her dress, heard a whisper that the President had supervised the dinner seating, found a chance to tell Mrs. George Marshall how profoundly I had admired her husband before dinner was announced.

President Kennedy had seated Mrs. Marshall on his right, me on his left and Dr. Carl Anderson, a winner in physics from California, on my left. After preliminary niceties I suggested to our host that the U.S. government's position toward Cuba was stupid, unrealistic, and worse, ineffective, especially—sotto voce—since the Bay of Pigs fiasco.

President Kennedy was looking irked and impatient. As the dinner courses were changed, he turned to Mrs. Marshall. I turned to Dr. Anderson and asked, "If an enemy were to bomb this room at this moment, how much, do you think, of our technological knowledge would be lost?"

"Not very much," Dr. Anderson said. "As you may have observed, most of us fellows here are elders. All those young scientists, working away in our laboratories, already know what we learned; they'll go forward with their research."

I was pinching salt from the President's salt dish, and when he turned away for a moment from Mrs. Marshall, I said, "I could jump into Cuba, you know. The Cubans liked my husband, and I know Fidel."

"Have you read Katherine Anne Porter's *Ship of Fools?*" the President asked.

"No. I'm sorry. If I talked to Fidel . . ."

"You are rated as politically unreliable," said the President.

"You haven't checked M.I. 5," said I, and subsided. I had never been a knee-deep member of any political party. The Robert Kennedys drove me to Bill Walton's house, where I was staying.

30

Beginnings

CLARA SPIEGEL'S SAFARI for a lion was due to leave Arusha, Tanganyika, on June 1, and a week earlier, squirming with anticholera and antitetanus shots, I flew to Rome with my beautiful Mannlicher-Schoenauer 6.5 rifle and my Winchester Model-21, 20-gauge shotgun, old outdoors companion. We left Rome at midnight and when the rising sunshine swept through our plane windows the next morning I awoke to find Mt. Kenya gleaming pink and white just off our port side and we descending. At the New Stanley Hotel in Nairobi, I went to bed again as soon as the luggage boy closed my door behind him.

Bathing and dressing five or six hours later, I remembered Rocky and Maria Cooper's stopping in at the Ketchum house that spring to show me a cutting from one of the fashion magazines. Beneath a photograph of a handsome young man, the caption said that Mr. Peter Beard, a recent Yale graduate, was working on a book about Africa, soon to be published with the arresting title *The End of the Game,* and that he had returned to East Africa to do final research. "Isn't he attractive? You must find him for me," Maria had said.

"Darling, there's quite a lot of East Africa. It doesn't even say which country."

"Oh, you can find him. Somebody there will know where he is," said Rocky. "Just put your mind to it. I'd like to meet him too."

Since I had last been there eight years earlier, the New Stanley Hotel had redone its interior. At the front desk I asked, "What have you done with the bar?"

"It's upstairs," said a blond boy at the far end of the desk. "I'll buy you a drink." Upstairs he introduced himself. "Peter Beard, from New York." It was an auspicious opening for the month of carefree adventure I had planned.

Ernest's middle son, Patrick, now one of Tanganyika's most successful white hunters, drove up from Arusha to collect me, and we were no more than half an hour outside of Nairobi when the magic of the high plateaus began seeping into me again, the African wind with its scent of wildflowers and antelopes and big cats, the mystery of thorn trees with who knew what creatures resting in their crowns or in the shade at the bases of their trunks, the anticipation of a month of mornings on which we would never know what strange delights or dangers we might encounter before nightfall.

Clara joined me at the New Arusha Hotel, and on June 1 we left Arusha almost on time, heading for the Serengeti Plain, the national park, and bordering its southwest boundary the 2,000-square-mile Maswa Reserve which had been closed to lion hunters for five years, and in which the Tanganyika Game Department was permitting Patrick to take a client for one lion. We would have the whole place to ourselves.

Patrick established our camp more or less in the middle of our hunting grounds, and on our first morning out from it, after the inevitable struggle of getting up—untuck mosquito netting hanging from the tent ridgepole, shake out boots to dispose of any possible dozing snakes, pull on shirt and pants icy-wet from dew, toss down hot tea and an antimalaria pill, pile guns, cameras, film, shells, books, sweaters into the Land-Rover—we explored eastward, Patrick driving. Beside him in the front seat was ancient Mumu, once a poacher and subsequently one of East Africa's best game trackers, wearing his good luck hat of a thousand patches, an inverted snobbery. Between Clara and me in the uncushioned back seat was Hamisi, Clara's hero with whom she had hunted on her earlier safari. Hamisi was of the Nyamwezi tribe, the same which a century earlier had escorted Livingstone to the coast and was still proud of that achievement.

Driving to the western end of our reserve the second day of the safari we assembled bicycle tires of grass and flower seeds blowing up our sleeves and down our necks to lodge above our belts, a phenomenon of that dry season. We emptied out the accumulations before lunching beside a small, chuckling stream. In a story *Life* published subsequently, I wrote about our return home that afternoon.

It was at the end of the long, hot, seed-ridden drive homeward that the Maswa Reserve presented us with the sort of luxury you get on safari and nowhere else. Skirting some 70-foot-high boulders of exfoliated granite, we saw a lioness stretched out on top, forepaws almost over the rock's edge, placidly surveying the countryside below, considering, doubtless, what to have for supper among the animals on the plain. We bumped around the boulders and, on the other side, the westering sun tinting their hides bright gold, lay nine lionesses and two young lions peering from the top like the gentry from boxes at the opera. They posed for their portraits by long-distance lenses until we noticed that the light was dimming.

In the trackless grass of the high plateau you must get home before dark or spend the night in the car, and darkness seeps swiftly over East Africa after sundown. Neither the headlights nor the landmarks which the Africans magically retain in their memories of the thousand turns each day can help you in the equatorial darkness.

We hurried homeward in the last light, found our last creek and forded it without breaking an axle and were nearly at the camp when the Land-Rover made noises of refusal. She was steaming and thirsty, and Hamisi and Mumu alighted to administer to her. Hamisi had the hood up and Mumu had opened the big water can when Clara said, mildly, "Look, there's a rhino."

There indeed was a female rhino with a large teen-age child beside her. We had inadvertently crossed the path they intended taking and they

654

had caught our scent. Nothing upsets a rhino more than having its path crossed. Mother and son suddenly stopped, chuffing with anger, heads lifted, seeking the enemy scent again. They found it, swirled in the bushes and came at us, big as boxcars and black in the twilight.

Hamisi slammed down the hood. Mumu jumped aboard on top of the cameras. I screamed and took pictures through the hatch. Clara screamed and sensibly hung on. Patrick flung the car over rocks and stumps. When we stopped again, the rhinos had lost us. But they picked up the scent another time and bellowing with rage again came at us, their heads going down to gore and toss us as they drew near. I imagined the Land-Rover lying wounded on its side and us broken and battered in the thorn bushes, four days' drive from a hospital. The rhinos were no more than ten yards away in the dusk when Patrick got the car restarted, and this time we went on to the safety of the campfire before we stopped.

Denis Zaphiro, Ernest's and my friend from 1953, had arrived and sitting tranquilly by our campfire listened to Clara's and my trembling, tumbled account of our near ambush.

"I thought I heard a ruckus out there," Denis said placidly.

Lolling in the warmth of my shallow bath in a canvas tub before dinner, I mused that it was the rarity value of being chased by a rhino which made it more exciting than being cut down by a New York taxicab. And I thought how lucky I was to be on that particular spot of Earth's surface that evening although Ernest was missing.

When I accepted Clara's invitation to share her lion hunt, I had wondered how the African landscape would look to me without Ernest in the center foreground of it. It would have a big gaping hole in the middle, I imagined. But now I was beginning to see the scenery around the hole, and that was good. At dinner Denis predicted that Clara would get her lion the next morning. I went to bed exhilarated but so lulled by good French wine that the morning arrived in a minute.

With our respective excitements barely under control, we got off from camp before 7 a.m., Denis and Patrick talking local politics like commuters from Connecticut in the front seat, Clara, Hamisi and I tense and quiet in back.

Patrick headed for the area where we had seen the nine lionesses sunbathing on the high rock. We were cruising slowly in sparsely treed country when simultaneously Hamisi from the roof hatch and Denis with my binoculars saw the lion with three lionesses and cubs at the foot of a tree. Clara on the back seat could not see him, but from the hatch I could, and saw the lionesses moving off to our right with the children and the lion, a great, blurred, dark patch, disappearing in the grass ahead of us. We waited, silent, but he must have heard our hearts beating. He moved again forty yards away and Pat, Clara and Hamisi got out of the car, Hamisi handing Clara her gun, then keeping one hand on her shoulder and making small sounds of reassurance. I needed a hand and reassurance, too, shivering with fear in the doorless unprotected back seat with the lionesses pausing ten yards away in their retreat, regarding me balefully, considering, no doubt, whether or not I looked good enough for breakfast. In the covered front seat Denis had no such concerns.

As the lion started forward again Pat whispered to Clara, "Shoot him if you like." After an eternity of five minutes Clara, barely visible herself in the high grass, shot one shot. The lion bounced into the light, fell down, bounced again and went down on his back with his great paws clawing the empty air. Pat whispered, "Give it a throat shot for insurance." Clara shot again. Later, doing the autopsy, Patrick found that her first shot had broken the beast's spine and lodged in his heart. In our 2,000 square miles of grass and forest Clara had hunted a mere three days and one hour for this beast complete with black mane, a hunter's dream.

At our second camp at Lolkisale south of Arusha, local tribesmen told Patrick that recently a leopard in bright daylight had come upon an African woman and her child squatting in the grass beside the road, had carried the baby in its jaws up a tree and devoured the baby's head while the frantic mother screamed helpless below. "You shouldn't mind killing a leopard," Pat said to me. I had made this trip to Africa for the purpose of enjoying the country, not for killing beasts. But in that child-eating leopard country, I would shoot one.

We shot a couple of gazelle and hung them in trees for bait and in the short evenings Patrick and I sat silent and motionless in the high grass waiting for the leopard to come to supper. We had a succession of unsuspecting visitors. A squirrel perched on a twig six inches from my head, furious about something, her tail jerking, her complaints raucous and interminable —an uncommon scold. A snake slithered past our boots. Birds darted down on us and a swarm of bees roared above us, loud as an air force armada in the silence.

On the fifth evening of our vigil Pat was reading mathematics and I was reading John Donne when I looked up to see a leopard bending over the bait forty yards in front of us, his hind feet on the branch of the tree, his forepaws on the bait fastened to the branch. I nudged Patrick. He nodded. I put the crosshairs of Clara's .270 Winchester precisely where the leopard's spine would be between his shoulders and softly squeezed the trigger. His forepaws relaxed and he slumped against the bait. Then he fell to the ground. He was a beautiful young male, pro-football-sized for his breed, and I hoped it was he who had eaten the baby.

There was the day I could have had a buffalo as easily. Cruising in the Land-Rover, Patrick, Denis, Hamisi and I saw him dozing on his feet beside a spindly thorn tree and afoot stalked toward him, I with camera at the ready for a closeup portrait. Thirty yards from him Pat stopped, incredulous, and whispered, "He's a tourist's dream. He's got a great head. You ought to shoot him."

"But I don't want to shoot him. I have no earthly use for him. I want to take his picture."

Pat was already sending back to camp for a gun to back me up in case I fumbled the shot. By the time

657

we were broadside of the buffalo, he had gone down on his knees for a siesta.

"I can't shoot a sleeping innocent beast," I protested.

Pat knocked on a tree trunk. The buffalo opened his eyes and in a flash turned and rushed away. I had not even raised my rifle. I felt good about the buff and bad about my lost picture.

On Sunday, July 2, in Nairobi, I chartered a little airplane and with Clara flew southeast to admire Kilimanjaro rising above its clouds like a frosted cupcake on a platter and to salute it for Ernest a year after he shot himself. After eight years East Africa had again given me the luxuries of sweet fresh air, miles of space unspoiled by man, time unbracketed except by the natural division of light and darkness, the absence of all but natural sounds, wind, rivers murmuring, birds, beasts, the anticipation each morning of the day's surprises waiting. Now it gave me another present, a sense of an ending to my past year of looking backward.

Back in New York, after finishing my story for *Life,* I could find no further excuses for failing to deal with Ernest's bulky manuscripts I had brought out of Cuba. Clearly Ernest had expected me to publish some, if not all, of his work. Malcolm Cowley, who subsequently read through pounds and pounds of manuscripts and gave me his calm, disinterested judgment on them, reminded me of the damage done by inept editors to some of Mark Twain's work which was published posthumously. Fanny Butcher, who had run the Chicago *Tribune*'s book review department for fifty years minus a few weeks, told me of similar mistreatment of some of Willa Cather's writing. I hunted around New York public libraries for guidebooks to the administration of literary estates and found no pertinent advice.

But somewhere between Tanganyika's Maswa Reserve and East Sixty-second Street two principles of procedure for the work sprouted in my head. One was that, whatever the temptations or persuasions, Charles Scribner's Sons and I would publish nothing we jointly considered to be of quality inferior to the work published during Ernest's lifetime as approved by him. The other was that nobody, including me, would be permitted to put his cotton-picking typewriter to work on Ernest's prose to "improve" it. Except for punctuation and the obviously overlooked "ands" and "buts" we would present his prose and poetry to readers as he wrote it, letting the gaps lie where they were. Where repetitions and redundancies occurred, we would cut. We would not add anything.

Since Ernest had expected his Paris memoirs to be his next published book, I dug out that manuscript, the first part of which I had typed for him five years earlier in Cuba. With the exception of a couple of chapters about which he had worried and which I felt not sufficiently germane to the tenor of the book, I thought it read well. So did Harry Brague at Scribner's. We worked together checking Ernest's final draft, making a few further cuts and switching about some of the chapters for continuity's sake.

As I wrote later for *The New York Times Book Review,* Ernest had walked me many times on the streets of Paris's Left Bank which he had known forty years earlier. In his book, they read accurately. But I was concerned that he might have put in a street where it did not belong. No matter if he left some out. I wondered how trustworthy Ernest's memory was, and in October of 1963 I flew over and retraced all the steps Ernest had written he took, first by myself, and later with Gordon Parks, the photographer, writer, film director, and my friend, who would make photographs of those long-remembered places for *Life,* which was going to publish a condensation of the book, finally titled *A Moveable Feast.* Ernest had made two mistakes in the spellings of street names. Otherwise his memory had not faltered.

A new apartment building was rising in my neighborhood in New York, and I leased one of its two penthouses. Large tracts of sky hung outside the little flat's windows, east, south and west, together with a couple of slices of Central Park and an oblique view of the Metropolitan Opera and New Jersey in the distances. It seemed to me an anchored bubble floating in the diverse and entertaining skies of New York. Just before Christmas 1963 I moved in, and on New Year's

Eve inaugurated it with a small dinner party, a few friends gathered around a low table in front of the dancing flames of the fireplace, sipping decent champagne, spooning down codfish, lobster and shrimp stew done in the manner of Pamplona, and at midnight swallowing twelve grapes, each with good wishes to an absent friend.

In the steadfast conviction that vacations, especially in new places, are with books the best stimulants for the head and spirit, I resisted for a full minute Dave Roberts's suggestion that I go along on a jaunt to Alaska. We took the 6 p.m. flight northwest from Seattle, cruising in bright sunlight above the mountainous, pine-dark islands along the Canadian and Alaskan coasts to Anchorage, I prudently wearing boots and black woolen pants for my introduction to the northern frontier. They looked ridiculous among the floating chiffon evening dresses and pink satin slippers crowding the lobby of the town's main hotel when we got there.

This was a salmon-fishing expedition, so we flew out over Kodiak and the misty Aleutians to a salmon camp nestled in a slope of myriad-tinted tundra. As the little plane descended to the landing strip, a moose with a beautiful big rack of horn came running to us out of the forest and our pilot and camp-owner had to pull up in order to miss him. When we disembarked after several passes with the moose blocking the runway, our host said, "That demented beast could tear us apart."

A few days later, tramping the tundra, entranced with the sensation of stepping on little coiled bedsprings, I came upon the moose's head, lying abandoned in the wind, a victim of misdirected love. I asked that the rack be sent down to New York. For years it has rested in a comfortable corner of my terrace, one of New York City's smallest minority groups.

Since Tina Roberts, Dave's beautiful wife, does not enjoy hopping over the curves of Earth's surface as much as he does, she recommended that I accompany him on another fishing trip, this time in March 1965 to New Zealand and Australia. The biggest trout in the world's rivers hang around rocks in some of New

Zealand's streams, and David dreamed of enticing them to his lures. Also, said the New Zealand consulate people in New York, some of our planet's best marlin fishing was available out of their Bay of Islands on the northeast coast of their North Island, and they made me an appointment for three days of fishing with Captain Leslie Tautori Blomfield, an impeccable fisherman with some native Maoris in his ancestry, aboard his sensible boat *Avalon*. Promptly at 8:30 on three successive mornings, Les pulled into the hotel's dock, and we turned east, first to pick up half a pailful of fresh, flopping kahawai fish to use, still wiggling, as seductive marlin bait, then to troll the Pacific Ocean. In three days of unremitting search, we found no marlin tail or fin, but watching our baits I amused myself imagining what exaggerated tales Les and Ernest, surely immediate friends, would have swapped about fish and storms and hapless fishermen.

Dave and I then flew to Melbourne, Australia, picked up Ernest's and my old friend from Cuba, Bill Caldwell, who was running the U.S. consulate there, and his lively, lovely wife Joss, and together we flew from 37 degrees south latitude to Cairns, a village on Australia's east coast at 16 degrees south latitude. Our objective was Green Island, a dot of foliage which had risen out of the Great Barrier Reef off eastern Australia.

I am an island idolater. As I wrote for *Holiday:*

> My heart thumps for Madagascar and Zanzibar and the silent islands in the tropical lakes of East Africa. . . . If anyone were to give me a year as a present, I'd squander half of it exploring the islands of the Dalmatian coast, the second half nosing around all those lovely empty islands with their beguiling beaches and probably no fresh water along the east coast of New Zealand's North Island, and the third half puttering among the Fijis.

> Island fanciers will probably find that Green Island approaches perfection in size, shape and inaccessibility. It is only one of the 679 islands of the 1,250-mile-long, 80,000-mile-square Great

Barrier Reef, and it may be the most felicitous of them all. It has thirty-two acres of greenery, white beaches and rocks—big enough for an hour's walk around it, and distant enough from populous places to stay off the tourist routes for a while longer.

A steel and concrete fish-viewing room was anchored beside Green Island's jetty three fathoms below the surface of the Pacific, and its windows gave us intimate but dry contact with a million finny creatures, an almost solid wall of fish hanging there, gills fluttering. Here were forty-two different kinds of coral—count them if you can—and fifty-two species of fish ranging from infant sardines hardly bigger than plankton to yard-long glum-mouthed groupers, a bullet-shaped creature dressed from nose to tail in red-dotted white organdy, Schiaparelli-pink coral trout. From the windows of the underwater observatory, marine life on the reef appeared to be so well ordered, if overcrowded, that it was difficult for us to remember that we were watching changing scenes of mortal combat even better organized than mankind's mutual slaughter. Morally the fish seemed superior. In the ascending scale of organisms, the larger devoured the smaller for purposes of survival rather than for power or greed.

31

Under Weigh

AFTER ANOTHER ISLAND trip—this one in 1966 to the Dalmatian coast—various projects awaited my attention in Idaho, among them "Papa's Birthday

Party" on July 21. A few years earlier I had decided it would be a pleasant gesture to arrange some kind of annual reunion of Ernest's Idaho friends for remembering him, however briefly, and immediately discarded the idea of a church service or any session of speech-making. He would like his friends to join in an evening of food, drink and music, I surmised, with his money paying the bills. Some eighty old friends assembled each year for a festive few hours at Sun Valley's Trail Creek Cabin where Ernest and I had given joint-jumping parties. Invitations and a menu and wines and music needed organizing.

Ernest's sister Ursula and her husband were coming from Honolulu for the birthday party, and after them my guest room would be occupied by a succession of other friends. That was the autumn we changed the road from our gate to go up a hill behind the house, instead of marring the view from the front windows. September 1 the work was finished and I gave a big lusty road-warming party to celebrate. Ernest's men friends had taken over the duties of host. The following spring we planted green lawn in front of the house, pleasant to the eye and sporting a croquet court.

In the winter months in New York patterns of obligations and pleasures were forming, and daily I followed orders scrawled or implied in my desk calendar: "Scalper—Man for All Seasons, Evelyn Duys; check to Leg. Def. Fund; 5-7 Architectural League; Ellisons, dinner—order car; flowers to Ilka Chase Brown; tickets, Star-Spangled Girl; Brunch, Fran Koltun; check to World Wildlife: 8:30 Rubinstein, Carnegie; call Jimmy Sheean; fly Miami, Dave, Tina Roberts; reserve La Caravelle; ducks here, Peter Schub; Janet Murrow, Westbury; Amory Thomas arriving, 5:00; Peter Vanderwicken's birthday; traveller's cheques; ballet, Sebby Littauer, lunch, Sports Illustrated; check to Audubon; W. Walton, dinner." On and on the reminders go, some new names appearing, old names happily recurring, blank pages signifying journeys taken and the calendar left behind unheeded.

In the summer of 1967 William White, professor of journalism at Wayne State University in Detroit, was assembling and sorting the mass of journalistic reporting Ernest had written from 1920 onward for newspapers and magazines. When Scribner's sent me the list of contents of the book, which would contain less than a third of his total output, I noticed the absence of Ernest's dispatches about China published in the long-defunct *PM*. Professor White and Scribner's reconsidered and added the stories about China to the book which came out that year as *By-Line: Ernest Hemingway,* with an amusing dustcover by Victor Mays portraying four decades of various means of transportation.

When *Holiday* decided in 1967 it would like a quick story about Harry's Bar overlooking the Grand Canal in Venice, I made a luncheon date by telephone with Giuseppe Cipriani for that December 5, flew to Milan on December 2, and by December 10 was back in New York with my little wad of penciled notes including Arrigo Cipriani's recipe for the renowned bar's fish soup with shrimp and mussels.

Early the next year Lester Cooper, writer, director and producer of TV productions at ABC, persuaded Alfred Rice, usually "Mister No," that an hour's documentary film, *Hemingway's Spain,* using quotations from Ernest's writings about Spain, would be a project worthy of our respective efforts. In mid-March Mr. Cooper and his wife Audrey and I made a rendezvous in the bar of the Palace Hotel in Madrid. Thereafter for three weeks the three of us in fair and foul weather examined the country north, east, south and southwest, I pointing out places similar to those imagined bare hills and forests, rivers and roads my husband had described in *For Whom the Bell Tolls* and *Death in the Afternoon.* It was a journey of serious intent and frequent joyous interludes, and we parted friends, to rejoin in Pamplona in July. The mayor of the town had invited me to the dedication of a sculptured head of Ernest outside the bullring on the opening day of the fiesta of San Fermín. Willie Walton came with me for this small ceremony, flying from New York, I sleeping on the floor beneath our seats in the crowded first class, first to London for a day or two at Claridge's, then to Paris and Biarritz where a rented car was waiting for our tranquil drive to the Basque provincial capital. In Pamplona we danced half the night in the streets, drank wine from a dozen friendly *botas,* yelled *olés* at the bullfights and departed from the din and crush a day before the fiesta officially ended. (On October 21 that year, ABC served up Lester Cooper's film *Hemingway's Spain* on TV screens and I thought it beautiful, honest and poetic.)

One reason we left Pamplona early was that Ketchum, Idaho, was calling loud and clear. Carlos and Dorothy Baker were going out to stay with me and meet Ernest's friends there. Ernest's Ketchum friends had secured from Sun Valley a little piece of woodland and sagebrush overlooking Trail Creek and had there installed on a simple rustic column the bronze head of him done by the sculptor Robert Berks, and Robert Manning, by now editor of *The Atlantic Monthly,* would be going out to speak at the dedication ceremony on Ernest's birthday, July 21.

The American Museum of Natural History was sponsoring a nature tour of the U.S.S.R. that September of 1968 for the particular purpose of bird-watching, I discovered in one morning's mail, and immediately sent an application to join it. Under the guidance of Dr. Charles Vaurie, one of the museum's ornithologists, the tour would skim over European Russia from top to bottom in three weeks, a handy device for an introduction to that vast region, I thought, and so it turned out to be. To my pleased surprise Dr. George Saviers mentioned that he had enrolled himself for the same journey.

Our group of twenty-five nature lovers took off from Kennedy airport September 3 on a night flight to Amsterdam and at the new, modern Sovietskaya Hotel in Leningrad we met the young woman who was to be our guide and interpreter for all the tour, Galina of the lustrous big brown eyes and a posterior of startling proportions, an industrious instructor, knowledgeable about her homeland. At dinner in the hotel that night—cucumber, pressed caviar, watery beef stew—we had a look at local highlife. A wedding dinner was progressing in the dining room, the bride in white chiffon with a demure headdress and veil, her gown cut off above her pretty knees, one bridesmaid wearing mauve stockings to match the mauve in her flowered dress. There was one good trumpet in the orchestra which played ancient American jazz, and the girl singer was on key but neuter-gender. Perhaps by decree, I guessed. My room overlooking a little park contained such western amenities as wall-to-wall carpet, a reading light at the head of the bed, plastic light controls, and outside streetcars thumping into the square until 1 a.m., and reviving again doggedly at five.

After two days of bussing about the city, we boarded the Murmansk Express, billed as a first-class train, for Petrozavodsk at Lake Onega and as gallant, stupid travelers froze through the night, uncomplaining.

From Petrozavodsk we high-tailed it in a hydrofoil forty miles to Kizhi Island for a day of birding, tramping around the treeless, 62 degrees north latitude, grass-covered gentle hills and valleys, photographing the wooden cathedral with its twenty-two onion domes each covered with shingles shaped like elm leaves, its ancient windmill, and wooden farmhouses brought in from other places to add to the island's tourist attractions. The vegetation reminded me of northern Minnesota with its wild columbine, ferns, goldenrod and mountain ash with red berries. The local birds had sensibly migrated southward. The night train back to Leningrad was just as cold and miserable as it had been on its northward journey.

On Sunday, September 8, we flew to Moscow, installed ourselves in the Hotel National, and that evening went to a ballet in the great wood-paneled, red-tweed-seated auditorium inside the Kremlin. The next morning we went back again to the Kremlin's yellow brick museum to gawp at the ostentation of its one-time residents, their jewels and costumes, their horse bridles and harnesses inset with inch-square emeralds, and 40-carat rubies and diamonds. I looked but failed to find any birds in Moscow.

That afternoon, conscientious, loving Frieda Lurie of the U.S.S.R. Writers' Union, who translated from Russian to English and back again as methodically as a metronome in motion, took me to the office of the

666

foreign literature magazine for tea, chocolates, chat and cognac. Later at the office of the Writers' Union, a number of writers and translators were assembled.

After a lengthy discussion of Ernest's work and my plans for further publications, I made a digression. They had been reading in their newspapers, I assumed, that a great many people in the U.S., both on the Eastern Seaboard and in the mountains of the West, were firmly against our country's commitment to the war in Vietnam. "We think it is immoral," said I, "and while I have not marched in the streets, I have protested in other ways.

"I can say this to you without concern that it may be published here or anywhere else," said I, "because, of course, we have freedom of speech in my country." The court reporter girl in the back of the room was putting it all down. The ensuing silence lasted a full minute.

Our group flew from Moscow to Rostov-on-Don in the Ukraine, visited some poor farms and poor farmers in the steppes, found blue and turquoise birds, rollers as in Africa, a crested lark and some cattle egrets, flew on to Pyatigorsk in the wooded mountains of the lower Caucasus, and by bus rolled through cornfields and orchards and hemp to Tbilisi, our birders noting swallows, saker falcon, buzzards, magpies, mourning doves and black warblers.

From Tbilisi we flew to Baku, reminding me of Ploesti, an Allied bombing target in World War II with its oil fields, and across the Caspian Sea to flowering Ashkhabad, just above the border of Afghanistan, went birding at an oasis with a lake in the vast surrounding desert, in which irrigation projects were now beginning, watched pretty Turkoman girls with shining flirty eyes and long black braids weaving Bukhara rugs of handspun, hand-dyed wool, making, they said, 400,000 hand-tied knots to the square meter, their hands darting like dragonflies at the looms. On we flew, almost due east, to Dushanbe, picnicked near there in a mountain pass beside a rushing stream, then to Tashkent in Uzbekistan, to Bukhara and Samarkand. Romantic names and Ernest would have appreciated their shining turquoise towers.

667

Flying to Alma-Ata in the state of Kazakhstan, the last stop on our tour, we could see the snow-capped range of the Tien Shan mountains in the Himalayas which extended into China. But Alma-Ata at 2,600 feet was abloom with autumn flowers and shrubs in park after park with their bustling fountains, the most decorative city of the U.S.S.R., I thought. "Not a scrap of paper blows in this country," I noted. "There are no cigarette butts in the gutters. A perplexing contrast to their filthy public toilets everywhere."

Reading Henri Troyat's excellent biography of Tolstoy, I was unaware on our 1,974-mile flight back to Moscow that we had sat in the airplane for six hours. That night I gave a dinner party in our hotel for the whole crowd, many of whom would continue as friends and correspondents for years. According to Dr. Vaurie, the tour saw one hundred eight species of birds in Russia. Our birders were industrious. I saw about thirty species. They all left for home the next morning, and I met Julian Semenow, a young Moscow friend, for an excursion to Yasnaya Polyana, Tolstoy's country house near Tula on the main road south from Moscow to Sevastopol.

On the way down in Julian's car we came to a high plateau with vistas of forests and plains and farmlands ebbing away on both sides for miles and 180 degrees of sky fluffy with little clouds and pulled into an empty field beside the road for our picnic lunch. Misha, the chauffeur, spread a newspaper on a board he found and Julian unpacked food and drink, I danced around the field, exulting in the fresh air, the tranquilty of the field and the charm of a copse of trees nearby, hollering, "Here I am in the middle of Russia. Not another tourist in sight. The first American to set foot on this field."

Julian kicked an object with his boot. It was an empty package of Marlboro cigarettes.

At Yasnaya Polyana the curator of the house, Nicolai Pavolich Pusin, a descendant of the poet Fet who was Tolstoy's contemporary and friend, was waiting to show us everything from the entryway leading to the dining room, the table set with silver and china, including Tolstoy's special bowl for his vegetarian soup,

668

to his surprisingly small study with his low chair so that, with his poor vision, he could sit closer to the papers on his desk, and to Tolstoy's bedroom with his flannel nightshirts hanging against the wall and a tin of biscuits from England among the bottles of medicine on his bedside table. Sonya's bedroom was much bigger, with a washstand in one corner, its walls studded with framed photographs and every flat surface filled with bibelots.

Nicolai Pusin told us how they had saved the Tolstoy house from German depredations in World War II. They had photographed every bit of it, including hinges on the doors and handles opening windows, then sent the 22,000 volumes of books, the furniture, china, silver, portraits, photos, the clothes, and the chessboard to a town in Siberia for safekeeping. The Germans had occupied the house, stabling their horses in the basement. When they departed finally, the place was re-established exactly as it had been originally.

Another day Frieda Lurie took me to see Tolstoy's town house in the middle of Moscow with its sixteen big rooms which the family used for nineteen winters. As we were looking at the dining room with its cuckoo clock, a little old woman who was standing guard pulled a chair from the table and stood on it to make the cuckoo chirp for us, and muttered to the young curator who was showing us around, "I know this house better than you do. I knew HIM."

Julian took me off to an eighty-mile nighttime drive to a duck-shooting club in Kalinin province at the confluence of the Volga and Unzha rivers. As they had promised, the club staff had remained on duty for us and served us hardboiled eggs and caviar, then steaks, potatoes and wine after midnight and lamented, just as in Idaho, there were few ducks because no cold wave had yet hit the country to the north where the ducks spend their summers. At 5:30 a.m. the club manager chuffed us across the water in a skiff, the wind rising, pulled into a bunch of weeds and poplar seedlings, and I clambered up to a wooden platform a foot above the river, Julian handing me one of his guns and a box of shells. No sign of ducks or sound of wings. Only the wind in the reeds. I jumped up and down on my platform to keep warm.

I saw a pair of what looked like widgeon flying downwind half a mile away. Gray daylight began to bring out the fall colors, soft browns and yellows of the near and far shore and gray yellows of my surrounding reeds. About ten o'clock, Victor, the club man, and Julian came to collect me and we headed back toward the club. As we crossed a wide stretch of the Volga, a big covey of mallards rose from the river, almost within gun range. Our guns were properly cased.

Sergo Mikoyan invited me to a stupendous lunch, and another day Konstantine and Larisa Simonov produced a sumptuous dinner at their apartment. They came to see me off the next morning at the airport. I could not remember any country—England, France, Spain, Kenya, Australia, even Italy—in which people so generously invited visitors to their homes. The approval of Ernest's work brought me extra attentions and courtesies throughout the U.S.S.R., but I could devise no remedies for the discomforts of traveling in a group on a strict schedule.

We had special guests and something absolutely new in entertainment for Ernest's 1969 birthday party at Trail Creek Cabin. People danced to our local steel band on the silvery grass but paused frequently to look up in speculation at the nearly full moon. Neil Armstrong and Buzz Aldrin, who had left the U.S.A. four days before, were walking around in the dust up there, gathering rocks.

Now, more than I had before I lost my closest friend, I cherished long-time pals and new ones. Twice I went to Winnipeg with my Winchester 20-gauge shotgun for the luxuries of duck shooting on the Delta Marsh and gorging on Clara and Jimmy Robinson's hospitality at St. Ambroise. Sarah Boyden buzzed out from Chicago to holler her delight at finding Jim Hill weed and other dusty treasures when she tramped the sagebrush with us duck hunters—Chuck Atkinson, Bud Purdy or Chuck and Gioia Larkin from Scottsdale who had taken a cattle ranch on Silver

Creek near Bud's property and were a valuable and edifying addition to our community.

One morning Betsy Douglas, who ran America House, the gift shop at Sun Valley Lodge, came out to show me something amusing her husband Luther had found in their mail. As a member of the Explorers Club in New York he had received a brochure outlining the delights of a tour to Antarctica aboard the new ship *Lindblad Explorer* of Lars-Eric Lindblad, the New York travel agent. Members of the cruise would have opportunities to interview penguins, sea lions and some of the scientists who work at weather stations on Earth's only ice-topped continent.

"Just the ticket. Let's go," said I, and we were among the ninety passengers aboard the scarlet and white motorship when she pulled out of Buenos Aires for the Falkland Islands and twenty-one days of roaming 3,810 nautical miles through the Roaring Forties, the Furious Fifties and the Screaming Sixties south latitude, ending in the classic tradition by rounding Cape Horn, which remained in character for us, the wind reaching Force 9 on the Beaufort Scale (12 is hurricane force), sending mountainous seas over the entire ship.

It was a remarkably congenial company, we discovered early on, and luckily so for various reasons. One was that Mr. Lindblad, to avoid complying with U.S. seaman's union rules, had hired English-speaking Swiss boys and girls as room and dining salon stewards and stewardesses, most of whom were so stricken with mal de mer when we hit heavy seas that they could not stay on their feet. Another was that since pack ice, wind and sea dictated our excursions ashore, the plans for any day, printed and distributed in the ship's daily program, were constantly altered or canceled or switched in midstream. When a brisk wind rose at Carcass Island in the Falklands, with most passengers ashore, the *Explorer's* captain ordered the gangway lifted. When the ship's crowded lifeboats came alongside, ship's winches raised the boats four decks above the water, ship and boats swaying in the wind, so that people could hop aboard.

From the Falkland Islands we headed south then

west to Admiralty Bay and King George Island in the South Shetlands, on to the Fildes peninsula where Chile and the U.S.S.R. maintain meteorological stations among colonies of chinstrap and Adélie penguins, to the Argentinian weather station at Hope Bay on the northeastern tip of the Graham peninsula which protrudes from the Antarctic continent like a beckoning finger, and on down and around.

Mr. Lindblad's southernmost target for the cruise was Adelaide Island, nearly 68 degrees south latitude, where the British maintain a weather station and emperor penguins live on the ice. We never made it. After four tries to slice through the pack ice and breach the Antarctic circle, we turned north to visit the U.S. Palmer Station at Arthur Harbor.

Subscribing to Mr. Lindblad's penchant for educating his customers as well as diverting them, we listened to hours of lectures in the ship's assembly hall and I learned more than I really wanted to know about the chronological and natural history of the area, also about penguins.

Having caught fish in the Caribbean, the Atlantic, the Indian Ocean, the Pacific and the Bering Sea, I wanted to catch a fish in Antarctic waters, but compromised. I found some ancient tackle at the U.S. Palmer Station just above 65 degrees south latitude and after fussing around finally caught a fish that looked something like a Gulf Stream grouper, a small beastie which would have dressed out at no more than two pounds. My fish's problem, and mine, was that nobody could identify him. Demeaning, until Keith Shackleton, the delightful British naturalist and painter of birds, found him in a fish book in the ship's library. He was *Trematomus bernacchii,* without any common name. Grilled for breakfast the next morning he was delicate and delicious.

On the way north we paused for an afternoon of playing with elephant seals on the beach at Potter's Cove at King George Island and after crossing the boisterous Drake Passage around the Horn, Betsy and I strapped in our beds, disembarked finally at Punta

Arenas, the southern-most city on our planet, with pretty girls in miniskirts making a big do of showing us the local sights. Back in New York, my bubble flat was so stable and secure that it seemed momentarily a bore. But Charlie Scribner produced a stimulus.

Having read and reread Ernest's manuscript about Bimini, Cuba and the sea chase of German survivors from a sunken submarine during World War II, I had taken it to Mr. Scribner before I left for Antarctica, suggesting we could make a book. It would need cutting, of course, I had said. When I got back to New York he was enthusiastic on the telephone. We should get to work right away on the manuscript. Working separately and together we cut out one whole section of the book which seemed irrelevant to us, but added nothing. Ernest would have written passages linking the three separate parts of the book, connective tissues. But as I had decided earlier, no one might anonymously add anything to Ernest's prose.

As usual, I was much concerned about the book's dustcover, and Mr. Scribner agreed with me that a correct marine chart of the waters off Bimini and the north coast of Cuba could provide a good theme for a dust jacket, and he went to New York's coast guard headquarters to find such a chart. A few days later the F.B.I. called on him at his office to say that he had better hire a U.S. battleship if he were planning to invade those waters. *Islands in the Stream* was published in August 1970 with its accurate chart dust jacket in beautiful green, and two of the critics I most respected, Cyril Connolly of the London *Sunday Times* and Edmund Wilson of *The New Yorker,* approved it.

Since then Scribner's has published *The Nick Adams Stories* (February 1972), including several previously unpublished stories, and in May 1974 the fat *The Enduring Hemingway, An Anthology of a Lifetime in Literature,* the first reassembled collection of Ernest's work in more than twenty years with a thoughtful introduction written by Charles Scribner, Jr. (I thought the dustcover unprovocative). All Ernest's papers—published and unpublished manuscripts, letters, notes—are going to the Kennedy Library at the University of Massachusetts in Boston.

But our editing chores are not yet finished. Two very long manuscripts remain unpublished, awaiting attention. One, set mostly on the Riviera in the 1920s and titled *The Garden of Eden,* concerns a writer and his triangular domestic arrangements and contains some good characteristically Ernest prose. The other big job is his original treatment of *The Dangerous Summer* dealing with rivalry in Spain's bullrings, condensed versions of which *Life* published in 1960. Many of Ernest's observations of Spain cut out by *Life* may merit publication, and many of his descriptions of work with the capes and muletas in the bullring might perhaps be put to rest. Also tucked away in New York are some short stories emanating from adventures in World War II, pieces Ernest liked when he wrote them, and his semifictional account of our African safari, excerpts of which were published by *Sports Illustrated.*

The trepidations that swamped me when first I heard of the enormous assignment Ernest had given me in his will, the administration of his literary estate, have eased away since then. Unexpectedly, learned professors of English literature around this country and abroad have helped me build a certain assurance about my job. The professors are invariably writing dissertations or articles for scholarly reviews on such ambiguous or abstruse topics as Ernest's "fish syndrome" or that *Across the River and into the Trees* is an "imitation" of *The Divine Comedy.* Did Ernest discuss Aristotle's *Poetics,* this scholar asked recently, and was he reading Dante and discussing him with me or others while he was writing the Venice book?

On my bookshelves I have twenty-some published books sent to me by their authors in the pastures of Academe. Many others have published without sending. Some of the interpretations I find frightening and somehow theatrical, as though I were enmeshed in a rope dangling from a rising balloon, absurdities overriding common sense. But it is comforting to find other people making mistakes of judgment, and I have grown grateful that Ernest trusted mine enough to relay to me the burden of responsibility for his work. It has given point and purpose to my days.

On a crystalline September morning my neighbor Sepp Froehlich in Ketchum took Sarah Boyden and Martha Vanderwicken and me up the twisty road to the rounded pate of Baldy, our 9,300-foot-high principal ski mountain, to look at Idaho a hundred miles in all directions. Baldy's protruding shoulders obscured our village, but I noticed a green pond far below where no pond belonged. It was part of a tennis court in a new resort, Sepp explained, the only unwelcome blot on our vast landscape. Otherwise only the pines, aspen, sagebrush and limpid sky comprised our view. We prayed it would not change. As time ticks away, I cherish continuities increasingly. With exceptions.

One such interlude occurred in March 1975 while Denne Petitclerc, Bruce Tebbe and I were fishing the bouncing currents off Cabo San Lucas at the tip of Baja California. In uncounted days of trolling baits through bucking seas, I had seen but never taken a broadbill swordfish. In the Gulf Stream off Cuba they feed only at night when the commercial fishermen catch them. In *Pilar* we never tried for them.

Now, only ten miles offshore in the Pacific, we counted dorsal fins and tails of a dozen fish at a time, both marlin and broadbill, waggled baits under their noses, coaxed, exhorted, begged, with no response. These beasts had a well-stocked larder somewhere else. That morning they were simply out for a swim. Until the boat's mate tossed a live bait at one of them and, accepting it, the fish caught his anal fin on my hook. With the help of Denne's strong left arm, I inched him in to the gaff, never letting the line grow slack so he might throw the hook, never jerking, never toughing it, pulling so hard that the hook would cut the fin's delicate membrane, my back, shoulders, forearms, wrists protesting the strain, my feet digging holes in the deck so that my legs could help more, resisting the fish's pull. The stupid fishing chair had no footrest. My lungs gasped, but my right hand failed to freeze, making turns and half turns on the little handle of the reel. In thirty-five minutes we brought that fish to gaff and I heard the most satisfying compliment of a decade. *"Qué buena pescadora!"* the boat's mate said to himself. My beast weighed 130 pounds hung from the scale on the beach, and that he was foul-hooked diminished my joy not a jot.

32

Generally Stormy, Locally Fair

SOME ACTIVITY INSIDE the head has accompanied my movements through space and time, producing questions without answers. I wonder how it is that *Homo sapiens* with his majestic achievements in the arts, philosophies and technologies, has paid so little attention to the preservation of his species that he continues, more vicious than almost all other animals, destroying his own breed, for power or pride or pelf. I wonder why he underrates the uses of decency and compassion while overrating machinery and its mystiques, devoting half a billion dollars and inestimable energies to a ballyhooed handshake in the sky— Apollo-Soyuz—while fumbling its meaning on Earth's surface. I wonder how it happens that the great brains of the U.S.A. have felt so little responsibility for the lesser brains that nineteen million of us are now discovered to be illiterate; that our vaunted economies have permitted deficit spending programs to enclose us in a mighty tower built mostly of sand and false reliance on the future; that with six percent of Earth's population we heedlessly consume forty percent of its goods. Where has foresight gone?

I wonder if *H. sapiens* harbors an unrecognized, built-in self-destruct mechanism, or if scattered warnings and the Club of Rome—altruism is not charity but necessity—will serve to correct our atrocious housekeeping. Can heuristic research and global action save one-third of our planet's people from malnutrition, with damage to brain as well as body, or starvation; prevent disastrous climatic changes—deserts spreading—or arrest the pollution of oceans, rivers and air, and the damage to Earth's ozone buffer? Will twentieth-century despoilers leave anything to posterity except our sphere's—oval's—empty shell?

Since the beginning of this century, man has devoured more natural resources than in all previous history. Can he or will he reverse that course? Who will instigate such global action? Are there members of our species broad enough of perception, deep enough of concern for mankind and strong enough in determination to persuade warring neighbors to live and let live and join an effort to rescue Earth? Not long ago R. Buckminster Fuller, a master in circles of such thinking, publicly reaffirmed his faith in man's capacity to adapt to changing environments, to develop new capabilities, and so to survive. "We have the option," he said. I find his cool appraisal solacing, even though an option may not imply hope.

Twenty years ago I sat alone one evening at Pauline's pool in Key West watching starlight flicker on the water and wondering how it was I got there, what unrolling skein of a life had drawn me there from northern Minnesota, a path disparate from those of my childhood friends. Our Professor Smith in Bemidji had said that the children of pioneers tend to move farther on, and most of my schoolmates had ventured farther, a day's drive or so. But few had ranged as far as I had, except in wartime service. Was I a maverick, an unintentional nonconformist? (My father had said, "Never be a sheep.")

In the gallimaufry of decisions which dictate a

677

life's direction, which one had landed me finally beside Pauline's pool, I wondered, and concluded that my opting, age twenty-eight, to see Paris on my summer holiday from the Chicago *Daily News* had been my most significant decision. It had dictated my wish to work on a London newspaper, and persuading Lord Beaverbrook that I should do so. From that step haphazardly sprang my job with the London bureau of Time Inc., then meeting Ernest and deciding to marry him. I remembered Lord Woolton's telling me that his reading sociology as a struggling social worker had changed his targets of intention and started him on a course which led him to the immensely difficult and responsible job of minister of food in World War II. There may be people who design a pattern for their lives and manage to follow it precisely. But I marvel that happenstance governs so much of the human condition.

Enough of editorializing, patient reader. I hope you have found this excursion half as agreeable in the reading as I have in the eight or nine years of writing it. . . .

"Hold on," some dear friends order me. "You haven't told us anything about yourself."

M.H.: "Whatdaya mean? Five hundred some pages."

Dear Friends: "No, no. About *you*."

M.H.: "Five feet two, eyes, blue, 35-27-35. Too thick amidships."

D.Fs.: "Not that nonsense. Why did you write the book, for instance?"

M.H.: "Who cares? Because I kept all those diaries, I suppose, and thought they were sometimes amusing."

D.Fs.: "So, why did you keep the diaries?"

M.H.: "A harmless eccentricity. Or, no. It was partly because I thought Ernest might find them useful—dates, places, people, weather. Which was ridiculous, because he had a tape recorder in his head. I don't remember his ever making a note in Africa, but after we got home he wrote 40,000 words or more about our safari. No dates, but places described and sharp characterizations of people, also dialogue. I found it entertaining."

D.Fs.: "You weren't disappointed that your work was wasted?"

M.H.: "No. Ernest wrote fiction mostly and the safari piece was fiction based on fact, more fun than my facts."

D.Fs.: "You say you're a reporter. But you don't report your feelings."

M.H.: "If events are properly reported, the reactions should be implied. What feelings haven't I implied?"

D.Fs.: "You imply little about the loss of your baby, for instance."

M.H.: "That would seem obvious, I think. At first I felt I was a slacker in the human race, being unable to contribute to it. But pining and keening couldn't rearrange my private plumbing. Later on, seeing how many of the children of my admired, intelligent friends were becoming autistic little monsters, I felt better. Or maybe it was the Duncan-Shaw syndrome."

D.Fs.: "Did you feel yourself 'slaving' for Ernest in Cuba, as you say?"

M.H.: "Hyperbole. I slaved at the Finca as that lovely man, Arthur Rubinstein, slaves at the piano. Most blessed are they who enjoy their work, I think."

D.Fs.: "You enjoy all your work?"

M.H.: "Within reason. Jousting with the English language to make it serve my purposes I enjoy the most. But entertaining friends, cooking for them with imagination, making my living places comfortable and happy—that's working with pleasure. Long ago I worked out devices for ignoring or eluding work I don't like. Such as fussing over bank statements."

D.Fs.: "Do you concur that men are chauvinist pigs?"

M.H.: "No more than that women are chauvinist sows. I'm thankful for almost every man I've known and the mother who produced him. I've been remarkably lucky with men friends, it seems to me. Through all these years only one fellow quote took advantage unquote of me, as I recall, and I don't include Noel's heisting our joint bank account. Otherwise those sweet, various alliances ended, for whatever reasons, with our continuing to be cheerful friends."

D.Fs. (a bit disgruntled): "How did you sustain the trauma of Ernest's suicide?"

M.H.: "I feel I've written plenty about that. Too much, maybe. First it was remembering to breathe in and out. Then it was learning to tackle problems in their logical sequences and to rely on my own judgments about people and situations. It tends to make a woman a bit arrogant, I'm afraid. Like men. But I don't know any recourse."

D.Fs.: "There were rumors that you wanted to sell the Ketchum house after Ernest died."

M.H.: "Rumors only, entirely false. I love the house and its views—folded brown mountains, space, brilliant skies and my river crooning over its stones. Ernest wouldn't have wanted me to sell it while it gives me so much pleasure. It enfolds me."

D.Fs.: "So you think you've coped well with widowhood?"

M.H.: "Don't be patronizing. Without points of reference, who knows? Living alone was the worst part for me. Rather like those years in London when my feet were forever cold. After a couple of years my feet continued cold, but I grew unaware of them. Now I no longer notice that I'm alone. And if I do notice, I'm sometimes pleased to be. There are no quarrels in my house. Nobody disagrees with me. It's selfish, of course."

D.Fs.: "You're self-sufficient, all the time, every day?"

M.H.: "No, darling. Going to bed alone is the toughest part for me. Not so much for the cuddling, but for the bedtime talk, the comfort. Books are helpful in bed. But they are not responsive."

D.Fs.: "How is it you haven't remarried?"

M.H.: "Nobody has asked me."

D.Fs.: "You must regret that."

M.H.: "Sometimes."

D.Fs.: "With this book finished, what will you do?"

M.H.: "I've been dreaming about the Seychelles, if I could find a decent boat, cruising with a few friends, exploring reefs and beaches. Must have a captain who knows the waters, and good fishing tackle. It could be glorious."

D.Fs.: "A life of leisure?"

M.H.: "Certainly not. Only a holiday. Knowing that there is work waiting spices the leisure. Then back to my desk and work, lovely, satisfying work."

Index

New York, 311-312, 328, 408, 549, 564, 614, 621-622

pets, fondness for, 193, 195, 196, 214, 220-221, 224-225, 234, 243, 244, 247, 268, 271, 272, 305, 308, 330, 336-339, 365, 388, 392-393, 396, 399, 441-442, 455-456, 517, 540, 543-547 *passim*, 558, 562, 566, 576, 578, 639

poems: EH for MH, 151, 542; MH for EH, 348

shooting and hunting, 244; Cuba, 196, 213, 234, 235, 396, 400; East Africa, 435, 436, 452, 460, 461, 511; guns owned by, 262-264, 270, 273, 570, 635, 636; Idaho, 240, 241, 242, 265, 267, 574, 575, 576, 580, 605, 606, 607; Italy, 284, 319

Hemingway, Mrs Ernest (Mary Welsh):

Alaska (1964), 660

Antarctica (1969), 671-672

art, interest in, 30-31, 147, 283, 288, 423, 553, 555, 564

Australia and New Zealand (1965), 660-662

Baja California (1975), 675

BBC, broadcasts for, 68-69, 86, 97

birth, 5

boating and fishing, 195, 213, 232, 234, 256, 330, 406, 672, 675; Cuba (*Pilar* and *Tin Kid*), 198-199, 256, 309, 333, 340, 362, 363, 368, 401, 404, 644; East Africa, 491-492, 494

childhood and early life, 3, 5-29 *passim*, 34

Cook, Lawrence Miller, marriage to, 34

cooking, interest in, 267-268, 294, 305, 372, 379, 429, 509, 522, 532, 542, 543, 627, 664, 679

correspondence, 196; Baker, Carlos, 645, 646; Berenson, Bernard, 291; Brague, Harry, 649; Cooper, Gary, 632;

Cowley, Malcolm, 646; Hemingway, John, 631; Hemingway, Patrick, 631; Hemingway, Pauline, 251, 266, 303; Jepson, Ursula, 631; Kerr, Mrs. May, 537; Schustedt, Fred, 533; *see also* parents *below*

Cuba, 603-605; Castro and closing up of Finca Vigía, 638-645

death of EH, 636, 637, 647, 680; annual reunion of friends in Idaho, 663, 665, 670; as executrix, 153n., 314, 539, 637, 638; as executrix, handling of manuscripts and property, 637-646 *passim*, 649, 664, 673, 674

East Africa (1962), 652-659; plans for trip, 648

Europe (1936; Ireland, England, and France), 37-40, 678

Europe (1948; Italy), 288-290

Europe (1954; England, France, and Spain), 487, 498-503

Europe (1956; England), 558-560

Europe (1963; France), 659

Europe (1966; Dalmatian coast), 662

Europe (1967; Venice), 664

Europe (1968; England, France, and Spain), 664-665

health: anemia, 549, 566, 571; broken bones, 294, 322, 596, 607, 609; car accident, 208-212, 216, 434; fever, 257; plane crashes, 482, 485, 489; tubular pregnancy, 235-238, 250, 679; ulcer, 647

and Hemingway, Pauline, 255-262 *passim*, 266, 303, 365, 366, 407, 540; *see also* correspondence *above*

Idaho, 631, 636-638, 645-649, 663, 665, 670, 675, 680

Kennedy, John F., and Nobel Prize dinner, 650-651

689

Key West, 257-258, 277, 303, 365, 406, 407, 540, 541, 648
languages, study of: Spanish, 196, 197, 202, 232; Swahili, 395, 429, 443, 481, 550
on men, 392, 679
and Monks, Noel, 50, 489; divorce, 208, 215; marriage, 51-52, 57, 58, 61-66 passim, 71, 73, 76, 77, 78, 84, 86, 87, 88, 92, 103, 104, 105, 116, 121, 122, 133, 158, 162, 182, 183, 184, 679
music, enjoyment of, 107, 108, 148, 149, 161, 226, 292, 343, 356, 398, 416, 418, 450, 493, 521, 550, 635, 636, 663
New York, 390, 615-621, 632, 649, 658-660, 663, 673
at Northwestern University, 30-31, 33, 34
and parents, 99, 100, 190, 203, 231, 232, 244, 269, 270; correspondence, 106, 122, 127, 182, 185, 197, 332, 357, 372, 393, 517; father, 1, 2, 4-30 passim, 45, 190, 528; father, correspondence, 269, 379, 390, 526, 527; father's death and burial, 527-528; father's illness and visits, 248-255 passim, 277, 278, 308, 329, 343-344, 346, 347, 359, 364-365, 379, 508-512, 526-528; and mother, 9, 10, 15, 16, 18, 19, 26, 28, 30, 45, 160, 250, 251, 255, 272, 363, 379, 529; mother, after Thomas's death, 529, 533-537 passim, 549, 557, 561; mother, correspondence, 344, 364, 529, 534, 549, 557; mother's death and burial, 566
reading, 10, 20, 23, 31, 35, 37, 86, 87, 98, 183, 240, 298, 321, 344, 380, 395, 419, 425, 427, 440, 441, 487, 541, 660, 668, 681
Seychelles, plans for trip, 680
shooting and hunting, 196, 203, 212, 234, 235, 265, 389, 550, 575, 576, 646, 670; East Africa, 444, 447, 449, 452, 460, 511, 652, 657
Soviet Union (1968), 665-670
will, 257
writing, 29, 30, 237, 272, 627; Chicago Daily News, 35-40 passim, 46, 47-48, 159, 349; Chicago newspapers, 34, 47-48; in Cosmopolitan, on marlin-fishing tournament, 333-336; diaries, 678; diaries, EH's entry in, 466-467; in Flair, on life at Finca Vigía, 346, 358; in Holiday, on Harry's Bar, 664; and on islands, 661-662; in Life, on East African safari (1962), 654-655, 658; London, freelance, 65-67; London Daily Express, 47-65, 678; London Daily Express, attempts to get job, 38-48 passim, 678; The New York Times Book Review, on background for EH's A Moveable Feast, 659; poem for EH, "For the Road, October 13, 1970," 348; in Sports Illustrated, "Holiday for a Wounded Torero," 594; in This Week, two pieces for "Words to Live By," 517; Time Inc., 66-143 passim, 147, 159, 161, 163, 171-178 passim, 180, 183, 185-190 passim, 192
Hemingway, Dr. Gregory (Gigi), 303, 338, 566
and father, 167, 185, 191, 239, 278, 303, 636, 637; and MH, 201-206 passim, 213, 226, 232, 240, 268, 400
and mother, 248, 257, 303, 406
Hemingway, Mrs. Gregory: see Danby-Smith, Valerie
Hemingway, Hadley Richardson (later Mrs. Paul S. Mowrer), 167, 324, 559
Hemingway, Joan (Muffet), 338, 402, 403, 563
Hemingway, John (Jack; Bumby), 210, 266, 303-304, 338, 566
and father, 228, 239, 303-304, 636, 637; and MH, 170-175

690

371, 378, 379, 380, 385, 388, 391, 398, 409, 410, 413, 414, 415, 417, 418, 536, 553, 597

James, Sidney, 394
Jensen, Anita, (Nita; Mrs. Walter Houk), 304
Jepson, Jasper, 360, 548
Jepson, Mrs. Jasper (Ursula Hemingway; Ura), 119, 286, 288, 360, 522, 548, 631
Johnson, Grace, 620
Johnson, Larry, 577, 626, 631
Josépha, 236, 314, 529
Juan, 194, 208, 209, 210, 212, 214, 223, 226, 228, 230, 255, 257, 273, 341, 348, 352, 356, 368, 373, 513, 515, 524, 528, 538, 582, 613, 638, 639, 642, 645
Justo, 201, 202, 214, 226, 233

Kechler, Alberto (Titi), 284
Kechler, Carlo, 497
Kechler, Count Federico, 281, 282, 497, 498, 503, 504
Keiti, 433, 440, 458, 465, 469, 472, 473, 494
Kennedy, Harry, 96
Kennedy, John F., 626-628, 650-651
Kennedy, Joseph P., 59, 76
Kennedy, Mr. and Mrs. Robert, 651
Kennedy Library: EH's papers, recipient of, 674
Kennish, Jacqueline Saix, 106, 499, 500
Kerr, Mrs. May, 537, 549, 557
Kirk, Grayson, 650
Kjerner, Dorothy, 626
Knickerbocker, Red, 65
Knox, Col. Frank, 35, 145
Kohly, Dr. Carlos (Cucu), 197, 209, 210, 227, 236, 250, 263
Kohly, Mrs. Carlos (Joy), 197, 214, 227
Kyungu, 441, 444, 491, 495, 526

Lahey, Edwin, 36
Lang, Will, 599, 600
Lanham, Col. Charles T. (Buck),

148, 155, 156, 184, 217, 220, 235, 238, 244, 303, 346, 376, 597, 598
Lanham, Mrs. Charles (Pete), 217, 220
Larkin, Mr. and Mrs. Charles, 670, 671
Laski, Harold, 83, 234
Leopoldina, 224, 258
Lerner, Michael, 648
Lewis, Lloyd, 35
Lewis, Sinclair, 295-296
Lindblad, Lars-Eric, 671, 672
Littauer, Sebastian, 33, 663
Life: EH: *The Dangerous Summer*, condensation, 599, 606-613 *passim*, 618, 620, 621, 674; East African safari, possible article, 393, 394, 397; *A Moveable Feast*, condensation, 659; *The Old Man and the Sea*, 373, 376, 382, 386
MH, on East African safari (1962), 653-656, 657, 658
see also Time Inc.
Lili (de la Fuentes), 569, 570, 645
Lucarda, Antonio (Tony), 292, 293
Lola (Richards), 504, 539, 571, 583, 605, 608, 609, 645
London *Daily Express*, 38, 39, 41, 42, 48, 51, 54
MH: attempts to get job, 38-47 *passim*, 678; writing by, 47-64, 678
LOOK: EH: East African safari, 394, 397, 404, 405, 435, 451, 452, 456, 489; follow-up ("Situation Report"), 547, 550-552
see also Theisen, Earl
Loos, Anita, 542
Lord, Joseph, 623, 624, 631
Low, Robert, 65, 76
Lowe, William, 404, 516
Luce, Henry, 89, 96, 101, 112
Luce, Mrs. Henry (Clare Boothe), 102, 163, 650
Lurie, Frieda, 666, 667, 669
Lyons, William, 229
Lyons, Mrs. William (Maruja; later Mrs. Luiz Meirelles), 229, 230

695